The Student Companion to
SOCIOLOGY

The Student's Companion to SOCIOLOGY

British Editors:
Jon Gubbay
Chris Middleton

American Editor:
Chet Ballard

BLACKWELL
Publishers

Copyright © Blackwell Publishers Ltd 1997

First published 1997

Reprinted 1997

Blackwell Publishers Ltd
108 Cowley Road
Oxford OX4 1JF, UK

Blackwell Publishers Inc
350 Main Street
Malden, Massachusetts 02148, USA

British Library Cataloguing in Publication Data
A CIP catalogue record for this book is available from the British Library

Library of Congress Cataloging in Publication Data
The student's companion to sociology/edited by Chet Ballard, Jon Gubbay,
and Chris Middleton.
p.   cm.
Includes bibliographical references and index.
ISBN 0–631–19947–0 — ISBN 0–631–19948–9 (pbk)
1. Sociology. 2. Sociologists—Vocational guidance. I. Ballard,
Chet. II. Gubbay, Jon. III. Middleton, Chris
HM51.S925   1997   96–33056
301—dc20   CIP

Typeset in 9.5 on 11pt Ehrhardt
at The Spartan Press Ltd, Lymington, Hants
Printed and bound in Great Britain
by T. J. International Limited, Padstow, Cornwall

This book is printed on acid-free paper

Contents

Part IV   Doing Sociology: Study and Research

Active Reading

Doing Sociological Research

Part V   Directory and Resources

Preface

We have tried to build into the *Student's Companion to Sociology* the sort of qualities you would hope to find in any companion with whom you were about to set out on a journey. We hope you will find it lively, full of enthusiasm, serious but user-friendly, and a source of guidance when you need advice. It is there to be consulted throughout your journey into sociology until the point at which you are ready to move into employment or higher level study.

This is not a book to be read all at once, or by starting at the beginning and working your way through to the end. Rather you can consult it as your needs or moods suggest – sometimes for inspiration, sometimes to be provoked, sometimes for information or guidance.

We have set out to achieve four objectives in this *Companion*.

- We hope to stimulate your sociological curiosity by emphasizing the discipline's attempts to "engage with" – to comprehend and explain – the pressing social problems facing the world.
- We hope to orient you in a discipline that is both complex and varied, helping you to understand the different values and traditions that have shaped sociology's development, and their relationship to each other.
- There is advice on how to practise sociology in ways that develop explanatory theory – primarily as a student, but also with an eye both to future employment and life as a citizen.
- Finally the *Companion* offers some sociological perspectives on the nature of sociological education itself. It provides information and practical reflections on sociology as a *profession* and as an *educational resource*, which we hope will assist you in your own personal engagements with the social world.

The *Student's Companion to Sociology* is not a textbook. The essays do not provide a systematic exposition of sociological knowledge. They vary greatly in their subject-matter, complexity and approaches. Many of the essays express personal convictions, often quite forcefully, or provide insights into their author's experiences as people trained in sociology. Sociologists, like everyone else, have their personal concerns and public agendas and, as well as depicting the discipline's intellectual concerns, the essays try to convey a flavour of what it is like to *be* a sociologist.

The *Companion* is organized into six parts. Part I sets the tone by illustrating how sociologists engage intellectually and politically with the social world, at their best seeking to understand and ameliorate the problems facing ordinary people. Part II develops this theme be locating the development of sociology within nineteenth- and twentieth-century history, and shows how its core concerns and concepts have been influenced by different social movements and political traditions. Part III provides a flavour of some of the most exciting and innovatory themes in sociological research today. Part IV offers practical insights into the practice of reading, theorizing and researching that may help *you* acquire and develop the skills of the sociologists' craft. Part V provides an introduction to some of the resources available to the professional or budding sociologist. Part VI offers insights, advice and information on employment and further study opportunities open to sociology graduates. We hope you will find the book good company.

Acknowledgements

The publishers and editors are grateful to the following for permission to use and for their help in supplying photographs: © Joe Miles (2, 6.1, 6.2, 13.1, 13.2, 14, 17.1, 17.2, 37 and 40); © C. Rodwell, Pacemaker (36.2); the authors (51). The photograph of the Wandsworth Prison Record, PRO 26082 (36.1) is Crown Copyright and is reproduced with the permission of the Controller of Her Majesty's Stationery Office. The source of (16) is unkown. The Clay Bennett editorial cartoon (21) is reprinted from *H. Clay Bennett: Best and Wittiest* and reproduced with special permission of © North America Syndicate. All other cartoon images (12, 16, 18.2, 22, 30) are taken from original postcards and reproduced with permission of © Leeds Postcards (0113-246 8649).

List of Contributors

Chet Ballard is Professor of Sociology at Valdosta State University in Valdosta, Georgia. He has served as president of the Georgia Sociological Association, vice-president of the Association for Humanist Sociology, and has produced over 20 scholarly articles and research reports. His most recent research describes how rural public school systems in Georgia are employing technology in efforts to prevent school violence.

Leonard Beeghley is Professor of Sociology and Graduate Coordinator at the University of Florida. He is the author of several books and many articles on theory, inequality, and gender roles. The most recent is *What Does Your Wife Do? Gender and the Transformation of Family Life*.

Paul Bellaby is Senior Lecturer in Sociology at the University of East Anglia. He has interests in the sociology of health and illness, and is currently working on the possible health effects of insecurity in employment.

Ted Benton is Professor of Sociology at Essex University. He has written extensively on the philosophy of social science, Marxism, the history of biology and green social theory. His *Natural Relations: Ecology, Animal Rights and Social Justice* was published by Verso in 1993. He has been involved in recent attempts to bring together Green and Socialist political groupings in the UK.

Randy Blazak is a Professor of Sociology at Portland State University, where he also teaches criminology. He earned his PhD in 1995 at Emory University and his research has involved studying how young people become involved in racist subcultures and gangs. For his dissertation, "the suburbanization of hate", he spent five years working undercover with skinheads in the USA and Europe.

Harriet Bradley lectures at the University of Bristol and was formerly Reader in Sociology at Sunderland University. Her latest book is *Fractured Identities: Changing Patterns of Inequality*. Her main research interests are women's employment and trade unions.

Phil Brown is a Senior Lecturer in Sociology at the University of Kent at Canterbury. He has written, co-authored and co-edited a number of books including *Schooling Ordinary Kids* (1987) and *Higher Education and Corporate Realities* (1994 with Richard Scase).

Robert Burgess is Professor of Sociology and Director of the Centre for Educational Development, Appraisal and Research (CEDAR) at the University of Warwick. His most recent publications include *Howard Becker on Education* (1995) and *Computing and Qualitative Research* (1995). He is a former president of the British Sociological Association and is currently president of the Association for the Teaching of the Social Sciences, and founding chair of the UK Council for Graduate Education.

Simon Cottle is Reader in Mass Communications at Bath College of Higher Education and the author of *TV News, Urban Conflict and the Inner City* (1993, Leicester University Press) and co-author with A. Hansen, R. Negrine and C. Newbold of *Mass Communication Research Methods* (Macmillan, 1997). He has also published numerous articles on news production and the reporting of diverse social problems. His recent research includes the production of minority ethnic TV programmes, news access, and methods of visual analysis.

Sheila Cross is Director of the Careers Service at the University College of Ripon and York St John, based at York. Sheila trained as a sociologist. After lecturing for some years she contributed to setting up adult educational guidance in the UK and in her 15 years as a university careers advisor has played a leading part in developing equal opportunities, in particular chairing committees and editing books to promote sex equality for women, as well as researching careers in the caring professions.

Mick Drake is a doctoral student at the University of East Anglia researching the military constitution of modernity.

Janice Eglin is a sociology graduate. She has a master's degree in post-16 education and training and a diploma in careers guidance. After working as a careers adviser in local government she is now employed in the careers service of the University of East London.

Mary Patrice Erdmans is an Assistant Professor of Sociology at the University of North Carolina at Greensboro. She is currently working on a book about Polish immigrants in Chicago and the construction of ethnic identity. Her previous articles, published in the USA and Poland, examined the differences between ethnics and immigrants, the employment of illegal immigrants in America, and the factors surrounding the decision to emigrate.

David Fisher is a Social Science Information Specialist at Nottingham Trent University. He studied at the universities of Durham, Cambridge and North London. He has worked previously at Essex University Library and the Squire Law Library, Cambridge.

Kay Freeland is the Director of Financial Aid and Veterans Affairs at Abraham Baldwin College in Tifton, Georgia. She earned a BA from Miami University, Oxford, Ohio, and an MSc from Valdosta State University, Valdosta, Georgia. She was awarded the 1995 Academic Achievement Award by the Department of Sociology, Anthropology and Criminal Justice at Valdosta State University. Her academic interests include social stratification and the study of organizations.

Dong-sook S. Gills is Lecturer in Sociology of Development at the School of Social and International Studies, University of Sunderland. She received her PhD for a thesis on rural women in Korean development at the University of Sheffield in 1995. Her main research interests are capitalist development, global inequality and women's work. She is currently engaged in research on economic liberalization and Korean agriculture.

Glenn A. Goodwin is Professor of Sociology at Pitzer College, Claremon, California. In addition to his long tenure at Pitzer College, Goodwin has guest lectured and taught at universities in England and the Middle East and his published work has appeared in numerous professional journals. His current (and long time) research interests include the history and development of sociological theory, humanistic sociology, the sociology of C. Wright Mills, and the sociology of existentialism.

Jon Gubbay is a Lecturer in Sociology at the University of East Anglia. He has a wide range of research interests including the sociology of higher education curricula, housing satisfaction, research methods and class analysis. He is the author, with Rosemary Crompton, of *Economy and Class Structure*.

Jackie Hammond graduated from the University of East Anglia in 1991. Jackie found employment as an administrative officer in an unemployment benefit office. She later trained as a teacher in primary education, but is currently working as a residential social worker for Barnardos where she also pursues her culinary and creative interests.

Nicky Hart is a Professor of Sociology at the University of California, Los Angeles. She served as a research fellow to the *Inequalities in Health Working Group* which produced the Black Report. Her publications include *When Marriage Ends* (1976), *The Sociology of Health and Illness* (1985) and various articles in the sociology of health and on gender and class stratification. She is currently completing a two-volume study of the sociology of human survival.

Frances Heidensohn is Professor of Social Policy, Goldsmiths' College, University of London. She is the author of *Women and Crime* (2nd edn, 1996), *Crime and Society* (1989) and *Women in Control?* (1992). Her current research is on comparative studies of policing. She has also been a member of several health authorities and is the chair of one.

Millsom Henry is the Deputy Director of SocInfo at the University of Sterling – the CTI Centre for the use of learning technologies in Sociology, Politics and Social Policy. Her research interests include: gender, ethnicity, culture and the new technologies and she is currently working on two projects in these areas.

Lori Holyfield is Assistant Professor of Sociology at the University of Arkansas. Her publications include (with Lori Ducharme and Jack Martin), *Drinking Contexts, Alcohol Beliefs, and Patterns of Alcohol Consumption: Evidence for a Comprehensive Model of Problem Drinking* (1995), and (with Gary Alan Fine) *Secrecy, Trust, and Dangerous Leisure: Generating Group Cohesion in Voluntary Organizations* (1996). Her current research concerns include sociology of emotions and culture.

Roger Homan graduated in religious studies from the University of Sussex before taking master's study in government in the London School of Economics and doctoral research in sociology at the University of Lancaster. He has published numerous articles on aspects of ethics and research methods and his *The Ethics of Social Research* is published by Longman. He is currently Principal Lecturer in religious studies at the University of Brighton.

Stevi Jackson is Senior Lecturer in sociology and women's studies at the University of Strathclyde. She is co-editor of *Women's Studies: A Reader* (Harvester Wheatsheaf, 1993), *The Politics of Domestic Consumption: Critical Readings* (Prentice-Hall/Harvester Wheatsheaf, 1995), *Feminism and Sexuality: A Reader* (Edinburgh University Press, 1996) and the author of *Christine Delphy* (Sage, 1996). She has also published a number of recent articles on romance and heterosexuality.

Charles Jaret is Associate Professor of Sociology at Georgia State University. He is the author of *Contemporary Racial and Ethnic Relations* and articles on urban ethnic issues. His current research is in two areas, racial–ethnic humour and income inequality between urban blacks and whites.

David Jary is Professor of Sociology and Dean of the School of Social Sciences at Staffordshire University. With Julia Jary, he is the editor of the widely used *Collins Dictionary of Sociology* (2nd edn, 1995). His other general works include (with Christopher Bryant) *Giddens' Structuration Theory – a Critical Appreciation* (Routledge, 1991) and (also with Christopher Bryant) *Giddens: Critical Evaluations* (four volumes, Routledge, 1996). He also writes on the sociology of sport and leisure and on higher education.

G. David Johnson is Associate Professor and Graduate Coordinator of Sociology at the University of South Alabama, in Mobile, Alabama, USA. A former editor of *Sociological Spectrum*, he is currently engaged in research on the health effects of work stress and economic dislocation on workers in the commercial seafood industry.

Liz Kenyon is Lecturer in Sociology at the University of Newcastle upon Tyne. She is currently writing her PhD thesis at Lancaster University, with wider research interests including: the changing student experience and identity; the meaning of home; and the importance of space and place for youth transitions. Forthcoming publications include an article in the *British Journal of Sociology* entitled: "Seasonal sub-communities: the impact of student households on residential communities".

Graham C. Kinloch is a sociologist at Florida State University where he has engaged in teaching and research for almost 25 years. His academic interests include sociological theory, the sociology of knowledge and comparative minority group relations. During the past five years he has served as Associate Dean of Academic Affairs in the College of Social Sciences.

Bill Kuvlesky gained his doctorate from The Pennsylvania State University, and is Professor of Sociology at Texas A&M University. His research and teaching specialities are theory, race and ethnic groups, rural communities and social stratification. He is a past president of the Association for Humanist Sociology and of the Southwestern Sociological Association.

Derek Layder is Reader in Sociology at the University of Leicester. His publications include *The Realist Image in Social Science* (1990), *New Strategies in Social Research* (1993), *Understanding Social Theory* (1994), and (with Julia O'Connell Davidson) *Methods, Sex and Madness* (1994). His current research concerns social theory and research methods.

David Lee studied at the London School of Economics and at the Universities of Liverpool and Birmingham. He lectured in sociological studies at the University of Sheffield and the University of Essex where he became Senior Lecturer in 1977. He has published numerous articles on social stratification, skills, vocational education, apprenticeship and industrial relations. With Howard Newby he wrote *The Problem of Sociology* (Hutchinson, 1993), and was co-author of *Scheming for Youth* (Open University Press, 1990) (with Dennis Marsden, Penny Rickman and Jean Duncombe). With Bryan Turner he has just edited *Conflicts about Class* (Longmans, 1996).

Frank Lyons is Director of the Partnership Programme, a work-based learning degree at the University of Portsmouth. Previously he lectured in sociology as well as working in staff and curriculum development. His current work involves the development of student-centred and independent-learning methods.

Chris Middleton lectures in sociology at the University of Sheffield, UK. He has written widely on the sociological history of class and gender and, more recently, on teaching in higher education. He is the principal editor of *The Sociology Teaching Handbook* a sourcebook produced collaboratively by and for university teachers with the support of the British Sociological Association.

Sheila Miles is Visiting Research Fellow at the University of London Institute of Education. She was formerly a Senior Lecturer in education at Homerton College Cambridge, and has also been an educational advisor for the London Borough of Haringey. She is currently a co-director of an ESRC-funded project on teacher education and has published widely in this and other areas of educational policy. She is also working on a European Commission-funded project on "gender and citizenship". She is an editor of the *Sociology Teaching Handbook*.

Steven Miles is a Lecturer in leisure, culture and consumption in the Department of Sociology at the University of Glasgow. He is presently writing a book concerned with "the sociology of consumerism" and his current research interests concern the relationship between consumption and identity among young people.

Steve Morgan is currently Campus/Subject Librarian at the University of the West of England, Bristol, having spent the previous five years as Social Science Librarian at the same institution. He is a regular contributor of journal articles to the literature of librarianship and has published two books entitled *Performance Assessment in Academic Libraries* and *Practical Strategies for the Modern Academic Library*.

Joanne Osborn graduated from the University of East Anglia in 1991. She is currently working as the geography project editor for Hodder & Stoughton Educational Books, and is in her second year of study for an Open University Geography degree. Previously she worked as a production controller for children's books and an assistant production editor, both at Simon & Schuster.

Stephen Papson is Professor of Sociology at St Lawrence University. He is co-author of *Sign Wars: The Cluttered Landscape of Advertising*. His current research is on advertising and nature texts.

Meeta Patel graduated from the University of East Anglia in 1991. She worked as an administration and computers manager in her first two jobs after graduating. Recently, she completed a Swedish massage and acupressure course, and is now running her own on-site massage service. Any spare time she has is filled with health and fitness interests.

David Phillips teaches research methodology and statistical methods at the University of North London, where he is Head of the School of Policy Studies, Politics and Social Research. His previous research concentrated on European social and political values. Currently he co-directs the Applied Social Research Unit, providing methodological advice and research support for colleagues and external organizations.

Momin Rahman is registered for a PhD at the University of Strathclyde where he also teaches the sociology of sexuality. He is currently researching issues of gay political representation.

John Rex who was born in South Africa has been engaged in teaching and research in sociology in Britain for 47 years. He was the founder and chair of the Departments of Sociology in Durham and Warwick and director of the Social Science Research Council's Research Unit on Ethnic Relations.

George Ritzer is Professor of Sociology at the University of Maryland. In addition to *The McDonaldization of Society*, which is in the process of being translated into ten languages, he is the author of *Expressing America: A Critique of the Global Credit Card Society* and the forthcoming *Consuming Society*.

Martin Scarrott is the Subject Librarian for leisure, tourism and hospitality management at the University of North London. He graduated in economic and social history and sociology in 1986, completed a postgraduate diploma in library and information studies in 1988 and became a chartered librarian in 1991. He has held posts at the British Library and the British Library of Political and Economic Science (London School of Economics).

Richard Scase is Professor of Sociology and Organizational Behaviour at the University of Kent at Canterbury. He has written several books including recently (with R. Goffee) *Corporate Realities* (Routledge); (with P. Brown) *Higher Education and Corporate Realities* (UCL Press); and (with J. Thirkell and S. Vickerstaff) *Labour Relations and Political Change in Eastern Europe* (UCL Press).

Joti Sekhon is Associate Professor of Sociology at Greensboro College in Greensboro, North Carolina. She received a BA degree from Delhi University, MA and MPhil degrees from Jwaharlal Nehru University in New Delhi, and a PhD from University of Waterloo, Ontario. Her research interests include comparative-historical sociology, social movements and democratization.

Martin Shaw is a sociologist and Professor of International Relations and Politics at Sussex

University. His books include *Post-military Society* (1991), *Global Society and International Relations* (1994) and *Civil Society and Media in Global Crises* (1996).

Simon Speight is currently Assistant Librarian (Law) at the University of Wales, Cardiff. Prior to this, he was Assistant Subject Librarian (Humanities and Social Sciences) at the University of Glamorgan. After completing a history degree at the University of Warwick, he gained an MA in librarianship at the University of Sheffield, where he studied the career patterns of MA librarianship graduates from Sheffield University. An article reporting these findings was published in the June 1996 issue of the *Journal of Librarianship and Information Science*.

Jerold M. Starr is Professor of Sociology at West Virginia University and a former president of the Association for Humanist Sociology. He has authored four books and numerous articles, principally in the areas of youth, education and social movements. He is currently writing a monograph, tentatively entitled *Public Broadcasting and the Public Interest.*

Jonathan H. Turner is Professor of Sociology, University of California at Riverside. He is the author of 24 books and many articles on sociological theory, ethnic relations, stratification, evolutionary sociology, American social structure and related topics. Several of his books have won awards. He has served in a variety of editorial positions, including associate editor of the *American Journal of Sociology* and *American Sociological Review*, editor of *Sociological Perspectives*, and is on the editorial board of the University of California Press.

Alan Walker is Professor of Social Policy, Department of Sociological Studies, University of Sheffield. He has researched extensively in the sociology of social policy and the sociology of ageing. His publications include *Social Planning* (Blackwell 1984); *The Caring Relationship* (with H. Qureshi, Macmillan, 1989); *The New Generational Contract* (UCL Press, 1996); *Ageing Europe* (with T. Maltby, Open University Press, 1996).

Tricia Lain White is a senior research officer in the Department for Education and Employment. She grew up in Canada and studied at the University of British Columbia. She graduated from the University of Sheffield in 1988 with a BA in sociology and politics and subsequently gained an MA in applied social research from the University of Manchester. She is married with two children, Cameron and Belinda.

Chas Wilson is Senior Lecturer in Criminology at the University of Portsmouth. He has published widely in the field of comparative criminology and is currently undertaking empirical research on the effectiveness of the European Convention on Human Rights in safeguarding the rights of prisoners.

Anne Witz is Senior Lecturer in Sociology at the University of Strathclyde and was the Marie Jahoda Visiting Professor in Feminist Studies at the Ruhr University, Bochum during 1996–7. Her publications include *Professions and Patriarchy* (1992), *Gender and Bureaucracy* (1992, with M. Savage) and *Gender, Careers and Organisations* (1997, with S. Halford and M. Savage).

Part I
Sociology: Engaging with the Social World

The opening part attempts to set the tone for the rest of the *Companion* by considering some of the different way sociology "engages" with the social world. The first three essays are accounts by leading sociologists in the UK and the USA describing how they were intellectually "turned on" by sociology and, in particular, how it enabled them to understand public issues with which they were concerned (Rex; Heidensohn; Kuvlesky). As John Rex tellingly puts it, the point may be to change the world rather than merely to interpret it, but "more effective strategies for changing it will be worked out if we first interpret it correctly". The next "pair" of essays by Goodwin and Shaw explores the relationship between individual and society by drawing on C. Wright Mills' (1957) famous distinction between "personal troubles" and "public issues" – the two essays coming at this relationship, as it were, from opposite directions. That the problematic connection between "personal troubles" and "public issues" is one that continues to exercise the minds of sociologists today is indicated by the number of contributors to this volume who independently chose to cite it, finding it an essential reference point when trying to communicate the distinctive character of sociological perspectives. Finally, another "pair" of essays, though very different from each other in tone and subject-matter, illustrate the practical application and impact of sociology in public debate and policy-making. One is about a government-commissioned, "top-down" survey of the social causes of health inequalities (Hart); the other describes a sociological input into a "bottom-up" community movement (Starr). Yet, in each, common concerns emerge regarding the scope and limits of sociology in promoting change in public policy.

Discovering Sociology – Personal Accounts

Discovering Sociology

John Rex

Karl Mannheim suggested more than 50 years ago that sociology was best done by outsiders and displaced intellectuals. He had in mind the contribution of Jewish refugees to European sociology and, more specifically, to British sociology. This, however, was an idea which appealed to many of us who were born and grew up in South Africa, allied ourselves with its liberation movement, and then came to England as quasi-refugees and tried to make sense of British society.

I was born as a poor White (actually not completely White but passing as such) in the political system of White Supremacy and my family was protected within this system by a colour bar which prevented non-Whites from competing for jobs and houses. None the less, by the time I reached university a number of influences, including serving in the British forces during the war and being in England for the general election of 1945, had caused me to see this as an evil system and one which should be overthrown.

"Philosophers," Karl Marx once said, "have hitherto only interpreted the world", but for him, "the point is to change it". My own view is certainly that the object of the exercise should be to change the world, but that more effective strategies for changing it will be worked out if we first interpret it correctly. The point about sociology in South Africa was that it led one to try to understand the actions and motivations of the contending racial groups and the sanctions which they had at their disposal.

South African society was, of course, deeply divided. In fact it stood on the edge of revolu-tionary change. When I came to Britain, on the other hand, I found a society in which gradua-list reform seemed possible and in which the state would take action to ameliorate the condition of the working classes. Sociologists, represented above all by David Glass and his colleagues at the London School of Economics (LSE), saw their task as one of exposing the inequalities of opportunity available to the children of non-manual and manual workers on the assumption that if the facts were known the government would put matters right. This trust in governments' benevolence, however, seemed to me at odds both with my experience of a more divided society in South Africa and with the world of my extramural students in Yorkshire who were steelworkers, miners and agricultural workers. They still believed in the class struggle and so did I.

My first target, in relation to which I defined my own position in sociology then, was the LSE tradition which I derided as "the book-keeping of social reform". Although I wasn't fully aware of it at the time this belief that we could simply gather facts in a scientific way, and that these facts would then be acted on, was generally referred to as "positivism". I said that what I wanted were not just statistical tables but some indication of why the people grouped together were so grouped, in terms of the ways in which they were likely to act. This seemed to me to be the basis of an alternative to positivism which would best be called a sociology of action. The mere fact that a group of people were earning £x thousand per annum was not particularly important unless those in the same category were likely to act together. Another label, which was attached to this approach, was that it was "phenomenological" as distinct from "positivist". I wasn't at first fully clear about either of these positions, but clearly my stand against "the book-keeping of social reform" was getting me into deep theoretical waters.

Perhaps even more important was the fact that there was actually some sort of theoretical perspective underlying British sociology. This was that of "functionalism", a notion familiar to me in the social anthropology of Malinowski and Radcliffe-Brown, but now imported in a more sophisticated theoretical form in the work of Talcott Parsons. I had actually given a lot of thought to the functionalism of the anthropologists and saw Malinowski, at least, as recognizing the importance of change and conflict. Parsons, however, seemed to me to have no place for conflict and an inadequate theory of change. In opposition to this new kind of functionalism I suggested that in any social relationship two actors might reject each other's expectations and fight to oppose them, and I was often associated as a conflict theorist with C. Wright Mills and Dahrendorf.

I wrote my first book, *Key Problems of Sociological Theory* in 1961 to state a position based on anti-positivist and anti-functionalist perspectives. Firstly, I argued that in studying human life we had to give explanations which were not only adequate as telling us about the "causes" of events, but which referred to the meaning of action for an actor. Secondly, I rejected the idea in Durkheim's *Rules of Sociological Method* that social facts were things, which suggested that there was no difference between studying societies and social relations and studying physical objects. What we had to talk about in sociology were structures of social relations and these were all unpackable in terms of the concepts of action and interaction. Thirdly, I also agreed with Weber that researchers' values influence the starting point of investigation, but that the researcher can and should ensure that his or her values do not affect the findings. Finally, it seemed to me that a so-called science of society had its limitations. It could not describe the world directly or with a kind of final certainty. The most that it

could do was to construct typical forms of action and interaction called "ideal types" which came as near as possible to describing as well as explaining the world.

In the popular British sociology of the 1970s this identification of my approach with that of Weber led to a new generation which saw itself as "Marxist" dismissing me for ideological reasons as some type of right-winger. In fact I always claimed to be a "left Weberian" with little sympathy for Max Weber's own nationalistic concerns. What seemed to me to be important was the fact that Weber helped to clarify concepts like "class" or "the state" in a way which Marxism did not, and that if one was interested in liberating people from class, racial or ethnic oppression, we had necessarily, if we were to be clear, to develop accounts of classes and racial and ethnic groups in Weberian terms.

My own sociology combined theoretical argument with empirical work in the sphere of what were called race or ethnic relations. As Britain came to have a substantial minority of West Indian and Asian immigrants, I was concerned to work out the relation between race and ethnic relations on the one hand and those based on class on the other. I did this in the context of Birmingham, Britain's second largest city. In 1963 the City Council, in which the Labour Party was in power, set up an elaborate system of indirect discrimination against immigrants in the allocation of publicly rented houses built or owned by the Council. Extending the use of the term "class" in a Weberian way, I suggested that local politics were based on a struggle between "housing classes" and that the system of discrimination in housing placed the new immigrants in a different housing class position from the indigenous working class.

As a result of this work I was made a member of the UNESCO International Experts Committee on the Nature of Race and Race Prejudice in 1967. This committee concluded that since racial differences, as the term "race" was used scientifically by biologists, could not explain the political differences amongst men (and women), it was up to sociologists to say what the real nature of the situations were which were called race relations situations. After the 1967 meeting I wrote a book called *Race Relations in Sociological Theory* in which I sought to answer this question. I argued that such situations had three elements: they were situations of severe conflict, oppression and exploitation going beyond that in normal labour markets: they involved not merely relations between individuals but between groups; and the dominant groups in such systems justified them in terms of some sort of deterministic theory which implied that existing differences were understood by scientists as natural.

As Director of the Social Science Research Council's Research Unit on Ethnic Relations I saw that the British case, in which discrimination was based on colour, was a special case, and that in Europe such discrimination was often based on culture and religion, particularly in France where the central problems arose in relation to Algerian immigrants. I therefore sought to set out, in a series of working papers published in 1995 under the title *Ethnic Minorities in the Modern Nation State*, the different ways in which European societies dealt with immigrant ethnic minorities and also what a society would be like in which all were treated equally, yet in which cultural differences were also respected.

This particular interest of mine has come to be one of the most important themes in the sociology of democratic welfare states in western Europe. Clearly, whereas previously the main theme of politics had been simply that of stratification and class struggle, the supersession of the large industrial enterprise as the basic unit of society in a new kind of society based on the control of knowledge, meant that classes as such were no longer the sole basis of what came to be called "exclusion" (a term whose usage was unclear but seemed to refer mainly to lack of access in labour markets). Some of those who wrote about these problems suggested that the new social movements, like the green movement, the women's movement or the peace movement, but also movements based on ethnicity, had nothing to do with class. In my own view this was not the case. Working-class immigrant ethnic minorities seemed to me to be in many respects like classes, but it was necessary to try to describe the complex relations between cultural factors and the defence of class interests which was involved in their structure.

On a more general theoretical level I had found during the 1970s that the way in which sociology developed turned attention away from many of my concerns and that both political intellectuals and theoretical sociologists were no longer providing the sort of sociological basis for political action which I wished to see. Much of the theoretical literature which came to be dominant and was reproduced in a popular form was based on French philosophical thought or on the argument about the quest for a better society which was reflected in the work of the Frankfurt School and its arguments about Marxism. Also the tendency was to replace sociology with philosophy rather than simply trying to ensure that sociology had a sound philosophical base. Although the issues here are complex and difficult, students of sociology today will no doubt be told much about the ideas of such authors as Althusser, Habermas and Garfinkel. It will therefore, I think, be useful to describe my own encounter with this body of ideas and to indicate why I insist on retaining a more Weberian perspective.

In terms of practical politics my own past in South Africa as well as my deep involvement in the Campaign for Nuclear Disarmament led me to join the editorial board of the *New Left Review*. This didn't present any great difficulty for me since the early board consisted of a number of left-wing academics and intellectuals who simply respected each other enough to be able to work together. What I found as time went on, however, was that the New Left group, like so many other groups in British politics, was dominated by Oxford and Cambridge intellectuals. They had little knowledge of sociology, but as part of their upper-class culture had strong interest in European and, particularly, French Marxism. When the board was handed over to the even more upper class and ideologically rigorous group led by Perry Anderson, I knew that I had no place in it.

The Phase Two New Left, however, had a profound effect on British sociology. Suddenly Robin Blackburn, who had played a leading role in supporting the student rebellion at the LSE, announced that the theory group of the British Sociological Association was to be reformed and that it would study the work of "the most important European sociologist, Louis Althusser".

If my position as a conflict theorist had led to my being labelled as a radical and Marxist, I now found that the Marxist position had been pre-empted by the Althusserians. What was striking about this version of Marxism, however, was that it was based on a kind of systems theory not all that different from that of Talcott Parsons, and that it had little place for class struggle. Poulantzas wrote that the problematic of "class in itself" and "class for itself" – which I always found useful myself in analysing situations of class conflict – was an unfortunate tendency associated with "Georg Lukacs and the historicist school".

The other aspect of my work which was overwhelmed in the early 1970s was its leaning towards "phenomenology". For me this had meant little more than trying to interpret observed behaviour in terms of its subjective meaning, but now this perspective became lost in the new efflorescent growth of "ethnomethodology". I had little interest in this development which actually had a highly empiricist technique for studying the creation of meaning and interpreting human behaviour, and which seemed to turn its back on any kind of intelligent political activity.

Garfinkel, the leading exponent of ethnomethodology, developed his work out of the peculiar version of phenomenology associated with the work of Alfred Schutz, but he also drew on the work of the later Wittgenstein with its interest in "following a rule", "language games" and "forms of life". In Britain too, a young Wittgensteinian philosopher, Peter Winch, wrote a book called *The Idea of a Social Science* rejecting the possibility of such a science. These ideas were very acceptable to British philosophers and very quickly a kind of philosophical discipline came to replace sociology in any empirical or Weberian form.

The lead in the development of this new discipline was taken by Anthony Giddens and no-one could possibly deny the degree of learning which has gone into the production of his many books. What he has done, however, is to enter into the European argument about philosophic issues. What is not often recognized, however, is that, although there is some kind of historical generalization to be found in some of his work, it does not connect with new detailed empirical research and involves a rejection not merely of the scientific method of positivism, but, no less, that of Weber. Weber's ideas on the philosophy of science, Giddens told us in one of his earlier works, were now obsolete in the light of new developments in philosophy. For my part I believe that sociology must have a sound empirical base and that the philosophy of social science involved in developing this must be that of Weber.

A great deal of contemporary European philosophy, of course, has concerns going beyond those of sociology. In France disillusionment with Marxist structuralism and the politics to which it led, has now resulted in the emergence of various tendencies described as post-modern. One feature of this post-modern ideology is the belief that politics, as we understood it in terms of conflicts of interest, are no longer possible. Modern social movements, including ethnic ones which have displaced classes, are said to be about identity. They are no longer to be understood in terms of some sort of theoretical account of history or "meta-narrative" about the supersession of this society by a new and better one.

Such a meta-narrative is of course central to the Frankfurt School and its successors in Germany. Its main empirical concern is that of discovering the situations in which new forms of moral consciousness will develop. Habermas is not simply an empirical sociologist. He is a philosopher, concerned, as he said in his inaugural lecture, with the pursuit of beauty, truth, and goodness. From a Weberian perspective such an enterprise is not within the scope of sociology. Weber does suggest that there is a continuous tendency in history towards increasing formal rationality, that is a rationality of means, but he cannot see any tendency towards substantive rationality or the choice of ends which are more "rational" or good. The result is that we appear more and more trapped in an "iron cage" of increasingly rationally organized social relations.

I have always shared Weber's pessimism and it does appear to me to be more appropriate in the world after the collapse of Communism than either the philosophy of postmodernism in France or the continuing belief in the Enlightenment idea of Progress in the work of Habermas. None the less I have also accepted another aspect of Weber's work, namely his belief that social facts are not things, but structures of social relations worked out by human beings in the course of their action and capable of being changed by human beings. In this perspective we are always responsible for the nature of the social world and can change it, difficult though this may be.

In working out these ideas in the particular sphere of race and ethnic relations, moreover, I found that I did not have the support of my sociological colleagues who called themselves "Marxists". There are many aspects to the criticism they made of my work, which was seen as a diversion from central Marxist ideas that set the question of "race" and ethnic relations within the context of the study of the capitalist mode of production. Often they misrepresented my work and saw it as simply part of what Gilroy called "managing the underclass". I think these criticisms are misleading and I would like my work to be understood as using precise Weberian concepts to describe the most important political actors in contemporary society, an enterprise which should form a central part of any Marxist theory. It is about the exploitation and oppression of groups of people and what they would have to do to liberate themselves and to win equality.

Having now been involved in doing sociology for nearly 50 years, I find the struggle for the kind of sociology to which I am committed as challenging as ever. Although my first work in Britain called for a greater philosophical sophistication in the use of concepts, and sought to lay emphasis upon the conflicts and possible compromises between contending groups including classes, I have been out of sympathy with many recent developments. The various kind of philosophically-based sociology outlined above came to be based first on the theories of structuralism, and then on the theories of post-structuralism, postmodernism and post-Marxism, and there was less and less interest in contending groups with conflicting interests. My hope is, however, that in the world after 1989, the kind of sociology which I have continued to do may come to play a more important role. As sociologists we need to interpret the world accurately. As political actors we may then seek effectively to change it.

John Rex: Bibliography of Main Works

Rex, J. 1961: *Key Problems of Sociological Theory*. Routledge & Kegan Paul.

—— with Moore, R. 1967: *Race Community and Conflict*. Oxford.

—— 1970: *Race Relations in Sociological Theory*. Weidenfeld and Nicolson (new edition by Routledge & Kegan Paul 1983).

—— 1973: *Sociology and the Demystification of the Modern World*. Routledge & Kegan Paul.

—— 1973: *Discovering Sociology*. Routledge & Kegan Paul.

—— 1973: *Race, Colonialism and the City*. Routledge & Kegan Paul.

—— with Tomlinson, S. 1979: *Colonial Immigrants in a British City*. Routledge & Kegan Paul.

—— 1981: *Social Conflict*. Longmans.

—— 1986: *Race and Ethnicity*. Open University.

—— and Mason, D. (eds) 1986: *Theories of Race and Ethnic Relations*. Cambridge.

—— Czarina Wilpert and Joly, D. (eds) 1987: *Immigrant Associations in Europe*. Gower.

—— 1987: *The Ghetto and the Underclass*. Gower.

—— 1990: *The Concept of a Multi-cultural Society*. Warwick: Centre for Research in Ethnic Relations.

—— 1991: *Ethnic Identity and Ethnic Mobilisation in Britain*. Warwick: Centre for Research in Ethnic Relations.

—— and Drury, B. (eds) 1994: *Ethnic Mobilisation in a Multi-Cultural Europe*. Avebury.

—— 1995: *Ethnic Minorities in the Modern Nation State*. Macmillan.

2

Discovering Sociology: Further Enquiries

Frances Heidensohn

The title of this part of the *Companion* is "Discovering Sociology" and that is a very apt description of what has been for me an adventurous quest, a journey to find things out, understand them too, and in some ways to change them. I began to explore sociology in the 1960s as an undergraduate student in London. This happened to be a very good time to study the discipline. The era itself was one of excitement and change in society, the arts and politics. At that time the civil rights movement in the USA was mobilizing and in eastern Europe the Prague spring flowered for a while. A series of social issues with equality, justice and freedom as their themes were widely discussed both in public and academic debate.

Protests about the Vietnam War, and the role played by the USA in it, as well as dissatisfaction with hierarchical forms of governance, led students into confrontation with authorities on American campuses and also in Britain. The London School of Economics, where I had studied and was by then on the staff, was closed for several weeks after one such episode in 1969.

It was a challenging and exciting time to be young and engaged in exploring sociological ideas. Yet I found that in the area of *women and crime*, a subject in which I was becoming particularly interested, even the most innovative thinking, such as that from the new sociology of deviance, could not fully answer the questions to which I sought answers – though these new vessels did enable me to embark on some exciting explorations and to make some important discoveries. Later on my journey I investigated the topic of *gender and social control* which took me to the heart of the central traditions of the discipline. Throughout this time I have been involved in social policy especially that relating to *health and social care*. Throughout I have been concerned to understand new social issues, to try out sociological concepts, and sometimes also to bring about changes.

Women and Crime: The Art of Asking Questions

Among the things that puzzled me as a student was the fact that, according to the statistics of offences known to the police and convictions in the courts, women and girls were responsible for very many fewer crimes than boys and men. Popular ways of expressing this have been to say that "females cause 10% of the trouble" or that women offenders are "just too few to count". In fact there is some variation according to the type of crime in the proportion of offences committed by females, with women contributing under 20% of the more serious types.

While I found this remarkable, since sex differences in most other aspects of life were nowhere near as great as these, there was another feature which also struck me. What we now call the gender gap in criminality has been observed for as long as crime figures have been kept. A few early observers had commented on and attempted to explain this curiosity, but their explanations were limited either to biology or to stereotypes; there was little that was *sociological* to them. I therefore set out both to try and explain women's low performance in recorded criminality and also why social scientists had ignored this most significant question for so long.

There were then no obvious ways of handling these topics within existing and familiar sociological frameworks. But at that very time we were being offered encouragement to re-think older ways of sociological "seeing". Howard Becker, for instance, had published a paper which challenged the idea that the definition of deviance was something fixed and essential and that everyone could agree on what it is. From Becker (1963), from Matza and from other American sociologists there came the ideas of deviance as a *process*, and of questioning the roles of other participants in that process such as law makers and law enforcers. Eventually, and some of this took a very long time, I saw that different questions had to be put and new terms and ideas brought in from outside the sociology of crime and deviance.

The new sociology of deviance encouraged us to recognize that "deviants" are not people who are essentially different from "normal" people, but that we are all capable of becoming deviant. When I came to write *Women and Crime* (1985) I had decided that the key query was not so much "why do men commit more crimes?" as "why were women so conforming?". "What social structures and processes, what cultural assumptions and patterns of socialization bring this about?". This approach takes us straight into important gender differences in freedom, authority and access. As you may have realized, I had now acquired from the second-wave feminist work which had come from the USA in the 1970s, a new range of ideas about gender, about "oppression" and "patriarchy", which I could apply to my original questions.

To those questions I now had some answers. Women, I suggested, were subject to special and additional forms of social control in ways men were not. (Mostly) male academics had avoided these topics because conformity attracted them less than crime did. An excellent

and very honest example of this was W. F. Whyte's classic account of his participant observation study of gangs in Boston's North End in which he describes his fascination with the lively, deviant gang members and his inability to observe domestic scenes and the lives of women.

Alongside my academic studies, which had involved me in empirical work in prisons and young offender institutions, I was also trying to make sense of my own experience as an academic. I argued vigorously for the recognition of gender in crime and criminal justice and that it was an unavoidable issue. Of course, all aspects of social life are gendered, so is academic life. In analysing the ways in which women as subjects and as researchers could be marginalized, key guides for my journey of exploration were early feminist studies. The American writer Kate Millett introduced a notion of patriarchy and challenged the assumptions of male writers in a humourous but nevertheless serious fashion. British writers Ann Oakley and Juliet Mitchell began a critique of society and scholarship. Oakley's work on the sociology of housework, on maternity and on the conduct of research itself all provided keys to unlock gates into new territories for me.

Gender and Social Control

The next piece of work and steps in my journey have gender and social control as the main theme. By the 1980s the world had changed a great deal and so had I. Once again I was teaching in the University of London, having spent some years as a part-time lecturer and five years as a full-time civil servant. During that time I learnt a lot about worlds previously unknown to me, especially the workings of central government and of powerful élite groups. In addition, I became increasingly fascinated by social policy and with obstacles to ways of achieving social change. As an academic and civil servant, I represented the then Social Science Research Council on a panel which, together with the Equal Opportunities Commission, commissioned a series of projects on barriers to equality for women.

By the late 1970s gender usually received a ritual genuflexion from social commentators, but it was rarely firmly-woven into their approaches. Gender was like a lean-to built on to the main structure of criminology (Heidensohn, 1986). My experiences had deepened my insight into the operation of power and the cultures and subcultures of professional life, and I had come to realize how central gender was to their functioning. An anthropological study of Whitehall, depicting it as a village and stressing the importance of the common histories and values of senior civil servants, crystallized and reflected some of my own experience there (Heclo and Wildavsky, 1981). I therefore decided to focus my next research project on a topic that would illuminate aspects of power and control, and also their interaction with gender (Heidensohn, 1986).

Years of observation of my professional colleagues had also instructed me in what counted as significant work for sociologists and might have an impact, might break the barriers to the recognition and incorporation of gender analysis. The canonical sociological studies were *international* in some way, they *initiated* and/or engaged in serious debates which usually fed back to the central traditions of the discipline. In *Crime and Society* (1989) I wrote about those traditions as they have developed in criminology and how they link to the themes – social order, authority, community – of the founding fathers. They can also be adapted and applied to current concerns about victims, urban crime and gender and crime.

For *Women in Control?*, my next empirical project, I embarked on a comparison of the history and experiences of women in law enforcement in Britain and the USA. There was an established and lively debate around the historic origins of the "new" police in Britain (defined usually as the founding of the Metropolitan Police in London in 1829) and parallels with the USA. The entry of women into policing had been carefully covered but not linked into wider debates. In my own

study, I tried both to explore the lives of the 50 women officers whom I interviewed in Britain and the USA, and to relate this to all the wider themes outlined above.

In recording the histories of the officers whom I interviewed, I used the understanding about processes and procedures in research which I had gained from modern feminist work. Feminist epistemological work, addressing questions of how we study and understand the people and subjects we research, had attained considerable sophistication and provided me with a framework. Carole Smart (1990) asked what criminology could offer feminism and concluded that criminology was a dead end. While not sharing all her views, I found her approach stimulating.

In terms applied by Smart I did not share a standpoint with the police whom I interviewed, yet I did try to give them the chance to express their own views and have outlined in a later article some aspects of this (Heidensohn, 1994a). Two sociological approaches (both from the sociology of deviance) I employed in this work were the "natural history" of a career, and the idea of subculture. Using the first approach I observed that the female officers shared with each other and to some extent with their male colleagues, common key stages and milestones in their professional lives. A fascinating and widespread event for many of them was the "transformation scene" in which a resented, rejected female officer was transformed into a valued colleague, usually through her own examplary action, just like Cinderella on her way to the ball. This "discovery" is one of many sociologists have made about people's strategies for managing and getting by in their lives.

Another pivot of *Women in Control?* is the idea of subculture. Throughout the accounts which I gathered from my interviewees and from my own observations during the project, male officers were described as resistant to women's entry into and presence in policing. Previous analyses had depicted cop or canteen culture (Reiner, 1986) and sought to explain it. Ideas which illuminated the analysis further came from Klofas and Toch (1982), who wrote about "subcultural guardians" acting as

Figure 2.1 *Women in Control?* Male officers are resistant to women's entry into policing.

self-appointed defenders of the *status quo*, and Bob Connell (1987) who had outlined notions of dominant and subordinated masculinity and linked these to the theme of power.

Women in Control? (1992) and related publications present a range of questions about gender, social control and equality as well as trying to set these in comparative contexts. This can be helpful, when, for instance, there is public disquiet about women officers and public order. In considering this topic (1994b and 1996) I was able to draw on my US and British data and show how the women managed violence and disorder in both countries and the apparent irrelevance of both guns and physique to the issue.

One of the sociological "discoveries" which I can claim some part in making is that of feminist perspectives in criminology. There can be a lively debate about what these mean, but in the mid-1990s it was clear that there were enough significant indicators of some real developments. In preparing a second edition of *Women and Crime* (1996) Marisa Silvestri and I identified hundreds of articles and picked out several key themes of debate. These include discussions about the female share of crime and the possibility of convergence between male and female rates; the appropriate treatment of women in the criminal justice system, whether "equitably" or "differently", and the growing discussion about masculinity as a problem for social order. In another project, Nicole Rafter and I, building on groundbreaking work by other feminist scholars, produced a survey of the impact feminism has had on criminology around the world (Rafter and Heidensohn, 1995). Altogether these form a special kind of "discovery" – that of finding a new way of looking at the world, which is sometimes called a paradigm shift. Thirty years on from my first steps in this direction it is very exciting to find that this is where we have got to so far, how many others share these perspectives and what impact they have had.

Health and Social Care

As well as being an academic sociologist for most of my career I have been for most of my life involved with social policies in various settings. Here I have constantly found that I both use sociological *ideas* and rely on *methods of analysis* drawn from social science. Working in the health service, for instance, I have found the repertoire of modern sociological ideas invaluable in order to make sense of the broader developments which have affected politics and policies and the state of society. Ideas about *globalization* and *localization* and the *hollowing-out* of the modern state all assist in comprehending the pace and complexity of change. The organization of the National Health Service has been in a process of perpetual change during the 1990s. This has parallels in other welfare delivery systems here and abroad, and also in other kinds of agencies.

At quite another level, the more classical range of concepts which sociologists have used in welfare analysis still serve very well. For example, the relationships between poverty, inequality and ill-health are well-documented (see Hart, Chapter 6 in this volume). A significant contribution to perceptions about carers and caring began with the work of Dulcie Groves and Janet Finch who highlighted the gendered nature of much social care, provided by women in families. They pointed out the apparently neutral concept of "community care" really meant care by families and that, in practice, was (unpaid) care by women. They linked this "discovery" to key social and demographic changes likely to reduce both the supply of available carers and their commitment to the task. This has since been much more fully elaborated and there have been some policy changes which reflect this.

....

My career as a sociologist has been a voyage of discovery. As well as enjoying such voyages for the intrinsic excitement of adventure – the search for knowledge and understanding – I have always sought to achieve two others goals as well. The trips I most enjoy are those shared with good companions, and so I have tried to share the findings from my own work with others, and to engage in sociological discourse about feminist work or the significance of gender. Most of all, it has been important to me to acquire the understanding and the techniques to effect changes and improvements in the society of which I am a citizen. When early in 1995 I gave my inaugural lecture on taking up the chair of social policy at Goldsmiths' College, I looked forward to the twenty-first century and tried to forecast future trends in crime and feelings of insecurity. Then I reviewed my own work and that of others in order to find some solutions to reduce the prevailing and growing sense of insecurity in modern society. In return for the opportunities and insights which the discipline has given me, to offer some discoveries and proposals for the (re)construction of reassurance was the least I could do.

References

Becker, H. S. 1963: *Outsiders*. London: Collier-Macmillan.

Connell, R. W. 1987: *Gender and Power*. Oxford: Polity Press.

Finch, J. and Groves, D. 1980: Community care and the family: a case for equal opportunities? *Journal of Social Policy*, 9(4).

Heclo, H. and Wildavsky, A. 1981: *The Private Government of Public Money*, 2nd edn. Basingstoke: Macmillan.

Heidensohn, F. M. 1968: The deviance of women: a critique and an enquiry, *British Journal of Sociology*, XIX(2), 160–75.

—— 1986: Questions for criminology? In P. Carlen, and A. Worrall (eds), *Gender, Crime and Justice*. Milton Keynes: Open University Press.

—— 1989: *Crime and Society*. Basingstoke: Macmillan.

—— 1992: *Women in Control? The Role of Women in Law Enforcement*. Oxford: Oxford University Press.

—— 1994a: Gender and crime. In R. Maguire, R. Morgan and R. Reiner (eds), *The Oxford Handbook of Criminology*. Oxford: Oxford University Press.

—— 1994b: From being to knowing: some issues in the study of gender and contemporary society

Women and Criminal Justice, 6(1), 13–37.

—— 1996: *Women and Crime*, 2nd edn. Basingstoke: Macmillan.

Klofas, J. and Toch, H. 1982: The guard subculture myth. *Journal of Research in Crime Delinquency*, 238-54.

Matza, D. 1964: *Delinquency and Drift*. London: John Wiley.

Millett, K. 1977: *Sexual Politics*. London: Virago.

Mitchell, J. 1971: *Women's Estate*. Harmondsworth: Penguin.

Oakley, A. 1974: *The Sociology of Housework*. Oxford: Martin Robertson.

—— 1980: *Women Confined: Towards a Sociology of Childbirth*. Oxford: Martin Robertson.

Rafter, N. H. and Heidensohn, F. M. (eds) 1995: *International Feminist Perspectives in Criminology*. Milton Keynes: Open University Press.

Reiner, R. 1985: *The Politics of the Police*. London: Wheatsheaf.

Smart, C. 1990: Feminist approaches to criminology or postmodern woman meets atavistic man. In L. Gelsthorpe and A. Morris (eds), *Feminist Perspectives in Criminology*. Milton Keynes: Open University Press.

Whyte, W. F. 1955: *Street Corner Society*, 2nd edn. Chicago: University Press.

3

Discovering Sociology

William P. Kuvlesky

The Early Years

Little Black Sambo![1]

My sister yelled these words at a small black boy who was passing us as we were going to school; she was in the first grade at the time. The boy appeared startled and ran away from us. This event marked the first time I consciously became aware of racial differences, as far as I can remember. Peter Rose (1981, pp. 116–19) calls these pejorative labels ethnophaulisms. The use of these labels are acts of negative social discrimination and cause minority group members pain. The language used in any society includes some ethnophaulisms. Currently in the USA such terms are "niggers" (Blacks), "chinks" (Asian –Americans), and "queers" (homosexuals).

The neighborhood in North Braddock, Pennsylvania where we lived at the time was ethnically mixed even though it was only about two blocks long. Blacks, Italian–Americans, Polish–Americans, and Lithuanian–Americans were the largest part of the mix. Even so, all but one of the black families lived together in brick row houses at one end of the street. Little interaction took place between them and the people of European origin. As I look back now, I can see that I was aware of these group differences but did not understand the significance of them. Even among the European origin groups the ethnic differences mattered; we each went to ethnic-specific churches nearby but outside the neighborhood.

One thing all of us in the neighborhood shared was being defined by others to be "poor people." We had limited contact with people in "higher" levels of the rank system and thought of them as being rich. Those we did have contact with – teachers, store owners, police – were often resented. We were prejudiced toward these middle-class people.

My father resented having never gone to college. He worked in a steel mill until the 1929 "Great Depression," which left him without a job. My mother, daughter of a coal miner, left school after the eighth grade. She worked as a maid in the home of a wealthy judge. I remember she brought leftover food when she came home. Also, I remember eating a lot of bread soaked in milk with sugar in it. Being poor was not something I remember thinking about a lot. I recall very clearly a recurring nightmare I had; I saw myself being smothered by dollar bills that were being dumped on me in great quantities.

My best friend in school was much better off than us because both of his parents had good jobs. I was crushed the day my mother denied my request to have my friend over for dinner, since he would see that our dinner was cabbage soup and bread. It is a good guess that these early experiences sensitized me to differing rank structures in the larger community of which our neighborhood was part. These experiences built the foundation for a world view that would ultimately lead me into the field of sociology.

Teenage Years

My father's highest aspiration was to own a farm. My mother came from a rural area and did not share his enthusiasm. During World War II my father had improved the family's economic status dramatically by working two jobs during the war years. By 1945 he had accumulated money to put a down-payment on a farm. We moved to a small 80-acre farm near Lake Erie in northwestern Pennsylvania. For a few years I experienced the most devastating poverty I could imagine. I recall being teased for wearing hand-me-down clothes from my uncle. One of these experiences that particularly stands out in my memory concerns a pair of work shoes, a number of sizes too big for me, given to me by one of my uncles following his military service. The farm became a bottomless pit, consuming great hunks of our family's resources. We had to buy animals and equipment.

Another problem surfaced when my family moved from a very large urban school to a one-room school with one teacher. Five or six other boys were in the school and, for the most part, had been together from the first grade. No doubt they were sensitive to "big city" people referring to them as "hicks" or "hayseeds." At any rate, they isolated me and taunted me continuously. This was the third kind of negative social differentiation I had experienced, one related to rural–urban status. I had never heard the word sociology, but this time I had analyzed the situation and knew what I needed to do: move my position in the local "pecking order." I targeted one of the taller boys. The next time he teased me I pretended to be in a rage and beat the hell out of him. I had changed my social ranking among my peers.

During high school rural kids like me were teased about smelling of manure and other demeaning characteristics. This situation motivated me to work hard on my studies in order to outdo the others. I did, and this led to a number of teachers becoming friendly with me. They provided me with support and recognition; things I sorely needed. Respond-ing to a teacher's suggestion, I joined an agriculture club that provided me with close friends and opportunities to develop my social skills, including leadership experiences.

Perhaps one of the most important things in moving me to anticipate the possibility of going to college was the fact that I chose the "vocational ag" teacher as my primary role model. I really admired him and wanted to be like him. To be like him I realized I would have to go to college.

College and Military Service

After high school I didn't go off to the teachers' college nearby like many of my friends; instead I decided to enroll in a state university miles from home and study vocational agriculture.

To earn money for college I took a job as "deckhand" on a ship that sailed the Great Lakes. With little expenses, I could save a lot of money quickly, although deckhand was the lowest ranked job on the ship. It was in this job that I experienced the great diversity of people in the USA for the first time. There was plenty of time on the ship to read and I found myself thinking about the different people in the world, their different ranks, and the inequalities which exist worldwide. As a result, I began to look at college not just as a way to become like my high school teacher role model, and I could see that a college education would broaden my horizons and lift me out of poverty.

After a good start at Penn State, my grades dropped and I found myself questioning why I was in college at all. How could I sit in college when buddies from high school were being drafted to fight the Korean War? How much did I really know about the world? I was a mixed-up youth and felt a pervasive anxiety. This discomfort led me to make a dramatic change in my life. I joined the Marine Corps during the summer of 1953. The experiences I had over three years in the Corps helped me mature and gain direction. One weekend I met a girl with big blue eyes and asked her to dance. That was one of the most important decisions I ever made. She became my wife and would become the mother of our five children. We were Roman Catholic and wanted a large family. How to support our goal of a large family impacted my college decisions.

Back to College

The three years I was out of college had changed very much my understanding of human beings and their diversity. I recall thinking about why groups of people were so mean to one another. Being, or not being, a member of a particular social category seemed to be the most important consideration in defining who one was. Certainly these concerns became part of my world view. Being married made me less self-centered.

Eileen worked to supplement the income we got from the government until she was about to give birth to our first child. Somehow we got through these first years of marriage, more poverty, and my decision to return to Penn State.

My studies were easy for me now and I made practically all A grades. My first sociology course was an elective in the last year of my undergraduate program. I took an introductory sociology course from a professor, who really turned me on to sociology, then a course in social problems. That course, and its teacher, gave me the idea that sociology could be used to make human conditions better. However, it was my agricultural economics teacher who suggested I enter graduate school. This was something I had never considered. With my teacher's recommendation, the rural sociology program offered me a graduate assistantship and I started the program in the fall of 1958.

Graduate School

In graduate school at Penn State I came across the first black professor I had in my college career. He taught a sociology of family course and he used so much sociological jargon that I had a terrible time deciphering what he had to say. My problems in the course prompted him to call me to his office where he said, "Kuvlesky, I am going to give you a B in this course, though you should get a C. You should consider getting out of the graduate program." His comments motivated me to work harder and persist in the program. I have used the same strategy to challenge students in my classes.

As I neared the completion of my master's degree, I started looking for jobs. Rural sociology as a discipline places a heavy emphasis on applied research. My thesis involved research on conflict over the role definition of public school teachers. My thesis advisor had the reputation of being one of the best teachers at Penn State and, as his teaching assistant, I got the opportunity to train to teach sociology as the instructor in several introductory sociology courses.

My new aspiration was to become a sociologist and a college teacher. I entered the doctoral program in rural sociology at Penn State immediately on completion of my master's degree. I worked on a 10-year longitudinal study of young people. This research provided me with a good paying assistantship and the study was a large survey of Pennsylvania teenagers with a 10-year follow-up in early adulthood which really interested me. The data attracted me because they had possibilities for investigating social stratification and upward mobility. What social factors helped youth climb the social ladder? My sociological interests became focused as a result of working on that study. Although I didn't realize it at the time, a seminar taught by Professor Jim Copp on rural communities opened up the idea of ethnic group and ethnic relations to me. This later triggered research interests for me at Texas A&M University.

Another teacher, Bob Bealer, turned me on to sociological theory during a seminar he offered on classical theory. My new interest in the core ideas of sociology, including inequality, social stratification, social mobility, and race and ethnicity, led me to explore these ideas in the works of Karl Marx, Herbert Spencer, Émile Durkheim, and Max

Weber. These "classic theorists" were inspirations as were the writings of more contemporary sociologists Marion Levy, C. W. Mills, and Talcott Parsons. I was not the typical rural sociology graduate student interested only in applied agricultural or industrial topics. My dissertation involved a longitudinal study of how adolescent aspirations relate to early adult achievements, and I found a way to integrate the core concerns of classical sociological theory with my interest in rural youth.

Off to Texas

With supporting my family foremost in mind, we decided that we would leave Penn State before I finished my dissertation. I started looking for a job. The market for sociologists was better than it is now; Texas A&M, North Carolina State, the University of Wyoming, and Wilkes College in Pennsylvania were some of the schools I considered. I chose Texas A&M for several reasons: one of my former students had gone there and spoke well of the place, they offered more money, and they gave me a spot on a regional research project they were involved in that fitted my interest in social rank attainment.

President Kennedy had been assassinated before we took the job in Texas. Friends kept asking why we were going to such a primitive place. It is hard now to picture how strong the negative prejudices were among people in Pennsylvania. Sociologically, it isn't hard to explain our friends' ethnocentrism, but it is still astonishing.

We were sad to leave central Pennsylvania, the mountains, streams, and forests, but were eager to start a new adventure. For the first time our prospects for climbing out of the poverty we had experienced since our first year of marriage looked good. Sometimes to move up, you must move on, geographically.

We moved to Texas in a Plymouth station wagon without an air conditioner during late August. That is not a good time to move to the south. We replaced three tires on the trip and had cranky children always wanting to stop for

one good reason or another. Moving across southern Arkansas on a two-lane highway during midday was a trial. We observed a lot of black people working the fields or sitting in the shade by "shotgun" cabins in which they lived. The Civil Rights Movement was not visible in this region yet. East Texas was no better. Restrooms were still labeled "whites only." We visited one restaurant where there were two rooms for customers: the front one for whites, and the back one for black people. The rigid segregation of residential areas was apparent all the way to Texas A&M and included the surrounding area. It was easy to be judgmental and to put down the culture of this region. Yet, it also came to mind how few blacks there were at Penn State, except for athletes, and the huge black-only neighborhoods I had seen in Philadelphia and Washington, DC. This experience was instrumental in my decision to focus my Texas research on the problems of disadvantaged minority groups.

Establishing myself as a teacher and researcher was probably the most intense and exciting period of my life. I was totally involved in my work. The period from 1964 through 1974 saw my greatest period of development intellectually. I organized and taught a wide range of courses: at the undergraduate level I taught introductory sociological theory, social stratification, and rural sociology; at the graduate level I organized a seminar in advanced sociological theory. I particularly enjoyed the undergraduate theory course which was a required senior-level course with 15–20 students. I expected a lot from students and most gave back a lot and really moved themselves forward in analytical skill as well as substantive knowledge.

At this time in sociology functionalist and conflict paradigms dominated and controversies were growing in the discipline. I came to believe that these two schools of thought complemented rather than contradicted each other. In the USA in the late 1960s, new paradigms of sociology were coming to the forefront: phenomenology, critical theory, language theory, and small-group theory were viewed as formal theory by experimentalists. I recall hearing Robert Merton say at an American Sociological Association meeting that this would be good for sociology – the "let all the flowers bloom" perspective. Having been trained in rural sociology I was also interested in more applied perspectives, particularly the "diffusion and adoption" theory of intended social change ("progress") first developed by Rogers (1983) and the application of social system theory by Loomis and Beegle (1957). I firmly believed that a sociological framework could have utility for everyone.

The graduate seminar I offered could be described as a "theory of sociological theory class." For 10 years or so, this seminar was considered the capstone of our graduate program. In fact, I remember the article published by one of the editors of this book (Ballard, 1980) which first appeared as a term paper for this seminar.

I began my independent research career focusing on problems related to my dissertation topic. At that time the "war on poverty" was beginning to catch the imagination of social scientists. The very first report I produced at Texas A&M dealt with rural–urban comparisons of the extent of poverty in Texas counties (Kuvlesky and Wright, 1965). It was a pretty primitive demographic analysis that led to the generalized finding that, proportionately, poverty was more extensive in rural Texas than in the urban areas. The most extreme poverty in the state can still be found in rural "colinas" (places where new Mexican immigrants settle) in south Texas and rural "ghettos" (historic residences related to old slave quarters for blacks) in east Texas. Policy-makers responsible for rural areas found this report very useful to counteract the tendency for the government funding of the "war" to go to large metropolitan cities. This project demonstrated how social research affects social policy.

About this same time, I worked on research sponsored by the US Department of Agriculture which sought to identify variables underlying the root causes of poverty. At this time little research knowledge about status aspirations and expectations existed. In fact,

almost all the sociological research findings on this subject involved white males. Eventually 15 years of research, involving about 15 graduate students partners, produced some of the earliest research providing comparative findings by race, ethnicity, and gender as well. It was commonly believed by educators and policy makers that disadvantaged youth had little success in upward mobility because they had low status aspirations. Our research brought this belief into question as it pertains to poor youth, Black, White, or Mexican–American, relative to male and female teenage youth. We found that in general, for all these categories of youth in Texas high aspirations for education, occupation and income prevailed. We also documented that, as a general rule, boys and girls did not differ much on levels of aspiration or expected status. At the same time, we reported that there were significant differences in types of jobs by gender; girls were more oriented toward jobs such as nurses and teachers, while boys tended to select much more often skilled trades or professional jobs (becoming a lawyer or doctor).

During the mid-1970s I broadened my research focus to look at the problems faced by low-income minority families and their communities and focused more directly on intergroup relations (Kuvlesky, et al., 1982). Our research findings challenged the "pathological subculture" theory, sometimes referred to as the "self-blame" theory, about why minority people did do well in status attainment.

My Later Career

During the late 1970s I became very active in a small group of sociologists led by Al and Betty McClung Lee organized around a new paradigm we labeled "humanist sociology" (Ballard, 1980). Al Lee was a well-known activist-oriented sociologist. At about the same time he was president of the American Sociological Association he wrote the book *Toward Humanist Sociology* (1973). He was critical about the scientism of sociology-for-sale that permeated the "normal" sociology of the time. I shared his belief that the brand of sociology which was being practiced in corporate sponsored graduate training programs across the USA was less courageous, less activist, than sociology's founders had envisioned. The humanist sociology movement involved, to a large extent, sociologists who were labeled as radical, including neo-Marxists, anarchy theorists, clinical sociologists, and a variety of other fellow travelers. The experience of interacting with the members of the Association for Humanist Sociology deeply influenced my orientations toward theory, research, and teaching. One thing I had in common with the others from the start was the belief that sociology should serve the needs of the socially disadvantaged, which "normal" sociology was not doing. I view this as my Marxist orientation. All of my life experience, as I have tried to show, led me in this direction. Also I was influenced to take a broader perspective toward theory, toward historical context, and toward notions of appropriate methodology. This began to influence my writing (Kuvlesky, 1980, pp. 3–9) and definitely the subject matter I used in my courses. I moved away from a narrow perspective of empiricism ("the facts and nothing but the facts") toward more interpretive and qualitative orientations.

To be honest, I have not published much in recent years. A report I did recently (Kuvlesky, 1992) shows how I have wed my interest in ethnic relations and my humanist concerns. For the past 10 years I have been mainly a teacher and department-level administrator.

My research over the last decade has mostly involved a study of a tradition-bound (even archaic in life-style) ethnic minority, the Old Order Amish, and how they relate to the larger society. My particular focus started with a small migration stream of Old Order Amish moving into Texas since 1981, but has expanded to include several communities in Oklahoma. In the process of this self-supported research I have met many Amish families and count several as good friends. It is remarkable that this separatist group (strong in-group orientation and a lot of ethnocentrism) has been able to continue to live without electricity, phones, cars, and tractors with which to farm. They dress in very simple standardized clothing that dates back to the mid-nineteenth century and will not allow their children to attend school beyond the eighth grade. Their language in the home is a unique blend of archaic German and a small amount of English. Yet, with this increasingly divergent subculture and strong value of remaining separate from others, their numbers increase strongly every year and, from my experience, they maintain a satisfying and enjoyable attitude toward their community and themselves. They do experience some negative discrimination and are subject to some negative prejudice, but they seem to absorb these things and turn them into functional results: ways of strengthening their boundaries and motivating themselves to remain apart from others. They are sociologically important far beyond their small numbers. They demonstrate that extreme separatists with a many-faceted divergent subculture can persist in a very modern society and thrive.

I hope to do more significant writing as I move through my twilight years. My greatest aspiration is to impact positively on the quality of life of the people we label the "disadvantaged." This aspiration can only be met in small ways by me, mainly by helping different groups to understand that there is a "human condition" we all share and that only by getting along with each other can we realize the optimal conditions of life. I guess that could be called a Utopian perspective. So be it; I believe that a Utopia gives us all something to motivate the "good" that is in all of us.

Note

1. This is the title of a book for children widely read 50 years ago. All I recall about it was a little black boy sitting behind a stack of pancakes with a tiger watching him.

References

Ballard, C. C. 1980: A metasociological examination of humanist sociology. *Humanity and Society*, 4(1), 10–28.

Kuvlesky, W. P. 1979: Youth in Northern Taos County, NM: no one cares. *Humanity and Society*, 3 (3).

—— 1980: Humanist sociologies: diversity and tolerance. *Humanity and Society*, 4 (1).

—— 1992: Ethnic groups and minorities: toward conceptual harmony. College Station, TX: Texas A&M University, Race and Ethnic Studies Institute, Report II-I.

—— and Wright, D. 1965: Poverty in Texas: the distribution of low-income families. College Station, TX: Texas A&M University, Department of Agricultural Economics and Sociology, Information Report, October.

—— Knowlton, Clark S., Durant Jr, T. J. and Payne Jr, W. C. 1982: Minorities. In D. Dillman and D. Hobbs (eds) *Rural Society: Research Issues for the 1980s*. Boulder, CO: Westview Press.

Lee, A. M. 1973: *Toward Humanist Sociology*. Englewood Cliffs, NJ: Prentice-Hall.

Loomis, C. P. and Beegle, A. J. 1957: *Rural Sociology: The Strategy of Change*. Englewood Cliffs, NJ: Prentice-Hall.

Merton, R. K. 1968: *Social Theory and Social Structure*. New York: The Free Press.

Rogers, E. M. 1983: *Diffusion of Innovations*. New York: The Free Press.

Rose, P. 1981: *They and We: Racial and Ethnic Relations in the United States*, 3rd edn. New York: Random House.

The Sociological Imagination

4

From Personal Troubles to Public Issues

Glenn A. Goodwin

Whatever you have heard, or have come to think, sociology is of vital importance to all individuals desiring to come to some workable terms with their world.

(Lemert, 1995, p. ix)

From the Beginning . . .

Since the founding of sociology in the nineteenth century, the discipline has had an abiding concern with understanding the relationship between the individual (the "inside") and social structure (the "outside"), or what some have called "conciousness and society." Such classical German sociologists as Karl Marx, Georg Simmel and Max Weber, British sociologist Herbert Spencer, and the French sociologists Émile Durkheim and August Comte all addressed this question in one form or another in their work. To be sure, some of these founding scholars of sociology differed in their approaches to the issue but their collective concern for *understanding* the relationship between the person and his or her society was always central. What has also been important to the discipline from its beginning has been the attempt to "frame" this understanding in terms of the realities and problems that real, living, existential human beings face on a daily basis and how these human beings construct their sense of self and their sense of meaning.

At the time of sociology's inception, the everyday realities of most of Western humankind rotated around problems of alienation, anomie, and rising rates of personal and social disorganization generally. Thus, when Marx (1971) attempted to understand the consequences of capitalism and its associated division of labor, themes which are still of intense contemporary concern, he zeroed in on the increasing alienation of the masses. The masses of humankind, Marx argued, were experiencing their labor as forced, as possessed and controlled by others, and not as something meaningful and/or satisfying to their needs ("inside"). This, he thought, contributed to the possibility of structural change through revolution ("outside"), arguing in his later work that common existential conditions and density of interaction ("outside") would generate a class consciousness ("inside") among the masses.

Durkheim too, in his writings on suicide (1951) and on education (1956) and morals (1957) clearly spoke to many of our everyday, taken-for-granted realities. His classic study of suicide represented an important attempt at linking human motivation ("inside") to the coherence or lack thereof of social groups ("outside"). Thus he argued suicide, that "most individual of all acts," was more prevalent among bachelors than among married men because bachelors lacked the integrative and positive effects of the family group, and it was more prevalent among Protestants as opposed to Catholics because Protestants experience a much more "individualized," solitary religious ethic than do Catholics who feel part of a wider, more encompassing religious "collective conscience."

Durkheim's study of religion (1965) accomplished a similar goal by linking the nature and meaning of religious symbols to social solidarity. Thus, Durkheim tells us, religious symbols (the cross in Christianity, the star of David in Judaism, etc.) take on important meaning ("inside") because collectivities of people (Christians, Jews, etc.) invest these objects with sacred values (i.e., there is nothing *inherently* sacred about two pieces of wood crossed or a six-pointed star). When these collectivities "worship" these symbols they are, in effect, worshiping their own collective beliefs and sentiments, the result of which is to bind them together into a moral community ("outside").

Simmel also focused on the individual in interaction with the society or social groups around him or her and, like Marx and Durkheim, "grounded" his analyses in the realities of everyday life. Thus, Simmel (1921) wrote about the role of the "stranger" in society, about the city and its effect on mental health (1936), and even about the role of "fashion" in everyday life (1904) (see Chapter 27). He also presents us with essays on superordination and subordination, essays on the role of secrecy and secret societies in human life (1906), and analyses of how society is even possible (1910). Simmel's work continued the tradition of superb testimony to the necessity for understanding the interrelationship between "inside" and "outside," whether it be understanding how our feelings ("inside") about strangers in our midst help determine our group identities or group structures ("outside"), or whether it be about how moving from a rural, tightly knit community to a large, anonymous urban environment ("outside") necessitates the formation of a "blasé" attitude or personality ("inside") in order to psychologically "survive" such a transition.

Among the most vivid examples of understanding the relationship between "inside" and "outside" by way of analyzing the world of everyday reality was the work of Weber who, like Simmel, focused on the individual actor but always an actor within a socio-historical context. Thus Weber (1958) explains, for example, what it is that motivates an individual (Protestant/Calvinist) to act ("inside") and what it is that gives him or her a sense of meaning, all within particular socio-historical circumstances ("outside"). By understanding the individual Calvinist's belief in predestination (i.e., the belief that God had chosen some to go to heaven while others are condemned to burn in hell), we begin to see why and how the Calvinist becomes committed to a rational, sober, work ethic. The Calvinist comes to believe that economic success may be a sign that they are in a state of religious "grace" (for after all, God could have made them an economic failure) and they commit themselves, accordingly, to hard work, frugality, economic planning, and making profit, all in order to achieve worldly success and, of course, to convince themselves (and others) that they are among God's "chosen."

These commitments to a rational work ethic, frugality, reinvesting to make profit, economic planning, etc., all motivated essentially by a set of religious ideas ("inside"), are also necessary conditions for the emergence and development of the economic institution of capitalism ("outside"). Thus, in Weber we see clearly how ideas ("inside") relate to and even help structure institutions ("outside"). Further, the tradition of framing issues around the everyday lives of men and women continues in the work of Weber when, for example, he warns of the increasing "disenchantment" ("inside") characterizing the lives of ordinary men and women in the Occident, due primarily to the institutionalizing of rationality and the rise of bureaucracy in the West ("outside") (Weber, 1919).

Even Herbert Spencer (1884), while stressing external, evolutionary forces as determinant of individuals, was also concerned with the relationship between these forces and such "inside" phenomena as ethics, morality, and consciousness (1892–3). Spencer attempted to apply evolutionary principles articulated by Darwin to the study of human beings and society (this perspective would catch on in early American sociology and come to be known as "social Darwinism"). Thus, as with Darwin, Spencer emphasized the importance of adaptation to external ("outside") societal developments as formative of such "inside" phenomena as morality, consciousness, and even ethical positions. Also, staying true to his (Darwinian) views that only the "fit" would survive a societal "struggle for existence" and that interfering with this "natural struggle" would only disrupt or postpone societal evolution, Spencer (1940), while recognizing the effects of poverty and rising rates of social and personal disorganization on human beings, thought the state should stay out of the lives of citizens and argued to the public accordingly, i.e., that there was little role for the state in ameliorating such conditions.

These dual notions of examining the relationship between the individual and society and focusing on the problems of ordinary men and women and how they construct their sense of self and their sense of meaning, then, has been an underlying part of sociology since its inception. These kinds of questions and issues have contributed over the years to defining a sociological perspective – a way of viewing the world sociologically. They are, accordingly, suggestive of what we as sociologists should be investigating and how we should go about doing our investigations. One could go so far as to say that there is a kind of "sociological imagination" embedded in these guiding questions and issues.

The Sociological Imagination

It was the American sociologist C. Wright Mills who, from about 1945 to his untimely death in 1962, drew our attention to the idea of the "sociological imagination." Interestingly, Mills (1961, p. 12) characterized his own historical epoch as a time of "uneasiness and indifference," a characterization that has much in common with the visions of the nineteenth century expressed by the founding scholars of sociology and that may have much in common with the the way in which many of us would characterize our lives today. Mills' work is particularly important because he explicitly reminds us that, if we wish to know about the ways human beings define and

create their sense of meaning, it is necessary to examine the interrelationship between the individual and society, or what Gella et al. (1978, p. 167) call "the dialectical interplay between objective conditions and subjective existence."[1] Further, it is the cultivation and use of our sociological imaginations that allow us to get a handle on these interrelationships.

Mills (1961, p. 5) referred to the "sociological imagination" as a quality of mind that helps us develop reason in order to accurately understand what is going on in our worlds; it is a quality of mind that ". . . enables its possessor to understand the larger historical scene in terms of its meaning for the inner life and the external career of a variety of individuals." Thus, as Mills makes clear, the sociological imagination stipulates that each of us can understand our own experiences and our own sense of meaning only by first locating ourselves within society and then by becoming aware of other individuals in the same societal and/or historical circumstances. What is essential here is the realization that knowledge about "self" depends upon knowledge about *others* and about *external societal realities*. The sociological imagination, then, becomes ". . . a quality of mind that . . . promise[s] an understanding of the intimate realities of *ourselves* in connection with larger social realities" (Mills 1961, p. 15, my emphasis).

There is perhaps no clearer way to understand how ordinary men and women are intricately connected to social institutions (society), how they are actors constrained by those institutions, and how they may negotiate and/or construct meaning in their lives than by examining what Mills called "personal troubles" and "public issues." In doing so, we will also be able to see how the study of sociology can be particularly helpful in making sense of our own lives.

Personal Troubles and Public Issues

Mills (1961, pp. 8–9) tells us that "troubles" are "personal" in the sense that they occur in the character of the individual and his or her social milieu; a "trouble" is a private matter, having to do with the self, as when the values of a *particular individual* feel threatened. "Issues," on the other hand, transcend one's self and one's immediate social milieu – they are *institutional* in nature, and oftentimes involve crises in institutional arrangements. "Issues," then, are *public* matters wherein the values of publics (e.g., a nation, a community) feel threatened. The distinction between troubles and issues may be seen more clearly by commenting briefly on two developments that face most of contemporary society: poverty and divorce rates.

According to a recent (October, 1993) US census report 36.9 million people – 14.5 per cent of the total population – lived below the poverty line in the USA (the poverty threshold for a family of four in 1992 was $14,335; for one person it was $7,143). These are extraordinary numbers for a country that has, historically, been a world leader in wealth and high standards of living. It prompts the sociologist, accordingly, to ask what is going on here. Now, if the number of folk living in poverty were much lower (a few thousand perhaps), one could confidently conclude that their poverty was indeed a "personal trouble," for example, that they have no desire to live any other way; that is they choose not to work, or they have a personal inability, perhaps due to mental or physical illness, to cope with the world of work.

When however, the number living in poverty rises to over 14 per cent of the total population, one is forced to look beyond "individual psychologies" (personal troubles) for an explanation. It is somewhat absurd to argue that millions of people are inherently lazy and/or that they *choose* a life of poverty for themselves or are incapable of coping with work. To explain such extraordinary numbers we need to look beyond the "personal" to the structural (and the relationships between the two), i.e., we need to ask questions about the structure of work, the control and distribution of wealth (power), and perhaps raise questions about such major structures as the family, education, and

economic institutions. This reasoning is strengthened even further when we discover that while more than one in eight Americans live in poverty, this figure rises to an extraordinary two out of every five children. Child poverty obviously cannot be attributed to their individual psychologies (laziness or whatever). Poverty needs to be conceptualized as a *public issue* as well as a personal trouble.

We see similar examples when we examine divorce rates in various developed nations. According to a 1990 report issued by the Population Council in the USA, approximately 55 of every 100 marriages ends in divorce in the USA. Sweden has a divorce rate of 44 per 100 marriages, England and Wales almost 42, and Canada 38. Italy, meanwhile, has a divorce rate of eight per 100 marriages, Greece a rate of 12, and (former) West Germany has a rate of 29. Looking at the divorce rate, say, in the USA, it is astonishing that over half of all marriages in this particular society will end in divorce and, again, prompts the sociologist to ask "why?"

As with the example of poverty, were there only a small number of divorces occurring for every 100 marriages, such as in Italy or Greece or even (former) West Germany, one could reasonably argue that these were probably the result of the personal biographies ("troubles") of the individuals involved (they couldn't get along, didn't like each other, one or the other was neurotic, etc.). When, however, almost 55 of every 100 marriages end in divorce in the USA or when nearly 42 of every 100 marriages end in divorce in England it borders on the absurd to argue that all of these failed unions are a result of individual/ psychological troubles. We need, rather, to raise questions about the structure of marriage itself and perhaps about other areas of the institutional order as well (e.g., the family, work, economic institutions). Such high divorce rates suggest that something *structural* is going on here, i.e., we need to analyze this phenomenon as a *public issue*, as well as a personal trouble.

There is a lesson to be learned from this truncated discussion of personal troubles and public issues and it is a lesson that could be very liberating, at least to the extent that self-knowledge and self-understanding is liberating.

Sociology as Liberating

Perhaps the greatest service sociology can offer to its students is to teach them to understand the ways in which what they perceive to be their "personal troubles" may in fact be "public issues", how their own biographies – their loves, their demons – are oftentimes those of many others. Even more importantly, once the student understands his or her connection to "others," to social structure, he or she understands the ways in which that structure both creates those demons and how that structure might be changed to alleviate them.[2]

The student who comes to understand that his or her feeling of intimidation in the classroom ("everyone is smarter than me," "my question is dumb") is a feeling shared by most of his or her peers is on the road to liberation and self-enlightenment; the student discovering that common experiences of alienation (powerlessness, meaninglessness, etc.) are related to the system of examination hurdles and college bureaucracy has exercised potentially emancipatory sociological imagination. Though they may not know it, they are also on their way to thinking sociologically – to using their sociological imaginations. For in both cases what students initially felt to be a "personal trouble" begins to get translated into a "public issue" and, before long, the student will begin to ask questions about the educational institution in contemporary society ("why is learning an alienating experience?," "what is there about the educational structure that promotes negative self-feeling?"). These questions, in turn, can lead to strategies that might be utilized to change this very institution.

A classic example of the "liberating" effects of such a sociological understanding occurred in the 1960s and 1970s among many women in the western world. Having felt for decades that it was their own individual peculiarity (their own "personal trouble") that they desired more than a husband and family (perhaps a career, equal pay for equal work, entrance into male dominated spheres of work and professions, etc.), women began to talk to each other. In doing so they discovered their "sisterhood," i.e., they discovered they shared similar feelings and aspirations and a movement (the "women's movement") was launched, a movement that began to press for institutional change in all areas of equal rights for women. The liberating of many women in the 1960s and 1970s was an exercise in the sociological imagination: *personal troubles had been translated into public issues*. Surely a field of study has no higher calling than furthering the cause of human emancipation as far as possible. The American sociologist Alvin Gouldner (1920–80) captured this vision of sociology when he wrote (1973, p. 126):

. . . sociology should be, on the one side, instrumental to the furtherance of human emancipation. On the other, such a sociology would be an end in itself, embodying the ancient human aspiration for self-knowledge. If that is not a high calling, than none is.

Practicing the craft of sociology, then, is about more than analyzing data and memorizing facts. In learning how to distinguish between personal troubles and public issues and, when justified, learning how to translate *personal troubles into public issues*, the student is empowered to work toward changing the conditions that give rise to many social problems and a great deal of human anguish. And, just as important, the student of sociology also acquires essential tools that can be utilized to make sense out of his or her own life or, as Max Weber put it, the student can learn to give ". . . himself an *account of the ultimate meaning of his own conduct*" (in Gerth and Mills, 1963, p. 152, emphasis in the original). One is hard pressed to find any more noble a calling for a craft than to be able to say that it is emancipating and self-enlightening for its students. This is part of the classic "promise" of sociology and anyone willing to seriously study its subject matter will be so rewarded.

Notes

1. I have argued elsewhere that this is also a fundamental tenet for what is referred to generally as "humanistic sociology" (cf. Goodwin, 1983, p. 229).

2. In an earlier article I developed this theme as to how it could impact the teaching of sociology generally (cf. Goodwin, 1987).

References

Durkheim, É. 1951: *Suicide: A Study in Sociology*. Glencoe, Ill.: The Free Press.

——1956: *Education and Sociology* (translated by S. D. Fox). Glencoe, Ill.: The Free Press.

—— 1957: *Professional Ethics and Civic Morals* (translated by C. Brookfield). London: Routledge & Kegan Paul.

—— 1965: *The Elementary Forms of the Religious Life* (translated from the French by Joseph Ward Swain). New York: The Free Press.

Gella, A., Jansen, S. Curry and Sabo Jr, D. F. 1978: *Humanism in Sociology: Its Historical Roots and Contemporary Problems*. Washington, DC: University Press of America.

Gerth, H. H., and Mills, C. Wright (eds) 1963: *From Max Weber: Essays in Sociology*. New York: Oxford University Press, Sixth Galaxy Printing.

Goodwin, G. A. 1983: Toward a paradigm for humanistic sociology. *Humanity and Society*, 7(August), 219–37.

—— 1987: Humanistic sociology and the craft of teaching. *Teaching Sociology*, 15(January), 15–20.

Gouldner, A. W. 1973: *For Sociology: Renewal and Critique in Sociology Today*. New York: Basic Books.

Lemert, C. 1995: *Sociology After the Crisis*. Boulder, CO: Westview Press.

Marx, K. 1971 [1848]: *The Communist Manifesto*, 11th printing. New York: Washington Square Press.

Mills, C. Wright. 1961: *The Sociological Imagination*, First Evergreen edition, 4th printing. New York:

Oxford University Press.

Simmel, G. 1896: Superiority and subordination as subject-matter of sociology, *The American Journal of Sociology*, II (2), 167–89.

—— 1936 [1902–03]: The metropolis and mental life. *Second-Year Course in the Study of Contemporary Society (Social Science II), Syllabus and Selected Readings*. Chicago: University of Chicago Bookstore, 221–38.

—— 1904: Fashion. *International Quarterly*, 10(1), October, 130–55.

—— 1906: The sociology of secrecy and of secret societies. *The American Journal of Sociology*, XI (4), 441–98.

—— 1921 [1908]: The sociological significance of the stranger, In Robert E. Park and Ernest W. Burgess (eds), *Introduction to the Science of Sociology*. Chicago: University of Chicago Press.

—— 1910: How is society possible? *The American Journal of Sociology*, XVI (3), 372–91.

Spencer, H. 1884: *First Principles*, 5th edition. London: Williams & Margate.

—— 1892–3: *Principles of Ethics*. New York: Appleton.

—— 1940: *The Man versus the State*, Coldwell, ID, The Craxton Printers.

Weber, M. 1919: Science as a vocation. In Gerth and Mills (eds), *From Max Weber: Essays in Sociology*. New York: Oxford University Press, 129–56.

—— 1958: *The Protestant Ethic and the Spirit of Capitalism* (translated by Talcott Parsons). New York: Charles Scribner's Sons.

Suggestions for Further Reading

Mills, C. Wright, 1961: Chapter 1, The promise; and Appendix, On intellectual craftmanship. In *The Sociological Imagination*. New York: Oxford University Press, pp. 3–24, 195–226, respectively.

Berger, P. Chapter 1, Sociology as an individual pastime; and Chapter 8, Sociology as a humanistic discipline. In *Invitation to Sociology*. New York: Anchor Books, pp. 1–24, 164–76, respectively.

5

From Public Issues to Personal Troubles

Martin Shaw

Humans are social beings. We live our lives in and through interactions and relationships with others. We fashion these interactions and relationships and with it our individuality. Yet we often perceive our lives to be structured by larger social forces. To many people "society" is something out there, an external force shaping their lives. This view is encouraged by the ways politicians and journalists talk about social issues. Individual problems are often ones about which it is argued that "society should do something". Alternatively it is sometimes claimed that many issues are nothing to do with society – in Margaret Thatcher's view "there is no such thing as society" – but are purely the responsibility of individuals. Either way, it is as though society was separate from the individual people who make it up.

This way of thinking has gained credibility because there are so many things that seem to *happen to* people and appear outside their control. A fundamental reason for this is that societies are highly complex. Many social relationships are now global in character: we are part of global markets, production systems and communication networks. World society and the world economy are so huge and varied that even the most powerful governments and corporations hardly seem to control what is going on. Ordinary people certainly cannot affect them, it seems. Another reason for the separation of "society" from "the individual" is, however, the fact that power is concentrated in élite groups. Ordinary people's sense of power-

lessness is heightened by the sense that the capacity to make key decisions belongs to small minorities, usually operating through highly complex bureaucratic structures. To most people, these structures seem barely penetrable. They see them as forces outside themselves.

The "big" questions about society seem so separate from small questions which people feel they can affect directly – what happens in their family, workplace and immediate locality – that they are seen as a "public" sphere distinguished from their "private" personal lives. Most people, most of the time, are concerned overwhelmingly with their private existence. The public sphere is distant, something of which they are aware through mass media but not actively concerned about. The minorities of people who are concerned enough to do something – "activists" who actually contest what governments, corporations and other big organizations are up to – are often seen as people apart.

In the next section I shall look further at how people experience public issues as something separate from individual actions and how this can often result in *mis*perceptions of the nature and causes of large-scale social structures and events. I shall illustrate this with different kinds of public issue, but will focus particularly on war, which is the public issue *par excellence*. Then in the final section I turn to the question of how sociological perspectives may enhance our understanding of public issues, enabling us to see how they are rooted in human actions and thus improving our chances of bringing them under control.

Public Issues and Personal Troubles

In this section I shall look at three examples of "public issues" each of which may be said to represent a different kind of issue. First I shall discuss unemployment which is a public issue constituted by the accumulation of individual personal troubles (poverty is another, closely related example). Then I shall look at environmental degradation, as a set of troubles caused – sometimes quite indirectly – by public economic activity. Finally, I shall consider war, which is a very different sort of public issue: a quintessentially collective action, undertaken traditionally by public authorities which are regarded as "legitimate", but also by other organized groups seeking to establish their power and make it legitimate.

Unemployment is generally discussed in terms of abstract representations, unemployment "figures" and unemployment "rates" (i.e. the percentages of the labour force registered as unemployed). But these notions clearly represent *individuals* who are out of work. You can't have unemployment without there being individuals who are unemployed, and by extension families and local communities which are blighted. These public issues are actually *constituted by* personal troubles.

Thus what is generally seen as an impersonal, large-scale structure (called "unemployment") actually refers to the way the individual experiences of large numbers of people are not purely random, but are patterned and organized. Although no individual's experience of unemployment is exactly identical to another's, it is useful to generalize about rises and falls in the level of unemployment in so far as this reflects some common elements in people's experiences of human interaction. This is what sociologists mean by "social structure", but as we can see from this example, "structure" is not just a problem for social theorists: ordinary people have pictures

of society and have structure-type ideas of how it works.

What is interesting, in these cases, is the way in which the representation of unemployment by numbers and ratios turns them into public issues in an abstract sense, while the real social misery involved is often hidden and unexamined. There are a number of things for sociologists to explore in such issues. One is the way in which many people relate to the plight of others – who are often their near-neighbours – through the strange mechanism of contemplating a rise or fall in the unemployment figures and percentages on the television news. Another, more fundamental, is the way in which the troubles of so many people are presented as almost "natural" problems, fluctuating like the weather. Although publication of the figures is usually accompanied by assertions and denials of government responsibility, the social processes which lead to millions of people being out of work – the policies of governments and employers, the operation of markets, etc. – are rarely explained.

"The environment" is a different sort of public issue. For a start, it is not one issue but many. There are some very big issues, like climatic warming and the depletion of the ozone layer, which are manifestly global in character. In principle, they affect all human beings, and this is what is meant by calling them "global". There are also some small, "local" issues, like the pollution of a river or the plan to build a road through a beauty spot. Although these are part of wider patterns of industrial activity or motorway development, they take the form of local issues because they affect people in a particular area in definite ways.

In fact, even "global" issues affect people very differently, and not just because of geography. People whose lives and lifestyles depend on the weather in different ways are variably affected by climatic changes. People who work indoors and live in solid brick-built houses in England may be hardly affected by climatic changes – or may even be affected for the better. For every "abnormal" climatic event, like the 1987 hurricane in southern

England, there may be numerous warmer summers and milder winters which improve the overall quality of life. For subsistence farmers on the brink of encroaching desert in Africa, however, climatic change may be literally a life–or–death matter. Or take the prospect of rising sea levels due to global warming. For people in low-lying districts of Holland, this may indicate the need to improve their sea-defences; for people in Bangladesh, where millions of the world's poorest people live in areas already regularly flooded by the sea, and where the government may not have the resources to erect huge barriers, rising sea-levels may spell disaster.

Environmental issues are "issues" precisely because of how they affect people. They may affect them either directly, or because they affect other life forms which people care about. Pollution matters not because of changes in nature as such, but because the changes affect people and the things that matter to them. Sociologists explore the ways in which communities are affected and how they articulate their protests against changes they don't like.

Part of sociological study is to examine the ideas and organization of social movements like environmentalism, including exploring the contradictions between abstract ideals like "saving the planet" and the realities of how people's lives are affected by environmental change. An important task for sociologists is to examine the kinds of circumstances in which people stop accepting the changes as "inevitable" and start to look for ways to affect outcomes. We try to identify the point at which people stop experiencing public issues as separate from their own lives or as completely beyond their control. We are interested in when they see public issues in a more positive light, as problems about which something can be done because they have been brought about by the interplay of human activities. Sociologists emphasize that humans are social beings: we live our lives in and through relationships with others. Moreover, social relationships are arenas for human creativity – which is limitless. This means that although social structures often seem univer-sal and invariable, they are in fact subject to human intervention and change.

Unemployment, poverty and environmental problems are on-going, permanent components of many individual experiences – and hence of society – in most parts of the globe. War, on the other hand, is generally seen as an exceptional experience, not a normal part of everyday life (although for people in some parts of the world it has been a part of everyday life for decades). Wars are seen as crises which happen to society, upturning normal patterns of life and throwing individuals and families into abnormal situations. As far as most people in the West are concerned, wars don't come from within society. They happen as a result of conflicts in international politics, *between* governments and societies rather than within them. We tend to forget that even England (in the seventeenth century) and America (in the nineteenth) have experienced civil wars centred on deep conflicts within national societies.

Often wars may seem inexplicable, and this sense is heightened by the fact that generally people know even less about international relations than other areas of politics. Domestic politics centre on issues that people often know about from their own experience – unemployment and environmental problems are examples – but international politics are exotic. They involve people in "far-off lands of which we know little" (Prime Minister Neville Chamberlain's notorious description of Czechoslovakia in 1938 could just as well describe Bosnia, Afghanistan or Angola today). They involve people who speak different languages, whose names we cannot pronounce and of whose politics and cultures we are largely ignorant. Even closely related cultures and polities can seem strange and impenetrable (as Northern Ireland does to most English people).

In the history of most western societies, wars have been either limited, distant events in which "our" soldiers have taken part, or major catastrophes engulfing the whole organization of society and all the individual lives within it. Some "limited" conflicts have of course had profound effects, as the Vietnam War did on

American society. It is "total" wars, however, in which both violence and social mobilization are maximized, which have been our chief source of memories of and beliefs about war. Twice in the twentieth century, world wars have catapulted the peoples of Europe, North America and Asia into total conflicts. Many regions of the world were invaded, conquered and fought over by land armies; others (like Britain) were threatened and bombarded from the air. Tens of millions of soldiers and civilians died, more were displaced and became refugees. The whole organization of society was radically changed by war-mobilization. The life experiences of survivors, whether combatants or civilians, were indelibly marked.

War has appeared as a traumatic experience in people's lives. The shock of war was most palpable after 1914, because prior to that there had been a long period without major European wars, and ways of life which had previously changed much more gradually were exposed to sudden upheaval. The pre-war order later became idealized in Western culture as a golden age, the "Edwardian era" or "la belle époque", the calm before the storm. The sense of dramatic change was important for individuals as well. For many young people who survived World War II – especially in victorious and uninvaded countries like the USA, Britain and Australia where many were spared the worst horrors which affected people in continental Europe and Asia – their war experience was one of heroism, danger and comradeship unmatched in their later lives. Despite the hardships and sheer boredom of war, survivors' experiences have often been idealized in personal memories and images. As these people have grown old, a culture of commemoration, centred on the many anniversaries of key events, has catered for their nostalgia for these formative experiences.

Despite this relatively cosy representation of war in some western societies, war maintains its capacity to shock and threaten. People still have deep fears of war, however far away, because wars still seem mysterious in origin and unknown in their capacity to involve us in

danger. The Falklands War of 1982, for example, erupted "out of the blue" so far as British people were concerned. Most probably did not know where the Falklands Islands were before Argentina invaded. Nor did most people in the USA or Britain have much inkling of Iraq's dispute with Kuwait before its armies invaded in 1990. And yet within weeks or months of these events, western forces were at war in the Gulf region.

Although both these conflicts were – to those who understood and knew what was going on – inherently limited conflicts, most people *did not* fully understand, and *could not* know for certain. Many fears were therefore generated. Research carried out by the present author showed that some schoolchildren worried that Saddam Hussein might actually launch missile attacks on Britain. They did not know that Iraq had no missiles with the capacity to reach British cities. Many students (and some of their parents) worried that if the Gulf war went on for any length of time, conscription would be reintroduced: young men would be forced to go and fight and would possibly be killed. They did not know that the war had been carefully planned to be quick, that sufficient professional troops were available, and that the British government and military alike would hardly want to reintroduce untrained conscripts during the conflict. Many old people, who saw in the enemy leader the reincarnation of Adolf Hitler (as many newspapers portrayed Saddam Hussein), feared a repeat of the aerial bombing and other horrors of 1939–45. They did not always understand that, however awful Saddam's regime, its military capacity and expansionist ambitions were far less than those of Nazi Germany (Shaw, 1996).

However irrational many of these views appeared from the point of view of the knowledgeable, they were highly intelligible given the way in which the events were depicted in the more popular mass media, the lack of prior knowledge and understanding, and the images of war left by the world wars. They highlighted the fact that, even in situations where saturation media coverage provided huge amounts of information, many people lacked the capacity to make sense of it. War, as a public issue, remained baffling and therefore profoundly worrying. Much of the anxiety at the beginning of each conflict, when the outcome was unknown, subsided somewhat as news reports reassured audiences that the campaigns were progressing successfully and without large numbers of casualties on "our" side.

The casualties on the "enemy" side were minimized, especially in the Gulf war where tens of thousands of Iraqi soldiers and thousands of civilians were killed. In each war, however, issues arose which punctured the sanitized picture of the effects of "our" campaigns: the sinking of the Argentine cruiser *General Belgrano*, and the bombing of the civilian shelter at Amiriya, a suburb of Baghdad. Military and politicians, with the aid of mass media, had to explain away the apparently unnecessary mass killings involved in these events, to make them less troubling to audiences.

Most wars today involve troops from western countries not as combatants but as peace enforcers. These are wars in which all sides are often mysterious, and in which media compound people's lack of comprehension by dismissing both victims and perpetrators as "the warring parties", or by labelling them in "ethnic" terms. So, for example, the genocide in which probably over half a million people were killed in Rwanda in 1994 was presented on western television largely as a tribal slaughter of Tutsi by Hutus. The politics of the conflict, and the fact that some Hutu who opposed the regime were also victims, were not explained. Even in the much-covered Bosnian war (1992–5), genocide was often obscured for most media consumers in western countries. The aftermaths of killings, rapes, dispossessions and abuses were sometimes shown, but they were often not very fully explained or discussed in mainstream news bulletins which "ordinary" viewers watch (still less in tabloid papers). Except for brief moments when particularly appalling events made the headlines, many members of media audiences remained largely in ignorance of what was happening. Even at these moments

they may have had difficulty in making sense of what was going on. This has been even more true of most other wars, which have had less coverage than Bosnia.

In the discussion of the Falklands and Gulf wars, above, I emphasized the insecurity and fear which stem from poverty of understanding. The genocidal character of recent conflicts, in which massacres and expulsions of civilians have been the main aims of violence, remind us however that knowing and understanding do not necessarily bring reassurance. Like the Nazi Holocaust against the Jews, Rwanda and Bosnia underline the fact that to know the full extent of the evils which one group of human beings can inflict on another only raises very difficult questions for those who know. Understanding things such as these is not easy, and coming to terms with them emotionally may still be a problem even when we believe we understand.

Despite these important reservations, knowledge and understanding are still very much to be aimed for. They are essential prerequisites for properly coming to terms with, and doing something about, the horrendous things which happen in war. In the remainder of this chapter I want to try to suggest some of the ways in which sociologists approach this task, and thus elucidate the personal troubles which these largest of public issues entail.

Explaining Public Issues

Sociological explanations of public issues generally centre on the concept of structure: how individual action is organized by social relations. The idea that social action is structured means that it is patterned and organized, not purely random. The problem that this concept poses is, however, the conflict between freedom and determinism. If social life is structured, how can individuals be free to make their own lives? Or if individuals can be creative in their relationships, how can we claim that social action is structured?

Much thinking has gone into trying to resolve these issues. Some writers have seen social structures as highly determining; others have emphasized freedom. Many have tried to catch the dynamic relationships between constraints and creativity. Marx wrote that "men make history, but only under conditions given from the past". More recently, Giddens (1984) has put forward his theory of "structuration", according to which structures are the patterns formed in people's action. In his view, there is a dual interaction: people's actions simultaneously shape and reshape the structures, and are shaped and reshaped by them.

Because of the importance of looking at social action from the point of view of the actors, and emphasizing creativity, many theoretical approaches in sociology privilege small-scale social contexts. These approaches often fail to get to grips with the macro-structures of modern society or explaining public issues of the kind we have been discussing. It sometimes seems as though to deal with large-scale processes inevitably reduces the significance of actors, and so there is reluctance to engage with these problems. It is as though "big" issues are opaque to some sociologists, just as they often seem to many "ordinary" members of society. In addition, among sociologists who deal with public issues, these are often matters of considerable controversy. Cross-cutting the more obvious political differences are often important intellectual disagreements. In this final section I cannot give a definitive account of major approaches, but I can provide some examples of the different ways in which sociologists explain macro–issues.

One approach which has no inhibitions about tackling large-scale issues is Marxism, which was very influential in social theory between the 1960s and 1980s. Marxism is still an important reference point in many debates even if fewer sociologists would now call themselves Marxists. Although there are major differences among Marxists as well as between them and other sociologists, they operate within a common theoretical discourse centred on concepts of the capitalist mode of production. Marxists have developed accounts of war, for example, which see it as arising from the conflicts generated by imperialism – the tendency of capitalist states, rooted in the dynamics of expansion in production, to spill over national boundaries (a classic statement is given by Sweezy, 1968). For Marxists, wars have arisen chiefly because of conflicts either between rival imperialisms (like the world wars) or between imperialisms and oppressed nationalities (wars of national liberation). Marxist accounts stress war's roots in political economy, but also include theories of the state and of ideologies like nationalism and racism through which states mobilize people for war.

Other macro-sociologists look more to Weber than to Marx and argue that Marxists are too prone to reduce states and ideologies to economic forces. Giddens (1985) sees war-making as a distinct "institutional cluster" of activities in society, separate from capitalism, industrialism and the internal "surveillance" side of the state. He is one of a group of theorists who have argued that we have to understand the distinctiveness of war-making as a social activity. Skocpol (1979), for example, has studied the three major revolutions of modern times – the French, Russian and Chinese. While other social theorists and historians, including Marxists, have explained revolutions in terms of class contradictions in these societies, Skocpol argues that warfare was a critical factor in precipitating them. War – and in the French case, the costs of war – produced crises of state power which made revolutionary upheavals possible. Mann (1986, 1993) is writing a major historical sociology of the state, and has argued that it is historically constituted by war – that is what state finances have been about throughout the last millennium. Kaldor (1982) makes Giddens' point in Marxist language, arguing that there is a "mode of warfare" analogous to but highly distinct from the "mode of production". For all these writers, the state as an organization claiming a territorial monopoly of legitimate violence (Weber's definition) is more important than economic factors.

Ironically, many people who study international relations would argue that the state has become relatively less important. Most wars today are not between states, but are civil wars, increasingly involving struggles for power in which leaders mobilize identity politics, understood in ethnic terms. Thus a different sort of explanation is becoming seen as relevant to explaining wars – and many other macro-social issues – today. The twin pivots of this new explanation are "modernity" and "globalization". Giddens (1991) has argued that modernity involves constant flux in which individuals have to re-invent their self-identities continuously. For some writers, this leads to what is called "post-modernity", since identities are no longer "objectively" determined by the key perameters of "modern" society (such as nationality and class) but are (subjectively) chosen from an infinite range within an ever-expanding and diverse cultural universe.

There is some agreement that new problems of identity have been reinforced by the processes of "globalization" of economic, cultural and political life. These dissolve old national boundaries and lead people to seek new definitions of who they are. This in turn may lead to people forming new political communities, and hence to conflict. Many would argue that these kinds of changes better explain "new" wars like that in Bosnia. There some people reacted to the collapse of the old state (with its dominant "Yugoslav" and "Communist" versions of identity) by reasserting old ethnic roots, while others (especially in the cities) affirmed new pluralist visions of society in which people might claim several different identities at the same time. The war could be seen not just as a conflict between "ethnic nationalisms" but also as a war of ethnic nationalism against pluralist democratic values.

In this brief overview of macro-sociological approaches we have seen an interesting shift from "systemic" approaches such as Marxism, which define change within closely structured perameters, to looser approaches offering more emphasis on flux and creativity in social life. Both sorts of approach offer people the possibility of understanding and controlling problems, such as war, which appear to be outside their control. Marxism suggests that control can come through asserting given identities, through developing working-class consciousness as an alternative to nationalism and war. Approaches based on modernity (in Giddens' sense) and post-modernity stress that identity is more open, and can be defined by the people involved. So nationalism and racism are choices which can be countered by democratic, cosmopolitan, feminist and many other kinds of alternative identities and values.

What all sociological approaches find difficulty in coming to terms with is the sheer violence and brutality of war. It is relatively easy to understand why someone should identify themselves as a Serb or a Croat, but why does this entail that he then joins in butchering people who have lived alongside him for decades? There are no easy answers to such questions. Sociological analyses have emphasized the roles of economic and political insecurities, peer pressure and the breaking-down of conventional morality and social constraints. But sociology will continue to be challenged, where the most demanding of public issues intersect with the worst personal troubles. The challenge is one for the reader, as well as the author, to take up.

References

Giddens, A. 1984: *The Constitution of Society: Outline of the Theory of Structuration.* Cambridge: Polity.
—— 1985: *The Nation-State and Violence.* Cambridge: Polity.
—— 1991: *Modernity and Self-Identity.* Cambridge: Polity.
Kaldor, M. 1982: "Warfare and capitalism". In

Thompson, E. P. et al. (eds), *Exterminism and Cold War.* London: Verso.
Mann, M. 1986, 1993: *The Sources of Social Power,* Vols I and II. Cambridge: Cambridge University Press.
Mills, C. W. 1961: *The Sociological Imagination.* London: Penguin.
Shaw, M. 1996: *Civil Society and Media in Global*

Crises: Representing Distant Violence. London: Pinter.

Skocpol, T. 1979: *States and Social Revolutions.* Cambridge: Cambridge University Press.

Sweezy, P. M. 1968: *The Theory of Capitalist Development*. London: Monthly Review.

The Public Impact of Sociology

6

The Black Report and the Politics of Health in Britain

Nicky Hart

Social Class and the Stratification of Health and Survival in Britain

The Black Report[1] is a study of class differences in health in the British population. Drawing principally on the government's own routine statistics of sickness and death, it shows that material living standards – wealth, income, work and living conditions are the principal determinants of health, sickness and death in Britain. It was published in 1980 and takes account of statistical trends from the beginning of the twentieth century up to the early 1970s. These data suggested a current worsening of class inequality in mortality risk, and further government statistics issued since testify to a continued widening of the gap in life expectancy between middle- and working-class men, women and children in Britain.

The Black Report was a government-sponsored review of health inequality. It was commissioned in 1977 by the government health minister who appointed a team of two sociologists and one epidemiologist to examine the persisting pattern and possible worsening trend of social class inequalities in health in Britain. The group was chaired by Sir Douglas Black, then chief government medical scientist in Britain, and assisted by a full-time research fellow – a medical sociologist on secondment from the University of Essex – myself. The membership of the working group might be called bidisciplinary – a collaboration of sociological and medical researchers. At its meetings, held at the Department of Health in London, the government's own technical specialists (social scientists and epidemiologists) were present for consultation and advice.

There was never any question that the final report of the working group would be anything other than sociologically oriented. It shows how far a sociological perspective and research tools can break through the particularities of individual medical experience to reveal health as a collective phenomenon shaped by processes of societal development and by policies of socio-economic distribution and redistribution. Max Weber introduced the term *life chances* to depict the *substance* of social class, to stand for all the interconnected aspects of material life distributed by the market mechanism of industrial capitalism. The Black Report demonstrates that even health and mortality (apparently biological attributes of human beings) are primarily the product of social and economic life – that besides identifying the material resources of individuals and households, *life chances* also encompasses the chance to exist itself. It achieves this by showing that measures of socio-economic inequality (wealth, income, living and working conditions) are the strongest determinants of human growth and of the risk of sickness and death in the population. In fact, social class is a far more powerful determinant of survival than access to the expertise of modern physicians or to the "high-tech" facilities of modern hospitals.

In the Black Report, social class is measured by occupation, a statistical indicator pioneered by social surveyors and government statisticians in Britain more than a century ago.[2] By dividing the British population into six broad occupation sectors arranged hierarchically according to working conditions, wages and salaries, it is possible to measure the incidence of sickness and death experienced in each sector.[3] The resulting averages are known respectively as class morbidity and mortality rates and in the latter case, have been calculated in the UK following every census so that trends in health inequality may be monitored throughout the twentieth century.[4] Because occupational class is routinely incorporated as a measure in British official statistics, it has always been among the central indicators employed by epidemiologists searching for the social correlates and causes of disease and premature death. For the same reason, British epidemiology ranks among the most *sociologically* sophisticated in the world. This is reflected in the sociological orientation of the Black Report which emerges not because sociologists outnumbered other experts, but because medical researchers in the UK are equally at home with measures of class and equally aware of its power to shape health and disease.

The twentieth century has witnessed tremendous improvements in the health of people living in industrial capitalist societies. Sociological techniques for studying the aggregate health properties of a population reveal that the human body has increased its stature and durability in response to the rise in living standards fuelled by the advancing capitalist economy. They also show that health, like wealth is shared unequally within national populations. The same pattern is found in all industrial societies where public authorities routinely gather and publish relevant data. Social inequality is not merely a matter of financial wealth or social honour. It enters into the growth and development processes of human beings from conception, through infancy, childhood and adult life shaping the chance for vitality and disease, programming the ageing of the body and setting the probable timing of its death.

Explaining Health Inequality and Conceiving Preventive Policies

Although the research for the Black Report was sponsored by the British government, its findings were to prove very controversial.

The working group had been set the following objectives.

(i) To assemble available information about differences in health status among the social classes and about factors which might contribute to these, including relevant data from other industrial countries.

(ii) To analyse the material in order to identify possible causal relationships, to examine the hypotheses that have been formulated and the testing of them, and to assess the general implications for policy.

(iii) To suggest what further research might be initiated.

In response to the first of these objectives, as already noted, the Black Report testified to the persisting even worsening trend of class inequalities in health in Britain. It assembled striking evidence of higher morbidity and higher mortality among manual (blue collar) classes in the population. A single statistic helps bring home the gravity of this inequality in the UK – measuring differences in the risk of death from birth to age 65, the child of the unskilled manual worker will die around seven years earlier than a counterpart born to professional parents. Between these two most and least privileged classes, further inequalities stratified the life chances of the intermediate classes. The health of the British people strongly conformed to a pattern of relative deprivation with additional increments of health advantage and disadvantage separating each of the six social classes. Figure 6.1, taken from the report, illustrates this pattern.

A gloomy conclusion emerges from this evidence, for it seemed to prove that the British welfare state had made little or no progress in equalizing life chances (in this most fundamental sense) in the post-World War II era. If anything the health gap separating the

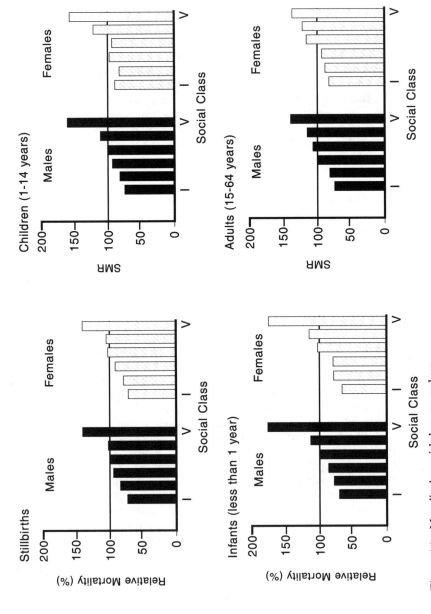

Figure 6.1 Mortality by social class, age and sex.
Source: *Occupational Mortality* 1970–2 (HMSO, London, 1978). Crown copyright 1995. Reproduced by permission of the Controller of HMSO and of the Office for National Statistics.

classes had widened over the preceding half century suggesting that the National Health Service which had been introduced in 1948, more than 30 years previously, had failed to achieve its promise to equalize opportunities for health and survival in the population.

This conclusion held implications for the second objective, the explanation of the causes of class inequalities in health. Orthodox health policies concentrating on widening access to skilled medical advice and treatment had not succeeded. In fact they might even have made inequalities worse. As health economist Julian LeGrand argued in his *Strategy of Equality*, it was the middle not the working classes that had derived most benefit from welfare state provision in housing, education and health because they made the most exhaustive use of their entitlements.[5] If equalizing access to medical care was not the answer, what was? The Black Report strongly favoured a materialist explanation. The working group argued that the continuing pattern of relative health deprivation could only be satisfactorily explained by differences of livelihood and living standards – *livelihood* in the sense of job type, working conditions and employment security, *living standards* in the sense of income and consumer power. Alternative explanations proposing that health advantage/disadvantage might be due to natural selection processes,[6] to psychological or behavioural traits, or lack of education were either judged to be peripheral or to be the secondary effect of underlying inequalities in command over material resources.

This led the working group to the conclusion that orthodox health policy initiatives in the sphere of medical care were insufficient to reverse the patterns and trends uncovered in the report. In their judgement, the growth and development of the human body was a material process inseparable from all other aspects of material life. A government pledge to equalize opportunities for health among citizens could therefore only hope to be fulfilled by policies which recognized the linkages between health and economic sufficiency and security. The working group recommended that government departments concerned with employment, income and the cost of living should be made aware of the implications of their policy decisions for the distribution of health in the community. Although the report recognized the need to conduct further research to document the mechanisms articulating material inequality and health deprivation, its authors accepted that enough was already known about the causal links between class and health to be confident that only policies addressing problems of livelihood, security and income maintenance would be capable of redressing the pattern of severe health deprivation they had revealed. Moreover, on the grounds that material deprivation in early life threatens the healthy development of the human body, they gave particular emphasis to the importance of ensuring that family households with children should be the primary target of strengthened initiatives in the sphere of income maintenance. Poverty in childhood was the surest foundation of health deprivation later in life and government would need to declare a "war on poverty", particularly child poverty, if it genuinely wished to see a narrowing of the gap in life expectancy between the social classes. Around this recommendation there was complete unanimity between the group's social and medical scientists.

Politics and Sociological Knowledge

The government's response to these recommendations was expressed in the foreword to the report authored by the minister responsible for health when it first appeared as a government publication in 1980:

I must make it clear that additional expenditure on the scale which could result from the report's recommendations – the amount involved could be upwards of £2 billion per year – is quite unrealistic in present or any foreseeable economic circumstances, quite apart from any judgement that may be formed of the effectiveness of such expenditure in dealing with the problems identified. I cannot therefore endorse the group's recommendations.

The minister's hostility to the working group's findings may seem strange considering that the report was a government commission and that the drift of its major empirical conclusions were anticipated. Health inequalities have been known in Britain since vital rates were first registered in the middle of the nineteenth century. The report's major findings were based on the government's own routine statistics, and there was never any doubt but that the working group would find disturbing evidence of persisting trends in health inequality. Indeed the Department of Health did not need to hire experts to interpret these data. Its own very able team of social and medical statisticians could have done the job perfectly well. What then was the point of setting up an inquiry into health deprivation, if there was never any political will to do anything about it?

The answer to this question partly lies in the changing political climate of Britain at the end of the 1970s. The interval between the commissioning of research and the publication of findings was a turbulent period in British politics. In 1979 the electorate dismissed the former Labour government whose health minister commissioned the study and swept into power a new look Conservative Party led by Britain's first female prime minster, Margaret Thatcher. The new government was dedicated to a programme of public expenditure cuts and economic liberalization. It was certainly *not* disposed to uncover, let alone remedy long-standing health inequities which had withstood the welfare state initiatives of the post-war era.

This reality was manifested in the new secretary of state's handling of the Black Report when it landed on his desk in April 1980:

(i) The publication of the report was delayed until August during the summer parliamentary recess at a time which seemed designed to minimize political and public debate of its contents.

(ii) The report was made difficult to obtain – a very short print run of only 250 copies were produced and then only made available on application to the Department of Health and Social Security.

(iii) No press conference was called to publicize the report, to increase its dissemination and promote discussion.

(iv) The secretary of state wrote a foreword to the report purporting to summarize the report's conclusions and alleging that the working group had declared the causes of health inequalities to be too numerous and complex to be disentangled.[7]

The working group responded to what it saw as a political attempt to silence its voice by organizing its own press conference as the report became available. The members of the group were remarkably unanimous and at this event they accused the government of attempting to hide the problem of health inequality by restricting circulation of the report and deliberately misrepresenting its conclusions "in the claim that health inequalities were complex and did not permit of simple solutions." If the government minister responsible for health intended to limit the report's circulation, his attempt backfired, for the national press, scenting a real controversy, packed their columns with stories of the report the government tried to suppress.

It is impossible to predict what the fate of the Black Report might have been had the Labour government retained power into the 1980s. It is unlikely that a Labour minister for health would have dismissed the working group's recommendations in so summary a fashion as his Conservative counterpart. At the very least the report would have been handled more sympathetically by a government drawing its main political support from the Labour movement who could not afford to ignore such damaging evidence of class inequality. Even so, it is doubtful whether in 1980, the working party's recommendations would have been enthusiastically embraced and implemented by a Labour administration. By this time economists were losing faith in Keynesian theory and the idea that economic growth could be compatible with high levels of public expenditure. The Labour government had itself initiated an austerity programme designed to curb the growth of public expenditure and every government department was feeling the pinch. In this context, every minister was in search of compelling support to resist cuts in their budget. This was perhaps the most important motivation for commissioning a semi-official study of inequalities in health. The minister concerned was certain to be rewarded with strong political ammunition with which to defend his departmental budget from a cost-cutting treasury.[8]

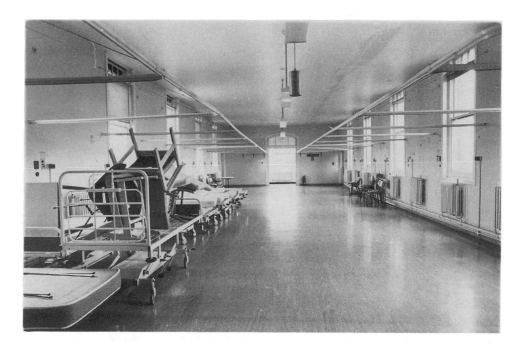

Figure 6.2 "The government was dedicated to a programme of public expenditure cuts." Sociologists investigate the effects of public policy on class inequalities in health.

Here lies the political motivation for a government-sponsored report on the state of the nation's health. The minister responsible knew perfectly well that it would have been difficult for a Labour government to introduce economies and cuts in health care services against the evidence of widening inequalities in health. This may also explain the membership of the expert working group, two of whom were well known for their interest in the study of poverty and their commitment to its eradication. J. N. Morris was a world-renowned epidemiologist who had demonstrated the inseparability of social and biological factors in infant mortality, using class as the primary social factor. In earlier research he had studied the links between unemployment and disease during the Great Depression. (Morris and Titmuss, 1944a, b). Peter Townsend was Britain's foremost poverty researcher, was president of the Child Poverty Action Group and currently completing a major study of income inequality in Britain when the working party was formed. (Townsend, 1979). The prominence given to the prevention of child poverty in the report's recommendations was predictable given the participation of Morris and Townsend, and the Labour minister for health knew it.

The political character of sociological knowledge comes out clearly in this narrative of the Black Report, for both its origins and its fate were politically determined. This is not a new phenomenon. The empirical evidence that human health is primarily a social product has always carried political implications. In the nineteenth century, as the disciplines of sociology and social statistics emerged in the midst of increasing urbanization, the first practitioners were known as *political arithmeticians* motivated to gather empirical data in order to guide the process of industrialization through creative public policy. More often than not political arithmetic was gathered specifically as ammunition by sanitarians (public health campaigners) and others struggling to bring some degree of rationality into the administration of society.

The technique of using occupation to measure the distribution of material well being in the population was conceived in this period and incorporated in the British Census. This is why a continuous series of class mortality data exist in Britain and indeed why the Black Report could be written. It is also the reason why epidemiological research in the UK has always incorporated occupational class as its primary social indicator. In this sense, sociological approaches and methods have never been confined within a specialized profession. It was only after 1950 that most British universities began to offer degrees in sociology and a distinctive profession began to emerge. However, long before this happened, the sociological imagination was at work shaping the intellectual consciousness of people struggling to make sense of the impact of a changing social environment on human experience.

The Legacy of the Black Report – Intellectual

The political controversy surrounding the publication of the Black Report had both positive and negative dimensions for those wishing to see its findings widely disseminated. The idea that the government had attempted to suppress the report generated a great deal of interest among journalists and newspaper editors. Sometimes the same reporters gave detailed accounts of the substance of health inequality though very often the issue of political censorship often got more coverage than the report's evidence. Among health professionals, especially those allied to rather than within the medical profession, the report had a major and continuing impact. Though epidemiologists, medical statisticians and health sociologists in Britain knew of the existence of class differences in health before 1980, the majority of practicing health professionals had only the haziest understanding.

In revealing the overwhelming power of class as a determinant of disease and death, the report drew attention to what Ivan Illich has termed the *limits to medicine*. In the twentieth century, as the medical profession consolidated its control over the definition of what constituted health and disease and persuaded national governments to make individual therapy in clinical settings the centrepiece of national health policy, the achievement of good health gradually became synonymous with medicine. Even for sociologists used to working with the conceptual language and measurement tools of class, the findings of the Black Report were revelationary. Health was widely understood to be a biomedical phenomenon. The argument that it was primarily determined by sociological factors, that disease was a social phenomenon, was a modern heresy. Yet this is exactly what the Black Report demonstrated.

The controversy surrounding the Black Report rumbled on in Britain throughout the first half of the 1980s. Though the government resisted all attempts to make health inequalities either a policy or research priority, the findings of the working group rapidly percolated into every regional health authority in the country. The report, soon after being republished as a cheap paperback, (Townsend and Davidson, 1982) found its way on to the medical and social science curricula in all the major universities. At the local level the estimation of health inequality emerged as a tool for measuring need, for evaluating the effectiveness of health care policy as well as a guide to the allocation of resources. Outside of Britain the Black Report became famous among epidemiologists and health-oriented social scientists. In western Europe, especially, a whole generation of researchers were stimulated to discover whether class inequalities in health similar to those documented for Britain were to be found in their own countries. The World Health Organization for Europe made the reduction of health inequalities a primary goal for the year 2000. Through the agency of the Black Report, social inequalities in health emerged as one of the great *public health* issues of the advanced societies in the last quarter of the twentieth century.

The Legacy of the Black Report – Practical

Although the Black Report helped transform political and even professional knowledge of the causes of health and disease, the scope for reshaping policy was limited. Since 1980 the political climate has become steadily more hostile to the idea of redistributing income to lessen health inequality. This is the lasting effect of the Thatcherite era. High marginal rates of taxation to fund a substantial social wage are no longer socially legitimate. Even parties of the centre-Left quake at the prospect of putting such policies before the electorate. The centre stage of Western democratic politics has moved sharply to the Right. In the immediate aftermath of World War II politicians in the Western liberal democracies, still conscious of the disastrous economic depression of the 1930s, were united by an economic consensus that government should play a directive and interventionist role in the management of national economies and that public expenditure was a necessary, even virtuous means of stabilizing economic life and keeping unemployment to a minimum. These policies fuelled a period of continuous economic boom in North America and western Europe (with knock-on effects elsewhere, especially Japan). The effect was the considerable increase in living standards.

The 1970s saw growing disillusionment with this kind of Keynesian economic policy as economists began to associate public investment with inflation. The new monetarist orthodoxy suggested that full employment strengthened workers' bargaining power and encouraged them to demand wage increases in excess of productivity gains – the gap being equal to the depreciation of the currency. In Britain, the retreat from Keynesian economics was initiated by the last Labour government in the late 1970s and massively accelerated after 1980 under Mrs Thatcher's administration, which was elected on a pledge to roll back the state and liberate individual economic initiative. Britain was not alone in this policy turnabout. In the USA, Reaganism represented similar initiatives, and elsewhere, in more muted form, the same kinds of policies were pursued. As a result the 1980s witnessed huge increases in unemployment all over the Western world, prolonged economic recession and de-industrialization. One effect on both sides of the Atlantic was to reverse the century old trend towards narrowing wealth and income inequalities as tax cuts made the rich richer and rising unemployment and falling wages made the poor poorer.

These government-managed economic trends did not occur in a social vacuum. The same period witnessed major shifts in the social, demographic and occupational structures of advanced capitalist societies like Britain and the USA, which further reinforced the trend towards greater inequality. The economics of family life shifted as married women increased their participation in wage employment and as opportunities for blue-collar males to obtain stable and well-paid jobs of the kind that had traditionally upheld the male breadwinner model declined. These trends affected blue-collar and white-collar workers differently. Middle-class families were much more likely to benefit. In the upper reaches of the occupational structure, new well-paid employment for people with professional qualifications and technical expertise created opportunities for dual-career couples to bring home two substantial salaries.[9] In manual working-class households, opportunities to raise living standards by sending both mother and father out to work were much less. New service sector jobs created in the wake of de-industrialization have tended to be casual and part-time and so low paid that, even when both partners work, take home pay is insufficient to raise the household above the poverty line. Overall the increase in female employment over the last three decades has made relatively little impact on household living standards. As Fuchs shows for the USA, it has greatly increased the work hours of women (paid and unpaid labour) for very little extra in the way of household income (Fucks, 1988). In other words, the average family household has only managed to maintain its standard of living by sending more of its adult members into the labour market. In so doing it has become more dependent on cash purchasing its everyday needs.

The employment trends of the late twentieth century have widened pre-tax inequalities in household income by enabling middle-class families to monopolize a larger proportion of worthwhile jobs in the economy. Alongside the lack of political will to redistribute national income through progressive income tax, the incidence of poverty has rapidly increased. In the UK in 1992 according to the government's own figures,[10] one in four people were living in poverty. The ratio in 1979 had been one in 10. The new poor are disproportionately found among the young and the old. The ageing of the population produced an increasing proportion of elderly people dependent on a diminishing tax base, and rising divorce and "out of wedlock" births have generated an increase in single-parent families. Both trends have swelled the ranks of the poor and particularly the incidence of children in poverty. In 1979 10 per cent of the poor were children, by 1990, this had increased to 33 per cent.[11] Exactly the same trends are found in the USA.[12] It is ironic that the Black Report called for concerted government action to prevent poverty early in life at just the moment when the conditions for stimulating a huge increase in inequality among children were being set in place. The human cost will be witnessed in a continuing trend of widening inequalities in health and survival.

The discipline of sociology has been called the child of industrialism. The new form of civilization revolutionized social life on a global scale in the space of less than two centuries (Nisbet, 1967). The rapidity of the industrial revolution and its dramatic social consequences forced an awareness of the scope for public intervention in human affairs and the need to both comprehend and manage change. This was how the intellectual tools and techniques of sociology emerged. Industrial society is inherently dynamic – its structure constantly shifting in response to internal (national) and external (international) pressures. The necessity to measure, evaluate and predict the course of industrialism's innate dynamism has never diminished even though the political willingness to act upon the knowledge fluctuates. The Black Report is an example of sociology performing its historic role *re-inserting* the evidence of health as a social product on the political agenda. Sociological knowledge is political ammunition. Though the will to "fire" it may vary from time to time, the necessity to maintain its production, to continuously chart the social fallout of public action and inaction will never be diminished.

Notes

1. The Report became known as the *Black* report after its chairman – Sir Douglas Black. The report is otherwise known as *Inequalities in Health – Report of A Research Working Group*. DHSS London, 1980.

2. Occupation is employed as a measure of class on the grounds that it is a good summary of material living conditions. Occupation is the most important determinant of wealth and income for the majority of the population in an industrial society. It is likewise linked to education and therefore offers in a single variable the best indicator of an individual's material circumstances.

3. The Registrar General's so-called social classes are constituted as follows: I = professionals; II = managers; IIIN = skilled white collar; IIIM = skilled blue collar; IV = partly skilled blue collar; V = unskilled. The classification has evolved over the last century being modified according to changes in the occupational structure of the labour market. As some occupations disappear and others emerge in response to technological change, government statisticians delete and incorporate new jobs, striving to preserve the integrity of the classification. Mortality risk by social class can be calculated in Britain because occupation is formally registered on death certificates. Using current census estimates of the size of occupations as the population denominators and the number of registered deaths in occupations as numerators, occupational death rates are readily computed. These methods produce their own distinctive problems of statistical interpretation (see OPCS, 1978).

4. There was no census in the war year of 1941, and between 1911 and 1921 a major change in methods of classification eliminated the basis of comparison.

5. See LeGrand (1982). In the case of health care, the National Health Service had definitely increased middle-class access to medical care disproportionately. Before free health care was introduced in Britain, the middle classes were the most deprived of contact with physicians. Their income was too high for them to be eligible for the voluntary hospitals set up in every town and city for the poor, yet they did not earn enough to pay the heavy costs of hospitalized medical care.

6. At the turn of the century eugenic theorists argued that class and race differences in mortality risk reflected genetic processes of health selection. For a discussion of medical racialism in the USA, see McBride (1991).

7. This is taken from the foreword by the then secretary of state for health, Mr Patrick Jenkin.

8. The alternative and no less political explanation for the appointment of the working group was the idea that by handing over the issue of inequalities in health to a team of experts to report at some later date, the government could move this embarrassing problem to the "back burner". Any report was unlikely to be ready before the next election and this would prevent the issue becoming a source of conflict and political disunity in the Labour Party on the eve of a general election.

9. This trend encouraged a new kind of household – the DINK (double income, no kids). The falling fertility of professionally qualified women was one factor underlying the increasing prosperity of the middle classes.

10. Defining poverty in relative terms as an income set at less than 50 per cent of the national average.

11. These estimates are taken from HMSO (1995). Child poverty is defined by membership of a household whose income is 50 per cent below the national average after housing costs. At 1995 prices for a couple with three children, this weekly income was £196 ($290).

12. In the USA, life expectancy of black males is around a decade shorter than whites. During the 1980s amid economic recession, black male life expectancy decreased, while white male life expectancy improved (see US Government 1992).

References

DHSS 1980: *Inequalities in Health – Report of a Research Working Group*. London: Department of Health and Social Security.

Fuchs, V. 1988: *Women's Quest for Economic Equality*. Cambridge, MA: Harverd University Press.

HMSO 1995: *Households below average income 1979–1992/3*. London: HMSO.

LeGrand, J. 1982: *The Strategy of Equality*. London: Allen & Unwin.

McBride, D. 1991: *From TB to Aids: Epidemics among Urban Blacks since 1900*. Albany: State University of New York Press.

McKeown, T. 1976: *The Modern Rise of Population*. London: Edward Arnold.

Morris, J. N. and Titmuss, R. M. 1944a: Health and social change – the recent history of rheumatic heart disease. *Medical Officer*, 26 August, 2 September, 9 September 1944.

—— 1944b: Epidemiology of peptic ulcer. *The Lancet* 841.

Nisbet, R. 1967: *The Sociological Tradition*. London: Heinemann.

OPCS 1978: *Occupational Mortality: Decennial Supplement 1970–72*. London: HMSO.

Townsend, P. 1979: *Poverty in Britain*. London: Penguin Books.

—— and Davidson, N. 1982: *The Black Report*. London: Penguin Books.

US Government Department and Human Services 1993: *Health USA 1992*. Hyattsville: US Government Printing Office.

7

The Public Impact of Sociology: Public Broadcasting and the Public Interest

Jerold M. Starr

Introduction

Sometime in April 1993 the front page of my daily newspaper headlined the troubles of the city's public service broadcasting corporation–two television stations, a radio station, and magazine serving almost 1.2 million people. Facing a $7.4 million loss of revenues, the chief executive officer (CEO) had dismissed 54 employees (about 25 percent of his staff) and, after 21 years, resigned his position.

Within weeks I had organized what the newspapers dubbed a "grassroots watchdog" group to press for reforms of the corporation. Over the next two-and-a-half years my group and I succeeded in raising public awareness of the issues, and getting ourselves placed on strategic committees to rewrite the corporation's bylaws, choose its next CEO, and advise on programming and services for the public. We were ordinary citizens seeking to change a corporation controlled by wealthy and powerful people. We surprised many with our accomplishments. In my view, however, while we won a few battles we have most of the war ahead of us. Nevertheless, the terrain has shifted and, in the final analysis, real social change takes time. As Thomas Jefferson warned, democracy requires constant vigilance.

My principal goal was to promote public awareness of the threat to public broadcasting and public participation in its reform. While many people see public broadcasting as simply a noncommercial alternative with relatively low ratings, a sociological perspective underscores its importance as a medium of communication crucial to the formation of public opinion to ensure democratic government. Sociological research has also been important to me in two other respects. It has informed my efforts to organize a social movement to impact station policy, including how to use the media in that campaign. And it has helped me to understand the institutional sources of the corporation's problems and the kind of restructuring needed to correct them.

Mass Society or a Society of Publics

The free expression of public opinion is essential to democratic government. Such opinion must be the autonomous creation of citizens acting as members of a public rather than the representations of elites who presume to speak on behalf of the public. Local matters can still be addressed through public discussions within organizations or even town meetings. However, on matters of larger social importance the size and complexity of modern society does not permit effective public opinion to form through direct participation.

On the other hand, the emergence of authentic public opinion on the big issues would be possible if the mass media of communications served as a vehicle for rational discussion featuring the full range of political and cultural perspectives (Blumer, 1966). However, this would never occur if such communications were controlled by a narrow political elite or by commercial interests seeking to maximize their audiences by excluding controversial issues or views that dissented from the conventional wisdom. Despite its congressionally authorized mission to serve as an alternative to the commercial networks, such censorship had seriously compromised public broadcasting in my city. My colleagues and I felt strongly it was imperative that we press for the sort of services that would help to foster a society of active publics rather than a passive mass.

In Europe, public broadcasting was established before commercial broadcasting was allowed. The original vision of first director-general John Reith for the British Broadcasting Corporation was that of a national service that would promote social unity out of a diverse population by broadcasting national events. French presidents dubbed their public broadcasting services "the voice of France." These early conceptions do suggest public broadcasting in the service of elite culture and government control. In recent years, however, the more democratic justification for public broadcasting has been that it is "the principal forum which enables the whole nation to talk to itself" (Keane, 1995, p. 7).

In Europe public broadcasting has been subsidized by independent funds created by such devices as an annual tax on television ownership or a license fee on the purchase of a new television set. Lately, public broadcasting has had to make compromises because such funds have declined due to the saturation of TVs and radios, government cutbacks, inflation and rising production costs (Avery, 1993, p. 20).

In the USA, noncommercial institutions like schools and churches pioneered the development of radio broadcasting. However the national commercial networks used their influence with members of Congress to achieve near monopolization of the airwaves by the 1930s (McChesney, 1993). This pattern became even more pronounced in television. A Carnegie Commission report in 1967 criticized a system dominated by commercial interests and argued that public broadcasting could provide a needed forum for "debate and controversy," a place to hear groups "that may otherwise be unheard" and a resource to "help us see America whole, in all its diversity" (Carnegie Commission, 1967, pp. 92–3). In short, public television "could have a central mandate to foster a viable, vital public sphere" (Aufderheide, 1991, p. 169).

The Carnegie Commission also proposed a plan for independent funding of public broadcasting, but the White House did not propose nor Congress authorize such. Congress did then establish the Corporation for Public Broadcasting (CPB) and its programming arm, the Public Broadcasting Service, but, unfortunately, this important resource has been under constant attack by conservative presidents and congressional leaders who have slashed federal funding and stacked the CPB board with directors who have refused to broadcast many programs critical of government or corporate practices on the pretext that they lacked "balance" (Twentieth Century Fund, 1993).

In the USA most of the federal support goes to covering the operating costs of 344 different channels in 175 markets. Failing to define an explicit public service mission and facing shrinking revenues and rising costs, stations have cultivated corporate underwriters, foundations and "customers." As a consequence there is much more of a commitment to "a broadcasting service" than to a "public project executed through broadcasting" (Aufderheide, 1991, p. 170).

In fact, in the USA the conservative majority in Congress is threatening to eliminate all federal funding for public broadcasting and is urging the Corporation for Public Broadcasting to sell its spectrum (i.e. government-reserved frequency) to private interests. The response in Europe has also been in the direction of "self-commercialization" – co-production deals, subcontracting programming and facilities, and international marketing ventures. In the UK, the 1986 Peacock Commission recommended that the pure public service model be replaced by "a partial, market-supplemented model, not unlike the one that shapes American public television today" (Avery, 1993, p. 20). In France, four out of six channels are already in commercial hands, while in Italy there is a battle over state control of Radiotelevision Italiana.

Humanist Sociology, Advocacy Research and Conflict Methodology

My research approach consisted of various strategies of participant observation, including direct observation of meetings, personal interviews, evaluation of organizational records, and content analysis of newspaper accounts. Data collection took place over a period of 30 months.

Consistent with the humanist tradition, the goal of my research was to enhance the social liberation of the powerless, rather than the social control of the powerful. This approach proposes that true value neutrality is never really possible anyway; that sociologists express personal interest in all phases of their research, starting with the selection and definition of the problem. Moreover, sociologists dependent on funding from government grants or corporate contracts, and/or on the cooperation of government or corporate officials in gathering their data, encounter real constraints on their freedom of inquiry. In fact, acknowledging one's values and interests, rather than pretending they do not exist, provides the researcher and his/her readers with the means needed to compensate for them. Although true "objectivity" is never possible, the researcher still has an obligation to ensure the greatest possible degree of validity and reliability in his/her methods and findings.

My research was "participatory" in so far as it represented scholarly activity in the service of goals set by members of the community (Petras and Porpera, 1994). My research was also participatory insofar as members of the movement suggested new directions and received and acted on my findings (Cancian, 1993). Since it was not always possible for community people to control my study or use my findings, my approach more closely resembled the "advocacy model" as articulated by Hondagneu–Sotelo (1993).

The research also had strong elements of "conflict methodology" (Lehmann and Young, 1972). Unlike the standard consensus methodology, conflict methodology recognizes that the interests of the government and large corporations are different from and often in conflict with the public interest and general welfare of all citizens. Such elites are "sophisticated in selling an ideology of service to the public by hiding the facts of power from those over whom power is exerted" (Lehmann and Young, 1972, p. 22).

By finding independent support for their research and dropping the establishment friendly pretense of value neutrality and detachment, sociologists become free to use different adversarial strategies to secure information about corporate activities that would otherwise be kept secret. Consistent with this academic-as-activist model I used the media extensively, writing letters to the editor, being interviewed for the newspapers and guesting on radio talk shows. We also used the threat of a Federal Communication Commission license challenge as well as media exposés (either written by us or leaked to the press) to pressure the corporation into opening meetings and records which were supposed to be public by law, but which were being kept secret.

Using the Media

Certainly, television is not the only medium capable of providing a public forum for democratic discussion. Mass circulation newspapers can also perform this function. Unfortunately, such newspapers, like the commercial TV networks, are privately owned big businesses which are heavily dependent on

Figure 7.1 Sociology provides insight into the biases of corporately-owned mass media. But mass media can also be used by community groups to promote change.

corporate advertising and the cooperation of government officials. These interests influence their reporting of events. Citizens of capitalist republics assume the press is "free" and rarely perceive such interest. Instead, most assume that there is an objective reality in the world to be described and that good journalists simply reflect that reality in the news.

In contrast, numerous sociological studies have demonstrated that the news reflects "the practices of those having the power to determine the experiences of others" (Molotch and Lester, 1974, p. 11). There are countless numbers of "occurrences," both planned and unexpected, in the world every day. Yet only a few of them become published or broadcast as news "events."

Certain agencies collaborate in constituting news events – news "promoters" who identify "an occurrence as special" for news "assemblers (newsmen, editors and rewritemen)" who transform such "promoted occurrences into public events through publication or broadcast," to news "consumers" (e.g. readers) who selectively attend to such material and, with others, create in their own minds a sense of the world out there (Molotch and Lester, 1974, p. 4).

It is a profoundly political process in which some people have advantage over others in determining what citizens know and can discuss. Those with extreme wealth or power have "habitual access" to the newsroom. In contrast, ordinary people can only have "disruptive access" to the news by creating events, like demonstrations, which cause a problem for those in power. However, such events are usually covered like crime stories. The emphasis is on the disruption and restoration of social order and reports of crowd size, scuffles, damage and arrests. Little or no attention is paid to the analyses presented in the speeches and literature of the demonstrators.

Historically, one major check on the conservatism of the press has been competition between dailies to "scoop" each other on stories that might sell more newspapers. Unfortunately, the trend worldwide and especially in the USA has been toward increasing monopolization of media (Bagdikian, 1992). Like 95 percent of cities in the USA, mine is served by only one major daily newspaper (approximate circulation 510,000 weekdays). This made it imperative that we utilize all alternative media. These consisted of a growing suburban competitor (approximate circulation 70,000), an independent newsweekly (approximate circulation 70,000–150,000), numerous community newsletters, and several radio news and talk shows. While these outlets reached many fewer people than the major daily, they did help us to mobilize active supporters for our campaign. The new members' visible participation, in turn, made us more newsworthy and led to better coverage by the major daily.

In addition, the station's financial mismanagement gave us a unique opportunity to raise public awareness. That is because the one exception to the domination of news by elites occurs in the wake of major accidents or scandals. Such events are unusual, dramatic, raise the question of responsibility and reveal some of the behind-the-scenes operations of those in charge. At such times "nonimportant

groups" like ours can gain access to the newsmaking process. The struggle then is waged over how the event is framed by the media.

Organizing a Social Movement

For years, my friends and I had been concerned with the increasing domination of Public Broadcasting Service (PBS) programming by corporate-sponsored conservative public affairs shows. The only three regularly scheduled programs are hosted by associates of the right-wing *National Review*. Scholars with dissenting views are rarely invited even to guest on such shows. The only program aimed at an African–American audience is hosted by a Republican. There are weekly shows for big business and Wall Street investors but not one regular program aimed at the lives and concerns of working people, environmentalists, or consumers.

Cultural affairs tend to be middle brow or imported, only rarely presenting the most creative American talent in film or the performing arts. In fact, the PBS and most of its local affiliates consistently refuse to show award-winning documentaries on significant social issues if they are critical of government or corporate policy. To add insult to injury many hours of programming are taken up with reruns of old commercial American TV shows and British situation comedies ("Britcoms"). Worst of all, the average PBS affiliate devotes only about 5–6 percent of it schedule to local programming. My city's station offered less than 2 percent local programming, much of it nostalgic fluff which did nothing to educate the community about the city's many problems.

In the USA each PBS affiliate must pay an annual fee for the national schedule. While optional programming must come out of their own budgets, they are free to choose alternatives and many programs are offered to them by satellite downlink at no charge. Federal law requires all public broadcasters to maintain a community advisory board to evaluate whether programming and services are meeting the "specialized educational and cultural needs" of the community. Unfortunately, the corporation's compliance was only perfunctory. It held only two meetings in 1992 and one in 1993. The meetings were not publicly posted. Only 13 of 23 members showed up in 1993. All but 10 minutes of the hour-long meeting were taken up by staff presentations. Two participants were later quoted as saying that station officials were not interested in their opinions.

Recognizing the enormous obstacles to influencing national program policy, my watchdog group, at least, sought to influence public television in our city. Even those scholars skeptical about the importance of the public sphere (e.g. Schudson, 1992) have urged consideration of ways to make representative institutions more "public." That was our goal. When the station's leadership jeopardized this community resource by their financial mismanagement, we had an issue and an opportunity.

Spurred on by anonymous letters charging fiscal improprieties and a growing corporate debt, reporters from the daily paper made frequent calls to the corporation to ask for comment. All allegations were denied as well as access to relevant records. At the point of the CEO's resignation, however, the corporation's leadership recognized they would have to meet the press.

In addition to the bad news already mentioned, the corporate establishment confessed that the outgoing CEO and his three top officers had cashed in $189,000 in insurance policies purchased for them by the board as deferred compensation in 1970. They had done this secretly in 1991 while openly taking 10 percent voluntary pay cuts as a public relations gesture.

The corporation's leadership tried to frame the story as an accident caused by market forces beyond their control. Their complicity, they alleged, was only in not acting quickly enough to limit the damage. They praised the outgoing CEO for making the station an award-winning national production center, but blamed him for failing to cut back staff

when the major corporations significantly cut back their program underwriting. The outgoing CEO defended the three-year delay as a necessary "gamble" since "positive program funding decisions" would have required the staff and facilities. The board chair told the daily press: "We were late coming to the problem [but] boards and auditors only know what is told to them by management." A former board member advised the *Wall Street Journal*: "I'm not sure how much any board member – even the officers – was aware of the nuts and bolts of what was going on over there. It was a big operation with a big board, and authority gets a little bit fragmented."

As the months passed, the acting CEO sought to present himself as a reformer whom the public could trust with their money. He criticized his predecessor's accounting methods as "very shoddy," his drawing additional salary from a for-profit subsidiary as "completely inappropriate" and failure to include depreciations in the corporation's bottom line as "misleading as can be."

The retired CEO, in turn, charged that the acting CEO himself, as former chair of the board's finance committee, was "fully informed" about the "station's financial position." In fact, he implied, the acting CEO may have been responsible for any misperceptions that might have occurred. Clearly, all this personal finger pointing betrayed an institutional problem – the board had failed to protect the public interest by exercising proper oversight over management practices.

Our movement began quite modestly with three people in my living room. We decided to use the media to organize a movement that would promote our perspective on the corporation's problems as a scandal which threatened an important community resource. I wrote an opinion editorial for the independent newsweekly that linked the corporation's fiscal problems – gambling with public contributions, huge executive salaries, unorthodox accounting methods, a rubber stamp board – with its conservative programming – pro-big business, anti-labor, commercial reruns instead of independent documentaries, etc. We defined the problem as too much corporate control and the solution as "putting the public interest back into public broadcasting."

The editorial and a mention in the local TV critic's column brought us about 20 volunteers. The research on social movements has found that most individuals require personal incentives in order to sustain participation (Downtown and Wehr, 1991) and that organizations must devise effective procedures for "role differentiation and assignment" in order to be effective. Right away I proposed projects that would provide opportunities for newcomers to participate selectively and receive recognition.

We organized a delegation to attend the corporation's regularly scheduled board meetings as observers. We were the first real members of the public to identify ourselves and, as such, attracted the interest of the media looking for another quote, conflict to spice up the story and leverage for getting more cooperation from the corporation for their own investigations. I negotiated with the corporation for five minutes to address the board. I then advised the media. Nine of us dressed up and met at the station. The corporation put us in a room with refreshments to wait until board members had finished lunch. The press was also referred there giving me about 30 minutes to stage my own press conference with photos. My "unprecedented" outsider speech to the board was also printed in the papers.

From that day forward I was routinely called by the press for comment on whatever the corporation claimed. Of course, we had to make ourselves accessible so we continued to send delegations to witness board meetings and to talk to the press afterward. As mentioned, we also promoted coverage in alternative media throughout the community. I worked hard at developing a cooperative relationship with all reporters, keeping in touch regularly with updates on our campaign, leaking information about the station and suggesting new angles they might consider. In addition, my scholarly knowledge about public broadcasting generally made me a re-

source they would call upon for background. For example, when the Corporation for Public Broadcasting (CPB) canceled a national town meeting in Pittsburgh to evaluate programming on the grounds that it would be diverted into a "local rage session" about the station's problems, I brought the story to the local press, complete with quotes from the CPB spokesperson and the executive director of Fairness and Accuracy in Reporting.

Almost immediately we also began planning a "Banned by PBS" film program featuring Academy Award winning documentaries that had been rejected for alleged "bias." We sent fliers to the mailing list of 3,000 maintained by a coalition of 46 public interest groups that endorsed our campaign. The film program sold out, generated more media coverage, increased our mailing list to almost 300 names, and showed people the kinds of public interest programs they were not getting on public broadcasting. I also published an opinion editorial in the daily paper to underscore the theme of our campaign.

A few months later, we created another news event by exploring a challenge to the corporation's license renewal with the Federal Communications Commission (FCC) for violating federal requirements to post and hold open meetings of all committees and to have certain records open for public review. Despite lack of interest by the FCC, this challenge was widely reported (including the national press) and ultimately gained us access to a crucial board retreat.

After my June speech to the board of directors I was invited to join a Corporate Governance Committee to rewrite the corporation's bylaws and I accepted. The whole endeavor and my invitation were clearly part of the corporation's public relations effort to control the damage of the scandal and restore confidence in its establishment. The sociological literature on social movements identifies "co-optation" as a social control strategy of elite groups in which prestigious but powerless appointments in the establishment are offered to leaders of protest groups. The intended effect is to separate protest leaders from their followers and to give the general public the impression of reform. Sensitive to this possibility I accepted the opportunity to work for change from the inside, but insisted on maintaining an independent base and public visibility at the same time.

Diagnosing the Institution's Problems

The Corporate Governance Committee consisted of 14 members, 10 of whom were recruited from outside the corporation. The appearance of an independent evaluation was essential to the station's credibility. Although identified as a critic, I found support for many of my ideas from other members, especially the three foundation directors for whom management accountability was an important value. I was the most active member of the committee and, by sheer persistence, had considerable influence on the outcome.

Using my social research skills, I compared the corporation's bylaws to seven other nonprofit-making organizations, including five other PBS affiliates. The differences were dramatic and easily explained how so many miscommunications, bad decisions and even abuses had been permitted.

First, the mission statement included only a simple reference to providing "suitable educational and cultural television programs." There was no specification of values, goals, or standards and, thus, no real basis for a strategic plan and performance evaluation by the board or management. While all organizations must remain solvent, nonprofit corporations unlike commercial businesses, do not measure their success merely by the financial bottom line. Instead, the nonprofit institution (school, library, museum, hospital, etc.) "has to judge itself by its performance in creating vision, creating standards, creating values and commitment, and increasing human competence" (Drucker, 1990, p. 112). Moreover, because the institution receives government funds, charitable gifts and volunteer labor, the board's responsibility goes beyond ensuring

program and fiscal responsibility to ensuring that the views of all significant public constituencies are reflected in organizational decision-making.

Second, given the importance of the board in representing the public interest, I noted that it was huge and dominated by affluent white males. Of the 57 members on paper, there were only 12 women and four African Americans. There were no representatives of organized labor. While directors were recruited to serve for two consecutive three-year terms, there were so many exceptions to these limits that some key figures had been around for 10–20 years. Nominations were solicited privately and approved without discussion, ensuring the insulation of the board from the broader community.

Third, the bylaws invited conflict of interest by not proscribing board membership for management. The National Charities Information Bureau recommends that the CEO be the only paid staff member on the board but, in addition to him, there were four vice-presidents on the board and 14 different staff people sat on 15 of the board's 18 committees. There was an Executive Committee "composed of the officers of the corporation and other board members" that in between board meetings could "exercise all the powers" of the board in directing and managing the corporation. This committee was composed of 16 people, four of whom were management.

Fourth, there were only four meetings scheduled per year and they typically lasted only an hour and a half over lunch. Despite their infrequency, fewer than half the members showed up for a typical meeting. With so many members, hardly any felt personally responsible for the board's decisions. Unlike other stations, there was no penalty for missing meetings. Attendance really didn't matter because only one-fifth of directors were required for a quorum (i.e. the minimum number required to make an official decision). Only five days' notice were required to call a meeting. The Executive Committee discussed and prepared recommendations on almost all of the important matters that came before the board, but these were rarely discussed. Voting was a mere formality.

Prescriptions for Reform

The thrust of the changes in the bylaws was to improve accountability of management to the board and of the board to the public. The new bylaws called for "diversity of occupation, race, gender, age and geographic community of residence." Furthermore, to "ensure such diversity," nominations were to be "actively solicited by the Membership Committee through the city magazine and otherwise." To promote more participation and personal responsibility, the size of the board was reduced from 57 to 20–25. Members could still serve two consecutive three-year terms, but would have to stay off the board at least two years before becoming eligible for membership again. The number of meetings was increased to six. A member would have to attend a majority of meetings or be asked to resign. Also, a majority was required to constitute a quorum. Perhaps the most significant bylaws reform was to strengthen the provisions for the community advisory board.

Unfortunately, the corporation's establishment rejected the committee's recommendation to contract with an organizational development consulting firm to work with the boards, management and staff to implement the proposed changes. This was considered essential by the committee because even organizations willing to change need help in unlearning old behaviors and learning new behaviors appropriate to changing relationships. In the absence of such a process, compliance has been selective and old attitudes have persisted.

Nevertheless, the new bylaws call for the board of directors to use various media to recruit a community advisory board which must be diverse by "race, gender, age and community of residence. Leaders of public interest organizations, including organized labor and those involved in community service, should have substantial representa-

tion." Members are charged with advising the directors whether the station's programming and services are meeting the needs of the various constituencies in the community and with making appropriate recommendations.

Months earlier our campaign began soliciting nominations for the community advisory board. Forty invitations were issued from an initial list of 100 possibilities. Finally, eight nominations were presented to the corporation. In exchange for my research assistance, the local papers made my nomination a public issue. Four of us were invited to serve and three accepted, including me.

In the past year the community advisory board has been tightly controlled by management and made little progress. However, some of us have spoken out and formed an alliance to challenge the leadership. At the same time I have mobilized support from organized labor in the area to propose a collaboration with the corporation on new programming and its promotion for working people. The proposal was framed explicitly in language taken from the bylaws and public relations statements made by the corporate leadership. I have kept the press informed of such communications.

Conclusion

This advocacy research case is testimony to the value of a sociological perspective in understanding social problems, like the importance of public service broadcasting and a free press in preserving the public sphere in a democracy. It shows how sociology provides valuable insights into how to organize a social movement to promote social change, including the role that the mass media play in such efforts. It demonstrates that many problems are deeper than personalities and their solution must lie in the restructuring of institutional relations. And it reveals the limitations of knowledge without power. Elites do not give up power willingly even when confronted with the truth. Finally, it illustrates that social change is a process that takes time, patience and persistence. We have not given up and walked away. We have made some changes and are in a better position to demand more.

Sociology has and will continue to make a public impact.

References

Aufderheide, P. 1991: Public television and the public sphere. *Critical Studies in Mass Communication*, 8, 168–83.

Avery, R. K. (ed.) 1993: *Public Service Broadcasting in a Multichannel Environment: The History and Survival of an Ideal*. White Plains, NY: Longman.

Bagdikian, B. H. 1992: *The Media Monopoly*, 4th edn. Boston, MA: Beacon Press.

Blumer, H. 1966: The mass, the public, and public opinion. In B. Berelson and M. Janowitz (eds.), *Public Opinion and Communication*, 2nd edn. New York: The Free Press.

Cancian, F. M. 1993: Conflicts between activist research and academic success: participatory research and alternative strategies. *The American Sociologist*, 24(1), 92–106.

Carnegie Commission on Educational Television 1967: *Public Television: A Program for Action*. New York: Bantam.

Drucker, P. 1990: *Managing the Non-Profit Organization: Practices and Principles*. New York: Harper Business.

Downtown, J. V. and Wehr, P. E. 1991: Peace movements: the role of commitment and community in sustaining member participation. *Research in Social Movements, Conflicts and Change* 13, 113–34.

Hondagneu–Sotelo, P. 1993: Why advocacy research? Reflections on research and activism with immigrant women'. *The American Sociologist*, 24(1), 56–68.

Keane, J. 1995. Structural transformations of the public sphere. *The Communication Review*, 1(1), 1–22.

Lehmann, T. and Young, T. R. 1972: From conflict theory to conflict methodology. Paper presented at the annual meeting of the American Sociological Association, New Orleans (August).

McChesney, R. W. 1993: *Telecommunications, Mass Media and Democracy: The Battle for the Control of U.S. Broadcasting, 1928–1935*. New York: Oxford University Press.

Molotch, H. and Lester, M. 1974: News as purposive behavior: On the strategic use of routine events, accidents and scandals. *American Sociological Review*, 39, 101–12.

Petras, E. McLean and Porpera, D. W. 1993: Participatory research: three models and an analysis, *The American Sociologist*, 24(1), 107–25.

Schudson, M. 1992: Was there ever a public sphere. If so, when? Reflections on the American case. In C. Calhoun (ed.) *Habermas and the Public Sphere*. Cambridge, MA: MIT Press.

Twentieth Century Fund 1993: *Quality Time? The Report of the Twentieth Century Fund Task Force on Public Television*. New York: Twentieth Century Fund.

Suggestions for Further Reading

Hoynes, W. 1994: *Public Television for Sale: Media, the Market, and the Public Sphere*. San Francisco, CA: Westview Press.

Lashley, M. 1992: *Public Television: Panacea, Pork Barrel, or Public Trust?* New York: Greenwood Press.

Ryan, C. 1991: *Prime Time Activism: Media Strategies for Grassroots Organizing*. Boston, MA: South End Press.

PART II
Sociology and its Traditions

"Sociological engagement" with the world operates at different levels. It refers both to our "political" engagement, as socially concerned beings, with issues of vital importance to humanity; and also to our intellectual engagement with problems of sociological description, categorization and explanation. These two forms of engagement are woven into the tapestry of sociological development in such intricate ways that the patterns are not always immediately apparent. This section sets out to help you recognize some of these patterns.

There is a dilemma at the heart of the sociological enterprise. As human beings we are born into a particular socio-historical setting, are shaped by the cultural norms of our childhood and share the understandings and concerns of our contemporaries. This social involvement leaves an indelible mark on our sociological imaginations: our intellectual endeavours reflect our experiences of the social world. Yet sociology seeks to engage intellectually with this self-same world, to describe and analyse it, and claims to do so in a *methodologically* dispassionate way. Even at its most vehemently committed it can be distinguished from prejudice and propaganda – for it does not make up its mind in advance. Its descriptions and interpretations are always open to modification in the light of new evidence or theoretical criticism. A sociologist should never start out on a research project saying "I shall demonstrate that this is true", but rather "I think that this may be true, and I will conduct research to check it out." *Intellectually*, sociological engagement paradoxically involves a degree of detachment.

Chapters 8–10 seek to convey sociology's distinctive character by three different routes:

(i) With reference to a set of individuals, traditions and debates which are acknowledged to have laid the foundations of the discipline and which continue, for the moment at least, to define contemporary sociological discussion (Turner).

(ii) As a distinctive "way of thinking" about the world which may be elucidated through a consideration of sociology's relationship with its intellectual neighbours – and also by asking what is it about the modern mind that makes us so bothered about differentiating disciplines in the first place (Lee).

(iii) By considering the special quality of sociology's subject-matter (human action and relationships) and the implications this has for the central dilemma of "objectivity" in sociological research and scholarship (Ballard).

The social world is a complex mix of cohesion and division, of continuity and disruption. On the one hand people identify with each other as "belonging" to the same nation, class, sex, ethnic group, etc. and form alliances on the basis of shared interests and outlooks. On the other hand social life is riven by conflicting interests, longstanding enmities, dissension over what constitutes the "good society" and disagreements on the best way to get there. Sociological controversies reflect these contests in the wider world, and this is the theme of the next few chapters which explore the impact of political and cultural influences on sociology's development. As Kinloch points out, sociologists who aspire to "scientific neutrality" often seem unaware of the impact personal values have on their work, while others knowingly locate their sociology within these wider social disputes and may even seek to serve directly some outside agency or social movement (Middleton; Witz). More recently a fragmentation of politics, culture and ideologies (associated with post-modernism) has seen itself reflected in the discipline (Papson) and even, according to some, threatens to tear the discipline apart (Turner). It is therefore appropriate to round off this discussion with a chapter that reflects on the significance of sociology's roots in European and North American culture for its subsequent development – from an author whose own social orgins lie in a very different region of the world (Sekhon).

Chapters 16–18 draw together the threads of intellectual and political engagement in an exploration of social divisions, power, and identity and the lifecourse (Bradley; Gubbay; Bellaby). The purpose of this selection is not to identify a short list of "key topics" such as you might find in a textbook, but rather to discuss some of sociology's most longlasting thematic preoccupations which permeate and contextualize the various disciplinary subfields and specialisms. The authors have attempted to show how these concerns have entered into sociological ways of thinking, rather than treating them as "objects of study".

Finally, the challenging essay that concludes this part is far more than a glossary of sociological jargon. Jary sets out to show the importance of precise and rigorous language to the sociological craftworker, and clarifies the meaning of key terms by relating them to their theoretical contexts.

The essays in this part are some of the most demanding in the volume because they deal with problems and issues which are probably unfamiliar to you. You may not comprehend or appreciate all the arguments and references on a first reading, but we think they will repay a return visit – or even several – as your sociological understanding deepens.

The Distinctive Character of Sociology

8

Founders and Classics: A Canon in Motion

Jonathan Turner

The Emergence of Sociology in Historical Context

The nineteenth century founders of the sociological canon saw themselves as part of intellectual and social currents dating back to the Renaissance. In their view, the Renaissance had liberated human thought from the restrictions of the "Dark Ages" in Europe (roughly the fifth through thirteenth centuries), and recaptured the classical cultures of the Greeks, Romans and Arabs. A rebirth of intellectual curiosity had occurred, culminating in the Age of Science in the seventeenth century. The hallmark of this new age was Sir Isaac Newton's law of gravity, first published in 1667.

The accuracy of these nineteenth-century scholars' retrospective examination of history is less important than their perceptions. They firmly believed that the Age of Science had created a new way to connect conceptual thinking to empirical observations. On the basis of this conviction sociology emerged as a distinctive mode of intellectual inquiry, perhaps as an inevitable response to three large-scale revolutions in economic, political, and intellectual life among western Europeans.

During the eighteenth century an economic revolution was well underway: the old feudal estates were giving way to markets and commercial activities, or themselves being converted into commercial enterprises; wealth and capital now existed independently of the landed aristocracy in the hands of the

bourgeoisie; industrial enterprises were being established; the hold of traditional guilds on craft occupations was loosening; the pools of urban labor who would work for wages in the new factories were expanding; the world-level trade in resources, financial instruments, and finished commodities was accelerating; the influence of religion was being eroded by markets, urbanization, state power, secular law, and industrial employment; the privileges of the old aristocracy were increasingly challenged; and the consolidation of bureaucratized state power was well underway. These kinds of changes – often labeled "modernity" – were transforming people's lives; and when traditional ways are disrupted, individuals begin to think about the world around them. Among intellectuals, this search for insight into the changes wrought by modernity led them to believe that theoretical and conceptual thinking could be used to reorganize society.

Political disruptions throughout Europe also caused intellectuals to perceive that a new, more democratic political order could be constructed. At first such thinking was speculative, evaluative, and moral in character, but by the beginning of the nineteenth century political commentary had become more rigorous, and some scholars were bold enough to assert that a "science of society" could guide the reorganization of the polity. To be sure, the earlier moralizing remained – indeed, as we will see, it has always been part of sociology – but there was a new confidence: What Newton had done in the seventeenth century for physics, and what evolutionary thinking was increasingly demonstrating in the nineteenth century for biology, would be possible for a new discipline studying the social universe.

The most immediate influence on the emergence of sociology, however, was an intellectual movement often termed "the Enlightenment." This movement grew out of the Renaissance, the Age of Science, and the changed political and economic order. Yet, it refocused intellectual inquiry on *social* processes, especially the societal transformations that were clearly evident to all.

Sociology and the Enlightenment

In both England and France (where sociology emerged as a distinct mode of inquiry) the central problematic was to understand the "forces" holding society together in face of the disintegrative pressures of modernity. The Enlightenment in England of the eighteenth and nineteenth centuries is often termed the "Age of Reason" which, in a sense, communicates the notion of rational thought about the social universe. Rationalism emphasizes efficiency and productiveness rather than established ways of doing things, even if these ways are sanctioned by traditional morality or religion. Much of this thinking in England was used to justify the highly disruptive and, indeed, brutal changes brought by industrial capitalism. For Adam Smith (1805), the basic issue was discovering the "forces" that could hold a rapidly differentiating society together. He was to propose an "invisible hand of order" arising out of rational and self-interested actions by individuals in open and free markets, although his work also recognized the importance of "moral sentiments" for integrating ever diversifying populations.

In France, the Enlightenment was dominated by scholars known as the "*philosophes*" who, in the eighteenth century, postulated the "natural laws" of humans as a critical foil against the existing political regime, although many of these same critics were shocked by the violence of the French

Revolution of 1789 that their works unwittingly encouraged. As political instability continued into the nineteenth century, scholars in France desperately sought to find the principles by which social order could be regenerated and sustained. And, by the dawn of the nineteenth century, some French scholars were committed to discovering the "laws" of human organization that would enable them to propose solutions to this basic problem of order.

As they followed up on this commitment they retained the metaphors of earlier Enlightenment thinkers. One key metaphor was the idea of "progress." Indeed, despite large-scale disruption to the social fabric, stages of human progress could be observed: the Renaissance had rediscovered the classical era and had brought a new curiosity about nature; the Age of Science had demonstrated the benefits of theory disciplined by empirical facts; and the dramatic changes in the political-economy of European social systems had initiated a top-to-bottom restructuring of the social order toward more democratic forms. The idea of "progress" was thus to be a dominant metaphor in the sociological canon.

A related metaphor was the notion of historical cycles, where the social world was seen to oscillate from one basic form of organization to another – as is the case, for example, when centralized and repressive political rule is replaced by less restrictive political forms. This idea of sociocultural cycles was often combined with arguments for long-term human progress, allowing scholars to see the social universe oscillating between states within a broad stage of development but eventually moving to an entirely new stage of development, within which there are further oscillations. In fact, for some, dialectical oscillations propelled societies to a new stage of evolutionary development.

These metaphors became mental templates for the first sociologists, as they sought to explain theoretically the transformations of the modern world. Their concerns about theoretical explanation of the changes wrought by modernity are still central to sociological theory today; and so, even as the sociological canon has moved, it has carried with it the legacy of The Enlightenment. Yet, this legacy is now a source of debate and acrimony among sociologists, especially with respect to two questions: (1) can sociology be a true science? and (2) what is the fundamental problem of sociological inquiry?

The Prospects for Scientific Theorizing in Sociology

The first founders of sociology firmly believed that a natural science of society was possible. Sociology could be like any other science, whether physics or biology, and with time it would take its place among the respected sciences. Indeed, the titular founder of sociology, Auguste Comte, preferred the label "social physics" to sociology and held Sir Isaac Newton's law of gravity as the ideal for this new kind of physics. Subsequent scholars – founders of sociology such as Herbert Spencer, Émile Durkheim, and arguably, Georg Simmel – were to carry the banner of science forward through the nineteenth century and into the twentieth century. Yet the view that sociology could be a natural science did not go unchallenged, although compared to current commentary on "scientific sociology" these challenges by scholars such as Max Weber and Karl Marx were rather muted.

The French Lineage

Auguste Comte sounded the call for a scientific sociology that could be used to forge a better society, as is exemplified by the title of his early 1822 essays on a "Plan of the Scientific Operations Necessary for Reorganizing Society." For Comte, who selectively borrowed and extended the ideas of the French *philosophes* as well as the problem of order inherited from Adam Smith, sociology was to be scientific in several senses which were subsequently spelled out in his great work, *Course of Positive Philosophy* (1830–42). First, sociology could develop abstract laws that explain the operation of social forces, with

Newton's law of gravity serving as the model. Secondly, these laws were to be tested against empirical facts, collected through careful observation, experiments, comparisons, and histories. Third, those laws that have stood up to empirical tests were to be *used* to forge a better society. In this advocacy for the use of science for human betterment, Comte (1851–4) went so far as to rekindle the organismic analogy of the classical Greeks, viewing society as a "social body" whose pathologies could be diagnosed and solved by "the physicians" of the social world, sociologists.

At the close of the nineteenth century, Comte's advocacy was repackaged by Émile Durkheim in his *The Rules of the Sociological Method* (1895). For Durkheim society was composed of emergent properties, or "social facts," that are not reducible to the features of individuals. The study of these social facts was to be conducted in terms of (a) their causes (antecedent social facts) and (b) consequences (functions) for the body social. And, like Comte, Durkheim firmly believed that theoretical explanations of the causes and functions of social facts were *to be used* to solve the "pathologies" of society.

Herbert Spencer's Earlier Advocacy

At the same time that Durkheim was repackaging Comte's advocacy, he was also engaged in a one-sided debate with the first sociologist in England, Herbert Spencer, whose ideas were lost under the impact of Durkheim's rather unfair criticisms. Perhaps more important than Durkheim's attacks, however, Spencer espoused a moral philosophy which today is considered "right wing" (although it was "liberal" in his time), and this advocacy made his work suspect to later sociologists who, on the whole, are left of center on the contemporary political spectrum. Yet, over twenty years before Durkheim's *The Rules* (1895), Spencer published his first work in sociology, a methodological treatise titled, *The Study of Sociology* (1873). This work had a significant impact in its time and, in fact, it was by far the most sophisticated methodological statement in nineteenth-century sociology. In this work

Spencer outlined in great detail the sources of bias in stating sociological problems, developing theories, and conducting empirical inquiry. For Spencer, biases such as public opinion, influence of the powerful, location of scientists in social structure, point in history and time of research, mental categories of researcher and subject, sources of funding, intrusion into ongoing social processes, distortion by research instruments, politics among scientists, and many other potential hazards to scientific sociology were very real. But, once known, he felt that they could be overcome.

Ambivalence in the German Lineage

Many key figures of sociology's first one hundred years sided with Comte, Spencer, and Durkheim, but others like Karl Marx, Max Weber, and perhaps George Herbert Mead did not fully embrace a "hard science" viewpoint. Yet the shrill anti-science mood of the contemporary canon was not evident in these skeptics who were ambivalent about, but not antagonistic toward, a rational-science model for sociology.

Karl Marx blended two basic Enlightenment ideas: a dialectical view of history (patterns of social organization will generate their opposite) and a developmental view of history as progress (as stages of social evolution move toward communism). For Marx, capitalism and modernity arose out of the dialectical cycles inherent in feudalism, and communism was to emerge from the contradictions of capitalism. Although Marx saw the long-term march of history as inevitable, he none the less stressed that individuals "make history" through their capacities for agency, but they do so under the constraints of the past. Yet, despite Marx's caution, this position has been converted to a more anti-science critique: as individuals exert their capacity for agency they change the *very nature* of social organization; hence, scientific theories seeking timeless "laws" about the nature of human organization are not possible. Marx did not go this far; and so, he compromised, arguing that each historical epoch contains its own laws of organization. Hence, feudalism and capitalism are different epochs of history with their own distinctive dynamics, but one can formulate in abstract theoretical terms the laws of each epoch. This compromise allowed Marx (1867) to theorize for an historical epoch and, at the same time, to retain notions of human agency and historical contingency, while mounting a critique of society.

Max Weber, who is often seen as carrying on a "silent dialogue" with Marx, argued against the view that there was an inevitable march of history toward some end point like communism. Weber (1904), like Marx, wanted to generalize about social structures and processes, but Weber did not see the actions of individuals and transformations of social structures as wholly predictable. His compromise was couched in terms of the "Methodenstreit," or methodological debate, that raged within German academic circles during the last decades of the nineteenth century. The poles of the debate were anchored in four specific issues (Turner et al., 1995, pp. 179–90):

(1) The relative merits of induction (i.e., generalizations arising from empirical observations) versus deduction (i.e., logical inferences to empirical events from abstract laws).
(2) The universality of phenomena (i.e., are there fundamental forces operating across all times and places?) versus the relativity of events (i.e., are processes tied to specific historical conditions or, at best, epochs?).
(3) The view of humans as rational (i.e., self-interested actors who calculate costs and benefits) versus the conception of humans as driven by morals, emotions, traditions, and customs.
(4) The view of social science, especially economics, as an ethical discipline stressing the morality of events versus the adoption of a scientific and ethically neutral stance in theoretical explanations.

Weber navigated a middle course between the points of this debate. He recognized the need for developing abstract statements about social processes, even though these processes were historically contingent on particular events and, at times, unpredictable; and so, he began to develop what he termed "ideal types" which analytically accentuated key properties that made a particular social structure or process distinctive. In this way, he could use a kind of conceptual yardstick for comparing different social phenomena, as measured against the points of the ideal type. Weber also wanted sociology to be value free and rational in the pursuit of knowledge; and he felt that the use of abstract ideal types would be a useful tool for accentuating the key properties of social phenomena without preaching about their merits or faults. In the end, Weber advocated what is a common theoretical strategy today: constructing conceptual frameworks for interpreting ongoing social events without making the presumption that these frameworks are universally true or law-like; instead, they represent an analytical accentuation of what are considered important social phenomena and are used for analyzing specific empirical and historical cases.

George Herbert Mead in America

George Herbert Mead's ideas are used by some to argue against scientific sociology, despite the fact that Mead's (1923, 1932) works were ambiguous about the prospects for social science. The reason for the ambiguity in interpretations of Mead's thinking about science is that he adopted a philosophical approach known as "pragmatism" which stressed that those properties of humans and patterns of social organization that facilitate adjustment and adaptation will be retained as long as they are useful. When they cease being useful, humans will construct new ways of making adjustments and adaptations. For Mead, science was just such an adaptive tool. Humans developed it because it was useful in making adjustments to the environment; and they would continue to employ science only as long as it continued to be useful. Mead's adoption of pragmatist philosophy raised questions about using Newton's mechanical vision of the universe to explain phenomena

who think, adjust, and adapt to the demands of the environment and who, therefore, reveal spontaneity and unpredictability (Mead, 1934, 1938). Anti-science critics of today who follow the Meadian tradition tend to emphasize this aspect of Mead's thinking. Yet, Mead (1934) clearly felt that the emergence of "mind" and "self" in humans revealed lawlike properties and that the maintenance of "society" occurred by virtue of fundamental processes made possible by mind and self. Moreover, Mead argued that science could be one of humans' most useful tools in reconstructing society. Thus, depending on one's biases, Mead can be used to draw diverse conclusions about the prospects for scientific sociology.

The Contemporary Canon: Acrimony and Debate

The giants of early sociology had all entered the debate over the prospects for social science but today, on the anti-science side, the controversy has become polarized. One line of anti-science critique takes Weber's effort to navigate a middle course to the extreme: social life is a contingent process in which unpredictable configurations and convergencies of forces specific to time and location determine the nature of social organization at any moment in history – thereby making impossible the formulation of universal abstract laws that cut across societies. Yet, despite this advocacy, the best-known historical sociologists of today – for example, Michael Mann, Theda Skocpol, Immanuel Wallerstein, and Charles Tilly – appear willing to make broad generalizations about social organization, although they are often reluctant to see these generalizations as immutable "laws" of human social organization.

Another line of argument pushes Marx's analyses of ideology and turns his sociology, which Marx himself saw as scientific (at least for a given historical epoch like capitalism), into an anti-science polemic: "scientific" laws and research legitimate the status quo and make current social arrangements appear as the way things *must* be; whereas, in fact, sociology should be used to criticize all forms of domination and to suggest more liberating alternatives to present-day social constructions. This line of attack has many branches, ranging from radical feminists who accuse science of being male-dominated and sustaining patriarchy through post-modernists who see science as "logocentric" to modern-day carriers of the Marxian tradition who wish to eliminate capitalism. For all of these critical theorists, science is a tool of domination, obfuscating alternative visions of how to restructure patterns of human organization.

A final major line of anti-science criticism is a composite of early sociologists' ambivalence about science: individuals interpret and assess their current situation and, as humans use their capacities for thought, they become active agents who can change the basic nature of the social world. Even the presumed "laws" of social science can, once known, be obviated by human agency.

The Post-modern Consolidation

The Enlightenment as it inspired science had emphasized that:

(1) Reality exists independently of human representations of this reality.
(2) Language is used to communicate meaning among thinkers as well as to denote the properties of an external reality.
(3) Truth is determined by the correspondence between (a) statements phrased in ever more precise languages and (b) empirical data collected with increasingly precise instruments.
(4) Knowledge is objective and self-correcting as conscientious efforts are made to increase the correspondence between empirical tests and abstract statements.

These are the basic tenets of what some have called "the western rationalist tradition"; and these tenets are taken as "articles of faith" by scientists. But now, a broad intellectual movement known as "post-modernism" magnifies the more muted doubts about social science in the early canon and, in extreme form, rejects all of the tenets within "western rationalism."

For most post-modern critics there are no objective truths. In its most radical form post-modernists argue that the "laws of science" and the "empirical facts" used to confirm these laws are merely one kind of "text" that is no better than any other. Hence, sociological theorizing produces statements or "texts" that represent interpretations, organizational politics, vocabularies, and location in historical time; and these "texts" have no "privileged voice" over those produced by other communities of individuals.

Among the proponents of science, post-modernism and the older lines of criticism that it codifies are viewed as extreme nihilism, subjectivism, and relativism. If there is no external reality and if there are no standards by which "texts" are assessed in terms of their capacity to explain this reality, then "anything goes." Thought becomes undisciplined, while cumulative knowledge and understanding of the social universe become mere word games among ivory-tower academics. For those who advocate social science, there is obdurate social reality "out there" that can be explained by value-neutral, self-critical, and self-corrective theories systematically tested against empirical data. The goal of such theories is to denote and explain the fundamental properties and processes of human organization; and the self-correcting nature of theories (as they are assessed against data) will mitigate against the issues raised by critics.

Currently, the debate between pro-science and anti-science factions in sociology is acrimonious, and far from settled. Early sociology's confidence in its ability to understand the basic dynamics of human organization has been shaken, although some social theorists today still believe that scientific analysis is the best approach.

Substantive Problems of Sociological Theory

The Enlightenment held the world view that human society was progressing, but thinkers saw the changes wrought by modernity as potentially ripping the social fabric apart.

Thus the Enlightenment's faith in "progress" had to be reconciled with the obvious signs of disintegration in modernizing societies. In different ways, all of the key figures in sociology's first century – roughly from 1830 to 1930 – worried about modernity, especially such matters as the loss of consensus and coherent meaning stemming from the differentiation of culture and social structure; the loss of cohesive communities in the face of rapid urbanization; the increase in inter-class conflict accompanying the destruction of the old feudal order; the impersonality of bureaucratization; the growth of state power; the use of secular law to replace more sacred symbols; the spread of markets and their capacity to commodify all realms of human thought and endeavor; the alienation of those who had lost control of what they produce or who were subject to the ruthless discipline of the marketplace; the isolation of individuals from cohesive structures in a world of specialization; the increasing rates of crime and deviance; and the many other trends that, to those schooled in the optimism of the Enlightenment, had undermined faith in progress.

As the masters of the early canon confronted these trends, they began to ask a more analytical question: How best to conceptualize these changes in terms of their underlying forces? This question was answered in different ways, and each answer spawned a diverse theoretical tradition that, to some degree, persists until the present day.

Functionalism

Functional theorizing was sociology's first clear conceptual orientation and began as an organismic analogy: society is a kind of organism whose parts can be seen as having functions for sustaining the "body social." Auguste Comte's original formulation of this analogy was to be carried through the nineteenth century by Herbert Spencer and Émile Durkheim; and the analogy was brought to midpoint of the twentieth century by anthropologists.

Functional theory saw modernity in terms of an underlying process of social differentiation (or the dividing of a society into ever more distinct and specialized units, positions, and roles) and rephrased questions about social order in terms of the "needs" or "requisites" necessary for sustaining this order in face of the disintegrative potential of differentiation. The French wing of functionalism championed by Durkheim emphasized the importance of cultural forces, backed up by interpersonal processes and rituals, as the key to integrating differentiated populations, whereas the British wing of Herbert Spencer stressed exchange in markets, interdependence, and moderate concentrations of power as the basic mechanisms for regenerating social cohesion.

As functionalism was carried into the twentieth century, a more "systems approach" became evident. It was suggested by theorists that the social universe can be analyzed as a series of interconnected systems, each operating to meet basic needs for survival and each serving as the environment for the others. The most influential theorist in this mode was Talcott Parsons (1951) and various collaborators (Parsons et al., 1953) who argued that social processes could be visualized for analytical purposes as four "action systems": a "cultural system" in which systems of symbols provide the necessary meaning and information for all other types of action; a "social system" in which actions are organized into social structures; a "personality system" providing the necessary attributes and skills for individual action in social systems as well as the motivation to give culture and social systems direction and purpose; and an "organismic" or biological system providing the physical features and energy necessary for humans to build and act in the other three systems. The goal of sociological analysis then became one of studying the effects of components within and between action systems for meeting basic survival requisites. As Parsons' work fell out of favor, however, a "neofunctionalist" movement sought to revive functional theory by downplaying notions of needs or requisites in action systems; and in particular, neofunctionalism began to stress the significance of culture in sustaining the viability of differentiated societies – a point of emphasis obviously taken from Durkheim.

Bio-ecological Theorizing

Virtually all early theorists had a view of basic human needs, drives, emotions, and other fundamental biological states that mobilize and direct human action. None of these ideas was well developed. Today, few theorists make explicit lists of biological need-states, but most still implicitly invoke them. For example, symbolic interactionists see needs for self-confirmation as fundamental to human interaction; exchange theories view needs to maximize payoffs or at least earn a "profit" in interactions as basic. More significantly, the early canon connected biology and sociology, and this connection has been revitalized over the last two decades. Conceptualizations of the bio-programmers pushing human action are being put back into the canon, but unlike earlier efforts to understand biological needs, the new bio-sociology uses models of natural selection from evolutionary theory as a means for determining how these bio-programmers came to drive human behavior and patterns of social organization (e.g., Lopreato, 1984; van den Berghe, 1979). This approach is widely disputed by most sociological theorists, but there is no doubt that it has regained a foothold in the contemporary canon (e.g., Turner and Maryanski, 1993).

Far more acceptable is another idea from early functionalism: any emergent social structure and cultural pattern can also be analyzed in terms of natural selection. A decade before Charles Darwin's theory of evolution by natural selection had been published in 1859, Herbert Spencer had made a moral argument about social selection with his famous phrase "survival of the fittest," but it was Durkheim (1893) who converted this idea into a sociological theory about modernity: Population growth, in-migration, and urbanization as well as new transportation and information technologies all reduce the "space" between individuals and groups, thereby escalating their competition for resources. This competition revolves around a struggle to find viable resource niches in which to survive; and as this competition intensifies, specialization of activities among individuals and groups (a kind of "social speciation") inevitably follows. Hence, the division of labor as a form of social differentiation is generated by a process of natural selection.

This Durkheimian analogy was championed between 1920 and 1950 by the "Chicago School" of American sociology. One branch of this school studied urban areas in cities in terms of competition for land and housing resources in real-estate markets (e.g., McKenzie, 1933). Today, "urban ecology" remains true to both Durkheim and the Chicago School in analyzing competition as a key force in the spatial distribution of populations (e.g., Frisbie and Kasarda, 1988). Similarly, a newer school of "organizational ecology" examines the rise and fall of various types of complex organizations in terms of competition for resources (e.g., Hannan and Freeman, 1989). And, even more in tune with Durkheim's societal level analyses are recent theories viewing the internal organization of whole societies as a process of competition and selection (e.g., Turner, 1995; Runciman, 1990; Hawley, 1986).

Conflict Theory

Karl Marx and Max Weber were the inspiration for what became known as "conflict theory" in the 1960s and 1970s. Marx had viewed the inequality and exploitation of industrial capitalism as leading to revolution by the proletariat, the destruction of capitalism, and the ascendance of communism (Marx and Engels, 1848). Max Weber (1922), although emphasizing many of the same processes as Karl Marx, was a political conservative, neither desiring nor expecting social revolution. On the other hand he was no enthusiast for capitalist modernity, being grimly pessimistic about the dehumanizing implications of the spread of rational-legal authority and the expansion of state power.

For a brief period in the 1950s and 1960s, the third German founder of sociology, Georg

Simmel (1903–4), also enjoyed currency as a conflict theorist, but his ideas were used to offer a more functionalist view of conflict as promoting forms of social integration (Coser, 1956). For example, conflict was seen by Simmel to increase the internal organization of protagonists; and, unlike Marx's prediction, Simmel felt that once parties to a conflict become organized, they are more likely to compromise and, thereby, avoid destructive conflict. Moreover, conflict was seen by Simmel to release accumulated tensions among the differentiated segments of a society. In Simmel's work, then, were some of the key ideas for why conflict in modern societies did not polarize and produce the class warfare that Marx envisioned.

Despite efforts to view conflict in functional terms, most theory in the late 1950s and 1960s was highly critical of functionalism which, it was argued, portrayed social organization as composed of complementary parts meeting basic survival requisites (e.g., Dahrendorf, 1958). The conflict theory critique became overdrawn, but it had merit and, in the end, led to the decline of functional theory. Yet, even as conflict theory ascended in the 1970s and 1980s, the Marxian wing had to confront the totalitarianism of existing communist regimes and, then in the 1990s, the apparent "victory" of capitalist societies in the world political-economy. In the wake of this intellectual crisis, some theorists reasserted the Marxian line, emphasizing that inequalities and exploitation in advanced capitalist modernity can still generate class conflict (e.g., Wright, 1985). Others shifted the level of analysis and time frame to a world system level, stressing that revolution and the collapse of the capitalist order cannot occur until the entire world becomes capitalist (e.g., Wallerstein, 1974). And, as we will see shortly, many moved into critical theory, taking a more philosophical stance and arguing that theory must expose all existing patterns of domination and suggest alternatives to the current status quo.

The less polemical Weberian line of conflict theorizing stimulated a revival of historical sociology, especially work on the conditions producing revolutions (e.g., Goldstone, 1990; Skocpol, 1979). Moreover, some historical analyses of revolution revitalized more general theorizing on social movements as a process of resource mobilization among protagonists (e.g., Tilly, 1978). Indeed, theoretically-oriented analyses of historical processes are among the most prominent and prestigious elements of the present-day canon – emphasizing, once again, Max Weber's continued influence on sociology.

Critical Theory

From sociology's very beginnings, most Enlightenment-inspired scholars felt that sociology should be used to forge "a better society." Of course, just what constituted a "better society" was debated, as was the role that theory was to play in creating more "humane" social arrangements. The positivists, following Comte's lead, saw theory as discovering the scientific laws that could be used to reconstruct society. Even Marx, who was the philosophical inspiration for the emancipatory thrust of much critical theory, saw his sociology in highly analytical terms: discovering the laws of capitalism so as to understand the internal contradictions that will lead to revolutionary class conflict. Only Spencer and American followers like William Graham Sumner felt that, once discovered, scientific laws "should be obeyed," although these thinkers clearly had what we would see today as a conservative activist agenda.

Critical theorizing is the essence of the Enlightenment: use knowledge in the name of social progress. Towards the middle of the twentieth century, philosopher-sociologists in Germany – sometimes termed the "Frankfurt School" because of their early work at the University of Frankfurt – pursued critical theorizing, but confronted the divergence in Marx and Weber's diagnosis of modernity. Marx's emancipatory project was clearly not coming true, especially with the massive repression and brutality of the communist regime under Stalin. Weber's pessimistic conclusions about a dreary world controlled by rational-legal bureaucracy seemed closer to the empirical truth, but violated members of the Frankfurt School's desire for humans to control their productivity, to be seen and treated as equals, to participate in cohesive social structures, and to be bound by common moral commitments.

What, then, were these thinkers to do as they tried to reconcile their diagnosis of modernity with their Enlightenment-inspired desire to create a new, more emancipatory society. Their answer was to criticize forms of domination and to suggest more liberating alternatives, even if these alternatives were not immediately practical (Held, 1980; Habermas, 1968). In this way, those inspired by the Frankfurt School could feel that they were contributing to the emancipation of humans, while actually side-stepping empirical contradictions to their emancipatory preachings.

This school has continued to the present day, although it enjoyed its largest following in the late 1960s and 1970s. More importantly, it paved the way for new varieties of critical theory. By the 1990s virtually any social and political cause could now be justified under the banner of exposing forms of inequality and oppression without having to be very practical about how to eliminate this oppression. Thus, some feminist theory became a broadside attack on patriarchy in human societies, with science being seen as a reflection of male domination and, hence, as part of the problem rather than its solution; some gay and lesbian activists could create a brand of theory unique to their needs and interest; and most significantly, these and other critical approaches increasingly came under a broad intellectual movement termed "post-modernism."

The Post-modern Turn of Critical Theory

As noted earlier, post-modern theory in the social sciences, and certainly in the humanities, takes an anti-science stance, seeing efforts to understand modernity in scientific terms as a "failed epistemology." At a more substantive level post-modern theory makes a series of empirical claims. One package of claims is that the trends evident in modernism have evolved to such an extreme degree that they now mark a "new stage" of human history – paradoxically a very Enlightenment-sounding assertion. This new stage of human development results from such forces as (a) highly dynamic and volatile markets in world-level capitalism that allow all objects, resources, ideas, and symbols to be converted into commodities that can be bought and sold, (b) the development of instantaneous communication technologies that can connect market transactions at any point of the globe, (c) the proliferation of reproductive technologies like cameras, videos, tape recorders and computers with imaging-processing chips that have created a world of images as much as material reality, (d) the expansion of the media to the point that what people experience is from video images as much as from real social relationships with specific people at particular times and places, (e) the collapsing of space, geography, and time as a result of new transportation and information technologies that can move ideas, images, people and resources around the globe so rapidly, (f) the declining salience of traditional symbolic markers of difference between distinctive groups and cultures that can now be mass-marketed and sold in world markets, and (g) the power of advertising in the media to stimulate needs and tastes and to define who and what people are.

In true Enlightenment fashion almost all portrayals of the post-modern condition are couched in terms of evolutionary stages, with the characteristics listed above as the distinctive features of a new stage that has developed out of modernity (e.g., Baudrillard, 1994; Gergen, 1991; Harvey, 1989; Lash and Urry, 1987; Jameson, 1984). All post-modern theorists are critical of this current post-modern stage; some see it as a permanent condition, whereas others see it as temporary. But, when one looks at the underlying concerns of these theorists, they are very much the same as those of the early canon. Marx's concern with the spread of markets and the commodification of everything is certainly present; Max Weber's worry about the efficiency and coldness of rationality is evident, although many post-modernists ignore his view on the growing concentration of state power; Émile Durkheim's recognition that communication and transportation technologies reduce the space and, hence, the time –space orientations among people is clearly represented; and even George Herbert Mead's portrayal of how self is defined in terms of "generalized others" can be found in the post-modern emphasis of identity fragmentation in a world of advertising and media images.

Exchange Theory

Despite Adam Smith's influence on the basic problematic of the early canon, his more technical works on the laws of supply and demand in markets inhabited by rational actors were never fully accepted by the first masters. Even Herbert Spencer, whom Durkheim attacked for adherence to Smith's views, did not develop a utilitarian theory. Indeed, most sociologists of the first 100 years reacted against a view of humans as rational actors who calculate benefits ("utilities") against costs ("utilities forgone" or "punishments" incurred) and who seek to maximize payoffs (i.e., utilities less costs). At the very least, the early canon wanted to view human calculations and actions as circumscribed by culture and social structure.

Durkheim reacted to the individualistic thrust of some utilitarian arguments, and his student, Marcel Mauss (1925) was to propose a view of individual exchange as symbolizing and sustaining social structural solidarities. Marx was also critical of Adam Smith's laws of capitalism, but he none the less saw his project as an extension of these laws and as a reconceptualization of a stage of history on the road to his communist Utopia. Max Weber recognized that "instrumental rationality" was a basic type of action, but he insisted that action was also guided by "value rational," "traditional," and "affectual" modes of orientation. George Herbert Mead accepted the utilitarian view of thought as calculation, but he filtered notions of rationality through the prism of pragmatist philosophy and saw humans' unique behavi-

oral capacities for thought and self-reference as learned adjustments and adaptations to ongoing social activity.

Among the early theorists in sociology only Georg Simmel (1907), in a work attacking Marx's view on money and capitalist markets, directly pursued what was to become an exchange theory of human action. For Simmel, money operates as symbolic medium of exchange to change the nature of social relations and, in contrast to Marx, he saw the use of this symbolic medium as increasing people's sense of value and breaking down parochial barriers to integration in differentiated societies. Yet Simmel did agree with Marx that power and conflict inhere in the very nature of exchange relations.

When exchange theory burst upon twentieth-century sociological theorizing, one line was clearly inspired by Simmel, another by behavioristic psychology, and a third by utilitarian economics. By the close of the twentieth century exchange theory has become a prominent theoretical perspective, and though it originally drew much from the canons of other disciplines, all these exchange theories have converged on the sociological problems enumerated in the early canon, such as how normative agreements arise, how differentiation occurs, how networks of interconnectedness develop and change, how power is used, and how conflict is activated. Thus, although the respective vocabularies of various exchange theories reflect the canons of other disciplines, they all address the basic problems posed by The Enlightenment as it inspired the first sociologists.

Interactionist Theory

In the first decades of the twentieth century, the University of Chicago philosopher, George Herbert Mead, established the conceptual base for theorizing about face-to-face interaction. Mead was not alone in turning sociological theory toward more micro-level social processes, but his genius lay in synthesizing a number of broad intellectual traditions, such as pragmatist philosophy, Darwinian arguments about natural selection, behaviorist assumptions about reinforcement, and utilitarian concerns about rationality, with specific concepts developed by other thinkers. For Mead (1934), human abilities for language-use, non-verbal gesturing, minded deliberations, self-reflection and evaluation, anticipating responses of others, and assuming group perspectives are all acquired behaviors, emerging as individuals seek to adjust to organized social activity.

Yet, even as Mead's concepts explained the fundamental nature of social interaction, his general philosophy addressed the same problematic as the early sociological canon (Mead, 1938, 1932): sustaining societies in the face of disintegrative pressures generated by social differentiation. Like Durkheim, he emphasized the capacity to use moral codes (which he saw as part of what he termed the "generalized other") to evaluate self and regulate conduct as an important force of social integration, but, unlike all other theorists of his time, he was able to specify the interpersonal mechanisms by which individuals assume the perspective of generalized others while, at the same time, responding to the gestures of others in their immediate social environment (Mead, 1934). This mechanism involved reading gestures to (a) assume the perspective of others, including generalized others, (b) to use this knowledge of others' expectations and likely courses of action to weigh alternative lines of conduct, and (c) to emit a response most likely to facilitate adjustment and, hence, social co-operation. Indeed, Mead followed the goals of the Enlightenment, seeking to find the interpersonal forces holding society together and hoping that the discovery of these forces would facilitate human adaptation and progress.

In the 1960s symbolic interactionism, as Mead's approach became known, often became bogged down in more philosophical debates over the possibility of developing general laws of social interaction and the kinds of research methods that should be given emphasis. Still, Mead's ideas were extended within the more positivistic wing of symbolic interactionism. Theories of self and identity represented important elaborations of Mead's work (e.g., Stryker, 1980). In these theories self was conceptualized as hierarchies of need for such gratifications as efficacy, esteem, and power. The emergence of role theory marked another creative extension of Mead's ideas. Here, the conceptualization of social structure as composed of interconnected status positions, roles, and norms provided a more precise conceptualization of the context within which interpersonal mechanisms operate (e.g., Turner, 1962). At the same time, the more experimental wing of social psychology was extending the concepts of self, status, and role into a variety of theoretical perspectives on how individuals evaluate themselves and others, how expectations for behavior develop and guide the flow of interaction, how authority and power are created and used, and how a sense of fairness and justice evolve during the course of interaction (e.g., Berger et al., 1974).

Yet, by far the most important conceptual breakthrough was Erving Goffman's (1959, 1967) blending of (a) Durkheim's analysis of norms and rituals, (b) Mead's conceptualization of mind, self, and role-taking, and (c) role theory. This blending became known as "dramaturgy" because emphasis was on how individuals strategically present themselves in face-to-face encounters and in more public places. Another major breakthrough involved the extension of Alfred Schutz's (1932) phenomenology into "ethnomethodology" (Garfinkel, 1967), where focus is on the interpersonal methods used by individuals to sustain presumptions of a shared interpersonal reality. A more recent theoretical breakthrough is the use of Mead's scheme in theories of emotional processes. And finally, in less spectacular fashion, the cumulative impact of experimental work in social psychology has produced an even wider variety of theories relating self, expectations, norms, perceptions of justice, and emotions to status processes within groups (e.g., Fisek, 1993).

Structuralist Theory

All early sociological theories offered a conception of "social structure", and though these were far from very precise, Émile Durkheim's and Georg Simmel's conceptualizations have exerted considerable influence inside and outside of sociology. For Durkheim, structure denoted *the nature, number, and arrangement of parts*, whereas for Simmel, structure was *the underlying form of social relations*. These ideas converge, but they were to be taken in very different directions during the course of the twentieth century.

By the turn into this century Durkheim and his followers, particularly Marcel Mauss, had begun to visualize mental categories of the mind as reflections of the nature, number and arrangements of the parts constituting social structures (Durkheim, 1912; Durkheim and Mauss, 1903). Two founders of modern-day linguistics, Ferdinand de Saussure and Roman Jakobson, began to borrow from Durkheim and argued that language reveals an underlying structure that can be analyzed independently of the meanings of words and the specifics of grammar. In particular, de Saussure (1915) appeared to visualize linguistic systems as reflecting social structural patterns. A fellow Frenchman, Claude Lévi-Strauss (1945) then turned Durkheim and, to a lesser extent, de Saussure on their heads, proclaiming that social and cultural structures were but manifestations of basic and, presumably, biologically-wired coding systems in the neurology of the brain. Out of this argument was born a broad intellectual movement known as "structuralism" and, as the movement lost steam, "post-structuralism." The movement penetrated sociology for a while in the 1970s and early 1980s, but it soon faded or became a part of the postmodern critique with its emphasis on "texts." The enduring contributions of structuralism were in the notions that systems of symbols evidence a structure of their own and that language as well as text-production can be analyzed independently of their producers. This is often termed "the decentering of subject."

More important than the drift into postmodernity was the creative use of Durkheim's views on social structure and mental categories. Here, emphasis turned to the analysis of how the structure of symbol systems, as reinforced by ritual activities among individuals, operate to shape ways of perceiving and acting that, in turn, sustain existing social structural arrangements. For example, Pierre Bourdieu (1989, 1984) in France has argued that class stratification is maintained by people's modes of classification, perceptions, choices, and behavior (termed "habitus"). Or, in America, Robert Wuthnow (1987) examined ideological movements in terms of their systems of codes and dramaturgical rituals. And, in England, Anthony Giddens (1984) developed a "structuration theory" that combines Durkheim's emphasis on codes and rules with a variety of other traditions in the canon. All of these approaches are critical of early structuralism, but all adopt the more enduring elements of this intellectual movement and give it substance in terms of face-to-face interactions, systems of power, institutions, and other sociological forces. Indeed, just as structuralism "decentered the subject" from cultural text, the newer theories have reconnected them, as Durkheim would have intended.

Simmel's legacy in the modern era has gone in a direction more in tune with Durkheim's original meaning: analyze *forms of social structure* in terms of the nature of arrangements among their parts. Modern network analysis uses this point of emphasis to develop mathematical models and computer algorithms for describing the underlying patterns of connectedness, *per se* (e.g., Turner and Maryanski, 1991). Within sociology the most developed network theories are combined with exchange approaches, explaining how forms of social structure are produced, sustained, and changed by the pursuit of rewards and utilities (e.g., Cook and Emerson, 1978). Another line of structural analysis by Peter Blau (1994, 1977) also blends Simmel with Durkheim. Here, abstract laws explain how symbols marking differentiation of discrete social categories and lines of inequality lower or increase rates of interaction and, true to the early canon, these rates of interaction are then seen as determining the level of social integration in complex societies.

Conclusion

The sociological canon has changed a great deal in the twentieth century, but it has sustained a concern with the epistemological and substantive issues raised by the early masters. In a very real sense sociology is at an important crossroads: the discipline has accumulated an enormous number of theoretical insights as the early canon has been extended and elaborated in many diverse directions. There is great potential here for new masters of theoretical sociology to unify the discipline. Indeed, more than ever, sociology can be what its first practitioners saw: a discipline that can explain the social trends of the modern world, including the post-modern condition, in terms of the basic underlying social forces that drive human behavior, interaction, and organization. Perhaps some do not want to go as far as to call the kind of explanatory effort "science," but the point is not what sociologists call themselves. Rather, despite disagreements among the early masters of the canon, they all presented one essential message: use of abstract and analytical thought to understand the social world and, if one is so disposed, to criticize social arrangements and propose alternatives based upon rational inquiry into the fundamental social processes driving the organization of society and the behavior of people. Just how these abstract explanations are to be formulated can vary, of course, but the essential goal of sociology is to analyze social conditions and processes.

For students of sociology today, or for those thinking about sociology as a career, there are great opportunities to bring together the diverse analyses of human behavior, interaction, and social organization into a body of knowledge that can not only inform but also guide efforts to deal with the problems of the present era. Such has always been the promise of sociology, as the early masters of the canon recognized. The key to the future of sociology is perhaps in the hands of the next generation. For those committed to sociology's future, the goal must be to tone down the epistemological debate over science and to focus, instead, on unifying the diversity of theoretical approaches into a more coherent substantive explanation of the social universe.

Disciplines that have a theoretical canon make a difference in the world. The founders of sociology provided a vision of what was possible; and indeed, gave us many of the critical insights to forge a contemporary canon that can be used to make a real difference in the quality of human life at the close of the twentieth century. What those who begin to practice sociology in the twenty-first century must do is consolidate the canon, make it ever more coherent even in the face of specialization in the academic world, and, if one is still guided by the goals of the Enlightenment, to use sociology to inform public debate, political policy, and social action to reconstruct society.

References

[*Note*: all references in this chapter are to the *original* date of publication.]

Baudrillard, J. 1994: *Simulacra and Simulation*. Ann Arbor: University of Michigan Press.

Berger, J., Conner, T. L. and Fisek, M. H. 1974: *Expectation States Theory: The Status of a Research Program*. Cambridge, MA: Winthrop.

Blau, P. M. 1977: *Inequality and Heterogeneity: A Primitive Theory of Social Structure*. New York: The Free Press.

—— 1994: *Structural Context of Opportunities*. Chicago, IL: University of Chicago Press.

Bourdieu, P. 1984: *Distinction: A Social Critique of the Judgement of Taste*. Cambridge, MA: Harvard University Press.

—— 1989: *Language and Symbolic Power*. Cambridge, MA: Harvard University Press.

Comte, A. 1875 [1851–4]: *System of Positive Polity*. New York: Burt Franklin.

—— 1896 [1830–42]: *The Course of Positive Philosophy*. London: George Bell.

Cook, K. S. and Emerson, R. M. 1978: Power, equity, and commitment in exchange networks, *American Sociological Review*, 27, 721–39.

Coser, L. A. 1956: *The Functions of Social Conflict*. New York: The Free Press.

de Saussure, F. 1966 [1915]: *Course in General Linguistics*. New York: McGraw-Hill.

Dahrendorf, R. 1958: Out of utopia: toward a reorganization of sociological analysis. *American Sociological Review*, 34, 127–38.

Durkheim, É. 1954 [1912]: *The Elementary Forms of The Religious Life*. New York: The Free Press.

—— 1938 [1895]: *The Rules of The Sociological Method*. New York: The Free Press.

—— 1947 [1893]: *The Division of Labor in Society*. New York: The Free Press.

Durkheim, É. and Mauss, M. 1963 [1903]: *Primitive Classification*. Chicago, IL: University of Chicago Press.

Fisek, M. H. (ed.) 1993: *Group Processes*. Chicago, IL: Nelson-Hall.

Frisbie, P. W. and Kasarda, J. D. 1988: Spatial Processes. *Handbook of Sociology*. Newbury Park, CA: Sage.

Garfinkel, H. 1967: *Studies in Ethnomethodology*. Englewood Cliffs, NJ: Prentice-Hall.

Gergen, K. 1991: *The Saturated Self*. New York: Basic Books.

Giddens, A. 1984: *The Constitution of Society*. Cambridge: Polity Press.

Goffman, E. 1959: *The Presentation of Self in Everyday Life*. New York: Doubleday.

—— 1967: *Interaction Ritual*. New York: Doubleday.

Goldstone, J. 1990: *Revolution and Rebellion in The Early Modern World*, 1640–1848. Berkeley: University of California Press.

Habermas, J. 1968: *Theory and Practice*. Cambridge: Polity Press.

Hannan, M. T. and Freeman, J. 1989: *Organizational Ecology*. Cambridge, MA: Harvard University Press.

Harvey, D. 1989: *The Condition of Postmodernity: An Inquiry into the Origins of Cultural Change*. Oxford: Basil Blackwell.

Hawley, A. 1986: *Human Ecology: A Theoretical Essay*. Chicago, IL: University of Chicago Press.

Held, D. 1980: *Introduction to Critical Theory*. London: Hutchinson.

Jameson, F. 1984: *The Postmodern Condition*. Minneapolis: University of Minnesota Press.

Lash, S. and Urry, J. 1987: *The End of Organized Capitalism*. Cambridge: Polity Press.

Lévi-Strauss, C. 1945: The analysis of structure in linguistics and in anthropology. *Word*, 1, 1–21.

Lopreato, J. 1984: *Human Nature and Biocultural Evolution*. Boston, MA: Allen & Unwin.

Marx, K. 1967 [1867]: *Capital: A Critical Analysis of Capitalist Production*. New York: International Publishers.

Marx, K. and Engels, F. 1971 [1848]: *The Communist Manifesto*. New York: International Publishers.

Mauss, M. 1967 [1925]: *The Gift*. New York: Norton.

McKenzie, R. 1933: *The Metropolitan Community*. New York: McGraw-Hill.

Mead, G. H. 1923: Scientific method and the moral sciences. *International Journal of Ethics*, 33, 75–85.

—— 1932: *The Philosophy of The Present*. Chicago, IL: University of Chicago Press.

—— 1934: *Mind, Self and Society*. Chicago, IL: University of Chicago Press.

—— 1938: *The Philosophy of The Act*. Chicago, IL: University of Chicago Press.

Parsons, T. 1951: *The Social System*. New York: The Free Press.

——Bales, R. F. and Shils, E. A. 1953: *Working Papers in The Theory of Action*. New York: The Free Press.

Runciman, W. G. 1990: *A Treatise on Sociological Theory*, Vol. 2. Cambridge: Cambridge University Press.

Schutz, A. 1967 [1932]: *The Phenomenology of The Social World*. Evanston, IL: University of Northwestern Press.

Simmel, G. 1978 [1907]: *The Philosophy of Money*. Boston, MA: Routledge.

—— 1903–4: The sociology of conflict. *American Journal of Sociology*, 9, 490–535, 672–89, and 798–811.

Skocpol, T. 1979: *States and Revolutions*. New York: Cambridge University Press.

Smith, A. 1805 [1776]: *An Inquiry into the Nature and Causes of the Wealth of Nations*. London: Davis.

Spencer, H. 1873: *The Study of Sociology*. London: Routledge & Kegan Paul.

Stryker, S. 1980: *Symbolic Interactionism: A Structural Version*. Menlo Park, CA: Benjamin/Cummings.

Tilly, C. 1978: *From Mobilization to Revolution*. Reading, CA: Addison-Wesley.

Turner, J. H. 1995: *Macrodynamics: Toward a Theory on The Organization of Human Populations*. New Brunswick, NJ: Rutgers University Press.

—— 1991: Network analysis. In Turner, J. H. (ed.), *The Structure of Sociological Theory*. Belmont, NY: Wadsworth.

—— and Maryanski, A. R. 1993: The biology of human organization. *Advances in Human Ecology*, 2, 1–33.

—— Beeghley, L. and Powers, C. 1995: *The Emergence of Sociological Theory*. Belmont, NY: Wadsworth.

Turner, R. H. 1962: Role-taking: processes versus conformity. In *Human Behavior and Social Processes*. Boston, MA: Houghton Mifflin.

van den Berghe, P. 1979: *Human Family Systems: An Evolutionary View*. New York: Elsevier.

Wallerstein, I. 1974: *The Modern World System*, Vol. 1. New York: Academic Press.

Weber, M. 1968 [1922]: *Economy and Society*. New York: Bedminister Press.

—— 1949 [1904]: Objectivity in social science and social policy. In *The Methodology of The Social Sciences*. New York: The Free Press.

Wright, E. O. 1985: *Classes*. London: Verso.

Wuthnow, R. 1987: *Meaning and Moral Order: Explorations in Cultural Analysis*. Berkeley: University of California Press.

9

Everything from Crabs to Islam: On the Relation between Sociologists and Their Intellectual Neighbours

David J. Lee

A few years ago I visited a sociology department which had just put two of its faculty members up for promotion. Both were extremely distinguished and well published scholars and in due course the university approved the promotions. Even so, the difference between the research interests of the two individuals raised a few eyebrows. The first had written several definitive treatises on the social and historical foundations of Islam. The second had for some years been observing the behaviour of hermit crabs in the local estuary. Could these individuals really be practising the *same* discipline? What, people asked, *is* sociology?

Many sociology students over the years, including myself when young, have ruefully asked themselves this very question. Their teachers and professors are generally unable to give a definitive answer because they themselves disagree about the aims and methods of the subject and the way it differs from neighbouring disciplines. Some people find this situation intellectually exciting, but for others it is all rather puzzling and perhaps disappointing. For their sakes, I hope this chapter will be helpful. All the same, the problem lies as much in the question ("what is sociology?") as in the answers. It is important to remember that studying any subject is itself a social process. We bring to it expectations shaped by our upbringing and in particular by the way in which we received our previous education. As we progress, these expectations can sometimes hinder our appreciation of more advanced work. So it is with studying sociology. We

need first to ask ourselves why we think that disciplinary identities and boundaries matter?

Misunderstanding Sociology and the Structure of Education

Educational systems are of course organized in many different ways according to a particular society's composition, history and culture. In a famous essay, however, Bernstein (1975) argued that despite this apparent variety, educational institutions in the modern world basically dispense knowledge in one or other of two contrasting ways. The first and more pervasive of these he called the "collection code"; the second, the "integrated code". The collection code is so called because it seeks to "collect" areas of knowledge together into categories with strong boundaries between them. At the centre of this collection process, in Europe especially, is the idea of a *discipline* in the sense of working within a curriculum of established knowledge or expertize. Under this system, too, the teaching and examination process emphasizes *what* the learner has acquired out of this established knowledge. Many of us, to a greater or lesser extent, have grown up with the collection code, and, arguably, it is this which feeds our doubts about sociology. Though it is not unique in this respect, sociology doesn't match up to what we expect: there isn't a standard curriculum or a body of established knowledge; and its practitioners seem not only suspiciously diverse in their interests but also inclined to pronounce on matters that seem to belong elsewhere – everything from crabs to Islam in fact. (And here am I, talking about *education*!)

There have, however, been periodic attempts in education to break away from the collection code. You have probably come across the idea of "progressive" education and "child-centred" teaching, in which fixed subjects and formal lessons are resisted and where the emphasis is on "discovery" learning. Though study materials may be linked by means of some topic or theme, the underlying emphasis is on *how* to learn rather than on *what*; i.e. on method rather than subject matter. Bernstein labelled the principles behind education of this sort the "integrated code" because its ideal is to stress the openness and unity of knowledge as against separating it into fragmented and exclusive specialisms. The development of public education in the US has supposedly been strongly affected by such ideas. If you yourself have experienced this sort of education, I suspect you may have found the "fuzziness" of sociology less of a problem. And, to anticipate what follows, I want to suggest that doing sociology is a matter of "how" rather than "what".

I should add, however, that I am not trying to join in the argument about which of these alternative education systems is "better". (Bernstein argued in fact that there were counter-productive features in both.) I merely want to suggest that the collection code, which has had some influence on most peoples' education, creates expectations about the nature of "disciplines" that may not be very helpful in studying sociology. Moreover, this is not just a problem for students but for scholars too. After all, the structure of education and the world of scholarship are pretty closely connected. To show the significance of this point I now want to talk briefly about how the idea of generating knowledge in "disciplines" came about and how it has hindered mutual understanding between sociologists and scholars working in cognate areas of study.

Sociology and the Hierarchy of Sciences

That there can be fundamental differences in the organization of scholarship is clear from the development of higher learning in the West over the last 200 years. Even as late as the early nineteenth century it was still common for "philosophers" – many of them scholars of independent means – to range at will across problems of physics, chemistry, nature, culture, history, economics, theology and morals. It is doubtful if these individuals would have found the fuzzy shape of contemporary sociology too troubling and they might indeed have regretted the extent to which it has become divided off from related fields of study like economics, politics or psychology. Since those times, however, right across the range of science and scholarship, successive specialist areas have in fact detached themselves from what they called "speculative" philosophy and set themselves up as individual "disciplines". This was, in part, simply the result of the success (and the growing scale and expense) of natural science. It also, however, reflected the growth of governmental and commercial bureaucracies, which created a demand for formally qualified staff; and, related to that, the vested interest of scholars and intellectuals in the growing professionalization of knowledge. Consequently the social institution of "the discipline" was increasingly emulated outside of natural science too. In most fields the amateur private scholar was edged out by bodies of paid specialists employed by publicly established colleges and learned societies, which began to confer "recognized" qualifications on the basis of examinations and tests (e.g. Perkin, 1989).

Furthermore, these developments came to be openly celebrated in what became known as the "positivist" account of knowledge. Here I am concerned only with nineteenth-century versions of positivism which, as you probably know, attempted to place a strict boundary between the speculative methods of traditional philosophy and what it saw as the certainties yielded by modern science, with its "disciplined" observation of empirical facts. The significance attributed to empirical observation in turn drew attention to the growing specialization of subject matter among scientists and scholars and the making of blueprints for the eventual structure of the intellectual division of labour. For example, both Comte and Spencer, who were important in the development of this early positivist outlook, ordered the individual sciences into an emerging hierarchy with each discipline having its appropriate body of facts and laws. The establishment of a "sociology", whose subject matter is the facts and laws of society, would be the culmination.

Nevertheless, two rather different conceptions of an intellectual "discipline" are muddled up in these writings. A discipline can be:

(i) an *institution*: that is, a pattern of social organization through which the activities of scholars are legitimated, focussed and controlled – for example, through professional associations and/or discipline-based departments in universities and schools. A discipline in this sense has a subject matter which is the intellectual property of "the experts". The latter typically seek to prevent encroachment from outsiders by encouraging collection code practices in education like the setting of approved curricula, and the use of formal credentials.

(ii) a *set of abstract principles and practices* constituting a method of analysis (e.g. the experimental method in natural science). A discipline in this second sense may be addressed to a particular subject matter, but attempts to impose restrictions on the kind of problem to which such analytical principles might be applied rarely prove sustainable. The extension of a discipline, in this sense, to a new topic may indeed disrupt the pattern of "disciplines" in sense (i) described above.

Sociology and Intellectual Property

During the twentieth century, the continual expansion of academies and mass educational systems, including of course the astonishing growth of sociology itself, in terms of teachers, courses and qualifications, right up to the present, has kept questions of the "intellectual property" of organized disciplines to the fore. Yet in sociology the attempt to stake out intellectual property has not in fact proved to be particularly easy or convincing. For one thing, the notion of a hierarchy of sciences, each with its own subject matter contrasts starkly with the untidy divisions which, by the beginning of the twentieth century, came to make up academic "social science" in practice. Perhaps the most relevant case in point is the co-existence of sociology with anthropology, whose practitioners have undoubtedly also claimed "society" as their intellectual concern. Admittedly the two subjects appeared to be fairly different at the outset because of anthropology's preoccupation with the traditional societies and tribal cultures encountered in the course of European imperial expansion. Arguably, however, the persistence of the division between them has had more to do with the politics of academia than with any real difference in principle.

Yet the difficulty of defining the intellectual property of sociology is not just the result of its history and of academic politics. In taking "society" as its object, positivist sociology tended to confuse "societies" with "countries", i.e. territorial entities or nation states. When stripped of these associations the concept of "society" becomes rather elusive. The everyday words "society" and "social" do not in fact have a precise meaning and certainly do not refer to anything that can be precisely observed or defined. (See also Jary's discussion of "society" in Chapter 19 in this volume.) This is not to argue that "there is no such thing as society" but to argue that in principle "society" cannot be used to define sociology's subject matter.

A further problem is that the question of "who studies what?" is really rather inappropriate outside of natural science (it may not work terribly well within natural science either, but that is another matter). Across the whole of the arts, humanities and social sciences, scholarship remains more like the openness of old style philosophy than like the stereotype of the experimental scientist investigating a strictly contained problem. More precisely, it resembles the "discovery learning" we described earlier. The work routinely involves "straying" across ritualized boundaries in the pursuit of some theme or topic: students of politics or literature get into historical questions; historians and anthropologists, for perfectly good reasons, start pronouncing about human psychology; the geographers of a region take up its anthropology and so on. All this means that the question "What is this subject about?" is just as difficult to answer definitively in, say, history, politics, literary criticism or geography as it is in sociology.

Lastly, the creation of "sociology" as an institutional discipline has involved putting together a particularly heterogeneous body of scholars, rather few of whom actually thought of themselves as contributing to the establishment of a new academic specialism. Marx, for example was a professed revolutionary and his followers since have continued deliberately to maintain some distance between themselves and the "bourgeois social sciences". Weber, who, by contrast, preached the need for scholars to avoid politics, thought of himself primarily as a comparative economic historian, accepting the title "sociologist" reluctantly (see Burke, 1992, p. 11). Of the other so-called "founders", only Spencer and Durkheim consciously sought an identity as "sociologist". Furthermore, outside of the American functionalist tradition, the adherents of the competing intellectual movements which have since been added to sociology, including feminism, have all too often thought of themselves as challenging the so-called pretensions of the academic mainstream and its (mostly male) practitioners. What they have typically offered is a new or heterodox sociology with its own distinctive preoccupation(s) or "subject matter".

Clearly, then, there are real difficulties in identifying sociology with any particular "intellectual property". We cannot conclude from this, however, that sociology isn't a discipline in the second of the meanings I described above, i.e. a set of abstract principles and practices constituting a method of analysis.

What it does mean is that, strictly speaking, talking about "sociology" is misleading and that we should instead be talking about sociological *analysis*, how it differs from other forms of intellectual practice and how it might be appropriate to an indefinite variety of subject matter.

From "What" to "How" – the Idea of Sociological Analysis

Sociological analysis evolved out of encounters with several formally separate fields of study: with history, with economics and the so-called "life sciences". It will, therefore, be helpful to say something about each of these encounters, if only in order to highlight the innovations in thinking about human society and human nature which lay behind them.

History and the Uses of Abstraction

The positivist blueprint for sociology has obscured the fact that sociology's so-called founders were not in fact grappling with a "scientific" problem at all, not as the positivists thought of science anyway. They were dealing with a concrete problem of west European *history*: namely the nature and origins of what we now call "modernity" and in particular a period of especially rapid change between the last quarter of the eighteenth century and the first quarter of the nineteenth. This was the period of the so-called "Twin Revolutions" i.e. the Industrial Revolution in England and the Democratic Revolutions in America and France, a time when all manner of commentators began to argue that a new form of social order was emerging. But why was this happening? And what *sort* of order was it? Such questions meant going past the details of concrete events as they unfolded toward an *abstract* account or theoretical "model" of the underlying causal processes involved.

This contrasted with and challenged the outlook of conventional historians. Though the idea of an abstract theory of history and historical change had been mooted as far back as the ancient Greeks, the ethos in historical writing around the time we are talking about was less and less favourable to abstraction. It became focused on concrete political events and showed minimal interest in society at large. During the nineteenth century, moreover, as history turned into a self-conscious discipline and enormous technical progress was being made in the use and evaluation of historical sources, historical scholarship became preoccupied simply with the aim of compiling a comprehensive record of "what happened". This encouraged the view that "scientific" history should prioritize the discovery and accumulation of objective *facts* about the past. It gave rise to the widely held view, even among historians themselves, that history is "without theory". Eminent historians commended the avoidance of abstractions in general and the wild speculations of sociologists in particular (Carr, 1961, Chapter 1; Jones, 1976).

Fortunately, over the past few decades more and more historical scholars have ignored these strictures especially as social history moved from being a peripheral specialism to its present prominence (Burke, 1992). Yet despite the many welcome points of contact which now exist between history and sociology, controversy continues as to their precise relation as "disciplines". It has been pointed out that even traditional historians can hardly help using what are in effect abstract ideas to select and explain the particular events and situations they study. On the other hand, the suggestion that history and sociology are really the same encounters resistance from both sides (Abrams, 1980; Jones, 1976). This controversy, which *appears* to be about disciplinary boundaries, is actually about an important methodological issue which also arises among historians and among sociologists themselves, as well as between sociologists and scholars in other fields such as geography and political science. What is really at stake is the appropriate use of abstraction in studying *any* set of concrete events or phenomena, not where to put fences between intellectual neighbours.

Structure, Action and Economic Theory

Abstraction is not unique to sociological analysis, of course, but is a common procedure across all theoretically based sciences. However, abstraction can be made in different ways as the history of the division between sociology and economics shows. The striking self-confidence and prominence of economics owes a great deal to the use of a particular kind of abstraction known as "rational choice" or "rational exchange" theory. Anyone studying sociology needs to understand at least the basic principles of this approach and its role as stimulus (or, perhaps irritant) in the development of sociological analysis.

The early economists (the so-called "political" economists) were one of the groups of intellectuals involved in the debate about western modernization which I described above. Much of their work is barely distinguishable in fact from early sociology in that they too acknowledged the abstract properties of institutions, customs and culture and the way in which these constrain and outlast the lives and actions of particular individuals. In modern sociological terminology we might say they had a remarkable sense of social "structure". On the other hand, when it came to the discussion of modern economic affairs, most of them had a particular viewpoint to put forward analogous to what today is called "free market liberalism". It depended on portraying economic phenomena and institutions as the outcome, not the cause, of individual choices and actions.

Gradually this focus on individual choice was detached from the rest and, shorn of its overt political baggage, became the basis of modern analytical economics. As a result, the use of abstraction by mainstream economic theory today is quite distinctive. It starts from a common general viewpoint in the philosophy of the social sciences called "methodological individualism": this argues that all explanations of social phenomena must be capable of being expressed in terms of the purposes, choices and actions of individuals. But in economics itself the many different purposes and meanings which individuals possess are merged into a single abstract notion of *utility*. Its measure is money, which after all is distinguished by the fact that it can express a diversity of wants and desires. This enables economists to work with an abstract concept of a "rational" economic actor who operates solely on the basis of maximizing personal utility from each transaction. The movement of supply, demand, prices and so on can then, it is argued, be explained in terms of calculations of advantage made by groups of such actors. Using these particular abstractions, then, rational choice theory has yielded a substantial body of formal propositions about economic phenomena, which these days can be expressed mathematically.

In contrast, (starting with Marx's notorious "critique of political economy") the sociological tradition, so diverse in other respects, is marked by a shared sense of the logical and empirical limitations of individualist economic theory. True, there are plenty who argue, as Max Weber did, that methodological individualism should be the basis for *all* social analysis. Of these, a relatively small number actually advocate extending rational exchange analysis from economic to non-economic phenomena. More usually, however, "methodological individualists" in sociology follow Weber against economics in two ways: (i) they recognize the importance of non-rational types of action; and (ii) they acknowledge that not all types of rational action are "utility maximizing". In fact, in the view of most sociologists, we lose a great deal, even in understanding *economic* life, by compressing peoples' diverse values and goals into a single notion of "utility".

Indeed, to talk about human individuals at all is already to take collective existence for granted (see for example Carr, 1961, p. 31; Craib, 1992, p. 127). So although methodological individualism may seem persuasive, it is actually more characteristic of the sociological tradition to start from the opposite principle, which I will call here "methodological collectivism". This means the view, to be found in both Marx and Durkheim, for example, that eventually social phenomena have to be explained by the behaviour of social structures, for example of power, community or belief. Structures and collectivities cannot simply be deduced from the actions and choices of individuals. Rather, actions and choices to some degree at least are *explained* by the structures. Some economists are in fact beginning to recognize (whilst trying to save as much of their method as they can) that the isolation of economics has caused them grossly to underestimate the role of institutional and cultural structures (e.g. Ormerod, 1995). There is also a vigorous tradition of economic sociology that has burgeoned in recent years, seeking to confront economic theory on its own ground (see for example Holton, 1992).

The Problem of Human Nature and Reductionism

The final stimulus to sociological analysis that I wish to consider has resulted from the encounter with certain ways of understanding "human nature" within the so-called "life sciences" of biology and psychology. You have probably already come across accounts of the so-called nature–nurture controversy and arguments about the role of heredity and environment in fixing, say, intelligence or personality. You may also have got the impression that most biologists and many psychologists tend to favour explanations in terms of nature and heredity whereas sociologists are all for "environment". Unfortunately, this is all too often not far from the truth – even though there is a strong case to be made that hard and fast distinctions between nature and nurture, or heredity and environment are very misleading (e.g. Benton, 1991; Jones, 1994). However, ever since the development of Darwinian evolutionary theory, with its emphasis on the hereditary transmission of characteristics, life scientists have been fascinated by the possibility of uncovering a common *material* explanation for both inorganic and organic (i.e. "life") processes. Under the influence of this prospect, biologists and psychologists have sought to understand the relation between (i) the behaviour and social organization of complex animals, including humans, and (ii) their genetic, biophysical or biochemical make-up. Sociobiology, human DNA research and neuropsychology are recent examples of such work and it is important to recognize that much of it is perfectly valid and carried out in a serious fashion. However, sociologists have always tended to be very dismissive of any hint of what they typically call "social Darwinism" in the study of human social behaviour. This is because *certain* life scientists periodically make excessive claims for genetic and biological analysis, often in ways that are tendentious, or conservative or racist – especially when put out for popular consumption (a notorious recent example is Herrnstein and Murray, 1994). Thus both sides have contributed to a sense that the respective approaches of the life-science disciplines and sociology and irreconcilable.

In this whole debate, questions of method are of critical importance. The sociological case against social Darwinist accounts of human nature centres around a problem called *reductionism*. Reductionism means trying to show that an existing set of explanations and theories about a particular subject area can be replaced with another set which (typically) has already had some success *outside* of that area. We could talk of reductionism, for example, if atomic physicists tried to substitute physical concepts for those now used in biology. In one sense reductionism is a virtue, for there is a principle in scientific work that a simpler or more economical explanation should always be preferred to one which is relatively complex. On the other hand reductionism can be a source of error if it leads scholars into oversimplification. For this discussion, the most relevant example of such oversimplification occurs when investigators try to explain something that is variable by means of something else that doesn't vary. Thus, it is a "reductionist" oversimplification to explain all of the immense variability of human societies and cultures in terms of the biologically and genetically *fixed* properties of human nature.

That is why successive generations of anthropologists and sociologists have sought to demonstrate the relative unimportance of bio-

logical factors compared with culture in shaping human nature and social relationships (for a brilliant example, see Sahlins, 1977). Some have even turned things round and accounted for biological and psychological states in terms of variations in, say, community structure, sub-culture or social class. Incidentally, something like this was behind the research on crabs which I mentioned above. These creatures, it seems, have community structures too! More celebrated examples include not only Durkheim's well-known study of suicide, but also much modern research in, say, the sociology of health and of education. All this does not mean that nature and biology are irrelevant to society. Rather, that the really important work waiting to be done is on the reciprocal interplay of social, mental and biological factors. So it is of some significance that there has always been hostility to "social Darwinism" and reductionist explanations within the life sciences themselves (Benton, 1991).

To sum up so far: among the chief features of sociological "analysis" as it has developed have been:

(i) Abstraction;
(ii) A sense of the relative permanence of social and cultural structures;
(iii) An emphasis on the cultural variability and relative openness of human nature.

Unfortunately, as we have seen, the deployment of these principles has become confounded with attempts to assert and defend the distinctiveness of "sociology" as an institutional discipline. Too often this has caused sociologists to overstate their case. In turn, sociology's neighbours have perhaps neglected the possibility that sociological approaches might be complementary to their own rather than in competition with them.

Sociology as Method: Philosophy or Science?

Some of the most intractable problems for sociological analysis, however, are presented by its relations with philosophy rather than with substantive fields of study. You will no doubt already be aware that many sociologists themselves have philosophical doubts about the suggestion that sociology should seek to establish objective scientific knowledge. Maybe you have read some of the vast amount that is written about this (see Chapter 10 by Ballard). To some extent, however, the whole debate can be seen as a further misfortune brought about by the ethos of "disciplines" and the expectations induced by the collection code.

I argued earlier that the collection code in education and scholarship makes studying sociology difficult because it leads us to expect a discipline to consist of "established knowledge", "facts" or expertise, in relation to which a large degree of certainty exists. Controversies about what makes knowledge *certain*, however, are as old as philosophy itself. The early positivists, as we have seen, thought (wrongly) that the scientific revolution had resolved such arguments for good. They made an invidious contrast between the uncertain speculations of traditional philosophy and the objective certainties supposedly yielded by systematic empirical observation as found in the scientific disciplines.

But what role, if any, then remains for philosophy itself? Not all members of the emergent philosophy profession accepted that philosophy should now be restricted to the task of what one account calls an "underlabourer", merely dealing with certain residual issues and conceptual confusions which the grand march of empirical science had failed to resolve (Winch, 1958). Philosophy, they argued, should be thought of as different from empirical science in a special way. For whereas the latter is merely concerned with establishing knowledge about particular kinds of subject matter or "being", philosophy is concerned with the nature of being *in general* and with the certainty of our claims to know things about it.

This gambit has seemingly restored to philosophy the right to review *all* forms of intellectual endeavour. It also has provided the basis for a concerted attempt to reclaim sociology, psychology and indeed the humanities as a whole from the clutches of empirical science. Different forms of this challenge to

positivism in the humanities have appeared over the years but almost all depend on an argument whose basic form can be traced back to the nineteenth-century philosopher Dilthey. Humanities scholarship, Dilthey argued, is dependent on understanding values and concepts held in individual minds or (as later philosophers were to stress) embodied in culture, language and "texts". It therefore necessarily involves the analysis and interpretation of thought and meaning, so it requires the use of philosophical methods rather than the "purely empirical" investigations of science. Furthermore, the validity of these interpretations will always be relative to the subjective values and circumstances of the interpreter. Dilthey himself saw this last as a puzzle to wrestle with, but many later writers have simply taken it as further proof that findings in subjects like sociology can never possess the objective and established *certainty* of science. The most alarming use of this theme today appears in the work of recent post-modernists where it contributes to a fashion for attacking, not just the idea of "disciplines" but of reason (that is disciplined thought) itself.

Arguably, however, all of this rests on a set of collection code inspired expectations that associate objectivity of thought with certainty of belief. In fact it is exactly the other way round. The certainty claimed, for example, by bigots, dogmatists, ideologues or uninformed common sense is based on prejudiced thought which is wholly personal or subjective. By contrast, the objectivity of science lies in the fact that it obliges us to submit the "certainties" we personally cherish, as well as the observations *and* interpretations we make, to the informed critical doubt of others. What passes as "established knowledge" in science is, therefore, constantly under revision, inductive and *uncertain*. To be scientific is to be more certain about *how* to think, than about *what* to think. Moreover, because of this matter of "how to think" there is an inherently philosophical element (i.e. methodology) at the very heart of all empirical science, not just in sociological analysis. Thus, the whole interpretative attack on the idea of social science is flawed by its own use of a crude and misleading positivist account of what empirical science is like. Once this is abandoned, no role exists for a separate "philosophy" to wage an anti-scientific crusade in sociology or any other subject. Philosophers and scientists should instead, perhaps, make common cause against attacks on reason.

Conclusions

My contention in this chapter, then, is that it is not very helpful to think about sociology as a self-contained discipline or to enquire "what" it is. We should rather be enquiring as to *how* sociological analysis approaches *any* substantive area of enquiry within its view. With this in mind I have tried set out what I consider to be some of its main characteristics and would resist the suggestion that there are strict or pre-ordained limits on how and where it might be applied. There is in any case, as we have seen, already a vast range of material to which it has been applied with interest and success.

References

Abrams, P. 1980: History, sociology, historical sociology. *Past and Present*, 87, 3–16.

Benton, T. 1991: Biology and social science: why the return of the repressed should be given a cautious welcome. *Sociology*, 25 (1), 1–30.

Bernstein, B. 1975: On the classification and framing of educational knowledge. In *Class, Codes and Control*, Vol. 3. London: Routledge & Kegan Paul, pp. 202–25.

Burke, P. 1992: *History and Social Theory*. Cambridge: Polity Press.

Carr, E. H. 1987 [1961]: *What is History?*, 2nd edn. London: Penguin Books.

Craib, I. 1992: *Modern Social Theory; from Parsons to Habermas*. New York: Harvester Wheatsheaf.

Herrnstein, R. and Murray, C. 1994: *The Bell Curve: Intelligence and Class Structure in American Life*. New York: The Free Press.

Holton, R. 1992: *Economy and Society*. London: Routledge.

Jones, S. 1994: *The Language of the Genes: Biology, History and the Evolutionary Future*. London: Flamingo.

Ormerod, P. 1995: *The Death of Economics*.

Perkin, H. 1989: *The Rise of Professional Society – England since 1880*. London: Routledge.

Sahlins, M. 1977: *The Use and Abuse of Biology*. London: Tavistock.

Steadman Jones, G. 1976: From historical sociology to theoretical history. *British Journal of Sociology*, 27, 295–305.

Winch, P. 1958: *The Idea of a Social Science*. London: Routledge & Kegan Paul.

10

Sociology as a Humanist and Scientific Discipline

Chet Ballard

In this chapter I identify two intellectual cultures – one scientific and the other humanist – and show how both have been influential in the development of sociology. Scientists have a devout belief that there is an objective reality to be known through controlled, systematic observation. *Positivist* scientists know the rules of nature which control events and can predict outcomes with certainty. The best and only way to know anything, according to them, is by use of the scientific method based on controlled, detached observation and systematic experimentation. The culture of humanism recognizes that the "natural order" of things, as it applies to human behavior, is *not* governed by nature nor by objective forces. Humanists know that people make their own laws although, as Karl Marx noted, they do not make them as they choose. Humanists are certain that there is no fundamental reality, only the one we choose to regard as such, and that every truth is limited in space and time. There are no universal laws to be "discovered" (Snow, 1959).

I will show that sociology, when practiced as a *solely* scientific or *solely* humanist discipline, is unable to generate the richness of insight that is possible when both traditions are combined in the service of humanity. When it draws on both, however, it is capable of producing powerful analyses of society such as are found in the great works of sociology's founders.

My argument in favor of a sociology that draws on both traditions is presented through the discussion of five points.

(1) Both traditions have contributed distinctive research methods and conceptions of the sociological enterprise.
(2) The unique subject matter of sociology demands different approaches from those of the natural sciences.
(3) Some important traditions within sociology have been modelled exclusively on the methods of natural science.
(4) Humanist sociologists reject this approach.
(5) The best prospects for sociology lie in the *combination* of scientific and humanist traditions.

Sociology's Scientific and Humanist Traditions

There can be no doubt regarding the respect in which science was held by the founders of sociology. Such thinking is evident in the writings of Auguste Comte, usually credited with founding sociology as a discipline, who believe that the methods of physics should be applied to society resulting in the establishment of a "science of society," and in the work of classical sociologists such as Karl Marx and Émile Durkheim. Marx's brilliant analyses of the social forces shaping industrial societies combined insights from across what would now be recognized as the disciplines of history, economics, theology, philosophy, and political science – yet he aspired to a "scientific" understanding of the origins, dynamics, and contradictions of capitalism (which he saw as leading to socialism). His understanding of "science" was very broad, encompassing all the above disciplines purged of ideology and unified with natural science. Durkheim was equally inspired by the goal of constructing a "science" of society and his analyses of society reflected in an exemplary way his insistence on careful, systematic observation. These analyses also drew widely on insights from what would now be regarded as the separate disciplines of anthropology, history, theology, psychology, and the classics, though he argued forcefully for distinguishing sociology from all other humanities and social studies.

But humanist traditions are just as evident in the works of classical sociologists as this enthusiasm for science. Humanist research methods aim to understand people by seeing the world through their eyes, and so they emphasize first-hand observation and direct fieldwork experience. This insistence on careful observation of social life in the real world, so as to understand people in the context of the social structures they create and act within, often results in the sociologist taking on the role of participant–observer. This creates a situation where the actors to be studied and the researcher interact and so reciprocally affect each other's behavior. The humanist tradition in sociology therefore employs a variety of methods including descriptive case studies, ethnographic field accounts of episodes, encounters, and events, reflexive understandings (often called "verstehen"), rhetorical arguments, and metasociological analyses of secondary source data.

The humanist tradition in sociology is value-committed and activist, not value-free (Scimecca, 1995). To paraphrase Marx, the point of sociology is not merely to understand social life, but to change social relations which oppress and harm people, or otherwise deny them freedom and dignity. Humanist sociology's unapologetic value commitment to the powerless, the forgotten, the less-valued members of society, means that knowledge produced from this perspective would have an applied goal – knowledge used in the service of humanity. As we shall see later, this guiding principle became problematic from the 1920s to the 1950s as sociology came to be dominated by a scientific ideology which made observation an end in itself (empiricism).

The Exceptional Subject Matter of Sociology

For students entering sociology with an expectation that there must be a core set of facts, definitions, and theories on which there is *de facto* agreement, the first course in sociology is disconcerting to say the least. Not only do students encounter multiple theories to explain the same behaviors, but there are very few, if any, "laws" or scientific principles to cling to as they proceed to learn the moving canon of sociological knowledge. Students struggle with apparently conflicting messages: on the one hand there is an underlying message that sociology is an objective, unbiased science; on the other it lacks the presumed certainty of the natural sciences and the moral concreteness of religious teaching. They learn that cultural differences are just that – differences, nothing more. It seems that nothing is fact forever. Everything is subject to change, to re-interpretation, to further scientific review. To the uninitiated, sociology may seem neither fish nor fowl.

Comparisons to the natural sciences are inevitable and, when compared, sociology may at first appear confusing, tentative, even trivial. I shall now put forward six points which rebut this kind of thinking, and will explain that because sociology has an "exceptional" subject matter it requires a different approach and method from the natural sciences.

(1) *The deterministic cause-and-effect model underlying the natural sciences does not apply to the subject matter of sociology.* For better or worse, people frequently act in irrational ways or ways that are even counterproductive to their self-interests. Since humans exercise free will and some measure of choice, there is a big difference between people (the subject matter of sociology) and things (the subject matter of the physical sciences). The human capacity to confound rational logic means that it will never be possible to formulate absolute laws of human behavior.

(2) *The experimental method, typical of natural scientific inquiry, is neither as effective or ethical when applied to people instead of things.* The classic experimental model of science, a given in the physical sciences, is rarely the best method for investigating social phenomena. Controlled laboratory experiments are not often appropriate or ethical for the study of people. It is impractical to expect people to interrupt their lives and submit to total control by an experimenter. The artificial lab environment yields few of the insights about the naturally occurring group behaviors that sociologists attempt to understand. Thus, given the exceptional subject matter of the discipline, sociologists find other methods, such as participant observation, content analysis, and survey research to be more productive and ethical.

(3) *The causes of social phenomena are not invariant, but change from time to time and place to place.* Just because the "causes" of a social phenomena, such as crime, are known to be true at one point in time, does not mean that they will still be true at another. Explanations of crime today may need to be profoundly different from what they were just a few years ago. Unlike the natural sciences, the exceptional subject matter of sociology is unstable and this makes the task of sociologists much more complex. Sociologists must constantly monitor changing societal conditions and explore how the reasons for behavior change over time.

(4) *Statistical data cannot tell us about important aspects of social phenomena, in particular the motivations of actors.* People can be counted and rates of particular behaviors calculated, but sociologists need to do *more* than that. Rates of behavior tell us things about systems and social structures, for example, but not about the underlying motivations which produced these behaviors.

(5) *The act of data collection can itself affect the behavior of the actors being studied.* A big difference between sociology and the natural sciences is the likelihood that the researcher will, merely by the act of studying social phenomena, have an impact on what is being observed. Certainly "the classic experiment" does not solve this dilemma, and sociologists have often used unobtrusive methods of observation, such as content analysis of human communications, and analysis of existing file data to eliminate the impact of the observer on the observed.

(6) *The publication of research may affect the population concerned, causing a reaction which may change, sometimes in a fundamental way, the behavior being studied.* The publication of findings in physics or astronomy has no impact on the behavior of the stars or planets, but sociological research has the potential to produce changes in the people being studied. For example, during the 1960s sociologists were deeply involved in research on racial desegregation of public schools in the US (the equivalent of state schools in Britain). Publication of their research results had an impact on political leaders, the general public, and most directly on the students who subsequently attended racially integrated schools, and their parents. Once again, this illustrates the interactive nature of sociology's exceptional subject matter, and is something which sociologists have to consciously anticipate.

For all of these reasons, sociology's subject matter differs significantly from that of the natural sciences, and requires different methods of scientific inquiry. The classic experimental model and the formulation of "invariant scientific laws" may not be available to sociologists but, recognizing the limits of experimental science for the study of human behavior, they have made explicit the interesting dilemmas involved when humans study humans, and the special impact the researcher has on the researched. Sociology's impressive methodology employs a range of humanist research methods as the tools which enable them to apply science to the study of social phenomena.

Scientism and Sociology

In the first half of the twentieth century the scientific tradition in sociology took a false turn towards *scientism*. An important dimension of this was the spread of positivism, a perspective which regards empirical, sensory data as the *only* credible data. The positivist tradition has two basic tenets. First it is "positive" in its belief that science can be certain about reality and "knowing things". It holds that through the careful observation and quantification of recurrent events, an objective, knowable reality may be *"discovered"* – leading to the formulation of universal laws of behavior on the basis of which future rates of different types of social behavior could be predicted. This value-free, objectified version of science "was passed to modern society via Parsons, Merton, Lundberg, and their followers." (Lee 1968, p. 2). Second it is "positive" in the sense of being the opposite to negative: the use of positivism would illuminate the "goodness," the positive aspects of institutions and social structures. Positivism combined this with an optimistic belief in progressive social evolution. These ideas were central to the development of functionalist thought.

Functionalism is a theoretical perspective which dominated sociology and sociological training during the early and middle decades of the century. Its origins can be traced to positivism's concern for the core values and beliefs which form the glue holding society together. Sociologists trained in modern structural-functionalism, (particularly the followers of Parsonian functionalism) blended a confidence in technological and social progress with a faith in the authority of social "science," by which they understood a detached, depersonalized, and dehumanized brand of sociology. They raised method and quantification to the status of a religion, concerned only to measure whatever could be measured, and assuming that whatever they discovered must be beneficial to social cohesion. This led them to celebrate the value of existing societal arrangements, a position which has obvious conservative implications.

The arrival of the computer reinforced this tendency to base methodology on what was technologically possible. The computer provided the means to handle large datasets easily. The availability of national and regional datasets, built mostly on the basis of survey research, and the ever more sophisticated statistical designs made possible by computers, lured sociologists into a fascination with technology for its own sake – while ignoring the perplexing problems facing society. They lost sight of the fact that no method,

no matter how sophisticated, can tell us "what it all means." As Cameron once said, ". . . not everything that can be counted counts, and not everything that counts can be counted" (1963, p. 13). Yet the domination of "scientism" in graduate training programs in sociology guaranteed that this brand of sociology would be practiced by subsequent generations. Indeed "scientism" is still evident in much sociological research and writing today.

Humanist Sociology's Rejection of Scientism

Scientific methods and techniques are the tools sociologists use to observe the world more carefully and more systematically than is the case with the commonsense methods used by people to make sense of their everyday lives. But these methods and techniques are, or at least should be, means to an end, not an end in itself. Humanist sociologists reject the excesses of scientism, but most do not abandon scientific methods. They accept the idea that research methods should be value-free, in the sense that sociologists should not be setting out to prove their own prejudices or ignoring evidence they would prefer not to have found. Indeed, they found the detached brand of sociology being practiced throughout much of the past 50 years to be too unquestioning, too supportive of the status-quo and the corporate class which controls the funding of research projects. They accused positivist sociology of being controlled by these elites, in fact of being nothing more than sociology-for-hire to the highest bidder. However, some humanist sociologists rejected not only mainstream sociology, but even its methods – including those of science itself. Finding the elitism and careerism of mainstream sociologists to be alienating, they felt science itself was not to be trusted.

Sociologists working within the prominent positivist paradigm countered by arguing the humanist tradition represented nothing more than left-liberal ideology. They rejected its qualitative emphasis and value-committed practice as unscientific and trivial. It was, they said, characterized by nonreplicable case studies, "touchy-feely" research designs, and given to overgeneralization.

It was many years, therefore, from the 1960s to the 1990s before those critical of mainstream sociology made a real impact on the discipline. Today, although positivist survey research methods still dominate, sociology is a more reflexive, self-critical discipline as a result of these struggles. In the final section I make the case for sociology as a discipline that, at its best, is at once scientific and humanist.

Sociology: A Different Kind of Science

A sociology that is both humanist and scientific is a sociology with an agenda to make sense of social reality *and* to act upon that knowledge. This "hands-on" sociology is a very different scientific practice from anything else out there at the present time. The activist orientation of the best kind of sociology has its roots in the revolutionary movements of the Enlightenment, the dismantling of feudal theocracy, and movements to establish democratic principles in Europe and North America. Thus the tradition of social reform in sociology is one which extends back to the earliest days of the discipline *as a science*. Armed with a sociology that is both humanist and scientific, students practice a reflexive brand of education that wants "to know" in order to "act upon and change" society. The power of this kind of sociology is captured by C. Wright Mills in his conception of the "sociological imagination" – an understanding that personal troubles are not purely personal, but are inextricably tied to public issues and social structures (Mills, 1959). The combination of empirical knowledge with an agenda of change poses a serious threat to the status quo.

But whose beliefs and values will set the agenda for change? Sociological knowledge, as discussed earlier, has consequences for people – but it can be used to liberate or to control, to protect human dignity or to destroy it. Revolutions don't always throw out the corrupt rascals and replace them with freedom-loving patriots. Some revolutions throw out the corrupt rascals and replace them with even worse rascals. The classical sociologists, Marx, Weber, and Durkheim, upon whose work sociology still rests, were not in accord on the form future society would take – and neither are contemporary sociologists. But a sociology that is both humanist and scientific takes responsibility for the production of socially relevant information, and also *for how that information is disseminated and used*. It is this dimension of sociology as a different kind of science that places different kinds of duties on sociologists as scientists. Sociological knowledge is not the sole objective of sociology. It must be produced with sensitivity for the people from whom data is collected, and on whose lives this knowledge will have impact.

I believe sociology, in its truest form, is a hybrid of humanism and science. Values such as equality, liberty, dignity and freedom guide us in how sociological knowledge, once produced, *should* be used.

References

Cameron, W. B. 1963: *Informal Sociology: A Casual Introduction to Sociological Thinking*. New York: Random House.

Lee, A. M. 1986: Sociology: humanist and scientific. In W. K. Fishman and C. G. Benello (eds), *Readings in Humanist Sociology*. New York: General Hall, pp. 9–23.

Mills, C. W. 1959: *The Sociological Imagination*. New York: Oxford University Press.

Scimecca, J. A. 1995: *Society and Freedom: An Introduction to Humanist Sociology*, 2nd edn. Chicago, IL: Nelson-Hall.

Snow, C. P. 1959: *The Two Cultures and the Scientific Revolution*. Cambridge: Cambridge University Press.

Recommended Reading

Elliott, R. D. and Shamblin, D. H. 1992: *Society in Transition: A Humanist Introduction to Sociology*. Englewood Cliffs, NJ: Prentice-Hall.

Goldenberg, S. 1992: *Thinking Methodologically*. New York: HarperCollins.

Johnson, A. 1991: *The Forest for the Trees: An Intro-duction to Sociological Thinking*. New York: Harcourt Brace Jovanovich.

Lee, A. M. 1978: *Sociology for Whom?* New York: Oxford University Press.

Yorburg, B. 1995: *Sociological Reality: A Brief Intro-duction*. Connecticut: Dushkin Publishing.

Values and Diversity in Sociology

11

Conservatism and Sociology: The Problem of Social Order

Graham C. Kinloch

Contemporary politics is often described as predominantly "conservative": "unencumbered market forces," "standing on your own two feet," "family values," and "respect for tradition" are a few of the more popular buzzwords. The term "conservatism" is, in fact, of relatively recent origin, arising in Europe as a negative reaction to the perceived destructive impact of the French Revolution (Kirk, 1981, p. xii). In contrast to "traditionalism", a psychological commitment to the past or "old ways" (Mannheim, 1986, p. 73), conservatism was a response to a particular historical situation. But what does the "conservative" label now imply? What are the major varieties of conservatism and how did they develop? What has been the influence of conservatism on sociology?

A number of writers have insightfully characterized conservative assumptions as respect for the sacred, defense of inequality, support for traditional institutions, a perception of contemporary disorder, skepticism concerning social progress and criticism of individualism (Nisbet, 1978, pp. 98–103, 1986, pp. 1–20, 75–93; Kirk, 1982, pp. xv–xvii; Frohnen, 1993, pp. 9, 205; Hirschmann, 1991, pp. 1–10). Bringing them together highlights the following orientations.

(1) There is a strong belief in the *sacred* dimension of life to ensure harmony between the individual and community. The need for some kind of moral unity is highly stressed.

(2) Within this approach there is a strong belief in the importance of *hierarchy* as vital to social unity. Inequality is viewed as an inevitable part of social reality, with some people more suited to authority than others. Trying to ignore this will only result in aggravating modern society's problematic condition, so egalitarianism is rejected.

(3) Central to the conservative approach is a strong belief in the *importance of traditional institutions* which attach the individual to society in a vital manner. Traditional types of social associations such as the family, guild, and church are all viewed as central to the maintenance of social order. The individual clearly needs to be institutionally integrated into the general community.

(4) Related to this strong devotion to tradition is the principle of *historical/social continuity*. Society's past is defined as crucial to understanding both its present and future condition. Few, if any, improvements over the past are expected. The present is viewed as an obvious extension and continuation of the past and should be understood as such.

(5) Also implied in this devotion to tradition is a view of the *contemporary world* as reflecting *disorder* and that there are severe limits to human nature. Pragmatic realism is an important part of the conservative perspective. Accordingly, conservatives act slowly, avoiding the risk of making matters worse in an imperfect world. Unrealistic expectations are seen as potentially destructive in effect.

(6) In their rejection of a society based on the individual and individual rights, conservatives underline the *importance of the "social"* or group instead. Society and its institutions rather than the individual are "real" in the historical and

institutional sense. Individual needs generally are de-emphasized in this approach.

(7) Finally, all elements of the "*social*" are viewed as *interdependent*. It is the institutional order, rather than the individual, which is assumed to be orderly or rational. Such an "order" is viewed as interdependent, equilibrium-oriented, and functional. Again, structural rather than individual reality is stressed.

Conservatism, as thus defined, may be viewed as an attempt by those who respond negatively to social change to cope with what they perceive as societal disarray, disorder and emerging social problems. They accomplish this by re-asserting aspects of previous social arrangements. This limited view of society assumed center stage both in Europe and the US, as we shall see.

However, before proceeding, it is important to draw attention to different uses of the term "conservatism." In introducing the chapter, I mentioned two buzzwords which fit very well with the above concept of conservatism, namely "family values" and "respect for traditions." But the other two, "unencumbered market forces" and "standing on your own two feet" do not seem to fit so well, appearing to clash with conservatism's belief in traditional institutions and historical continuity, its rejection of social progress and hostility to the individual. Yet, paradoxically, it is these sorts of elements that appear most typical of people such as Margaret Thatcher and Ronald Reagan, who are usually viewed as conservatives. In fact, in the nineteenth century those who were thought of as conservatives regarded advocates of the unbridled free market as "economic liberals," threatening established elites and undermining the bases of differential consent by the masses. Thatcher and Reagan may have subscribed to the "family values" and "respect for traditions" buzzwords, but they combined this with attempts to mobilize popular support on the basis of rampant individualism and hostility to the "welfare state." Their views which combine individualistic populism with economic liberalism may thus be viewed as a highly distinctive variant on traditional conservatism, or as

an heretical departure from it. However, for purposes of this chapter, conservatism is conceived as embracing all the seven items listed earlier.

Conservatism in Europe and the United States

Examining the rise of conservatism in Great Britain, Nisbet highlights the significant presence of an anti-modernity reaction evident in the general opposition to the destructive effects of industrialization and the rising working class. The decline of traditional bonds, so central to feudalism, was decried, as was the development of new religions such as Wesleyanism, interpreted as a potential danger to the "established church," and new ideologies such as Bentham's utilitarianism which emphasized individual self-interest and "hedonism" (Nisbet, 1986, p. 12). All of these developments were viewed as having contributed to social heterogeneity and disorganization.

Specific political leaders during this era tended to be oriented to the past (for example, Cobbett), in search of a new moral basis for leadership (Coleridge), concerned with creating an "organic industrial society" through a new economic aristocracy (Carlyle), advocates of a "landed elite" as the basis of "One Nation" (Disraeli), and generally in favor of continuing inequality (Salisbury) (see O'Sullivan, 1976, pp. 82–118). Reflected in all of this is a common reaction – a negative view of the emerging industrial society as disorganized and individual-oriented, requiring reinforcement of social order through new moral leadership and the maintenance of inequality.

In the US, the Federalists were viewed as anti-Enlightenment and critical of the French Revolution (Nisbet, 1986, p. 6), emphasizing instead the importance of a "natural aristocracy," "progressive" rather than radical change, the need for a "strong central government," the political "dangers of liberty," and the rejection of government based on "abstract ideas" (Kirk, 1982, pp. 49–84). Nisbet also perceives conservatives as anti-

Enlightenment and devoted to the more traditional aspects of society such as family, community and the rights and obligations of private property (Nisbet, 1986, p. 38). American institutions such as the Federal Reserve and Supreme Court, given their relative independence of the electorate, are defined as conservative forces also, reflecting indirect government, with the constitution providing important checks and balances. Issues such as the campus rebellions of the 1960s, defense of institutional racism under the guise of "states' rights" and opposition to the dominant federal government fed into a number of right-wing movements which shared some of the features of conservatism as defined earlier. Reagan's rise to the presidency is a major example. Finally, conservatives on the Far Right tend to glorify localism, decentralization, and the private sector (Nisbet, 1986).

To a significant degree, then, both the foundation and development of American politics reflect an ongoing concern with previous conservative values such as traditional institutions, historical continuity, gradual change, and social integration. In many respects, American society was designed to embody conservative values as the colonists, responding to an unfamiliar environment, applied traditional ideas to the "new society." Such ideas had a major influence on sociology's development on both continents.

Conservatism and Sociology

Sociology's European origins have often been depicted as the reaction of Enlightenment philosophers to the "moral crisis" produced by the French Revolution, particularly the destructive effects of proposed equality on social order (Nisbet, 1978, p. 80). What emerged was a new science of society, identifying traditional institutions with natural law and rights, highlighting the *social* nature of reality (for example, social statics/ social dynamics, social evolution), distinguishing between the traditional and modern and rejecting the view of industrialization as progress (Nisbet, 1986). Many of these early sociologists came from

wealthy backgrounds and equated social problems with the negative effects of industrialization on their societies (Abrams, 1968, pp. 102–3).

Early writers likened society to an evolving organism, so the disintegrating effects of industrialization were seen as injurious to the social body's ongoing health. Comte, for example, stressed that society was a moral organism facing possible disorganization in the wake of France's post-Revolutionary developments (Kinloch, 1977, pp. 70–6). Spencer viewed society as an evolving, functional self-regulating organism, and concluded that attempts at amelioration were futile (Abrams, 1968, pp. 66–76). Views of this "organism" varied: Durkheim conceptualized it as essentially "coercive" and "restraining" (Durkheim, 1947), while Tönnies emphasized that society was a motivational organism risking the destruction of traditional *gemeinschaft* or community based on "natural will" (Tönnies, 1957). In general, then, many of sociology's founding figures reacted negatively to what they felt were the destructive effects of the French Revolution, spurning more progressive interpretations, and embracing instead the importance of traditional institutions as the foundation of the new social order. Their acceptance and application of Enlightenment philosophy clearly differs from earlier types of traditionalism; however, there are obvious similarities in the continuing concern with religion, inequality, traditional institutions, historical continuity, the denial of progress, and assumed reality of the "social." Modern social order, according to this perspective, is based on the scientific understanding of the social organism and its evolution.

Sociology in the US was similarly developed in response to the perceived destructive effects of industrialization and urbanization on traditional social order. Again, there is an emerging emphasis on institutional development, the search for community, and the stress on group consensus and cohesion. Many of these early sociologists were clergy from rural backgrounds who reacted negatively to the problematic nature of the industrial/urban context with its lack of "primary" ties and high levels of social problems (Bramson, 1961).

As American society and education moved away from being predominantly religious, sociology emerged as a secularized notion of the sacred – a shift from theodicy to sociodicy. As advocates of social science or the "ministers of positivism", sociologists moved from religious unity to social transcendence as the foundation of social order, replacing God with "functional equilibrium" in the case of structural functionalism, and identifying the "social system" with American society Vidich and Lyman, 1985, pp. 281, 288, 302. In this way, traditionally conservative ideas such as the sacred, hierarchy, the "social", and interdependence became part of the foundation of this new "social science." Conservative values became an integral part of the sociological model of society.

Talcott Parsons, as a major architect of structural functionalism, based much of his work on the earlier ideas of Spencer. This is reflected in his concern with the evolution of society as a system always tending towards equilibrium – as a functional, homeostatic, adaptive organism or social system – one system among "all living systems". He also identifies Western industrial democracies as "modern" – by which he means they are the most functionally evolved, i.e., the most successfully adaptive form of social system within the course of general societal evolution (Parsons, 1970; 1971). Traditional conservative concerns with historical continuity, the danger of social disorganization, the priority of the social, and functional interdependence are all clearly reflected in his work. Continuing order is achieved, according to him, through ensuring the normative integration of the individual into the (assumed) functional social system (Kinloch, 1981a). Social crises are to be avoided by limiting individual freedom through maximizing the person's commitment to *system* needs and goals. For Parsons, normative integration is vital to society's ongoing development and welfare – indeed, to its very survival. Consequently, deviance and other social problems are viewed as threatening its equilibrium. Other structural func-

tionalists such as Robert Merton (1957) and Kingsley Davis (1949) have elaborated the notion of systemic rationality or social order through their emphasis on the importance of social structures, underlying functional requirements, orientation towards equilibrium, and need for individual conformity to system needs. Merton is particularly concerned with adequate "means for goal achievement" to strengthen general societal conformity. Davis, on the other hand, highlights the importance of adequately "placing" people in the social hierarchy and ensuring their functional "motivation" to contribute to society's welfare.

More recently, sociobiology has attempted to link societal, environmental, and biological necessities through its view of human organization as reflecting our genetic adaptation to a dynamic environment. This approach is largely based on applying the major traits of "lower organisms" to human social organization (Wilson, 1978, pp. 1–12).

In these ways, the assumptions of traditional conservatism have been redefined as the functional, adaptive, modern social system founded on the normative commitment of the individual to system needs and their ongoing dynamics. Earlier ideas regarding the moral, functional, restraining, and motivational organism are reconceptualized in the form of "the general social system." Such a reconceptualization of conservative ideas attempts to highlight the need to protect the "system" at all costs, but in terms which are abstract, general, and defined as "scientific."

Conservatism and Sociology's Professional Development

In both Great Britain and North America sociology was originally part of the emergence of the social sciences – responding to the major problems engendered by the increasing dominance of an industrial-urban environment (cf. Abrams, 1968; Furner, 1975). While slow to establish itself as a discipline, sociology eventually emerged as a separate, specialized profession, clearly differentiated from related fields such as economics, political science, and social work. The primary basis on which this differentiation occurred was sociology's self-definition as a social *science* committed to gathering data on contemporary social problems for the state's political use, sharply separating itself from less empirically-oriented disciplines (Furner, 1975, pp. 14–17). Social data were to be used in the creation of empirically-based social legislation.

The above process had a number of implications for the development of conservative sociology. First, there was a shift in emphasis from a concern with historical continuity (viewing traditional institutions as the foundation of the new social order) to one in which "society" and "social change" are looked at in a general way, abstracted from their historical and economic contexts, and where the preservation of the kind of system in which the sociologist happens to live is defended on the grounds that it represents a "higher" form of functional evolution. Second, sociology's scientific, objective approach to social problems was contrasted to the allegedly more "political" and "subjective" views of others. Third, under this guise of objectivity, the sociologists' own values were projected as a solution to social problems.

Beginning with North America, the continuing effects of conservatism may be seen in the manner in which many professional sociologists tend to project their own values, such as consensus, gradual reform and the American form of democracy, as scientific solutions to the problems posed by social conflict (Kinloch, 1981b). When society appears to be faring well, this is identified as evidence of a general developmental trend; when situations arise that are more conflict-ridden it merely provokes attempts to implement normative integration. Either way, the arguments are justified on "scientific" grounds. In all of this, the notion of "society" or the "social" is reified, or treated as though it possessed a real or independent existence (Kinloch, 1987). Furthermore, when addressing more controversial issues such as the Vietnam War or other matters of public policy, many argue that taking public stands is unscientific, unrepresentative, inappropriate, and more typical of

lobbying groups than a professional association (Kinloch, 1985). Professional sociology emerges as the normative projection and scientific rationalization of one's own values, reification of the social, and portrayal of the discipline's direct involvement in social issues as essentially subjective and unscientific. While claiming scientific validity and objectivity, it is clear that such a perspective is equally as subjective as the views it attacks.

Sociology in Great Britain was also relatively slow in separating itself from more applied endeavors such as eugenics, civics, and social work (Abrams, 1968). Once professionally established, however, it experienced significant growth and specialization, rapidly becoming an important part of the modern state, particularly in its use of social surveys (Shaw, 1975). When confronted by different or more radical ideas, some British social scientists, in similar vein to their North American counterparts, contrast their own perspectives as "open," pluralistic, more "logical" and empirical than the ideological, intolerant, negative, and subjective views of the "radicals" critiquing them. The views of the latter, in fact, are often seen as constituting a general "attack on higher education" and its underlying premises (Gould, 1977, pp. 5–7). Here, opposing views are portrayed as threatening the general welfare of education, rather than being encouraged as the basis for healthy debate and reflecting academic pluralism.

Two major views of sociology are contained in the above controversies: the scientific versus the reformist. The former is more conservative and latter more radical, despite their common use of empirical methods in their research. While these disagreements may be shrill and highly emotional at times, it would be inaccurate to portray conservative sociologists as right-wing extremists or their radical opponents as left-wing ideologues. Both groups share a common desire to understand modern society, its major developments and social problems as thoroughly and scientifically as possible, despite differences regarding the profession's societal role and type of methods to be used. Modern sociology is generally concerned with the problem of contemporary social order irrespective of differing professional models. While subgroups of academics may engage in debate which is occasionally vitriolic and highly controversial, the commitment of most members of the discipline to professional values continues to maintain sociology's general stability. Right-wing conservative extremists in the profession are the exception rather than the norm.

Conclusions

In this discussion, we have made a number of major points as follows.

(1) The current political era as well as sociology's historical foundation have often been portrayed as "conservative." We asked the question, "what does this mean?"

(2) Conservatism emerged as a negative reaction to the effects of industrialization on traditional society as well as the disturbing ideas brought about by the French Revolution.

(3) We portrayed conservatism's predominant orientation as involving the attempt to maintain important aspects of the traditional social order in the face of significant social changes in modern society.

(4) Conservatism played a significant role in sociology's foundation as the latter applied enlightenment ideas to the scientific study of society as an evolving social organism.

(5) Conservatism was part of emerging sociology in its development as a specialized, social science involving the projection of social values as the scientific basis of modern social order in contrast to the more allegedly subjective and political views of others.

This is *not* to conclude that sociology is inherently conservative, nor are all members of the profession. Indeed, other discussions in this *Companion* attest to a diversity of perspectives within the discipline. Rather, we are emphasizing that conservatism was an integral part of sociology's foundation and is present in the reaction of *some* of its practitioners over time, as indicated in their critical, structural reaction to ongoing social change. Furthermore, emphasis on the relevance and importance of the "social" dimension of human existence makes an important contribution to our understanding of contemporary society and the social problems within it. The search for some kind of objective basis to contemporary social order is clearly relevant to our attempts to cope with increasingly exponential social change and its major effects on every aspect of our daily lives. However, it is also important to point out this perspective's limitations in its obsession with the structural and social. This results on occasion, in an inadequate appreciation of the complexity of the individual, social heterogeneity, the major significance of continuing inequality, and the complex dynamics of social change. While conservatism represents an important part of sociology, it is clearly *not* the whole "story" and students should be aware of its limitations as such. However, this perspective remains an important part of sociology's professional foundation and ongoing development, particularly as members of the discipline continue to grapple with the problem of social order during a very dynamic century. While perspectives on this topic vary over time, the conservative viewpoint remains central to the discipline and profession.

References

Abrams, P. 1968: *The Origins of British Sociology: 1834–1914*. Chicago, IL: University of Chicago Press.

Bramson, L. 1961: *The Political Context of Sociology*. Princeton, NJ: Princeton University Press.

Davis, K. 1949: *Human Society*. New York: Macmillan.

Durkheim, É. 1947: *Division of Labor in Society*. Glencoe, IL: The Free Press.

Frohnen, B. 1993: *Virtue and the Promise of Conservatism, The Legacy of Burke and Tocqueville*. Lawrence: University Press of Kansas.

Furner, M. O. 1975: *Advocacy and Objectivity, A Crisis in the Professionalization of American Social*

Science 1865–1905. Lexington: University Press of Kentucky.

Gould, J. 1977: *The Attack on Higher Education: Marxist and Radical Penetration*. London: Institute for the Study of Conflict.

Hirschman, A. O. 1991: *The Rhetoric of Reaction: Perversity, Futility, Jeopardy*. Cambridge, MA: Belknap Press of Harvard University Press.

Kinloch, G. C. 1977: *Sociological Theory: Its Development and Major Paradigms*. New York: McGraw-Hill.

—— 1981 (a): *Ideology and Contemporary Sociological Theory*. Englewood Cliffs, NJ: Prentice-Hall.

—— 1981 (b): "Professional sociology as the basis of societal integration: a study of presidential addresses." *The American Sociologist*, 16, 2–13.

—— 1985: "The tension between scientific and reformist sociology reflected in professional debate." *Journal of Thought*, 20, 50–58.

—— 1987: "American professional sociology as reification of the 'social.'" *The California Sociologist*, 10, 9–21.

Kirk, R. (ed.) 1982: *The Portable Conservative Reader*. New York: Viking Press.

Mannheim, K. 1986: D. Kettler, V. Meja, and N. Stehr (eds), *Conservativism: A Contribution to the Sociology of Knowledge* (translated by D. Kettler and V. Meja). London: Routledge & Kegan Paul.

Merton, R. K. 1957: *Social Theory and Social Structure*, New York: The Free Press.

Nisbet, R. 1978: "Conservatism" in Bottomore. T. and R. Nisbet (eds), *A History of Sociological Analysis*. New York: Basic Books, 80–117.

—— 1986: *Conservatism: Dream and Reality*. Milton Keynes: Open University Press.

O'Sullivan, N. 1976: *Conservatism*. New York: St Martin's Press.

Parsons, T. 1970: "Some problems of general theory in sociology." In J. C. McKinney and E. A. Tiryakian (eds), *Theoretical Sociology: Perspectives and Developments*. Englewood Cliffs NJ: Prentice-Hall, pp. 27–68.

—— 1971. *The System of Modern Societies*. Englewood Cliffs, NJ: Prentice-Hall.

Shaw, M. 1975: *Marxism and Social Science: The Roots of Social Knowledge*. London: Pluto Press.

Tönnies, F. 1957: *Community and Society* (translated by C. P. Loomis). Lansing: Michigan State University

Vidich, A. J. and Lyman, S. M, 1985: *American Sociology: Worldly Rejections of Religions and Their Directions*. New Haven, CT: Yale University Press.

Wilson, E. O. 1978: "Introduction: What is Sociobiology?" In M. S. Gregory et al. (eds), *Sociobiology and Human Nature*. San Francisco, CA: Jossey-Bass, pp. 1 –12.

12

Sociology, Social Reform and Revolution

Chris Middleton

Problematizing the Idea of "Social Order"

The previous chapter showed that traditional conservatives[1] value social order more highly than any other aspect of our secular existence. Accordingly, their sociological accounts – those of functionalism in particular – pay the closest attention to the mechanisms by which social order is maintained. This concern will strike a chord in all of us. Every day media images convey the misery and suffering that follow in the wake of any serious breakdown of social order – Rwanda, the former Yugoslavia, post-Soviet Russia with its high inflation, unemployment and spiralling crime rates, or the more gradual disintegration of community networks in our own areas of urban decay. The refugee crises of the late twentieth century are nothing if not crises of social order – a breakdown in the habitual, the regular and routine expectations that give shape and meaning to people's lives. In the light of such disasters Peter Berger's (1979) warning against "upsetting the fragile structures that protect men's lives from the terror of chaos" seems almost unanswerable. Isn't our bottom line the need to feel safe in our beds, secure in the knowledge of where our next penny is coming from? Such is the force of this notion that it has become a sociological commonplace to use "society" and "social order" as interchangeable terms.

But many critics of conservatism argue that its perspective on social order represents a particular rather than a general social interest.

To call *tout court* for the preservation of social order is to do more than affirm the desirability of social order as a general principle. For social order can never be maintained in the abstract. It is always *this or that particular* social order that has to be defended in practice. So, for example, to call for the preservation of social order in the contemporary West (the focus of this chapter) is to seek to secure a set of social relationships built around capitalist notions of private property, the dominance of white ethnic groups and so on, in a way that glosses over the choices that have to be made between alternative ways of organizing society.

In public discussion a society is conventionally deemed to be stable (i.e. orderly) if there is little evidence of social unrest, if the means of violence are firmly in the hands of a central political authority,[2] and if macro-economic indicators (such as the rate of inflation or national output) are reasonably steady. But what this in fact represents is a one-dimensional understanding of what constitutes "social order", and a refusal to scrutinize the experience of "order" from all perspectives. It may be totally at odds with the experiences of those at the bottom of the social and economic pile – millions of people who find it impossible to plan ahead because they lack essential resources and have little control over the social forces that govern their lives. For individuals, families and communities experiencing low wages, factory closures and redundancies, irregular employment, racial or sexual violence, and dispossession, life is anything but predictable and orderly. Yet these conditions have been integral to the routine functioning of that capitalist social order whose preservation is so assiduously defended.

Conservatives do not regard such conditions as incompatible with "social order" unless, of course, discontents accumulate and spill over into industrial conflict, protests on the streets, or insurrection. Indeed since, for functionalists, the key to prosperity resides in a social system built around rewards for enterprise, competence and effort, rather than one that is directly responsive to social needs, the plight of the most disadvantaged can only be alleviated at the margins – and then only in deserving cases. Moreover, when the dispossessed do engage in active struggle, functionalists look to see what mechanisms exist for "conflict-adjustment" (i.e. for "cooling out" dissent in a way that does not threaten social order) rather than how the structural causes of discontent might be eliminated. Thus the conventional (conservative) view of order rests on a paradox: social order is alleged to exist despite the contradictory experiences of many groups who comprise this "order", and the collective strivings of these groups for greater security is attacked as at best irrational, and at worst a *threat* to "social order".

In its single-minded emphasis on the fragility of ordered social existence, conservative sociology effectively treats "society" as an entity embodying the concerns of all its "members". Its message is one of a fundamental harmony of interests: "We're all in this together – so don't rock the boat!" But progressive sociologists who pay attention to social divisions based on inequality or oppression see beneath the surface of stability. What is represented as "functional to society" may not be functional to everyone within it. They recognize that while the boat's officers are comfortably quartered, the rest of the crew work below decks in less enviable conditions, some still indentured as slave labour, with thousands clinging desperately to the gunwale in fear of being cast adrift. They ask whether there isn't a better way of ensuring seaworthiness.

....

"Progressive" sociological opinion ranges all the way from liberal and social-democratic reformism at one end of the spectrum through to revolutionary thought at the other. The disagreements between them are often as great as any views they hold in common. In the following discussion I shall, at the risk of being over-schematic, distinguish between a reformist and a radical tradition, reserving the latter term for work that provides a fundamental critique of the structures of capitalist, patriarchal or racist orders.

Reformist Sociology: Social Reform from Above

An early contribution to the development of British sociology was made by investigative reformers who wished to bring the extent and severity of urban poverty to the attention of government legislators. In numerous local studies they documented in fine detail the misery of Britain's poor and dispossessed during a period of generally rising prosperity. One key methodological innovation, associated with Seebohm Rowntree (1941), was the construction of an "absolute" poverty line, based on what was intended to be an objective measure of basic subsistence needs (covering essential nutrition, clothing, fuel and shelter). The line drawn was very stringent: no allowance was made for inefficient spending (Rowntree's dietary recommendations assumed a knowledge of nutrition that even educated people would be unlikely to possess) or expenditure on items he considered non-essential.

In retrospect this "scientific" approach seems profoundly *un*sociological in conception, since an absolute poverty line tries to ignore the influence of social expectations and relationships. By the 1960s researchers such as Harrington (1963) in America and Townsend in Britain (1979) were arguing for "relative" definitions of poverty that were sensitive to social context – which recognized, for instance, the social and psychological degradation that arises when *communal expectations* of material "decency" cannot be met. Sociologists have increasingly sought to link the experience of poverty to wider structures of inequality, often working within a framework of "social citizenship" where the focus is on the individual's capacity to participate fully in the life of the community (Oppenheim, 1993).

What is most interesting about this tradition is the political premise on which it was built. The early poverty investigators exemplified Comte's belief that a positivist social science could be enlisted for purposes of social amelioration. But in practice the "scientific" measuring instruments they developed were not free of political calculation. Rowntree's poverty line was drawn harshly not on the basis of "scientific objectivity" (though this was how it was publicly legitimated), but out of a reformer's sense of political "realism". By drawing the line at a meagre level he could not be accused of being "soft" on the feckless and "undeserving" poor – precisely the charge levelled at more recent generations of reformers.

But if this tradition of poverty research has always been politically motivated, its assumptions have generally been reformist rather than radical. It sees no *essential* conflict of interest between the poor and the privileged, assuming that the problems of the former can be tackled without "rocking the boat". Indeed it calls directly on the officers to look after those less fortunate passengers and crew. If the public authorities could be alerted to the true facts of deprivation, and persuaded that indigence was due to social circumstances rather than individual idleness or waste, they could confidently be expected to take steps to remedy the problem. This strategy might be described as the "social face of Keynesianism", its success predicated on a bureaucratic stratum of enlightened experts managing social reform from above in the best interests of society (Skidelsky, 1979). The role of sociology in improving the lot of the disadvantaged was to establish "the facts" and set them in a realistic policy framework.[3]

It was recognized, of course, that a positive response was more likely to be forthcoming from a reformist party of government, so the message was directed primarily towards progressive political parties (the Liberal and Labour parties in the UK, the Democratic Party in the US). In some cases the sociological messengers became senior party advisers: there are, for example, direct links between Rowntree and the reforms which underpinned the post–1945 Welfare State in Britain, and between Harrington and President Johnson's "War on Poverty" in the 1960s.

There is clear evidence that state welfare does contribute to the alleviation of hardship, and also inhibits the market-led tendency for social inequalities to widen. The remorseless onslaught on welfare provision over the past 20 years, under the banner of "free market" deregulation, has resulted in a real, not just a relative, fall in the standard of living of the poor, while homelessness has grown on an alarming scale. The gulf between rich and poor has simultaneously deepened (Taylor, 1990). Yet even in its ascendancy the strategy of "reform from above" was unable to eliminate poverty and notoriously failed to achieve a positive *redistribution* of wealth and incomes (Westergaard, 1995).

Reformist Sociology: Equal Opportunities

Sociology's development has also been conspicuously influenced by another cornerstone of social democracy: the pursuit of equal opportunities – while the findings of sociological research have reciprocally been fed into the framing of equal opportunities policies.

One might be forgiven for thinking there is nothing especially progressive about the demand for equal opportunities. Nowadays it is an objective for which there appears to be broad political support. Long gone are the days when the idea of an "open society" – where social position is determined by individual merit and achievement rather than the circumstances of one's birth – would provoke outrage in the ranks of the ruling strata. As Westergaard has put it "the call for 'careers open to talent' is one expression of the spirit of capitalist rationality" (1995: p. 87) and today's corporate employers ostensibly demand access to the best available talent regardless of class origins, race or gender.

The privileged are, as a general rule, keen advocates of economic efficiency and therefore, as a matter of public principle, supportive of equal opportunities. But in their private capacity as parents and consumers they may wish to hang on to their privileges, so from this angle an effective equal opportunities programme will be viewed in a less favourable light. Conservative sociological arguments propose a way of resolving this tension. On the one hand it is claimed that institutional barriers to personal advancement have already been removed and that anyone who wishes to rise in the social hierarchy has the opportunity to do so. The relatively low proportion of women, blacks, and people from working class origins found in "elite positions" is then explained *individualistically*, i.e. by alleging that individuals from these groups are genetically less able than the rest of the population, or otherwise lack the necessary ambition and enterprise to "get on".

Progressive sociologists, on the other hand, have stressed the continuing salience of institutional and cultural barriers to equal opportunity (Halsey et al. 1980). They emphasize especially:

- the *cultural* sources of educational deprivation whether located in the home or the school;
- the capacity of privileged classes to pass on material, educational and cultural "capital" from one generation to the next. Children from these backgrounds are given a headstart over others through the inheritance of wealth, help in acquiring credentials, access to influential networks, and immersion in the "appropriate" linguistic and behavioural codes necessary for advancement;
- widespread discrimination, open or covert, against members of disadvantaged groups (especially those that are "biologically visible") even when their achievements and qualifications match those of individuals from more favoured categories. (For summaries, see Bilton, 1996, Chap. 11; and Grint, 1991, Chap. 7 on race.)

The struggle for equal opportunities clearly reflects a wider history of progressive social movements as marginalized groups struggle for recognition, rights and equitable treatment. As such its emancipatory potential is substantial. But the "equal opportunities agenda" also reflects the accommodation of progressives to the pervasive conservative mood. There are two aspects to this. First, many campaigns and research studies focus exclusively on *only one* dimension of inequality. The effect is not merely a narrowing of scope but, crucially, to render invisible those who are the most oppressed of all. An illustration may be helpful in clarifying this point. In researching the impact of the 1988 Education Reform Act on girls' education (Miles and Middleton, 1995), it was found that the gender-focused equal opportunities literature tended to treat girls as a homogenous category, failing to address the importance of class divisions. The Act was predicted to improve girls' access to the whole curriculum (especially to science subjects) and so was greeted in many quarters as a progressive measure. However, on closer examination it became evident that the main beneficiaries of the curricular changes would be girls from higher socio-economic categories, whereas the Act taken as a whole would certainly prove damaging to the life-chances of girls educated in under-resourced, inner-city schools. This was an outcome that gender-focused "equal opportunities" perspectives had largely failed to register. The wider implications of the Act for *working-class girls* were not "seen" because their interests had been subsumed under the far broader categories of "gender".

But a more fundamental limitation to the equal opportunities agenda (which would not be overcome even by a sophisticated multivariate analysis) arises from its failure to challenge the hierarchical structures within which occupational and other forms of competition take place. Equal opportunity discourses *presuppose* a framework of inequality and are bounded by it. Their concern is with the terms on which different categories of people compete for the more highly rewarded positions in an unequal world, rather than with the extent of inequality or the structures of organized power. Their interest is in the opportunities available for some individuals (regardless of race or gender) to "escape" their class origins, whilst paying scant attention to the fate of those who get "left behind".

Radical Sociology: Capitalism and Class Conflict

In the 1960s a more radical tradition of sociology re-emerged, heavily influenced by Marxist ideas (but highly critical of Soviet Marxism) and expressing dissatisfaction with the limitations of reformism. To pursue the nautical metaphor, they examined the capitalist boat's structure and found that, having been built without a rudder, it was sailing along out of control. They observed that essential repairs could not be carried out because of rivalry among the officers and irreconcilable conflicts of interest with the crew. And finally there was the small matter of the ship's encounters with other voyagers on the high seas. It turned out this was a pirate ship. Mutiny seemed the only solution.

Radical sociologists went beyond the documentation of inequalities to claim that there are inbuilt mechanisms such that the privileges of the powerful are secured *at the expense of* the mass of ordinary people, denying them any real say over their own lives. Thus radical sociology proposed a solution to the "paradox of social order" outlined earlier, arguing that the conservative emphasis on stability and order is a screen behind which lurk the interests of a powerful capitalist class. Attempts by dominant class interests to ensure "order" characteristically serve to aggravate the conditions of the majority. In the global economy corporate profitability is secured by the creation of "flexible" labour markets, i.e. by *removing the workers' security* of employment. On the day of writing (18 April 1996) my morning paper carries a report that the International Monetary Fund is looking for cutbacks in public services in order to restore confidence on the financial markets. Last month the Dow-Jones Share Index got the jitters because the latest figures showed a *fall* in US unemployment (since this might give US labour the confidence to demand wage

rises), and so on. Abroad, conditions are even more serious. IMF loans designed to restore "economic stability" to impoverished Third World countries are made conditional on "structural adjustments" involving cutbacks in basic education, health and housing programmes, while the requirement to earn "hard" western currency to pay off earlier debts forces small farmers off the land as agribusinesses move in to produce cash-crops. For some "economic stabilization" spells destitution.

According to this view, then, the capitalist system is riven by deep structural conflicts. Marxists dismiss all optimistic scenarios of sustained and unproblematic capitalist growth such as those which fuel reformist hopes that the welfare of the majority can be significantly and permanently improved within the framework of a market economy.

Needless to say radical sociologists seek to identify with and further the interests of subject populations (Sherman and Wood, 1989). There is an issue, however, as to what these interests are and how they should be determined. Marxists allege that social relations are not always what they seem on the surface, believing that our direct or "lived" experience of the world belies a deeper "structural" reality. They argue, for example, that although the labour contract in a market economy has all the semblance of a voluntary exchange between equals ("I'll work for you if you're willing to pay a fair rate for the job"), it is actually and invariably a coercive relation based on unequal exchange. Profit is based on the exploitation of the employee's labour, but this relationship is not transparent in the everyday interactions between employer and worker. Similarly western state aid to underdeveloped countries is not, as it might seem on the surface, a form of official charity, but on the contrary a means by which the rulers of Western nations seek to make Third World economies dependent on their own.

In particular, social relations are often experienced as though they had an independent existence – a life of their own – rather than being created and sustained by human practice and interaction. The most famous example discussed by Marx is the capitalist market itself whose "laws" of supply and demand appear to us as a "fact of life" quite as irreversible and beyond human control as the movement of the planets. Given their external and "law-like" character there is a compelling force to the argument that the only sensible course of action is to work "with the grain" of market forces (see Figure 12.1). Margaret Thatcher, the right-wing Prime Minister of Britain during the 1980s, once proclaimed that "you cannot buck the markets" – meaning to say that if the state or trade unions tried to interfere with market forces, for example by setting a minimum wage or subsidizing unprofitable enterprises, they would only be storing up trouble for themselves and others. The long-term outcome would not be greater prosperity for low income families or more viable industries, but higher unemployment and a chronic drain on the public purse. Eventually, she believed, the markets must "have their way". Marx believed that such "reification" of market forces (i.e. treating them as "things" independent of human

creation) was illusory – but it was an illusion with immense power because it was based in our everyday experience of capitalist relations. It is an illusion, in other words, to which we are *all* prey. In our day-to-day living we have no sense that our economic actions, whether at individual, firm or national level, could ever escape the constraints imposed by impersonal and irresistible forces – the "economic laws" of supply and demand. We find it hard to envisage an alternative way of organizing a modern economy governed, not by these "laws", but by moral and co-operative values.

Marxists do not see it as inevitable that advanced industrial economies should be organized around market relationships. The market is not some neutral (still less benign) mechanism for the allocation of scarce resources – a universal force governing economic relations everywhere. Indeed, for them, there is no such thing as "the market"; only different markets which vary in the way they function and the relations of dominance they sustain. Markets are constructed socially

Figure 12.1 A radical view of how market forces work. (*Rich more/poor less*, artwork: Angela Martin.)

through the cumulative force of repetitive human actions, and the capitalist market is just one particular historical form of market relationship built around the competitive buying and selling of human labour-power. It has led to the creation of an unprecedentedly powerful dominant class, whose decisions and actions have massive repercussions across the globe. Yet, paradoxically, it is a class which is ultimately unable to control the destiny of the system from which it benefits.

In stressing the *opacity* of capitalist relations, Marxist sociologists have claimed a very clear and important role for intellectuals. For if our everyday experience fails to give us a true and valid picture of the society in which we live, a heavy responsibility falls on those who, whilst continuing to identify closely with working-class struggle, have the education and the time to *expose* these relations for what they are. This then is seen as the function of Marxist sociology. In contrast to social reformers who turned their lanterns on the poor to bring their plight to the attention of the powerful, Marxists shed light on the workings of capitalism exposing the underbelly of the powerful to those who lack influence and resources, that they may take collective action to bring about fundamental change.

Radical Sociology in the Global Age

Marxism's dominant influence over radical sociology from the 1960s to the 1980s has visibly waned in recent years. Its decline is not attributable primarily to the collapse or internal attrition of Communist regimes in Eastern Europe and Asia (from whom Western Marxists had long maintained a critical distance), though it has suffered from the general loss of confidence in the efficacy of social planning. But it has, crucially, been accused of marginalizing the experience of those, such as minority ethnic groups and women, whose oppression does not "fit" its historical schema. This last criticism has led to a renewed emphasis on *subjectivity*, with radical sociologists advised to listen to and reflect the diverse experiences of differently oppressed peoples. In fact this shift of focus reflects the convergence of several lines of thought, not all of them radical, which are represented in Figure 12.2.

1. The fragmentation of forces for change

Let us begin in the top right-hand corner of Figure 12.2. Marx was extraordinarily prescient in forecasting developments that persist to this day – for example the globalization of capital and the accumulation of power in capitalist hands (Bottomore and Brym, 1989). Moreover, the key problem he identified remains unresolved: despite its unprecedented productive capacity capitalism continues to generate misery because establishing secure conditions for profit-making *requires* the creation of insecurity at the personal level. But in other respects the Marxist account currently looks less plausible – especially its identification of a progressively homogeneous and solidaristic working class having both an interest in and the capacity for overthrowing the social order based on capitalist exploitation and competition. For a period during the twentieth century, as Western labour established mass trade unions and political parties to represent its interests, and "proletarian" and "peasant" revolutions affected a third of the world's population, it was not unreasonable to believe that this represented a realistic possibility. But, apart from the fact that Communist parties, once in power, regularly established coercive rule over the oppressed masses on whose behalf they claimed to be acting, it became evident that "proletarian unity" often served as a cloak for racism, national chauvinism, sexism and the marginalization of less-skilled or organized workers. The divisions within the working class, material and cultural, were *structurally* rooted and not to be overcome by spurious calls to unity.

By the late twentieth century the growing conviction that the working class was internally divided and that, indeed, class domination was not the only form of contemporary oppression, had led to a proliferation of social

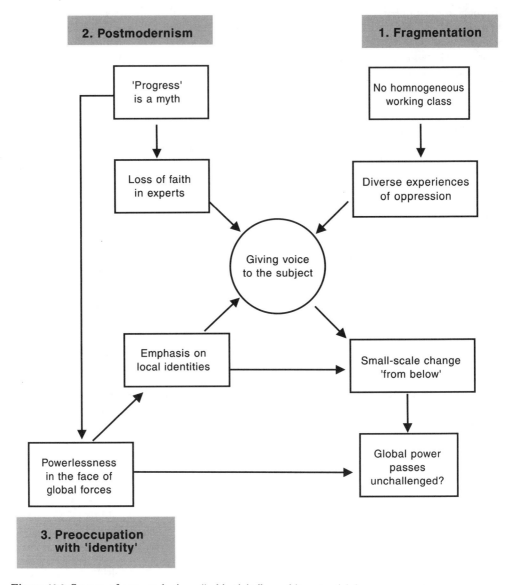

Figure 12.2 Sources of new emphasis on "subjectivity" – and its potential dangers.

movements appealing to women, those subject to racism, native peoples, youth, the elderly, ecologists, gays and lesbians, people with physical disabilities, learning difficulties and so on. Radicalism, far from becoming centripetally organized around an ever more coherent labour movement, had now become centrifugal with new social movements spinning off at a rapid rate. Radical sociologists (and those in related disciplines) reflected that if in the past, the experiences of different oppressed groups had not been adequately represented, this was because sociologists had sought to stand "above" the research process, imposing their own values and agendas on it. The solution was a more reflexive sociology drawing on the researcher's own experiences of oppression (e.g. Stanley and Wise, 1993), and/or a more democratic relationship where sociologists placed their research skills at the service of oppressed groups. Marginalized groups could be assisted in the recovery and preservation of endangered cultural traditions; those with little power or influence over the policy-making process could be supported in getting their voices heard (e.g. Starr, this volume).[4] Above all it was necessary to listen to and respect differences in peoples' social experience and values. The Marxist intellectual as the expert unlocking the secrets of reality is thus replaced by the sociologist acting as a conduit through which the socially disenfranchised might be empowered.

2. Post-modernism: questioning the idea of progress

The validation of personal experiences and cultural difference, even when these run counter to the views of "experts", has found favour among many progressives because "scientific knowledge" has come to be seen, not as a neutral force, but as reflecting the dominant cultural values and interests of the West, of men, and of white ethnic groups. This "shift to subjectivity" has been a vital force in the extension of emancipatory struggles to include previously marginalized groups, and has thus led also to a broadening of the remit of progressive sociology. But, for all that, in certain forms it can become a Trojan Horse – admitting into the conceptual heart of sociology a post-modernist philosophy whose logic must be to debunk the very idea of social progress.

Whatever their disagreements regarding the prospects for tackling the evils of capitalism, or the best means of effecting social change, reformist and radical sociologists are both creatures of the Enlightenment. In other words they share a belief in the possibility of progress brought about by planned intervention in social and economic relations on the basis of a rational, enlightened understanding of how the world works.[5] It is this belief in the ameliorative power of conscious, *organized* action, and the knowledge-claims that underpin it, that attracts post-modernist scorn. Since all knowledge is socially located and therefore relative, post-modernist thinkers argue that it is epistemologically untenable to claim that one kind of knowledge is more certain or valid than others, or indeed to privilege any one set of normative values over another. There are simply no external criteria on which to base a judgement of the comparative merits of alternative views (for an excellent summary see McLennan, 1992). In fact post-modernist ideas in the intellectual domain have a close affinity with "free-market" philosophies in the field of economics – where we find a similar denial of any "external" criteria for evaluating the relative merits of different wants such as clean piped water to an African village versus the demands of international tourists.

3. The preoccupation with identity in the face of globalism

Finally the emphasis on subjectivity is given additional impetus by the sense of powerlessness which frequently accompanies globalization. There are two key aspects here. First the prospect of any social movement or organization being able to control the forces that generate personalized insecurity seems more remote in the era of global economics. What hope is there for ordinary people when even an institution as powerful as the Deutsche Bundesbank cannot prevent the devaluation of national currencies on the international finance markets! Secondly, as global culture – Coca-Cola, Sky TV, packaged tourism, and so on – increasingly penetrates our daily lives, the survival of local and national traditions appears to be at risk. Faced with the combined threat of these two factors many view the revitalization of the *local* dimension as the route to salvation in the global era. "Localism" in the late twentieth century takes many forms – resurgent nationalism, regional development as a framework for economic regeneration, the ecological movement's advocacy of local economies and communities, or the search for territorial "roots" in diasporic cultures – but it invariably holds out two promises. It offers hope that while the world "out there" is beyond control, we can at least create one small corner of it where we have a modicum of control over our destiny: and it provides a source of "identity" in the face of cultural rootlessness. But that identity – be it national, ethnic, religious or whatever – has to be continually re-created and re-articulated. It has to find its subjective voice.

....

The implications of the greater emphasis on subjectivity, often defined as the hallmark of radical reconstruction over the past 20 years, are in fact highly equivocal. First, while the democratic impulse to listen to the disparate voices of the oppressed has enabled socio-logists to gain a deeper, more comprehensive understanding of the processes of oppression, the cultural relativism implicit in the injunction that all views should be equally respected can result in moral and political paralysis. Second, focusing on the personal, the subjective and the "politics of identity" may both reflect and help sustain a situation where many progressive sociologists have abandoned the terrain of collective global struggle as a lost cause. (Giddens, 1994.) But if the concept of "social order" is to acquire any real meaning for those whose present insecurities are a precondition for capitalist viability, that global struggle is the ground on which radical sociology must engage (Sherman and Wood, 1989). The challenge is to discover ways in which diverse groups and local forces can be mobilized around the global, as well as the particular, causes of oppression.

Notes

1. Sociological conservatism has to be distinguished from the neo-liberal ideas that have been so influential in right-wing circles over the past 25 years. The implications of neo-liberalism are often socially disruptive, rather than orderly (Giddens, 1994). The two traditions are held together in uneasy alliance by the need to secure, respectively, the economic and the social conditions for continued capital accumulation.
2. Or small arms, if available to individual citizens, are only for self-defence.
3. This "Mandarin" approach was also evident in many other areas of social policy such as health inequalities, housing, and education.
4. Much of this methodological renewal took place within Marxism itself. See, for example, the success of the *History Workshop* movement and journal in Britain.
5. As we have seen reformists tend to view intervention as the responsibility (and preserve) of an elite, while radicals emphasize the possibilities of democratic participation.

References

Berger, P. 1979: "Intellectual conservatism: two paradoxes". In *Facing up to Modernity*. Harmondsworth: Penguin.

Bilton, T. et al. 1996: *Introductory Sociology*, 3rd edn. Basingstoke: Macmillan.

Bottomore, T. and Brym, R. J. (eds) 1989: *The Capitalist Class: An International Study*. Hemel Hempstead: Harvester Wheatsheaf.

Giddens, A. 1994: *Beyond Left and Right: The Future of Radical Politics*. Cambridge: Polity Press.

Grint, K. 1991: *The Sociology of Work*. Cambridge: Polity Press.

Halsey, A. H., Heath, A. F. and Ridge, J. M. 1980: *Origins and Destinations: Family, Class and Education in Modern Britain*. Oxford: Clarendon Press.

Harrington, M. 1963: *The Other America: Poverty in the United States*. Baltimore, MD: Penguin.

McLennan, G. 1992: The Enlightenment project revisited. In S. Hall, D. Held and T. McGrew (eds), *Modernity and Its Futures*. Cambridge: Polity Press.

Miles, S. and Middleton, C. 1995: Girls' education in the balance: the ERA and inequality. In L. Dawtrey et al. (eds), *Equality and Inequality in*

Education Policy. Clevedon: Open University Press.

Oppenheim, C. 1993: *Poverty: The Facts*. London: CPAG.

Rowntree, B. S. 1941: *Poverty and Progress: A Second Social Survey of York*. London: Longmans.

Sherman, H. J. and Wood, J. L. 1989: *Sociology: Traditional and Radical Perspectives*, 2nd edn. New York: Harper & Row.

Skidelsky, R. 1979: The decline of Keynesian politics. In C. Crouch (ed.), *State and Economy in Contemporary Capitalism*, London: Croom Helm.

Stanley, L. and Wise, S. 1993: *Breaking Out Again: Feminist Ontology and Epistemology*. London: Routledge.

Taylor, I. (ed.) 1990: *The Social Effects of Free Market Policies: An International Text*. Hemel Hempstead: Harvester Wheatsheaf.

Townsend, P. 1979: *Poverty in the United Kingdom*. Harmondsworth: Penguin.

Westergaard, J. 1995: *Who Gets What? The Hardening of Class Inequality in the Late Twentieth Century*. Cambridge: Polity Press.

13

The Feminist Challenge

Anne Witz

Women entering sociology in the 1970s experienced a problem: they saw the actions and experiences of men reflected in sociological writings, but not that of women. Traditionally sociology has been both gender-blind and gender-biased: gender-blind because its practitioners have not regarded gender difference and gendered power relations as a significant element in the constitution of the social; gender-biased because most sociologists have been men, have looked predominantly at men in their research, and have seen men as the active, thinking subjects inhabiting the social terrain. In short, men's lives have been the stuff of which sociology is made. Since the 1970s feminists working within sociology have been correcting this partial image and the main impact of their work has been to gender our understanding of the social, so that the gender of people is always made explicit in sociological analysis, and men can no longer be taken to represent humanity as a whole.

Any assessment of feminism's impact on sociology needs to consider a number of different, though interrelated, aspects of its critique of sociology. First, feminists have argued that the epistemological basis of traditional sociological knowledge (i.e. the basis on which evidence and ideas are regarded as valid and/or significant) bears the fingerprints of its male producers: sociological theory has been written from the particular standpoint of men, whilst masquarading as an objective and disinterested account of the social. This spurious claim to universality must be challenged.

Second, gender relations are not simply the expression of benign "differences" between men and women but are constituted by a system of gendered power relations. All sociological research (not just that explicitly "concerned with women") must build on a recognition of this. Third, the characteristic research methods of existing sociology which distance themselves from the subjects of research in order to make "objective" claims about the social world, are symptomatic of a particularly male way of thinking that feminists find unacceptable. Together these arguments pose a severe challenge to sociology's traditional view of society as existing independently of the researcher and capable of being known in an objective, disinterested way. We shall consider each argument in turn.

Feminists have worked both within and against the existing body of sociological knowledge and interpretation. Some do both simultaneously – asking feminist questions (such as how we can document, understand and improve women's lives) but drawing upon the sociological heritage of concepts, theories and methods to explore women's lives and gender relations. Others believe that feminism works with a distinctive epistemology and so aim to produce sociology from a "feminist standpoint" using methods that tap into women's subjectivity and experiences. The priority for them is to understand the social world as women know and experience it – producing a "feminist sociology" that is different from the masculinist version in form, content and intent (for feminists hope their research will change women's lives for the better). At the risk of some simplification we could follow Harding (1987) in calling the first approach "feminist empiricism" and the second "feminist standpointism".

Feminism and Sociological Paradigms

One way of carving out a distinctive feminist perspective is through the critical re-evaluation of existing sociological theories and paradigms – a paradigm being a framework of assumptions and questions on the basis of which the social world is interpreted. Sometimes feminists criticize these paradigms "from a distance", seeking to debunk the paradigm as a whole and showing how it precludes the asking of feminist questions. At other times feminists work critically within a particular paradigm, seeking to develop it as a way of exploring the specifically gendered nature of society.

To begin with feminists have examined the historical legacy of sociology's "founding fathers", exposing the fact that the key actors which they placed at the centre of the stage of modernity were male rational actors: in the new social class relations of production (as in Marx), in civil society and civic associations (Durkheim), or in new bureaucratic organizational forms (Weber). In contrast what little the founding fathers had to say about women was heavily coloured by the "naturalistic" assumption that women are less social beings than men – that is closer to biologically determined nature.

This was especially true of the once dominant paradigm in Western sociology: "structural-functionalism". Feminists were particularly critical of its implicit biological reductionism when accounting for distinctive gender roles in modern society. Functionalist research into "sex roles", looking at ways in which men and women are socialized into different behaviours, attitudes and social orientations, generally concluded that women display "expressive orientations" through their family roles and men "instrumental" ones

through their work roles. Feminists argued that the "role" concept was unsatisfactory since it de-politicized experience by stripping it from its historical and political context, neglecting issues of power and conflict (Stacey and Thorne, 1985). Feminists began to distinguish between "sex" as a relatively fixed biological property and "gender" as socially and culturally more variable (Oakley, 1974). The idea that gender relations are neither natural nor immutable marked the emergence of a specifically feminist sociological paradigm. Moreover the distinction between "sex" and "gender" opened up the way for a third term to enter feminist sociology: "sexuality" referring more explicitly to forms of power centering around desire and identity, and also seen as socially constructed.

Many feminists concerned to debunk the dominant structural-functionalist paradigm, and desiring a theoretical home for the new analyses of women's oppression, became increasingly engaged with Marxism in the 1970s. Working both within and against the existing Marxist paradigm feminists have used the concept of gender ideology to explain how women's oppression is secured within capitalist societies, and that of "social reproduction" to pinpoint the specifically gendered ways in which the daily and generational reproduction of class society is ensured (through, for example, women's domestic work) (Barrett, 1988). Other feminists, whilst continuing to conduct their analyses at the broad level of structural and systemic social relations, have adopted a more critical stance towards Marxism, focussing on patriarchy rather than capitalism as the system in which men dominate women (Hartmann, 1979; Walby, 1990; Delphy, 1984).

All these paradigms, and the feminist responses to them, operate at the structural or macro level – delineating commonalities and differences between women, explaining why these social patterns exist and change and, most significantly, locating them within a systematically ordered set of power relations between men and women. But other feminists have preferred to explore the micro-processes of social life, grounding their feminist sociology in the everyday negotiation of the social world and the on-going production of social meanings by its participants. This work, which is informed by traditions such as symbolic interactionism, phenomenology and ethnomethodology, focusses less on structures of gender and power, and more on the everyday accomplishments of gender. It relies heavily on detailed empirical documentation to reveal how we "do gender" or "do difference" as we engage in social interaction (West and Zimmerman, 1987).

What impact has feminism had on traditional sociological paradigms? Regrettably it has been pretty minimal. To take but one important example, the "stratification agenda", which revolves around the theory and analysis of social class, has proved highly resistant to feminist accusations of "intellectual sexism" on the grounds that the class position of wives (and children) was derived from the husband's occupation. Instead of seeing major shifts in traditional paradigms, we have seen rather the development of a new feminist paradigm of gender, sexuality and power. In the above case, for example, feminists have responded to the sexism of class analysis by going their separate ways, concentrating instead on how gender inequalities and divisions are generated, sustained or changed (Walby, 1990).

Indeed some feminists regard any kind of abstract theorizing as a peculiarly male-centred way of doing sociology. They have argued that only particular ways of doing sociology provide the means of developing a specifically feminist sociology and have adopted a "feminist standpoint" position (Smith, 1988; Stanley and Wise, 1993). Smith advocates "a sociology for women" rather than a sociology of or about women, urging that the everyday social world as women experience and know it should form the subject matter of feminist sociology, and that in working from the standpoint of women it is important not to erase the subjectivities of those women who are the subject of feminist sociology. This view is based on a critique of white male sociology as a patriarchal discourse located in the "relations of ruling", and is underpinned by a notion that since women experience the

world in ways that are fundamentally different from men, so their knowledge of the social world will be different. It is men who enter the abstract disembodied, conceptual mode precisely because women attend to the concrete, embodied, material everyday world. Sociological conventions are man-made, and therefore consist of objectifying practices which subdue local positions, perspectives and experiences (Smith, 1988). The task of feminist sociology is to work outside these objectifying practices, in the everyday world where women live out their lives, understanding and interpreting the world in gender-specific ways.

Feminism and Substantive Sociology

Many feminists work within a particular substantive field and focus specifically on women's lives or on gendered social relations. This approach has generated a vast amount of empirically based knowledge by asking feminist questions, and then proceeding to investigate them using the inherited methodological and conceptual tools of the sociological trade, i.e. "doing sociology as usual". This is perhaps the route by which feminist sociology has made the greatest impact on sociology generally, an impact that has been felt in several different ways.

First, feminists have "gendered" our understanding of many substantive areas of social life such as education, work, the family or crime (on the last, see Chapter 2 by Heidensohn). These subfields have felt the full force of feminist arguments because they demonstrate, quite simply, that gender matters in these areas, and show convincingly that a gender-inflected sociological analysis contributes to a better understanding of what is going on. The feminist focus on the gendering of jobs and hierarchies shows, for example, how male careers are carved out at the expense of women's. Feminist analysis of male violence against women has led to an explicit recognition of the links between masculinity and crime.

Second, feminists have established the

sociological significance of areas of experience previously overlooked by sociologists or dismissed by them as trivial. These new areas include motherhood, pregnancy and childbirth; resource distribution in families and households; housework and forms of caring work in the family and community; sexuality, romantic love and friendship; violence (sexual harassment, domestic violence, rape) in both the public and private spheres; and new reproductive technologies. This means that the sweep of topics regarded as the legitimate subject matter of sociology has been considerably expanded by feminist work. Of particular importance is the way feminists have opened gendered activities in the private sphere to sociological scrutiny, and have used sociological concepts to analyse these activities – for example, treating housework as work, and showing that it is distinguished not by the tasks involved but by the social relations of marriage within which it is performed; examining gendered power relations and decision-making processes in relation to household finances; looking at how parenting work is gendered, and so on. In opening up the whole topic of domestic violence against women, feminist sociologists have taken C. Wright Mills' notion of turning "personal troubles" into "public issues" (see Chapter 4 in this volume) considerably further than before. They have shown that domestic violence is not to be understood in terms of the aberrant behaviour of a few men, and that it is not a "private matter" between husband and wife. It is rather a means by which men exert power over women within patriarchal household relations, and is therefore a public issue amenable to sociological analysis.

Third, feminists working empirically have felt compelled to re-work many of the conceptual tools of sociology. Concepts may be seen

 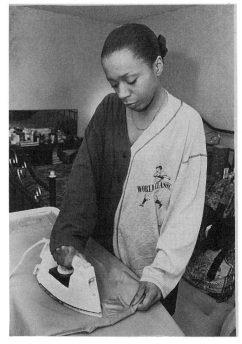

Figure 13.1 Women experience the "double-day" of employment and domestic labour. Feminism exposed the masculinist connotations of "work" that were prevalent in sociology.

as intellectual tools for "naming" aspects of the social world which we wish to think about sociologically, and to explain. Feminist empiricism poses challenging issues when studies of women's lives reveal that existing concepts do not provide the means to analyse typical forms of female sociality. "Work", for example, has long been a core sociological concern, but when feminists came to investigate the nature of women's work they began to fill the concepts of "work", "labour" and "the worker" with gendered, sexualized and embodied content that had hitherto been unacknowledged. The masculinist connotations of the previously existing concepts were brought to the surface and exploded. Sociology, and particularly Marxism, had operated with concepts which assumed a disembodied, abstract social actor living out a life of labour in the public sphere of employment, where the only real worker was one able to contract freely with an employer and "go out to work". Thus the concept of "worker" had become virtually synonomous with a "male worker" (Acker, 1990). This became most evident when sociologists fleshed out the disembodied abstract worker in research studies – it was working men (coalminers, car assembly workers, managers and bureaucrats) who manned the pages of sociological texts.

One response, as mentioned above, was to name housework as "domestic labour". This represented an attempt by Marxist-feminists to de-naturalize housework (i.e. to challenge the assumption that it was essentially the same in all times and places and was "naturally" women's work) and to analyse its relation to capitalism in the same way as waged labour. But, even more radically, the analysis of women's work led to the development of new concepts to "name" the gendered and sexualized content of work: for example,

- "emotion work" to analyse the management and control of emotions, disposition and demeanour of airline stewardesses (Hothschild, 1983 – see Chapter 28 in this volume)
- "caring work" to name gender-specific forms of unpaid work in the family and community, and paid work in occupations such as nursing (Finch and Groves, 1983)

- "sexual work" to describe how women in many service occupations are required to "sell" their sexuality, constantly presenting themselves in ways defined as attractive to men, responding to sexualized demands for women to smile, flirt, etc. (Adkins, 1995).

Feminism and Sociological Research Methodology

Feminist sociologists have also been critical of received ways of researching the social. The critique of "objectivity" in sociology led to a rejection of quantitative in favour of qualitative methods. Feminists argue for reflexivity in the research process, meaning that women sociologists should not adopt the "hit and run" techniques encouraged by standard textbooks, but should think about the relationship between the researcher and the women who are the subjects of the research, both in terms of the interview itself and the ownership of data gathered during the course of research. Feminist sociologists are, after all, attempting to produce knowledge-from-below, as well as ensuring that this knowledge will be of benefit to women. The attitude of feminist researchers is "involved" rather than "detached" (Fonow and Cook, 1992). Feminists have pioneered new kinds of reflexivity in research, reflecting on the research itself as a social process, and advocating practices that empower rather than disempower women subjects of research.

Qualitative rather than quantitative methods have been advocated as a means of tapping into women's experiences and emotions on their own terms rather than replicating masculinist attempts to order and objectify the world in measurable categories. However, some feminists have begun to re-think this position recognizing that, for all their problems, quantitative methods may be appropriate for some purposes. Certainly these have been extremely important in demonstrating what factors influence women's health; the extent to which women, as single mothers or pensioners, are particularly vulnerable to poverty; and patterns of gendered occupational segregation in labour markets.

Unsettling Sociology/Unsettling Feminism

Any assessment of the impact feminism has had on sociology has to take into account the different ways in which feminists have worked. Feminist standpointism advocates an autonomous path of constructing "a sociology for women" through accounts of women's lives that are epistemologically and methodologically quite different from male-stream sociological practices and accounts. Other feminists look to a paradigm shift in sociology, pressing it to acknowledge that social processes are gendered to the very core (Acker, 1989).

Certainly a vast amount of feminist sociology remains ignored or resisted by the male-stream. But at the same time, in specific subfields of sociology, the innovative work done by feminists has reverberated throughout the area, not only forcing a recognition that gender is important but also identifying new kinds of questions and developing new kinds of conceptual tools. In addition the role played by feminist sociologists in pioneering more reflexive modes of research has been considerable.

But we end on a note of reflexive uncertainty. Concerned to establish its different voice, feminist sociology often failed to recognize the "difference within", i.e. it worked with universal and ethnocentric categorizations of "woman". Most importantly, in claiming its own distinctive voice within sociology, feminist sociology did not hear itself speak solely of gendered whiteness, and thus created the conditions for its own critique by Black feminists, and the emergence of a distinctive Black feminist standpoint (Hill Collins, 1990). Ironically the feminist critique of sociology has generated the grounds for its own unravelling. The argument that social knowledges are situated has opened the way for a cacophony of different voices all claiming a hearing. Many claim an intellectual affinity between feminism and post-modernism and the challenges they pose to the nature of sociological explanation and theory.

Thus feminism has unsettled sociology and, in so doing, has unsettled itself. Nonetheless, as I have tried to show, it has in the process not only challenged received ways of thinking and doing sociology, but also enriched sociology. It has critically and reflexively taken up the tarnished tools of the sociological trade – methodological, conceptual and theoretical – polished them up, and added new tools of its own.

References

Acker, J. 1989: Making Gender Visible in R. A. Wallace (ed.) *Feminism and Sociological Theory*. London: Sage.

—— 1990: Hierarchies, Jobs and Bodies: A Theory of Gendered Organisations, *Gender and Society*, 4(2), 139–58.

Adkins, L. 1995: *Gendered Work*. Milton Keynes: Open University Press.

Barrett, M. 1988: *Women's Oppression Today*. London: Verso.

Delphy, C. 1984: *Close to Home*. London: Hutchinson.

Finch, J. and Groves, D. 1983: *A Labour of Love*. London: Routledge & Kegan Paul.

Fonow, M. M. and Cook, J. A. (eds) 1992: *Beyond Methodology: Feminist Scholarship as Lived Research*. Bloomington: Indiana University Press.

Harding, S. 1987: Introduction. In S. Harding (ed.) *Feminism and Methodology*. Milton Keynes: Open University Press.

Hartmann, H. 1979: Capitalism, patriarchy and job segregation by sex. In Z. R. Eisenstein (ed.) *Capitalist Patriarchy and the Case for Socialist Feminism*. New York: Monthly Review Press.

Hill Collins, P. 1990: *Black Feminist Thought*. London: Routledge.

Hochschild, A. R. 1983: *The Managed Heart*. Berkeley: University of California Press.

Oakley, A. 1974: *Sex, Gender and Society*. London: Temple Smith.

Smith, D. 1988: *The Everyday World as Problematic*. Milton Keynes: Open Universtiy Press.

Stacey, J. and Thorne, B. 1985: The missing feminist revolution in sociology. *Social Problems*, 32(4), 301–16.

Stanley, L. and Wise, S. 1993: *Breaking Out Again: Feminist Ontology and Epistemology*. London: Routledge.

Walby, S. 1990: *Theorizing Patriarchy*. Oxford: Blackwell.

West, C. and Zimmerman, D. H. 1987: Doing Gender. *Gender and Society*, 1, 125–51.

14

Mr Faust meets Mr Bateman: Mapping Post-modernity

Stephen Papson

From Grand Narratives to Empty Plots

Faust and the Modernist Vision of Progress

> If there be spirits in the air
> That hold their sway between the earth
>   and sky,
> Descend out of the golden vapors there
> And sweep me into iridescent life.
> Oh, came a magic cloak into my hands
> To carry me to distant lands,
> I should not trade it for the choicest
>   gown,
> Nor for the cloak and garments of the
>   crown. *(Goethe, 1963, p. 145)*

In his analysis of modernism Marshal Berman (1982, p. 39) argued that Goethe's *Faust* expressed the "modern world-system coming into being." Alienated from a world defined and bounded by tradition, religion, and superstition, Faust experienced overwhelming restlessness. He made a pact with Mephistopheles who promised him an infinite number of new sensations. A world without limits was his to experience. But, the rush of new experiences was not enough. Faust wanted more. He wanted to create a social world in which persons were liberated from tradition and could experience the wonders which he did. His quest for self-development had been transformed to the desire for social development (Berman, 1982). Faust recognized that

meaning and purpose for his own individual life were anchored in the social project of human liberation from need and suffering. He turned the knowledge which he attained from his experiences into a project to benefit humanity. Faust commenced to build a city. Even at the moment of his death Faust imagined the development of a modern world.

> For millions I shall open regions
> to dwell, now safe, in free and active
>   legions.
> Green are the meadows, fertile; and in
>   mirth
> Both men and herds live on this newest
>   earth,
> settled along the edges of a hill
> That has been raised by bold men's
>   zealous will.
> A veritable paradise inside,
> Then let the dams be licked by raging
>   tide;
> And as it nibbles to rush in with force,
> A common will fills gaps and checks its
>   course.
> This is the highest wisdom that I own,
> The best that mankind ever knew:
> Freedom and life are earned by those
>   alone
> Who conquer them each day anew.
>   *(Goethe, 1963, pp. 469–470)*

When Goethe wrote *Faust*, Europe was undergoing widespread social transformations. The theories and methodologies of the Scientific Revolution not only redefined the nature of the physical universe but also under-mined the religious worldview which shrouded agrarian society for centuries. Disrupting familial and communal life, the Industrial Revolution unleashed the forces of capitalism, industrialization, and urbanization. The Enlightenment and the French Revolution marked the end of traditional political authority. These transformations were both liberatory and destructive. On the one hand, individual rights or the concept of citizen were now anchored in a conception of the state legitimized by the will of an electorate. On the other hand, changing economic relationships meant that individuals increasingly had to confront a marketplace defined by the logic of capital. Here, economic competition and the quest for profit reduced the value of work to the lowest wage necessary to maintain a work-force. Marx's analysis of capitalism paints a world of industrial disorder in which workers were exploited economically, spent their lives in unsafe and unhealthy work conditions, and who were easily discarded. Out of these social upheavals both modernity and sociology were born.

Organized around the Enlightenment principle that social institutions could be transformed through reason, modernist discourses embraced and unified the themes of technological progress, social justice, and utopianism. In response to these social upheavals, modernist discourses empowered humanity with the hope that a humane social world, the good society, was attainable. Sociology emerged as a modernist discourse. We locate the birth of the discipline with Auguste Comte whose vision of sociology was both positivistic and humanistic – a science of and for humanity, a vision which paralleled Faust's. Against the chaotic world of early modernity, moderns constructed universal projects based on reason, logic, and science. These projects ranged from building dams to supply power for vast regions to conceptualizing a Utopian society. Despite the insecurity and change associated with the coming of modernity, the modern mind visualized a Utopian future based on universal humanism, a philosophy which attempted to expand the benefits of

science and technological progress to all (Berman, 1982). Modernity is based on grand narratives: visions which both conceptualized a higher quality of life and mapped ways for attaining it. Just as Faust envisioned the construction of a Utopian city, Comte envisioned a discipline able to discover the social laws which govern human behavior. He believed that social institutions could be designed according to these laws. Comte's vision of a positivistic sociology mimicked the grand narrative of science and technological progress, that humans can master the physical universe. In this respect even narrative and interpretative traditions that set themselves up in opposition to Comte's scientific positivism, such as Marxism or Critical Theory, shared his modernist faith in the possibilities of human improvement. Both Marx's narrative of economic and social justice, that the proletariat will develop a revolutionary consciousness and transform a class society into a classless one, and Rousseau's narrative of self-actualization, that humans can construct social institutions which support authentic human development, map a route for human evolution. Sociology participates in these grand narratives of modernity and these grand narratives legitimize sociology. The modernist view of the world presumes the possibility of progress, in the sense that social and technological changes lead to ever greater economic plenty, justice and the development of each individual's human potential.

Located in modernist social narratives was a conception of self associated with authenticity, depth, knowledge, and reason. Faust's identity emerged along a narrative for self-development – experience, alienation, reflection, creation. This conception of self permeates Western bourgeois culture and is expressed as the *auteur*, the artist whose creative power rises from the innermost depth of his being. Faust is the model of the *auteur*. He experienced both the exhilaration and the contradictions of modernity, and he attempted to give meaning to his existence through the act of creation. In sociological discourse this conception of self was most fully articulated by Critical Theory in its critique of the commodification of culture (Horkheimer and Adorno, 1982). Critical Theory, a modernist view of the world, maintained a notion of self based on the categories of authenticity and depth, qualities achieved through acquiring knowledge located in the philosophical traditions of bourgeois high culture. According to Critical Theory, however, the vision of an autonomous reflective individual which emerged in the Enlightenment had been undermined by the transformation of high culture into mass entertainment. The proliferation of mass culture particularly via television jeopardized the development of a reflective self capable of acting with moral purpose. As commodification or the consumer society advanced, individuality, critical thought and authenticity declined. Critical Theorists argued that the Enlightenment project of self liberation conflicted with the logic of capital. For example, Adorno and Horkheimer (1982) theorized that art in its various forms, i.e. music, film, painting, theater, or writing, was increasingly governed by the laws of the market. Like any commodity under the logic of capitalism, art had to be produced to sell. The larger the audience, the more profits could be made. Repetitive structures, the use of themes of violence and sexuality, and the simplification of plots or the moral dilemmas they embodied were viewed as some of the ways in which artistic forms were made palatable to a mass audience. Even now we oppose authenticity to commodification. When we say a musical group has sold out, we are referring to changes in a style which make the music more marketable. When this happens, the *auteur* status of the artist is lost. Critical Theory associated the loss of individuality with the consumption of these mass produced commodified cultural forms. These theorists argued that each individual's ability to think critically was undermined by the pervasiveness of capitalistic economic relations. Essentially, they extended Marx's critique of capital to include consumption as well as production. Yet, despite this pessimistic vision of the future, they maintained some hope. As long as one could establish critical distance from this onslaught of commodified culture, authen-

ticity was possible. Critical Theorists such as Herbert Marcuse tried to find solid ground from which to criticize. But, as culture became increasingly commodified, that ground eroded. The success of capitalism, measured by the ability of the economic system to produce goods and services profitably, resulted in a commodified world in which the construction of an autonomous reflective self was called into question. Located within modernity were both a conception of selfhood which celebrated reason, authenticity and depth, and the social forces which undermined that ideal.

Patrick Bateman: The Post-modernist Self

Patrick Bateman is the yuppie anti-hero of Bret Easton Ellis' controversial novel *American Psycho*. Bateman describes himself:

In bed I'm wearing Ralph Lauren silk pajamas and when I get up I slip on a paisley ancient madder robe and walk to the bathroom. I urinate while trying to make out the puffiness of my reflection in the glass that encases a baseball poster hung above the toilet. After I change into Ralph Lauren monogrammed boxer shorts and a Fair Isle sweater and slide into silk polka-dot Enrico Hidolin slippers I tie a plastic ice pack around my face and commence with the morning's stretching exercises. *(Ellis, 1991, p. 26)*

In contrast to Faust who prayed for a magic cloak to send him to all lands, Patrick Bateman displays his Ralph Lauren silk pajamas. His life is organized around consuming signs produced by the marketing apparatus of corporate capitalism and distributed and circulated through a range of media. Bateman is Critical Theory's nightmare, a self constructed out of the commodity signs (the objects plus the meanings attached to them) which he consumes. Since the value or the meaning of these signs is constantly changing, Bateman is engaged in a war against his colleagues and his friends to appropriate and display the most up to date signifiers of status. It is not the pursuit of signs, however, that makes this novel controversial. Patrick Bateman is also a serial killer. The lists of commodity signs are paralleled by lists of body mutilations. While Ellis' book was criticized for its "death of affect" style and its ethical distance from the cool horrid descriptions, the exaggerated use of these extensive lists (a post-modern literary technique) foregrounds not only the pervasiveness of signs but the internalization of signs into what we think of as our own identities. Ellis constructs a self which slides across the slippery surface of a commodified culture, privatized and isolated, unable to experience emotion or empathy, without authenticity or depth, without ethics or meaning, a self constructed solely out of the consumption of free-floating rapidly circulating commodity signs.

Faust made a pact with Mephistopheles in order to experience the world, yet he used these experiences not only to develop his inner self but also to engage the social world with a vision of social progress. While his actions resulted in the death of others, his intentions were humanistic. Bateman, however, inhabits a world in which there are no new experiences. Everything has been done. As Bateman states in one of his few self-reflexive moments:

There wasn't a clear, identifiable emotion within me, except for greed and, possibly, total disgust. I had all the characteristics of a human being – flesh, blood, skin, hair – but my depersonalization was so intense, had gone so deep, that the normal ability to feel compassion had been eradicated, the victim of a slow, purposeful erasure. I was simply imitating reality, a rough resemblance of a human being, with only a dim corner of my mind functioning. Something horrible was happening and yet I couldn't figure out why – I couldn't put my finger on it. The only thing that calmed me was the satisfying sound of ice being dropped into a glass of J&B. (Ellis, 1991, p. 282)

Bateman, our yuppie serial killer, kills out of boredom, out of narcissistic delusions of grandeur, and without emotion. He inhabits a world in which all that is left is the celebration of perversity. I am not arguing that to live in a post-modern society is to become a serial killer, nor am I arguing that there are even tendencies that orient persons towards such action. I am arguing that Ellis' construction of Bateman's experience of depersonalization propels us towards a fascination with the perverse.

What happened to the modernist vision? How did our modern man with his hopes of constructing a rational social world turn into a yuppie serial killer? How does one go from Faust, the modern, whose restlessness sends him on a quest for experiences, sensations, and meanings to Bateman, the post-modern, whose boredom with experience and sensation results in the thrill of serial killing? From the hope of the Enlightenment to contemporary cynicism? From Utopian dreams to the fascination with the perverse? How does a sociology reconstruct its vision of the relationship of self to society when confronted by literary characters like Bateman who appear to reflect a growing cynicism and a growing fascination with "perversity?"

Post-modernity and the Realm of Signs

Post-modernity is a condition in which signs, the raw material of culture such as images, sounds, words, video clips, and artifacts and the meanings associated with them, are freed from their socio-historical referent systems and circulate at ever increasing velocities through our lives. Privileging signification over experience, information over production, and simulation over reality, post-modernism expresses an emergent global culture in which the cognitive, affective, and evaluative codes that we use to map the social world are in disarray (Best and Kellner, 1991). Phrases such as "the death of subjectivity," "the lack of affect," "the loss of meaning," and "the death of authenticity" are used to describe our responses to the disorienting nature of this cultural formation. Post-modern social theory suggests that the resulting fragmented nature of culture makes it difficult to construct a coherent identity, one in which an individual has affective links to other particular humans or to a notion of humanity in general. It posits this crisis of self as a "crisis" of culture and it locates these crises in the changing nature of signs – their pervasiveness, their construction, and their relation to referent systems, sites of production, technology, and one another. Post-modern social thought conceptualizes these new sign relations in four ways: *decontextualization*, the separation of signs from their historical or geographical sites of production; *acceleration*, the increased velocity with which signs pass through our lives; *fragmentation*, the incoherent relationship that signs may have with one another; and *virtualization*, the separation of signs from reality itself.

The Separation of Signs from Actual Time/Space Referents (Decontextualization)

Sociology defines culture as a system of norms, values, and beliefs which are historically derived and which provide the cognitive, affective, and evaluative criteria necessary for a group to adapt to its physical environment. It associates culture with geography and history. For post-modernists, this notion of culture has increasingly lost weight. We now live in a swirl of signs, images and texts which have been freed from space and time. While all cultures signify, the quantity of signs to which we are asked to respond continually increases. While the traditional self was anchored by a culture which emerged in relation to a physical geography, and the modern self had narratives which tied action to a collective future, the post-modern self is constructed as a surface for the play of floating or decontextualized signifiers. In the process of decontextualization a signifier which has meaning in a particular context, a referent system, is taken out of that context and used for another purpose. We can see this process operate by looking at advertising. This discourse appropriates

signifiers from referent systems and attaches them to commodities in order to increase the value, that is the desirability of the commodity. For example, rap is a style of music which emerged in hip-hop culture in the New York City ghettos. Rap is an expression of struggle, economic hardship, racism, police brutality, and the socio-historical conditions of ghettoized Afro-Americans. Signifiers of the ghetto such as rap, basketball courts surrounded by chain link fences, and slam dunks are used in a Reebok's commercial for a basketball shoe named Blacktops. The function of these signifiers is to increase the value of the commodity (Goldman and Papson, 1995). In the process rap as well as other signifiers were decontextualized from their site of production. Moreover, by using the product we appropriate the meanings associated with these signifiers, i.e. coolness, hipness, resistance. We use commodity signs to construct our identity. Commodity signs have overwhelmed Patrick Bateman's life. His identity is a function of sign consumption and the value which advertising discourse confers on the signs he consumes. As Lee (1993, p. 176) notes, "Bateman's consciousness itself is assembled from nothing other than fragments of the commodity-form; it is a consciousness from which all social meaning has been evacuated save that evoked by the endless succession of commodity-signs through which Bateman's experiences are channeled." Post-modern social theory argues that our identities are nothing more than the ensemble of commodity signs which we consume, the sum of the labels and logos which cover our bodies (Featherstone, 1991) (see Figure 14.1).

Operating by the logic of capital, commodification infects all signification and spreads to all spaces. Commodity signs, as well as information and images in multiple forms, circulate globally at faster rates. Invading all cultures, these signs are transported by media, by tourists, and by commodities. No culture is immune. Likewise, signs are appropriated from all cultures and circulated through this global information system. Advertising even uses signifiers of resistance (Goldman and

Figure 14.1 Post-modern social theory argues that identities are nothing more than the ensemble of commodity signs which we consume, the sum of the labels and the logos which cover our bodies.

Papson, 1996). Rap sells Sprite. Hendrix's music has been appropriated by Chevrolet. Converse, a shoe company, sends its researchers into street cultures in order to find new styles. Presently, skateboard culture is seen as a hot subculture. The "authentic" styles of everyday life are instantly appropriated and transformed into commodity signs. Once a signifier is appropriated it enters the general flow of signs to be used by whomever in whatever context. The notion of advertising as existing in the in-between-spaces, the commercial breaks, has been replaced by the integration of brand signs into events and institutions such as schools, museums, and playgrounds. For example, think of advertising and sports events. GM donates money in honor of "the Player of the Game"; Office Depot owns the foul poles at many major league baseball stadiums; Reebok presents the half time report; the US army takes us back into the past to give us highlights of great moments in sports suggesting that these highlights have something to do with joining the army; Rolaids presents its relief pitcher of the year award; Nike Swooshes are everywhere. Often the event itself is so spectacularized it becomes a sign in itself. The Super Bowl is a Super Bowl for advertisers as much as a football game. Are there any spaces left? It has been suggested that outer space could be the next space to be invaded with huge inflated orbiting logos. Post-modern social theory collapses the categories of signification and commodification. It conceives culture as a vast array of ever-changing decontextualized signifiers flowing through the electronic circuitry of a global information system.

Post-modernists associate the pervasive commodification of the culture to disorientation. Olalquiaga (1992) contends that the breakdown of spatial and temporal boundaries caused by the diffusion of information technologies and by the logic of capital weakens cultural referents. Cultural artifacts, such as food, dress, music, clothing styles, etc. are now free-floating entities, which are both commodified and homogenized. She refers to this process as the breakdown of referentiality. In place of a system of perception organized in categories based on lived experience, it is now based on simulative, intertextual and vicarious associations.

A more extreme form of the breakdown of referentiality is exemplified by corporate word construction. An *Advertising Age* advert reads:

Making names
At NameLab, we've made product and company names like *Acura, AutoZone, Compaq, Geo, Lumina, Renova, TrueVoice*, and *Zapmail* by constructional linguistics.

The result of a NameLab project is a report presenting and analyzing registrable names expressing your marketing ideas. We quote costs accurately in advance and complete most projects within four weeks. *(1995, p. 12)*

In the novel *White Noise* Delillo comments on the construction of language:

A long moment passed before I realized this was the name of an automobile. The truth only amazed me more. The utterance was beautiful and mysterious, gold-shot with looming wonder. It was like the name of an ancient power in the sky, tablet-carved in cuneiform. It made me feel that something hovered. But how could this be? A simple brand name, an ordinary car. How could these near-nonsense words, murmured in a child's restless sleep, make me sense a meaning, a presence? She was only repeating some TV voice. *Toyota Corolla, Toyota Celica, Toyota Cressida.* Supranational names, computer-generated, more or less universally pronounceable. *(1985, p. 155)*

Corporatized word constructions are determined by the logic of capital. Words are designed to add sign value to the commodity. These constructions take on meaning in relation to an inbred culture which is governed by media technocrats and which circulates through mainstream media, particularly television. Words and images such as these are designed to either market products or to legitimize corporate practices. Their meanings are a function of their position on the chain of signifiers in the product category. Nevertheless, this institutional language construction seeps down into our everyday lives and mediates the relationship between our perceptions and reality. For Olalquiaga (1992), when the signs we use to guide us through everyday life are decontextualized and dehistoricized, it is difficult for us to locate our positions on a cultural map. Using "the lost in space" metaphor, she argues that psychasthenia, the psychological condition in which self and surroundings fuse, is a consequence of post-modernity.

The Circulation of Signs (Acceleration)

Hyper is a post-modern prefix – hyperreality, hyperspace, hypercommodification, hyper-signifiers. How many images flow past our eyes as we surf the increasing number of television channels? How many sound bytes, those chunks of information used to construct a news story pass through us daily? More information is crammed into smaller spaces and time segments, i.e. commercials have been shrinking in length. For post-modern social theory speed is everything. Lyotard (1984) describes post-modernity as an epoch in which the flow of information is over-whelming. The self is reduced to a node on the information superhighway through which the continuous but uneven flow of information passes at ever increasing rates. For Lyotard (1984, p. 51) those who have the "operational skills" to navigate this flow will be the one's who are rewarded.

Post-modern social theory associates acceleration with two factors. On the one hand, new communication technologies not only distribute signs globally but also increase the velocity at which signs, images and information flow. Post-modernists often refer to Marshall McLuhan's communication theories. His conception of the global village has now been extended into a vision of a digitally integrated information system, a superhighway on which all transactions and communications take place. As new technologies appear which are able to compress and unpack information faster, the velocity at which signs circulate will continue to accelerate. On the other hand, velocity is seen as a function of the logic of capital (Harvey, 1989). The faster commodity signs circulate, the more profits are to be made. To stand still is to be rendered obsolete by competitors. As the half-life of commodity signs continually shrinks, new ones instantly appear and vie for our attention. The logic of capital drives technological development and in the long run will determine the shape of the information system.

Post-modernists theorize that the accelera-tion of signs creates a crisis of self. As the flow of signs accelerates, meaning evaporates (Baudrillard, 1983a, 1987). When signs are decontextualized, all we can do is wait for a more spectacular sign. Like Bateman, our identities flow along these chains of signifiers. Meaning requires depth, and depth requires time for reflection. In a post-modern society, the velocity of information flow does not allow it. The surface reigns. The man on the street becomes the expert; Oprah Winfrey a sociolo-gist. Knowledge based on reflection and con-textualization is replaced by the factoid, an isolated, fragmented, spectacularized bit of information. Our response is distant non-affective fascination. As Olalquiaga (1992, p. 35) states, "it is the quality of permanently living at a second remove that underlies our time, raising it to an almost artistic level of detachment-hence its inevitable fascination with the baroque and the decadent."

In his introduction to *Crash*, J. G. Ballard (1985, p. 1) writes "voyeurism, self-disgust, the infantile basis of our dreams and longings – these desires of the psyche have now culminated in the most terrifying casualty of the twentieth century: the death of affect." The death of affect is regarded as a post-modern trait (Jameson, 1984). The sheer ac-celeration of images has created a continuous stream of signs. Reacting to a particular sign with depth, coherency, and concern is difficult. The flow is just too fast. Take the evening news which mixes death scenes from Bosnia, hemorrhoid and denture cream com-mercials, victims of natural disasters, and a human interest story about a chimp at the zoo. How does one emotionally respond to the juxtaposition of death and consumer happi-ness? In a short period of time we are asked to respond with a range of disparate emotions to a range of images which we do not control. When the stream of images calls forth radic-ally different responses, the consequence is reciprocal inhibition, an emotionless response.

Accelerated commodification leads to cyni-cism. Once the boundaries of a culture are permeated by commodity signs, they be-gin to hemorrhage and the hierarchy of meaning associated with culture collapses.

Commodification overwhelms cultural authority and replaces it with the logic of the spectacle. In order for signs to circulate they must be more salient, more fascinating, and more spectacular than the previous sign. Media violence, particularly, attracts an audience. But the ante must rise in order to circulate the product – slasher films become the fiction of choice. *Faces of Death* and its many sequels are enjoyed by adolescents; the mystery story is replaced by spectacle of the serial killer. Think of the number of recent movies about serial killers: *Silence of the Lambs*, *Henry: Portrait of a Serial Killer*, *Kalifornia*, *Natural Born Killers*, *Seven*, *Serial Mom*, and *Man Bites Dog*, or the television series such as A&E Biography and American Justice which regularly show episodes on serial killers. There are even serial killers trading cards. Post-modernists theorize that the death of affect and, more importantly, the inability to empathize result from this bombardment of spectacularized signs.

The Lack of Coherence (Fragmentation)

Once signifiers have been dislodged from their socio-historical site of production and begin to circulate freely through the communication system, their relationship to one another becomes increasingly tenuous. Composed of disparate signifiers post-modernist texts are eclectic. Post-modernist cultural forms such as Las Vegas, *Blade Runner*, *Tank Girl*, MTV, and Kathy Acker novels, are concocted out of dead styles, remnants, retro fashion, kitch, and junk culture. Jameson (1984) refers to this aesthetic formation as pastiche, a collage which brings together styles from earlier periods without necessarily making reference to the historical periods from which they were drawn. Post-modern aesthetics abandon historical continuity. History is plundered for its signifiers which are reassembled into new forms. Creativity has been replaced by bricolage, the act of assembling and combining disparate elements.

Fragmentation extends beyond specific forms and refers to culture in general. Faust's vision reflected the Enlightenment narrative that science and reason could liberate humanity from unnecessary suffering by constructing social institutions which would allow humanity, nature, and society to coexist harmoniously. Lyotard (1984) theorized that the *grand narratives* of humanism, Marxism, and scientific progress which legitimized Western society have collapsed leaving Western culture without a center or direction. In place of these grand narratives a plurality of discourses such as Third and Fourth World, feminist, gay, ethnic, and alternative, have arisen. For Lyotard discourses are language games in which each discourse has its own rules, structures, and moves. No discourse can make universal claims to values, principles and morals. No theory can explain or describe the social world. No art form or style has more legitimacy than any other.

For post-modernists the central issue is "how much fragmentation?" On the one hand, post-modern theory celebrates fragmentation as the decline of bourgeois "legitimate" or high culture and the Euro-patriarchal codes associated with modernism (Aronowitz and Giroux, 1991). Cultural balkanization is synonymous with multi-culturalism. This position constructs the world as a mosaic of cultures which are located in the history and the struggles of different ethnic groups. It argues for a world which recognizes, respects and promotes local cultures. It sees the contemporary resurgence of interest in national cultures as evidence for cultural formations in which identity construction is located in the heritage of ethnicity. It argues that new nomadic social formations such as immigrants and refugees are in the process of forging new hybrid cultures and new sources of identities (Said, 1994). On the other hand, post-modernism argues that fragmentation is leading to a global culture consisting of decontextualized signs circulating through communication circuits without historical or geographical reference points (Harvey, 1989; Olalquiaga, 1992). This disembedding process leaves no cultural history intact. This totally commodified culture mimics the marketplace. Like the shopping mall it is composed of decontextualized signs plundered from a variety of referent systems – nature, history, and exotic cultures. The corresponding self is described as de-centered, lacking both depth and affect. Post-modern theorists use schizophrenia as the dominant metaphor to describe the construction of the post-modern self. Jameson (1984) suggests that when culture is composed of isolated, disconnected, discontinuous signifiers, constructing a coherent identity becomes increasingly difficult. Like words without a sentence, or a novel without a narrative there is no organizing principle for the self. In the age of continuous signification the problem is one of mapping, of locating oneself in this chaotic ever shifting cultural landscape. What is left is the present, the hallucinogenic experience, fascination, the spectacle. Like surfing the internet, there are no coherent maps, no ultimate authority, just a cultural world in a permanent state of flux (Collins, 1995).

"The End of the Real" (Virtualization)

As post-modern social theory evolved it argued that the relationship of representation (how we describe and theorize) to reality (what's out there) has become increasingly suspect. Debord (1977) noted that an ever increasing proportion of our experiences are not of physical sensual reality but are of mediated reality – representations. He stated that "everything that was directly lived has moved away into a representation." (Debord, 1977, p. 1) Furthermore, these representations followed the logic of the spectacle. The celebrity, the model, the cinema in general, the Super Bowl are sensationalized versions in which non-eventful reality is edited out. The spectacle presents itself as an exciting version of existence. Everyday life cannot compete with the spectacle. It will always appear dull.

Eco (1987) used the category hyperreality to describe the construction of social reality in which signifiers of the real are reproduced and assembled to resemble the original. Spaces such as restaurants, malls, and tourist sites splice together signifiers from a range of referent systems – street subcultures, native cultures, ethnic cultures, and nature. Williamsburg, Virginia publicizes itself as an "authentic reproduction." What does this oxymoron mean? (Huxtable, 1992). Generally, we enter these spaces as tourists. Who can tell what's authentic and what's not? This process of Disneyfication, or the theming of spaces, results in contrived hypercommodified spaces (Wakefield, 1990). When this happens the traditional categories of fiction/documentary, original/copy, authentic/fake collapse. Likewise, this process has taken place in media in the form of docudramas and simulated crime shows. Baudrillard (1983b) suggests that the simulation model often precedes reality and validates it. Even photographs which we generally assume are representations of an actual physical reality can be computer-generated. If we see an image of a model in a magazine should we assume the equivalent exists? Or, is it a paste-up, a mixture of body parts or simply a computer simulation, or a hybrid?

Virtuality refers to the synergistic combination of the above factors. It's when hyper becomes cyber, when velocity and simulation reach the point that Baudrillard's metaphor of "zero gravity" is the appropriate allusion. It's cyberspace, cyberpunk, the net, virtual reality – all sooner or later reduced to cybercash, the new medium of exchange, virtual money. Cynically capturing the meaning of virtual reality, Kroker and Weinstein (1994, p. 162) state "where flesh goes to die and the electronic body struggles to be born at the fin-de-millennium. Strap on a head-mounted scanner, wire your flesh with digital trodes, slap smell patches on your data suit and take an out of-body flight across the outer galaxies of cyberspace." For these authors the human sensory system is extended electronically into a reality which lacks physicality – experiencing without having the experience. Virtuality refers to the absence of a referent located in time and space. What happens to values and ethics when actions have no consequences – like a video game in which you can rip your opponent's head off or destroy the universe at a whim? Virtual sex, virtual relationships, virtual death. Think of the possibilities. What is the relationship between virtual experience and identity? Is it liberating? Does the contrived nature of these experiences deaden the possibility of experience in real time, in real space? How will post-modern social theory map virtual reality? How will it construct the relationship of self to society as an increasing proportion of our experiences become virtual?

Rethinking Sociology

The discipline of sociology is not immune to the hyperanomic conditions post-modern social theory describes. Sociology emerged as a modernist discourse and was motivated by the modernist vision of social progress. It embarked on a project to construct social theories supported by research strategies which mimicked the natural sciences. Like any discourse, it created shared categories, concepts, and practices and made the claim that it had the right to speak about the social world. It attempted to construct a coherent vision of society. Most importantly, it was institutionalized in the academy and so gained legitimacy to make statements about the social world. In post-modernity the view of sociology as a legitimate and privileged discourse has been increasingly challenged. First, grand theorizing as a practice has been called into question. Baudrillard (1983a) has even suggested that the notion of society itself is perhaps an outdated construction. Second, interdisciplinary discourses are gaining ground in the university. Cultural studies may

be better positioned than sociology to study and speak about a world which is increasingly fragmented; communication studies better positioned to speak about cultural forms which travel through the circuits of the information superhighway. Third, commercial discourses such as talk shows, news programming, and infoentertainment series make sociological statements to much larger audiences than sociologists could ever hope to have (Bauman, 1988). Fourth, increasingly emergent Third and Fourth world discourses question the right of outsiders to speak about their cultures in a jargon which emerged with European practices of colonization. Finally, sociology itself has become increasingly fractured. Even its center, classical social theory, has been attacked by feminist theory and non-Western discourses as theory constructed from the perspective of great white men.

Where does sociology fit in the post-modern world? What is its role, its function, and most importantly how does it legitimize itself? How does sociology make a claim to speak about the social world when other discourses make the same claim or question the legitimacy of sociology? If grand theorizing is no longer possible, will sociology be absorbed by the growing interdisciplinary field of cultural studies? These are some of the questions the discipline must face. Sociology is an historical discourse. It emerged under specific historical conditions and may also disappear when those conditions change.

References

Advertising Age 1995: Making names. September 11.

Aronowitz, S. and Giroux, H. 1991: *Postmodern Education: Politics , Culture and Social Criticism*. Minneapolis: University of Minnesota Press.

Ballard, J. G. 1985: *Crash*. New York: Random House.

Baudrillard, J. 1983a: *In the Shadow of the Silent Majorities . . . Or the End of the Social*. New York: Semiotext(e)

—— 1983b: *Simulations*. New York: Semiotext(e).

—— 1987: The year 2000 has already happened. In A. and M. Kroker (eds), *Body Invaders: Panic Sex in America*. New York: St Martin's Press, 35–44.

Bauman, Z. 1988: Is there a postmodern sociology? *Theory, Culture and Society*, 5,(2–3), 217–238.

Berman, M. 1982: *All That Is Solid Melts into Air*. New York: Simon & Schuster.

Best, S. and D. Kellner. 1991: *Postmodern Theory: Critical Interrogations*. New York: Guilford Press.

Collins, J. 1995: *Architectures of Excess: Cultural Life in the Information Age*. New York: Routledge.

Debord, G. 1977: *Society of the Spectacle*. Detroit: Red & Black.

Delillo, D. 1985 : *White Noise*. New York: Viking.

Eco, U. 1987: *Travels in Hyperreality*. London: Picador.

Ellis, B. E. 1991: *American Psycho*. New York: Random House.

Featherstone, M. 1991: *Consumer Culture & Postmodernism*. Newbury Park, CA: Sage.

Goethe, J. W. 1963: *Goethe's Faust*. Kaufmann, W. (trans.). Garden City: Doubleday.

Goldman, R. and Papson, S. 1996: *Sign Wars: The Cluttered Landscape of Television Advertising*. New York: Guilford.

Harvey, D. 1989: *The Condition of Postmodernity*. Cambridge, MA: Basil Blackwell.

Horkheimer, M. and Adorno, T. 1982: *Dialectic of the Enlightenment*. New York: Continuum.

Huxtable, A. 1992: Inventing American reality. *The New York Review of Books*, 24–9.

Jameson, F. 1984: Postmodernism, or the cultural logic of late capitalism. *New Left Review*. 146, 53–92.

Kroker, A. and Weinstein, M. 1994: *Data Trash: The Theory of the Virtual Class*. New York: St Martin's Press.

Lee, M. 1993: *Consumer Culture Reborn: the Cultural Politics of Consumption*. New York: Routledge.

Lyotard, J. 1984: *The Postmodern Condition: A Report on Knowledge*. Minneapolis: University of Minnesota.

Olalquiaga, C. 1992: *Megalopolis: Contemporary Cultural Sensibilities*. Minneapolis: University of Minnesota Press.

Said, E. 1994: *Culture and Imperialism*. New York: Random House.

Wakefield, N. 1990: *Postmodernism: Twilight of the Real*. Winchester, MA: Pluto.

15

Putting Sociology in its Place

Joti Sekhon

After obtaining an undergraduate degree in English literature, I enrolled in the master's program in sociology at a university in New Delhi, India, in 1976. At that time, I did not know what sociology was. What I did know was that much as I enjoyed reading English literature, it did not provide me with an understanding of the complexities of Indian culture and society. The discipline of sociology, I felt, would help. It did, to an extent. A review of my course titles and readings is revealing. Nearly all the readings for courses on sociological theory and methods were written by Europeans and North Americans. Courses focusing on various aspects of Indian society were dominated by theoretical works by European and North American scholars and studies of Indian society by them. There were a few studies by Indian scholars, most of whom were schooled in the Euro-American sociological traditions. Much of what I learned about Indian society came from a Western intellectual and cultural perspective. At that time, this did not seem problematic. I was socialized in a country that had emerged as an independent state in 1947 after two centuries of British colonial rule. Indian political leaders accepted political, administrative, legal and educational institutions introduced by the British as the appropriate framework within which to develop India as a modern industrial society. The discipline of sociology also developed in India within the context of British colonization. Only gradually did I become aware of the debates within Indian sociology challenging the dominant Western theoretical and methodological traditions and arguments for a distinctively Indian approach to sociology.

My own development as a sociologist, therefore, was influenced by where and when I studied sociology. This statement underscores the point that the development of sociologists, and accordingly of the discipline of sociology itself, is profoundly influenced by the spatial and historical contexts in which these processes take place. In the rest of this essay I will substantiate this point in three distinct, but related, ways. First, I will discuss sociology's European origins and the way this has influenced comparative sociology and analysis of non-Western societies. Second, I will comment on the neglect of the concept of place or space as an explicit and analytical variable in conventional sociology. Finally, I will consider the struggles within selected non-Western regions of the world to develop their distinctive sociologies through interplay between indigenous intellectual traditions and experiences and Western influences.

Sociology's European Origins

Sociology developed in Western Europe within the context of the eighteenth century Enlightenment and the political, economic, technological and social transformations associated with the French and Industrial Revolutions of the late eighteenth and nineteenth centuries. Society came to be viewed as continuously developing and progressing, and as an entity that could be transformed and perfected through human will and reason (see Turner, Chapter 8). The growing scientific and technological developments led to the belief that scientific research and observations would uncover "natural laws" governing human social behavior. These discoveries could then be used to change and improve human societies. This optimism, however, was tempered by a fear of chaos and disorder brought on by the political and economic changes. Early sociologists, particularly French sociologists Auguste Comte and Émile Durkheim, focused on searching for social conditions and factors that would contribute to social stability and an orderly transition from a traditional to a modern industrial society. They believed that research using methods modeled on those of the natural sciences would assist in this project. Evolutionary theories of social change emerged as the dominant framework to understand and analyze the processes of change. In this view, all societies evolve and change from simpler to more complex forms. Change was, therefore, viewed as unilinear, progressive, cumulative and as proceeding from uniform causes (Nisbet, 1969).

This sociological perspective, geared to the analysis of Western industrial and capitalist societies, also influenced the analysis of non-Western less-industrialized societies. Western societies became the standard against which non-Western societies came to be compared and judged. Accordingly, all societies were placed along a continuum from the "traditional" to the "modern." Non-Western less-industrialized societies were believed to be at lower stages of evolutionary development and were expected to become socially and culturally similar to Western societies as they industrialized. Economic and socio-cultural changes associated with industrialization were believed to be responsible for the transformation of societies from traditional to modern. This transition was seen as beneficial and progressive because it would lead to an increase in material wealth, individual freedom, equality of opportunity and democratic rights. Any strains arising inevitably as part of the

change process would, it was assumed, be resolved through institutional means developed within these societies to manage conflict, such as occupational associations, educational opportunities and voting rights. If they failed to do so, it was due to their traditionalism and resistance to change (Giddens, 1987, pp. 25–33).

These views became dominant in Western sociology during the twentieth century and became the basis for the modernization theory of development that emerged during the 1950s. According to this theory, in order to become more "developed," the less developed societies needed to adopt "modern" or Western economic, institutional, psychological and cultural characteristics such as industrialization, advanced technology, high level of education, desire to work hard, goal-oriented thinking, representative democracy, etc. During the 1950s and 1960s, modernization theory became the basis for stipulating conditions for assistance given by Western government and development agencies to the less industrialized countries of Latin America, Asia and Africa. Development in these countries was and continues to be, measured in terms of statistical measures developed and based on economic, social and political conditions characteristic of Western industrialized countries, such as gross national product, per capita income and the human development index. Non-quantifiable economic and cultural practices were ignored as sources for meeting human needs, being viewed largely as obstacles to economic devlopment (Bradshaw and Wallace, 1996, pp. 40–4; and McMichael, 1996).

The main alternative to modernization theory, world system theory, was associated with the Marxist critique of industrialization within a free enterprise capitalist framework. According to this theory, economic underdevelopment in less industrialized countries is the *result* of the development of the capitalist world system. European countries colonized and exploited these regions of the world and expropriated raw materials and cheap labor in order to develop industrial manufacturing in Europe and North America. They imposed

Western economic, political and cultural institutions at the expense of local ones, which
were often destroyed. This led to an unequal
and dependent relationship between industri-
ally advanced and less developed countries.
This inequality has persisted due to economic
policies promoted by Western industrialized
countries in the post-colonial era. According
to the world system perspective, therefore, it is
unreasonable to expect all non-Western
societies to follow the Western path and
achieve the same level of capitalist development and industrialization (Bradshaw and
Wallace, 1996, pp. 44–53).

In both modernization and world system
theories the Western industrial societies are
used as the reference point for comparing
other parts of the world. This is not problematic in itself. Most parts of the world have
been impacted to some degree by industrialization and capitalism. What is problematic is that development continues to be
identified with industrial development and the
focus is primarily on the economic level of
production, distribution and consumption of
goods and services. Analysis of the political
system and the variety of cultural practices
that form the basis of people's lives is limited
to the extent to which they promote or hinder
modernization and capitalist economic development. Within modernization theory,
non-Western cultural practices are viewed as
traditional elements that need to be modern-
ized and Westernized. For example, it is
suggested that beliefs and values associated
with practices such as subsistence production
(for example, wealth-sharing, communal
ownership of property and decision-making,
group or family loyalty) need to be replaced by
qualities that are more conducive to capitalist
economic development and modernization,
such as individualism, competitiveness,
goal-oriented decision-making, and private
ownership of property. And in world system
theory cultural characteristics of societies
are mainly viewed as elements that are
manipulated in the quest for economic power
and exploitation (Bradshaw and Wallace, 1996;
McMichael, 1996).

Recently, some researchers have attempted
to move beyond the orthodoxies of both
theories (see Bradshaw and Wallace, 1996;
McMichael, 1996; Sanderson, 1995). They
argue that analyses of societies should examine both factors internal to particular countries and also the ways in which they are linked
as part of the world system. There are also
calls to acknowledge the cultural, economic
and regional diversities within different
countries that account for variations in their
incorporation into the world system as well as
resistance to capitalism and Westernization.
This opens up the way to comprehending the
variety of forms of knowledge that people have
used to live their lives without viewing them
ethnocentrically. The numerous grassroots
movements for resistance to Western cultural
imperialism, capitalist development projects,
political domination and ecological destruction launched by racial/ethnic groups, women
and the poor have also exposed the limitations
of traditional theories used as the basis for
comparing non-Western and Western societies. These movements are not just strains in a
unilinear course of development but conflicts
rooted in the global *interaction* between processes of development in some parts of the
world and underdevelopment in others. While
the West is still often used as the basis for
comparison, there is now more debate on
these issues and more of a tendency to guard
against over-simplistic universal generalizations about social change across time and
space. As part of this debate, there are now
calls for explicit acknowledgement and analysis of the concept of place or space in social
science research.

Place as an Analytic Variable

As already noted, the aim of the dominant
Western sociological tradition was to uncover
the laws governing human social development
through scientific research. European and
North American sociologists searched for
general concepts and theories that could be
used to categorize and explain all types of
societies and human behaviors. One consequence of this process has been the

marginalization and devaluation of the relevance of *place* as a distinct variable in sociological research.

Agnew (in Agnew and Duncan, 1989, pp. 9–29) argues that in nineteenth century conventional social thought societies were placed along a continuum between community and society. The concept of community was associated with place or physical setting for social relations as well as the traditional way of life. And the concept of society came to be associated with national state boundaries. Within this perspective, thinkers focused on the loss of community, and attachment to place, as part of the process of industrialization and urbanization. As individuals moved from place to place in search of new opportunities and material wealth, they were expected to lose ties with any particular spatial community. This view of the transition from community to society orientation was incorporated into modernization theory. As part of the modernization process, attachment to the spatial community was associated with parochialism and localism and was expected to be replaced by loyalty to the national state which was viewed as the legitimate context for the development of a modern industrial society. The transition from community-orientation to society-orientation was viewed as natural and universal. Modernization theorists assumed and expected that with the diffusion of modern technological innovations and industrialization, people in all parts of the world would be exposed to the same material conditions as well as ideas. There would, then, be less cultural diversity and increasing similarity in lifestyles and values. Spatial location, therefore, was assumed to be less significant in determining social lives. And with increased disciplinary specialization in twentieth-century Western social science, analysis of space was delinked from sociology and subsumed as part of the regional studies wing in geography. Place, therefore, was marginalized as an explicit sociological variable structuring human diversities.

Marxist critiques of conventional sociology focused on the development and worldwide spread of capitalism. Analysis centered on the ways in which all parts of the world were incorporated into the capitalist world system. In this process people were detached from their spatial location as land and labor became commodities to be bought and sold in the market. Hence place was assumed to be of less value as an independent structuring variable influencing capitalist social relations.

In reality, however, the spatial variable continues to be significant in understanding modern capitalist societies and the uneven spread of capitalism around the world. The historical and cultural characteristics of different places are associated with variations in the goods manufactured, cost of labor, level of unionization, regulatory laws, etc. Furthermore, alternative modes of social organization continue to survive and emerge in specific spatial-temporal contexts. Conventional Western sociological and Marxist paradigms continued until recently to assume a decline in cultural variations and standardization of societal practices due to the processes of modernization and/or the rise of the capitalist world system. Only recently has there been increased recognition that human actions are always rooted in spatial-temporal contexts. Now efforts are being made to include spatial location as a significant factor mediating and structuring human social life in non-Western and Western societies. Giddens (1984) and Agnew and Duncan (1989), for example, argue that spatial settings form an integral part of socio-cultural practices and interactions. These efforts are emerging alongside the recognition that social science concepts and theories are also abstractions rooted in space and time. Several articles in Agnew and Duncan, for instance, illustrate the ways in which North American and European social scientists have thought about places when analyzing human lives. This observation leads to the consideration of the third theme related to the significance of place in sociology: the development of sociology in non-Western parts of the world.

Non-Western Sociology

As noted earlier, sociology emerged in Western Europe and it spread to other parts of the world through colonialism and the development of the global state system. It took with it the commitment to a science of society aimed at discovering laws of societal development. In most instances, then, the sociological enterprise became associated with the development of universal theories, concepts and research methods. However, the nature of the different political, administrative and cultural variables clearly impacted on the growth and legitimacy of sociology in different countries. Also, there were varying degrees of resistance to acceptance of Western conceptual tools from those advocating indigenous intellectual traditions and experiences as appropriate frameworks for sociological analysis. I will illustrate this process by outlining the development of sociology in three non-Western areas of the world: Latin America, Russia and India.

Lower levels of industrial development compared to the United States and Europe, unequal distribution of wealth and power, and Euro-American neocolonialism and cultural imperialism have contributed to a focus on the definition and creation of national identities and culture as one key element underlying the development of sociology in Latin America. In addition to traditional university departments, several semi-autonomous sociology programs affiliated with universities were established with the assistance of European and American governments, aid agencies and universities as part of the modernization and development projects that emerged from the middle of this century. The overall socio-cultural and political environment in Latin America, however, has often been hostile to independent sociological thinking particularly during the 1960s and 1970s when many countries, such as Brazil, came under authoritarian rule. Several sociologists chose to focus on social engineering and applied sociology, and assist in the solution of urban and rural social problems within the framework of the modernization theory of development. For instance, several

Latin American governments were concerned with providing economically viable landholdings and increasing agricultural productivity through mechanization and efficient use of resources. Agrarian reform, therefore, emerged as an acceptable and important area for research to provide policy guidelines for rural development. More radical sociologists, however, critiqued the unequal power structure and assumptions underlying capitalist industrial development. Much of this critique took place from within the Marxist and neo-Marxist dependency and world system theories that grew in popularity in the 1970s and 1980s, times of economic crises and decline in the standard of living of the middle and working classes. However, with the decline in popularity of Marxism related to failures of communist regimes, along with realization of the failures of Western-style capitalism, internal sources of knowledge may emerge as appropriate theoretical frameworks for sociological analysis. Some sociologists are analyzing liberation theology as a mode of resistance using religious symbols and images as well as the various indigenous cultural traditions. They are also questioning ecologically destructive economic development programs such as mining and farming in the Amazon Basin (Bluhm in Mohan and Wilke, 1994, pp. 255–76).

As sociological ideas spread to Eastern Europe during the nineteenth century, they were critiqued in the light of unique conditions operating there such as cultural differences, peasant economies and feudal states. While East European scholars and intellectuals were also concerned with the evolution toward modernity and adaptation to industrialization, Marxism – in many different variants – emerged as the key tool for sociological analysis in Eastern Europe. Soviet Marxism, as defined by Lenin, was institutionalized in the Soviet Union in the years after the Bolshevik Revolution in 1917. The evolutionary approach to social development and a faith in the scientific reconstruction of society was inherited from the Enlightenment project. However, social transformation was linked to the Marxist-Leninist plan for societal development through "scientific communism." With the consolidation of Stalin's rule during the 1930s and the spread of "state socialism" to other parts of Eastern Europe after 1945, Soviet Marxism was used to justify Soviet domination. Any opposing intellectual thought was labeled as "bourgeois" sociology and suppressed. Within this context, sociology in other East European countries developed through a complex struggle for autonomy from Soviet domination. Ironically, the very hostility to Western sociology in the Soviet Union exposed Soviet sociologists to Western ideas, and after Stalin's death there were increased contacts with foreign sociological institutions. Diverse trends emerged within Soviet sociology. For instance, some engaged in intellectual debates with Western sociological ideas, some focused on empirical research using "neutral" statistical models, while others devoted themselves to developing and promoting "scientific communism." There were struggles for legitimacy within and between these currents, the outcome often relating to the degree of control by the Communist Party. Diversification has only increased since the fall of the Soviet Union and other changes in Eastern Europe since 1989 and, consequently, sociology is now characterized by theoretical eclecticism and pluralism (Batygin and Deviatko in Mohan and Wilke, 1994, pp. 436–58).

Sociology in India is a product of India's indigenous cultural traditions and Western cultural influences that derived from colonialism and its aftermath. British administrators encouraged and sponsored widespread research on various aspects of Indian society in order to assist them with colonial rule. The discipline of sociology, however, developed during the first half of the twentieth century when several European scholars undertook research and analysis of Indian society. Many Indians also studied in Europe and played a significant role in establishing departments of sociology and social anthropology in several Indian universities. After independence from Britain in 1947, the influence of British and American structural-functionalism and positivism became predominant alongside plans for the modernization and development of the country. Critiques of Western sociological traditions have increased since the 1970s and diverse trends are now identifiable in Indian sociology. While several sociologists continue to apply Western concepts and empirical research techniques to the study of Indian society, calls for the development of conceptual tools rooted in Indian intellectual and cultural traditions are emerging as dominant. Sociologists such as D. P. Mukerji, Radhakamal Mukerjee, Yogendra Singh and Satish Saberwal argue that Indian society reflects a unique combination of indigenous cultural, religious and philosophical traditions and outside influences. Indian sociology, therefore, should be based on a critical evaluation of Western influence and a creative synthesis of aspects of Western and Indian intellectual traditions in order to understand, analyze and transform Indian society. Critiques of conventional sociology and Indian social structure from within a Marxist framework have also emerged as a significant trend. With the rise in economic and political crises and popular discontent among the poor, women, tribal groups, etc. in the last two decades, many sociologists from different theoretical standpoints are also calling for social scientists to be more practical and responsive to the search for a more just and democratic society. There is an increase in research on activities and voices of people at the local levels, particularly those in subordinate and powerless positions. Contemporary debates in Indian sociology, therefore, reflect a diversity of viewpoints and research agendas corresponding with diversities in Indian society as well as recent trends in Western sociology (Mohan and Pillai in Mohan and Wilke, 1994, pp. 673–700).

Conclusion

It is within this spatial-temporal and intellectual environment that I was initiated into sociology. Familiarity with Western sociological and cultural traditions made for an easier transition to graduate school in Canada. However, exposure to critiques of dominant Western sociology assisted me in maintaining a critical outlook as well as developing the capacity to view social phenomena from both non-Western and Western perspectives. The point here is not to dismiss the entire Western sociological enterprise. It is, however, essential to be conscious of the ways in which spatial and temporal contexts affect sociology and how theoretical and methodological ideas emerge through engagement with the social world and not through an artificial detachment from it. It is also essential to be aware of the ways in which time and place affect human lives. As sociologists we must always be open to the various forms of knowledge and experience and work to overcome spatial and cultural ethnocentrism.

References

Agnew, J. A. and Duncan, J. S. (eds) 1989: *The Power of Place*. Boston, MA: Unwin Hyman.

Bradshaw, Y. W. and Wallace, M. 1996: *Global Inequalities*. Thousand Oaks, CA: Pine Forge.

Giddens, A. 1984: *The Constitution of Society*. Berkeley: University of California Press.

—— 1987: *Sociology*, 2nd edn. San Diego, CA: Harcourt Brace Jovanovich.

McMichael, P. 1996: *Development and Social Change*. Thousand Oaks, CA: Pine Forge.

Mohan, R. P. and Wilke, A. S. (eds) 1994: *International Handbook of Contemporary Developments in Sociology*. Westport, CT.: Greenwood.

Nisbet, R. A. 1969: *Social Change and History*. London: Oxford University Press.

Sanderson, S. K. (ed.) 1995: *Sociological Worlds*. Los Angeles, CA: Roxbury.

Focal Themes of Sociology

16

Social Divisions

Harriet Bradley

Harriet Bradley

Divided Societies

As we approach the end of the twentieth century, most Western industrial societies are deeply divided. In the context of an increasingly global, harshly competitive economic environment cleavages between propertied and non-propertied classes, between the employed and unemployed, men and women, old and young, minority ethnic groups and the white majority are becoming more apparent. Conflicts of interest over scarce resources are more naked in an intensely consumerist society, where glamorous possessions are daily paraded before us on our television screens. Is it surprising that these covert conflicts periodically explode into the more overt forms of social conflict: rows between parents and children, industrial action by unions representing working people, protests by fathers required to pay child support to estranged partners, inner-city riots often involving racial issues, environmental protests backed by disaffected young people, demonstrations over taxation or the dismantling of the welfare system? These events certainly do not surprise sociologists who have long argued that social divisions and conflicts are built into the structure of modern industrial societies.

Throughout the past two decades the income gap between the rich and the poor has been steadily growing in most Western societies. Fat corporate salaries along with taxation policies favouring the wealthy have helped promote a rich elite who enjoy all the delights and luxuries of an advanced consumer society; while the decline of manufacturing industry has left many in working-class communities, such as the mining villages and shipyard areas of the north-east of Britain or the "rustbelt" towns of the American mid-west, without jobs or prospects of finding new employment.

Consolidation of poverty and unemployment in particular communities has led to talk of the growth of an "underclass" made up of people permanently excluded from employment and dependent on state benefits for subsistence. American sociologist Charles Murray believes that this underclass has developed values quite different from those of the broader society. To back up this view he points to the increasing number of illegitimate births, with young women bringing up babies on state benefits because jobless young fathers are unable to support them. Without family responsibilities to teach them maturity, the young men drift into an aimless life of violence and crime (Murray, 1990). Others are fiercely critical of this view. They deny that an underclass exists or, if they accept the idea, argue that it is a structural phenomenon rather than a product of different cultural values. They link the emergence of an underclass to government policies which trap the disadvantaged in a vicious cycle of poverty (Field, 1989). Wilson (1993) has applied the term to the minority ethnic communities in cities such as Chicago, describing how the life of social isolation in ghetto areas remorselessly pressurizes some African–Americans into demoralization, thence to violence and crime.

The underclass scenario depicts a deprived (and possibly depraved) minority set against a comfortable and affluent majority. But other accounts suggest a more complex view of modern societies. Will Hutton (1994) uses the term "the 40–30–30 society" to describe the social divisions thrown up by the current phase of economic development in Britain: 40 per cent are doing very well, 30 per cent are marginalized and excluded while, in between, another 30 per cent are in employment but in jobs which have recently become insecure. The demand by firms for "flexibility" in their employment relations means that increasingly people are working part-time, or on temporary or short-term contracts, or are threatened by redundancy. As people lose the stability of a "job for life", many are forced into early retirement. With public provision of pensions being cut there is increasing risk of falling into poverty in old age.

Inequalities of this kind spring from class relations but, as the example of poverty in old age shows, class is closely linked to other aspects of social cleavage. People from minority ethnic groups, especially those of colour, are economically disadvantaged relative to the majority; they are under-represented in managerial and professional occupations and are much more likely to face unemployment. They constantly have to contend with racism, shown in prejudice, insults, and sometimes physical assaults, especially if they live in deprived urban areas where community tensions run high. Age divisions are also increasingly evident: young people are especially vulnerable to unemployment, while older people struggle to maintain living standards as welfare services are cut. A report by the charity Age Concern (1995) found that a third of pensioners were having difficulty in managing on their incomes, while another 50 per cent said they were only just succeeding in getting by. Whilst women's employment has been steadily rising over the past decades and well-qualified women are now better able to compete with men, there are still few women in top posts and many women find themselves in part-time work, with its characteristic low pay and poor conditions. Any equalization between women and men in the workplace has not been matched by an equalizing of tasks in the home. Overall, women in most societies continue to perform about 70 per cent of housework and child care; the domestic burden is a major disadvantage to married women who wish to develop a career.

All these types of social divisions mean that as individuals we face very different "life-chances". The son of manual parents who grows up in a run-down area (a council estate on the fringe of Bristol, Newcastle, or Glasgow, or an inner-city ghetto in Los Angeles or Washington) finds himself faced with restricted opportunities for self advancement. As a result of under-resourcing his neighbourhood school may suffer a poor academic record and problems of truancy and discipline. He will experience pressure to associate with a group with an anti-school culture and the temptation to drift into vandalism, joy-riding, drugtaking or theft, which appear to offer more than the limited local employment options. He may end up leaving school early with minimal qualifications, finding himself unemployed, hanging around with other "dolies". He may join the high proportion of young men who get into trouble with the law, the more so as class and skin colour expose him to police stereotyping as a "troublemaker". His sister has marginally more chances to enter the labour market, obtaining a low-paid job in retail or as a care assistant. But, finding her job boring and opportunities limited, she may opt to start a family as an alternative to uninspiring employment and as a way to show that she has achieved adult status. Once she has children, she finds her employment chances further restricted. While many young people from poorer backgrounds escape these traps and make a success of their lives, it is a harder struggle for them than for their more affluent fellows.

Very different experiences await the young man born into a business or professional family, who attends a well-funded private school, with smaller classes, a better academic record and tighter discipline. His parents have the money to allow him expensive leisure pursuits and opportunities to develop his intellectual skills in the form of "cultural capital" – access to books, films, music, art which will help him to succeed in school. His parents might celebrate his twenty-first birthday by buying him a car, which will contribute to the good time he is enjoying with his mates at one of the older elite universities such as Oxford, Cambridge, Harvard or Yale. While he may be tempted to join in the mildly deviant activities associated with youth subcultures (raving, drugtaking, heavy and rowdy drinking), he will be careful that it does not jeopardize his promising career chances. If he does commit an offence sociological studies show that he is more likely to get off with a caution than his working-class counterpart. When he gets his degree he has a good chance of finding employment in stockbroking, in accountancy, medicine or law or even in the media; here he may be joined by his sister. Middle-class young women have been the greatest beneficiaries of the expansion in higher education, using their qualifications to compete with male contemporaries for jobs where feminine attributes are now being seen as assets. Young middle-class women tend to delay having children till their careers are established. But, if she does have children when young, she and her husband can afford nannies and minders to enable her to return to her career as soon as she wishes. Of course, it is possible to "drop out" from an affluent background. But the statistical odds are against it.

Sociology and Social Divisions

Gathering information about inequalities (such as those I have just described) and seeking explanations for them have long been tasks central to the sociological endeavour. This was linked to the first sociologists' attempts to define the nature of the emerging modern society. Classical social theorists Karl Marx and Max Weber provided the discipline with two influential models of a divided society which have been under discussion ever since. Marx spoke of class divisions as emerging

from the way society organized its production system. In the capitalist form of production, Marx believed that the most important features were the concentration of economic power in the hands of corporations which made major decisions about economic development and investment, and the emergence of a labouring class excluded from the ownership and control of the means of production but which actually produced the goods which brought wealth to society. Thus he identified the fundamental axis of social cleavage as between these two classes: bourgeoisie (capitalist owners) and proletariat (wage labourers), although he pointed to the existence of other classes. Weber, however, while acknowledging the divide between the propertied and non-propertied, offered a more complex model of social divisions, identifying multiple class groupings which developed on the basis of the particular assets people had to offer in the capitalist market, such as different skills and qualifications. He emphasized that these exist alongside other divisions, resulting from status rankings and from the mobilization of groupings to obtain political power. There is still fierce debate about the definition of class: but we can define it broadly as referring to relations arising from the way the production, distribution and consumption of goods and services are arranged in any given society.

In the 1950s, 1960s and 1970s a familiar way of classifying sociological theory was in terms of the "sociology of order" and the "sociology of conflict". Sociologists of order, such as Talcott Parsons and Robert Merton, were influenced by the writings of Émile Durkheim and his exploration of the forces which act to keep complex societies stable and integrated. They developed the idea of a "social consensus" – a set of core values held by all in a society which could smooth over the clashes of interest between individuals and groups and prevent societies fragmenting. Conflict theorists, on the other hand, followed the ideas of Marx and Weber and asserted that complex societies were inherently conflictual: clashes of values and interests arose from the way societies were organized, notably the unequal distribution of wealth, privilege and power. Conflict theorists accepted that social order was maintained by a variety of devices, such as political oppression, or the compensations provided by the welfare state, or the spreading of consensus values by the mass media, but suggested that interest and value clashes could never be ultimately resolved. Overt conflicts of various types might erupt at any moment. As Weber said, our societies are at the mercy of "warring gods" (Weber in Gerth and Mills, 1991, p 153).

Currently an important division among sociologists is between the adherents of "modernity" and of "post-modernity". Broadly speaking, modernists are concerned to develop the insights of the classical sociologists and refine their models to fit more recent social developments. They portray modern societies as characterized by inbuilt social divisions; many see the capitalist production system as the major force which generates social divisions. By contrast, postmodernists present societies as fluid and deny that there are underlying forces which create rigid patterns of differentiation. They accept that societies are divided, but suggest that there are numerous different sources of division, and that these are always changing. There is no inevitability that people will identify themselves in terms of fixed interest groups such as classes or "races"; instead, people are seen as continually redefining their interests and relocating themselves in different groups according to their specific individual experiences. While the modernists still tend to see class as the most significant form of social division, post-modernists see society as made up of a plurality of groups jostling for social position.

Class: a Sociological Obsession?

As I have implied, class was the primary form of social division studied within sociology. Indeed, those who are suspicious of sociologists (often seen as undermining the status quo by those who would prefer to see it unchallenged) sometimes accuse them of being obsessed with class! It has certainly

been a major topic of sociological research in the post-war period. Sociologists such as John Goldthorpe, A. H. Halsey, David Lockwood and Peter Townsend explored how class relations were changing as a result of post-war prosperity. Had the expansion of white-collar jobs and consequent upward mobility brought a merging of classes? How open and meritocratic were modern societies? What was the link between class background and educational attainment? How was class related to poverty, ill-health and crime? This important research contributed crucially to our knowledge of modern social life.

Yet looked at from the vantage point of the late twentieth century (especially if one espouses a post-modernist stance) the preoccupation with class at the expense of other forms of social division such as age or gender seems a little odd or misguided. However, if we place this interest in historical context it is easier to understand. Marx and Weber in using the language of class were only reflecting social concerns of their times. In Britain the question of the "condition of England" centred on the disruptive effects of industrialization upon the labouring classes. The French Revolution had roused the spectre of popular revolt causing alarm to ruling groups. Waves of protest were experienced in Britain throughout the nineteenth century: rioting by angry citizens when food was scarce or expensive; industrial strikes which sometimes brought whole towns to a standstill; violent demonstrations by agricultural workers demanding a living wage; mass meetings of the Chartists demanding universal suffrage (for men only) and other political rights. While government policies slowly began to address the problems of poverty and deprivation experienced by many working people, the outbreak of mass unemployment across the world in the 1920s and 1930s, brought the plight of the working class to centre stage again. Government concern about public order in capitalist industrial democracies was exacerbated by the communist takeover in Russia. The journal *The Economist* warned in 1943 "if liberal democracy is not compatible with full employment, then it is liberal democracy that will go" (quoted in Deacon, 1980, p. 62). These social preoccupations fed into the sociological concern with class, seen as the major form of conflictual social division. Moreover, the political organizations that arose to redress these ills, such as the Labour Party in Britain, the trade unions and the co-operative movement, explicitly presented themselves as fighting on behalf of the working classes.

The post-war period saw the rise of welfare systems and state provision in most industrialized societies and brought in its wake two decades of relative prosperity and social stability. American sociologist Seymour Lipset declared "the fundamental political problems of the industrial revolution have been solved" (Lipset, 1960, p. 406). Yet this was the heyday of class analysis in Britain. Debates centred around whether post-war changes were indeed bringing an end to class inequality or radically altering the nature of the class structure. The theory of embourgeoisement, for example, stated that the barrier between middle and working classes was breaking down in face of a shared affluent consumer lifestyle. By and large American sociological orthodoxy was that modern societies were fairly open and classless, while most British sociologists argued that class inequalities persisted, despite greater social mobility.

Recently the interest in class has become less predominant within sociology. This is partly because of the rise of post-modernism, which tends to reject the type of structural theories used to explain class divisions. But just as importantly, new political and social movements have emerged representing other interests, such as those of gender and "race". Such movements present these social relationships as being as oppressive as those of class, if not more so. Moreover, in a time of rapid economic growth people are confused about their own personal class positions. Long-held class identities seem less relevant, especially as the old class-based organizations have lost some of their social influence. In Britain, the Labour Party and the unions are now concerned to play down their class origins and appeal to broader constituencies. Only small ultra-Left groups, such as the Socialist Worker Party or Class War, continue to use the political language of class.

This does not mean that class as a form of social division has no relevance. Class obstinately refuses to lie down and die. At least three aspects of class division and inequality mentioned already in this chapter are currently causing immense social concern.

(1) *The continuance of mass unemployment.* Unemployment is rising in most advanced industrial societies. Ray Pahl (1984) has argued that unemployment is now the major source of social cleavage. He distinguishes between "work-rich" and "work-poor" households, haves and have-nots. Pahl suggests that this form of division is replacing class, but he is surely mistaken here. By the broad definition offered in this chapter, unemployment is an aspect of class, referring to the way the work required to produce goods and services is organized and allocated.

(2) *The debate over the underclass.* Many sociologists reject the idea of an underclass, arguing that the term is a rhetorical device used to pin the blame for poverty on the poor themselves and distract attention from its real social causes. But most accept that the presence of a large minority of people dependent for subsistence on state benefits and excluded from employment is a major social problem and an aspect of changing class relations.

(3) *Flexible employment and the post-industrial economy.* The shift away from manufacturing to service employment in all the advanced economies is creating new employment problems and hierarchies. A growing insecurity for most employees is one result. A TUC survey carried out in 1995 found that 52 per cent of British workers expected greater job insecurity in the next year, while three quarters expected greater pressure in their work (Guardian, 28 December 1995). Only the elite of top executives, managers and financial experts are gaining from these changes, with massive increases in income, pensions and other benefits. Again this is an aspect of changing class relations.

Gender, "Race" and Ethnicity: Current Preoccupations

Since the 1980s, though, sociologists have concentrated more on other forms of social division, notably gender, "race" and ethnicity. Gender divisions are not an entirely new topic in sociology, but post-war sociologists gave little attention to women workers or to issues such as women's under-representation in politics or public life. Study of gender was mainly confined to the sociology of the family, where the unequal domestic division of labour and its effects on women's working lives were topics of discussion, but were often taken for granted as "natural" consequences of women's childbearing role. The view of biology as destiny was little challenged, although optimistic sociologists such as Bott (1971) or Young and Willmott (1975) suggested that a more egalitarian relationship based on "joint conjugal roles" was developing in some families, especially among the middle classes. This was linked to a view that since women had gained the vote old inequalities of gender had largely disappeared. Women and men were (formally at least) equal as citizens.

It was the emergence of second-wave feminism in the 1970s in North America and Europe that caused the proliferation of studies of all aspects of gender relations. Feminists argued that contemporary gender relations were far from egalitarian; men held greater social power and women were oppressed by prevailing gender roles and ideologies. Radical feminist Shulasmith Firestone (1971) argued that gender was the original form of social division from which all others sprang. While nineteenth- century feminists had exposed gender inequalities and pioneered exploration of women's lives, their exclusion from higher education meant that the study of gender made little headway within the university curriculum. The past three decades have brought notable changes. Within most disciplines gender is now a major concern, while women's studies, gender studies and even men's studies are now academic programmes in their own right.

Towards the end of the twentieth century gender relations are in a state of flux, leading some to speak of a "post-feminist" era. It is true that in all western societies women have made advances into some (not all) areas of male-dominated employment and are catching up with men in educational achievement. But the domestic division of labour remains little changed; women are in a minority in most positions of power, political, economic or social; male violence to women is widespread and apparently increasing; and around the globe women bear the greatest burden of poverty, deprivation and disease. Struggles over gender are set to continue in the twenty-first century.

So are those of "race" and ethnicity. Racial inequality received earlier attention in sociology than gender inequality. Sociologists have long been concerned to deconstruct the term "race", arguing that there is no scientific validity to the idea of genetically or biologically distinct racial groupings. Rather, certain social groups are "racialized", that is defined as being of distinct racial origin and thereby inheriting distinctive physiological traits and associated behavioural characteristics (such as lower intelligence, greater athleticism or whatever). On the basis of such ascribed "racial" characteristics, minority groups are discriminated against and disadvantaged.

Post-war study of racial disadvantage often linked it to class. Some Marxists suggested that "race" was a false social construct designed to obscure the realities of class divisions and the injustices of capitalism. More recently, however, racial divisions have become a topic of study in their own right. It is recognized that racial inequalities cannot be reduced to class. Sociologists have also become increasingly interested in the broader concept of ethnicity. While skin colour has been central to the idea of "race", the notion of ethnicity encompasses other aspects of differentiation in groups claiming some kind of common geographical origin: the idea of a "homeland", a common culture, a common language, the right to political autonomy or a distinct territory.

Various factors have contributed to the

heightened interest in racial and ethnic inequality. In many countries anti-racist movements have kept the issue of racial hierarchies and racial injustice to the fore, especially as post-industrial change and economic restructuring have hit minority groups particularly hard, exposing them increasingly to redundancy and unemployment or to insecure and illegal forms of employment. In Britain and North America growing numbers of intellectuals come from minority ethnic groups and those of African and south-Asian descent in particular have been concerned to explore more fully their own history and culture, both in the colonial past and the post-colonial present, and to link them to present experiences of racism and disadvantage. The connection between gender and ethnicity has been an increasingly popular topic following criticism by black feminists of the ethnocentrism of white-dominated feminism. The breakup of the former Soviet empire led to outbreaks of nationalist conflict which focused the attention of sociologists on ethnic rivalries. A greater public awareness of ethnicity has promoted the revival of distinctive ethnic cultures and practices, sometimes linked to the re-emergence of fundamentalist religions.

These trends seem set to continue in a world where economic production and communications are increasingly globalized, generating new patterns of migration and new ethnic divisions of labour, both national and international. Wars around the globe have contributed to the complexity of migration processes as refugees seek asylum, often in former colonizing powers. But rather than accepting the idea of the "melting pot" in which distinct ethnic traditions would be fused into a generalized modern social identity (dominated by American consumption goods and popular cultural forms), minority groups and migrants seem increasingly concerned with the right to maintain traditional ways of living and retain cultural differences. At the same time minority ethnic groups occupy the bottom positions in economic hierarchies, and face prejudice and racial hostility in all advanced Western nations. In some countries xenophobic political parties are growing in strength and calling for the adoption of stricter immigration controls or even the repatriation of migrant groups. In the USA many states are starting to dismantle the equal opportunities legislation designed to help black minorities improve their social position, a move encouraged by a backlash among white Americans who claim that they are now victims of discrimination (a claim increasingly being made by some men in response to the women's rights movement). Ethnic and racial struggles are likely to heighten.

New Concerns: Sexuality, Disability and Age

Gender and ethnicity have been sharply in focus in the 1980s and 1990s. But there are other forms of social division which may be seen as submerged, in that they have received little sociological attention or are just emerging as a topic of importance. Three such are sexual orientation, disability and age.

Sexual orientation is a classic case of an issue brought to the attention of sociologists by a political movement. The vigorous gay and lesbian movement which sprang up in the USA to defend its members against persecution and prejudice and to win the right for them to live their preferred lifestyle openly and in public has spread around the world. The movement has prompted an academic exploration of homosexual history, culture and literature, along with an analysis of homophobia and the discrimination gays and lesbians face within "straight" heterosexual culture. The problems of individuals "coming out", acknowledging their homosexual orientation or identity in a world which still generally fears and refuses to accept homosexuality, have been studied, along with issues of discrimination in the workplace, the difficulties faced by gays and lesbians who wish to be parents, and homophobic legislation which reinforces the stigmatization of homosexuals.

Another growing movement is that around disability. People suffering from physical impairments of all kinds have come together in Britain to campaign for legal rights for disabled people and for the opening up of access to all aspects of social life by the provision of aids, such as wheelchairs, ramps, more suitable transport services, and devices to help blind or deaf people enjoy artistic events. Linked to this, a new interest is awakening in sociology in the way society itself acts to "disable" those who depart from its physical norms. The exploration of the social divisions that surround bodily differences is still in its infancy, but if the movement continues to thrive disability is likely to prove a topic of growing importance within sociology.

By contrast the study of age differences has been long established in sociology. In the post-war decades American functionalists considered age as a distinct form of social stratification. However, age divisions and inequalities have never preoccupied sociologists as class and gender have done. Perhaps this is because the growth of political bodies designed to promote age interests has been limited, although there are now signs of greater militancy among pensioners' organizations.

However, age divisions and conflicts are growing sharper. Industrialized societies are grappling with the problem of the costs of an "ageing population", an increase in the proportion of people over retirement age. Older people, especially women, are among the most vulnerable to poverty and are seriously affected by welfare cutbacks. Younger people are growing up in a more competitive economic world which offers them fewer opportunities than those enjoyed by the post-war younger generation. Younger age groups are most likely to be unemployed or to work in low-paid service jobs, such as cooking burgers in McDonalds. In defence one response has been for young people to develop their own powerful culture, which has different values from those of their elders. Studies indicate, for example, that taking soft drugs is a norm rather than deviant behaviour for older adolescent party-goers. Some young people

Figure 16.1 The Study of new social movements such as those around disability rights will be of growing importance in sociology.

go further, abandoning altogether the adults' world with its unpromising prospects, and finding their own ways to survive in a world where "a job for life" is becoming a thing of the past. Attempts by the British government to use legislation to restrict the activities of ravers, New Age travellers and environmental protesters may be pointers to a future of increased age conflicts.

Conclusion: Changing Society?

So what does the future hold? This chapter has shown how the exploration of social divisions has always been a key part of the sociological enterprise. But according to changing economic, political and theoretical contexts, different forms of division take sociological priority. In this chapter I have suggested that social divisions, far from diminishing as is sometimes suggested, are increasing. But your guess may be as good as mine which of the currently studied or emerging types of division will become the next sociological preoccupation.

Currently, however, most sociologists are particularly concerned to study the way inequalities of class, gender, ethnicity and so forth are interconnected and act upon each other. An account of current inequalities which disregarded class entirely would be as inadequate as earlier class theories which marginalized other forms of division. For example, the labour market chances of women from manual and professional backgrounds are vastly different, as are the solutions they take to the problems of childcare. Similarly it is a different experience being old and poor from being old and prosperous. Mike Davis has shown how class, ethnic and age divisions come

together in the ghettoes of California to create a major problem of poverty among the young (Davis, 1990).

Because of the interest in division and inequality lay people often muddle up sociology with social policy or social work – or even socialism! While these other disciplines have taken it upon themselves to design policies for society, or to provide blueprints for a better type of society, sociology proper has tended to see itself as an analytic discipline whose task has been to describe and explain how societies *do* work, rather than prescribe or advise how they *should* work.

But this view of the sociologist as an objective observer has continually been debated. Marx declared, famously, "the philosophers have only interpreted the world in various ways; the point, however, is to change it" (Marx and Engels, 1968, p. 30), and many radical sociologists have espoused this position. Weber, writing firmly from an academic not a political standpoint, argued by contrast that sociology could never answer those crucial questions, "what shall we do and how shall we live?" (Weber in Gerth and Mills, 1991, p. 143). All it could do was indicate what would be the likely outcomes if particular actions were implemented. Yet since, as sociologists, we are so much a part of what we study, we tend to be drawn to explore those social injustices about which we as individuals happen to feel passionately. The study of social divisions will continue to be a key sociological task, whether carried out by postmodernists seeking to give a voice to the victims of some of the more neglected forms of social division, or modernists seeking to demonstrate the power and persistence of longstanding inequalities of class and gender.

References

Age Concern 1995: *Just About Coping*. London: Age Concern England.

Bott, E. 1971: *Family and Social Network*. London: Tavistock.

Davis, M. 1990: *City of Quartz*. London: Vintage Books.

Deacon, A. 1980: Unemployment, and politics in Britain since 1954. In B. Showler and A. Sinfield (eds), *The Workless State*. Oxford: Martin Robertson.

Field, F. 1989: *Losing out*. Oxford: Blackwell.

Firestone, S. 1971: *The Dialectic of Sex*. London: Jonathon Cape.

Gerth, H. H. and Mills, C. W. 1991: *From Max Weber*. London: Routledge.

Hutton, W. 1994: *The State We're In*. London: Cape.

Lipset, S. M. 1960: *Political Man*. London: Heinemann.

Marx, K. and Engels, F. 1968: *Selected Works*. London: Lawrence & Wishart.

Murray, C. 1990: *The Emerging British Underclass*.

London: Institute of Economic Affairs.

Pahl, R. 1984: *Divisions of Labour*. Oxford: Blackwell.

Wilson, W. J. (ed.) 1993: *The Ghetto Underclass*. London: Sage.

Young, M. and Willmott, P. 1975: *The Symmetrical Family*. Harmondsworth: Penguin.

Further Reading

Abercrombie, N. and Warde, A. 1988: *Contemporary British Society*. Cambridge: Polity. An introductory textbook which focuses strongly on social divisions.

Bradley, H. 1995: *Fractured Identities*. Cambridge: Polity. Introductory discussion of the analysis of four aspects of social divisions: class, gender, ethnicity and age.

Hudson, R. and Williams, A. 1987: *Divided Britain*. Belhaven. A Survey of empirical data on social inequalities, dealing with class, gender and "race".

Anthias, F. and Yuval-Davis, N. 1994: *Racialized Boundaries*. Routledge. This shows how racial inequality interacts with gender and class.

17

Power: Concepts and Research

Jon Gubbay

For anyone who wishes to understand their own society, or any other, power must be a central matter of concern. The questions abound: where does power lie? why is power structured as it is? what are the consequences of power? These sorts of questions are usually discussed in terms of the individuals, organizations and institutions who are conventionally regarded as being involved in "politics" – that is politicians, parties, pressure groups, parliament and congress. Thus there is endless speculation, for example in the mass media, about whether prime ministers or presidents have the power to implement their policies, resist demands of others or overcome threats to their continuation in office. Although these matters are of considerable interest, sociological approaches characteristically view power much more widely as a pervasive element of social relations well beyond those of formal politics. Attention is focused at least as much on the social contexts of power as with its manifestation in actions.

There have been many insightful sociological contributions which apply to contexts other than political institutions and organizations. For example, Max Weber identified bureaucratic power as embodied in a supervisory hierarchy of offices, each with its own sphere of responsibility and with duties carried out according to impersonal rules and on the basis of the application of trained expertise (Weber, 1967, pp. 196ff.). This notion has been shown to be relevant to the understanding of armies, churches, businesses and educational institutions. Another seminal sociological study of power is *Political Parties*, first published by Robert Michels in 1915, where it was argued that even the most democratic political parties are actually dominated by elites; the punch line of this argument is that this *must* be true of *all* large complex organizations. As you might expect, these grim conclusions have been vigorously debated subsequently.

Another stream of sociological studies has focused on the networks of personal and institutional connections between politicians, state officials and those who own and control business (Mills, 1956; Domhoff, 1967; Miliband, 1969; Scott, 1991). This fascinating research throws light on the extent of uniformity of economic elites in respect of background, lifestyle and values and the means through which, whether or not deliberately, they constrain those who are constitutionally responsible for determining state activities. There are many other contexts of power which have been studied including relations of race (see Rex, Chapter 1) and sex (see Witz, Chapter 13 and Jackson and Rahman, Chapter 22).

Typically, the conclusions of empirical studies of power have been vigorously disputed among sociologists, sometimes concerning the "facts", but also as to what "facts" are significant and, indeed, what is meant anyway in stating where power lies. The conceptual problems have severe implications for how power is portrayed. Let us consider why this should be so. If there were some essential meaning of power embedded in a single tradition of writing and talking about the subject, then our first task would be to distill that essence into a clear and coherent concept. Although we would still be faced with technical challenges in devising observable indicators of the concept and making the corresponding measurements, empirical investigation of power could then proceed in an orderly fashion. However, it is argued here that the premise of such a project is false: there is no essential meaning of power but rather a complex web of meanings. To pursue some essence is not just fruitless but blinds us to the interplay of different aspects of power. Accordingly, this chapter attempts to untangle some of these meanings, showing the sorts of insights each meaning can provide and their associated research procedures. In order to make some of the difficult conceptual issues more concrete, I have limited most of my examples to the context of the workplace. Six clusters of concepts are considered in turn — the exercise of power, the formation of intentions, the imputation of interests, the posses-

sion of power, the legitimation of power and disciplinary power.

Exercising Power

Let us start with what appears to be a fairly straightforward example of the exercise of power. Imagine that an employee regularly arrives five minutes late for work but then, after being instructed by his manager to be punctual, starts coming in on time. Here we have evidence that the manager has exerted power over her employee because the employee's change in behaviour is plausibly explained by the order to mend his ways. It is possible, of course, that this explanation is wrong (for example, it might simply have happened that the commuter train had been rescheduled to arrive earlier) but, this possibility apart, we have here an example of a way of conceptualising power, as propounded by the American political scientist Robert Dahl. "A has power

Figure 17.1 Authority confronted. Sociologists enquire into the structures underlying the visible manifestions of power.

over B to the extent that he can get B to do something that B would not otherwise do" (Dahl, 1957, p. 202).

Accordingly, Dahl argued that the only way of proving that one person exercises power over another is to observe situations where B's behaviour varies according to how A acts. However, this is evidently an inadequate basis for assessing power because it only applies to situations where the supposed exercise of power occurs within a repetitive sequence of behaviour, as with the tardy employee who mended his ways after being reprimanded.

One way of developing the concept of power to make it more widely applicable is to consider the actors' intentions explicitly, as does Weber in defining power as the "chance of a man or number of men to realize their own will ... even against the resistance of others" (Weber, 1967, p. 181). Taking up the previous example, if we were able to establish that the employee disliked being at work one moment more than necessary but, as a result of his manager's instruction, had resolved to be punctual in future, then we would be able to clinch the claim that the manager had exerted power. That is, we would have established that a change in intention was the reason for the difference in the employee's behaviour. The case for bringing intentions into account can be seen even more clearly when we turn our attention to the manager. It would surely be perverse to say that the manager exercises power if effects are produced, but not those that she intended. For example, if she had complained about lateness in the hope that the employee would "take the hint" and quit the job without having to be formally dismissed, then an improvement in the employee's punctuality would be the result of the manager's action but not in accord with her intention. Dahl, building intentions into a subsequent analysis (1958), proposed that power relationships must be proven or disproved by examining situations of overt conflict of wills – and identifying whose will prevails.

Note that to insist that this is the *only* valid research procedure leads to agnosticism about many conventionally asserted views about the distribution of power. It would be invalid to claim that somebody is powerful on the grounds that they are thought to be powerful, or because they have a top position in some organization or institution. Presidents and prime ministers are widely assumed and constitutionally defined as standing at the head of political administration, but there remains the possibility that we are deceived by appearances, that they are buffeted by forces beyond their control and possess only the trappings of office.

Unfortunately, evidence of the full range of conflicts and their outcomes required for using Dahl's research method is rarely available to researchers, let alone the public, especially among those whom we suspect are most powerful. Conversely, there may be others who are rarely on the public stage but who routinely take important decisions covertly and do their arm-twisting behind closed doors. Because researchers are most unlikely to discover anything like a representative sample of conflicts, Dahl's proposed method cannot produce the evidence that its own rationale requires in order to judge where power lies. Furthermore, parties to conflicts characteristically put "spins" on those relatively few conflicts which are brought to public attention, and will often put up a smokescreen of "false" demands as the basis for negotiation. That is, demands are deliberately introduced as bargaining points on which "concessions" can be made in exchange for the other party acceding to one's real demands. A naive observer who recorded all the points "won" and "lost" in a negotiation might well be misled into believing that the outcome was more equally balanced than was in fact the case.

It might seem good scientific research design to insist on *observing* the exercise of power, whether in terms of behaviour or of expressed intentions. But some forms of exercising power are virtually invisible. Suppose for example, employees wish to propose measures to reduce stress at work but the manager rules this as beyond the remit of the works safety committee. This surely is as effective an exercise of power as if the issue had been raised at the committee but the manager had then vetoed the employees' proposals. The sociological researcher sitting in on committee meetings or analysing the minutes might not be aware that the employees' desired outcomes had been excluded from consideration before the agenda had even been set. But if we want to comprehend the exercise of power it is obviously important to know who has the capacity for such agenda-setting – be they committee chairs, newspaper editors, budget controllers or whatever – and for thus determining what issues become "live".

I hope it is apparent that researchers who focus exclusively on observable decision-making processes (and insist that all other forms of research are speculative) tend to understate the extent of entrenched power and thus overstate the extent to which power is distributed between rival groups and individuals. Such a research procedure tends to encourage pluralist conclusions: that there are competing centres of power which are forced, by the very fact of their competitive relationship, to seek support from non-elites (Bachrach and Baratz, 1962).

The attempt to dig beneath the visible surface of social relations requires complex and sophisticated research procedures. Now we also have to listen to voices off-stage, that is attend to the actions and interactions that do *not* happen and to seek out explanations for their non-occurrence. The efforts made by one person to try to raise an issue and another person preventing this from happening are often separated in time and place and the process of agenda-setting may be concealed. A battery of more indirect methods of research is thus required, with the results being cross-checked. These might include case studies of those who have faced obstacles when trying to raise issues, identification of formal institutional barriers, and the testimony of "insiders" on the processes of deciding on agendas.

Forming Intentions

The above discussion has been based on situations where a conflict of wills has been expressed. But what if no such conflict is expressed? What if both parties appear to desire the same ends? Does this mutuality mean that no conflict, and therefore no power relationship, exists between them? Many sociologists would be reluctant to draw that conclusion.

Firstly, a person may be *persuaded* by another because of the latter's superior resources, be these personal (superiority of rhetoric, browbeating or appeal to higher status) or organizational (e.g. control over the media).

Secondly, a person may be *induced* to go along with the wishes of another – "If you work harder you'll get promotion – and if you don't you'll get the sack!" – but the employee concerned does not openly express opposition. It might be argued that where partners to a relationship freely enter into an exchange, such as a labour contract, inducements cannot be considered an aspect of power. The argument is that this is an agreement by both parties under which an employer pays a wage to an employee in return for the latter working under the employer's direction. Workers are not slaves, for they can exercise choice over whether to sell their capacity to labour and then only do so on a temporary basis without being tied to any particular employer. However, the implication that the labour contract is an equal exchange, and thus that the employee's submission to the employer is voluntary, can be challenged on the grounds that the only choice he has is to be impoverished – or submit to another very similar employer.

A third situation where differences of intention may fail to surface comes in cases of *anticipated reaction*. For example, employees may refrain from taking unscheduled days off work for fear of displeasing their manager – even though there may be no rules or instructions to this effect. It is possible that a manager will attempt to create the sort of climate, whether through fear of repercussions or encouraging a sense of a common fate, where employees will anticipate her wishes and act accordingly. It is also possible that such a climate is the unintended consequence of the interplay of many past actions. Either way, the managers' wishes are met effortlessly and without any overt conflict.

Finally, we need to consider *habituation*. This is the case where a person has become so used to complying that it is done automatically. The origin of compliance, perhaps in the dim and distant past, might have been in more blatant exercises of power, but progressed through phases of reluctant acquiescence and then resignation to unthinking obedience. Similar considerations apply to *socialization*, that is processes of learning socially expected behaviour, knowledge, desires and values. The employer effortlessly benefits insofar as employees' learned self-control, politeness, deference to authority and respect for property entail dispositions to act in ways that she desires. Is this not an amazing form of power, that someone's desires are met without having to do anything? (Lukes, 1974).

Imputing "Real Interests"

We are now in the seemingly paradoxical position of suggesting that power relationships exist even where there is no disagreement between the parties. Continuing the workplace example, a possible way out of this paradox is to consider what employees *might* have wanted to do if they had not anticipated the employer's reactions or become habituated or socialized into compliance. In other words, we can make a judgement on what their "real interests" are. But can sociologists make a judgement about a person's "real interests" which the persons themselves do not recognize?

The move can in fact be justified though it does raise complex issues of interpretation and judgement. Let us imagine a situation where A has control over what B can know or how B can think. In those circumstances it would be unreasonable to accept B's thinking at face value. An extreme example here might be "brainwashing" techniques using sensory deprivation. If the victim "changes his mind" under such circumstances, do we simply accept this as representing his "true" opinions? Similar considerations are raised in less violent but more sophisticated form by the way our tastes and opinions are affected by

advertising and news management. These considerations show that there is nothing inherently absurd in insisting that there can be a difference between expressed wants and "real interests" and, indeed, refusing to countenance this possibility leads to ridiculous or naive conclusions. But specifying "real interests" in a positive fashion is much more difficult.

There are several ways of defining interests by specifying counter-factual conditions under which a person would choose how to act – having all relevant knowledge; being an autonomous individual; thinking, feeling and articulating in ways undistorted by power relations. (Perhaps such conditions are ideal for academic debate!) Unfortunately all such approaches are open to the objection that they are purely speculative since there is no way to investigate what would have happened if conditions were so radically different than what they are. That said, the notion that a person has interests of which they could be unaware is perfectly coherent, although any particular attributions of interests may be contestable.[1] Consider an example where an employee readily agrees to operate a new machine even though knowing that this is likely to result in some workmates being made redundant. One view of the situation is that he is acting in his own interests, perhaps because such compliance earns the manager's goodwill and thus the likelihood of job security or promotion. A quite different interpretation is that the workers as a whole constitute a collective entity whose interests are damaged when members of this entity comply with the employer's wishes without corresponding guarantees, such as that there be no consequent redundancies. These very different attributions of where interests lie draw upon rival theoretical perspectives, notably liberalism and Marxism, respectively.

Possessing Power

In order to simplify the exposition, the above discussion was presented in terms of the power of persons but this is to abstract drastically from the social arrangements on which power is grounded. Power is rooted in socially structured abilities and resources – necessary technical knowledge and skills, means of coercion, economic assets and organizational positions. It is not Murdoch the person, but Murdoch the media boss of News International and multi-millionaire, who possesses power. The foreman may shout his orders, but he does so according to rules and goals assigned to his position and determined though a hierarchy stretching up to remote figures. Moreover, it is not only positions with a single occupant that are agents in power relations, but also organizations or particular parts of them which behave as single entities. Indeed, at the societal level they are far more important.

Now, it can be argued that positions and organizations are wedded to "real interests", structurally imposed upon them quite apart from the will of the persons who occupy positions and make up organizations. For example, the interests of business management includes profit maximization, though it is perfectly possible that individual managers have quite different personal priorities. Note that these considerations signal a shift in the questions we might ask about power from "who exercises power and how?" to "what positions and organizations are powerful and why?". Thus has concern been transformed from action to structure.

This switch in focus has important implications. Since persons (but not positions or organizations) can have will or desire, reformulating the concept of power in terms of positions and organizations must mean abandoning both reference to intentions and conflict of will. This completely reverses the argument advanced in support of the definitions of power proposed by Weber and Dahl. Since the term "act" involves the sense of behaving with intention, we need to signal the shift of focus by a change of terminology. Let me use the term "performance" to refer to the socially structured meaning of acts carried out by one or more persons by virtue of their positions. For example, a teacher may write a fail grade on a student assignment with the

intention of failing it, but the performance only comes off effectively if it was carried out according to established rules and conventions by someone who has the *position* of teacher. In short, identifying the agents of power as positions rather than persons entails a shift of attention from some persons triumphing over others to the relative capacities inherent in positions or, in other words, from the exercise of power to the possession of power (Benton, 1981).

With this redefinition, the research agenda is again transformed. Firstly, the capacity to engage in a repertoire of performances depends upon the resources and abilities associated with positions and organizations; these need to be documented and their social distribution discovered. Secondly, investigation is required of the conditions under which mobilization of resources and abilities produce particular outcomes. Thirdly, the conditions need to be explored under which an organization, or even a looser category of persons, constitute a collective entity capable of being an agent in a power relationship. Fourthly, there is a need for a type of theorization of social structure and social processes that identifies interests as linked to positions. Clearly, if no acceptable theory of this sort can be constructed then the above concept of power collapses. This is a profound and controversial matter that cannot be properly addressed within the confines of a short essay.

Legitimation of Power

As discussed above, reasons for compliance include calculation and habituation but there may also be acceptance that it is *right* to obey, that a request to behave in a particular way is legitimate. For example, many employees may be opposed to particular policies of the employers but accept their right to manage, perhaps on the grounds that they are the owners of the business (or agents of the owners). Thus does the legitimacy of the principle of rights to unfettered use of private property translate into the acceptance of the management's general rights to command. (Critics might argue that the legitimacy of this principle, so convenient to the economically dominant class, flows from their political and social dominance.)

It is of considerable importance to the effectiveness and security of those who possess power that it is legitimate and unchallenged – but this is never guaranteed. Power that is not legitimated tends to be insecure. (Note that even habituation does not mean that compliance is unconditional because it is typically sustained by routines of action and indulgences. If these change, deference is betrayed and defiance may result.) The problematic nature of legitimation is indicated below by considering how it can fail and how threats to legitimacy may be offset.

Let us start with a definition. The power of A over B can be said to be legitimate if it is acquired and exercised in conformity to rules which can be justified in terms of beliefs and values common to A and B[2] (Beetham, 1991, p. 16). Now consider how legitimacy can fail by taking the example of relations between government and citizens. If government power were usurped, for example seized without due process as in a military coup, then at least initially it would have been illegitimate. Also, the government's power becomes illegitimate in so far as it violates, and is seen to violate, supposedly generally binding rules (e.g. rules against corrupt use of office), whether these be formalized as in the case of laws or informal custom and practice. Even if the government abides by the rules, its power would be deficient in legitimacy if there are insufficient or inappropriate common beliefs and values to justify these rules. Consent also plays a vital role in the legitimation of power. Typically, citizens' expressed consent to government power derives from its legitimation, but consent is also a means of reinforcing it. Overt display of willing submission is, symbolically, an affirmation by citizens that the government has the right to command and thus commits not just those who participated in the display but also witnesses of it. (Hence

Figure 17.2 Power has become routine and impersonal.

the importance to dictators of loyal public parades and intolerance for dissent.) Contrariwise, publicly withholding consent, or only consenting with obviously sullen resignation, undermines legitimacy.

The basic reason for the fragility of power which is not legitimate is because power relations inherently involve negative features which are potential sources of disobedience. Thus, employees are typically socially and materially disadvantaged relative to employers, both as a result of and as a condition for the power relationship between them. On the other hand, were employees and employers to share beliefs in the latter's superiority in some relevant respect, then their relative advantages and disadvantages could be justified. Furthermore, the power of employers is legitimated by employees' beliefs that employers possess special skills and knowledge that make them peculiarly fit to direct the labour process or simply that they have rights in this respect by virtue of property ownership and/or their position as employers.

One possible line of explanation for how power is legitimated is to argue that those who are most powerful possess the motive and means to propagate ideas which justify their power through their control of the ways by which consciousness is formed, such as mass media and the education system. It is certainly possible to show how business elites and politicians seek to influence educational curricula and that mass-media moguls are intricately linked to other parts of the business – political establishment. Nevertheless, the capacity of these various elites to act collectively is questionable, as is their effectiveness in "thought control" over the masses. A more satisfactory line of investigation is to trace *indirect* effects of the existing structure of power in legitimating itself, as people adjust to the everyday practical realities of the social order. For example, the lived reality of needing a regular wage, working to get it, the necessity of compliance in order to avoid the sack and so on may make submission to the employer seem natural – and, as noted above, expressing consent reinforces the legitimacy of power.

Disciplinary Power

In any given society relations are structured in such a way that some organizations or groups possess power seemingly without having to become self-conscious agents in defence of their power, inasmuch as the normal workings of the society continually reaffirm and reproduce the existing power structure. Every time an employee goes into work and acts in conformity with tacit and explicit duties, existing power relations are confirmed and reinforced. Since the eighteenth century there has been an enormous growth of new forms of disciplinary power, operating intrusively and continuously by means of registration, inspection, certification, surveillance and individuation – and thus promotion of *self-discipline*. Such power is manifest in families, schools, hospitals, churches, social work, workplaces and prisons – habituating us to orderly routines and subjecting those who deviate to medical, psychological, educational or penal training. Paradoxically, disciplinary power at its point of impact on the daily lives of individuals is nowadays usually quite impersonal. Routine conformity to the rules and goals occurs much of the time without instruction. Rather people become self-disciplined by the physical arrangement of machinery and workstations, systems of payment, record keeping and monitoring, timetables of tasks and work breaks, job evaluation and procedures for promotion. But those who are relatively powerless need to exert themselves even to become agents.

In the earlier discussion of possession of power I mentioned the research problem of investigating the conditions under which a group might be constituted as an agent in a power relationship. Now it might well be argued that the constitution of agents is itself a power process. For example, the transformation of an unorganized category of workers into a trade union branch requires them to engage in actions which define their identities as jointly constituting that entity. Typically such a project involves conflict among themselves and with their employers – and the outcome depends on who wins. Moreover, individuals can only be agents insofar as society is organized in such a way as to acknowledge them as possessing independent will and autonomy. Recognising that power and agency are interdependent undercuts the concepts of power considered from the beginning of this chapter. The A and B of a supposed power relationship are only contingently constituted *by power* as agents, rather than being pre-existing agents that exercise or possess power.

The workings of disciplinary power are best discerned at the micro level of mundane routine through examining the effects of rules and techniques embodied in institutions. Accordingly, it might be argued that appropriate research methods for the exploration of rules and practices are ethnography and historical investigation of their origins and development. However, there is a danger that such a research strategy loses all sense of agency and is blind to the ways in which rules and techniques might serve the interests of social entities whose existence is structurally determined. Although the As and Bs are constituted through power relations, they thus become relatively empowered agents. Whilst it is true that claims about the constitution and interests of social entities are contestable, that is not a

good reason for refusing to entertain them as hypotheses, provided that appropriate research is then undertaken to test them. Failure to do so leads back to the pluralist overemphasis on the play of power at the expense of its structure.

Conclusion

In this chapter, I have traced out a number of different and conflicting understandings of power, each of which suggests its own insights and research programmes. The dominant tradition of theorizing, is concerned with the exercise of power by an active agent. However, the development of this tradition dissolves the power of agents into structural causation. Attention to disciplinary power breaks with structural causation but restores agents only contingently as constituted entities rather than inherently autonomous participants in power relationships (Clegg, 1989). As I have hinted above, my own view is that there are social entities, notably classes, whose existence and interests can be established on the basis of a theory about the working of the (capitalist) system as a whole. However, I also readily accept that any such theory is contestable.

Notes

1. A relativistic view, often associated with "post-structuralism", is that there is no sense in which a person or persons can be either correct or mistaken about where their interests lie. All one can say is that some claims about where their interests lie have been made to stick. Power is manifest in defining such discursive reality.
2. Note that I have followed Beetham in departing decisively from the well-established Weberian

definition that A's power over B is legitimate if and only if B believes in A's legitimacy. Rather, the crucial point is that what B (and A) believe justifies A's power. I have not followed Beetham in another respect. He takes B's expression of consent to A's power as part of his definition of legitimacy whereas I see it as (both) a means of establishing it and as an indicator of it.

References and Suggestions for Further Reading

Bachrach, P. and Baratz, M. 1962: Two faces of Power. *American Political Science Review*, 56, 947–52.

Beetham, D. 1991: *The Legitimation of Power*. London: Macmillan.
Benton, T. 1981: "Objective" Interests and the

Sociology of Power. *Sociology* 15(2), 161–84.

Clegg, S. R. 1989: *Frameworks of Power*. London: Sage.

Dahl, R. A. 1957: The concept of power. *Behavioural Science*, 2, 201–15.

—— 1958: A critique of the ruling-elite model. *American Political Science Review*, 52, 463–69.

Domhoff, G. W. 1967: *Who Rules America?* Englewood Cliffs, NJ: Prentice-Hall.

Edwards, R. 1979: *Contested Terrain*. London: Heinemann.

Foucault, M. 1977: *Discipline and Punish: The Birth of the Prison*. Harmondsworth: Penguin.

Lukes, S. 1974: Power: A Radical View. London: Macmillan.

—— (ed.) 1986: *Power*. Oxford: Blackwell.

Miliband, R. 1969: *The State in Capitalist Society*. London: Weidenfeld & Nicolson.

Mills, C. W. 1956: *The Power Elite*. New York: Oxford University Press.

Scott, J. 1991: *Who Rules Britain?* Cambridge: Polity.

Weber, M. 1967: *From Max Weber: Essays in Sociology* (translated, edited and with an introduction by H. H. Gerth and C. W. Mills). London: Routledge & Kegan Paul.

18

The Life Course

Paul Bellaby

Of all things, commonsense is the most evenly shared, for everyone thinks they are well supplied with it.
(René Descartes, Discourse on Method, *1637*)

Commonsense is what most people think the life course amounts to. In one way they are right. Everyone is passing through the life course and knows it from within. The life course is growing up, becoming an adult, ageing – a process started with birth and ended with death.

However, Descartes spoke with irony. He wanted us to be sceptical, not commonsensical. This chapter will show that it is a mistake to *dismiss* the life course as if it hardly merits a second thought. To begin with, there is a paradox in our experience of the life course which commonsense cannot resolve:

- for each individual the life course is a *becoming* and *unique* – she or he is uncertain of the future, must make choices and must adjust to the unexpected;
- and yet much of the life course is *repeated* from individual to individual – from a bird's eye view, humans seem to be following paths through a maze, that are finite and predictable even when varied.

This chapter explores the life course from three points of view:

(1) some of the factors that shape the course of lives;
(2) how individuals give accounts of their own life courses;
(3) how sociologists might set about researching the life course.

Factors that Shape the Life Course

Of all the topics in this book, the life course is the one where the imprint of *nature* seems likely to be strongest. However, nature is not the only factor that shapes the human life course: *culture* and *social relations* affect the life course too.

The Biological Foundation of the Life Course

Like all other living things humans are generated, grow to maturity, age and finally die. Biologists speak of this as the "life cycle" of each species. Moreover, reproduction of the human species is sexual, as in other complex organisms, rather than by cell division, and so, from the biological perspective, age and sex seem to be the main sources of difference between individuals.

Genes, which encode our biological development, are a source of both repetition across generations and the uniqueness of each individual. Each gene is a replica of one found in the individual's parent and so a source of repetition, but since genes are transmitted to the foetus from both parents, the combination of genes in each individual is unique and the outcome is usually indeterminate. For instance, only rarely may a syndrome be predicted from the parents' chromosomes (as in Down's Syndrome) or a terminal disease from the presence of a single gene (as in Huntington's chorea).

In summary, nature creates *repeated processes* in the form of the life cycle and genetic continuity between generations, *repeated structures* in the form of age and sex differences between individuals, and also *indeterminacy* with the effect that each individual is unique.

Culture and the Life Course

While genes regulate how individuals develop they are not alone in doing so, for in all species external environment determines which genes will survive. For humans that environment has two aspects, natural and cultural.

Culture covers the ways of life, including technology, that humans have developed in response to nature. The biological foundation and the natural environment together provide part of the "programme" for the human life course, but it is incomplete without culture. Culture is modified by each generation and handed on to the next. Moreover, through their ways of life, humans have played a major part in *shaping* the *natural* environment itself (and indeed that of other species on the planet), and this tendency has become stronger as the pace of change in technology has intensified. The present generation almost has within its grasp the awesome power to engineer genes and so directly affect the biological foundation of the life course.

As in nature, cultural forms are repeated. But there are two key dissimilarities. First cultural forms are repeated wilfully, not simply because nothing has happened to change them. Second, nature's repetition applies to the whole species of *homo sapiens*, whereas the cultural aspect of repetition varies significantly around the world today and between past and present.

Rites of Passage and the Life Course

Throughout history and no doubt pre-history, people have built "traditions" and tried to live up to them. Many such traditions are to do with the life course. Van Gennep, a pupil of Durkheim, famously drew together examples of these from ethnographic accounts of non-modern societies that were based on hunting and gathering or agriculture, and that were without writing and so had oral records (van Gennep 1960). Here people were graded by age. As they grew older, indeed when they died, they moved from one well-defined status to another. So fundamental was the transformation, that the end of each stage was treated as if a death, the beginning of the next as if a rebirth. Physical death was no less cultural than the status passages of the living, for it was the prelude to a new birth into the world of the spirits or ancestors.

Status passages were fraught with uncertainty. The continuity of society depended on children becoming adults, women giving birth to live infants, kin finding a successor to one who had died or the dead passing to the world of the ancestral spirits. To negotiate these passages people must observe ritual, because only by this means could accidents of nature be brought under the control of society.

Ritual took place in a domain considered separate from the everyday world, and thus sacred. Punctilious repetition was essential to the effectiveness of the rituals that van Gennep wrote about: each inflection, each piece of dress, each artefact was packed with symbolism.

According to van Gennep, rites of passage fell into three parts:

- rites of separation from the old status;
- rites of exclusion while in process between old and new (or "liminal");
- rites of aggregation into the new status.

Liminality (literally being on the threshold between old and new) was the most charged of the three. Until the issue was settled people and corpses in process were sources of the unexpected – threats to good order, fertility and health. They must be segregated and avoided, except by ritual specialists, whose duty was to initiate them into their new status.

The Emergence of the Modern Life Course

It may be obvious, even from this thumb-nail sketch, that the courses of modern and non-modern lives are different. Modern life courses are *individuated*. They are also divided between private (family) and public (employment) spheres, quite unlike lives in van Gennep's societies. Movement through life is a gradual process rather than one of abrupt change, and even when change is relatively abrupt – say, on retirement – the individual remains the same person throughout. However, the generations of van Gennep's societies moved through life and death together, not as individuals.

In modern society rites of passage apply *in life* only in exceptional cases, notably on entry to such total institutions as the army, boarding school or prison, and such closed groups as religious sects and secret societies. While ritual survives *after death*, it has all but disappeared from dying (e.g. the priest has been supplanted by the doctor), and funeral rites themselves are low key as if to indicate that most moderns suspect that death is the end of the person, not the prelude to rebirth in an afterlife (Ariès, 1983).

How, then, did the distinctively modern life course come about? The details of this history are beyond this short account, but their flavour is conveyed by the metaphors of the life course (Frankenberg in Bryman et al., 1987) contained in the following series of quotations.

Late Medieval Life as Seven Ages

> All the world's a stage,
> And all the men and women merely players:
> They have their exits and their entrances;
> And one man in his time plays many parts,
> His acts being seven ages. (William Shakespeare, *As You Like It*, c. 1599)

Shakespeare's depiction of the life course is tongue-in-cheek, but it draws on ideas that would have been familiar to his audiences. He defines the "seven ages" as infancy, schoolboy, lover, soldier, justice, pantaloon (foolish old man) and second childishness. As in van Gennep's societies the life course is broken into steps but, unlike the situation there, the same soul or person continues

through each step, a concept that Christianity had long ago made its own.

To the modern mind, the second age, that of "schoolboy", seems unremarkable, but it was actually an invention of the period in which Shakespeare lived. Schools themselves were not new. They had been developed by cathedrals from the twelfth century for training clergy to read and write Latin, the common language of Christendom, and were for pupils of all ages. But in England after the Reformation many grammar schools were established independently of the church. Though they taught the elements of Latin *grammar* (hence their name) and of reading and writing in English, their objectives were as much to educate morally as to train in useful skills. These schools were aimed at the young and so were developing the *modern* concept of "childhood" – as a period in life in which as yet unformed adults should be separated from all adults bar specialist teachers, and exposed to the higher things of the common culture (Ariès, 1960). Only middle-class boys were affected. Poor boys and all girls continued, as before, to receive a practical training within the household, much as did children in the non-modern societies that interested van Gennep, while children of the aristocracy and gentry had private tutors.

Proto-modern Life as a Pilgrimage

> From this world to that which is to come, wherein are discovered the manner of his setting out, his dangerous journey and his safe arrival at the desired country. (John Bunyan, *The Pilgrim's Progress*, c. 1677–9)

If Shakespeare's age kept the medieval view that the life course was a series of ordered stages which all passed through, the seventeenth century emphasized the idea that individuals made their own destiny. Bunyan, a devout Puritan, thought of the course of life as a spiritual (rather than a literal) journey, full of trials and temptations that one needed high courage to negotiate. The desired journey's end was in an unknown eternity, not in the space and time of mortal beings. It was far from certain that even the most valiant pilgrim would reach this destination. God alone, who called him to take the journey, knew who would reach the eternal life.

This sense of an individual journey into the unknown was reflected in a shift in the themes of the arts and literature. Before Bunyan written (and pictured) "lives" were homilies about the miraculous power of the Godly (as in numerous medieval lives of saints) or the character of men famed in politics or war. For Bunyan life was a calling from God, and, following in his wake, countless novelists, biographers and autobiographers wrote about lives that were a personal struggle to discover meaning (or its absence) or to realize a purpose.

Modern Life as a Trajectory

The official is set for a *career* within the hierarchical order of the public service. He moves from the lower, less important, and lower paid to the higher positions. The average official naturally desires a mechanical fixing of the conditions of promotion: if not of the offices, at least of the salary levels. He wants these conditions fixed in terms of *seniority*, or possibly according to grade achieved in a developed system of expert examinations. (Max Weber, *Economy and Society*, 1970, originally, in 2nd edn, 1925)

From the late nineteenth century, large organizations imposed a new pattern on the life course. Bunyan's pilgrim had his calling (or vocation) from God. The office-holder in the public services, the professional in law or medicine, the manager in industry and commerce made their job their vocation. The organization gave them the opportunity to make a success of their career, which they took to the best of their ability.

In due course the uncertainty of personal salvation to which Bunyan was condemned by the doctrine of predestination (God alone knows!), was alleviated by secure employment and insurance against the uncertainties of the world, i.e. the market, ill-health and old age (Man in control!). The course of life was recast as a trajectory, which rose steadily from birth, through education and learning on the job; falling precipitately with ageing, as one ceased to be a useful employee; and to earth with death.

Towards a Post-modern Life Course?

. . . a transition is occuring . . from a uniform system of lifelong full-time work organized in a single industrial location, to a risk-fraught system of flexible, pluralized, decentralized underemployment . . .

The relation between family and individual biography loosens . . . Each person lives through several family lives as well as non-familial forms of life . . . and . . . lives more and more his/her own biography. (Ulrich Beck, *The Risk Society*, 1992)

In the 1980s and 1990s, the course of lives has come to seem more reflexive or self-determined, less pre-determined, than it had become in the course of the previous hundred years. This has been encouraged by employing organizations. As markets have become more competitive, so organizations have slimmed down numbers employed on secure contracts. The "flexible" employee is one who is treated as autonomous and responsible for his or her own career. Such employees are also expected to carry much of the risk that is entailed, rather than look to the state or their employer for insurance against that risk. At the same time, with increasing rates of divorce and family formation, more children and adults are encountering risks in their private lives than at any time since women ceased to die in childbirth and children ceased to die in the early years of life in significant numbers. Individuals often have to remake their lives, in both public and private spheres.

Social Relations and the Life Course: Gender and Class

The cultural factors discussed so far have affected almost everyone in the societies to which they have applied. Other factors make for different life courses in the same society, among them the social relations of gender and class.

In the early modern period the male head of household was treated as if the sovereign in his own domain. He alone had property rights and his power over the women and children of his household was virtually absolute. Like Shakespeare's seven ages, Bunyan's pilgrimage implied male heads of household, not women or children.

Class played a part too. If girls' or boys' fathers were too poor to maintain them, they would become servants in the household of a richer man and might remain celibate. In effect a servant could remain "the boy" or "the girl" until they died. Typically, daughters of richer fathers awaited an alliance that would be useful to the family before they married. Thus they moved from their father's to their husband's households. The sons of sufficiently affluent fathers waited until their fathers died or were ready to retire before inheriting the farm or workshop and then they married (Segalen, 1986). Thus the course of lives was crucially dependent on gender and class.

The spread of wage labour loosened the old regime. In the course of the eighteenth and nineteenth centuries many men and women were able to leave their father's household or the household in which they were servants, and marry relatively early because they had money in their pockets. In short, they became relatively autonomous adults – "free labour" indeed – almost as soon as they became sexually mature. In this first flush of the agricultural and industrial revolutions women and children of the working class were drawn into paid employment alongside men, and often this meant work outside the home.

There was a conservative reaction, led by aristocracy and gentry, against the employment of women and children in factories, mills and coalmines. It took several forms. Schools were, for the first time, provided for the sons and daughters of the poor, thus extending everywhere the institution of childhood, founded for the sons of the middle class, aristocracy and gentry in Shakespeare's time. Women's employment in certain trades, such as deep mining, was banned and their hours restricted in many others. It was considered indecorous for women of the upper and middle classes to seek employment and even to leave the home except with an escort, and, though this stricture did not apply in practice to all working class women, it became a mark of respectability among them. The sphere of the home came to be defined in opposition to that of employment: the private to the public. Women "belonged" in the private sphere and Victorian biological science considered that their natural destiny was fulfilled in rearing children, caring for the sick and infirm and keeping house. Males belonged there when very young but, as they grew older, they were to enter the public sphere and, on marriage, to become "breadwinners" for their families.

From the late nineteenth century, birth control did something to alleviate the unequal position of women. Yet women stayed in the home long after the decline in fertility made their continual presence there unnecessary. Since the industrial revolution women have typically taken full-time employment before having children, but only from the late 1950s have women with children returned to employment in significant numbers, and then chiefly if they have partners and frequently to part-time jobs (Tilly and Scott, 1978).

Today there is variation from country to country in the way life courses are shaped by gender and class, depending on social policy. In Britain and the USA (as opposed to, say, France and Sweden) the late development of maternity leave, high marginal tax rates on low incomes, and inadequate public provision of childcare, have ensured that women returners continue to be a peripheral element in the labour market, readily called in and readily laid off. As a result women are less likely to return to employment than in Sweden and less likely, if they are employed, to work full-time and without a break of service than women in

France. The lower cost of child-care in both Sweden and France encourages women with lower incomes to enter employment, whereas they would not do so in Britain or the USA. These include single mothers.

In an economy based on wage labour, workers depend on income from employment to accumulate capital for their old age. To the extent that women have part-time jobs and less continuous service than men, they have less than men to call their own on retirement. This predicament is only aggravated by the tendency of women to survive men and to live on into old age in greater numbers. Among men continuous employment and full time work helps make up for low wages, but in the USA and UK in recent years there has been expansion of employer-provided occupational benefits, such as pensions and sick pay, principally for the higher paid. This has led to a situation in which, while some are relatively prosperous after retirement, others are dependent on low, basic state benefits.

Thus, even after women have entered employment outside the home in substantial numbers and most men have become dependent on selling their labour to earn a living, there are substantial differences in life courses that arise from gender and class.

The Life Stories of Individuals

We have been outlining some of the many factors that shape the life course. However, sociologists have to make a distinction between the actual life history of a person and its representation in the stories of individuals reviewing their lives. Bertaux (in Dex, 1991) argues that the latter, "life stories", are dictated by interests in the here and now. These *interests* are of many kinds and arise quite frequently: seeking a job or getting a place at university; striking up a friendship with an attractive stranger; answering questions about the course of a long illness or a

Figure 18.1 Each of us belongs to a generation that has lived through a similar history. This common experience affects the life stories we tell.

varied medical history; writing up memoirs as an eminent politician, soldier or intellectual; reviewing in old age the experiences of a long life and coming to terms with impending death – to mention a few. Plainly the life course itself provides pretexts for life stories.

Life stories are also literary forms or *genres*. Narrators must choose the one that fits the occasion. The CV required for a job application is not at all the same as the response expected to "tell me about yourself" from an attractive stranger, and to mistake either request for the other would cause embarrassment.

Life stories can be expressed in several *media*. Since the marketing of cheap cameras and camcorders many people have kept photographs or videos, especially of their children's early lives. Personal diaries – handwritten or audio-taped – remain typical of those for whom either self-awareness or self-justification is a driving concern. In their pioneering study of Polish peasant immigrants to the USA, Thomas and Znaniecki (1984) made much use of letters between migrants and those left at home. The medium un-

doubtedly influences the message, for all those mentioned here have a feel of immediacy that is lacking in, say, the CV or edited memoirs.

Another pretext for telling life stories is that of social regulation. Life stories are told and often kept on file by organizations, not only by those who have lived the lives. A common source of anxiety about files is whether they will be kept confidential. Yet, authenticity is perhaps a more crucial issue, for recall of lives is invariably partial and selective. Doctors, for example, may honour confidentiality and still hold a different version of the truth of a life from that of the subject who has lived it.

Bertaux is right about present interests dictating our life stories. However, two aspects of time past also play a part. Life courses unfold in their own individual time – biography – and also that of the wider society – history. Each of us forms part of a *generation* that has lived through similar *history* – industrialization, war, full employment, recession – and our reaction to the present is conditioned thereby. Thus, today, employment is becoming less secure for more people. But people's reaction to this will vary depending on the

Figure 18.2 Life stories as social regulation. A "smart" ID card could contain 3000 words of information about you. How would you find out what was on it? Who would have access to it? How would you get it corrected if it was inaccurate? (*This is your life* design by Artworkers.)

history they have lived through. A generation raised at a time when their parents' jobs were secure, who themselves entered the labour market when work was plentiful, is likely to react differently to the new circumstances from a generation that has never known any other.

Movement from place to place is a source of varied *biography*. People may migrate for higher education or employment, whether within or from their country of origin. They often bring to their new society a different way of defining realities. This was a consistent theme of the sociologists of the inter-war Chicago school, including Thomas and Znaniecki (1984). The migrants' variant definitions were, as Thomas put it, "real in their consequences". Typically, these definitions led first-generation migrants to encapsulate themselves in an American version of the society back home.

There is a multiplicity of stories that may be told about any one life. They can be approached either as observations from different angles of the same life history, or as stories told from different interests and coloured by variant experience – but not from both viewpoints at the same time (Bellaby in Dex, 1991).

Researching the Life Course

The subject has an interest in how his or her life story is told and recorded; officials and professionals in organizations almost certainly have a different interest in that story; and – needless to say – sociologists who research the life course have distinctive interests too.

Telling It As It Is

But what *are* the sociologist's interests? The Chicago school tradition aligns itself with the subject. It seeks to *tell it as it is* from the actor's point of view. This favours qualitative use of documents of life and life-history interviews, in the manner that Ken Plummer advocates in his excellent *Documents of Life* (1983).

Such a decision simplifies the sociologist's

choices, but does not remove all the dilemmas. First, as we have seen, the narratives that subjects offer are conditioned by present interests. Are sociologists to privilege an account that reconstructs the actual history, simply because it is the account that suits the subject here and now? Second, as we have also seen, messages are affected by the genre and the medium in which they are told. Even a verbatim transcript from a tape-recorded interview mediates the original intention of the story-teller, and when this is edited and quoted selectively with a commentary, the subject's "primary" account is transformed into the sociologist's "secondary" account. The outcome usually is that the subject ceases to be *the* case study, but is transformed into an example of one *type* of several compared in the academic paper. Arguably the dictum "tell it as it is" is not realizable in the final analysis.

Theorizing the Structures

An alternative, perhaps the opposite, approach is to start, not with the subject, but with the structures that constrain and enable her or his actions: for instance gender or class. An example of this approach is the presentation and interpretation of life story interviews with Boston working men in *Hidden Injuries of Class* by Sennett and Cobb (1972). As the title suggests the men who were interviewed tended not to refer directly to class. Instead they spoke of personal ambitions, the standards they thought others expected of them, and their successes and failures. Since the men thought of getting on in American society and the "badges of ability" they must wear to succeed and, when they felt they fell short, sometimes spoke wistfully of the dignity of manual labour, the authors developed the theory that social class played a part in shaping their thoughts and deeds. Clearly social class, or any other aspect of social structure, is not directly observable, but has to be *theorized*. A plausible case can be made for its existence if a pattern of observations conforms to the concept. At the outset of the interviews Sennett and Cobb had an explicit model of the USA as a class society though, perhaps usefully, different views of how it had developed and why. It is unlikely that they would have been able to sustain their argument from the evidence had they interviewed only one person, but a persuasive case was made on the basis of some 200 life stories of people from the varied mix of ethnic groups that makes up Boston. They reinforced their argument by using evidence that their subjects did not provide and may not even have been aware of – about the history of emigration, ethnicity and class relations in the USA.

Whatever approach the sociologist takes to researching the life course, she or he will be concerned to make the account *reliable*. If the aim is to get as close as possible to the way the subject sees her or his life, then reliability is a matter of avoiding errors of interpretation. There must be checks within interviews to ensure that the response to any single question is understood properly by the sociologist. When an approach is taken from the other direction, starting with theoretical concepts such as class and gender, reliability remains important but *validity* also becomes an issue. The account is no longer viewed as a story; it becomes a history. Now it is necessary to seek external corroboration for the account the subject gives. Typically, the subject's account will be compared with those of other people and may also be cross-checked against other sources, such as diaries, produced by the subject herself.

Lives Viewed in Retrospect and Prospect

Life story and life-history interviews alike are retrospective. If treated as history the accounts depend heavily on the subject's power of recall, but techniques are available that make recall more likely and more reliable. There are certain events and times in any life that tend to get prominence and may be routinely recalled – such as when the subject left school, was married, had children, etc. Sociologists who want to construct a life history from the interview will ask at an early stage for a series of dates when these life events occurred. They may also remind the subject of major historical events which his or her generation has lived through. Other, less readily recalled life events can then be fitted into this chronology. Another useful technique is to produce a grid or matrix on which life-events are arrayed by type and given dates (e.g. births of children). This is then used by both interviewer and subject as a resource for recalling and adding in details that would otherwise be missed, for example changes of job, or periods of unemployment.

The collection of life-history material can be prospective rather than retrospective. Studies of cohorts of similar age follow their members over a number of years, sometimes from birth, and even into old age. If new data are gathered every few years, dependence on the respondent's recall of the distant past is reduced. Such studies depend upon the long-standing cooperation of large numbers of people who are ready to answer regular enquiries about changes of address, occupation and household arrangements, and to be investigated far more intensively at intervals. Individuals can refuse of course. But having entered the process, they are under moral pressure to continue and play the game.

The Ethics of Researching the Life Course

The *ethics* of research seeks a set of rules of the game which all can assent to and abide by. Sociological research is rarely so invasive as to put the physical health and safety of its subjects at risk, but it may well venture into psychologically painful areas of people's lives. Moreover, research on the life course is often open-ended, in the sense that it follows where the subject leads rather than having an entirely predetermined plan. In the interview situation, subjects can make revelations that they later regret. Researchers have a responsibility to ensure that subjects understand the purposes of the project and any risks they may carry in taking part. Subjects need to know in advance that they can withdraw, review what has been recorded and cause items to be taken off the record. In other words, subjects should give "informed consent".

An experienced researcher spares the subject from embarrassing themselves, if only because this often leads to the untimely end of the interview and may forfeit the chance to interview that person again.

Conclusion

In *The Sociological Imagination* (1970, originally 1959), C. Wright Mills argues that in modern society people feel trapped, swept up by forces they do not understand and cannot control, but that the forces *are* intelligible and *are* controllable. In principle, sociology is able to make them so. Sociology must set up its intellectual camp, not in abstruse questions of grand theory or scientific method, but where biography and history intersect – throwing light both on the private troubles to which individual lives are prone and the public issues that make history, and demonstrating how they are linked.

Mills also urges sociologists to approach with scepticism issues that are generally perceived to be the social problems of the day. A current example of such a "social problem" is the so-called "demographic time bomb" of many old people being dependent on few younger people able to generate wealth. It is a useful topic on which to end this chapter as it shows how the biographies and histories of groups of different ages intersect and affect each other.

The claim is not without foundation. The present generation now 75 and over was the last to be born into families with numerous children. They themselves had small families (in the inter-war period). A similar imbalance will occur when the baby boomers of the Second War and its aftermath reach 75, for they too had smaller families of their own. Problems arise because pensions and health and social services are not funded out of the contributions which those who are now old made when they were earning. Rather they are funded out of current tax revenues from those earning today.

However, there are positive as well as negative natural factors. While the old are often not as fit as younger people, more are fit than infirm. Many care successfully for partners who are infirm; many couples are both fit. This historically high level of fitness among the old has been obscured by a trend to earlier and earlier exit from labour markets and a tendency to enlarge the boundaries of what counts as "invalidity". Before the late 1950s men over "retirement age" were employed in significant numbers; but by the 1990s men under retirement age were taking early retirement and, in yet larger numbers, were being invalided out of employment.

Thus what appears at first as a natural or demographic problem actually conceals a shift in the organization of labour markets and the way health and social services define fitness for employment – that is, changes in social relations and perhaps, in the longer term, in culture itself. It shows too how much the life course is both a public issue that sociology can help explain in macro terms and a personal trouble that sociology can help each of us understand.

References

Ariès, P. 1973: *Centuries of Childhood*. Penguin.
—— 1983: *The Hour of Our Death*. Peregrine.
Beck, U. 1992: *The Risk Society*. Sage.
Dex, S. (ed) 1991: *Life and Work History Analyses*. Sociological Review Monograph 37. Routledge.
Bryman, A., Bytheway, B., Allatt, P. and Keil, T. (eds) 1987: *Rethinking the Life Cycle*. British Sociological Association/Macmillan.
Mills, C. W. 1970: *The Sociological Imagination*. Penguin.

Plummer, K. 1983: *Documents of Life*. Allen & Unwin.
Segalen, M. 1986: *Historical Anthropology of the Family*. Cambridge University Press.
Sennett, R. and Cobb, J. 1977: *The Hidden Injuries of Class*. Cambridge University Press.
Tilly, L. A. and Scott, J. A. 1978: *Women, Work and Family*. Holt, Rinehart & Winston.
Thomas, W. I. and Znaniecki, F. 1984: *The Polish Peasant in Europe and America* (edited and

abridged by E. Zaretsky). University of Illinois Press.

van Gennep, A. 1960: *The Rites of Passage*. University of Chicago Press.

Weber, M. 1970: Bureacracy. In H. H. Gerth and C. W. Mills (eds), *From Max Weber*. Routledge & Kegan Paul.

The Language of Sociology

Conflict theory Critical theory **Culture**
Decentred   self
Deconstruction Dialogical model
of truth   **Double hermeneutic**
Duality of structure **emic**
and   etic   Epistemology
Ethnomethodology   Feminist
theory   Foundationism
Functionalism Lange and parole
Methodology   Ontology   Post-
modernism   POST-
STRUCTURALISM Social interaction
Social institutions social system Social
action   Social   structure
Socialisation   Society   structuralism
Structuration   **Symbolic interaction**

19

A Brief Guide to "Difficult" Sociological Jargon and Some Working Resolutions

David Jary

Introduction – Why Sociology needs "Jargon"

No jargon, no sociology! The Plain English Society might be quite happy with such an outcome. But sociology could not exist without jargon, and, at least in part, sociology exists because sociological jargon *is* useful.

The fact is that there are two main dictionary definitions of the word "jargon" which must be clearly distinguished: (i) jargon as "unintelligible gibberish or debased language", and (ii) jargon as the "specialist or scientific language of a discipline, science or profession". If jargon in the first sense is obviously best avoided, jargon in the second sense is not only unavoidable but *necessary* – which doesn't mean, of course, that *all* sociological jargon is justified or that sociologists should not always try to write as accessibly as possible even when using jargon.

A prime reason why, as a discipline, sociology needs jargon is to extend our common language and the everyday understandings of social reality that are associated with this common language, to provide the basis for new descriptions and novel explanations of this reality.

The aim of this chapter is to provide a brief guide to some of the most "basic" concepts in sociology, together with a consideration of some of the more esoteric but widely used concepts in sociology – including some currently fashionable but controversial and difficult concepts. As well as this, the chapter also proposes a working resolution of some these controversies and difficulties.

"Basic Concepts" and Different Theoretical Approaches in Sociology

The concepts identified in Box 19.1 are those which most sociologists would probably agree are the basic concepts which define the discipline of sociology.

While not as inherently difficult as some in sociology, these concepts do present problems in that different sociologists utilize them in different ways, leading to different "approaches" or "schools of thought" within the subject (see Box 19.2). For example, while *symbolic interactionists* particularly emphasize "social action" and "social interaction" and tend to play down the value of concepts like "social institution", "function" and "system", *functionalists* emphasize these above all. Whereas *symbolic interactionism* and *functionalism* have tended to dominate the mainstream of modern sociology, *conflict theory* has been as concerned with whole societies as the latter, but highly critical of its overemphasis on "values" and "consensus". *Structuralism, ethnomethodology* and *feminist theory* constitute important further recent shifts of emphasis on the basic focus of previous mainstream sociology.

Two contrasting views exist on the occurrence of different approaches in sociology: either they can be seen as "opposing" approaches, presenting alternative views of the social world, or they can be seen as complementary, with different approaches dealing with different aspects of social reality. For

Society   The largest self-sustaining, relatively bounded human groupings (today typically based on nation-states), identified by their possession of distinctive patterns of *culture* and distinctive *social institutions*. Sociology itself is often defined as "the study of human societies". There is some debate, however, as to how far, in a globalizing world, this definition of society is becoming outmoded, leading sociology to neglect the highly important relations between societies.

Culture   The socially transmitted patterns of behaviour, knowledge and practices – including language, knowledge, technology, artefacts, values, etc. – that are the basis of the social complexity and the growth of human societies, and the crucial differentiating factor between human *societies* and the rest of the animal kingdom.

Social institutions   Established areas of *society* possessing a relatively stabilized, relatively differentiated, existence, e.g. family, religion, education.

Socialization   The processes by which societies pass on and individuals acquire *culture*, e.g. child rearing, formal education and peer influences.

Social action   Socially motivated action, which is distinguished from merely physical action or "behaviour". As such, social action usually involves conscious goals and is guided or governed by cultural concerns. Either way, all such action possesses either a particular or a general cultural context.

Social interaction   The mutually attuned, including the face-to-face, exchanges between individuals. Given the social expectations which "govern" such interaction, Goffman refers to the existence of an "*interaction order*."

Social structure   Any relatively stable pattern of social arrangements or *social institutions* (e.g. "family structures" or "social stratification").

Social system   The relatively persistent operation and interrelation of *social institutions*, in which social activities and institutions are sometimes also seen as performing *social functions* which maintain the system. It is usually recognized, however, that the degree of "systemness", the self-maintaining features, of social systems is highly variable and rarely attains the level of integration, internal unity and tendency to self-maintenance found in some biological or physical systems.

Box 19.1: Basic sociological concepts

example, an "action" approach may be seen as appropriate for "micro" phenomena and "structural" approaches for macro phenomena. However many sociologists would see this as far too simplistic (see Mouzelis, 1995). And even if complementarities are acknowledged, many issues remain about the relative importance and appropriate and inappropriate use of basic sociological concepts and the developments from these.

Contested Conceptual Terrain

At least to some degree, the previously heated disputes in sociology between social action and social structural approaches, and between functionalist and conflict theory *have* become more muted. They now seem, at least in part, like phoney wars, with the key issue now seeming to be how conflict and consensus, and interaction and social structure – and also micro and macro – interrelate. However, this outcome has also emphasized the complexity and fluidity of social action and social

Symbolic interactionism An emphasis on social accounts and explanations – often of "micro" social contexts – couched simply in terms of the socially purposive or "meaningful" actions and interaction of social actors. Sometimes presented in opposition to functionalism, symbolic interactionism on the whole avoids holistic conceptions like "system".

Functionalism Theories which explain the persistence (if not the origins) of social institutions in terms of the social functions they perform. "Values" are sometimes emphasized at the expense of power and "consensus" at the expense of conflict – but these should not be seen as essential features of functionalism.

Conflict theory Approaches (including Marxism) which emphasize the importance of conflicts of interest in human societies, especially over resources, but also over values. These conflicts and "contradictions" (inherent incompatibilities of structure and "interests") are seen as the crucial source of social change and social development and potential social progress.

Structuralism Approaches which identify different structural "levels", and "explain" the more readily observable or measurable social structures and actions as the outcome of "deeper" underlying, *generative structures* – much like grammar has the capacity for generating sentences (see also Box 19.3). (Note. The apparently similar terms "*social structure*" (Box 19.1), "*generative structure*" (Box 19.3) and "*structuration*" (see Box 19.4) are easily confused. It is especially important to note carefully the distinctions involved.)

Ethnomethodology An approach which emphasizes the importance of understanding the social actor's "competence" and "methods" in undertaking social action – something other approaches to sociology are seen as failing to do.

Feminist theory Theories which focus on issues and areas neglected in mainstream sociological theory which, for the most part, is regarded as having been either gender-blind or "malestream".

Box 19.2   Main theoretical approaches in sociology.

structures and, if anything, has increased the complexity and difficulty of sociological concepts.

The rise to prominence of *structuralism* and *ethnomethodology*, (and also feminist theory) in the 1960s, 1970s, and 1980s, each of which is critical of previous "conventional" approaches to sociology, has compounded this complexity, leading to some notoriously difficult, but now central, new concepts in sociology.

The conceptual innovation and the resulting conceptual complexities introduced by structuralism (and later by post-structuralism) are indicated in Box 19.3. In the jargon of structuralism, particular social occurrences (like particular language-use, Saussure's *parole*, the so-called *etic* aspect of language) can be read-off from underlying "generative" (in Saussure's terms, *lange*-like or grammar-like) structures, as seen in Levi-Strauss's (1969) account of kinship. Structuralism, however, is far from being the final word on these matters.

Structuralism has been widely recognized as innovative and valuable in its emphasis on the importance of underlying generative structures, including those which structure the "unconscious". It emphasizes the "emic" at the expense of the "etic", thus providing a strongly rule-determined account of language and social action. However, these very achievements are open to criticism. As will be

Structure(s) (structuralist sense) The underlying – grammar-like – generative sources of social action and social regularities.

Lange and parole; emic and etic Distinctions in structuralism drawn between the grammatical structure of a language (*lange*, its *emic* elements) and the particular utterances made using a language (*parole* or *etic* elements). With this distinction there is no reason in principle, why structuralism should not support both structural and individual explanations. Nevertheless structuralism is widely associated with an under-emphasis on the "*agency*" of the individual person, and an over-emphasis on the determining influence of structure. As for Althusser, social actors are often presented as merely the "supports" for structures.

Deconstruction The "method", especially associated with Derrida (1976) and *post-structuralism*, in which it is assumed that the ever present possibility of new interpretations of any writing (or "text") mean that essentialist claims to truth (especially, for example, in traditional "foundationist" *epistemology*) can always be subverted.

Decentred self (post-structuralism) A conception of the "self" in which the self is no longer regarded as a unitary entity or basis of individual continuity, as assumed in action theory or in traditional *epistemology*. Instead, the self becomes an unstable point within ever shifting structural contexts, e.g. within the flow of language or in the multiple interpretations of any "text".

Members' methods (ethnomethodology) The general "methods" of carrying out and bringing-off social action (e.g. "turn-taking", "glossing" meanings) seen as routinely possessed by "members" within social settings. Ethnomethodology is especially effective in elaborating conceptions of an actor's tacit knowledge ("*knowledgeability*") and social competence.

Box 19.3 Structuralist, post-structuralist and ethnomethodological key concepts.

discussed in the next section, structuralism reinstates the division between action and structure that in part previous sociological theorizing had attempted to transcend. Two lines of criticism have been particularly important – first, that structuralism is excessively static and over-deterministic in its explanations and, second, that it understates the creativity of the social actor and the degree of autonomy sometimes open to the *self*.

The *post-structuralist* response has been to embrace the first criticism – making "*deconstruction*" its central theme (see Box 19.4), but respond to the second by portraying the self as *decentred*, that is actually deconstructing the self. On this view, the "self" is nowhere and among other things can no longer be assumed

as the basis of the "knowing subject" as in traditional epistemology (see Box 19.5 later) – a collapse of previous epistemological conceptions that is the core of Derrida's (1976) claims for "deconstruction" . Thus the outcome of post-structuralism can be portrayed as leaving "only movement". The conceptual (and analytical) Pandora's box opened-up by structuralism and post-structuralism cannot easily be closed. There can be no question of a return to simpler conceptions of "self" and of "structure".

As a further critique of conventional sociology, the innovation and conceptual complexity introduced by *ethnomethodology* is markedly different from that involved in structuralism and post-structuralism and arises from a focus

Duality of structure Giddens' model of the relation between social action (or *agency*) and *structure*, in which "structure is the medium and outcome of the conduct it organizes", where *structure*, refers to the "rules and resources" implicated in the production and reproduction of social systems and social structures.

Structuration The processes – involving "rules" and "resources" – by which *social structures* and *social institutions* come into being.

Structuration theory This refers to both the general recommendations about the subject-matter, and the means of study, of the processes of structuration.

Box 19.4   Structuration theory – a successful synthesis and a resolution of some conceptual difficulties?

on social actors' "methods" (or "competence") in undertaking and "bringing-off" social action as the central "topic" (see Garfinkel, 1967). Based especially on the social phenomenology of Alfred Schutz among others, when first introduced ethnomethodology was presented as implying a radical break with all forms of "conventional" sociology which were seen as simply failing to explore the groundedness of all social reality in "actors' knowledgeability". Today, ethnomethodology is acknowledged as promoting important attention to previously neglected dimensions of social conduct which, once again, means that older conceptions of social action and social structure must be recognized as far too rigid and no longer adequate as a basis for sociology.

In a word, what both structuralism and ethnomethodology can be said to lead to is a deconstruction and transformation, and an increase in the "difficulty" of, sociology's key concepts.

The "Structurationist" "Synthesis" – Duality of Agency and Structure

The importance of *structuration theory* to which we now turn is that it offers an important synthesis and reconciliation of different approaches, including both structuralism and ethnomethodology (see Box 19.4, based especially on Giddens, 1994).

Centrally Giddens proposes to resolve the tendency of sociologists, as he sees it, to operate with a dualism of agency and structure. Giddens addresses the theoretical dilemma: "are we the creators of society, or created by it?". His conclusion is that posing the issue as a choice is mistaken. The real issue is to ask: "How are the two aspects of social life – 'action' (or agency) and 'structure' interrelated? and to treat structure and agency not as a dualism but as a *duality of structure* in which structure is the medium and outcome of the conduct it organises."

As well as offering a reconciliation of different approaches, the virtue of structurationism in the above terms is that, to a degree, it also simplifies the complexity that has grown up around key sociological concepts. It especially utilizes ethnomethodology (and in doing so fills out previous conceptions of individual "agency") while accommodating this to the mainstream of sociology and, *at the same time* seriously addresses the issues and new complexities raised by structuralism and poststructuralism. As well as this, it also strives to take account of feminist critiques of malestream sociology and the previous frequent invisibility of gender in the discipline. While sometimes criticized for adding too many neologisms and for some loss of the nuances of different approaches (see Craib, 1992), this can be seen as a price worth paying for the clarification, simplification and integration achieved, given that nuances can always be built back in as and when required for particular purposes.

Epistemology   Theories of how knowledge is gained and "truths" established. Compared with the reliable foundations suggested by traditional epistemologies, recent decades have seen an increasing ascendancy of "post-foundationist" epistemologies (including the deconstructions of "self" and "structure" associated with post-structuralism) seriously challenge previous foundationist epistemologies (such as empiricism and positivism).

Ontology   Accounts of the basic kinds of thing which exist and how these interact. Thus a social ontology proffers an identification and an account of the basic nature of social reality. It is the character of some current accounts of social ontology (see Box 19.3) that they undermine previous epistemological accounts. Thus, modern *social* ontology and epistemology are interconnected.

Methodology (and *methods*)   Although these terms are sometimes used interchangeably, properly used, *methodology* refers to epistemological issues and to general issues of concept formation and theory construction, while research *methods* (or perhaps *research methodology*) refers to the more specific methods employed in carrying out research (e.g. the use of questionnaires or interviews).

*The "double hermeneutic" (*and *critical theory)*   The presence of a double set of understandings involved in any sociological account – "the meaningful social world as constituted by lay actors and the languages invented by social scientists" (Giddens, 1994). The continuous "slippage" between these two worlds has important methodological implications – not least, that sociological theory will sometimes be *"critical theory"*, leading to radical reappraisals of existing social practices.

Dialogic model of truth,   Habermas's conception that the *only* forum in which claims to "truth" can ultimately be upheld is the forum of all with the inclination and capacity to debate the issue; there are *no* other general epistemological prescriptions (see also Feyerabend, 1975).

Box 19.5   Socially located socio-methodological concepts

It *is* a problem with structuration theory, as commentators have pointed out, that it doesn't *automatically* resolve all issues of structure and agency, but against this it is a part of the theory's argument that many agency/structure questions can *only* be resolved *within* specific studies. What structuration theory provides, and provides well as indicated by its increasing use by sociologists, is a conceptual framework within which questions can be appropriately and readily posed. Furthermore, what it has to say on methodological issues includes both issues of substantive research (see Giddens, 1994) *and* central *epistemological* issues, in relation to which the conception of a "duality of structure" proves especially useful, particularly in overcoming some of the "hiatus" on

issues of "truth and falsity" and the problems of radical relativism, associated with post-structuralism and also sometimes with ethnomethodology.

Central Methodological Concepts – Conceptual Proliferation and Agreement in Sociology

What the somewhat forbidding philosophical terms *epistemology* and *ontology* mean is really quite straightforward (see Box 19.5). The issues they relate to are more complex, involving the fundamental identification of both the subject-matter and the *methodology* and *methods* appropriate to knowledge and study in general and also to particular areas of knowledge and study.

Any detailed answer to the question "what subject-matter and methods are appropriate for sociology?" is bound to be complex because sociology's subject-matter must necessarily include the physical environment of social action, including the physical bodies of social actors as well the realm of social selves and social structures. As Comte indicated in coining the term "sociology", as the "Queen of the Sciences" standing at the head of a hierarchy of the sciences, sociology is potentially heir to all of the problems and complexities of sciences at lower levels in the hierarchy.

Post-structuralist (sometimes referred to as "post-foundationist") assaults on previous epistemological and methodological foundationism now mean, in addition, that epistemological questions about the basis of truth and falsity and appropriate methods of study can *only* be answered provisionally and within a circle of meaning in which an identification of ontology and method raise *interrelated* issues, answerable only from the "inside" of an ongoing social discourse in which *sociological* insights are now utterly central (*crucially* involving issues of the role of agency and structure in the production of knowledge). It should be noted, although not discussed further here, that *all* scientific knowledge can be regarded as subject to this new sociological understanding, a viewpoint known as the "strong version of the sociology of science" (see Jary and Jary, 1995).

There is no space to discuss further here all the many ramifications of the above. However, there is room to briefly discuss two key "resolutions" of these issues, each of which can be seen as vital as a source of working assumptions in sociological analysis and research.

The first of these resolutions arises from Giddens' concept of the "*double hermeneutic*" – the identification of the presence of the double set of understandings involved in any sociological account (see Box 19.5). (The term "hermeneutics" refers to the process of interpretation.) The issue of the relation between the meaningful social world as constituted by lay actors and the languages invented by sociologists gives rise to a number of recommendations concerning methodology. Three aspects are important:

- In formulating their own explanations, sociologists must first seek to grasp ethnographically a world that has already been conceptualized by the social actors being studied.
- The descriptions and explanations devised by the sociologist can be "tested" at one level for acceptability among those studied.
- Since a disjunction will sometimes exist between sociological and lay accounts (e.g. institutional accounts, accounts of the unintended consequences of intended actions), sociology will sometimes also possess a role as "*critical theory*", leading to a reappraisal of existing social practices and helping potentially to change these.

The second methodological resolution of considerable value is Habermas's "*dialogic*" model of "*truth*" (Box 19.5). This arises both from the existence of the *double hermeneutic* and the overall context of "post-foundationism". Based on his model of "ideal discourse", what Habermas argues is that the *only* ultimate forum in which claims to "truth" can be upheld is the forum of all who wish to debate the issue; there are *no* other methodological prescriptions. Giddens also adopts much the same position.

The possibility of dialogic resolutions of conceptual or theoretical disputes in sociology (and in social life) is a vital step in combating the post-structuralist (and post-modernist) conceptions of a world in which there is *only* flux and profusion. Nevertheless, it is important to end by noting that there exist many reasons why conceptual proliferation in sociology (or indeed elsewhere) *cannot* be expected to end, *not least* because, as pointed out by the iconoclastic methodologist Paul Feyerabend (1975), conceptual variety and theoretical proliferation *are* often an advantage, not only in preserving the richness of knowledge and in creating "new" knowledge, but also in protecting individually or collectively "preferred ways of life" from unjustified persecution. It should also be noted that both Habermas and

Giddens accept such points, and recognize the importance of the retention of what can be termed a dialectic of "the universal and the plural" and the "global and the local" in discussion of many important issues of the day, not least nationalism or tendencies to cultural globalization. The framework provided by structuration theory and by Habermas is intended to allow "resolutions" without asserting either a dogma of universalism or falling into a relativist trap.

Because this is so, a final caveat about this chapter is also in order. The view expressed in it has obviously been ecumenical, emphasizing for the most part the relative unity of sociology and the complementarities of different points of view within the discipline. It should *not* be ignored that, like any sociology, the ideas expressed in this chapter remain a *point* of view, which obviously would not necessarily be accepted by all sociologists. Nor, therefore, should it be accepted without careful further thought by the reader. Nonetheless, the author *does* believe that a conception of the discipline of sociology that recognizes its unity as well as its undoubted pluralities has much to recommend, not least today at a time of attacks on reason and universalism. At the very least, it is a point of view that any student of the subject should not dismiss lightly.

References

Craib, I. 1992: *Anthony Giddens*. London: Routledge.

Derrida, J. 1976 [1967]: *Of Grammatology*. Baltimore, MD: Johns Hopkins University Press.

Feyerabend, P. 1975: *Against Method*. London: New Left Editions.

Garfinkel, H. 1967: *Studies in Ethnomethodology*. Englewood Cliffs, NJ: Prentice Hall.

Giddens, A. 1994: *The Constitution of Society*. Cambridge: Polity Press.

Habermas, J. 1981: *The Theory of Communicative Action* (2 vols). Boston, MA: Beacon Press.

Jary, D. & Jary, J. 1995: *Collins Dictionary of Sociology*, 2nd edn. Glasgow: Harper-Collins.

Levi-Strauss, C. 1969: *The Elementary Structure of Kinship*. Boston, MA: Beacon Press.

Mouzelis, N. 1995: *Sociological Theory – What Went Wrong?* London: Routledge.

PART III
Contemporary Sociological Engagement

Within sociology there is a never-ending movement of the pendulum between value-commitment and detachment. The essays in the previous part swung towards the more "detached" end of the arc even as they discussed the centrality of human engagement. Whatever their own views the authors of those chapters were asked to observe how the values and perceptions of others had influenced the development of sociology, the way it came to define its field of study, and its characteristic modes of explanation. Their essays also included an important historical dimension.

We have organized Part III around the two senses of "engagement" distinguished in the introduction to Part II, with the emphasis here firmly on *contemporary* engagement: first, as sociological engagement with issues of current public concern, and then as intellectual engagement by a rising generation of sociologists with the traditions they are inheriting. The distinction, of course, is just a basic principle of selection. It is in no way meant to suggest that the two senses are mutually exclusive.

The six chapters on *contemporary social issues* focus on areas of intense public interest and debate. The authors were invited to be provocative and, if they wished, to eschew notions of "balance" in favour of closely argued sociological polemic. The result is a series of vigorous essays that provide an insight into the high quality scholarship that marks contemporary sociology. They offer new slants on familiar controversies and, in so doing, demonstrate the continuing power of the sociological imagination to re-cast our mental frameworks.

Sociology to fire the imagination comprises six short essays from the "new" generation of sociologists (recently appointed lecturers and postgraduate students) on works that had an "eye-opening" effect in their own intellectual development – transforming the way they looked at the social world or their own place within it; articulating ideas that were already forming in their own mind; or else providing them with significant insights into how sociologists set about the task of investigating the social world. The sense of exhilaration that accompanies personal intellectual growth is vividly conveyed – and we hope you will be sufficiently enthused to hunt down some of these works for yourself.

Social Issues

20

Higher Education and Employment in a Post-industrial Society

Phillip Brown and Richard Scase

The relationship between higher education and employment in a post-industrial economy is undergoing fundamental change. In the past, bureaucratic forms of organization offered an educated elite security of employment and careers through personal promotion. A graduate could look forward to a career which might be defined as progression in an ordered, predictable sequence through a succession of related jobs arranged in a hierarchy of prestige. This pattern of career progression was embedded in a relatively stable organizational structure – the system was maintained over more than one generation of recruitment (Wilensky, 1960, p. 554). But in most advanced countries there has been a shift from an elite to a mass system of higher education and, at the same time, both private and public sector organizations are being restructured in ways that challenge the conventional assumptions about managerial and professional careers – assumptions which also underwrite the criteria of *personal success* in contemporary society. Within these alternative organizational structures, which are often described as *flexible, post-bureaucratic* or *post-modern* (Brown and Scase, 1994) it is no longer possible for university graduates to plan their futures on a long-term basis. It is becoming increasingly difficult for them to assume that their work, and hence broader life styles, can be *anchored* within stable organizational structures of the kind that existed in the past. For virtually all employees the future consists of uncertainties and anxieties, and requires the ability to cope with the unpredictable nature of the world of work. Compared with earlier generations, today's university graduates are likely to experience periods of unemployment at various stages during their working lives. Forces of corporate restructuring are also likely to force them to move more frequently between jobs within the same organization as well as to make more frequent shifts between employers (Confederation of British Industry (CBI), 1994; Carnevale and Porro, 1994). Moreover, far more of today's graduates are likely to be found in self-employment, to be engaged in business start-up ventures and to be working in small businesses at different periods in their working lives.

Unlike in the past, then, the occupational future of university graduates is likely to be characterized by uncertainty, a variety of work experience and a *discontinuous* experience of employment. Hence graduates have to be more "flexible" in their attitudes towards work and more "adaptive" in their behaviour in the labour market. They require a broader portfolio of technical, social and personal skills than the more job-specific skills which were previously emphasized by employers. In earlier decades, graduates would leave universities to join employers who would train them to exercise specific organizational tasks on the basis of narrow technical expertise. While the acquisition of technical expertise has not diminished, organizations are now demanding that university graduates acquire such skills as part of a broader portfolio of personal competences. This is not only a necessary requirement given the increasing emphasis on team and project work approaches to work in innovative organizations, but also because the acquisition of generic skills is essential for graduate employees to maintain their *employability* in both the organization and the external market for jobs. In place of bureaucratic careers, graduates are now required to make incremental progression by gaining the skills, experience and contacts necessary to construct a "value added" curriculum vitae in order to progress within and between organizations. This pattern of occupational advancement is inevitably contingent and unstable. Hence they need to be able to use their expert "core" skills within a variety of work settings which, at various stages within their labour market biographies, will incorporate working in both large and small businesses, and in companies that are constantly being rationalized and restructured because of global competition, technological innovation, corporate mergers and acquisition. At the same time, maintaining one's *employability* is also needed in order to be able to trade as "independent" and freelance consultants (Goffee and Scase, 1995).

The psychological and sociological consequences of these changes for university graduates are far-reaching. It is no longer possible to plan ahead in the sense of pursuing personal career agendas. In the past, notions of personal success and failure were closely based upon age-related achievements (or not) in relation to such factors as organizational position, level of earnings and material standard of living. Hence self-evaluation of personal performance – as well as that of others – could be based on a series of steps or stages in a sequence which had to be achieved by certain ages in order to be regarded by oneself and by others as successful. Graduates could, therefore, "benchmark" their achievements against others and also in relation to their own personal plans.

Equally, from a sociological point of view, it was possible for graduates to "plan" the nature of their personal relationships. Within a context of personal progression in a highly-ordered future, they could plan various life-cycle patterns in terms of when to have children (and how many), whether or not to foster partner relationships, and how to plan projected (and reasonably predictable) earnings. In such a framework graduates in relatively safe and clearly-defined career jobs could make substantial financial commitments to long-term loans for house purchase or other purposes. The organizational career, therefore, was the pivotal axis around which middle class lifestyles were structured (Whyte, 1965). Indeed, it sustained the ideals of western capitalism in nurturing the opportunity of social mobility for all, in which effort and talent would be rewarded both psychologically and materially. Accordingly, it legitimated wealth (insofar as it was achieved through personal career success) and poverty (made up of those who had failed in the meritocratic race). In the days of the Cold War (1945–89), when Europe was divided between the countries of Western capitalism and East European state socialism, the former was often portrayed as being morally superior because of its meritocratic, achievement-related rewards by comparison with the system of individual sponsorship characteristic of state socialist regimes. Although these images owe more to rhetoric than to reality – as contrasting types of society – they were important as ideologies that sustained competing forms of social order for more than four decades. Moreover, meritocratic career progression within bureaucratic organizations played a key role in the social control of the middle classes in the West. As Wilensky has suggested "they give continuity to the personal experience of the most able and skilled segments of the population – men [*sic*] who otherwise would produce a level of rebellion or withdrawal which would threaten the maintenance of the system" (1960, p. 555).

However, such ideas of "personal achievement" and "career progression" have depended upon the bureaucratization of public and private sector organizations since the late nineteenth century (Gerth and Mills, 1958). Within the sociological literature most discussion of the nature of bureaucracy stems from the ideas of Max Weber. As a German philosopher–sociologist, writing at the turn of the twentieth century, Weber argued that the growth of the modern organization was leading to the increasing bureaucratization of the world (Jacoby, 1973). By this he meant that large organizations were becoming increasingly structured according to a number of related principles. First, there is the clear delineation of work tasks so that all organizational participants know what is expected of them in terms of their duties and responsibilities. There are job descriptions and people are expected to achieve their aims according to the procedures stipulated in these. Second, these jobs are hierarchically arranged so that organizational coordination is achieved through chains of command in which people appointed to positions of authority control the actions of subordinates, and where those lower down the hierarchy are accountable to their "superiors", but not vice versa. Third, the hierarchical structuring of specialized work tasks in bureaucratic organizations offer personal careers as part-and-parcel of the reward system. Appropriate performance is rewarded through promotion through the formally-structured hierarchy. Equally, adequate performance requires personal commitment or loyalty and this is obtained by offering organizational members relative security through (more or less) life-long tenure (Merton, 1967). Further, the specialization of work tasks leads to skill enhancement such that both individual participants *and* the organization operate at an optimum level of efficiency. It was for this reason that Weber considered bureaucracies to be *rational* forms of organization compared with pre-industrial, traditional forms of administration. But this model of organizational efficiency is presently breaking down as it ceases to be relevant for the structuring of organizations. This in turn is leading to a "crisis" in the traditional assumptions, values and motivations of the middle class and of university graduates in particular.

In bureaucracies, the overriding goal was to select those who are prepared to undertake tasks in a compliant, dutiful and reliable manner. Staff recruitment therefore focuses upon those who can demonstrate a willingness to play by the "rules of the game", and who are able to cooperate with others in a functionally inter-dependent division of labour. They are not expected to be "creative", "entrepreneurial" or "individualistic" since such behaviour undermines the essentially conformist cultures that bureaucracies require to be effective. Thus, there is an organizational requirement for mass recruits to lower-level positions where there is a demand for compliant employees in the *usual* bureaucratic manner. On the other hand, there is also a need for quite different sorts of person who have the potential to fill the top senior managerial positions. Such people do need to be creative and analytical in terms of their ability to formulate and implement organizational strategies. The result of this dual requirement is the emergence of a higher education system which, although structured on a unitary basis, is bifurcated in terms of this bureaucratic occupational order. What emerges in most advanced economies is an "elite" group of institutions which provides the human resources for the senior organizational positions and a broader framework of institutions providing the training for those who will fill the great mass of technical, managerial and professional positions within bureaucratic structures. However, this neat fit between higher education and the occupational order becomes less relevant as organizations de-bureaucratize.

The shift to a "flexible" paradigm of organization has been driven by a number of factors including a recognition that bureaucracy is inappropriate in an innovative environment; that "downsizing" organizations could make substantial savings on labour costs, especially among the mass ranks of supervisors and middle managers; that job-redesign and job enlargement could not only make the organization more efficient but allowed greater potential for employers to exercise discretion, responsibility and creativity; and that the widespread application of information technology will allow organizational decision-making to be undertaken through non-human monitoring and communication processes. Hence the need for large numbers of compliant employees who undertake their tasks in a highly routinized and predictable manner is severely reduced. According to the flexible paradigm of efficiency, there is an increased need for those who are able to be creative within ill-defined and ambiguous work settings. It is a form of organization that is decentralized on the basis of administrative units and operating processes. Each of these will be empowered to achieve their goals according to whatever means is most appropriate. *Results* are monitored rather than the *means* and reward systems are structured accordingly. In the flexible organization there is a small core of key staff who may still be able to make a career within the organization, although this is likely to be limited, involving horizontal as well as vertical mobility, given the absence of an extensive corporate hierarchy (Handy, 1989; Kanter, 1989). These core workers are supported by those on fixed or short-term contracts which offer little prospect of progression within the organization. Many of these workers are "contracted in" when required and will include technicians and professional consultants. The flexible organization will also make extensive use of "contracting out" to other companies who will undertake tasks which were previously provided in-house. Therefore, if the bureaucracy was characterized by stability and order, the flexible organization epitomizes constant change and uncertainty.

As a result of these trends, employers state a preference for graduates who are able to cope with these new demands. It needs employees with good interpersonal skills who are able to engage in "rule-making" rather than "rule-following" behaviour. What we are currently witnessing, therefore, is a significant change in the "cultural capital" required for entry into middle class occupations (Bourdieu and Passeron, 1964). Within classical economics "capital" is defined in material terms such as equipment, materials, goods and labour costs. A more complete concept of capital, which includes "human" capital, was outlined in Irving Fisher's *The Nature of Capital and Income* (1927) and marked the beginning of attempts to measure the

economic returns of investments in education and training. Fisher's definition of capital treats "all sources of income streams as forms of capital" (see Schultz, 1968). In this sense it is not only possible to talk about "codified" and "certified" knowledge and skills as a potential source of capital, but also as "cultural" capital (Bourdieu and Passeron, 1977). Not everyone has access to the same cultural resources, in the sense of cultural identities based on different patterns of socialization, language codes, and cultural artefacts. The cultural disposition of a child or student, for instance, can be capitalized in the school in terms of the harmony (or lack of it) between what is taught, modes of transmission, and motivation to learn school knowledge as a result of parental, teacher or peer group pressures. Cultural capital in school takes the form of access to qualifications which can ultimately be traded in the labour market for jobs offering high status and income. An important feature of the cultural capital required for entry into managerial and professional positions within "flexible" organizations, however, involves a shift in emphasis from the recruitment of those who exhibited evidence of "bureaucratic" to "charismatic" personality characteristics. (Brown and Scase, 1994; Brown, 1995). The idea of the charismatic personality is one which values those who seek to break the structures of routine actions and rule-following, to replace them with patterns of innovative and creative behaviour. "The charismatic person is the creator of a new order as well as the breaker of routine order" (Shils, 1965, 1968).[1] In essence, the charismatic personality is the opposite to the bureaucratic in that it is primarily based on personal and interpersonal skills. The ability to get on with others and to identify with a strong corporate culture is paramount. Consequently, it is no longer enough to acquire the appropriate credentials and to show evidence of technical competence. It is now the whole person who is on show and at stake in the market for managerial and professional work. It is the "personality package" (Fromm, 1962) based on a combination of technical skills, qualifications and charismatic qualities, which must be sold.

As a result, employers will nowadays translate their need for flexible, innovative and creative employees into concerns about how "personalities" fit into the changing interpersonal dynamics of the flexible organization. It might, therefore, have been expected that the shift to flexible forms of organization would lead to more "pluralistic" approaches to corporate recruitment so as to exploit the talents of graduates from different social and ethnic backgrounds, as well as of women. Paradoxically, however, the increasing importance attached to teamwork and project work has in reality become translated into the need for "safe bets" – that is people with the appropriate cultural capital (white, middle class and predominantly male).

This tendency for flexible organizations to recruit "safe bets" is motivated by at least three factors. Firstly, when emphasis is placed on teamwork, negotiation and interpersonal skills, organizations are increasingly concerned to recruit people with the appropriate "personal chemistry" which allows them to fit easily into existing teams. Secondly, given that flexible organizations are designed to give employees greater room for individual discretion and responsibility, the problem of organizational control is addressed, at least in part, by ensuring the recruitment of those the organization is likely to be able to "trust". In other words, they are likely to recruit people like themselves. Thirdly, at a time when organizations are looking to cut overheads and unit budgets, there is considerable pressure on recruiters to select people who will stay with the organization for at least two years. Given that the retention of new recruits is an important performance indicator within personnel/human resource departments, this again reinforces the propensity for "risk avoidance", by rejecting those who do not conform to the usual criteria of appointment, i.e. someone from outside of the elite university sector; a person of colour in a predominantly "white" organization, and so on.

Moreover, as the market for graduate labour has become flooded through the rapid expansion of higher education, a degree may unlock but does not open doors – especially into highly-paid senior organizational positions which remain "earmarked" for those with the cultural capital that is difficult to acquire without attending an elite institution. Employers increasingly target the elite "old universities" (Oxford, Harvard, Berkeley) in the belief that, since access to them is extremely competitive, they are most likely to contain the best intellectual talent and the students with appropriate cultural capital. Hence the often stated claim by employers that, whilst they would like to select graduates from a broad university base, their experience unfortunately [sic] confirms that it is only in the elite universities that they are able to find the type of person that suits their corporate needs (Brown and Scase, 1994).

There has recently been a proliferation of initiatives, especially in the "mass" university sector, which aim to furnish students with the personal and social competences required of the flexible organizations. Undergraduates in the mass universities are encouraged to develop their "leadership" and "teamwork" potential, while at the same time to be more "creative" and "entrepreneurial" in their approach to studies. Courses have become more project-focused, requiring students to exercise their ability to work *both* independently and in cooperation with others. However, despite these attempts by the institutions of "mass" higher education to nurture such skills, their graduates continue to be perceived by employers as lacking the necessary cultural capital (Brown and Scase, 1994). Ironically, indeed, such initiatives are viewed by employers as the latest version of "compensatory" education for disadvantaged students. Hence, instead of the opening up of opportunities to traditionally disadvantaged youth, the expansion of higher education has involved an assessment by employers that "more means different" (Ball, 1990), exaggerating the existing hierarchy of academic worth which favours the elite universities.

This is not to argue that university education is worthless and that those from less privileged backgrounds do not benefit or enhance their market value by studying for degrees. Clearly, the great majority do gain. The extent to which employers will rely on elite universities will depend on the job in question. For jobs requiring specialized vocational training the "mass" institutions of higher education are able to compete with the elite institutions by tailoring the curriculum to meet the technical needs of large companies. In this way a degree within the mass university sector provides a route into the labour market whereby employment in low-paid, unskilled jobs can be avoided (albeit, given the financial difficulties faced by students, not until after their studies are complete). Overall, however, the traditional hierarchy of universities is left intact.

Of course, all this presupposes that the role of the university system *is* to prepare people for employment, whether they be school leavers or, increasingly in a post-industrial society, those who are already in the labour market. Indeed, this is a questionable assumption despite attempts by governments to introduce policies to make university education more relevant to the needs of industry. Certainly, the role of higher education is becoming increasingly ambiguous as a result of broader societal transformations. Compared with only a couple of decades ago, universities have lost their position as monopoly providers of knowledge in a number of areas, particularly within the humanities and the social sciences. It is no longer necessary to leave home, to rent uncomfortable accommodation and get a low-paid, part-time job in order to attend university to understand, for example, issues of social and economic inequality. The traditional mode of delivery of such information via the 50-minute lecture is now challenged by information technologies which are able to offer various forms of distance learning through the use of computers, television, video, teleconferencing, and so on. Moreover, 20 years ago, there were few social scientists working in the media. Today, most newspaper, magazine, television and radio journalists, editors and producers will have studied at least some of the social sciences whilst they were at university. With the use of media technology, they have been able to build upon their own knowledge and "beat the universities at their own game". Those interested in

poverty, inequality or employment trends, for example, can often get more up-to-date information and analysis through newspapers, magazines and computer databases than from academic books or journals. Even in the natural sciences, developments in information technology are destroying the need to attend university. The growing use of such innovations as the internet could enable students to construct a broad portfolio of courses selected from those offered by eminent professors on a world wide basis. The learning process can be undertaken on an interactive basis *without* the need for face-to-face relations in a specific geographical location. Hence, the seminar room, the lecture theatre and the university campus is no longer a necessary condition for in depth academic study. So why have universities expanded precisely at the time when the monopoly of academic knowledge is most under threat? The reason is simply that the transmission of knowledge is only a part of the university's role in society. Perhaps of equal importance is the fact that universities have largely maintained a monopoly over the award of high status credentials.

Indeed, so long as universities can maintain a monopoly over the examination process, where and how students learn is of diminishing importance, although of course it does make a difference whether or not it is an elite university that awards the degree. Universities have become key players in the provision of distance learning and the franchizing of course materials, if not the university's imprimatur to institutions around the world. What is crucial to universities is that they maintain or seek to enhance their "reputational" capital in order to maximize the market value of their products (i.e. diplomas, BAs, MScs, PhDs) relative to the "branded" certificates of other higher education institutions. After all, what is important to students in the competition for jobs is how an individual is judged relative to others. If only five per cent of the population have a university degree, it matters far less what reputational capital is attached to the qualification than in a situation where 30 per cent of labour market entrants have an equivalent qualification.

Hence, although a university education can offer the prospect of a middle class "career" to a reduced proportion of students in higher education, there is little to suggest that the demand for higher education will decline in the coming decades. The decline of bureaucratic careers and the absence of relative employment security means that a university education offers the opportunity to avoid long-term unemployment or a life in low-waged, low-skilled work. To express this more formally, investment in tertiary education has become a form of "defensive" expenditure, especially for those who have not gained access to elite colleges and universities. Thurow and Lucas suggested that "education becomes a good investment, not because it would raise an individual's income but because it raises their income above what it will be if others acquire an education and they do not" (cited in Hirsch, 1977, p. 51).

A further expansion of higher education can also be anticipated because it offers governments in post-industrial societies a partial solution to youth unemployment. With the increasing application of information technology modern societies require less in the form of human labour. Accordingly, not only are rates of unemployment likely to continue to be high beyond the year 2000 but also there is less need for individuals' working years to be as extensive as they were in the past. In order to reduce the demand for labour force participation, therefore, university participation delays entry into the labour market just as early retirement fulfils a similar function for older age groups. Indeed, access to higher education for young people keeps alive the meritocratic ideal of a middle class career. For older or more mature students, universities offer opportunities for retraining and career change. But equally as important is their role for the purposes of *identity reconstruction*. They offer a context within which mature students are able to "step-out" of their everyday taken for granted identities and review their life experiences. It is not surprising, therefore, that for some of these students attending university is associated with the break-up of

partner relationships and the reconstitution of personal networks, cultural interests and socio-political activities. Hence, although access to higher education can have significant benefits associated with individual self-development, the nurturing of middle-class occupational aspirations at a time when these are likely to remain extensively unfulfilled suggests that in the next decade the problem of "over-education" will become a major political issue.

The fact that we remain some way from a "virtual" university system is also explained by the fact that the mode of transmission and the social context in which it takes place is often as important as curriculum content. As employers in flexible organizations emphasize personal and social skills, the university as a "finishing school", nurturing the appropriate forms of cultural capital, has become even more important to students aspiring to enter professional and managerial "careers". The importance of the university as a source of social education was clearly recognized by mature students in a study about higher education and corporate restructuring we conducted in the early 1990s (Brown and Scase, 1994). They realized that having to leave the campus after lectures in order to fulfil work and family obligations deprived them of the opportunity to socialize with other students and develop contacts which could prove to be extremely useful once they enter the labour market. Hence, a key role of campus universities is to manufacture personal and social identities which modern learning technologies cannot supersede. In conclusion, it can be suggested that the relationship between systems of higher education and the occupational orders of advanced economies are increasingly ambiguous, despite attempts to make them vocationally more relevant. The growth of flexible organizations has reinforced the divide between "elite" and "mass" forms of higher education. Notwithstanding this, they have fulfilled other sociological as well as psychological functions which have emerged as modern society has evolved from the stage of industrialism to the age of information.

But, with the exception of the most prestigious institutions, they may no longer be the gateway to social mobility that they were in the past!

Note

1. The use of the term charisma in this context differs from the idea of an elite of extraordinary people such as religious prophets, military heroes or political leaders. Our use of the term recognized that the qualities of charisma are more attenuated and accessible to a much larger proportion of the population (Shils, 1965, 1968).

References

Ball, C. 1990: More means different: wider participation in better higher education. *Journal of the Royal Society of Arts (RSA)*, October, 743–57.

Bourdieu, P. and Passeron, J. 1964: *The Inheritors: French Students and Their Relation to Culture*. London: University of Chicago Press.

—— 1977: *Reproduction in Education, Society and Culture*. London: Sage.

Brown, P. 1995: Cultural capital and social exclusion: some observations on recent trends in education, employment and the labour market. *Work, Employment and Society*, 9, 29–51.

Brown, P. and Scase, R. 1994: *Higher Education and Corporate Realities: Class, Culture and the Decline of Graduate Careers*. London: UCL Press.

Carnevale, A. and Porro, J. 1994: *Quality Education: School Reform for the New American Economy*. Washington, DC: US Department of Education.

Confederation of British Industry (CBI) 1994: *Thinking Ahead: Ensuring the Expansion of Higher Education into the 21st Century*. London: CBI.

Fisher, I. 1927: *The Nature of Capital and Income*. London: Macmillan.

Fromm, E. 1962: Personality and the Market Place. In S. Nosow and W. Form (eds), *Man, Work and Society*. New York: Basic Books.

Gerth, H. and Mills, C. W. 1958: *From Max Weber: Essays in Sociology*. New York: Oxford University Press.

Goffee, R. and Scase, R. 1995: *Corporate Realities: The Dynamics of Large and Small Organizations*. London: Routledge.

Handy, C. 1989: *The Age of Unreason*. London: Hutchinson.

Hirsch, F. 1977: *The Social Limits to Growth*. London: Routledge & Kegan Paul.

Jacoby, H. 1973: *The Bureaucratization of the World*. Berkeley: California University Press.

Kanter, R. 1989: *When Giants Learn to Dance*. London: Simon & Schuster.

Merton, R. 1967: *Social Theory and Social Structure*. New York: The Free Press.

Schultz, I. W. 1968: Human Capital. *International Encyclopedia of the Social Sciences*, 2, 278–87.

Shils, E. 1965: Charisma, order and status. *American Sociological Review*, 30, 199–213.

—— 1968: Charisma. *International Encyclopedia of the Social Sciences*, 2, 286–300.

Whyte, W. 1965: *The Organization Man*. Harmondsworth: Penguin.

Wilensky, H. 1960: Work, careers, and social integration. *International Social Science Journal*, 12, 543–60.

21

Inequality and Affirmative Action: Sociological Perspectives

Charles Jaret

Introduction

This chapter provides a sociological analysis of social inequality and a policy supposedly designed to reduce it – affirmative action. It is a multi-perspective analysis, offered in the belief that having several distinct conceptual perspectives for examining social phenomena is a strength, not a weakness, of sociology. I will show how three paradigms each provide insights into inequality and affirmative action: functionalism, conflict theory, and symbolic interactionism. My goal is to show that socio-logical thinking is very helpful in understand-ing the origins of affirmative action and useful in clarifying the assumptions and viewpoints adopted, consciously or unconsciously, by in-dividuals, interest groups and state officials who have supported or opposed affirmative action. Although affirmative action (or positive action/discrimination as it is called in some countries) can seek to address various forms of social inequality this discussion is limited to inequality between racial–ethnic groups (often termed "minority groups") in the USA.

Inequality and Affirmative Action: An Overview

Before beginning we should clarify our central concepts: inequality and affirmative action. Social inequality occurs with regard to dif-ferences in (a) income, wealth, and occupa-tional position; (b) educational level and mental or physical health; (c) respect, honor, and prestige; and (d) political power and influence in decision-making. For example, there are some blacks with high incomes and some whites with low incomes but the average income of blacks is much lower than the average income of whites.

Affirmative action refers to special efforts to improve the opportunities and outcomes for minority groups suffering disadvantages such as higher rates of poverty, unemployment, and deprivation than the rest of society. These disadvantages are often seen as the result of discrimination and, accordingly, affirmative action is supposed to reduce current dis-crimination against minority groups or redress the effects of past discrimination. Its effective-ness, for example with regard to occupational achievement, would be measured by a decline in the difference between the percentages of blacks and whites in prestigious or well-paid occupations (which does not necessarily lead to society having less occupational inequality overall).

Modern affirmative action began during Presidents Kennedy's and Johnson's adminis-trations and was intended to mean bringing minorities into the applicant pool but hiring and promoting on criteria of merit (Graham, 1992, p. 55). The words "affirmative action" appeared in the 1964 Civil Rights Act (Title 7 outlawing employment discrimination) and in Executive Orders for fair employment by Kennedy (1961) and Johnson (1965). By 1968, however, the Department of Labor's Office of Contract Compliance requested companies to provide them with "specific goals and timetables for the prompt achievement of full and equal employment opportunity" and report on the status of their "Negro," "Oriental," "American-Indian," and "Spanish-American" employees (Glazer, 1987). It also began insisting that employers known for or suspected of racial discrimination must try to hire more minority workers to reach a target percentage of their employees or else they would lose federal contracts (e.g., the employment goal in the "Philadelphia Plan" for construction jobs was 30 per cent, the metropolitan area workforce's percentage black). In ensuing years pressure to award more benefits to minority groups produced stiff resistance to affirmative action in some quarters. It generated conflict as it was extended to new areas (e.g., education, voting rights) or as changes were proposed or made in the groups receiving affirmative action benefits. Law suits and legislative and administrative efforts are currently in process that may greatly reduce the legal and practical status of affirmative action.

Much affirmative action policy comes from federal, state, or local government initiatives in response to grievances and protests by groups claiming they were and still are subject to racism and discrimination. Affirmative action remedies have been prescribed by judicial decrees, legislative acts, presidential executive orders, and municipal ordinances. These include requiring companies to interview, hire, or promote people from certain minority groups, requiring voting district boundaries that almost guarantee a candidate from a particular minority group will be elected, or requiring city agencies to purchase a certain percentage of their goods and services from minority-owned businesses. However, not all affirmative action plans result from governmental efforts; some are adopted by businesses, labor unions, and universities either on their own volition or through negotiation and conflict resolution (e.g., preferences for minority applicants to college or law school; job training programs that take equal numbers of blacks and whites).

Sociological Perspectives on Inequality and Affirmative Action

We now explore inequality and affirmative action from three sociological perspectives, each of which provides distinctive insights and questions.

Inequality and Affirmative Action From a Functionalist Perspective

From a functionalist perspective social phenomena are explained in terms of their purposes or the effects they seem to have for society as a whole, and are evaluated in terms of their contribution to the "health" and viability of society. Both inequality and affirmative action may be evaluated from this perspective. If either performs a vital service for society efficiently and without harmful side-effects it is considered valuable or perhaps essential to society. If either detracts from society's well-being then it is considered pathological. If either performs a useful purpose inefficiently or with bad side effects it is seen as problematic – to be reformed or replaced with more effective functional alternatives that enable society to achieve its optimal level.

Functionalism has strongly influenced both the analysis of inequality in the USA and the shaping of early affirmative action policy, as we now show.

Davis and Moore's (1945) functionalist theory argues that inequality (i.e., people holding certain jobs receiving more money or prestige than other people) is necessary for the well-being of society. They contend that in any society certain positions or activities are more important to the general welfare than others, and that many of these also require greater skill, ability, or diligence than the average member of society has. Giving people in these vital positions higher rewards (e.g., more money or prestige) than other people is a way of inducing and motivating the "right" people (those with the most potential talent) to work to develop the necessary skills and then take up those essential but more demanding tasks.

Thus the functionalist position is that inequality serves an essential purpose in society. The functionalist interpretation, however, does *not* say that *all* forms of inequality are essential or "good" for society; instead inequality is necessary if, and only if, it results in channelling the "best qualified" individuals into the important social positions that need their rare talents. If a system of social inequality prevents or inhibits talented individuals in a particular category (e.g., blacks, women) from being recruited into important positions, then a functionalist would say that this particular system is dysfunctional. In other words, from the functionalist perspective, the "healthy" society is a meritocracy, not an aristocracy.

During the policy's formative years (the 1960s and 1970s) supporters and opponents of affirmative action both argued from a functionalist perspective, but they differed on the key issue of whether such action contributes to the well-being or detriment of society. Supporters claimed it was needed in order to improve the functioning of society by opening up jobs to talented and capable minority group members and shrinking the "cancer" of racism. They pointed to evidence that discrimination prevented minority group members from getting good jobs for which they had talent or credentials. They further argued that racial discrimination contradicted central American values of fairness and equality – it was like a dangerous infection which if not eradicated would hurt society in many ways. In the mid-1960s however most supporters of the Civil Rights Act and Executive Orders conceived of affirmative action in its mildest form – as a way of making job opportunities more available to minorities by seeking out minority applicants and being fairer in hiring and advancement decisions. Congressional leaders carefully cast affirmative action and equal employment opportunity in "color-blind" terms – discrimination against *any* racial-ethnic group was not permitted and no group was to be favored or given "preferential treatment" (Glazer, 1987; Graham, 1992).

It was not long, however, before the idea that African-Americans needed or deserved special considerations above and beyond simple "equality of opportunity" was broached in the context of affirmative action. Some observers take President Johnson's 1965 Howard University speech, where he said the real issue is "equality as a fact and as a result" (meaning more and faster movement of blacks into better jobs and schools), as an early sign that affirmative action would move towards encouraging preference for blacks in workplaces, schools, and political positions.

Opponents claimed that affirmative action programs would be dysfunctional because they lead to hiring and promoting less qualified or even incompetent people, which would lower overall productivity. They feared that pressure to have "appropriate" percentages of minority workers would cause employers and colleges to pass over the best qualified person (presumably white) and take a less well-suited minority group member for the job. To buttress their argument affirmative action critics showed that most members of minority groups protected by affirmative action did worse than whites on various tests that allegedly measure a person's qualifications or talent for a job (e.g., job placement tests, SAT scores, medical school exams). Supporters argued back that these tests were not valid, perhaps because they are culturally biased, or that the results should be dismissed on other grounds. They asserted that affirmative action beneficiaries could do well on the job or in school and that by adding needed racial-ethnic diversity they make the company or school better able to adapt to America's changing social and demographic environment.

In the above discussion, the imprint of a functionalist perspective is clear. When affirmative action plans were being formulated the most popular images crafted for American society (Kennedy's "New Frontier," Johnson's "Great Society") were functionalist. They held that society's "best and brightest" could create social programs to produce the optimal society and that a new value system – one really committed to a racially integrated society free of discrimination – was emerging. The massive 1963 March on Washington symbolized this alleged new value consensus supporting social and political change to attain racial integration and equality.

A purely functionalist interpretation of affirmative action, however, is inadequate. As it became a more controversial and sharply contested issue, arguments and insights about inequality and affirmative action derived from other viewpoints were used by people on all sides of the issue. The rest of this chapter discusses two, conflict theory and symbolic interaction, that are helpful in analyzing the subject.

Inequality and Affirmative Action From a Conflict Perspective

In contrast to the functionalist image of society having a strong consensus on basic values and consisting of cooperative parts striving for optimal performance, a conflict perspective sees society as like a battlefield where individuals, groups, and classes vie for material goods, economic resources, prestige, and power. By adopting a conflict viewpoint we observe that in any society or organization, certain individuals, types of people, or groups gain control over important social institutions and use this power to give themselves more material rewards, more rights and privileges, and other advantages that yield better life chances than are available to the rest of the population. Less advantaged people also organize into interest groups that compete and struggle over "a piece of the pie." The resulting societies are stratified by class, sex, age, spatial, and racial-ethnic categories.

A conflict perspective directs our attention to the ways socioeconomic inequality is created and maintained. Most important, vis-à-vis affirmative action, are coalition-building, divide and rule tactics, gate-keeping, and ideological hegemony. A conflict perspective also shows that the "normal" workings of the system reproduce existing inequality, so reducing inequality may require doing things that contradict what the dominant system defines as just, legal, or fair.

To illustrate a conflict perspective applied to racial inequality, we summarize James

Blackwell's (1990) ideas. He proposes that achieving racial equality requires changing the power relations among groups. Dominant group members (whites) benefit from the creation and maintenance of inequality and devise ways of consolidating, protecting, or expanding their benefits and privileges. They control valuable resources and important institutions, use them to serve their own needs first, and also use their power to limit the access other groups have. One way they do this is by establishing authoritative standards and procedures that serve a "gate-keeping" function (screening out all but a select few of the subordinate group).

From these ideas come four observations. The first is explicit recognition that ethnic groups *compete* with each other. Ethnic groups can be thought of as interest groups with competing claims for power and resources rather than groups with distinct subcultures that coordinate to perform vital functions for society as a whole. In his Howard University speech President Johnson said, "You do not take a person who, for years, has been hobbled by chains and liberate him, bring him up to the starting line of a race and then say, 'you are free to compete with all the others,' and still believe that you have been completely fair." Affirmative action was begun as an adjustment in the "foot race" (socioeconomic competition) to make it fairer for blacks – to take away the advantage whites had and create a "more level playing field." As such, affirmative action was applied to the full occupational range, not just society's "top" positions. Besides affecting who goes to medical school, affirmative action plans helped decide which unskilled factory workers receive training for new skills so they can be promoted, who are hired as police or fire-fighters, and which companies get government contracts for everything from legal and financial services to installing toilets in city buildings.

Second, the conflict perspective highlights the idea that change does not come without pressure. Martin Luther King Jr (1963) wrote: "History is the long and tragic story of the fact that privileged groups seldom give up their privileges voluntarily." Affirmative action plans were established only after civil rights groups convinced American political leaders in the 1960s that promises not to discriminate and laws making it illegal were not having much effect, and then pressured them by pointing out that minority communities were angry enough to cause massive disruption and damage unless something was done to open up more employment and educational opportunities for them. In the late 1960s and early 1970s, lobbying and political pressure on or by government officials in bureaucratic agencies like the Equal Employment Opportunity Commission, the Office of Federal Contract Compliance, and the federal courts resulted in the adoption of minority hiring goals and timetables. Employers who resented interference in their discriminatory hiring and promotion practices and many whites who felt that affirmative action narrowed their own employment prospects resisted it via political pressure, law suits, and evasive behavior.

The third observation is that the competitive system in the USA is unfair because it really does *not* give people an equal opportunity for socioeconomic success. Institutionalized unfairness of biased gate-keepers and "American apartheid" (Massey and Denton, 1993), which isolates poor racial minorities in the worst neighborhoods and schools, "screens out" all but a select few. Many job opportunities are advertised in a "word of mouth" fashion within social networks containing few blacks or other minorities, so they do not have a fair chance to obtain these. Great discrepancies are allowed in the funding of public schools districts attended by poor blacks and affluent whites. Housing discrimination makes it hard for blacks to move to areas with better schools, so many receive inferior educations and do poorer on tests or other measures used as criteria for hiring or acceptance decisions. These realities lead affirmative action supporters to argue that it is a myth that all Americans have equal opportunities to succeed and until there really is a fairer system that does not favor the dominant group a policy like affirmative action is needed.

Fourth, a conflict perspective suggests that groups in competitive situations seek allies or coalitions with others who are willing and able to assist, or they try to weaken their adversary by creating divisiveness within the opponent's ranks. Coalition building occurred in the battles over affirmative action – other groups (Hispanics, women, people with disabilities) sought to benefit from it; they joined with blacks and formed a stronger "civil rights lobby" calling for affirmative action. Attempts at weakening an adversary by trying to fragment it also occurred, and account for a puzzling aspect of affirmative action's history. Although affirmative action is mainly supported by Democrats and opposed by Republicans, some key decisions that pushed it towards using racial quotas were made in Republican President Nixon's administration. Part of the reason is that Republican leaders thought affirmative action might be used to weaken the Democratic labor union-black coalition (Graham, 1992). Specifically, they supported the "Philadelphia Plan," an affirmative action program Republicans thought might weaken construction unions and split white and black workers; they also felt that if affirmative action produced a larger black middle class much of it could be attracted away from the Democrats to become Republican voters.

That affirmative action might widen divisions between groups is a real concern. Cynical critics argue that it is a perfect policy for getting groups to fight with each other over the limited opportunities that now exist instead of uniting to demand more opportunities for everyone in need. But supporters answer that what is needed is both a "larger pie" and careful scrutiny, via affirmative action, to insure that minority groups get a "fair share" of the pie.

Finally, we note that conflict over affirmative action occurs on two levels. One is direct competition for jobs, places in good universities, business contracts, etc., and involves the pressure of public protests, law suits, votes, and other forms of political influence. The other is ideological and involves competition among opposing voices for the "moral high ground." It is a battle for people's hearts and minds and is fought out in essays, lectures, editorials, radio talk shows – anywhere people argue over whether affirmative action is "the right thing to do." To elucidate this issue a third sociological perspective, symbolic interaction, is useful since one of its strengths lies in analyzing the symbolism and rhetoric found in disagreements over the interpretation and definition of contested situations.

Inequality and Affirmative Action from a Symbolic Interaction Perspective

The symbolic interaction perspective on inequality, which is given insufficient attention in most sociology textbooks, suggests that "social reality" is more a product of fluid processes than concrete structures. Inequality is created and reproduced during interaction processes as we compare and argue about our subjective understandings and definitions of the situation and as we negotiate and manipulate our identities using symbols and other impression management devices (Collins, 1994). Thus inequality is a "socially constructed arrangement," *not* an automatic or pre-ordained outcome based on inherent superior or inferior qualities of certain kinds of people. For example, Everett Hughes studied the privileged status enjoyed by doctors and lawyers and found that it was due to these professions' control of their credentialing system and their proficiency in occupational "impression management" (i.e., how they shaped the public's perceptions and beliefs about these occupations).

Symbolic interactionism also shows us that even our personal identity (sense of self) emerges and is constructed through subtle and obvious social interactions and comparisons, so that being perceived and treated as inferior, unequal, or undeserving by significant others in one's reference groups could negatively affect one's self-concept. Finally, symbolic interactionists argue that the maintenance or disruption of any system of inequality is based ultimately on people's feelings and beliefs about how much wealth, income, or status they have a right to have and

what, if any, redistributional schemes are possible or rational. Conflicting beliefs or "definitions of the situation" on these matters often emerge. Symbolic interactionists say the one that "sticks" or dominates usually depends on the disputants' relative power ("He who has the bigger stick has the better chance of imposing his definitions of reality" [Berger and Luckmann, 1966, p. 109]), though sometimes less crude means of persuasion succeed.

Regarding affirmative action, a symbolic interaction perspective highlights three issues. The first concerns how racial–ethnic groups are defined, and which groups should receive benefits. This is a complicated matter since racial or ethnic categories are social inventions based on custom, law, ideology or political considerations, which are re-appraised and renegotiated over time. In the context of affirmative action the issue of who is to be counted as a "group member" can become contentious. For example in the process of establishing an affirmative action benefit (e.g., deciding what percentage of jobs should be made available to members of a minority group) the group may lobby to be enumerated in a way that enlarges its size. Thus Hispanic leaders succeeded in having people who are black and of Spanish ancestry officially counted as "Hispanic" rather than "Black." But once the benefit is established people may try to minimize the number of "qualified" minority group members in order to increase their own chance of receiving benefit. (In San Francisco a Chicano candidate for promotion in the fire department filed a law suit to exclude "Spanish–Americans" from affirmative action benefits slated for "Hispanics." His definition of the situation was that Spanish-American firefighters never suffered discrimination and are "not real Latinos" because they lead "a totally white life"; critics said his motive was self-interest – the elimination of rival candidates.) Thus the very existence of affirmative action generates lively and divisive discourse about group identity and which groups should receive benefits (other racial-ethnic groups that have become involved in debate over whether they deserve affirmative action benefits include Asian-Indians in the USA and Italian and Polish Americans).

A symbolic interaction perspective also looks at how claims about the rightness or wrongness of affirmative action (or its extension to specific groups) are framed and communicated. This is the battle for the "moral high ground," where "authoritative" definitions of the situation, rhetoric, and accounts based on statistics, facts, and analogies are bandied about to justify or attack affirmative action.

On the pro–affirmative action side we find assertions that white males received preferential treatment for over a century so now it's the minority groups' turn; evidence advanced that negative stereotypes are common, that employers still discriminate and that minorities suffer particularly high rates of unemployment; and claims that academic success of minority students depends on there being minority teachers as mentors and role models.

The anti-affirmative action side includes: accounts of groups that say they succeeded without receiving preferential treatment; substitution of negatively loaded words like "reverse racism" for affirmative action; charges that affirmative action rewards the less competent at the expense of better qualified people; assertions that it's impossible to make a fair decision about which groups deserve preferential treatment; contentions that affirmative action doesn't help minority group members who are in the most need and that attempts to do so lead to the "balkanization" of American society.

Perhaps the most successful part of the pro–affirmative action definition of the situation was the link it made between minority groups' lower socioeconomic condition and institutional racism. As long as policy makers and judges maintained that racially unequal results were produced mainly by the "normal" operations of "the system," they could prescribe "color conscious" affirmative

Figure 21.1 Reprinted with special permission of North America Syndicate
© North America Syndicate.

action remedies (Graham, 1992). But when, under President Reagan's administration, the importance of institutional racism was challenged, great publicity was given to minority group members who disapproved of affirmative action: their criticisms could not be dismissed as due to racism or self-interest, and thus made for powerful impression management in the fight for the moral high ground.

The final issue a symbolic interaction perspective highlights is how affirmative action can affect individuals' self-concept. Critics claim that doubts and suspicions about the abilities of affirmative action beneficiaries inevitably arise. Do they really deserve to be accepted, hired, or promoted, or are they undeserving and only getting it because they have "the right" racial-ethnic background? A number of minority authors have written poignantly about the repeated doubts and negative impressions from others as making it hard to maintain a good self-image.[1] Defenders of affirmative action respond to this using rhetorical "turn-around," asking, with mock-exaggerated concern, about the self-esteem of all the mediocre whites who received opportunities when better qualified minorities were passed over (see Figure 21.1).

Conclusion

Sociologist Nathan Glazer, in the late 1970s, wrote that a powerful "civil rights lobby" held the "moral advantage" and was so strongly entrenched in mid-level government agencies that it could force preferential treatment for minorities even if Presidents and Cabinet officers opposed it. He said affirmative action policies were unlikely to be abandoned soon (Glazer, 1983). But conditions can change, as was emphasized in our sections on conflict and symbolic interaction perspectives. It now seems opponents of affirmative action have gained the upper hand and these policies will be cut back sharply. While Glazer deemed such a change unlikely, he perceptively stated that it would only happen if the courts took the lead by reversing earlier reasoning and rulings on affirmative action cases and if a shift in both elite and public opinion on civil rights occurred. The appointment of more conservative judges to the Supreme Court during the 1980s has caused a reversal of this sort, and both elite and popular attitudes are less receptive to affirmative action than they were two decades ago. Will affirmative action disappear or will the tide turn back in its favor? That is an open question, but an understanding of inequality and affirmative action from the sociological perspectives outlined here can help you decide the stance and role you take in influencing the future outcome.

Note

1. Examples include Richard Rodriguez, *The Hunger of Memory*; Stephen Carter, *Reflections of an Affirmative Action Baby*; Shelby Steele, *The Content of Our Character*; Yolanda Cruz, "A Twofer's Lament."

References

Berger, P. L. and Luckmann, T. 1967: *The Social Construction of Reality*. Garden City, NY: Doubleday.

Blackwell, J. E. 1990: Current issues affecting Blacks and Hispanics in the educational pipeline. In G. E. Thomas (ed.) *U.S. Race Relations in the 1980s and 1990s*. New York: Hemisphere pp. 35–52.

Collins, R. 1994: *Four Sociological Traditions*. New York: Oxford University Press.

Davis, K. and Moore, W. E. 1945: Some principles of stratification. *American Sociological Review* 10, 242–249.

Glazer, N. 1983: *Ethnic Dilemmas*. Cambridge, MA: Harvard University Press.

—— 1987: *Affirmative Discrimination*. Cambridge,

MA: Harvard University Press.

Graham, H. D. 1992: The origins of affirmative action: civil rights and the regulatory state. *Annals of the American Academy of Political and Social Science*, 523, 50–62.

King, M. L. 1963: Letter from Birmingham city jail. In H. A. Bedau (ed.), *Civil Disobedience: Theory and Practice*. New York: Pegasus, pp. 72–89.

Massey, D. S. and Denton, N. A. 1993: *American Apartheid*. Cambridge, MA: Harvard University Press.

22

Up Against Nature: Sociological Thoughts on Sexuality

Stevi Jackson and Momin Rahman

Within Western societies it is often taken for granted that sexuality is "natural", guided by instincts derived from our animal ancestry, encoded in our genes and driven by our hormones. Frequently sexuality is reduced to an urge to reproduce (a view endorsed by some evolutionary biologists) even though more effective contraception has now made it possible to think of heterosexual activity as "recreation". From this perspective – known as biological essentialism – sexuality is an essential, innate, universal and pre-social element of the human constitution. Essentialism has other variants, notably the older idea that the ordering of sexual relations is "natural" in the sense of being "god given". In either case, social regulation is seen as repressing, controlling or channelling drives or urges which already exist. The single most important contribution that sociology has made to our understanding of sexuality is to critique this essentialism. Sociologists have argued that sexuality is not merely regulated, but is itself socially constructed: sexual desires, identities, activities and relationships are as much a product of a particular society and culture as any other aspect of social life. Moreover, scientific "knowledge" about the sexual is also a social product: it is constructed within specific historical contexts and encodes specific cultural assumptions about masculinity, feminity and sexuality (Fausto-Sterling, 1992; Oudshoorn, 1994). Rather than treating biology as a set of scientific "facts" existing outside the social realm we should, as sociologists, consider how our society "represents 'biology' to itself" (Delphy 1993, p. 5).

Very particular representations of biology are evident in the language we use to talk about sexuality. In everyday usage the words "sex" and "sexual" have two meanings, denoting both the physical distinction between male and female and intimate erotic activity. This linguistic confusion mirrors the social privileging of heterosexuality within which "sex" both defines men and women as two distinct categories and is what brings them together – "the sex act" means heterosexual coition. Fundamental to the essentialist paradigm is the idea that sexual difference provokes desire, that men's and women's bodies are made for each other, that sexual "normality" requires the appropriate organ being placed in the appropriate orifice (Gagnon and Simon, 1974). As in a toddler's activity centre, only certain shapes can be put into certain holes. The straight mind can conceive of men being sexual with each other only in terms of something being forced into the "wrong" hole, hence the conflation of gay male sex with anal sex. Lesbian sex is discounted because two women have *nothing* to play with (Rahman, 1994).

But once "sex" is no longer equated with heterosexual penetrative sex, it is not so easy to define. It becomes clear it is not a matter of what we do with particular parts of our bodies, but the erotic meanings which we associate with particular acts (Richardson, 1992). "Sex" – erotic activity – and "sexuality" – the totality of our erotic desires, practices and identities – then become fluid concepts, because what is deemed erotic varies historically, culturally and contextually. Sex, let alone sexuality, cannot be reduced to organs and orifices, since our bodily functions and activities are themselves invested with complex cultural meanings. Far from being fixed by nature, human sexuality is extremely variable.

Early anthropologists recorded an enormous array of diverse sexual practices existing in human societies (see Ford and Beach, 1952). More recently anthropologists have gone further, suggesting that there is no way of defining what constitutes a sexual act outside its cultural context (see, for example, Herdt, 1981). In Western societies, sexuality has a history: it has not existed unchanged over time. According to Michel Foucault (1979), sexuality as we understand it today was constituted as an object of discourse in the nineteenth century. This was not, as is commonly thought, an era of repression in which sex could not be talked about openly, but one in which there was an incitement to discourse, a deployment of power through which diverse sexualities were produced, classified and catalogued. These discourses made it possible to differentiate between "normal" and "perverse" sexualities and think of sexuality as an intrinsic attribute of each individual. Once sexuality was located as part of our inner selves, acts once considered simply as sins (to which we were all susceptible) came to define the essential character of those who engaged in them. For example, it became possible to *be* a homosexual.

The idea that sexuality is a matter of biological drives dates from this era, as does the idea that men are more sexual than women. Nineteenth-century discourses were highly gendered. Active sexuality was thought of as a masculine force, as opposed to feminine passivity and responsiveness. Paradoxically, while "normal" women were deemed incapable of autonomous desire, they were also seen as saturated with sexuality in that they were governed by their reproductive capacities. Modesty and chastity, however, were regarded as defining features of normal femininity. These ideas continued to circulate within early twentieth-century sexology in which

men's sexual response was understood as ready and spontaneous, whereas women's should only emerge in response to male tutelage (Jackson,1994). There has long been another side to this idea of feminine sexuality, an opposition between the virgin and whore. Even in Victorian times, an older model of women's sexuality as dangerously unruly lurked beneath the surface of the chaste ideal. The dualistic opposition between good and bad women has still not been entirely eradicated.

Another feature of essentialist discourse in the modern era is that it disguises moral and political judgements as scientific fact. In Western culture there is a long tradition of binary thinking in which socially approved "natural" sex is opposed to reprehensible "unnatural" sex, thus endowing nature with moral meaning (Connell and Dowsett 1992; O'Connell Davidson and Layder, 1994). This idea was originally shaped by Christian teaching in which otherwise sinful lust was acceptable only when placed in the service of God within monogamous heterosexual marriage. Non-reproductive sex, particularly acts such as sodomy, were "against god" and "against nature". Later scientific discourses incorporated this existing binary structure, translating the rationale for the positive evaluation of "natural" sexuality into a medical language of "health" and psychological functionality and an evolutionary language of species survival. Sexual desires deemed "unnatural" are still regarded as immoral but they are now also regarded as a sign of some underlying pathology.

These discourses have most often been mobilized in the defence of the patriarchal and heterosexist *status quo* – to emphasize "essential" differences between men and women and to claim that lesbian or gay sex is "unnatural". But there are other variants of essentialist thinking which have been pressed into service for different ends. One such is the "1960s" libertarian-left argument that sex is natural and good (for both men and women) and that we should all seek freedom from sexual repression. A few feminists, too, have taken up this theme arguing men and women are differentially repressed, that patriarchal control holds women's natural sexuality in check (see, for example, Sherfey 1973). Another example is the recent attempt to reclassify homosexuality as "natural" rather than "unnatural" – and so to use science to shift it across the moral divide.

But the essentialist model is too deeply flawed to serve progressive ends. In the first place, it conceptualizes the social regulation of sexuality as a repressive force and hence does not allow for the productive effects of cultural prescription (as opposed to proscription) in shaping our sexualities: our sexual lives are shaped far more by what we learn to do than what we are told not to do. In the second place, it rests on something unknowable, a hypothesized "natural" sexuality somehow uncontaminated by cultural influences. This means that it cannot adequately encompass the diversity of human sexuality. Essentialist perspectives can only account for differences in masculine and feminine sexuality in terms of "natural" differences or differential repression. Either women and men are innately different and nothing can change this, or women's sexuality is seen as more repressed than that of men. The appeal of the concept of repression is that it can carry a sense of the damage which women and gays experience within a patriarchal and heterosexual society, our sense of the difficulties we have in defining a sexuality for ourselves. But it actually takes current definitions of male sexuality as the bench-mark of unrepressed sexuality, in other words what sexuality should be like or would be like in the absence of social constraints. Subsumed within this paradigm is an equation of normal sexuality with heterosexuality, thus it is fundamentally, and not merely accidentally, both sexist and heterosexist.

It is for this reason that most feminist and gay theorists have rejected essentialism and have played a leading role in developing alternative perspectives, enabling us to think in terms of sexual oppression rather than repression. Whereas the concept of repression suggests the holding back of some underlying force, oppression focuses attention on social relations of power and domination. A socio-logical understanding of sexuality also offers us more hope of change than does the idea of repression. If sexuality is socially constructed it can also be transformed-male dominated heterosexuality is not an inevitable fact of life. In what follows we will draw on the work of these scholars in order to argue that a sociological analysis is crucial for our understanding of sexual oppression and of feminist and gay responses to it.

Our position is that gender and sexuality, while analytically distinct, are empirically interrelated. The hierarchical division between men and women profoundly affects our sexual lives – whether we are lesbian, gay, bisexual or heterosexual. These sexual categories can only exist because we think of sex in gendered terms, defining people's sexuality by the gender of those they desire. Conversely, conventional masculinity and femininity are validated through heterosexuality; hence, for example, gay men are not "real" men and gayness is conflated with effeminacy. Moreover, male domination is sustained, in part, through the institutionalization of "compulsory heterosexuality" (Rich, 1980) and its association with patriarchal marriage. We also recognize that gender and sexuality intersect with other social divisions such as those based on "race" and class, so that we each live our sexuality from different locations within society.

Questioning Compulsory Heterosexuality: the Challenge of Feminism

Sexuality has been an area of fierce debate among feminists (see Jackson, 1996; Jackson and Scott, 1996a), but there is not the space here to consider the issues which divide them. Rather we will focus on a theme common to most feminist analyses: that the current ordering of (hetero)sexual relations is detrimental to women and implicated in their subordination. The questioning of patriarchal definitions of "normal" sex highlights the capacity of feminist sociology to problematize what is taken for granted in the everyday world and thereby reveal the social processes underpinning individual sexual encounters.

As we have already noted, the "sex act" or "having sex" usually means heterosexual penetration, thus privileging this one sexual act above all others as "the real thing". Anything else is either "foreplay" (a prelude to "the real thing") or "petting" (a substitute for "the real thing"). Moreover, this act has conventionally been spoken of as something men do to women, casting men as sexual subjects and women as objects; it prioritizes male pleasure and defines women's sexuality as existing to serve male sexual "needs". Early feminist critics of "the myth of the vaginal orgasm" (Koedt, 1972) drew on mainstream sexological research which demonstrated that female orgasm centred on the clitoris rather than the vagina. Feminists turned this "discovery" to their own ends, calling for a rethinking of sexual practice and a deprioritizing

of penetrative sex (Campbell, 1980). More radically, if the vaginal orgasm is a myth then the penis ceases to be essential to female sexual pleasure and lesbian sexuality becomes a viable and attractive alternative. Many feminists, however, continue to have sexual relationships with men and strive to find new ways of conducting these relationships in keeping with a critical stance on conventional heterosexuality.

The critique of heterosexuality goes far beyond discontent with male sexual selfishness. Heterosexuality is a social institution not just a sexual preference, an institution through which men acquire rights over many aspects of women's lives, not just their bodies. Moreover, participation in heterosexuality is neither natural nor a choice. As Adrienne Rich (1980) pointed out, a whole array of social and cultural constraints persuade or coerce women into compulsory heterosexuality. Hence for some

Figure 22.1 Heterosexuality is a social institution, not just an individual sexual preference. As such it constrains how we can act. (*Pink cross code* by Angela Martin.)

women becoming a lesbian was an act of resistance: it signified solidarity with other women and constituted a refusal to service men domestically, emotionally and sexually. As Monique Wittig put it, lesbians are "escapees" from patriarchal domination, just as runaway slaves were "escaping slavery and becoming free" (1992, p. 20). For many feminists, egalitarian heterosexual relations seem an impossibility within patriarchal societies.

Heterosexual sex has indeed proved resistant to change. While information about women's sexual response is now widely available through magazines and sex manuals, this has not had the effect of transforming the meaning of sex. Despite increased emphasis on women's pleasure and ever more elaborate variations in sexual practices, the idea of penetration as the final goal is still a pervasive feature of most mainstream sex advice. This obduracy is also evident in public health information on HIV transmission. Feminists were quick to respond to new concerns about risk and sex, pointing out that sex had never been safe for women and had always been associated with fears of pregnancy, disease and sexual exploitation. Safer heterosexual sex could, they argued, be better sex ordered around more egalitarian alternatives to penetration (Coward, 1987; Richardson, 1989). However, health promotion for heterosexuals has continued to focus on penetrative sex (sex as usual, but with a condom). It is clear from recent research that young heterosexual women still find it difficult to define and demand their own pleasures, to negotiate safer sex with men and to resist being coerced into sexual activities they do not enjoy (Holland et al., 1990, 1991, 1994). Power remains a pervasive feature of intimate relations between men and women (Ramazanoglu and Holland, 1993; Ramazanoglu, 1994).

The issue of sexual coercion is another, and central, element of the critique of heterosexual practice, calling into question the construction of both male and female sexuality. Feminists have drawn connections between routine forms of sexual coercion in which women "give in" to male demands and more extreme forms of sexual violence. They have highlighted the continuities between diverse forms of sexual violence, arguing that sexual harassment, rape and sexual abuse are products of a society where men are expected to initiate and control sexual encounters, to dominate women sexually and overcome their resistance – and where women are expected to serve male needs. Hence feminists have sought to supplant individualistic accounts of sexual violence with a sociological understanding of it. In the case of rape, for example, they have not asked why some men rape, but how rape becomes possible under current social conditions. In the process they also deconstructed many of the myths which arise from essentialist understandings of sexuality – particularly the idea that male sexuality is an uncontrollable force, that if a woman is "provocative" a man "can't help himself". Here essentialist discourses have very real, material effects on women's lives since they provide men with justifications for sexual violence (Jackson, 1978; Scully, 1990) and inform the processing of rape cases by the police and courts (Clark and Lewis, 1977; Smart 1989; Brown et al., 1993; Lees, 1993).

These are by no means the only sexual issues which feminists have addressed. However, most feminist writings on sexuality have entailed a critique of institutionalized heterosexuality or of contemporary heterosexual practice. This critique continues to be elaborated and debated and informs both theory and political activism (see Wilkinson and Kitzinger, 1993; Richardson, 1996). The same is less true of gay politics. While there is a great deal of interchange between feminist, lesbian and gay theorists in the academic world, some gay activists have turned away from social constructionist perspectives and the critique of heterosexuality.

Towards a Queer Nation or Just Some Queer Notions?

Three hundred of us took over the escalator at Nordstroms – this incredible spiral thing that goes on for ever. It was like Tiananmen Square meets Busby Berkeley ... it was amazing. A whole store full of us chanting "We're here, we're queer and we're not going shopping". (Armistead Maupin, *Suddenly Home*, 1991)

In the 1970s Gay Liberation burst onto the scene with the Stonewall riots in New York, creating a new positive identity – *gay* – and a new attitude – *Gay Pride*. Since that time political priorities have changed. We now live in an age of angry Queer politics fuelled by AIDS activism and a not-so-angry Queer politics focused on the "pink dollar" and the freedom to party (Evans, 1993; Maddison, 1995). Going shopping has become as central to the maintenance of gay identity as political activism. In course of these shifts, there has been a move towards the pursuit of minority rights coupled with the endorsement of biological explanations of homosexuality. It is ironic that the name "Stonewall" is now associated with the reformist gay lobby in the UK and here, at least, no longer conjures up an image of militant direct action.

Gay liberation *was* radical. It challenged patriarchal constructions of sexuality (Edwards, 1993; Watney, 1980) and shared with feminism the assumption that sexuality was socially constructed. Its radicalism profoundly influenced the development of academic debate but has proved less resilient at the level of grass roots politics. In both the USA and the UK the alliance between the gay movement and feminism was short lived; many lesbians, disillusioned with the male dominated agenda of gay politics, turned their attention to the women's movement (Stanley, 1982; Jeffreys, 1990; Edwards, 1993; Evans, 1993). As the revolutionary fervour of the early 1970s died down, many gay activists began to retreat to a more liberal, reformist position which drove gay politics further away from feminism and an interest in the politics of gender.

At the same time, new lifestyles became possible within the commercial scene which burgeoned during the 1970s in major conurbations in the USA, UK and Australia

(Altman, 1980). The tales of *these* cities came to be based on hedonism, disco, gay pride and gay *identity*. These scenes were, and remain, male dominated – and ordered around the relatively privileged lives of affluent, predominantly white, men. With many of these gay men enjoying the economic advantages over women that heterosexual men do, they were able to build communities based on exclusively gay clubs, bars and a range of services provided for gays by gays – not to mention creating a target for the "niche marketing" of mainstream advertising companies. Gay men have come to exemplify a form of consumption founded on a self-consciously constructed identity (Evans, 1993). Their lifestyles, and the ghetto locations of the world's "gay villages", have fostered a sense of an essential, "ethnic" gay identity (Weeks, 1980; Mort, 1980; Epstein, 1992).

This "ethnic" identity has had a deradicalizing effect on gay politics, creating a more receptive audience for biological accounts of homosexuality as an innate product of the "gay brain" or "gay gene". Such accounts of gay identity can in part be understood as a response to a version of social constructionism which has found favour among the moral right (demonstrating that sociological arguments are not invariably associated with progressive politics). This is the idea that homosexuality is something which can be *promoted* by subversives and misguided liberals – that the threat thus posed to "family values" must be averted by depriving homosexuals of the chance to "corrupt" others. In the hostile climate of the 1980s, when New Right political executives were in place in both the USA and the UK, the assertion that homosexuality was "natural" became a means of claiming political rights, but it also located gays as a permanent minority. This further reinforced ethnic identification (Epstein, 1992) and rendered any critique of heterosexuality obsolete (since it became the "natural" condition of the majority). In this context many gay activists restricted their aims to the pursuit of minority rights, the quest for equality *with* heterosexuals (see, for example *Liberty*, 1994).

Activists of any kind must, of course, work

within given institutional contexts and the present social and political climate is far from supportive of Utopian ideals. Moreover, basic human rights are a necessary first step in freeing lesbians and gays from discrimination and from intrusive surveillance and regulation. Yet to frame the quest for rights in terms of equality *with* heterosexuals is to lose touch with a basic sociological insight: that homosexuality is constructed in opposition to heterosexuality, as the deviant "other" which confirms the heterosexual norm. The reliance on the assumption of an innate "difference" as the basis for claiming rights leaves heterosexuality untroubled and turns attention away from the intersections between hierarchies of gender and hierarchies of sexuality.

The AIDS epidemic has both served to reinforce the moral boundaries erected against those outside heterosexual normality and to inspire an upsurge of radical activism. The long period of official inaction on AIDS was largely due to the perception of it as a problem affecting despised and excluded "others" – gay men, Africans, drug users. When the heterosexual population was eventually seen to be at risk, there was still a reluctance to adopt the strategies for safer sex promotion which had proved effective within gay communities. As we saw earlier, there is an unwillingness to destabilize the heterosexual model of "real sex" – even when it might be a matter of life or death.

The anger provoked by heterosexist responses to the tragedy of AIDS, however, helped fuel a revival of radicalism and has facilitated a partial re-alliance of lesbians with gay men. In this context a new "Queer" politics spearheaded by groups such as ACT-UP, Queer Nation and Outrage! has emerged. Yet one of the ironies of Queer politics is that it has tended to affirm identity categories rather than to destabilize them, and is hence out of step with its academic incarnation as Queer theory. Queer theory, which is associated with post-modernist perspectives, retains a commitment to an anti-essentialist stance, to deconstructing the binaries between gay and straight, men and women, to subverting the "heterosexual matrix", the "com-

pulsory order of sex/gender/desire" (Butler, 1990, p. 6).

It is possible to see the growing diversity of dissident sexual identities, and the redefinitions of masculinity and femininity which they sometimes entail, as evidence of an emerging pluralism which will itself threaten the stability of the binary oppositions which divide us into men or women, gay or straight. This trend may be a sign of resistance, but it is doubtful it will unduly disturb basic patterns of social advantage and disadvantage. While it may be possible to maintain a diversity of gay or queer identities within specific enclaves, these will remain marginalized while heterosexuality retains its privileged place and while material inequalities between men and women persist.

What has gone awry in gay activism is that the social and cultural context in which identities are forged has been forgotten. In particular the politics of sexuality has come adrift from the politics of gender. There are those, such as Gayle Rubin (1984) who maintain that this separation is necessary for a radical politics of sexuality. We, on the other hand, see the oppression of lesbians and gays as inextricably interconnected with the oppression of women through institutionalized heterosexuality. The critique of heterosexuality might seem a queer notion, but it is central to a sociological perspective on sexuality. We should continue to defend and develop the basic sociological insight that sexuality is socially constructed. Without this we cannot hope to understand, let alone challenge, the hierarchies of gender and sexuality through which the subordination of women, lesbians and gays are perpetuated.

Conclusion

The tendency for gay politics to become lifestyle politics should not, perhaps, surprise us. One characteristic of late modernity noted by sociologists is the tendency for the self to become a project to be consciously worked on, part of an "individual" lifestyle constructed from the consumer products available to us. There is now a huge market in magazines and advice books on how to improve our health, bodily apperance, speaking skills, confidence – and, of course, our orgasms. Sexuality has become central to the reflexive project of the self (Giddens, 1992) and being "good at" sex has become a mark of distinction (Jackson and Scott, 1996b). In making our sexuality central to both personal style and the pursuit of individual fulfilment, however, we are potentially falling prey to what Steven Heath (1982) has called the "sexual fix", which encourages us to focus on our personal lives rather than wider social critique.

References and Further Reading

Altman, D. 1980: What Changed in the 70s? In Gay Left Collective (eds), *Homosexuality, Power and Politics*. London: Allison & Busby.

Brown, B., Burman, M. and Jamieson, L. 1993: *Sex Crimes on Trial: The Use of Sexual Evidence in Scottish Courts*. Edinburgh: Edinburgh University Press.

Butler, J. 1990: *Gender Trouble: Feminism and the Subversion of Identity*. New York: Routledge.

Campbell, B. 1980: Feminist Sexual Politics, *Feminist Review*, 5, 1–18.

Connell, R. W. and Dowset, G. W. 1992: The unclean motion of the generative parts; frameworks in western thought on sexuality. In Connell, R. W. and Dowsett, G. W. (eds), *Rethinking Sex: Social Theory and Sexuality Research*. Melbourne: University of Melbourne Press.

Clark, L. and Lewis, D. 1977: *Rape: The Price of Coercive Sexuality*. Toronto: The Women's Press.

Coward, R. 1987: Sex after AIDS. *New Internationalist*, March.

Delphy, C. 1993: Rethinking sex and gender. *Women's Studies International Forum*, 16(1), 1–9.

Edwards, T. 1993: *Erotics and Politics: Gay Male Sexuality, Masculinity and Feminism*. London: Routledge.

Epstein, S. 1992: Gay politics, ethnic identity. In E. Stein (ed.) *Forms of Desire*. New York: Routledge.

Evans, D. T. 1993: *Sexual Citizenship: the Material Construction of Sexualities*. London: Routledge.

Fausto-Sterling, A. 1992: *Myths of Gender: Biological Theories about Women and Men*, 2nd edn. New York: Basic Books.

Ford, C. S. and Beach, F. A. 1952: *Patterns of Sexual Behaviour*, London: Eyre & Spottiswood.

Foucault, M. 1979: *The History of Sexuality: Volume One*. Harmondsworth: Penguin.

Gagnon, J. H. and Simon, W. 1974: *Sexual Conduct: The Social Sources of Human Sexuality*. London: Hutchinson.

Giddens, A. 1992: *The Transformation of Intimacy: Sexuality, Love and Eroticism in Modern Societies*. Cambridge: Polity Press.

Heath, S. 1982: *The Sexual Fix*. London: Macmillan.

Herdt, G. 1981: *Guardians of the Flutes*. New York: McGraw-Hill.

Holland, J., Ramazanoglu, C., Scott, S., Sharpe, S. and Thomson, R. 1990: *Don't Die Of Ignorance – I Nearly Died of Embarassment: Condoms in Context*. London: Tufnell Press.

Holland, Jo, Ramazenoglu, C., Sharpe, S. and Thompson, R. 1991: *Pressure, Resistance, Empowerment: Young Women and the Negotiation of Safer Sex*. London: Tufnell Press.

—— 1994: Power and desire: the embodiment of female sexuality. *Feminist Review*, 46, 21–38.

Jackson, M. 1994: *The Real Facts of Life: Feminism and the Politics of Sexuality c. 1850-1900*. London: Taylor & Francis.

Jackson, S. 1978: The social context of rape: sexual scripts and motivation. *Women's Studies International Quarterly*, 1(1), 27–38.

—— 1996: Heterosexuality as a problem for feminist theory. In L. Adkins and V. Merchant (eds), *Sexualising the Social*. Basingstoke: Macmillan.

Jackson, S. and Scott, S. 1996a: Sexual skirmishes and feminist factions: twenty-five years of debate on women and sexuality. In Jackson, S. and Scott, S. (eds), *Feminism and Sexuality: A Reader*. Edinburgh: Edinburgh University Press.

—— 1996b: Gut Reactions to Matters of the Heart: Reflections on Rationality, Irrationality and Sexuality. Unpublished paper.

Jeffreys, S. 1990: *Anticlimax: a Feminist Perspective on the Sexual Revolution*. London: The Women's Press.

Lees, S. 1993: Judicial rape. *Women's Studies International Forum*, 16(1).

Koedt, A. 1972: The myth of the vaginal orgasm. In Koedt, A. (ed.), *Radical Feminism*. New York: Quadrangle.

Liberty 1994: *Sexuality and the State: Human Rights Violations Against Lesbians, Gays, Bisexuals and*

Transgendered People. London: National Council for Civil Liberties.

Maddison, S. 1995: A Queered Pitch. *Red Pepper*, February 1995, 27.

Maupin, A. 1991: Suddenly Home. In White, E. (ed.), *The Faber Book of Gay Short Fiction*. Boston, MA: Faber.

Mort, F. 1980: Sexuality: regulation and contestation. In Gay Left Collective (eds), *Homosexuality, Power and Politics*. London: Allison & Busby.

Oudshoorn, N. 1994: *Beyond the Natural Body: An Archeology of Sex Hormones*. London: Routledge.

O'Connell Davidson, J. and Layder, D. 1994: *Methods, Sex and Madness*, London: Routledge.

Plummer, K. 1995: *Telling Sexual Stories: Power, Change and Social Worlds*. London: Routledge.

Rahman, M. 1994: *Sexuality as identity*. Unpublished paper.

Ramazanoglu, C. and Holland, J. 1993: Women's sexuality and men's appropiation of desire. In Ramazanoglu, C. (ed.), *Up Against Foucault*. London: Routledge.

Ramazanoglu, C. 1994: Theorising heterosexuality: a Response to Wendy Hollway. *Feminism and Psychology*, 4(2), 320–1.

Rich, A. 1980: Compulsory heterosexuality and lesbian existence. *Signs*, 5(4), 631–60.

Richardson, D. 1989: *Women and the AIDS Crisis*. London: Pandora.

—— 1992: Constructing lesbian sexualities. In Plummer, K. (ed.), *Modern Homosexualities*. London: Routledge.

—— 1996: *Theorising Heterosexuality: Telling it Straight*. Buckingham: Open University Press.

Rubin, G. 1984: Thinking sex: notes for a radical theory of the politics of sexuality'. In Vance, C. (ed.), *Pleasure and Danger: Exploring Female Sexuality*. London: Pandora.

Scully, D. 1990: *Understanding Sexual Violence: A Study of Convicted Rapists*. London: Unwin & Hyman.

Sherfy, M. J. 1973: *The Nature and Evolution of Female Sexuality*. New York: Random House.

Smart, C. 1989: *Feminism and the Power of Law*. London: Routledge.

Stanley, L. 1982: "Male needs": the problems and problems of working with gay men. In Friedman, S. and Sarah, E. (eds), *On the Problem of Men: Two Feminist Conferences*. London: The Women's Press.

Watney, S. 1980: The ideology of the GLF. In Gay Left Collective (eds) *Homosexuality, Power and Politics*. London: Allison & Busby.

Weeks, J. 1980: Capitalism and the Organisation of Sexuality. In Gay Left Collective (eds), *Homosexuality, Power and Politics*. London: Allison & Busby.

—— 1995: *Invented Moralities: Sexual Values in an Age of Uncertainty*. Cambridge: Polity.

Wilkinson, S. and Kitzinger, C. (eds) 1993: *Heterosexuality: A Feminism and Psychology Reader*. London: Sage.

Wittig, M. 1992: *The Straight Mind and Other Essays*. Hemel Hempstead: Harvester Wheatsheaf.

23

Whither Welfare?

Alan Walker

Reference to the "crisis in the welfare state" became a familiar feature of public discourse in the 1980s and, during the first half of the 1990s, an economic orthodoxy has emerged in all Western societies which favours restrictions on public expenditure and the reduction of tax rates. There are undoubtedly global pressures behind this new orthodoxy, especially the drive for international competitiveness and the market-oriented policies of the international economic agencies such as the IMF, OECD and World Bank. However it would be mistaken to conclude that the policies adopted by Western governments are all the same or that their impact on national welfare provision has been similar. Thus the key task for the sociologist in approaching the controversial and value-laden topic of welfare is to disentangle rhetoric from reality. We must examine the ideological components of the dominant discourse on welfare in any society in order to understand both the goals of different commentators and the differences in approaches to welfare between countries. So, rather than attempting to crystal-ball gaze, this short essay will focus on the three sociological insights which help us to interpret different perspectives on the future of welfare: that "welfare" has a variety of meanings, that there are variations in the institutional forms of welfare provision between countries, and that there are also contrasting ideological perspectives on welfare.

What is Welfare?

In its most basic form welfare means well-being and, as such, is relatively unproblematic. However, the term was appropriated long ago by policy-makers and is used most commonly to refer to specific public policy measures such as income maintenance, health, housing, education and personal social services. It is highly revealing that such positive terms as welfare or social welfare are used to describe these public services. The impression is thereby conveyed that such services have a beneficial impact on well-being. In fact such idealistic and value-laden terms are frequently employed within the field of social policy and they tend to obscure more than they reveal. A typical example is "community care", which may evoke a warm glow among politicians but, in practice, can mean neglect by public services following de-institutionalization or the often hard labour involved in caring for a sick or disabled relative by women within the family (Walker, 1982: Finch and Groves, 1983).

The term "welfare state" itself is one that conveys a particularly misleading optimism about both the level of social development in a country with this label and the role of the state in the provision of welfare. The origins of this sociological critique of welfare are to be found in the work of Titmuss (1968, 1974). He always employed quotation marks when referring to the "welfare state" in order to emphasize that it was an aspiration rather than an achievement. Perhaps, as Mishra (1984) has argued, it is best to regard welfare state as having two meanings: on the one hand policy intention, the idea of the state taking responsibility for welfare and, on the other, the institutions and practices for actually delivering benefits and services.

Titmuss recognized the dangers inherent in taking for granted the dominant discourses on welfare and argued that public welfare may, in fact, be ill-fare for some. In particular he alerted us to the ideological components of these discourses which may disguise the true intentions of welfare and conceal who really benefits or loses from welfare provision. His sociological analysis focused on the functional similarities between different forms of welfare provision both within and beyond the state. Thus social or *public welfare* represents only one of three elements of the "social division of welfare", and is, therefore, simply the more visible part of the real world of welfare. At the same time there are other social policy measures, which although not labelled as "social welfare", share similar objectives. In particular he called attention to *fiscal welfare*, as represented by the allowances and reliefs provided through the taxation system, and *occupational welfare* consisting of all the non-wage benefits provided by employers to their staff. Fiscal and occupational benefits represent alternative methods of making social transfers (i.e. redistributing income from one group to another) but they are perceived quite differently from public welfare benefits by recipients, policy-makers and the general public. For example the receipt of public welfare may attract stigma and public accusations of scrounging whereas tax reliefs (e.g. for owner occupation) and occupational "fringe" benefits (e.g. pensions and company cars) are usually regarded as earned rights. Despite this major insight into the nature of welfare in modern capitalist societies most accounts of the welfare state still solely focus on public welfare and, therefore, this prevents a rounded picture of welfare transfers and, particularly, the impact of welfare provision on the distribution of income.

The identification of social divisions of welfare was extended later by the political economy of welfare (O'Connor, 1973; Gough, 1979; Offe, 1984). The political economy perspective identified three functions of welfare in a capitalist society – accumulation, reproduction of the workforce, and legitimation and control. For example, contracting-out of public services and privatization of public assets provide direct opportunities for private sector profit-making and thus accumulation of capital (Le Grand and Robinson, 1984; Goodin and Le Grand, 1987). Welfare-state benefits, such as child benefit, and services such as education contribute to social reproduction. With regard to legitimation and control, the social security system, for example, reinforces the primary role of the market as the main source of income, and unemployment benefits are usually tied to tests of availability for paid employment with strict regulations concerning job seeking behaviour. Some sociologists have gone so far as to argue that these functions of the welfare state make it an indispensable part of capitalism (Offe, 1984).

While the political economy perspective broadens the meaning of welfare to contextualize it in conflicting class interests it tended to ignore other divisions in society, such as gender, race and age. In recent years feminists in particular have been analysing the gendered nature of welfare provision (Dalley, 1988; Langen and Ostner, 1991) and some have begun to link patriarchy and racism (Williams, 1989) and, thereby, have opened up the possibility of understanding the processes of social exclusion from a wide variety of perspectives.

One of the implications of this multidimensional analysis of welfare in capitalist societies is that the future of welfare may imply very different things to different groups in society. For example public welfare may be cut back at the same time as fiscal and occupational welfare are enlarged. The accumulation functions of welfare may be extended by means of privatization, a process that may also widen gender and race inequalities by emphasizing ability to pay as an access criterion for welfare, because women and people from ethnic minorities are particularly likely to experience poverty and low incomes.

Which Welfare State?

Having established that welfare conveys different social meanings and outcomes for different groups and that welfare provision performs various functions, it is important to recognize, secondly, that it is unwise to generalize about the future of the welfare state for the simple reason that it takes a variety of different forms. Thus the future of a particular welfare state will depend in large part on the nature of the welfare state itself, the historical tradition behind it and the socio-political context within which it is located. The realization that the welfare state takes a variety of different forms provides an antidote to simplistic functionalist theories of convergence and globalisation. Over the last decade, the comparative sociological analysis of the welfare state has made rapid progress.

For example Therborn and Roebroek (1986) have classified welfare states according to their commitments to the core goals of full employment and social security. Their typology puts Sweden at one extreme, as a "strong" welfare state, and the USA at the other as a "weak" or "market-orientated" one. In between are four other types, with Britain being classified as a "state of socio-economic mediocrity". Esping-Andersen (1990) has contributed the most sophisticated comparative analysis so far. His starting point is T. H. Marshall's (1950) proposition that social citizenship represents the core idea of a welfare state and, as such, comprises three key elements: social rights; social stratification; and the relationship between the state, the market and the family in welfare provision.

First, the granting of social rights entails decommodification – the provision of goods and services outside of the market. This opens up the possibility of variations in the *level* of decommodification. For example some residual or minimal welfare states may promote only partial decommodification such as the provision of free education up to a maximum age. Secondly, drawing on Titmuss' social division of welfare thesis, Esping-Andersen argues that the welfare state does not only

intervene in a structure of inequality in any society, but is itself a system of social stratification. In other words, the welfare state is a *source* of inequality, for example with regard to social class, gender, race and age. The provision of social rights by the welfare state may reinforce or compete with an individual's social class position. Thirdly, there are a range of possible configurations between welfare states in the relationship between the state, the market and the family and these are clustered into three welfare regime types: "liberal" (Australia, USA, Canada), "corporatist" (Austria, France, Germany and Italy); and "social democratic" (Norway, Sweden, Finland and Denmark). Esping-Andersen does not classify the British welfare state in these clusters, but it may be seen as a hybrid lying between the liberal and corporatist clusters and, during the 1980s and early 1990s, moving closer to the liberal one (see below).

A key problem with Esping-Andersen's framework is that it fails to acknowledge the assumptions made by welfare regimes about the different positions of men and women in the labour market and the role of women in the "decommodified" domestic sphere. Thus his concept of welfare regimes is ungendered because it excludes the private/domestic sphere and, therefore, fails to recognize that women's entitlements to welfare have often depended on their roles as wives and mothers. Again this feminist critique can be taken on board in comparative analyses. For example welfare-state regimes may be seen in terms of the extent to which they reinforce or counteract the gender division of domestic labour. Thus Lewis (1992) argues that the idea of the male-breadwinner family has been an important influence in shaping welfare states and distinguishes "strong" male-breadwinner states (Ireland and Britain) which lack child-care services and maternity rights and have longstanding inequalities between husbands and wives within their social security systems, "modified" male-breadwinner countries (France) which gives women greater social rights than found under the first type; and "weak" male-breadwinner states (Sweden and Norway) which have pursued policies which give women equal status in the labour market.

Given this wide variety of welfare state forms it is obvious that both the current meaning of welfare and the impact of future changes in welfare differ significantly between different groups within one society and between societies. There are major variations in the extent and form of the provision of state welfare between different countries and, as a consequence, in the level of well-being of citizens living in different welfare states. Therefore an increase or reduction in such provision will have varying consequences. For example the effect of social security and related provision in the USA is to reduce the proportion of households below the poverty line by only around 10 per cent. This is much less than in any European Union (EU) country where the average figure is around 30 per cent and, even in Greece which has the least effective system, social transfers reduce the proportion in poverty by around 18 per cent (CEC, 1994). This means that a cut in social security in the USA would most likely hit the very poorest who rely on its minimal welfare provision whereas, in Europe, a similar cut need not necessarily be borne disproportionately by the poorest. However, the USA tolerates higher levels of poverty and deprivation than would be countenanced in western Europe and, therefore, reductions in social security may be easier to implement – a point I come back to later.

So, the future of welfare will depend to a large extent on the starting point and these differ between capitalist societies. Certainly there is no developed society without some form of state welfare provision and even the rapidly developing Asian "tigers" (Hong Kong, Korea, Taiwan and Singapore) have their own state welfare systems. Indeed classifications of welfare regimes, such as those discussed above, may be criticized as being ethnocentric for ignoring these Eastern welfare systems (Walker and Wong, 1996).

A Neo-Liberal Welfare Strategy

The second major influence on the future of welfare is the ideology of national governments. A clear demonstration of the relationship between political ideology and national welfare strategies is provided by the social policies pursued by the Conservative governments in power in Britain since 1979. In effect Britain has been used as a test-bed for a neo-liberal-inspired welfare strategy and we can observe its impact.

The New Right or neo-liberal ideology which inspired the Thatcher and Major governments in Britain combines distinct liberal and neo-conservative discourses. The market liberal dimension is concerned with the conditions necessary for a free economy, while the neo-conservative dimension gives priority to the maintenance of authority in society. At the heart of the New Right's philosophy are a commitment to individualism and a belief that state intervention in the operation of the market is damaging to its free and effective operation.

The welfare state has been a particular bone of contention for the New Right because it embodies the interventionist and egalitarian preferences of social democratic ideology as represented in the post-war Keynes-Beveridge settlement. The British government's neo-liberal-inspired strategy towards the welfare state, in essence a strategy of inequality, consists of five main interwoven strands. First, cutting expenditure on the welfare state. Second, state-subsidized privatization and marketization (the extension of market principles such as charges for services) within the welfare state. Third, replacing universal benefits and services, such as unemployment benefit, with selective or "targeted" (means tested) ones. Fourth, reducing taxation to provide incentives to encourage the growth of alternative forms of private and voluntary welfare. Fifth, centralization of resource control and decentralization of responsibility for operations, thereby reducing pressure to increase public expenditure on welfare and diverting popular criticism towards those with the task of implementing its policies.

The first Thatcher government came to power in 1979 committed to rolling back the frontiers of the welfare state. It insisted in its first public expenditure white paper that "higher public expenditure cannot any longer be allowed to precede, and thus prevent, growth in the private sector" (HM Treasury, 1979, p. 2). The specific objective has been to limit the growth of public spending and, thereby, to reduce it as a proportion of national income. Because expenditure on the welfare state (excluding fiscal welfare) makes up around two-thirds of total expenditure (social security alone comprises one-third of the total) a policy of constraint could not avoid these programmes even if ideology had not placed them in the firing line. Moreover, because the government has increased expenditure to promote its own authority (e.g. defence, police, prisons) and that of the market (e.g. subsidies to the private sector) and has maintained a high level of unemployment as a consequence of its deflationary monetarist economic strategy, public welfare has had to yield a much larger than average proportion of spending cuts. This results in greater need for welfare just as the tax base for financing it has been reduced.

During the Thatcher government's first two terms of office, measures affecting the traditional realm of the welfare state were largely confined to the overall policy of constraint on spending, piecemeal privatization and limiting the scope of social security by targeting benefits towards the poorest. Some programmes were cut directly, particularly public sector housing provision which has been reduced by more than three-fifths since 1979 (though spending on that aspect of social security linked to housing has trebled). Growth in other areas has been held back relative to inflation and the rise in need for welfare spending resulting, for example, from demographic changes such as the ageing of the population. The health service and the personal social services have been systematically underfunded in this way.

The most significant cut in social spending occurred within the social security system when, soon after coming to office, the government altered the uprating role for pensions and related benefits so that they were no longer linked to rises in average earnings, only prices. This change of policy has had a cumulative impact on the basic national insurance pension received by the vast majority of older people in Britain. For example, the pension for a single person is worth £22.55 less per week in 1996 than it would have been if the uprating link with earnings had been maintained, a sum that represents more than one-third of the value of the current pension. However, most of the big changes in the distribution of income and life chances were implemented outside the traditional welfare state by fiscal and employment policy. This consisted of a strategy of reducing income tax, particularly at the higher rates, ostensibly to encourage enterprise, and the shift from an active demand-side programme of job creation to a more passive supply-side one focused on training and reductions in unit-labour costs.

With the advent of Mrs Thatcher's third term of office, following the 1987 general election, the attack on the welfare state was stepped up considerably. Thus a barrage of major policies was introduced in the late 1980s in all sectors of the welfare state which represented a concerted move against what was seen as the last important challenge to the spread of neo-liberal values in civil society. These included the creation of an internal market in the health service, the establishment of GP (family doctor) fundholders and the provision for the opting out of schools from local authority management. There was also a sustained rhetorical onslaught against the welfare state accusing it of creating dependency and stifling initiative and responsibility. Direct taxation was reduced but the emphasis shifted to indirect taxation so the overall tax take did not change.

There is not space here to examine the full impact of this strategy of reducing public welfare and increasing fiscal welfare (see Walker and Walker, 1987; Johnson, 1990; Walker, 1990). Certainly the moral justification that was used throughout the 1980s was that of "trickle-down": tax reductions for the rich would result in increased entrepreneurial activity which would benefit the poor. The reality was quite different because, in fact, inequality increased substantially during the 1980s. Between 1979 and 1992/93 the government's own statistics show that the real incomes of the poorest tenth of the population (including the self-employed) fell by 18 per cent after the deduction of housing costs. At the same time there was an average rise of 37 per cent for the whole population and an increase of 61 per cent in the real incomes of the top tenth (DSS, 1995). During this period there has also been a major rise in poverty. In 1979, 14 per cent of the population were living on or below the level of social assistance (then supplementary benefit) or the "official poverty line". By 1992 this proportion had risen to 24 per cent of the population. According to the alternative measure of low incomes favoured by the government, 9 per cent of the population were living below 50 per cent of average income after housing costs in 1979 and, by 1992/93, this had risen to 25 per cent (Oppenheim and Harker, 1996).

Of course there were in this period and continue to be global economic pressures towards increasing inequality, but one effect of the neo-liberal social and economic strategy adopted by successive Conservative governments in Britain between 1979 and 1996 has been to accelerate and accentuate those trends. As a result inequality has grown more rapidly in Britain than in any other European country (Atkinson et al., 1995). Welfare policies have played an important role in this wider strategy of inequality and, in a nutshell, they have been designed to reduce the role of the state as a direct provider of welfare and to enhance the role of the private sector. The intention has been to residualize state welfare and, thereby, to turn the British welfare state into something that more closely resembles the market-orientated systems of Australia and the USA.

The British government has had considerable success in reducing the role of the state as a *direct* provider of welfare services and in importing market principles into the welfare state. Ironically the impact of the government's social and economic strategy, such as increased poverty resulting from greater unemployment, has meant that social security spending has increased, from £48 billion in 1979 to over £80 billion in 1994/95. As a consequence of the increased demand created by its own policies, together with those resulting from socio-demographic changes such as population ageing, and the rising cost of subsidizing the private provision of welfare, the total welfare budget has not been cut substantially. However, from the perspective of those reliant on public welfare, the government's neo-liberal strategy has meant increased means-testing and social exclusion as benefits and pensions fall further and further behind average living standards.

But this welfare strategy, especially its most far reaching proposals, has met with resistance from public opinion (though in political terms this has not as yet proved salient). Since the early 1980s a political consensus has emerged and gradually strengthened among the British public supporting increases in taxation in order to devote more public expenditure to the welfare state. In 1983, 32 per cent of the population held this view and by 1993, the proportion had risen to 63 per cent (Lipsey, 1994). Thus the British government's anti-welfare-state ideology and preference for market-orientated welfare provision is not shared whole-heartedly by the general public. In their attitudes towards welfare and the role of the state the British public are more like their European counterparts than, for example, citizens in the USA. While Britons and Americans share some attitudes in common, such as the importance of extensive police powers to combat crimes, when it comes to welfare and the question of state intervention to promote welfare there are striking differences between the two populations. The average response in Britain to questions about whether the government should take responsibility for various welfare issues (such as providing health care for the sick) is more than twice as high as in the USA in stating that it definitely *should* be the government's responsibility (Davis, 1987).

There is some suggestion in this data that the residualization of the British and other European welfare states would be difficult to achieve. Though it must be pointed out that it is only the British government that has attempted to introduce a far-reaching neo-liberal welfare strategy, the rest of western Europe remains strongly committed to the welfare state. This means that the extreme neo-liberal policy prescription for welfare, such as that proposed by Murray (1984) to scrap the entire welfare state machinery, is not likely to be taken seriously in Europe. Indeed there is no sign of any widespread enthusiasm in the USA for this sort of draconian policy. Equally there does not appear to be any prospect of liberal or even corporatist welfare systems adopting Scandinavian style social democratic approaches. On the contrary, the platform of the recently elected left-wing coalition in Italy included proposals to limit the scale of state welfare provision. Similarly the Labour Party in Britain has been reluctant to promise any increases in public spending and has accepted some aspects of the welfare strategy of the Conservative government.

Because of the neo-liberal social and economic strategy pursued in Britain over the last 17 years the issue of the future of the welfare state is particularly critical. The French, Germans, Dutch, Danes and Swedes pay around 25 per cent more tax than the British and they do so largely to fund welfare provision. The question facing Britian therefore is does it want bigger and better state welfare and higher taxes or poor benefits and services than in those other European countries and the lower taxes that go with them?

Conclusion: Whither Welfare?

So where does this leave the future of welfare? A precise answer depends, as I have argued, on a particular country's starting point and the welfare ideology of the government in power. Thus it will be difficult in the USA to further residualize an already minimalistic state-welfare system. There is more scope in Europe but, apart from the recently democratized ex-Communist bloc countries, there is no indication of a rush to follow the British example. However, the global pressures towards greater competitiveness and the convergence criteria for monetary union in the EU will encourage some similarity in welfare policies over the next decade. For example, further attempts to limit public expenditure seem certain and these are likely to focus on the welfare state and particularly the largest item, pensions. This will mean the greater encouragement of private personal pensions, despite the well-known risks associated with them (Townsend and Walker, 1995). In some cases state provision of welfare will give way to a more pluralistic orientation (Johnson, 1987) such as in the care of disabled people. Transitions such as these may be interpreted as reflecting the shift from Fordism to post-Fordism (Burrows and Loader, 1994). The Keynes–Beveridge welfare state was clearly a construction of Fordism, and the transition to more flexible forms of production and the individualistic orientation that accompanies it obviously challenges the collective assumptions on which the welfare state is based. The political power base of the public sector is also challenged by the power of private sector interests, such as pension and insurance companies. Arguably however the economic security provided by a collectively organized welfare system is even more necessary in a more flexible and, therefore, insecure labour market. It is the mixture of these individualistic and collectivist policy paths that will determine the future of both the welfare state and the welfare of citizens. Thus we can say with certainty that the welfare state has a future, but what kind of future has yet to be determined.

References

Atkinson, A. B., Rainwater, L. and Smeeding, T. 1995: *Income Distribution in OECD Countries.* Paris: OECD.

Burrows, R. and Loader, B. (eds) 1994: *Towards a Post-Fordist Welfare State?* London: Routledge.

CEC 1994: *Social Protection in Europe.* Luxembourg: Office for the Official Publications of the European Communities.

Dalley, G. 1988: *Ideologies of Caring.* London: Macmillan.

Davis, J. 1987: British and American attitudes: similarities and contrasts. In R. Jowell, S. Witherspoon and L. Brook (eds), *British Social Attitudes,* the 1986 report. Aldershot: Gower, 89–114.

DSS 1995: *Households Below Average Income 1979–1992/93.* London: HMSO.

Esping-Andersen, G. 1990: *The Three Worlds of Welfare Capitalism.* Oxford: Polity Press.

Finch, J. and Groves, D. (eds) 1983: *A Labour of Love?* London: Routledge.

Goodin, R. and LeGrand, J. 1987: *Not Only the Poor.* London: Allen & Unwin.

Gough, I. 1979: *The Political Economy of the Welfare State.* London: Macmillan.

HM Treasury 1979: *Public Expenditure.* London: HMSO.

Johnson, N. 1987: *The Welfare State in Transition.* Brighton: Wheatsheaf.

—— 1990: *Restructuring the Welfare State.* Brighton: Harvester Wheatsheaf.

Langan, M. and Ostner, I. 1991: Gender and welfare. In G. Room (ed.), *Towards a European Welfare State?* Bristol: School for Advanced Urban Studies, 127–50.

LeGrand, J. and Robinson, R. 1984: *Privatisation of the Welfare State.* London: Allen & Unwin.

Lewis, J. 1992: Gender and the development of welfare regimes. *European Journal of Social Policy,* 2, (3), 159–74.

Lipsey, D. 1994: Do we really want more public spending? In R. Howell, J. Curtice, L. Brook and D. Ahrenott (eds), *British Social Attitudes,* 11th Report. Aldershot: Dartmouth, pp. 1–12.

Marshall, T. H. 1950: *Citizenship and Social Class.* Cambridge: CUP.

Mishra, R. 1984: *The Welfare State in Crisis.* Brighton: Wheatsheaf.

Murray, C. 1984: *Losing Ground.* New York: Basic Books.

O'Connor, J. 1973: *The Fiscal Crisis of the State.* New York: St Martin's Press.

Offe, C. 1984: *Contradictions of the Welfare State.* London: Hutchinson.

Oppenheim, C. and Harker, L. 1996: *Poverty – The Facts.* London: CPAG.

Therborn, G. and Roebroek, J. 1986: The irreversible welfare state: its recent maturation, its encounters with the economic crisis, and its future prospects. *International Journal of Health Services,* 16, (3), 319–38.

Titmuss, R. M. 1968: *Commitment to Welfare.* London: Allen & Unwin.

—— 1974: The social division of welfare. In *Essays on the Welfare State.* London: Allen & Unwin.

Townsend, P. and Walker, A. 1995: *The Future of Pensions.* London: Fabian Society.

Walker, A. (ed.) 1982: *Community Care: The Family, The State and Social Policy.* Oxford: Blackwell.

—— 1990: The Strategy of Inequality. In I. Taylor (ed.), *The Social Effects of Free Market Policies.* Brighton: Harvester Wheatsheaf, 29–48.

Walker, A. and Walker, C. (eds) 1987: *The Growing Divide,* London, CPAG.

Walker, A. and Wong, C. K. 1996: Rethinking the Western construction of the welfare state. *International Journal of Health Services,* 26 (1), 67–92.

Williams, F. 1989: *Social Policy: A Critical Introduction.* Cambridge: Polity.

24

McDonaldization and Globalization

George Ritzer

I created the term "McDonaldization" to refer to

the process by which the principles of the fast-food restaurant are coming to dominate more and more sectors of American society as well as of the rest of the world. *(Ritzer, 1996, p. 1)*

The idea is derived from Max Weber's famous theory of the rationalization of the Occident and ultimately the rest of the world. (Weber, 1968). Weber believed that the West was coming to be increasingly dominated by what he called "formal rationality," or a series of rules, regulations and structures that increasingly constrain people to seek the best possible means to whatever end they are seeking (Kalberg, 1980). His paradigm for this type of rationality was the bureaucracy with its hierarchy of offices, its well-defined spheres of competence, its codified rules and its unique capacity to handle the demands of mass administration. The McDonaldization thesis asserts that while bureaucracies continue to be important today, a better paradigm of the rationalization process is the fast-food restaurant. As well as being the epitome of formal rationality, its success has led to it becoming a model to be emulated not only by all sorts of businesses, but many other organizations and institutions as well. McDonaldization is my term for the way the rationalization process is made manifest as we move towards the twenty-first century.

McDonaldization may be further specified in terms of its five basic dimensions.

Efficiency

The first element of McDonaldization is efficiency, or the choice of the optimum means to a given end, whatever that end may happen to be (and sometimes without regard for the wider social consequences). For the fast-food restaurant efficiency might be defined as serving the largest number of customers with the smallest number of employees. Many aspects of the restaurant illustrate this such as drive-through windows, or turning customers into unpaid laborers. For example, customers are expected to stand in line and order their own food (rather than having a waiter do it) and to "bus" their own paper, plastic and styrofoam (rather than having it done by a busperson). Fast-food restaurants have also pioneered the movement toward handing the consumer little more than the basics of the meal. The consumer is expected to take the naked burger to the "fixin bar" and there turn it into the desired sandwich by adding such things as lettuce, tomatoes and onions. While we may have some control (within strict limits) of how much of these "extras" to put on, it means therefore that we are all expected to log a few minutes a week as sandwich makers. In a more recent innovation, we are now handed an empty cup and expected to go to the fountain and fill our cups with ice and a soft drink, thereby spending a few moments as what used to be called a "soda jerk." In some ultra-modern fast-food restaurants people are met by a computer screen when they enter and they must punch in their own orders. In these and other ways, the fast-food restaurant has grown more efficient (often by imposing inefficiencies on the consumer).

Calculability

The second dimension of McDonaldization is calculability. McDonaldization involves an emphasis on things that can be calculated, counted, quantified. In terms of the latter it means a tendency to emphasize quantity rather than quality. This leads to a sense that quality is equal to certain, usually (but not always) large, quantities of things.

As in many other aspects of its operation, McDonald's emphasis on quantity (as reflected, for example, in the *Big Mac*) is mirrored by the other fast-food restaurants. The most notable is Burger King which stresses the quantity of the meat in its hamburger called the *Whopper* and of the fish in its sandwich called the *Whaler* (recently renamed, not surprisingly, *Big Fish*). At Wendy's, we are offered a variety of *Biggies*. Jack in the Box has its *Colossus*, Pizza Hut its *BIGFOOT* pizza, and so on. In recent years the tendency has been for the fast-food restaurants to push ever-larger servings. For example, McDonald's now offers a *Super-Size* fries which is a portion 20% larger than a large order. Then there is the advent of the *Double Quarter Pounder* and the *Triple Cheeseburger* (Elmer-DeWitt, 1995, pp. 60–5). (It is worth noting that fast-food restaurants sometimes design packaging that gives the misleading impression of large quantities.) This emphasis on quantity in a McDonaldized society is not restricted to fast-food restaurants. To take one example, United Airlines boasts that it serves more cities than any other airline.

What is particularly interesting about all this emphasis on quantity is the seeming absence of interest in communicating anything about quality (except, perhaps, when they fear a loss of business [quantity] because of adverse publicity about the quality of their burgers or the ecological damage alleged to be caused by some of their packaging). Thus, for example, United Airlines does not tell us anything about the quality (for example, passenger comfort) of their numerous flights. The result is a growing concern about the decline or even the absence of quality, not only in the fast-food business, but in society as a whole. Were fast-food restaurants interested in emphasizing quality, they might give their products such names as the *Delicious Mac*, or the *Mac with Prime Beef*, or the *All Beef Frankfurter*. But the fact is that typical fast-food customers, or more generally those who patronize McDonaldized systems, know they are *not* getting the highest quality food.

Predictability

Rationalization involves the increasing effort to insure predictability from one time or place to another. In a rational society people want to know what to expect in all settings and at all times. They neither want nor expect surprises. They want to know that when they order their *Big Mac* today it is going to be identical to the one they ate yesterday and the one they will eat tomorrow.

The fast-food industry perfected things like replicated settings, scripted interactions ("Have a nice day") with customers, predictable employee behavior, and predictable products. As Robin Leidner puts it, "The heart of McDonald's success is its uniformity and predictability . . . [its] relentless standardization" (Leidner, 1993, pp. 45–7). Later she argues, "There is a McDonald's way to handle virtually every detail of the business, and that doing things differently means doing things wrong" (p. 54). While McDonald's allows its franchisees and managers to innovate, "the object is to look for new innovative ways to create an experience that is exactly the same no matter what McDonald's you walk into, no matter where it is in the world" (p. 82).

Control Through Non-human for Human Technology

Two further elements of McDonaldization – increased control and the replacement of human by non-human technology – are closely linked so I will discuss them together. Non-human technology is used both to replace human labor as far as possible, and to control the behavior of those people (both workers and customers) who remain. The great sources of uncertainty and unpredictability in any rationalizing system are people – either the people who work within the systems or who are served by them. On the production side it is most likely to do this by steadily replacing people with non-human technologies. After all, technologies like robots and computers are far easier to control than humans (except, perhaps, for fictional computers like HAL in *2001: A Space Odyssey*). Those who continue to labor within McDonald's are better controlled by these new technologies. These non-human technologies also exert increasing control over people served by the system (for example, uncomfortable chairs in some fast-food restaurants make customers want to get up and leave after 20 minutes).

McDonald's has developed a variety of machines to control its employees. When a worker must decide when a cup is full and the soft drink dispenser needs to be shut off, there is always the risk that the worker may be distracted and allow the cup to overflow. Thus, a sensor has been developed that automatically shuts off the soft-drink dispenser when the cup is full. When an employee must watch over the french-fry machine, there is the danger that misjudgment may lead to fries that are undercooked, overcooked, or even burned. Ray Kroc (the founder of the McDonald's chain) fretted over the problem of human judgment in the cooking of french fries: "It was amazing that we got them as uniform as we did, because each kid working the fry vats would have his own interpretation of the proper color and so forth" (Kroc, 1977, p. 131–2). Kroc's dissatisfaction with the vagaries of human judgment led to its elimina-tion and the development of french-fry machines that ring or buzz when the fries are done, or that shut the machine off and lift the french-fry baskets out of the hot oil.

Irrationality of Rationality

As Weber recognized in his analysis of bureaucracy, the rationality of work and or-ganizations may ultimately lead to irrational systems. We can conceive of the irrationality of rationality in several ways. At the most general level, it is simply the overarching label for all of the negative aspects and effects of McDonaldization. More specifically, it can be seen as the opposite of rationality and its several dimensions. That is, McDonaldization can be viewed as leading to inefficiency, un-predictability, incalculability, and loss of control. Most specifically, irrationality means that rational systems are *unreasonable* systems. By that I mean that they serve to deny the basic humanity, the human reason, of the people who work within, or are served by, them. In other words, rational systems are dehumaniz-ing systems. Thus, while in other contexts rationality and reason are often used inter-changeably, here they are employed to mean antithetical phenomena.

There are a number of ways in which the health, and perhaps the lives, of people have been threatened by progressive rationaliza-tion. One example is the high calorie, fat, cholesterol, salt and sugar content of the food served in fast-food restaurants. Such meals are the last things the vast majority of Amer-icans (and western Europeans) need. Many Americans suffer from being overweight, having high cholesterol levels, high blood pressure, and perhaps diabetes. The kinds of meals typically offered at fast-food restaurants only serve to make these health problems much worse. Even more worrisome, they help to create eating habits in children that contri-bute to the development of these, and other, health problems later in life. It can be argued that with their appeal to children, fast-food restaurants are creating not only lifelong dev-otees of fast-food, but also people who will grow addicted to diets high in salt, sugar, and fat.

The fast-food industry produces an enormous amount of trash, some of which is non-biodegradable. Many people have been critical of the public eyesore created by litter from innumerable fast-food meals strewn across the countryside. Even greater criticism has been leveled at the widespread use by the fast-food industry of virtually indestructible styrofoam. Styrofoam debris piles up in landfills creating mountains of waste that simply remain there for years, if not forever.

McDonaldized institutions not only have a negative effect on our health and on the environment, but also on some of our most cherished institutions, most notably the family. For example, a key technology in the destruction of the family meal is the microwave oven and the vast array of microwavable foods it helped generate. In fact, the microwave in a McDonaldizing society is seen as an advance over the fast-food restaurant. Said one consumer researcher: "It has made even fast-food restaurants not seem fast because at home you don't have to wait in line" (Visser, 1989, p. 42). This emphasis on speed has, of course, brought with it poorer taste and lower quality, but people do not seem to mind this loss.

All of this is not to deny the many advantages of McDonald's, but it is to point to the fact that there are counterbalancing and perhaps even overwhelming problems associated with the fast-food society. These problems, these irrationalities, need to be understood by a population which has been exposed to little more than an unrelenting set of superlatives created by McDonaldized institutions to describe themselves.

Perhaps the ultimate irrationality of McDonaldization is the possibility that we could come to lose control over the system and it could come to control us. Already, many aspects of the lives of most of us are controlled by these rational systems. However, it at least appears that these systems are ultimately controlled by people. But these rational systems can spin beyond the control of even the people who occupy the highest level positions within those systems. This is one of the senses in which we can, following Max Weber, talk of an "iron cage of McDonaldization." It can become a system that comes to control all of us.

There is another fear here and that is that these interlocking rational systems can fall into the hands of a small number of leaders who through them can exercise enormous control over all of society. Thus, there are authoritarian and totalitarian possibilities associated with the process of McDonaldization. We may come to be increasingly controlled by the rational systems themselves or by a few leaders who master those systems.

This kind of fear has animated many science fiction writers and is manifest in such futuristic classics as *1984*, *Brave New World*, and *Fahrenheit 451*. The problem is that these novels described a feared and fearsome future world, while McDonaldization is with us now, has been with us for decades, and is extending its reach throughout American society and much of the rest of the world.

McDonaldization and Globalization

McDonald's, and the process of McDonaldization it played a key role in spawning, are global phenomena. McDonald's is making increasing inroads around the world (McDowall, 1994). For example, in 1991, for the first time, McDonald's opened more restaurants abroad than in the United States (Shapiro, 1992). This trend continues and as we move toward the twenty-first century, McDonald's expects to build twice as many restaurants each year overseas than it does in the United States. Already, by the end of 1993 over a third of McDonald's restaurants were overseas. As of the beginning of 1995 about half of McDonald's profits came from its overseas operations. As of this writing, one of McDonald's latest advances was the opening of a restaurant in Mecca, Saudi Arabia (*The Tampa Tribune*, 1995). As if to counterbalance things, there is a new McDonald's in Jerusalem, one of 14 now in Israel (Lancaster, 1995).

Other nations have developed their own variants of this American institution (Israel has a chain called Burger Ranch), as is best exemplified by the now large number of fast-food croissanteries in Paris, a city whose love for fine cuisine might have led one to think that it would prove immune to the fast-food restaurant. India has a chain of fast-food restaurants, Nirula's, which sells mutton burgers (about 80% of Indians are Hindus who eat no beef) as well as local Indian cuisine (Reitman, 1993). Perhaps the most unlikely spot for an indigenous fast-food restaurant was then-war-ravaged Beirut, Lebanon; but in 1984 Juicy Burger opened there (with a rainbow instead of golden arches and J.B. the clown replacing Ronald McDonald) with its owners hoping that it would become the "McDonald's of the Arab world" (Leigh Cowan, 1984).

Other countries not only now have their own McDonaldized institutions, but they have also begun to export them to the United States. For example, the Body Shop is an ecologically sensitive British cosmetics chain with, as of early 1993, 893 shops in many countries; 120 of those shops were in the United States, with 40 more scheduled to open that year (Elmer-DeWitt, 1993, pp. 52ff.; Shapiro, 1991, pp. 35, 46). Furthermore, American firms are now opening copies of this British chain, such as the Limited, Inc.'s, Bath and Body Works.

This kind of obvious spread of McDonaldization is only a small part of that process's broader impact around the world. Far more subtle, and important, are the ways in which McDonaldization and its various dimensions have affected the way in which many institutions and systems throughout the world operate. That is, they have come to adopt, and adapt to their needs, efficiency, predictability, calculability and control through the replacement of human by non-human technology (and they have experienced the irrationalities of rationality).

While McDonald's and McDonaldization are global in character, they do not fit well what has come to be called globalization theory. While there are significant differences among globalization theorists, most if not all

would accept Robertson's advocacy of the idea that social scientists adopt "a specifically global point of view," and "treat the global condition as such (1992, pp. 61, 64).." Elsewhere, Robertson talks of the "study of the world as a whole" (1990, p. 13). More specifically, Robertson argues that we need to concern ourselves with global processes that operate in relative independence of societal sociocultural processes. Thus, Robertson argues, "there is a general autonomy and 'logic' to the globalization process, which operates in *relative* independence of strictly societal and other conventionally studied sociocultural processes" (Robertson, 1992, p. 60). Similarly, Featherstone discusses the interest in processes that "gain some autonomy on a global level (Featherstone, 1990, p. 1)."

While the reach of McDonaldization is global, it does not fit the model proposed by globalization theorists. The differences between them are clear when we outline those things rejected by globalization theorists:

1. A focus on any single nation-state.
2. A focus on the West in general, or the United States in particular.
3. A concern with the impact of the West (westernization) or the United States (Americanization) on the rest of the world.
4. A concern with homogenization (rather than heterogeneization).
5. A concern with modernity (as contrasted with postmodernity).
6. An interest in what used to be called modernization theory (Tiryakian, 1992, pp. 89–97).

The fact is that while McDonaldization *is* a global process, it has all of the characteristics *rejected* by globalization theorists – it does have its source in a single nation-state, it does focus on the West in general and the United States in particular, it is concerned with the impact of westernization and Americanization on the rest of the world, it is attentive to the homogenization of the world's products and services, it is better thought of as a modern than a postmodern phenomenon (because of its rationality, which is a central characteristic of modernity), and it does have some affinity with modernization theory (although it is not presented in the positive light modernization theory tended to cast on all Western phenomena). Thus, McDonaldization is a global phenomenon even though it is at odds with many of the basic tenets of globalization theory.

References

Elmer-DeWitt, P. 1993: Anita the agitator. *Time*, 25 January.

—— 1995: Fat times. *Time*, January 16.

Featherstone, M. 1990: Global culture: an introduction. In M. Featherstone (ed.), *Global Culture: Nationalism, Globalization and Modernity*. London: Sage.

Kalberg, S. 1980: Max Weber's types of rationality: cornerstones for the analysis of rationalization processes in history. *American Journal of Sociology*, 85, 1145–79.

Kroc, R. 1977: *Grinding It Out*. New York: Berkeley Medallion Books.

Lancaster, J. 1995: Jerusalem's beef: Is McDonald's one Americanization too many? *Washington Post*, 1 August, A14.

Leidner, R. 1993: *Fast Food, Fast Talk: Service Work and the Routinization of Everyday Life*. Berkeley: University of California Press.

Leigh Cowan, A. 1984: Unlikely spot for fast food. *The New York Times*, 29 April, 3: 5.

McDowall, W. 1994: The global market challenge. *Restaurants & Institutions*, 104(26), 1 November.

Reitman, V. 1993: India anticipates the arrival of the beefless Big Mac. *Wall Street Journal*, 20 October, B1, B3.

Ritzer, G. 1996: *The McDonaldization of Society*, revised edn. Thousand Oaks, CA: Pine Forge Press.

Robertson, R. 1990: Mapping the global condition: globalization as the central concept. In M. Featherstone (ed.), *Global Culture: Nationalism, Globalization and Modernity*. London: Sage.

—— 1992: *Globalization: Social Theory and Global Culture*. London: Sage.

Shapiro, E. 1991: The sincerest form of rivalry. *The New York Times*, 19 October, 35, 46.

—— 1992: Overseas sizzle for McDonald's. *The New York Times*, 17 April, D1, D4.

The Tampa Tribune 1995: Investors with taste for growth looking to golden arches. *Business and Finance*. 11 January, 7.

Tiryakian, E. A. 1992: Pathways to metatheory: rethinking the presuppositions of macrosociology. In G. Ritzer (ed.), *Metatheorizing*. Newbury Park, CA: Sage.

Visser, M. 1989: A Meditation on the microwave. *Psychology Today*, December, 42.

Weber, M. 1968 [1921]: *Economy and Society*, 3 vols. Totowa, NJ: Bedminster Press.

25

Green Futures?

Ted Benton

Planning for the Future

All human activities are in some way oriented to the future. Whether we put on a coat or take an umbrella when we go out will depend on our expectations of the weather. When we plan a day out or, in the slightly longer term, book a holiday, we are taking actions now on the basis of expectations both about what the future will be like, and the kinds of things we will want in that future. But many of us (not all) plan for much longer term eventualities. We talk of "planning" families and careers, take out housing loans which commit us to repayments over 20 or more years, invest in pension schemes, take out insurance policies and so on. Some of these decisions express a faith in the stability and continuity of existing external conditions of life – that we will continue to have jobs which provide enough income to maintain a family, that our relationships will survive the tests of parenting, and so on. Others, such as investing in a pension scheme, are based on expectations about change in our future life-course: that at a certain age our earning-power will cease and we will need some other source of income. Yet other decisions, such as taking out an insurance policy express anxiety about risks we face, and from which we are not otherwise (e.g. by public health and welfare provision, compensation entitlements and so on) protected.

So, sometimes we act now to achieve things we want in the future, on the assumption that the future can be predicted with some

confidence. But there are areas of life where we are much less confident of our ability to predict, and so we try to allay our anxiety by doing what we can to protect ourselves from the consequences, *if* things should go wrong. However, in each of these types of case the future is still thought of as predictable in a wider sense. We assume the continuity of our own personal identity, with roughly our current pattern of fears, wants and needs. Even in the "insurance" type of case, we assume that some reasonable assessment of the scale and type of risk to which we are vulnerable can be made. Someone with a rusty old "sit up and beg" bike (like mine) would be less likely to get it insured against theft than the proud owner of a brand new mountain bike. And, fundamental to all these cases of planning for the future is the assumption that our deliberate actions now can make a difference to how the future turns out for us – that we have at least some degree of control over our fate, and are not just at the mercy of external events.

However, there is something suspicious about my use of "we" in all this. I write as someone whose lifestyle is informed by a lot of reading – including sociological reading! – an extensive academic training, enough leisure time to be reflective about my aims and priorities in life, and, above all, the financial resources and autonomy in my working life to be able to put into practice my chosen options. Increasing numbers of people, even in the "advanced" capitalist societies of the West, are very much at the mercy of circumstances over which they have no control. A company take-over, or a shift of commercial strategy on the part of the firm they work for can shatter all their plans and expectations overnight by taking away their job. For those who have regular work, high levels of unemployment, the increasing globalization of economic activity, and the associated weakening of defensive organizations such as the trade unions mean that they are under constant pressure to intensify their efforts at work, accept declining conditions, and still face the anxieties of job insecurity. In these, and many other respects, we live in societies in which the practical power to plan ahead and to live according to one's chosen aims and values remains severely unequally distributed. Whether you are male or female, white or black, working class or middle class, employed or unemployed, fully abled or "disabled" will make a vast difference to your "life-chances" in this sense. Planning ahead is a privilege – and those who lack the privilege are increasingly being denied protection against the vicissitudes of life as the welfare state comes under unprecedented attack.

So far I've talked about planning for the future as an activity which individuals, or perhaps the members of a household might do together. In this sort of context, we normally work with a set of assumptions about what we can do something about, and what we can't. The things we can't do anything about set the conditions in terms of which we choose courses of action. We have to do our best to find out about and make reasonable predictions about those present and future conditions of action, and our choices will be largely circumscribed by the "room for manoeuvre" which those conditions allow for. Such conditions might include: expectations of the job market, the state of the housing market, one's own health and that of other members of one's household, the rate of inflation or of interest, future government tax policies, and so on, depending on the type of decision. But these "conditions of action" have a definite pattern. As we saw above, different individuals and households are differently placed in relation to them. When interest rates go up, creditors benefit, while borrowers suffer: who benefits

or suffers is to a large extent a consequence of how they are placed in relation to these wider "social structures". This is not to say that such structured conditions of action completely determine individual life-chances. If that were so, then the practices of planning in every day life that I've just been analysing would have to be seen as some kind of delusion. However, there can't be any general answer to the question "how much room is there for agency?". As I've just argued, it isn't just the costs and benefits that are conferred unequally on individuals by social structures, it is also the "room for manoeuvre" itself which is conferred unequally. Everyone is constrained by the social structure to some degree, but some people are more constrained than others. What sometimes, from the point of view of the privileged, look like self-destructive life-style "choices" (such as smoking or risky sexual activity) on the part of people with few options in life may in fact be understandable responses to that very situation of powerlessness.

But we still have to ask, where do the social structures themselves come from? Some traditions in social theory treat them as if they were rather like "facts of nature", to which we have to do our best to adapt, but which we can't change. Many people do, indeed, experience some areas of social life, such as the future state of the housing or job market, as if they were external "facts of nature". This sort of view, which excludes human agency from any role in shaping the pattern or structure of the *conditions* within which individuals live and plan their lives, has several variants. One of the most influential has been a common interpretation of Hegel's philosophy of history, in which "reason" realizes itself in the historical process, acting "through" what are experienced as the intentional acts of individual people. Another example of such a view is the idea of the "free market" often advocated by politicians of the New Right. On this version, the market is an impersonal set of "forces" which translates the chaos of individual self-interested decisions into an outcome which maximizes the aggregate welfare. On this view, we *can* intervene to alter the workings of the market, but to do so will always be self-defeating: "you can't buck the market". Yet another version of the "structures do it all" vision is called technological determinism. On that view, science and technology have their own, autonomous developmental logic. This shapes and re-shapes social structures in ways we can't prevent. This sort of view is implicit in phrases in common use, such as "you can't turn the clock back", or "you can't stop progress". People are expected just to adapt as best they can to the unstoppable demands of new technologies as they transform working lives, transport, communications and commerce. Technological determinist theories reflect this experience of powerlessness in the face of technical change, but they can be combined with various different value-orientations. Some traditions of thought, with their origins in the eighteenth century Enlightenment, give positive value to technological change, as liberating humans from vulnerability to the forces of nature, and giving them rational control over social life. For this sort of approach, scientific and technical advance either in themselves constitute "progress", or they are a necessary condition (in doing away with irrational beliefs, justifications of authority based on superstition, etc.) for progress towards rational self-determination in human affairs. For other traditions of thought, including some "greens", the technological determinist picture is retained, but the valuation of it is negative. The emphasis is put on the costs of scientific and technological "progress": the loss of human autonomy, the hierarchical systems of power and rule by "experts", the disenchantment of the world, and impending ecological disaster.

But there are other traditions of social thought, especially in sociology, which challenge structural determinism. They offer evidence and arguments to show that agency is also at work in shaping, regulating, reproducing and, sometimes, transforming the wider set of social structures which form the context of every-day life. Institutional economists, for example, argue that there is no such thing as a "free" market. Markets are social institutions, subject to legal and cultural regulation and

political direction (see Jacobs, 1994). The economic policies of the new right have been no less forms of political intervention than their Keynesian predecessors. They have been geared, among other things, to the political aims of weakening the organized power of workers *vis-à-vis* management, and individualizing employment conditions. Similarly, sociologists of science have drawn on both historical studies and philosophical arguments about the nature of science to establish the role of social and economic interests in shaping scientific research programmes, and of the wider culture in providing scientists with the crucial metaphors at the core of any scientific theory (see Webster, 1991).

So, if there is no onward march of reason, no "hidden hand" operating market forces, no autonomous logic to scientific and technical development, we are back to the question "where do the structures come from?". Sociologists influenced by Marxism or elite theory (see, for examples, Mills, 1956 and Miliband, 1973) are likely to bring the idea of agency back into the picture, but not, now, agency in the every-day life contexts analysed above. If some actors have more room for manoeuvre in relation to the structures than others, it seems a reasonable hypothesis that such relatively powerful actors, either individually or collectively, may also have powers to shape, reshape or even transform the structural conditions within which the rest of us live our lives. Boards of directors of transnational companies, institutional shareholders, government ministers, heads of state, policy-makers in business lobbies, trade unions and political parties, chiefs of staff in the armed forces, and scientific elites and other individual and collective occupants of positions of power do have power to alter the "rules of the game". Of course, even for them there is no "absolute power". They are often up against one another, as well as system-properties which may or may not be modifiable at any particular historical moment. If we find this way of looking at things convincing, then structural determinisms can be seen as a form of ideology: as so many ways of distracting attention away from the power relations and actual decision-making which shape our lives, and limit our options. Sociological studies of elites or ruling groups (see, for example, Scott, 1991) thus play a vital role in opening our minds to possibilities of democratic control which might otherwise be experienced as "fate".

These insights are of particular importance for the supporters of social movements committed to radical change – such as feminists, greens and socialists. In each case there are visions of the future, and action in the present, oriented to bringing about such a future. But unlike the "every-day" contexts of planning, some wider collective agency is evoked as the "subject" of the planned changes, and the aim is to change the structural patterns of social relationships – rather than predict and adapt to them. Any such radical social movement needs some way of understanding what it is about the present order of society which needs to be changed, some vision of the future society it wishes to create, and some idea of the grouping or alliance that can be put together to bring about the desired changes. In addition, any such movement needs some set of organizational forms and associated tactics and strategy through which the potential power of the movement can be brought to bear on existing power-structures. Traditionally, reform or revolution have been seen as the available alternatives: either to bring pressure to bear on the existing power structure from within, or to develop widespread social conflict to a level at which an overthrow of the existing powers becomes possible. For both feminist and socialist movements the reform strategy has had immense, if ultimately fragile and reversible, success: the winning of the franchise, legal rights at work, welfare provisions, universal education and so on. But two things should be noted here. One is that ruling groups arguably made concessions to "moderate" insiders only because they faced a more fundamental challenge from more radical movements. The other is that the gains from the reform strategy, especially in the case of the labour and socialist movement, have proved to be highly vulnerable to changing economic conditions and the associated

weakening of the political power of the labour movement to affect policy at the level of nation states.

Green Strategies

The contemporary green and environmentalist movement faces a similar dilemma. For some, the urgency of the ecological crisis is such that pressure must be exerted on those currently with power – national governments, businesses, policy-makers in the mainstream political parties and the like. For others, the ecological crisis calls into question the basis of the whole civilization: to call on government and business leaders to resolve it is like putting a fox in charge of the chicken-coup. A helpful way of thinking about this division is to see it in the light of a debate that took place in the early 1970s, in response to a report commissioned by the elite "Club of Rome". This used a systems-approach developed at the Massachusetts Institute of Technology to devise a computer model of the world as a limited physical system, faced with ever-growing demands from human activity: population growth, demand for raw materials, industrialization, agricultural production and pollution. Under the title *The Limits to Growth* (Meadows et al., 1972), this report had a dramatic international impact, with its forecast that exponential growth in these key areas of human activity would lead to catastrophe sooner or later. Some strategy for containing growth on a global scale had to be found. For ecological radicals, it was clear that growth was an imperative of the system itself: no amount of tinkering with the details could save us or the planet.

However, the method used in the *Limits to Growth* research, and many of its assumptions were vigorously criticized in the subsequent debate (see Cole et al., 1973). Most "establishment" opinion was converted to the view that the ecological impact of economic growth and "development" had to be taken seriously, but that this could be done by research and policy which addressed particular issues *within* the existing political and economic order. The idea that there were basic features of the system taking us to catastrophe was dismissed. Most Western governments now have environment ministries, and have on the statute book substantial swathes of environmental legislation. There are also bodies of international law, bilateral agreements over transboundary problems, international conventions and declarations, as well as an institutional framework for policy-making and implementation, largely conducted by the United Nations and its agencies (see Grubb et al., 1993). Social movement organizations, or Non-Governmental Organizations (NGOs as they are known) have played an active role in defining the issues and mobilizing public concern, both at the level of individual nation states and in the international arena. High levels of public concern have given organizations such as the World Wide Fund for Nature and Friends of the Earth a legitimate status in the policy communities which have shaped environmental legislation in most western countries. At the same time, these organizations have moderated or downplayed the political radicalism of their environmental message as a condition of acquiring influential "insider" status.

There is a parallel here with the adoption of an "insider", reformist strategy by the dominant traditions of the Western labour and socialist movements. Indeed, there may even be a substantive connection. The revolutions which took place under the banner of socialism, first in Russia and then in China, parts of south-east Asia, Central and South America and Africa throughout the twentieth century have failed to inspire confidence in the revolutionary project. Having survived civil war, military intervention and economic destabilization, the resulting regimes have tended to consolidate themselves as intolerant and oppressive state centralisms, abusing civil rights and as ecologically destructive as their capitalist rivals. Any renewal of the project of fundamental social transformation will have to confront that legacy with convincing reasons for believing it will not be repeated. In the light of all this, it is hardly surprising that environmental social movement organizations

have opted to take the "insider", reformist route where it has been available.

Under the current buzz-phrase of "sustainable development" there is a widespread consensus at least about the basic strategy for dealing with environmental problems. It is accepted that there is a link between poverty and environmental destruction at the global level, and growth is no longer seen as inherently incompatible with environmental protection. It is argued that economic growth is needed to address the urgent problems of poverty which persist in much of the "south". But the idea of "sustainable" development implies that this growth must be targeted at the relief of poverty, and regulated by environmental considerations. In the classic formulation of the "Brundtland" report (World Commission on Environment and Development, 1987), it must be growth which meets the needs of the present generation without compromising the ability of future generations to meet theirs. Of course, the verbal consensus conceals huge disputes about what sorts of transfers of capital wealth between the generations would be needed to satisfy the criterion of "sustainability", not to mention the institutional forms and financial resourcing which would be required to make sustainable development a feasible project on the global scale (see Grubb, 1993 and Redclift, 1987). However, the assumption, which even the NGOs now seem to have acknowledged, is that the future sustainable society may be achieved on the basis of continuing pressure and policy development within the existing institutional order – without, in other words, radical transformations in structures of economic, social and political power.

The Green Radicals

Set outside this consensus, and largely marginalized from the political mainstream, are radicalized minorities who remain committed to visions of fundamental social transformation, and to forms of direct action which are sporadically capable of capturing the public imagination, and drawing into action large and disparate coalitions of support (see Dobson, 1990, Chaps 4 and 5). The roads protests, and local campaigns against live exports of farm animals are recently topical examples in the UK. The people who are active in these campaigns are very diverse in their backgrounds and views – what they have in common often does not go much beyond the "single issue" which brings them together. Even the committed activists, who may be involved in a succession of campaigns over many years, often refuse to spell out any wider vision of a future society. However, there are networks of activists, and also more-or-less full-time intellectuals who do try to say why it is that the existing social and economic system needs to be radically changed, and what sorts of patterns of social relationship might replace it. In addition to the continuing presence of minority organizations which remain committed to a traditionally Marxist view of social transformation, there are also social movements and associated theoretical perspectives which have been fundamentally affected by the rise to prominence of the issues of environmental destruction: the intensification of agriculture, with its implications for animal welfare and human health; the pollution of drinking water; marine pollution from toxic waste disposal, agricultural run-off and oil spills; the destruction of the earth's most important reservoirs of "biodiversity", the tropical moist forests; the problems of urban decay, transport, energy generation, and the exhaustion of resources. These problems have recently been combined in media coverage with what are recognized as "global" environmental issues, such as the so-called "greenhouse effect" and associated climate change, and the measurable depletion of the ozone layer in the upper atmosphere which protects us from damaging levels of ultra-violet radiation.

What we might call the "ecological radicals" connect all these problems together as so many symptoms of a civilization in deep crisis. The source of this crisis is in our relationship to our naturally given "life support systems": a relationship of domination and exploitation

which is bound to lead to catastrophe for both humans and the other species with which we share the planet. They would argue that the materialist and consumerist vision of the "good life", the imperative to economic growth, the influence of private capital on state policy, as well as the role of transnational companies and the global "free" trade system are deep-rooted features of contemporary society. Though they are generally well-meaning, such activities as global declarations at UN conferences, attempts to reduce pollution from car exhausts, and green consumerism can have only minimal effects, and are constantly undermined by a social and economic world order which is driving in the opposite direction (see Lang and Hines, 1993). For the ecological radicals, our planning for the future must be far more long-term than both our everyday life and conventional public policy thinking. But it also must call into question not just the pattern of social relationships between humans, but also *their* relationship to the rest of nature.

Ecological radicals, as well as some of the academics who have been influenced by them, sometimes seek to emphasize the radical newness of their moral and political vision, and claim to go beyond the old political divisions between left and right (for example, Giddens, 1994). This is an understandable claim to make. Before the 1970s the mainstream parties of Left and Right tended to compete with each other in promising ever-rising standards of living, with little if any recognition that the massive industrial growth this required imposed equally massive burdens on the environment. This was possible in part because the environmental costs of economic expansion and rising average living standards in the richer countries have been paid mainly by the peoples, and especially the poorest, in "underdeveloped" parts of the world: the export of toxic waste, the environmental devastation associated with oil and other mineral extraction in countries which desparately needed the inward "investment", the economic pressures to convert to intensive production of export crops, and so on.

Also, the new agenda of ecological issues

generates new controversies, and throws into confusion some well established political alliances. For example, the German sociologist Ulrich Beck argues that the environmental consequences of industrial modernity have contributed to the emergence of a "risk society" (Beck, 1992). Political conflict is increasingly shifting from a concern with the distribution of "goods" to that of "bads", i.e. the risks and costs incurred by the industrial phase of development. In Beck's view, new technologies are generating risks which are qualitatively different from those encountered in previous historical periods. The risks associated with nuclear and genetic technologies, for example, operate on a time-scale which may be many thousands of years, may be irreversible, are potentially global in their impact, and are literally incalculable. A recent example is the risk that the fatal nervous disease affecting British cattle, BSE, might enter the human food chain, and infect humans who consume beef or beef products. Changes in cattle feeding, together with "deregulation" of the rendering industry at the end of the 1970s were defended on the basis of "official" scientific assurances that there was no risk to human health. Early in 1996, a government-sponsored scientific committee reported on ten cases of a new form of fatal human nervous disease that its "most likely" source was BSE-infected beef. There has been a great deal of public controversy since about the "rationality" or otherwise of consumer boycotts and international bans on beef exports. The point, however, is that the situation is in many respects unprecedented, and the disease-mechanism is not understood. No reliable epidemiological predictions can be made: it could be that only 10 individuals will be affected; it could be that many millions will die.

Beck and those who share his view would make the point that such incidents take us beyond the stage of social development in which risks could be calculated and people protected either by government welfare planning, or by the insurance industry. The authority of expert opinion is also at stake: scientists can no longer be reliably presented to the public as authoritative sources for policy decisions. This is not just because, as in the BSE case, they can be shown to have got it wrong. Rather, it is because scientific uncertainty is underpinned by value judgments and interests so that opposing political groups can often call upon their own rival "experts". Finally, in Beck's view, the prominence of this new order of risk is at least potentially the basis for new political alliances. Whereas an earlier phase of class politics meant that parties represented sectional interests, the whole population is vulnerable in the "risk" society: environmental politics can justifiably claim to represent a universal interest.

However, against this sort of argument, it is worth remembering that by no means all of the risks and costs of industrialization are of this nature. The impacts of industrial emissions, motorway extensions, air pollution from car exhausts, decaying urban infrastructure and so on can be avoided by the well-off who have choices about where they live and work. Even the risks from BSE are believed to be less for the consumers of prime steaks than they are for the down-market burgers and pies! More significantly than this, however, is that the "risk" debate distracts our attention from the power relations and class interests which are at work in *generating* the risks in the first place. Again, in the case of BSE a highly integrated industrial coalition of farming, chemical, animal feed, food processing and distribution firms is powerfully represented in the UK agriculture and food ministry (see Newby and Utting 1984; Newby, 1985 and Goodman and Redclift, 1991). The power of this "lobby" is such that agribusiness interests drive state policy in ways which change little as governments come and go. The same ministry is charged with responsibility for ensuring food safety standards. In this case, clear warnings in a Royal Commission Report from 1979 that the new methods of cattle feeding carried a risk to human health were ignored. An incoming Conservative government committed to eliminating "red tape" lowered safety standards in the industry, and continuing "outsider" scientific concerns were dismissed. Even when orthodox scientific opinion conceded that the risk was real, if not calculable, the issue was very speedily shifted from a matter of public health to one of defending the interests of British and European agribusiness: a redefinition with which the mainstream media in the UK complied without hesitation.

The picture, here, is one of powerful industrial, financial and political interests introducing innovations in production regimes without concern for the wider public interests and risks, and largely succeeding in setting the terms of media representations of the issues at stake. Of course, this is one example from one country. It does not show that a comparable pattern is necessarily present in other cases of environmental risk or degradation. However, studies of the institutionalization of scientific and technological innovation do show some striking patterns of change in recent decades throughout the industrialized world. An increasing proportion of research is being conducted in the research and development laboratories of the big transnational companies, rather than in publicly funded and regulated institutions such as universities. At the same time, public sector research (even in the social sciences) is being subordinated to the competitive requirements of private capital (Webster, 1991). If this broad picture is right, there are two important implications. One is that the technological determinist account of "progress" as somehow beyond our control, presenting us with both benefits in the shape of higher living standards, and environmental costs and "risks" to which we have to adapt as best we can, is shown to be mere ideology. The risks and costs (as well as the rising living standards for *some*) are the outcome (intended or not) of the strategic action of coalitions of powerful collective actors.

The second implication is that the claim made by some greens and academic sympathizers to have left behind the old political divisions of Left and Right starts to look a bit thin. It is certainly true that some parts of the labour movement are compromised by their defence of the short-term interests of groups of workers in environmentally damaging industries. However, these workers and their families are also at risk, often especially so,

from the industries in which they work. The broader situation can justly be described as one in which dominant political and economic collective actors pursue their interests through the institutional structures of the economy, state and media, with little regard for the lives and well-being of subordinate groups. All of this confirms the traditional emphasis of the left on structures of domination and power in capitalist societies, and the need for radical transformation in the direction of social justice, enhanced civil liberties and broad popular participation in decision-making. However, the new agenda does not simply confirm the traditional analysis of the left. It also presents powerful challenges to it. The new agenda of environmental issues requires the left to deepen and broaden its analysis, and to think in an imaginative way about potential alliances in opposition to the existing power-structure. It also requires of the left that it radically re-thinks its vision of what the future, post-capitalist society might be like: in other words, it needs to imagine and begin to build "feasible Utopias".

But even in the depths of this challenge, there are sources of strength. The radical movements which have arisen in response to the perception of an ecological crisis in modern civilization are very diverse, and also deeply sceptical about both of the main strategies of the traditional left: the "vanguard" party of the revolutionary tradition and the social democratic politics of the "parliamentary road". In several countries, dialogue is going on between ecologically influenced feminists, green socialists, anarchist greens, deep ecologists and others whose main concerns are with campaigning issues.[1] Green and anarchist hostility to state centralism converges with socialist rejection of the bureaucratic centralism of earlier versions of socialism. Out of this convergence are emerging new visions of decentralized economic organization, and ecologically benign technology in which people can have direct participation in the shaping of their social life together. Moreover, this is a dialogue which is at least aware of the limitations of the traditional Left's tendency to act as if the voices of all the oppressed and excluded could be included under the banner of class struggle. It is a dialogue which respects and values difference, and attempts to build coalitions which allow for continuing dialogue and renegotiation. Whether these new visions will take shape in the emergence of a social movement capable of challenging currently dominant global forces of oppression, exploitation and ecological destruction remains to be seen.

Note

1. In the UK this dialogue is going on within and between such groupings as the Red-Green Network, the Red-Green Study Group, the Green Socialist Network: the Way Ahead supporters in the Green Party, the Socialist Movement and others. Ideas and information is communicated in the bulletins of these groups, and also in the magazine Red Pepper. The booklet *What on Earth is to be Done?* (Red-Green Study Group 1995) sets out ideas for a red/green/feminist coalition. The US-based journal *Capitalism, Nature, Socialism* provides an international forum for this exchange of ideas, and now has several sister journals in other countries. A selection of book-length contributions to this dialogue is included in the References and Further Reading section.

References and Further Reading

Beck, U. 1992: *Risk Society*. London: Sage.

Benton, T. 1993: *Natural Relations: Ecology, Animal Rights and Social Justice*. London: Verso.

Benton, T. (ed.) In press: *The Greening of Historical Materialism?* New York: Guilford.

Bookchin, M. 1991: *The Ecology of Freedom*. Montreal: Black Rose.

Cole, H. S. D., et al. 1973: *Thinking about the Future*. Brighton: Sussex University.

Dickens, P. 1992: *Society and Nature*. Hemel Hempstead: Harvester.

Dobson, A. 1990: *Green Political Thought*. London: Unwin Hyman.

Eckersley, R. 1992: *Environmentalism and Political Theory*. London: University College.

Giddens, A. 1994: *Beyond Left and Right*. Cambridge: Polity.

Goodman, D. and Redclift, M. 1991: *Refashioning Nature*. London: Routledge.

Grubb, M. et al. 1993: *The Earth Summit Agreements: A Guide and Assessment*. London: Earthscan.

Hayward, T. 1994: *Ecological Thought*. Cambridge: Polity.

Jacobs, M. 1994: The Limits of Neoclassicism: Towards an institutional Environmental Economics. In M. Redclift and T. Benton (eds.) *Social Theory and the Global Environment*. London and New York: Routledge.

Lang, T. and Hines, C. 1993: *The New Protectionism*. London: Earthscan.

Martell, L. 1994: *Ecology and Society*. Cambridge: Polity.

Meadows, D. H. et al. 1972: *The Limits to Growth*. London: Earth Island.

Mellor, M. 1992: *Breaking the Boundaries: Towards a Feminist Green Socialism*. London: Virago.

Miliband, R. 1973: *The State in Capitalist Society*. London: Quartet.

Mills, C. W. 1956: *The Power Elite*. Oxford: Oxford University.

Naess, A. 1989: *Ecology, Community and Lifestyle*. Cambridge: Cambridge University.

Newby, H. 1985: *Green and Pleasant Land?* London: Wildwood House.

—— and Utting, P. 1984: Agribusiness in the United Kingdom: Social and Political Implications. In G. M. Berardi and C. C. Geisler (eds) *The Social Consequences and Challenges of the New Agricultural Technologies*. Boulder, CO: Westview.

O'Neill, J. 1993: *Ecology, Policy and Politics*. London and New York: Routledge.

Pepper, D. 1993: *Eco-socialism*. London and New York: Routledge.

Redclift, M. 1987: *Sustainable Development: Exploring the Contradictions*. London: Methuen.

Red-Green Study Group 1995: *What on Earth is to be done?* 2, Hamilton Road, Manchester.

Ryle, M. 1988: *Ecology and Socialism*. London: Radius/Hutchinson.

Scott, J. 1991: *Who Rules Britain?* Cambridge: Polity.

Shiva, V. 1989: *Staying Alive*. London: Zed.

Soper, K. 1995: *What is Nature?* Oxford: Blackwell.

Webster, A. 1991: *Science, Technology and Society*. Basingstoke: Macmillan.

World Commission on Environment and Development 1987: *Our Common Future*. Oxford: Oxford University Press.

Acknowledgement

This chapter was made possible by the award of a senior research fellowship from the Economic and Social Research Council, grant HI2427505494.

Sociology to Fire the Imagination

26

Leaving Home by Gill Jones

Liz Kenyon

"What I really like about sociology is that it takes some of the most everyday things that people never really think about, and makes you look at them in new and exciting ways". This enthusiastic and insightful comment, which provides an effective introduction to this chapter, came from a sociology undergraduate who sat opposite me on a recent train journey.

Gill Jones' book *Leaving Home* (1995) is one work which has recently inspired me in a similar way. As a researcher and lecturer in the contemporary British "youth" experience, I am very aware of the dated nature of many of the theories which are taught in this field. These often operate with notions of smooth and predictable life-course developments from "youth" to adulthood; explaining departures from this norm as deviant or even failed transitions. However, like many social experiences, the youth experience is a fast changing phenomenon, affected both by wider socio-economic, cultural and global changes, and how each new generation of "youth" reacts to these. Jones' work presents a challenge to such common-sense perceptions of "youth"; especially images of linear, non-stop transitions from youth to adulthood. In place of the dualism of normative or deviant transitions, she provides an alternative account of a variable process via which adulthood is reached. The shape and direction that this process takes is influenced by the journey that the individual travels along a continuum of unequally distributed risks and opportunities.

However, what differentiates this text from others is that not only does Jones recognize that changes are occurring in the transitional experiences of youth, but that she analyses such changes using empirical and theoretical data about a neglected, yet indisputably important "rite of passage" to adulthood: leaving the childhood home. Jones asserts that in recent years the failure to recognize that leaving home is not as straightforward as folk-images and earlier theories would suggest, means that sociologists, politicians and the general public alike, are not facing up to the variety of leaving-home experiences of today's youth. The young people in her study are faced with an uncertain future, where housing and jobs are no longer guaranteed to those approaching adulthood. As a result, it is recognized that today's young people are often forced to rely on the childhood home as a safety net for longer than their parent's generation. Those who do not have this safety net can therefore be doubly disadvantaged.

Leaving aside the wider arguments of the book, *Leaving Home* teaches us to think critically and differently about some of the common-sense assumptions and experiences which have impacted on many young people's lives in recent years. My own leaving home trajectory was extended in a way that, looking back, I would not have believed could have happened when I packed my bags for the first time. After a brief "year out" in France, followed by three years alternating between home and university, succeeded by what I believed to be a "brief" return home after graduation, my childhood home again became my permanent home whilst I was a post-graduate student. At the time this "inability" to leave home permanently was viewed by my parents' generation, who had left childhood and moved into adulthood in varying but generally smooth ways, as a strange and unusual phenomenon. I was *still* at home: poor me, poor parents! Jones' book reveals to us that in classifying transitions from childhood home to independent home as deviant or normative in this way, we as sociologists, and as human beings, are doing few favours for today's young people.

Reference

Jones, G. 1995: *Leaving Home*. Buckingham: Open University Press.

27

Fashion by Georg Simmel

Steven Miles

Classical pieces of sociological thought can often provide inspirational insights into what appear to be the most contemporary of social phenomena. Simmel's article on "Fashion" is one such example. Written at the turn of the century, this article illuminates the tensions that exist in modern life between the need to retain a sense of individuality, and yet to feel part of a social group. Simmel could just as easily be writing about young people buying the latest model of training shoe in 1990s Britain or America, than the fashions of early twentieth-century Berlin.

Simmel sees social life as a battleground, "of which every inch is stubbornly contested" (p. 543). The individual is therefore seen to balance the psychological tendency towards imitation with the personal desire for differentiation. In a capitalist society the things people consume arguably become important resources in the battle to construct identities. Presciently Simmel anticipates the extent to which fashion acts as a cultural resource in establishing who we are as individuals in a social context. He saw social life in the modern world as restless and ambivalent, and fashion as providing stability in an essentially unstable world.

Simmel's insights can be profitably applied to the analysis of contemporary fashion, a useful example being "retro" forms of clothing. My own research has looked at the meanings with which young people endow the goods that they consume. "Retro" clothing, and in particular sporting wear, originally popular in Britain during the late 1970s and early 1980s, and in the United States during the 1950s, was a topic that came up time and time again in my interviews with young people. What fascinated me about this was that young people very rarely talked about the specific qualities or aesthetic appeal of "retro" products. Indeed, despite constant references to the fact that such goods were fashionable and gave them a feeling of confidence in a group context, they continued to insist that only they personally could retain a sense of individuality; whilst their friends were perceived as no more than the victims of consumer culture. By buying a common model of training shoe, for instance, albeit in an alternative colour scheme, young people appear to be able to have their *communal* cake and yet eat their *individual* slices.

Fashion, then, acts as a sort of "mask" which, in effect, shields individuals from the everyday risks of the outside world. Arguably, in today's society the everyday threats impinging on personal identities are far more extensive than even Simmel could have envisaged. As such, traditional sources of identity such as class position, community, and the nuclear family, have been broken down, resulting in the individual becoming increasingly dependant upon secondary sources of identity, such as fashion. In effect, the individual cannot take the risk of constructing his or her identity completely freely; but craves the stability that fashion can offer. As the adage goes, we are – at least to an extent – what we buy.

Despite the language of this piece being complex in parts, Simmel is sometimes criticized for the fact that his work amounts to little more than his personal impressions of the modern world. However, I would suggest that through these impressions, Simmel manages to bring the sociological project to life. That is, he highlights the complex relationship that exists between the individual and his or her cultural experience, and how it is that in the modern world such an experience plays a crucial role in maintaining his or her psycho-logical well-being. To read this article is to realize that apparently common-sensical issues, such as fashion, have important socio-logical meaning. It is a tribute both to the insights of Simmel's work and to the value of sociology as a discipline, that Simmel identified the context in which these meanings operate, nigh on a hundred years ago.

Reference

Simmel, G. 1957 [1904]: Fashion. *American Journal of Sociology*, 62, 541–8.

28

The Managed Heart by Arlie Hochschild

Lori Holyfield

When I read Arlie Hochschild's *The Managed Heart: Commercialization of Human Feeling*, I was an undergraduate in sociology. At the time, I was not even aware that a sociology of emotions existed. I would later realize that not only has the sociology of emotions gained great credibility in the past two decades, but this book in particular, popular among both academics and non-academics, has had great influence on works since then.

Hochschild argues that our employers often exert a subtle form of social control over our emotions. In certain types of jobs (e.g.: service occupations where workers interact with the public), employers require workers to manipulate their own feelings as part of their job. Hochschild uses the concept of "emotion work" to describe how we act in certain ways, display certain facial or body gestures, and feel certain feelings, all in the line of duty. In essence, we exchange our emotions for wages.

Combining interviews and observations of airline recruitment procedures and flight attendant training sessions, Hochschild discovered that flight attendants were expected to display certain "positive" emotions on a regular basis. The company aim was to provide customers with a pleasant experience (e.g., "service with a smile"). Attendants were required to be cheerful. Moreover, they were expected to enjoy their tasks and to do so with little effort. Hochschild argues that one may "fake it" but not for very long before the company norm of not just acting, but feeling pleasant, takes over. Thus, if a flight attendant

came to work in a bad mood, he or she would be expected to *muster* the necessary feelings that coincide with company aims. Required to change one's actual emotional state, the individual engages in what Hochschild calls, "deep acting." She explains:

Some institutions have become very sophisticated in the techniques of deep acting; they suggest how to imagine and thus how to feel . . . As a farmer puts on blinders on his workhorse to guide its vision forward, institutions manage how we feel. (p. 49)

Emotion "work" is distinguishable from emotion "control", that is situations where it is held that emotional feelings could interfere with the adequate performance of the job. Emotion "work" involves the *generation* of desired emotions or "evocation" as Hochschild calls it, and "suppression" of undesirable feelings by one's self, not others. This has important implications for social control over our emotional lives because when we experience a disjuncture between our real feelings and those required of us, we may come to perceive ourselves as artificial, creating a feeling of alienation. This may lead one to try harder to actually feel the emotions required by the organization. In the end, we become powerless as we are encouraged to believe that it is us that must change and not the organizational practice of enforcing norms of artificiality. She quotes a teacher at a training session to illustrate this:

When you get mad at some guy for telling you that you owe him a smile, you're really mad only because you're focusing on yourself, on how you feel. Get your mind off yourself. Think about how the situation looks to him. (p. 196)

After reading *The Managed Heart*, I asked myself what the organizational control of emotions might look like in a non-work setting and how it might affect customers since they are an integral part of the service encounter. Already interested in commercial adventures, I conducted research in companies that produce organized trips and outings for profit, such as white-water rafting. I found in each setting that the emotions of both customers and employees were influenced by company norms. There were patterns, such as employee use of humor in situations of potential danger or norms requiring self-control in

fearful situations. Often excitement was generated through stories and anecdotes when the activities slowed and became potentially boring.

Like Hochschild, I found evidence that organizations do indeed intervene in our emotional lives. Even in outdoor adventure, a sphere that many have deemed the last bastion of spontaneity and authenticity, a setting in which nature plays a necessary and important role, emotion work can be found. Just like the airlines, a happy customer is a return customer and companies work behind the scenes to generate certain emotions (e.g., excitement) and constrain others (e.g., fear). To conclude, organizations are present in our work worlds but they remain with us in our leisure as well. Indeed, we live our emotional lives via the organizations with which we interact.

Reference

Hochschild, A. 1983: *The Managed Heart: The Commercialization of Feeling*. Berkeley: University of California.

[*Editors' note*: for further discussion of Hochschild's book, see Chapter 33 by Layder.]

29

Crime and the American Dream
by Steven F. Messner and Richard Rosenfeld

Randy Blazak

One of the most exciting parts of being a sociology student, for me, was learning to see private troubles as public issues. Topics like job opportunities and racism were gradually plugged into larger social patterns. My "Introduction to Sociology" course was like an intellectual therapy session, leading me to believe that macro-level social change was the best way to help people with their daily micro-level hassles. Now that I'm a sociology professor, the challenge is to help students to see how that even the smallest human interactions have a huge societal component.

Nothing seems more personal than the issue of crime. If you've ever been a crime victim (and there's a good chance that you have), you know how easy it is to start believing that some people are "just plain evil", that is regard criminals as inherently bad. Criminologists, on the other hand, without seeking to relieve criminals of responsibility for their actions, have been looking for sound societal explanations of crime for most of this century. One of the most exciting contributions to the debate is the recent book by Steven F. Messner and Richard Rosenfeld called *Crime and the American Dream* (1994). The authors update Robert Merton's concept of anomie, the sense of normlessness, when the rules don't make much sense or where their actions aren't guided by accepted norms of behavior. Merton used the concept to explain lower-class youths whose opportunities were blocked and who therefore engaged in crime as the only way of "getting ahead" in a society where the "American Dream"

focused on values of achievement and individualism. Thus Merton did not query the positive light in which the American Dream is generally seen – only the barriers to achieving it. But Messner and Rosenfeld expand the concept to explain a state of our culture. The American Dream, they argue, has a dark side. In a society where we are judged by what we own, the ends ("getting paid") begin to outweigh the means (legitimate ways of getting paid). In other words, "by any means necessary" makes crime as American as apple pie. It's not *how* you got there, but *that* you got there that counts.

Messner and Rosenfeld do a great job of dispelling other American myths, including our high crime rates. One method is to use cross-national comparisons. If we could blame the US crime rate on capitalism alone, we would expect comparable rates in other capitalist countries. Not so. Japan's homicide rate is 1/10 of the US's. Although guns are the #1 weapon of murderers, their availability doesn't explain Americans' love for violence. If we take the guns out of the picture and just look at *non-gun* murders, the US homicide rate is still greater than the *total* homicide rates of other developed nations. Another myth they explode is that the high US crime rates are the result of our racial diversity. Over 90 per cent of homicides are *intra*-racial ("black on black", "white on white," etc.). If we only look at white-on-white murders, the homicide rate is still *four* times the average rate in developed countries.

What is it that makes America so criminally

inclined? Where other criminologists make arguments about economic opportunities, or perhaps the lack of them, Messner and Rosenfeld argue that it is the "economicness" or "materialism" of our culture that creates the problems – and makes the question of "opportunities" such an issue in the first place. The weak emphasis on means and the "fetishization of money" explain why a poor person might steal your TV *as well as* why a rich person might embezzle from your bank. It also helps us to understand the maleness of crime, as men especially are rigorously socialized from childhood to desire economic success. Making matters worse, non-economic institutions like the family and school have been penetrated by the economic value system. If you're in college "to get a good job"

rather than "to get a good education" you would be illustrating the authors' point about the priorities of American culture.

Easy to read (only 111 pages). *Crime and The American Dream* is crammed with fascinating information to give sociology students the fuel they need for endless discussions. Highly critical of both conservative and liberal attempts to control crime, Messner and Rosenfeld offer hope in the regeneration of the non-economic parts of our lives to create a "mature" society. Their book is filled with the insights of a wide variety of personalities from Émile Durkheim to basketball star Charles Barkley. Messner and Rosenfeld have ignited my sociology students to look for broader answers to the issue of crime. What was once "micro" to them is now "macro."

Reference

Messner, S. F. and Rosenfeld, R. 1994: *Crime and the American Dream*. Belmont, CA: Wadsworth.

30

Civil War by Hans Magnus Enzensberger

Mick Drake

Hans Magnus Enzensberger is a cultural critic whose work can loosely be related to the German intellectual tradition of critical theory. In three very readable essays published under the title *Civil War*, he reminds us through the "Europe in Ruins" of 1945 of the fragile construction of Europe and of modern civilization in general. Thus, even our recent history disallows judgement based on a distinction between (Western) civilization and the "barbarism" of Others. Our reaction against the new world disorder – to enclose ourselves behind secure frontiers – is thus not only futile, but also misplaces the source of what we seek to secure ourselves against.

In the title essay of the book, Enzensberger likens state disintegration and warlordism on the periphery of global society to social crisis and gang warfare in the urban heart of the "civilized world". Afghanistan and Rostock, south-central Los Angeles and Bosnia should thus be considered examples of the same distinctive phenomenon – a new mode of violence. The "molecular" civil wars of our cities and the regional civil wars of the periphery, he argues, are perpetrated without regard for legitimation, for self, or for consequences – a generic condition of action which Enzensberger characterizes as "autism". We usually consider violence as an instrument, a means to an end, but this violence, without hope and without future, seems beyond such reason. Violence today, he says, ". . . has freed itself from ideology" (Enzensberger, 1994, p. 20). It is *end-less*.

Drawing critically upon the terms of liberal,

conservative, marxist and reformist analysis he sketches an explanation of this phenomenon as a negative complex comprised by the displacement of individual self-responsibility, the failure of modernization to universalize its value-system, the inherent irresponsibility of capital, and acculturation to violence through the mass media. He suggests that treatment of the problem should restrain itself within limits of local and interpersonal relations if it is to be effective, but this would not escape the tendency to deny responsibility and erect security zones around ourselves.

Despite the psychological terms Enzensberger uses, the idea of a generic condition of post-modern violence provides a useful alternative to the limits of conventional sociological approaches to violence. Since sociology itself derives from Enlightenment perspectives which measured violence against reason, our conventional approaches to the problem of violence in society – in terms of environmental determinism, pursuit of interest or individual pathology – misrecognize and even facilitate a new form of violence which is "liberated" from ideology and from rational self-interest, but irreducible to individuals.

The development of our discipline is inextricably bound up with the discipline of a modernity which simultaneously sublimated and extruded violence from its very beginnings. The monopolization of violence by the state historically provided and enforced non-violent ways of resolving social conflicts and disputes. State monopolization bifurcated violence, so it became either politicized –

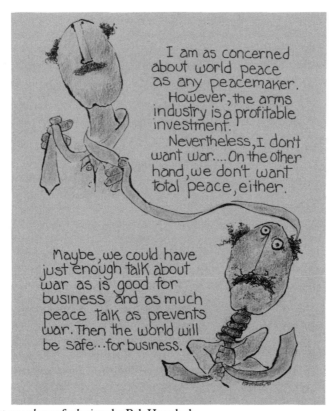

Figure 30.1 *Just enough war for business* by Bob Haverluck.

oriented toward power in the state – or criminalized. Civil society thus appeared as a space from which violence was absent in either its instrumental (political), or its deviant (criminal) forms. Violence was confined to struggles between or over states, or took place outside society altogether. Sociological explanation thus reduces violence to an instrumental means for political ends supposedly beyond violence, and "civil war" is reduced to the instrumental expression of conflicts of interests, ideologies and structures originating in civil society but having their end in the state (e.g. Giddens, 1985, pp.121 and 184; Shaw, 1991, pp.10-11). Having revealed the violence of the state, however, we seem unable to accept that "civil society" is not necessarily very civil at all.

Enzensberger fails to provide resolutions in these essays, but the problematic he maps out is one which sociology can no longer evade. If we are to come to terms with post-modern violence in some way, we may need to accord conceptual autonomy to violence in our analyses and to suspend our modern distinctions between military and civil society and even between states of war and peace. We can only hope to manage this violence as an aspect of our world if we can learn to acknowledge as social what we have hitherto misrecognized, after Hobbes, as the antithesis of society.

References

Enzensberger, H. M. 1994: *Civil War*. London: Penguin Granta.

Giddens, A. 1985: *The Nation-state and Violence*. Oxford: Polity.

Shaw, M. 1991: *Post-Military Society: Militarism, Demilitarization and War at the End of the Twentieth Century*. Oxford: Polity.

31

From Reproduction to Production
by Claude Meillassoux

Dong-sook S. Gills

When I began my PhD research on economic development and rural women in Korea, I was preoccupied with the question of the "backwardness" of the rural sector in South Korea's "miraculous" economic development. My main working hypothesis was that the agricultural sector was neglected in Korea's industrialization strategy and that therefore rural women are exploited *more* because they are not integrated with the *industrial* economy. I assumed that women were more highly exploited in the rural agricultural sector than in the industrial wage-labour sector precisely *because* the peasant economy was not well integrated with the industrial economy, being more of a separate appendage to the national export-oriented strategy.

In framing this hypothesis I had been influenced by Marxist approaches which, although they might disagree about the future development of capitalism, are heavily dependent on the same evolutionary assumptions as are found in liberal economics – that is, the idea that capitalism is the historical product of social evolution and is therefore one of the inevitable stages of the development process. The standard Marxist evolutionary approach presupposes that all societies are defined by their distinctive production relations. Different modes of production linearly follow one after another, with each particular mode being characterized by its own "internal logic". Thus capitalist social formations succeed *pre-capitalist* social formations, and are structured and organized by "the logic of capital".

It was, then, my initially unquestionable belief that South Korea is a capitalist society, solely governed by the economic rationality of capitalism. However, as the research progressed, confirming the "backward" features of the peasant economy and the grave way of life of the people in it, a new question began to emerge. I observed that the peasants keep on producing even when their products are sold at well below the cost of production. So why is it that peasants keep producing when it does not make any "economic sense" for them to do so?

It was Claude Meillassoux's article, A Marxist approach to economic anthropology, which enabled me to answer this question. Reading Meillassoux was the turning point which radically changed my research direction and re-cast my analytical framework. In this article Meillassoux not only repudiates the linear evolutionary process of the modes of production, but directly challenges the fundamental assumption that the capitalist mode of production is governed solely by capitalist relations of production (i.e. by the class relations between capitalist and free wage-labourers). He argues instead that different modes of production co-exist. Even more importantly, he emphasizes "the way in which capitalism utilizes agricultural communities to provide, in part, for the reproduction of labour-power in the modern wage-labour economy".

Meillassoux begins his analysis of modes of production with some essential questions: "Who is working with whom and for whom? where does the product of the labourer go?

who controls the product? how does the economic system reproduce itself?". He defines non-capitalist agricultural production, such as a peasant economy, as a *non-exchange system* where the major concern is not production but *reproduction*. The relations of production here consist of a redistributive system which is reciprocal between the current working generation and retired and future generations of workers.

Within this framework it began to make sense why the peasants keep producing at an "economic loss". It is because the nature of subsistence production is not governed by the capitalist logic of production – that is, the logic that capital must maintain accumulation via continuous realization of profit, and therefore the object of capitalist production is to maximize the level of profit through market exchange. To use the jargon of economics, subsistence farmers are not "utility or profit-maximizers". Their land, tools, seeds, fertilizers, etc., are not utilized to maximize profits, but to subsist, i.e. to reproduce themselves. That is why they continue production as long as their labour "pays" for their own human reproduction. They act rationally – but according to principles which are not those of capitalist rationality.

Meillassoux's allocation of production and reproduction as the elements of prime importance in, respectively, capitalist and non-capitalist production relations, also sheds a new light on my concern for the extreme exploitation of peasant women. Reproduction includes not only the reproduction of subsistence production as a way of life, but also reproduction of the life of the human producer. The relations of production in a subsistence economy are not founded upon control of the means of production, but on control of the "means of reproduction", i.e. *of subsistence and of women*. Korean rural women had long been subordinated in the home both as workers and, sexually, as reproducers of the next generation. With the onset of capitalism, as urban-industrial development bled the rural economy of both labour and resources, the difficulties of maintaining the subsistence economy became all the greater and peasant women are now required to work even longer and harder than they did in the past.

After reading Meillassoux I stopped viewing the agricultural sector as a backward appendage. I was able to see the farming villages as a distinct social formation in themselves, but nevertheless as tightly articulated into dominant industrial capitalism. Once I looked at the relations between Korean industrial and agricultural production in this way, the mechanisms of the super-exploitation of women and the role of "patriarchal social relations" in the peasant economy were revealed more clearly. I believe this framework is useful not only in the analysis of core-periphery relations and women in the Third World, but also for understanding women's domestic work in the advanced capitalist societies.

Reference

Meillassoux, C. 1972: From reproduction to production: A Marxist approach to economic anthropology. *Economy and Science*, 1 (1), 93–105.

PART IV
Doing Sociology: Study and Research

Thinking and doing, theory and practice, are often presented as alternatives. It is part of our common currency that there are those who "think" and those who "do"; there are people who live in ivory towers, and there are practical people who don't mind getting their hands dirty; things work "in theory", but not "in practice", and so on. Within sociology, as in many other walks of intellectual life, it is sadly not uncommon to hear those who favour one kind of activity make disparaging remarks about the other.

By concentrating on sociology's engagement with a social world that is constantly changing, this book tries to counter these false polarities. It sees reflection and evidence-gathering as necessarily complementary aspects of doing sociology properly. Sociology, crucially, is about finding out and interpreting, not rehashing some Old Master's thoughts for the purposes of a course grade. As Part II showed this does not lead us to disregard "the canon" — sociological knowledge builds upon the work of previous scholars. But it should do so on the basis of their insights which are of contemporary relevance. Research (finding out new things or looking at old things in new ways) and scholarship (being aware and keeping abreast of what others

have found out and argued) are the twin arteries of sociology's lifeblood, and they are not things in which only "qualified sociologists" engage. They are as essential for students to practise as they are for faculty staff.

"Doing sociology" then is broader than simply "getting your hands dirty" (which in a sociological context usually means field-work). You are engaged in sociological scholarship in the library or lecture hall if, instead of memorizing without understanding, you read and listen actively: "what does this mean?" "has good evidence been advanced for that proposition?" "is the argument logical and coherent?" "what are the implications of these findings?". The first three chapters by Erdmans, Layder and Beeghley offer guidelines for active reading and attempt to dispel the aura of mystery that often surrounds "theory". The capacity for analytical interpretation and theoretical construction are skills that can be acquired, not attributes with which some people happen to be endowed. These essays show how you can build creatively on the understandings you have achieved to imagine resolutions for the problems you encounter.

The theme of "learning through doing"

is continued through the next set of essays on research. Research is the royal road to learning. It is through our attempts to discover and explain that we come to make knowledge our own – not simply adding another brick to the pile, but fitting it into a construction (and, as necessary, shifting some of the bricks already there). But to do effective sociological research the imagination has to be rigorously focused. General interests have to be transformed into sharp sociological questions. How to set about this is the theme of the chapter by Lyons and Wilson. There then follow four chapters that show the importance of applying your sociological imagination in the research process – whether working in the field (Burgess) or with archives (Cottle), solitary or in collaboration with others (Phillips). The chapters give practical advice on how to do research, but resist any temptation to treat techniques in isolation from the formulation of sociological questions. Vitally, the sociological imagination must be extended to include empathy with the human subjects we study. Researchers (whether professionals or students) must refrain from manipulating people in order to get "a good result", and be sensitive to the complex ethical issues which social research entails (Homan).

Finally there is a chapter on the use of computers that is relevant both to your essay writing and your research activities (Henry). It also provides a link to Part V as it discusses locating and using sources of data through the Internet.

Active Reading

32

How to Read Sociological Texts

Mary Patrice Erdmans

This chapter offers suggestions on how to read different types of sociological texts. I hope that you approach your reading in an active and questioning way, seeking in a book or article the "aha" experience that will help you understand some aspect of your own life and social world that surrounds it. I am realistic enough, however, to recognize and appreciate the fact that you will sometimes find reading tiresome and boring. There may be several reasons for this: your previous education and life experience have not equipped you with the skills in and habits of reading complex texts; you are reading particular material in which you have little interest; the reading assumes that you have knowledge which, in fact, you do not yet possess; it is written in a dry and tedious style or is full of jargon. So, in giving you advice on how to read I will keep in mind that, as Howard Becker and his colleagues have found, students are often interested primarily in "making the grade." I hope this chapter will help you make a better grade. That said, I also know that many students are avid readers, and that a well-written sociological text can be entertaining as well as informative. A good ethnography that tells a story and reads more like a novel is fun to read, especially if it has to do with your life (e.g., Donna Gaines' book *Teenage Wasteland* about middle class white kids committing suicide in suburban America, or Douglas Foley's *The Great American Football Ritual* about high school sports in a small town). When reading less approachable texts, it helps if you read in an active, critical manner and tell yourself that the payoff may not be immediate.

It may be that you, like myself and many of my students brought up in our dazzling television, film, and electronic culture, find reading to be less stimulating, perhaps even dull and boring. Given the choice between seeing an exciting film like *Pulp Fiction* and reading Bebe Campbell's novel *Brothers and Sisters* you would find the film more enjoyable. Or your idea of entertainment is more likely to be watching the season premier of *Seinfeld* rather than reading the newest edition of *Harpers*. When books have to compete with film and TV they often lose. This holds true for me as well. I love TV and movies, but I also read. I don't see them necessarily as competing with each other – in fact, the activities take place in different arenas. At home I watch TV in the living room and I read in the study, bathtub and the bedroom. They are two different forms of pleasure. So, the second part of what I want to accomplish in this chapter is to try and explore some ways to get more pleasure from reading.

One argument given for why we prefer to watch rather than read is that watching is often thought to be an easier activity – the viewer is defined as passive, while the reader is often defined as active. I think this argument is unreliable. Some viewing may be passive, but certainly not all. When we talk back to the television or radio, when we discuss the merits of a television documentary or the moral of a movie with our friends, when we yell at our favorite soap opera victim "Don't believe him, he's lying to you," this indicates that in fact we are actively engaged in the viewing process. Moreover, if we view with what bell hooks calls an "oppositional gaze" then we are viewing critically, viewing to see how the media and the images it presents are shaped by the Anglo-dominant, patriarchal, capitalist society. The oppositional gaze requires that we think about who is behind the camera presenting these images to us and who in society benefits from representing reality in this manner. For example, watch the evening news in America with an oppositional gaze to see how the concept "crime" is defined in our culture. Crime is something that happens on the street, not something that happens in corporate offices. Crime is often shown with a dark face in the USA. Actions are most often defined as crime when we can point to a specific victim (e.g., a homicide) rather than a vague more general destruction of human life (e.g., toxic waste dumping). Viewing with an oppositional gaze is an active, not passive process. Furthermore, when we watch TV and think to ourselves, "this guy has it all wrong, people don't dress this way in real life," or "people of my class [race, gender] don't talk this way" then we are viewing actively. When we view with an eye that says "this guy has it right" or "this woman has it wrong" then we are viewing critically.

In fact, I think in some cases people are much more passive as readers, in part because there is a (false) blanket legitimacy invested in the printed word. People believe that if something is in print, and if the teacher assigned it, then it must be important and true. On the other hand, TV is much less legitimate. We know that a lot of junk is on TV, so we watch TV with an eye that distinguishes between good shows and junk. I want to suggest that we should do the same thing with reading. We need to read critically, and by this I mean we need to read with a mind that says I accept or reject some or all of this. We need to read with the attitude that bad stuff is published and that teachers do not always make wise decisions in what they assign. We need to read with the idea that some people (and many sociologists) are bad writers, and that they don't always get

it right all the time. For example, when we read a chapter about crime and deviance in a sociology textbook ask yourself how crime is being constructed – does it include corporate or white-collar crime? does it spend an excessive amount of space discussing minorities and crime? Don't be awed by the authority of the written word and a writer with a lot of credentials. Even when you like a book, you need to read with a critical eye. I myself forget this sometimes. For example, in my reading group we were discussing Mitchell Duneier's book, *Slim's Table*, which focuses on working-class black men in Chicago. I loved the book, and because I have a particular interest in the topic of working-class culture I sort of swallowed the book without really reflecting on it. I accepted it as a "good" book simply because it discussed working-class culture – a topic I feel given too little attention in sociology these days. At our discussion group, however, one member was very critical of the book. She found it offensive that the author spent so much time showing us that working-class people are honest, respectable, and dignified, as if he was surprised to find this. Moreover, she pointed out that there was almost no mention of women in this book, which she perceived as a gross oversight, and asked "how can you explain the lives of men without discussing their familial relations?" This women demonstrated the type of critical approach to reading that I am suggesting you adopt.

To summarize, I write this chapter with the assumption that you are reading sociological texts because you are a student concerned with your grades. This is not a bad thing – it shows that you are rational intelligent beings. Grades do matter, and our educational system puts a premium on grades. In addition, even those of you who love reading will probably concede that you enjoy reading non-academic material more than academic material. Finally, many of you read passively. In the remaining sections I examine several types of sociological writing and show you how to read them to improve your grade, to get more enjoyment out of reading (or at least minimize the pain), and to read critically. Not all writing is the same, so all reading should not be the same. Sociologists write for different purposes and to different audiences; you should read for different purposes and recognize that you were not always the author's intended audience. The different types of reading discussed are textbooks, books, ethnographies and articles. In the final section I will tell you how to use these different texts to help you do research and write papers.

Textbooks

Textbooks are often boring. Writers have tried to make textbooks more accessible to students by using everyday language and examples and including pictures. These attempts, however, do not counteract the boring nature of textbooks which stems from their efforts to present a diverse group of viewpoints and place them within a unifying framework. The middling effect that results from this process takes out some of the excitement found in the production of knowledge. The controversial topics, the newer (more explosive) theories that are not yet confirmed, and the radical thinkers on both sides are usually given, at most, a passing nod. Textbooks, because of the goal of presenting a lot of material, end up glossing over controversies, homogenizing diverse ideas, and "ironing out" the wrinkles of contradiction in a particular field. Many professors are loath to use textbooks but do so anyway for several reasons: they feel the textbook gives a good summary or survey of the literature in a field; the ratio of students to teacher is too high and textbooks with their test banks and teaching guides helps the time-stressed professor; it is less expensive for the student to buy one expensive book rather than six or seven moderately priced books. For these reasons, and others, textbooks are used.

The first thing you need to know when you are assigned a textbook is how you will be tested on the material. If you have in-class exams with lots of multiple choice questions then you will read differently than if there is a take-home exam with a few essay questions. Assuming the first type of exam, which is the easiest way for teachers to test students on this material, you will have to read with the goal of remembering certain things: new words (concepts and their definitions), key theorists or the scholars who use these words, and facts in the form of numbers and dates. Read a textbook quickly, most chapters can be read in less than an hour. Moreover, you do not have to read it all in one sitting; this is the sort of writing that can be broken down into parts. You can read one section on the bus or train (a good reason to take mass transit) and another section between classes. Your concentration level does not have to be perfect. Read actively – by highlighting certain points, but also by thinking of your own examples for the concepts as they are being presented. Write your examples in the margin of the text (only do this if it is your own textbook, please do not mark up library materials). Highlight only the key things; try not to underline complete sentences, just the key words. Remember that the textbook is designed to give you a little bit of information about a lot of things. You can minimize the pain of reading boring textbooks by learning to read them quickly to get an overview of the concepts, names and facts.

Books

There are different types of books. Most of them are about a particular topic based on some type of research. Authors have agendas for their books; that is they have a point to make. They often provide logical arguments and evidence to convince you that what they say is true. You should read these books as if you are a juror – have they convinced you beyond a reasonable doubt? The burden of proof is on them. Sometimes they are not very skillful in presenting the material – they may be bad writers and their main ideas may be buried in the middle of a text. Other times they may be masterful rhetoricians (that is they can use words skillfully and persuasively) but they do not have very good evidence. They may tell you over and over in convincing terms that a point is true, but they do not really give you enough evidence to support it. Simply ask yourself if the data presented convinced you. If not, try to figure out why. Don't be fooled by the use of a lot of numbers and statistics – numbers are no more legitimate than words. If you do not understand the statistics or a particular table in a book ask your professor or tutor to explain it. Question, don't just accept! Furthermore, when you read books, make note of what the authors are not saying as well as what they are saying. Remember the example of my colleague's comment that the author did not discuss the women or families in his discussion of working-class men.

When I sit down to read a book I start by guessing what the author is going to do. I first read the back jacket cover or the title and guess. For example, when I picked up Cornell West's book called *Race Matters* I immediately thought of a book written more than a decade before by William Julius Wilson called *The Declining Significance of Race*. Wilson's book argued that by the 1970s class (rather than race) was playing a more significant role in determining life chances for African–Americans. Wilson's book sparked controversy among some black scholars who argued that race still mattered for middle-class African–Americans. So, even before I began reading West's book, by the title alone, I guessed he was somewhere in this argument. What I did was place the book in context – something that teachers can do better than students *simply because they have read more*. Teachers can help students by giving them this context. Sometimes my students treat these introductory remarks as not worthy of note-taking, thinking that the teacher is just warming up to the lecture). Authors, however, often provide the context in the first chapter of the book. The first chapter will explain why the book was written, what the current debate is, and to whom they are responding; this chapter reveals to the reader the intended audience, the main debates, and the author's position. Read this chapter carefully!

Sometimes readers misunderstand the thrust of an author's argument. They will start by saying "Many people believe X" and discuss the merits of X theory. But then, ten pages later, the author says "X is wrong and I propose theory Y." Still, some students will come into the classroom (or exam) believing the author supports theory X. They show me the passages where the author is in fact talking about theory X. They did not see the rhetorical device the author was using; they did not understand that authors have to build a context for their work; they did not understand that knowledge is produced in a community. Scientists are always writing off of other people's work – we borrow people's theories; we reject theories and suggest new theories; we take bits and pieces of theories to build our own theories; we say that everyone before us has gotten it wrong; or that everyone before has gotten it right (a much less interesting book). So the first thing about reading a book is to figure out what community of scholars the author lives in.

Also in the first chapter(s), authors will tell you how they are going to support their point, how they collected the data, and what the following chapters are going to show. This becomes their contract with the reader. When you read the subsequent chapters you should continually be asking yourself, do I believe this?, is there enough evidence?, what are they leaving out?, and hey, what about those other theories dismissed in the beginning? When you read in this way you are reading in an engaged active way. Sometimes authors present exhaustive examples of one point. You do not have to read every single example. Once you have figured out the main idea of a section, move on (especially if the exam is tomorrow).

Reading books requires a different level of concentration than textbooks. Usually longer blocks of time are necessary. At least, you should try to read a whole chapter in one sitting, and sometimes it's useful to set an agenda of trying to read the whole book in a couple of days. Doing this will help you understand the main arguments and see the book as a whole.

There are different kinds of books. Some books are based on standard research practices which include quantitative, qualitative or historical data (e.g., Émile Durkheim's *Suicide*, Lillian Rubin's *Worlds of Pain*, or

Theda Skocpol's *States and Social Revolutions*). These authors are writing for other social scientists who study in this particular field, and as a result they use theoretical arguments and sociological terms (much to the dismay of students). These books are difficult to read if you do not have a large store of knowledge about this area. Keep the book at a distance – don't get hung up on each word, but try to grasp the overall theme. They are the opposite of textbooks in that they often present a lot of information about a narrow topic. As a result, authors will repeat ideas and use an assortment of data. Read these books to see the forest rather than the trees.

Another type of book is referred to as an ethnography. The work is based on data collected through fieldwork or participant observation – which I think of as sociologists acting like anthropologists (e.g., William Foote Whyte's *Street Corner Society* or Elijah Anderson's *Street Wise*). These books are very readable. They usually tell a story about a group of people (e.g., an ethnic group or urban community) and describe the way this group sees the world. Similar books are those that provide a journalist's account of something – usually an event (e.g., William Chafe's *Civilities and Civil Rights* which describes the sit-ins in Greensboro, North Carolina during the civil rights movements). The authors of these books are not always social scientists. They write for a broader audience, and as a result they have few (if any) theoretical arguments in the book. Nonetheless, they usually still try to make a point; that is, they have an agenda. Why was the book written? In the political climate of the day (always note what year the book was written), what does the book mean? Whose side is the author on?

Ethnographies are easy and enjoyable reading. You do not have to highlight theorists and facts and the writing is often engaging so ethnographies can be read quickly. Try to read these books in a few long sessions – give yourself an afternoon or a rainy morning to curl up on the couch and take a big chunk out of the book.

Articles

Articles are like books in that authors have an agenda (a thesis) and they usually try to present data to support it. Read the abstract of the article before plunging in to the main text (and again after you have completed the article). The abstract will give you a miniature blueprint to what the article is all about (theoretical argument, methods, findings, and conclusion). I think of it as the skeleton of the article. Read articles in the same way you read the book – trying to find out who the authors' audience is (often other scholars in the speciality field), where the authors are situated in that field (what side of the debate are they are), and which theories are rejected or supported. This discussion is usually found in the very first section. In the next section authors present the methods used to collect data and test theory. This should be noted and understood very generally. Oftentimes there are nit-picking details about the methodology (especially in quantitative studies). Read to get a general idea of the sample (e.g., how large, from what region, age, gender, race group) and how the researchers collected data (e.g., surveys, interviews, secondary sources). The next section is usually a description of the findings. Skim this section. Look at the tables first and try to make sense out of them. Take from this is a general understanding of the findings and not the specifics. Spend more time on the discussion section where the authors use their theories to explain findings. Do the theories fit? Did they prove or disprove their thesis outlined in the first section?

Always read articles in one sitting, in a place and frame of mind that allows you to concentrate. This will decrease the time it takes you to read an article. Reading a scholarly article in front of the TV at 10:30 in the evening when you have been up since 6:30 in the morning will take you twice as long than if you read it at 10:30 in the morning in the library. Reading it as one piece allows you to better see and evaluate how the theory and data hang together.

Finally, conference papers are (if they are

any good) really just draft forms of published articles. They are most useful for getting current information in a field because often it takes several years for an article to get published.

Using these Texts to Write your own Papers

Textbooks are a good first source of information for key concepts, theories and facts. They also help you find more information. Plan to spend a few hours at the library on your first trip there to research for your paper. Find a textbook and make a list of key names and concepts related to your topic and then do a literature search using one of your library's computer systems or the old card catalogue section if your library still has one. Use a reading list supplied by your professor or tutor not only to find particular books or articles she or he suggests but also to look for closely related material on nearby shelves. Do the search and write down the library call numbers. Now look at this list – do you find that several books have similar call number prefixes? This is the mother lode, or key area of the library for this particular subject. Go up to that section of the library. Find some of the books on your list and then look at other books that are around them. Sit on the floor (or at a table if you prefer) right in this section and start reading them; read the table of contents and parts of the introductory chapters – remember that the introduction will tell you what is inside the book. Begin the narrowing process in the library instead of hauling home all the books and deciding later which ones to use.

Two other good first sources are in the *Annual Review of Sociology* and *Current Socio-*

logy which publish overview articles about a specific field. These articles give you the landscape of the debates and research in this area. The article will also provide you with a good bibliography (the best source for finding further sources). Try to narrow down your topic and then choose only a few books and find other journal articles. Articles are often miniature books. You probably will not have enough time to read ten books if you are simply writing a term paper for a course; but you could read a few books (especially if one of them is an enjoyable ethnography) and several articles. Also, make use of a good reference book for numbers (e.g., statistical abstracts) to get some macro level data on your topic.

Some Final Summary Points

First, before you begin to "read" a text, look it over, flip through it, skim the introduction, take note of the chapter headings and any tables. Try to guess what the book is about and what types of data will be presented. After this first quick read, go through the book again in more detail. This is an especially useful way to read articles and even textbook chapters. Read it through once quickly, and then the second time more thoroughly. Second, read in different moods. Quick snatches of time are good for textbooks, bathtub and nighttime reading are good for fun ethnographies, intense periods of reading with high levels of concentration are needed for journal articles and especially the beginning chapters of a book. Finally, read with an attitude of disbelief, with a challenging mind that says, "Prove it to me!"

References

Anderson, Elijah 1990: *Streetwise: Race, Class, and Change in an Urban Community.* Chicago, IL: University of Chicago Press.
Becker, Howard 1968: *Making the Grade: The Academic Side of College Life.* New York: John Wiley.
Campbell, Bebe 1994: *Brothers and Sisters.* New York: Putman.
Chafe, William 1980: *Civilities and Civil Rights: Greensboro, North Carolina, and the Black Struggle for Freedom.* New York: Oxford University Press.
Duneier, Mitchell 1992: *Slim's Table: Race,*

Respectability, and Masculinity. Chicago, IL: University of Chicago Press.

Durkheim, Émile 1951: *Suicide: A Study in Sociology*. Glencoe, IL: Free Press.

Foley, Douglas 1990: The great American football ritual: reproducing race, class, and gender inequality. *Sociology of Sport Journal*, 7 (2), 111–35.

Gaines, Donna 1991: *Teenage Wasteland: Suburbia's Dead End Kids*. New York: Pantheon Books.

hooks, bell 1992: *Black Looks: Race and Representation*. Boston, MA: South End Press.

Rubin, Lillian 1992: *Worlds of Pain: Life in the Working-class Family*. New York: Basic Books.

Skocpol, Theda. *States and Social Revolutions: A Comparative Analysis of France, Russia, and China*. Cambridge: Cambridge University Press.

West, Cornel 1994: *Race Matters*. New York; Vintage Books.

Whyte, William Foote 1955: *Street Corner Society: The Social Structure of an Italian Slum*. Chicago, IL: University of Chicago Press.

Wilson, William Julius 1978: *The Declining Significance of Race: Blacks and Changing American Institutions*. Chicago, IL: University of Chicago Press.

33

Deciphering Research Reports

Derek Layder

Sometimes reading research reports can seem to be a daunting proposition even though the subject matter of the research may be interesting and attractive. In this chapter I want to suggest ways of overcoming some of the initial difficulties involved in reading and understanding research reports by indicating the main things to look for and by outlining methods of reading or examining them which may help in identifying and understanding their contents. Both of these are directed to the task of "deciphering" – or clarifying the meaning of – research reports. First I shall say a bit about the general nature of research reports and the possible approaches we may take to reading them.

Research reports vary in their length and form and there are two main types. First a report may appear in the form of a book whose chapters deal with different aspects of the research. As an example, throughout this chapter I shall refer to Arlie Hochschild's (1983) book *The Managed Heart* which focuses on jobs that require "emotional" (as well as physical and mental) labour. (See also Chapter 28.) In particular the book describes her research into airline flight attendants whose job requires them to smile and enjoy themselves while performing their hectic flight-deck service. The research investigates the social and psychological consequences that follow from this kind of emotional labour. Secondly, a research report may appear as an article in an academic journal or as a chapter in a book which brings together a number of such reports. As my main example of this I shall refer

to a journal article by Ackroyd and Crowdy (1990) which focuses on the behaviour and attitudes of a group of slaughtermen working in an abattoir (Slaughterhouse) in the UK. The authors aimed to investigate the extent to which the occupational culture of the slaughtermen could resist attempts by management to change or manipulate it from the outside.

With a book, it is probably best not to attempt to read it from start to finish but to do some preliminary "research" on it in order to identify which "bits" (sections, chapters, paragraphs and so on) are the most important for your immediate purposes (an essay, a dissertation, background reading for a lecture course). Only after examining the layout and organization of what you are going to read is it possible to be sure that you will use your time wisely when you attempt a more thorough reading. Although articles or chapters may seem an easier proposition in this regard the same principle of preliminary "selective" reading of the overall report may well help you to avoid later confusion (and consequent wasted time).

With a book, a serious (rather than a quick and superficial) examination of the contents page should reveal exactly where important information is stored in the text such as "who where the subjects of the research?" or "what methods of data collection and analysis were used?" Also it is often worth scanning the chapter titles of a book for clues as to its overall organization and content. Spending some time scrutinizing the introductory chapter (and preface, if the book has one), as well as the concluding chapter will give some feel for the report as a whole and exactly where in the text one might find discussions of key elements of the research. Also you should consult the index on topics for which you may have some immediate interest and then flip through some of the sections it refers to. With article length reports there is often an "abstract" at the beginning which provides a summary of the nature of the research, the sequence of the argument and the findings. This may be invaluable as a means of deciphering the whole article and identifying different aspects of the research. Not every article or chapter has an abstract to provide a key, so a quick look through the whole thing before tackling it in detail can be an important aid. Some articles provide a key in the opening and/or concluding section or paragraph and so it is worth scanning these. Particular attention should be directed to the sub-headings used throughout the report since these provide important clues about the sequence of the discussion and the presentation of results.

So when you first pick up the report, ask yourself:

• What are the purposes of the research?
• What information does it contain?
• What do *I* want to get out of the research?
• Can I read it selectively? What is the best way to do this?

Research reports differ in terms of the amount of emphasis that is given to key elements of the research process such as the sampling procedures, selection of informants, analysis of findings, the theoretical framework and so on. Also there is variation in the order in which various aspects are discussed. Sometimes findings or results of the research may be presented at earlier stages of the discussion than expected. Another variation concerns the amount of attention devoted to the theoretical implications of the research. As a result discussions of theoretical matters may appear in one or several sections of the report depending upon its relevance to the research project as a whole. The key point is that there is no *inevitable* sequence or organization of the presentation of research reports and thus it is important to be aware of the potential variations in advance. There are several ways of deciphering research reports and extended discussions can be found in Rose (1982) and Layder (1993). What follows is a brief guide to the key elements of research reports.

What to Look for in Research Reports

The Research Problem and the Influence of Theory

Research always relates to and is affected by the state of existing knowledge in the field so finding out about the background of existing knowledge will provide important clues as to the basic problems and research questions which the research project tries to answer. To find out about this background we can look at the text itself to see what information it provides about the context of the research. For example, Ackroyd and Crowdy reviewed existing studies and empirical information on other types of work groups and organizations and theoretical ideas about the nature of organizational culture. This gave rise to the basic research question which was "can workers attitudes be changed by management tinkering with the 'organizational culture'?" Hochschild reviews theories and research on emotions both in the main body of her book and in some of the appendices, and this helps to define her specific problem focus which centres on the the psychological effects of the commercialization of feeling.

In examining this background knowledge it is important to be aware of the relation between empirical and theoretical material since this can help us evaluate whether the research has achieved its purposes. Theoretical knowledge is expressed in the form of abstract ideas or concepts (such as "emotional labour" in Hochschild's study or "organizational culture" in Ackroyd and Crowdy's report). Alternatively the body of knowledge that forms the context may consist mostly of empirical information (data) that has been previously gathered in other research projects (such as, in Hothschild's research, the socio-economic backgrounds of flight attendants, or other occupational groups that require emotional labour such as nurses, social workers or teachers,). Empirical knowledge gives us basic information about the area (such as the types of jobs requiring emotional labour and the gender composition of the workforce), while theoretical knowledge offers explanations of what is going on, what social processes are indicated by the empirical data (such as how employee feelings may be put to the service of company efficiency and profitability). Both types of knowledge provide the context from which the basic problems and research questions arise and which the research project itself tries to solve or answer. Although the basic problems and objectives of the research are often formed from a combination of empirical and theoretical information, it is important to be aware of the fact that research reports vary in terms of their stress on one or the other of these types of knowledge.

To some extent this will depend on the amount and quality of knowledge and information that is already available. If there is very little known about a particular area or topic then research around it will be more exploratory in nature and driven by the need for basic information. For example, McKeganny (1990) chose to study the extent and meaning of needle-sharing among drug users partly because so little was known about this aspect of drug use and the danger of HIV infection through needle-sharing. Research in other areas about which there already exists quite a bit of data and knowledge, such as the behaviour of schoolchildren in classrooms or employees in work organizations, will tend to be driven by the need to check-out or test in some way existing knowledge and assumptions. For instance, one objective of Ackroyd and Crowdy's work on slaughtermen was to test the assumption in some of the literature that work cultures can be controlled or shaped by management. The findings of their case study along with other case studies, suggests that some work cultures are very resilient and resistant to change. In the case of the slaughtermen this was because their attitudes, beliefs and values are linked to, and shaped by,

factors external to the workplace such as class, regional and national cultures, and core values such as "aggressive masculinity" and "realism" in their attitudes towards the killing of animals.

Depending, then, on the existing state of knowledge in an area or topic, research will be more or less exploratory, or more or less concerned with confirming or disconfirming previous findings. The more exploratory in nature it is, the more research will concentrate on the accumulation of basic data and the construction of theories and concepts to explain the empirical information. The greater the amount of information already gathered, the more ongoing research will be geared towards the development and elaboration of existing theories or adding to the corpus of empirical data.

The Techniques of Data Gathering

The initial ideas, assumptions, objectives and problems with which the research is concerned have to be transformed into practical procedures so that they can be adequately studied and analysed. In this sense concepts and ideas important to the research have to be "operationalized" by deciding what empirical evidence they correspond to and how this evidence will be gathered. All research reports therefore contain some reference to the techniques used to gather the data. There are a whole range of possible techniques sociologists can use such as interviews, questionnaire surveys, various types of observation, case studies, the analysis of documents, the use of data collected by other researchers for their own purposes such as official statistics (like census data), and so on (see O'Connell et al., 1994). Hochschild used a variety of techniques and data sources. She gave a questionnaire survey to a group of 261 students to obtain preliminary information on how men and women from different social classes felt about and dealt with their emotions. She used census data to provide her with background information on jobs requiring emotional labour and their gender composition. She also interviewed flight attendants and observed training sessions in order to focus on the ways in which they aquire skills, such as calming and dealing with anxious or troublesome passengers, and to aquire information on how a company's image is projected through the flight attendants' demeanour. Only by using observational and interview techniques could Hochschild obtain data which represents the attendants' experiences with regard to their deployment of emotional labour.

Ackroyd and Crowdy's case study employed one particular technique of close observation wherein the researcher "participated" in the work activities and everyday lives of the research subjects. Although the other slaughtermen knew that the researcher was gathering material to "write a book" they eventually accepted his presence both in the work situation and in their leisure activities and homes. In this manner "some interesting material concerning the social milieu and non-work lives of the slaughtermen could then be gathered" (Ackroyd and Crowdy, 1990, p. 5). So then these two examples of research reports indicate that the kinds of data gathering techniques will vary from report to report depending on the kinds of problems they are tackling. However reports should discuss the reasons for the choice of techniques as that will enable the reader to judge whether they were properly used and appropriate to the research problem.

The Types of Data

These two studies also highlight the fact that the information or data of the research can take two forms. First *quantitative* data is information that can be expressed in numerical form and represents counts of various things such as how many people said "yes" to a particular survey question, or how many women there are in particular occupations. Secondly, *qualitative* data give us a broader and deeper impression of the texture of social life. One type of qualititative information provides us with an impression of the way people think and feel about their lives and is usually in the form of extracts from interviews with them or descriptions of their behaviour as it has been observed by the researcher. Such information, however, is subject to qualitative processes of selection and interpretation as it is in the second type of qualitative data which comes in the form of the researcher's interpretations of various documents that are relevant to the topic or area. For example, Hochschild examined airline company documents to find out whether and/or how official company policy was geared to the encouragement of emotional labour in their flight attendants as a result of economic competition between airlines. In distinguishing between quantitative and qualitative data it is important not to overstress the differences between them. For example, counting always requires prior decisions about which categories of people or events are to be included in the count, and which are not. Conversely, simple counting techniques may be used to summarize qualitative data.

Ackroyd and Crowdy's study relied solely on qualitative information gleaned from conversations with the slaughtermen and observations of their behaviour at work, home and in leisure time activities. In order to be able to decipher research reports (that is to understand and evaluate them) it is necessary to be aware of the kinds of data that they use and what they are trying to achieve. Just as some research like Ackroyd and Crowdy's relies exclusively on qualitative information, other kinds of research concentrate exclusively on quantitative data. Studies of rates of social mobility, social class composition, occupational structure, the concentration of wealth, ownership and control of companies, and labour market analysis, typically – but not always – use quantitative data and present their findings in statistical form. Other studies, like Hochschild's, use combinations of quantitative and qualitative data (see Layder, 1993).

The Empirical Sample

Research reports always refer to the *sample* (of people, events or situations) that has been used in the study to gather information and produce their findings. Careful choice of a sample to study is necessary because it is not possible to study everything or everyone even within a clearly defined area. For example, it is not possible to study all slaughtermen or all flight attendants, so one has to settle on a restricted number who will "stand for", or "represent" the whole group from which they are drawn. If the aim of the study is to generalize about the whole group, then representativeness of the sample is crucial in determining the success of the study and in evaluating the results of the research. If the sample chosen is not typical of the group as a whole then the validity of the findings may be undermined. For example, a sample of flight attendants must reflect what we know about the gender composition of the work force as a whole. If 70 per cent of the workforce were women then approximately 70 per cent of the sample should be women.

The size of the sample is often, but not always a crucial issue, and this depends upon the initial methodological approach. Large samples are more important for research that tries to identify large-scale processes (like rates of social mobility) or to make generalizations about large groups of people (like the attitudes of men or women, or the educational achievements of people from different social classes). In a case study like Ackroyd and Crowdy's, which relies on qualitative information about the nature of people's attitudes, beliefs and feelings, the size of the sample is less significant because the purpose of the

research is to obtain in-depth information on a closely defined area or group of people. Thus more extensive and personal knowledge is required of those who are being studied. Very often researchers engaged in this kind of research will include additional interviewees and observations until they are satisfied that they have enough information to answer the research questions they have set themselves.

Evaluating Findings and Results

In deciphering research reports it is necessary to bear in mind the following points concerning how we assess the success of the research and the validity of the conclusions and findings that are presented. First we should examine those parts of the report that describe how the data was collected and the problems that were encountered in so doing. For example, there may have been difficulties involved in getting hold of interviewees, or problems of access to a research site (a school, a hospital, a government agency), or of failure to obtain crucial documents. It is important to bear these problems in mind in assessing the claims the researchers make in the presentation of their findings.

Secondly, we should ask whether the important concepts and theoretical ideas have been clearly defined in relation to the empirical information that was gathered. For exam-

Table 33.1

	What to look for in research reports
The research problem and influence of theory	What is the relative emphasis on theory- building and theory-testing?
Techniques of data gathering	What techniques are used to collect data? Were they used properly? Were the techniques appropriate to the research problem?
The types of data	Is the data quantitative or qualitative – or a combination of the two? Is the type of data appropriate to the research problem?
The empirical sample	Is the sample appropriate to the aims of the research for generalizability or in-depth study in a closely defined area?

ple, how do we *identify* emotional labour in social life (or more formally what are its empirical "indicators"?). If we see a flight attendant smiling at another cabin crew member, does this count as emotional labour or does the concept only apply to interpersonal exchanges between flight attendants and passengers? The adequacy of the links between concepts and indicators is important in evaluating research reports.

Thirdly, we should ask what kind of contribution the research makes to our knowledge of the area in question. Does it furnish us with new empirical information? Does it develop new theoretical (explanatory) approaches or does it mainly extend or develop existing theory? Does it help clarify our thinking about particular concepts? Many research projects attempt to address several of these issues simultaneously, but it is important to be clear about the different aspects and their contribution to the overall project.

Finally we have to evaluate the findings and results of the research in terms of its initial objectives and questions. Does the information uncovered by the research and its analysis answer the questions or resolve the problems it set out with? Is the evidence presented adequate to support the conclusions and findings? Knowing what the objectives of the research are in relation to existing empirical and theoretical knowledge of the area or topic enables us to assess the adequacy of the research procedures. Thus we can evaluate whether the techniques and process of data gathering were suitable and properly conducted, and whether the sample of people or events was truly representative or otherwise appropriate to the research problem.

References

Ackroyd, S. and Crowdy, P. A. 1990: Can culture be managed? *Personnel Review*, 19, 3–13.

Hochschild, A. 1983: *The Managed Heart*. Berkeley: University of California Press.

Layder, D. 1993: *New Strategies in Social Research*. Cambridge: Polity Press.

McKegany, N. 1990: Drug abuse in the community: needle sharing and the risks of HIV infection. In S. Cunningham-Burley and N. McKegany (eds), *Readings in Medical Sociology*. London: Routledge.

O'Connell Davidson, J. & Layder, D. 1994: *Methods, Sex and Madness*. London: Routledge.

Rose, G. 1982: *Deciphering Sociological Research*. London: Macmillan.

34

Demystifying Theory: How the Theories of Georg Simmel (and Others) Help Us to Make Sense of Modern Life

Leonard Beeghley

Imagine putting a jigsaw puzzle together without using the edge pieces. To make the task even harder, imagine doing it without looking at either the box cover or the pictures on each individual piece. These bits of information are important because they provide a useful frame of reference for understanding the puzzle. As such, they guide us in putting it together by helping us to see relationships among the pieces that might otherwise go unnoticed. Without such orienting cues, assembling the puzzle becomes much more difficult, perhaps impossible. I would like to suggest that the edge pieces, box cover, and pictures on the pieces are analogous to a theory in that they provide a way of making sense out of what would otherwise seem chaotic.[1]

A theory is an abstract explanation of diverse observations. As the puzzle analogy implies, it serves as a frame of reference, a guide to key issues, and a vehicle for seeing non-obvious connections. A theory, in short, provides a way to understand what is going on around us. People develop theories all the time, usually based on their everyday experiences. When your parents say "you need an education to get ahead in this world," they have a theory – not a very abstract one, but a theory none the less. Scientists do precisely the same thing, usually based on more systematic observations (or tests) than are available in everyday life.

In this chapter I am going to extrapolate a simple theoretical statement from an essay by Georg Simmel in order to illustrate some of the characteristics and benefits of theory. In so doing I hope to make theory less mysterious,

indicate some of its benefits, and suggest how to read the classical theorists in sociology. At the end, I will present an exercise designed to help you develop theoretical skills.

Along with such people as Max Weber and Émile Durkheim, Simmel belonged to the first generation of academic sociologists. Between about 1890 and 1920, these early sociologists tried to account for (i.e., to theorize about) the transformative impact of modernity on social life. Everything, it seemed, was changing: the economy became industrialized, urbanization occurred, more people obtained advanced education, and families became smaller, among many other changes (Schlereth, 1991). The problem of understanding modernity was (and remains today) a key theoretical and practical issue. The essay I am drawing on reflects on some of these changes; it is titled "Conflict and the web of group affiliations" and was originally published in 1908 (Simmel 1955). In it Simmel examines how the increasing complexity of social life affects forms (or patterns) of interaction.[2]

According to Simmel, the social structure in which people participate influences forms of interaction regardless of individuals' purposes. Thus, he showed in the "web" that the number of groups people belong to and the principles on which groups are organized affect people's behavior apart from the content of their goals. Put simply, form exists independently of content.

One of the most important factors affecting people's web of group affiliations is the degree of "social differentiation." This is a jargon term, of course, referring to how complex a society is. For example, in a hunting and gathering society, almost all tasks are done in and by the family (gathering and producing food, educating children, worshipping gods, making law, and the like). Thus, people have only few roles in an undifferentiated society. This simplicity means that everyone they know is just like them; they do not interact with others different from themselves. By contrast, in an industrial society, many important tasks are divided up. This increase in complexity, which sociologists call differentiation, affects interaction. People still produce goods, worship, educate, and adjudicate; but they do so differently. They play a far greater number and variety of roles and, in so doing, meet others who differ from themselves.

The process of social differentiation produced, Simmel said, two fundamental changes in patterns of interaction.

First, the principles underlying group formation changed, in his words, from "organic" to "rational" criteria. As Simmel uses it, the term "organic" is a biological metaphor suggesting that a family or village is like a living organism in which the parts are inherently connected. Thus, when groups have an "organic" basis, people belong to them based on birth and they are so strongly identified with the group to which they belong that they are not seen as individuals in their own right. In Shakespeare's play, *Romeo and Juliet*, for example, Romeo did not have an identity apart from his family and village; they constituted who he was. This is why his banishment was so devastating. In contrast, the term "rational" suggests the use of reason and logic. Thus, as Simmel uses the term, when groups have a "rational" basis, people belong by choice.[3]

Second, social differentiation also leads to an increase in the number of groups which people can join. When groups have an "organic" basis, people can only belong to a few primary (i.e., small, intimate, face-to-face) groups: their family, their village, and that is about it. By contrast, when groups have a "rational" basis, people can join a greater number and variety of them, based on skill,

mutual interests, money, and other types of commonality. Moreover, many of these groups are larger and more formal than primary groups. As often occurs, what people can do, they in fact do: Simmel observed a trend in modern societies for people to join lots of groups and for such affiliations to be based on conscious reflection. And this tendency applies even to intimate relationships, such as marriages. Indeed, as I have commented elsewhere, the story of the last few centuries is of increasing choice in all areas of social life.[4]

The problem is how to express these observations. Simmel, like the other classical theorists, wrote in a discursive format that is rather imprecise. Today, sociologists emphasize the desirability of stating theories in propositional form, as in the following extrapolation from Simmel's work:

The greater the social differentiation, the more choice people have in group affiliation and the more groups to which they belong.

This simple statement displays all (but one) of the components of good theory. First, it is abstract, independent of time and place. Thus, if it is accurate, observers ought to see the impact of social differentiation in many nations as they modernize – not only in England or the USA in the nineteenth and early twentieth centuries, but also in Third World nations today. Second, the proposition includes concepts that are clearly defined; that is, their meaning is as precise and clear as possible. This is why I made the definition of social differentiation explicit a few moments ago. Third, the concepts used in the proposition express co-variation, so that change in one phenomenon (social differentiation) is linked to change in another (the degree of choice and number of groups). There is a fourth component of theory which is not displayed in this example: complete theories usually comprise sets of interrelated propositions linked together in a systematic way. This last component of theory is enormously difficult, however, and remains rare in sociology.[5]

None the less, even discrete propositions,

such as Simmel's, can lead to new insights about the nature of modern societies. He suggests, for example, that when groups are formed by choice and people belong to a large number of them, the possibility of role conflict arises because groups place competing demands on people. Thus, it is now common for people to have multiple obligations: as spouse, parent, employee, club member, student, and so forth. Sometimes these duties lead to hard choices. This happens, for example, when sorority, fraternity, or other social commitments conflict with studying for an examination. Usually, Simmel says, people try to balance their competing responsibilities by keeping them spatially and temporally separate. None the less, the impact of conflicting expectations can lead to psychological stress and, hence, influence behavior.

One example of the impact of role conflict and the resulting stress occurs in gender relations – although this is not a topic about which Simmel had much to say. It has been my observation, for example, that husbands do not like cleaning toilets; they think wives ought to do this. And, in fact, data exist on this issue. Studies show that even when they have full-time jobs, wives either perform most home-related tasks or make sure they get done (Blair and Lichter, 1991). This situation makes the comic's assertion that "a man around the house is an inanimate object" seem all too real. More to the point, employed wives usually have two jobs (roles) that are often incompatible: keeping house (defined broadly to include nurturing family relationships) and earning a living. One way married women resolve this conflict is by sacrificing career ambitions, working part-time, and other stratagems designed to make their lives a little easier. Another way is to get a divorce. After all, Simmel's analysis implies that a marriage is simply one group among many in modern societies; it remains special to be sure, and intimate, but one that people choose to form and sometimes choose to leave – as they do other groups (Beeghley, 1996). Some inanimate objects are not worth keeping around the house.

The problem of role conflict in gender relations seems to be a negative consequence of modernity, a perception that leads some observers to wishful thinking. If, it is said, we could return to a time when men's and women's roles were assigned at birth and expectations were clear, we would not have so many problems today. There might be fewer divorces, for example. This kind of argument suggests that modern societies are de-moralized in two senses: we lack moral guidance and we lack morale (Himmelfarb, 1995). As the poet William Butler Yeats put it, "Things fall apart; the centre cannot hold; Mere anarchy is loosed upon the world . . . " (Jeffares, 1989, p. 294). Regardless of whether you agree with such judgements (I do not), note that our understanding of the source of role conflict in today's world stems from a simple theoretical proposition that specifies the impact of differentiation: increased choice in both group affiliation and the number of groups to which people belong. Moreover, I would suggest that the connection between differentiation and the divorce rate is interesting and not obvious – until one thinks through the implications of Simmel's ideas.

Moreover, Simmel's proposition leads to other important insights about modern societies, insights that reveal some of the positive consequences of modernity. For example, if the proposition is accurate, people now play many different roles in contexts that are spatially and temporally separated. I am a husband, parent, son, (erstwhile) athlete, employee and political activist, among other roles. This list, which could be extended, gives me a distinct identity in relationship to other people. And these others also have a unique set of characteristics (roles) that make them distinct. Thus, Simmel's theory implies that the changes produced by social differentiation lead to greater individuality (what he called a "core of inner unity") that makes each person unique. Unlike the situation in Verona, where Romeo and Juliet lived, the group no longer absorbs the whole person and geographical mobility occurs often. In Simmel's words, "the objective structure of society provides a framework within which an individual's non-interchangeable and singular characteristics may develop and find expression" (1955, p. 150). Such a result is impossible when everyone resembles everyone else. It is an irony, then, that modernity not only produces role conflict and psychological stress, but also creates the conditions under which individuality emerges.

It emerges precisely because people in modern societies can, indeed must, make choices. Moreover, they must adjust their behavior to different people in different situations – an insight that carries many implications. For example, as people make choices and become aware of their uniqueness they enjoy greater personal freedom. In Simmel's words, while "the narrowly circumscribed and strict custom of earlier conditions was one in which the social group as a whole . . . regulated the conduct of the individual in the most varied ways," such regulation is not possible in differentiated societies because people belong to so many different groups (1955, p. 165). It is not accidental, from this point of view, that the ideology of personal freedom as an inalienable right of every adult arose during the last two centuries. Its structural basis, Simmel said, lies in social differentiation.

Other observers have added to Simmel's insights. In *Social Theory and Social Structure*, for example, Robert K. Merton notes that when people play many roles and face conflicting expectations, they develop the capacity for empathy – the ability to identify with and understand another's situation or motives (1968, p. 436). This capacity can sometimes reduce the level of conflict between people. Thus, the increasing complexity of modern societies provides a structural basis for an important personality characteristic. Note two important implications of Simmel's and Merton's arguments: First, role conflict now appears to be a positive feature of modern societies. Second, the distribution of psychological characteristics in a population (people's sense of individuality and empathy, for example) do not happen by chance; they reflect the social structure.

Rose Laub Coser illustrates these implications in her book, *In Defense of Modernity*. She observes that while role conflict burdens individuals, it also forces them to make choices and thereby encourages creativity (1991). After all, in a complex society, roles cannot be taken for granted, they must be negotiated; so people have to consider both their own and others' situations and be creative. Moreover, the aptitude for thinking imaginatively and originally extends to all arenas of life as people confront problems. As Coser summarizes: In modern societies, "the development of mental ability takes place together with the grasp of the complexity of social roles" (1991, p. 7). The logic of this analysis suggests that modernity results from and, at the same time, produces a spiral effect such that, as societies became more complex, more people became creative; and as more people became creative, societies became more complex, etcetera. A big etcetera.

Once again: these additional insights follow from a simple theoretical statement taken from Georg Simmel's work. As with using the edge pieces and pictures in putting together a puzzle, the theory provides a way of understanding relationships that are not at all obvious. Thus, the possible connection between increasing social differentiation and the development of individuality becomes clear. In addition, the potential impact of differentiation on personal freedom, empathy, and creativity is now explicit. I would like to suggest not only that these are some of the key issues for understanding modern societies, but also that the connections between them remain impenetrable without theory as a frame of reference.

These considerations lead to the conclusion that reading the classical theorists continues to have pay-off. After all, even if the proposition considered here turns out to need modification, we will have learned a great deal. This is because it raises important issues that help us to make sense of modern life and implies some non-obvious empirical connections. Yet students often find (or define) studying Simmel, Durkheim, Weber, and the others as rather difficult and of little relevance; hence, they are reluctant to do such reading. I am going to conclude this chapter by offering some suggestions about how to read and what to read for.

There is no question that any text by the classical theorists will be difficult reading. With the exception of Herbert Spencer, they are read in translation. This means that questions about an accurate rendering of an author's meaning arise. More importantly to students, the use of language often seems old fashioned, the sentence structure complex, and the references to unfamiliar authors and issues off-putting. In addition, the classical theorists came from a variety of cultural traditions. This diversity means that they each had a different notion of what science ought to be like; indeed, Durkheim, Weber, and Simmel all developed distinct conceptions of the appropriate questions that should be asked.[6] Finally, the classical theorists had few role models. This means that they were often groping for the right way to say things. Often, it seems to me, when Simmel or Durkheim appear confusing, it is because they are confused.[7]

Taken together, these problems require you to have a strategy for deciphering the text. Here are some suggestions:

(1) *Consider a second reading.* The "web of group affiliations" is not long and, while (like Simmel's work generally) it is disorganized, much more is often learned the second time through. With longer works, which make a second reading more difficult, break up the material into manageable sections.

(2) *Talk to one another.* Sometimes just a few minutes trying to explain what you have read, and hearing another person's take on the same thing, helps to increase understanding and aids in preparing for classroom participation.

(3) *Use secondary sources as guides.* Since these tend to fall into several categories – summaries, critical evaluations, and polemics (for or against) – it is essential to know the author's orientation. Be wary of those taking cheap shots; as I have indicated with the Simmel example here, the point of reading the classical theorists is to learn, not indict.[8]

(4) *Take reading notes.* I like to place the essential points of a piece on one sheet of paper, preferably in outline form. Now I do not always succeed, but the effort forces me to confront the writer's most basic ideas. When taking reading notes, ask yourself very simple questions. What are the key concepts? What do the concepts mean? Where is the variation? These kinds of questions will often lead you to an author's point. But in performing this task, do not be afraid of being wrong. Too often, I think, students are taught to approach the classical theorists' writings as holy writ. This is shortsighted. You are generally better off ransacking their works for good ideas that relate to your concerns, rather than trying to figure out "what Simmel really meant." The latter requires more knowledge than most undergraduates have and, in any case, varies from one interpreter to another. You will see this latter fact clearly if you consult more than one of the secondary sources referred to in the footnotes.

Here is a personal vignette that illustrates the approach you (and instructors) ought to take: As an undergarduate enrolled in introductory philosophy, I wrote a paper on Plato's *Republic* that received an "A" grade. Alas, when a subsequent course revealed that the premise of my paper was absolutely wrong, according to dominant interpretations of Plato, I went back to the earlier instructor and asked why I had received an outstanding grade. The reply went something like this: "You dealt with key ideas in an interesting way and I rewarded you for that. The fact that you were unaware of the literature was less important." Much of modern life remains a puzzle, the contours of which we remain ignorant even today. For this reason, I think it is more important for students to think creatively than to worry too much about being mistaken.

Although there remain important disagreements about what the nature and goals of theory in the social sciences ought to be (see Turner, 1991), the more general point is not in doubt. Our understanding of social life is not merely enhanced by theory, it is impossible without it. As the example from Simmel's work reveals, theory supplies a way of linking disparate observations and identifying the underlying principles involved. As a result, we are led to new insights. In this regard, the classical theorists continue to be read because they provide models for good research and deal with fundamental issues that remain important today. Like the edge pieces of a puzzle, they provide us with vehicles for understanding how human beings interact in modern societies.

Exercise

I mentioned earlier that Robert K. Merton adds to Simmel's work by observing that when people have multiple roles and, hence, must cope with conflicting expectations, they develop the capacity for empathy (1968, p. 436). One result is a reduction in interpersonal conflict. Think about this issue as a theorist and, in so doing, consider the following questions.

- How would you phrase this argument in one or more propositions that are abstract and express co-variation?
- How would you define each concept such that it is clear and unambiguous?
- How would you determine whether some people played more roles or faced more conflicting expectations than others?
- How would you determine whether some people displayed more empathy than others?
- How would you determine whether the level of conflict between people had been reduced?
- How would you explore the theoretical and empirical implications of this argument?

Notes

1. The puzzle analogy was suggested to me by Professor Kathleen Lowney of Valdosta State University.
2. The following paragraphs are adapted from Turner et al. *The Emergence of Sociological Theory* (1995, p. 254–8).
3. I emphasize Simmel's use of the terms "organic" and "rational" because the classical theorists in sociology often used the same (or similar) concepts with quite different meanings. For example, Simmel's notion of "organic" is the opposite of Durkheim's. Developing a clear understanding of the major concepts is often the key to comprehending the entire work.
4. In *What Does Your Wife Do? Gender and the Transformation of Family Life*, I take some simple ideas from Durkheim, Weber, and others, and use them to help us understand how relationships between women and men have changed over time (1996).
5. For a chapter length explanation of the components of theory, see Jonathan H. Turner's, *The Structure of Sociological Theory* (1991). For a more detailed, but quite readable, analysis, see Jerald Hage, *Techniques and Problems of Theory Construction in Sociology* (1972).
6. See Christopher Bryant's *Positivism in Social Theory and Research* (1986), and Lewis Coser's *Masters of Sociological Thought* (1978).
7. Jennifer Lehman reveals Durkheim's confusion in "The question of caste in modern societies: Durkheim's contradictory theories of race, class and sex" (1995).
8. In addition to the texts cited previously, some useful secondary sources are: Raymond Aron, *Main Currents in Sociological Thought* (1968; 1970), Randall Collins, *Four Sociological Traditions* (1994), Robert Nisbet, *The Sociological Tradition* (1968), and George Ritzer, *Sociological Theory* (1992).

References

Aron, R. 1968: *Main Currents in Sociological Thought, I.* Garden City, NY: Anchor Books.

—— 1970: *Main Currents in Sociological Thought, II.* Garden City, NY: Anchor Books.

Beeghley, L. 1996: *What Does Your Wife Do? Gender and the Transformation of Family Life.* Boulder, CO: Westview.

Blair, S. L. and Lichter, D. T. 1991: Measuring the Household Division of Labor. *Journal of Family Issues,* 12, 91–113.

Bryant, C. A. G. 1986: *Positivism in Social Theory and Research.* New York: St Martin's Press.

Collins, R. 1994: *Four Sociological Traditions.* New York: Oxford University Press.

Coser, L. A. 1978: *Masters of Sociological Thought.* New York: Harcourt Brace Jovanovich.

Coser, R. L. 1991: *In Defense of Modernity.* Stanford, CA: Stanford University Press.

Hage, J. 1972: *Techniques and Problems of Theory Construction in Sociology.* New York: John Wiley.

Himmelfarb, G. 1995: *The De-moralization of Society: From Victorian Virtues to Modern Values.* New York: Knopf.

Jeffares, N. A. 1989: *Yeats' Poems.* London: Macmillan.

Lehman, J. 1995: The question of caste in modern society: Durkheim's contradictory theories of race, class, and sex. *American Sociological Review,* 60, 566–85.

Merton, R. K. 1968: *Social Theory and Social Structure.* New York: The Free Press.

Nisbet, R. A. 1968: *The Sociological Tradition.* New York: Basic Books.

Ritzer, G. 1992: *Sociological Theory,* 3rd edn. New York: McGraw-Hill.

Schlereth, T. J. 1991: *Victorian America: Transformations in Everyday Life.* New York: Harper-Collins.

Simmel, G. 1955: *Conflict and the Web of Group Affiliations.* New York: The Free Press.

Turner, J. H. 1991: *The Structure of Sociological Theory,* 5th edn. Belmont, CA: Wadsworth.

——, Beeghley, L. and Powers, C. 1995: *The Emergence of Sociological Theory,* 3rd edn. Belmont, CA: Wadsworth.

Doing Sociological Research

35

How to Formulate a Student Research Project or Dissertation

Frank Lyons and Chas Wilson

For many students, writing a dissertation or research project is the climax to their university studies, representing both their greatest challenge and reward.

The aim of this chapter is to help you in the process of writing a dissertation and become aware of the learning you are expected to demonstrate. Careful preparation, research and presentation is essential if you are to maximize the chances of delivering a creditable end product.

A Note on Terminology

The terminology used by North American and British universities can be very confusing as identical terms are used to mean different things. Thus the word "dissertation", which refers to undergraduate or master's level work in the UK, is used exclusively for PhD level work in the USA. The word "thesis" is used in exactly the reverse order, i.e. it refers to work *below* PhD level in the USA, but only to PhD level work in the UK! However, as in the present chapter, "thesis" can also be used more generally to refer to the presentation of an argument.

American students may be unfamiliar with the term "dissertation tutor". The equivalent term in the USA is normally "thesis advisor".

Please note that this chapter is about work at undergraduate or master's level. UK terminology has been used.

What is a Dissertation?

A dissertation is an extended academic study which has clear and specific aims, and is based on the writer's own study, learning, research and original thought. Methods employed in the production of your work should reflect academic rigour, and the content should demonstrate substantial knowledge of the chosen topic area and the literature associated with this. (University of Portsmouth, 1996, p. 3)

A dissertation can be thought of as a piece of writing or report that has the content of four or five essays. It requires you to systematically research in depth and have something to say about your chosen topic. The length will vary according to the specific regulations of your university, but will probably be between 8,000–10,000 words (i.e. three to four times as long as this chapter).

When writing your dissertation you will be expected to:

(1) take greater responsibility for determining your aims and objectives, managing your time and resources, and in making effective use of your tutor;

(2) formulate and write a thesis relating to a social issue or problem that argues or has something to say about the topic (it is not enough just to describe or map out a field of study);

(3) interpret and explain the most appropriate theories, concepts and methodologies, and apply them to your subject;

(4) select and analyse relevant social data, case studies and social scenarios using appropriate research techniques;

(5) be able to evaluate others' and your own research findings;

(6) write, criticize and then re-write your work as you produce successive drafts of the different sections;

(7) draw your arguments together by making conclusions, recommendations, policy suggestions and/or action plans;

(8) submit a coherent, logically ordered finished product, which may need to be word-processed if this is a requirement of your university.

You may find it helpful to think of these eight points as *expected learning outcomes* (your department may even present them formally to you in this way, allocating a specified proportion of the potential marks to each outcome). You should study the above points, write out what they mean to you and what you think they are telling you to do. Next, it would be a good idea to discuss your interpretation with friends, fellow students (particularly those who have written dissertations), and the tutor responsible for dissertations (you could check whether your view of these expectations matches those of your department and tutor). Later, as you are researching and writing, you should ensure you address all of the required expectations, think how well you are attaining them, and make the adjustments necessary to improve your grade.

Choosing your Dissertation Topic Area

Choosing the right area to work on may take longer than you think. Remember that this topic will be occupying you for a long time, so you need to be sure that it will sustain your interest. Here are some ideas on how to go about the task.

Explore your Past Interests

You could start by thinking about social issues or subjects that have already captured your interest. Previously you may have researched work in an appropriate area. You might find it useful to go over your notes from lectures and your own reading, as well as essays or seminar papers you have written. These should remind you of issues you found interesting, puzzling and about which you want to find out more.

Look at Current Affairs

You will find a ready source of dissertation topics in media discussions and contemporary social debates. While such sources need to be approached with care, as journalists and commentators usually have an axe to grind, they do link into real-world concerns that make good areas for academic study. For example, local media discussion of vandalism might suggest an argument about media representations of juvenile crime, or debates about punishment and crime prevention.

Look Ahead to Future Work Plans

Choosing a topic related to a possible career will give you a chance to explore the area and it might well boost your chances at a future job interview. For example, if you wish to enter the police or community corrections service, selecting a crime-related topic will certainly give you a talking point at a future interview.

Look at Other Students' Past Dissertations

Dissertations written by other students are usually available from the library, and provide another source of ideas. Even if there appear to be several dissertations already written around your chosen area, you need not look for another topic. Your job will be to develop your own perspective and argument.

Developing your Initial Proposal

Once you have decided on your topic you will need to work out what it is you wish to say about it. At this point in your thinking it is a good idea to ask yourself, or discuss with others, why you are interested in your chosen topic. Asking "why?" helps you realize what you think about the topic, what you want to

A student's (Susan's) account of how she started to frame her dissertation thesis

I wanted to do my dissertation on nursery education. When I went to inform my tutor of my choice of topic our discussion went something like this.

Tutor: Nursery education, that sounds interesting and feasible, but why do you want to research this area?

Susan: Well I have a daughter in the nursery on campus.

Tutor: Well that's a good reason for choosing a topic – it helps in sustaining interest. But it wasn't what I was really getting at. What I meant to ask was, what is your *sociological* interest in this issue? What problems do you think you might be able to clarify by conducting research? For example, are you more interested in nurseries from the point of view of the quality of the educational environment they offer children, or are you more interested in the kind of deal they offer parents, or are you coming at it from an equal opportunities angle?

Susan: Well, the last of those I suppose. Yes, definitely – the equal opportunities angle. I had a lot of trouble trying to find a nursery place for Paula. It seems you're okay if you have money, because then you can always afford to get your kids into a nursery. But there are a limited number of places in affordable nurseries, and they often have priority lists for who is eligible. We are always being told that society needs our skills and that the opportunities are there for women to get the educational qualifications they require. But there are not enough cheap nursery places, on-campus or anywhere, for everyone who needs them. I'm not well off, and quite honestly before I got Paula in, I had to skip lectures because I couldn't find anyone to look after her. I've just managed to get her into the university nursery, but its been a real struggle. I'm wondering if other women have the same problems that I've had. Is it the same everywhere?

Tutor: Right. So you'll need to find out about the various provisions that exist in different universities and whether the number of places available per head of population varies from one university to another.

Susan: I guess they're all on tight budgets, but maybe some colleges, schools and universities put nursery education at the top of their spending list. I wonder what sort of factors affect the way they decide their priorities?

Tutor: Hold on, this is getting too big! You could compare nursery provisions in universities, or colleges within this region, but not all of them everywhere. It's too much. And remember you have other coursework to do!

Susan: Really I am interested in universities, so scrap the schools and colleges.

Tutor: Perhaps availability depends on the kind of university it is: whether it's in an urban area with lots of other problems, or if it's an established elite university, or it enrols students with money and other demands on university funds are not so great. The age-profile of the typical student population will also make a difference.

Susan: Yes, maybe it has something to do with the local economy, and campus politics? I'd also like to know how university nurseries allocate places. What discretion do they have? Do they take into account the needs of the parents – especially mothers – whether they're working and studying, or full-time students?

Box 33.1

research and say about it, and can give initial shape to your argument or thesis. You might try brainstorming ideas and comments about your selected topic and discuss this initial thinking with student peers and tutors, as did the student in the following case study (see Box 33.1).

Through the discussion in Box 33.1 we see how Susan's dissertation topic develops from a general interest in nursery education to a set of much more specific questions. As Susan thinks about her particular reasons for being interested in the topic, its scope begins to get focused. Thus the discussion helps clarify and define the *social problem* being considered, appropriate *research strategies* and the beginnings of an argument (see Box 33.2).

Susan's dissertation thesis takes shape

Social problem: The inconsistency between public encouragement for women to further their education and the apparent lack of support providing the practical means for women with children to do so.

Research strategy: In the first place to find out whether this is in fact a widespread problem, or whether the student's experience is atypical. If a general problem, to find out whether any special provision is made for mothers who are combining study with work.

Thesis: Structures maintaining unequal opportunities for women seeking access to universities vary in relation to the economic location of the university, the socio-economic status of the typical student and the policies of the different universities.

Box 33.2

After your first ideas have taken shape, you will find it useful to draft (and formally may be required to submit) a dissertation proposal. Such a proposal should define the orientation of your study in a clear, focused and un-ambiguous way. You should attempt to write a short summary, of no more than one paragraph, of what it is you are intending to argue about your chosen topic. This will be your first attempt at getting your thesis on paper. To this you should add a working title, first ideas about chapters or sections, research ideas, a list of the writing and other resources you are planning to use, and a work schedule (remember that it is best to plan backwards from the date specified for submitting your dissertation). You may be encouraged or even required to undertake an element of research for your dissertation, i.e. to collect your own data or undertake an investigation that involves more than just an examination of existing literature. Your research might involve interviews, observations, questionnaires, or the analysis of statistical evidence, reports, diaries or other documents. It is easy to be over-ambitious in your research, so remember that it is the quality of the research approach, rather than the scale of your research that is important. Do not attempt anything that is over-ambitious, devise a methodology that is appropriate for your selected topic and discuss with your tutor whatever research you decide to undertake. This research must conform to accepted ethical standards (see Chapter 39).

As your thinking and planning matures your proposal should become more detailed, covering the following areas.

- *Proposed title*, which should accurately convey your area of interest in an imaginative, but unambiguous way. You could check out your title with a friend: they should be able to understand what you are planning? If your completed dissertation does not match your title you will have problems, and might even fail.
- *Synopsis or summary*, which should provide a clear and concise outline of the main question or questions to be addressed and indicate the major

stages in your argument (ie. what you are trying to say and in what order you will say it). The synopsis or summary directs attention at what you are doing in your dissertation, whether this be an "assessment", "comparison", "analysis", "evaluation", "explanation", etc. Note here that including an "Abstract" might well be a formal requirement. An abstract is often found at the beginning of academic articles (find one and examine it carefully) and should summarize your thesis clearly and accurately. It is typically one paragraph and might begin: "In this dissertation it is argued that . . ."

- *Chapter or section headings*, with well thought-out titles, should be used to "signpost" the logical development of your argument. You will need to think carefully about the order in which you present your ideas and you might try moving the chapters or sections around until the order appears logical. You should also remember to think about introductions and conclusions to each section. Ultimately these will help the reader by indicating what you have done and where you are going.

- *Research approach*, indicating what research you propose, how you intend to collect and analyse your data and how your results will fit into and support your thesis. It is very easy to be over-ambitious here, so ensure that your plans are manageable. Also remember that all research raises ethical issues. Consider how you are going to be an ethical researcher, ensuring that your approach takes into account issues of privacy, race, gender, confidentiality of data, etc., and remember to fully acknowledge and reference anyone else's work you use.

- *Sources of information*, indicating what organizations and individuals you intend contacting for information or assistance and what books and articles you feel will be most useful.

- *Bibliography*, including a fully referenced reading list, which should include all the latest available sources to demonstrate the feasibility of your proposal. Readings should be focused and directly relevant to your topic.

- *Work schedule* outlining the meetings to arrange, literature to read and data to collect and analyse. Include time to write and get others to read draft chapters, as you proceed. Leave sufficient time to edit and finally redraft and produce the finished product (this final rewriting can take up to a quarter of the time available). If your dissertation involves contacting outside organizations or individuals, do this quickly as obtaining responses can take time. Whilst waiting for information to come through get on with another part of your dissertation.

The production of an effective dissertation proposal will provide you with a working plan to which you should constantly refer. It will become an invaluable tool for the management of your work.

Using your Tutor

You should consult with your tutor (and anyone else you can get to listen) at all stages in the development of your dissertation, from the moment you discuss your initial thinking, through the discussion of your formal dissertation proposal to the writing of the final draft. The best way to use your meetings with your tutor is turn up with a clear agenda, test your ideas, discuss plans, and seek advice on source material or research techniques. Make good notes during or after your tutorial, as ideas discussed soon get forgotten. If you then copy these to your tutor, they provide both of you with a reminder of earlier discussion next time you meet. Remember to remain flexible; your plans are necessarily provisional and will need constant monitoring and review.

Writing your Dissertation

Always write-up as you go along, chapter by chapter and submit drafts of what you write to your friends and tutor. Keep a fully referenced record of any sources and quotations you might use, as it is an enormous waste of time to have to go back later and find out. Your bibliography should emerge as your dissertation develops. As you write, check that you are not straying from your thesis or line of argument. Writing as you go helps clarify ideas and is the best way to ensure the production of a coherent dissertation. Always keep a backup copy of all you write in a safe place. Accumulating huge amounts of material

The Excellent Dissertation

Excellence is proven by demonstrating high standards in relation to all of the following criteria.

- The ability to select and draw together a broad range of up-to-date theoretical, empirical and primary research data in support of a tightly argued thesis with clear and specific aims that is relevant to a current debate.
- Accurate and critical understanding of theory, recent relevant debates, the quality and significance of appropriate research and the ability to use this understanding to present a thesis containing logical and insightful conclusions and recommendations.
- Presentational skills including: adherence to the required house style (e.g. word processed, correct margins, use of prescribed citation system, etc.); use of anti-discriminatory language; clear and appropriate data presentation; correct syntax, grammar and paragraph construction, use of sections and section headings; use of an introduction that states the thesis and approach taken, indicates the structure of what is to follow, and ends with a summary and conclusions (recommendations, action plans, policy ideas, etc.) that logically follow from the previous argument.
- Effective time and work planning evidenced by: the original project proposal (which should contain a work schedule); use of the library for research and the dissertation tutor as a consultant; and the on-time delivery of the dissertation.

Lower grades are awarded where the student does not demonstrate the above high standards in all aspects of their learning. Hence an on-time and excellently presented dissertation will be awarded a lower grade if the dissertation has no argument and merely describes a field of study. Lower grades will also be given where theories are misrepresented, the information used is not the best available, where the account is little more than a personal life history, where research techniques are misapplied, or the conclusion is just a summary. The message is know the expectations, consult with your tutor and then you can plan, manage, deliver and be assessed having given of your very best.

Box 33.3

and attempting to write up at the last moment is the biggest possible mistake. As successive drafts and sections are completed, written in accordance with the appropriate house style rules, you should evaluate them yourself with reference to the above eight *expected learning outcomes*. Doing this will ensure that your dissertation is the best that you can achieve.

Now that you have read this chapter try answering the following questions:

(1) What is a dissertation?

(2) What are the eight Learning Outcomes that you might be expected to achieve?
(3) How might you go about selecting a dissertation topic?
(4) What is the purpose of a dissertation proposal?
(5) What is "primary research"?

If you can answer these questions, you are well on the way to understanding what you need to do. Overcoming the uncertainty about what is necessary is half the battle. Best of luck!

References

Dunleavy, P. 1986: *Studying for a Degree in the Humanities and Social Sciences*. London: Macmillan.

Hampson, L. 1994: *How's Your Dissertation Going? Students share the rough reality of dissertation and project work*. Lancaster: Lancaster University.

University of Portsmouth, 1996: *Research Management BSc (Hons) Sociology, Resource Book*. Portsmouth: School of Social and Historical Studies.

Acknowledgements

The authors would like to thank colleagues in the School of Social and Historical Studies for their ideas which have informed and helped shape the writing of this chapter. Particular thanks to Martin Giddey for his quoted definition of a dissertation.

36

Society as Text: Documents, Artifacts and Social Practices

Simon Cottle

This essay aims to encourage you to engage in sociological thought and enquiry. It invites you to look more closely, more sociologically, at the documents, artifacts and social practices that continually surround us and, furthermore, to widen your understanding of what "documents", "artifacts" and "social practices" can be. Contrary to popular belief, sociological enquiry does not necessarily involve a large survey, a questionnaire and a researcher with more degrees than a thermometer! All of us are perfectly capable of engaged sociological thought – at any time, in any place. Constantly surrounded as we are by a ready supply of documents, artifacts and social practices the sociologist can always find a rich and plentiful resource for his or her sociological imagination. As discussed in earlier chapters, C. Wright Mills' classic statement on the "sociological imagination" continues to provide a useful vantage point from which the changing nature of society and the social can be approached. Informed by a historical sense of change, a cross-cultural or anthropological understanding of difference, and a critical and questioning stance to the nature and forms of contemporary society, the sociological imagination helps us to see and understand social processes – no matter how seemingly matter-of-fact or mundane. Moreover, it can help us relate "personal troubles of milieu" to those wider "public issues" involving changing social structures. When directed at documents, artifacts and social practices the sociological imagination takes us into fascinating, often uncharted, territory, prompting new ways of

seeing and even new departures for further sociological inquiry.

Documents Record and Represent

Documents, as a sociological resource, are typically thought of as written records "containing" or "storing" information awaiting analysis and interpretation. The popular image is that of official or government papers, musty and encrusted with dust: perhaps of Karl Marx poring over the British civil service's so-called "Blue Books" or Émile Durkheim interrogating reams of official statistics on suicides. For sociologists, however, the term "document" has come to mean a much wider range of written texts than this. John Scott usefully classifies documents in relation to two dimensions: authorship and access (Scott, 1990, p. 14). He reminds us that authorship can be personal (for example, letters, diaries, household accounts, and so on) or official and, if official, whether it is produced by a private bureaucracy or part of the State. The origins of "private" or "public" documents are of importance, revealing different purposes and intentions. They can also help illuminate the changing roles and responsibilities of "personal life" and "public administration" and the historically changing relation between the two.

Scott further categorizes documents according to whether access to them is closed, restricted, open-archival or open-published. Again, issues of purpose and intention are raised, now in relation to their degree of openness or availability for public scrutiny. Whereas a diary normally remains a "closed" document with access restricted to its author, following their death it may be made available by relatives, say, on a "restricted" basis to trusted interested parties. In some instances it may even be placed in an "open-archive" and thus made available to those enthusiastic enough to seek it out, or "openly" published and made easily available to the public at large. The changing forms of access can thus reveal much about the changing social values placed upon the document, irrespective of the possible motivations informing its production in the first place. That said, diaries like other documents can be produced for different purposes and may not always be what they seem; while most diaries are written for strictly private purposes, some are undoubtedly written for an anticipated future audience. The sociologist's interest in documents, then, is not confined to matters of "content" but extends to consideration of their possible purposes and uses, the interests they reflect *and* forms of subsequent availability, or reasons for their denied access and secrecy.[1]

Documents, therefore, need not be approached solely as sources of information; they have other dimensions and insights to

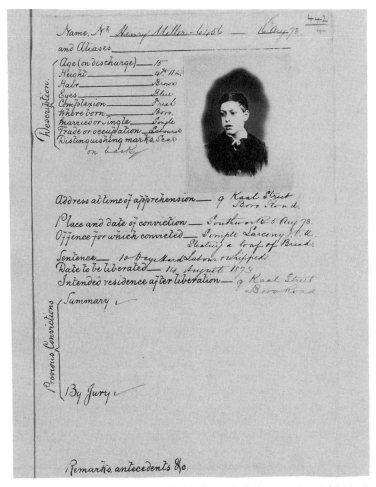

Figure 36.1 Wandsworth Prison record, 1873 (Public Records Office, London, PCOM 2/291).

offer us. Documents do not simply report and record; they also *represent*. For example, a patient's medical card, as well as telling us something about this particular person's medical history, can tell us about the sort of information that is collected, stored and used by doctors and even about the sort of society that encourages such documentation. That is, documents invite us to use our sociological imaginations to recover aspects of their social context which those who produced the document may never have intended or even thought about.

However, reading documents in this way is often far from straightforward because words and phrases change their meanings and may be used in a technical, ironic or metaphorical way. Thus making sense of what we read also requires *interpretation*, in which we bring to bear our existing knowledge of the social and cultural circumstances under which the document was produced, the purposes of its production and the way it was used. Such knowledge is essential if we wish to "read" documents, that is to decipher what they represent beyond the literal meanings of the words they contain, but it also creates problems because of the preconceived ideas we inevitably bring to bear on interpretation.

To put some flesh on these ideas and to demonstrate how the sociological imagination can be deployed on documents, let us look at a specific example. Consider the Wandsworth Prison record of 1873 shown in Figure 36.1. A straightforward response to such a document would be to approach it as a record. Approached this way, the particular record can be viewed as one of countless others which, taken together, provide an overview of the social composition of prison inmates in this particular prison in the late nineteenth century, placing on record what crimes were committed by them and what punishments were officially meted out. This record thus provides one small piece of "documentary" evidence in our attempt to build an overview of crime and punishment in this period. In more personalized terms the individual record may also prompt reflection on the biographical details of the inmate, perhaps his young age

and the severity of the punishment received, and may even prompt further documentary searches in pursuit of a more complete biographical picture of this hapless young boy. Approached in another way, however, this record may yet tell us other, perhaps more sociologically profound, things about crime and society in this period.

John Tagg, for example, when discussing this same image in relation to the early use of photography, argues, "What we have in this standardised image is more than a picture of a supposed criminal. It is a portrait of the disciplinary method: the body made object; divided and studied; enclosed in a cellular structure of space whose architecture is the file-index ... When accumulated, such images amount to a new representation of society" (Tagg, 1988, p. 76). What we have here, then, is an interpretation of how the early use of photography within the penal system exemplified its incorporation more widely into the institutional means of social surveillance and control. In other words, this "record" along with countless others, does not simply record the social composition of prison inmates, their various crimes and forms of punishment – interesting as this undoubtedly is; and nor does it simply demonstrate the involvement of early photography in the penal system – though this too is of interest. Subject to interpretation the document now provides profound insight into the changing, increasingly bureaucratized, nature of society and systems of social surveillance and control – sociological themes developed most forcefully by Max Weber and, more recently, Michel Foucault. Approached historically, comparatively and critically, all key vantage points of the sociological imagination, this record can thus help illuminate the changing nature of modernity and its forms of institutional and disciplinary control.

Documents, it would seem, can tell different stories to those originally intended. On occasion documents can also misrepresent. Consider, for instance, the newspaper photograph in Figure 36.2 which was widely used by the British press in expectation of the momentous 1994 declaration by the IRA (Irish

Figure 36.2 *Daily Mirror*, 31 August 1994 (photograph courtesy of PaceMaker).

Republican Army) of a ceasefire in its "long war" to reunite Ireland. Figure 36.2 illustrates the benefits sometimes gained from having access to alternative sources of information (in this case knowledge of the full slogan), and also demonstrates the value of having a wider *comparative* understanding of the social and policital viewpoints informing "the troubles" in Northern Ireland.

Here we have an image seemingly expressing

a general hope for peace. A boy throws a tennis ball up against a wall on which the slogan "Time For Peace" has been written. The *Mirror*'s subheading states "The Writing's on the Wall" and "Peace With No Strings". It subsequently became known that the full slogan in fact read "Time for Peace: Time To Go" (i.e. meaning time for British troops to go). The decision to crop the photograph omitting those final words prompts a very different understanding of the peace process. Whereas "Time For Peace" invites an interpretation of a generalized, perhaps liberal-humanist, concern for peace, the omitted words raise a less generalized, more conditional, prospect for peace based on the particular viewpoint of Northern Ireland's republican community – "Time To Go" indicates that for some peace may remain conditional on the withdrawal of the British from Ulster. Again, the point here is that pictures often don't simply record, but rather "represent" in particular ways (Cottle, 1997).[2]

This raises consideration of the symbolic appeal, in contrast to the informational content, of social texts. To help illustrate this let us look again at the newspaper photograph in Figure 36.2. If the photograph and its news interpretation provides an example of what could be termed "news distortion" (where the graffiti artist's "document" appears to have been deliberately misread by the photographer and/or newspaper editor as they created a secondary document), its visual impact and appeal invite further comment. This "document" works at a highly symbolic, in contrast to informational, level. A young boy playfully throwing a ball up against a sloganed wall, arm outstretched, feet in mid-air, has become a potent symbol of peace, hope and the future. Children and the idea of childhood, it has often been observed, are invested with historically variant meanings, values and societal aspirations and fears. When approaching news visuals what we often find is that they work at a symbolic as well as referential level. That is, they don't simply record and document in an evidential way, but aim to condense and convey social meanings through a symbolic image. The concrete scene represents abstract ideas; the individual stands for the collective. Further, they often invite not simply rational or analytical engagement but emotional and affective response, encouraging bonds of moral or social solidarity and identification. The capacity of documents to build, as well as portray, social relationships thus points to their representational complexity and social richness, a dimension that needs to be attended to carefully.

Artifacts: Material Culture with Meaning

A narrow view of documents as written texts may blind us to the rich and increasingly plentiful, non-written texts that are produced, circulated and consumed in society. If a "text" is understood to be anything, written or non-written, that is capable of sustaining or being invested with meaning, clearly society itself becomes a "text" composed of a multitude of texts, promising to reveal much about its characteristic social nature, changing social relations and processes.

Many "texts" have, of course, been produced to convey meanings, for example postcards, street signs or compact disk (CD) covers; they make use of visual imagery and language. But society is also suffused with objects and materials which are not designed principally to convey meaning in this way. Here things and objects may come to have abstract meaning for people through association and common experiences, thus becoming part of material culture (Hodder, 1994, p. 396). These too are of potential interest for sociologists. If the term "document", as conventionally understood, can usefully be expanded to encompass different "texts", so too can the idea of "artifact" be extended to encompass material culture more generally. The term "artifact" conventionally refers to products of artisans and craftsmen and is often used in the context of discussion of past societies. However, "artifact" can here usefully be approached as any produced material object which has become invested with meaning and therefore become part of material culture.

In the news photograph (Fig. 36.2) a brick wall is depicted. Walls, of course, are invariably built for functional purposes, typically protecting gardens, property and people from the weather and other people. They can also, however, be attributed with and sustain diverse social meanings. In the context of Northern Ireland walls have physically separated communities and symbolized the extent of communal antagonism, mistrust and fear. Walls more generally serve to mark out social space, territories and social distinctions of social power, wealth and status. Those who live behind high walls may physically demonstrate to their neighbours ideas of social exclusivity or, as in the case of prison inmates, their ascribed social unacceptability. Here questions of meaning often depend literally on which side of the wall you find yourself. This is important in that it points to possible competing interpretations of the same social text, as well as the role of social interests within these "readings". Material objects, then, can sustain diverse meanings for those who encounter them and readily become part of material culture. These "meaningful" material objects can reveal much about the nature of the social formation from which they derive and provide rich pastures for sociological grazing.

So far you have been invited to recognize how material objects, as well as documents, can convey meaning. However, the meanings sustained by these "texts" do not simply reside within the texts themselves, but must be actively interpreted by the "reader". This, as we have seen, may well involve a consideration of the text's origins, purposes and its subsequent uses. The conditions under which it has been produced, circulated and consumed can all influence our interpretation, as can our own value position and interests. No wonder, perhaps, the meanings of texts are often found to be equivocal and highly contested; responses that once again provide insights into the social relations and conflicts characterizing a particular society at a particular point in time.

Social Practices as Texts

Finally sociologists do not have to restrict themselves to studying "hard" evidence, whether documents or artifacts. The claim made at the outset was that anything, with the help of the sociological imagination, can be found to have deep sociological interest. Even the most mundane, ordinary, taken-for-granted documents, artifacts *and* practices can reveal much about the changing social nature and social relations that characterize societies across both time and space. Consider, for example, that most seemingly inconsequential practice of blowing one's nose. Most of us probably assume the need to occasionally blow one's nose is an unavoidable and shared biological fact of life, and rarely grant it a second's thought. On reflection, however, things are not so simple; this apparently "meaningless" act may hold more social significance and insight than first assumed. Reactions to people who have running noses, but who fail to take "appropriate" behavioural reactions, whether the "green-sleeved" child or handkerchief-less tramp, are revealing in this respect. Social meanings evidently do, implicitly, inform this taken-for- granted social practice. Furthermore, such meanings are by no means universal but vary through time and across cultures.

Norbert Elias has convincingly demonstrated, for example, how in Europe blowing one's nose has been invested with a wide range of social meanings across the centuries. Moreover this is no trivial matter, but provides an insight into the massive historical "civilizing process" of self-discipline operating at a cultural level and also manifest in, amongst others, table manners, spitting, attitudes towards natural functions, behaviour in the bedroom, and sexual relations (Elias, 1994, original 1939). Elias's historical recovery of the practice of blowing one's nose proves fascinating reading and exemplifies how period documents, the artifact of a handkerchief *and* the social practice of blowing one's nose can provide deep insights into the changing social nature and meaning of behaviour.

The following, taken from Elias's cited period documents, including books on courtly behaviour, social manners and etiquette, make reference to the introduction of the handkerchief in relation to the evolving practice of blowing one's nose (1994. pp. 117–21.

It is unseemly to blow your nose into the tablecloth (15th century)

In the fifteenth century people blew their noses into their fingers, and the sculptures of the age were not afraid to reproduce the gesture, in a passably realistic form, in their monuments. Among the knights, the plourans, at the grave of Philip the Bold at Dijon, one is seen blowing his nose into his coat, another into his fingers.

To blow your nose on your hat or clothing is rustic, and to do so with the arm or elbow befits a tradesman; nor is it much more polite to use the hand, if you immediately smear the snot on your garment. It is proper to wipe the nostrils with a handkerchief, and to do this while turning away, if more honourable people are present (16th century).

In 1599, after her death, the inventory of Henry IV's mistress is found to contain "five handkerchiefs worked in gold, silver and silk, worth 100 crowns".

You should avoid making a noise when blowing your nose . . . Before blowing it, it is impolite to spend a long time taking out your handkerchief. It shows a lack of respect towards the people you are with to unfold it in different places to see where you are to use it . . . After blowing your nose you should take care not to look into your handkerchief (18th century).

Evidently there is more to blowing one's nose than dispatching unwanted snot! A close reading of the above reveals how the historical development of manners was informed by a wider "civilizing process" involving social relations marked by distinctions of wealth, class, gender and status, distinctions that inform both the behaviour of, and the meanings ascribed to, blowing one's nose. All three of our identified social "texts" – documents, artifacts and social practices – have here been found at work and each has revealed meanings of deep sociological significance. You may want to check out for yourself to what extent social distinctions of wealth, class, gender and status continue to inform the practice of blowing one's nose in today's society!

Conclusion

Hopefully, this short discussion will encourage you to look anew at the "documents", "artifacts" and "social practices" that surround you and seek out the sociological significance contained therein. Of course, entirely different examples could have been selected from the near infinity of documents, artifacts and social practices available. But that is the point. Anything, and everything, can be read as a social text. Approached as text, society can indeed prove fascinating and insightful reading.

Notes

1. For a useful introduction to "using documents" see Macdonald and Tipton (1993). A more detailed but also accessible discussion is Scott (1990).

2. A detailed discussion of ways of analysing media visuals is Cottle (1997).

References

Cottle, S. 1997: Analysing visuals: the poor relation in mass communication research. In A. Hansen, S. Cottle, R. Negrine and C. Newbold, *Mass Communication Research Methods*. London: Macmillan.

Elias, N. 1994: *The Civilizing Process*. Oxford: Blackwell.

Hodder, I. 1994: The interpretation of documents and material culture. In N. K. Denzin and Y. S. Lincoln (eds), *The Handbook of Qualitative Research*. London: Sage.

Macdonald, K. and Tipton, C. 1993: Using documents. In N. Gilbert (ed.), *Researching Social Life* – London: Sage pp. 187–200.

Scott, J. 1990: *A Matter of Record – Documentary Sources in Social Research*. Oxford: Polity Press.

Tagg, J. 1988: *The Burden of Representation*. London: Macmillan.

37

The Researcher's Craft: Observing, Listening and Note-taking

Robert G. Burgess

How do you decide what methods to use in a research project? There is no one best method of social investigation but, on the other hand, choosing a method on the grounds that you like the idea of doing some interviews or participant observation is not a recommended strategy. The methods you choose depend upon the research questions posed, for without research questions and problems, research itself is arid. What this means is that all sociologists who are actively involved in the conduct of research need to have a knowledge of methodology and to be able to evaluate different methods in order to select those that are most appropriate for their work. An important element of this is knowing how research is done, as opposed to the methodological purism found in some specialist works on methodology. Some methodologists are so concerned with the elegance of the method and the search for perfection that they fail to consider the way in which a range of methods can be used to resolve problems that occur in practice. As the American sociologist Howard Becker wrote at the beginning of his book *Sociological Work* (Becker, 1970, p. 3), "Methodology is too important to be left to methodologists." Thinking about research methods is an activity in which all sociologists are actively involved when doing research projects. Indeed, many sociologists have now produced autobiographical accounts about how they have chosen research methods and conducted their research projects (Burgess, 1992; Bryman and Burgess, 1994).

Choosing Methods

As many sociologists have shown, the link between the research question and the method of investigation does not mean that a particular research question automatically *dictates* the choice of a particular method. Instead it is essential for sociologists embarking on a project to consider using a wide array of methodological approaches. Let me give an example from my own research. At the time of writing I am engaged in a study of training needs in the areas of Coventry and Warwickshire. The project is sponsored by the Coventry and Warwickshire Training and Enterprise Council who are interested in the training needs of managers and their employees in small and medium sized enterprises in the area. The project is funded for one year and employs one and a half researchers. We are focusing on policy issues concerning training, an analysis of training needs, and the ways in which training is implemented in some companies. The way in which we are approaching this study depends on several issues. First, sponsorship; that is the amount of money that is available in order to buy research time. Secondly, the geographical area that is to be covered. Thirdly, the industrial and commercial enterprises that need to be covered. In these circumstances a range of approaches seem to be appropriate, as the sociologist needs to think about the ways in which different methods can provide complementary sets of data to address the research problem that has been posed. We are using a combination of survey research and case study approaches and the key issue is how the data generated by these different methods fit together. We are conducting a large-scale survey in order to have a general idea of the training needs being specified by managers in a broad range of companies. The data generated by the survey is being used to frame questions for six case studies drawn from different sectors and based on companies of different size. These case studies provide more detailed insights into the training needs of managers in the different sectors, and so complement the survey data. Thus the case studies lend qualitative depth to our interpretation of the survey findings, while the survey data provides a useful indication of the statistical "representativeness" of the detailed case studies. Furthermore, the case studies are being used to tap into different levels in the company hierarchies, so that we gain a range of different perspectives that complement those of the training managers obtained through the survey data. The scale of these studies may be different, but the data need to be complementary. The methods used need to complement each other in order to focus on the issues and problems posed by the research team in this investigation.

Many research commentators have talked about the importance of using different methodological approaches in their work (Stacey, 1969; Denzin, 1970; Burgess, 1984). Here, the focus is upon the principle of combining different methods, or of checking out one method against another using different strategies of social investigation. In funded research projects it is often helpful to check quantitative data against data acquired by qualitative methods (as we have done in the "Training Needs" project). But because large-scale quantitative surveys usually require large resources, students working on collaborative projects or writing dissertations will tend to use a series of qualitative methods in order to handle their small scale study. It is to these approaches we now turn.

Approaches to Qualitative Research

Many methods used by researchers engaged in qualitative studies tend to have an everyday quality about them. Some researchers are involved in observing the activities of participants. Others are engaged in talking with the people they are studying. Some collect the documents that the individuals produce, which may include records, notes, diaries and photographs. So what is distinctive about the way in which a *sociologist* engages in these approaches when observing, listening, talking and recording? No matter what approach is used, it is essential that the sociologist works in a systematic way. Firstly, the researcher has to think about what is to be observed and who is to be engaged in conversation and interview. Secondly, the researcher has to consider what is to be recorded, and how it is to be analysed and reported, for the sociologist who engages in observation, interview and conversation has to return time and time again to the material that has been recorded to consider various ways in which it can be analysed and interpreted to generate articles and books for a range of different audiences. Finally, the sociologist also needs to consider the effect that he or she has upon the situation that is being studied, as the researcher is part of the situation that is researched. It is these activities that we now examine.

Observing

Traditionally, observation and participant observation have been associated with the work of anthropologists such as Malinowski dating from the first decades of this century (Burgess, 1982, 1984). Certainly, observation was often equated with research workers going to live among individuals in distant parts of the world where the tendency was to focus upon exotic behaviour rather than upon day-to-day practice. In recent years this emphasis has undergone considerable change. There is now much interest in the way in which observational methods can be used by anthropologists and sociologists to study behaviour within reach of their own universities. Situations in schools, hospitals, factories, trade unions, youth centres, churches and community centres all become appropriate sites for observational study.

It is important that the researcher who intends using observational methods asks himself or herself a series of questions: why? who? what? when? and where? The most fundamental question is the first, "why use observational methods?". There could be a number of good reasons, according to the particular research questions being investigated. These may include providing basic data on fundamental social processes that need to be studied over a period of time, providing the context for other aspects of an investigation and complementing research data that are generated using other methods. Then there is the question, "what is to be observed?". Within any research site there are a number of different research locations and observing at those different locations will influence the kind of data

that are obtained. For example, a researcher studying in a school may make observations in a classroom, in a laboratory, on the sports field, in the staff room and in the dining hall. Each location provides a different social context for sociological study and has an influence on what the researcher can study. The question "who is to be observed?" has a bearing on the choice of location and the events to be observed. It also focuses the researcher's attention upon principles of selection. The researcher needs also to consider when observations are to occur and, finally, where they occur. All these questions need to be evaluated by the researcher to overcome bias and to ensure that a study is conducted which draws on a wide range of evidence to address the research problem.

Accordingly, the activities of an observer do not merely rest upon the art of observing. Instead, observation relies on a variety of skills which were neatly summed up by Howard Becker when he wrote:

Figure 37.1 Observation involves watching carefully what occurs within a social situation, talking to the participants and interpreting what has been observed.

The participant observer gathers data by participating in the daily life of the people or organization he studies. He watches the people he is studying to see in what situations they ordinarily meet and how they behave in them. He enters into conversation with some or all of the participants in these situations, and discovers their interpretations of the events he has observed. (Becker, 1958, p. 652)

This statement points to four important aspects of participant observation. Firstly, the importance of participation as well as observation. In this respect, the researcher has to evaluate the influence that he or she has upon the situations that are observed. Secondly, participant observation involves watching what occurs within a social situation. Thirdly, observation is complemented by talking with people in order that conversations complement the observations that are made. Finally, the researcher has a responsibility to interpret those events and activities that have been observed and discussed.

Speaking and Listening

It is important to be aware that interviewing is not just a matter of reading questions from a schedule, but requires good interpersonal and, especially, good listening skills. Only by careful listening will the interviewer be able to probe successfully, drawing out opinions and nuances that are not immediately apparent. In this respect, student researchers may have more complex motives for conducting research than trained researchers. While those working on a funded research project are primarily concerned with the findings of an investigation and how they are to be disseminated (so that individuals who are aware they do not make particularly skilful interviewers may choose to leave this part of the research to others), as a student you will additionally be concerned with your own development as a researcher, and so should be keen to get experience in as many aspects of the research process as you can. Only through practice will you get to know your own strengths and

weaknesses as a researcher, and thus learn how you are best able to make a contribution in team settings.

All these skills are developed through the use of interview approaches when structured or unstructured interviews are conducted with individuals in the field (Burgess, 1984). A structured interview is used when the identical questions are asked in the same order to a range of individuals in a study. In contrast, unstructured interviews draw on the art of conversation as the interviewer develops an agenda of interview topics which are not discussed in a particular order with the people in the study. Once again, a similar set of questions to those that arose in the conduct of observation come into play. The researcher has to begin by asking: why conduct interviews? Here, it is essential to consider the group of people that are being studied in order to decide whether interviewing them is the most effective strategy to obtain data. Interviews are very time consuming for the interviewee, and also for the interviewer who not only has to conduct the interview but find the time to record, transcribe, and analyse it. However, the interview may provide data that cannot be provided by documentary sources and observational methods. Indeed, interviews allow the researcher to follow up issues that have been observed or identified in documents. Interviews provide a setting in which the researcher can ask people about their reasons for engaging in certain activities.

If the researcher decides that an interview approach is most appropriate, then a series of other questions come into play. Firstly, where to interview. Is it appropriate to interview in an office as opposed to interviewing in someone's home? Certainly, the trade-off between public and private settings is essential to consider if confidentiality is to be maintained. But having decided where to interview leads us on to consider who might be selected for interview. Once again, a sampling issue arises as those researchers who can engage in small-scale qualitative studies have to think about the principles of selection. Accordingly, the researcher has to think about the categories of individuals that are to be interviewed in any study. Fundamental to it all is the researcher deciding on what basis people are to be selected. In turn, appropriate strategies have to be devised to obtain and record the data. Often, research involving unstructured interviews does not rely on lists of questions, with the result that topics are discussed with an individual in some considerable depth. However, having decided what data are to be collected, it is essential that the researcher considers how these data are to be recorded.

Recording, Note-Taking and Writing

In the literature on social research and research methodology, great emphasis is placed on the design of projects and the collection of evidence, with great stress being placed on the methods that are used to obtain data. Consequently little attention is paid to ways of recording data, or to strategies for analysing the material, especially data derived from observation and interview (Bryman and Burgess, 1994). Moreover, relatively little has been reported on the writing process, which has only recently come into view (Atkinson, 1990). Yet without a careful approach to data recording there will be nothing for the researcher to analyse and interpret. Investigators are often involved in writing throughout their projects when they produce notes, log books, diaries and working papers. These documents are used to develop concepts and so contribute to the understanding of the situation being studied, and, as mentioned earlier, researchers need to think about how they can express their research questions, report on their activities and develop elements of their investigation in order to produce writing for dissemination to different kinds of audience.

Many interviews are now tape-recorded, but the researcher has to remember that if the data are tape-recorded arrangements need to be made about how these data are to be transcribed (by the researcher or by a secretary), and an appropriate amount of time needs to be set aside for the transcription to occur (a one hour tape usually takes about seven hours to transcribe unless the re-

searcher has decided only to focus on particular topics or themes that were discussed in the interviews).

A second approach to data recording is the use of notes. These may be recorded in log books, field note books, diaries and journals (Burgess, 1981; Holly, 1984, 1989). A log allows the researcher to keep notes on situations and circumstances. It is an *aide-mémoire* rather than a continuous piece of writing. Diaries are less structured and, as Mary-Lou Holly comments, also include reactions from the writer.

Because diary writing is interpretative, descriptive on multi-dimensions, unstructured, sometimes factual, and often all of these, it is difficult to analyse. It is not easy to separate thoughts and feelings from facts and, as the writer, to extricate yourself from your writing. (Holly, 1984, p. 5)

Diaries allow the researcher to engage in writing on a regular basis. Each entry can be used to clarify the project, to report findings, to comment on the methodology and discuss the way in which the research is being done as well as suggesting the concepts and categories that can be developed to analyse the data. However, Holly goes a step further by distinguishing logs and diaries from journals which she argues are structured, descriptive and contain objective notes as well as some commentary. This may be useful in terms of methodological analysis that can contribute to different types of writing on the research process. When a researcher uses these different approaches to record data in what I would call a diary, they can include all the activities and decisions in which he or she has been involved, a commentary on the activity of doing research, and a record of a situation or event in which the writer has been involved (Burgess, 1994, p. 301). Fundamental to this approach is the way in which the researcher records data that will subsequently be used for data analysis.

The researcher's diary can be complemented by sets of material that have been produced and recorded by those who are studied. But many more documents are available for use. Almost every research site that is the subject of investigation involves groups of people who are involved in the production of documentary material. These ready-made documents can be used alongside documents that the researcher generates or requests others to develop in the course of an investigation, including diaries that those who have been observed and interviewed have been encouraged to keep (Burgess, 1994). This material can be used to produce the articles and books that are the product of the research process.

In the course of developing a research project, the investigator needs to consider the structure of the final report including the sections that are to be developed, and the ways in which these sections can be configured and reconfigured. This may involve a consideration of the relationship between the research design and the final report as well as between data collection, data analysis and writing. In this way, the process of structuring and writing the final report does not remain until the end of a project, but instead is integral to every phase of it. In these circumstances, the researcher is involved in drafting and redrafting material throughout the study in order to do justice to the evidence that has been collected, recorded and analysed.

Conclusions

The focus of this chapter has been on conducting research and the way in which researchers need to ask questions, not only of those who are being studied, but also of themselves. This is the nub of intellectual craftsmanship where the researcher is continually reflecting upon the dynamic interplay of problems, theories and methods (Mills, 1959; Burgess, 1995). Methods of social investigation need to be examined in the context of doing sociological work, being a sociologist and developing the craft of sociology. Certainly, methodological skills are essential to become a sociologist, but such skills are also dependent upon good ideas. Central to the conduct of sociological research is the ability of the sociologist to pose questions and consider methods which can be used to collect, record, analyse and produce data that will contribute to sociology as well as to the development of policy and practice.

References

Atkinson, P. 1990: *The Ethnographic Imagination.* London: Routledge.

Becker, H. S. 1958: Problems of inference and proof in participant observation. *American Sociological Review*, 23, 652–60.

—— 1970: *Sociological Work.* New Brunswick: Transaction Books.

Bryman, A. and Burgess, R. G. (eds) 1994: *Analysing Qualitative Data.* London: Routledge.

Burgess, R. G. 1981: Keeping a research diary. *Cambridge Journal of Education*, 11(1), 75–81.

—— (ed) 1982: *Field Research: A Sourcebook and Field Manual.* London: Allen & Unwin.

—— 1984: *In the Field.* London: Allen & Unwin.

—— (ed.) 1992: *Learning from the Field.* London: JAI Press.

—— 1994: On diaries and diary keeping. In

N. Bennett, R. Glatter and R. Levacic (eds), *Improving Educational Management.* London: Paul Chapman, pp. 300–11.

—— 1995: Problems, theories and methods in the work of Howard Becker. In R. G. Burgess (ed.) *Howard Becker on Education.* Buckingham: Open University Press, 1–15.

Denzin, N. 1970: *The Research Act.* Chicago, IL: Aldine.

Holly, M. L. 1984: *Keeping a Personal Professional Journal.* Deakin: Deakin University Press.

—— 1989: *Writing to Grow.* Portsmouth, NH: Heinemann.

Mills, C. W. 1959: *The Sociological Imagination.* New York: Oxford University Press.

Stacey, M. 1969: *Methods of Social Research.* Oxford: Pergamon Press.

38

Team Research

David Phillips

Introduction

Much sociological research is conducted by teams of social scientists combining their skills and efforts in joint projects. Research teams can take different forms and sizes, from two or three researchers in the same institution up to groups of specialists working in different countries on a cross-national study. There are significant practical and methodological advantages in working together but there are also problems to overcome – such as communicating, developing common perspectives, and confronting issues of power relations and equality within the team.

Until recently, the dominant image in research methods texts was the solitary sociological investigator. Team research received little attention, which is surprising since most practising social researchers acquire their skills through working with others. A capacity to work effectively and cooperatively within a team is a priority for social research employers seeking new staff. Team working is an effective way for students to learn about the realities of research and to gain practical experience of research techniques. The final section of this chapter looks in more detail at how students can enhance their research skills through small group projects.

The principal advantages offered by a team-based approach are:

- *creativity and generation of ideas* through collective discussion and "brainstorming" activity;
- *division of labour* permitting the sharing of re-

search tasks, often in terms of functional specialization;
- *extending the scope* of a research study in various ways;
- combining the *multiple perspectives* of team members in ways that can strengthen research methodology, analysis and interpretation.

Problematic issues associated with team research include:

- appropriate *practical organization* to manage the logistics of cooperative working;
- *team structure* and formal roles, with a choice usually between hierarchic (pyramid-like) or non-hierarchic (collective) ways of working;
- *power and equality* within the team;
- *potential for conflict* between team members.

Advantages of Working in Teams and Overcoming Problems

An immediate practical benefit is the opportunity to share the burden of the work with others, and this can extend to all aspects of the research process. For example, preliminary ideas can be developed and refined through discussion and shared insights. Data may be gathered in greater volume and detail, contacts with informants and subsequent interviews can be pursued more rapidly, data processed and research findings produced more quickly. Bringing researchers together can enhance the scope of research in terms of geographical coverage, enlarged sample size, extended time span or inclusion of different settings.

Division of labour within a team can be arranged to exploit the particular strengths and skills of individual members: for example, some individuals are more effective at depth-interviewing, others may have particular statistical or computing expertise. Often team roles will be linked explicitly to functional specialization, with responsibilities differentiated by technical requirements. This is typical of large-scale surveys, with different team members responsible for each stage of the research under the coordination of an overall project director. Lead researchers plan the research strategy and draft the survey questionnaire; specialists advise on sample design and selection methods; information is gathered by a field force of interviewers, trained and coordinated by a fieldwork manager; data returned to the research office is coded and checked by data preparation staff prior to entry into the computer; subsequent analysis may call on the expertise of statisticians or academic specialists; research staff and project director will prepare a final report.

Certain research topics positively require a team-based approach. An example is international comparative research where data is collected within a standardized framework from different countries, for subsequent analysis of underlying similarities and national differences. In the 1980s the European Values Systems Study Group adopted this approach to examine the structures of core social values and value change (see Harding and Phillips, 1986). Initially a large-scale survey carried out in 10 European countries in 1981, the study was eventually extended to over 20 countries world-wide and repeated with modifications in the early 1990s. Careful planning and design of the initial survey required a sizeable coordinating team drawn from participating European countries; within each country local teams were responsible for data gathering, relations with survey agencies, and initial analysis. Before the research could begin, the coordinating team had to spend considerable time and effort reconciling the interests of participants from diverse cultural backgrounds and with differing sociological priorities.

Many other research situations may call for a team approach. Research across ethnic boundaries is likely to encounter less suspicion and achieve greater success where the team includes participants from target communities. Community action research, which seeks to initiate policy change and action through research-based intervention, requires joint involvement and planning between researchers, community activists and representatives (see Starr, this volume).

Combining researchers with different skills can permit development of multi-level research designs, perhaps combining the findings of a survey with follow-up participant observation to explore certain findings in depth. More complex methodological approaches and more advanced forms of analysis are possible. The multiple viewpoints of different members can strengthen methodology as well as stimulating research ideas. Separate observations and interpretations can be compared in an attempt to corroborate the reliability and validity of data through *investigator triangulation* (see Burgess, 1984, pp. 158–9; Fielding and Fielding, 1986, pp. 23–6; Kellaher et. al., 1990). We all have the potential for seeing situations differently, so where two separate observers arrive at the same interpretation this increases our confidence in the findings. Conflicting interpretations can be a stimulus for further research questions. *Disciplinary triangulation* might be built into the team through combining subject specialisms to explore a topic from different angles: for example, research into gambling might combine ideas and insights from sociology, psychology and economics.

Forming teams entails logistical problems and steps must be taken to organize the research effectively. Decisions must be taken on when the group is to meet, how the research work is divided, how differing viewpoints are reconciled. Each stage of the research design needs to be addressed explicitly so there is a common understanding. Discussing these practical aspects is of particular benefit to the research process since alternative theoretical and methodological perspectives are made explicit which might otherwise remain unconsidered.

Of particular importance is the structure of the team and the formal division of roles and tasks. The hierarchic model is particularly associated with functional specialization and tends to be the dominant form in commercial social research. Overall responsibility is assumed by the project director, with specific tasks delegated to appropriate subordinates. This facilitates efficient decision-making, but unequal participation may not always encourage the best use of potential contributions from the team. Observations of subordinate staff – field interviewers, for example – are less likely to inform the research account. A non-hierarchic approach, with members working collectively, offers the possibility of more equal participation but also brings different sorts of difficulties: more prolonged discussion, postponement of decisions, greater potential for conflict.

Linked initially to criticisms of gender-based inequalities within the sociological profession, issues of power and the potentially detrimental effects of inequality within research teams have been highlighted by feminist methodologists. Ramazanoglu (1990) describes the experience of an all-women research team where, despite a shared feminist approach, differences of theory and interpretation surfaced as the project developed. It became essential to make explicit the theoretical standpoints of participants, to monitor tensions within the team, and relations between researchers and researched, so that implicit assumptions and conflicts could be addressed. In this way, disagreement became a springboard for positive development of the research.

Learning about research methods by working on a team project

Small-scale group projects offer an excellent means for students to gain experience of team research. Often, sociology courses include this type of project within the formal curriculum, with groups of students working together under a tutor's guidance on a self-contained piece of research. Projects tend to be small-scale although more ambitious projects are possible, sometimes attracting funding from external agencies. The role of the staff supervisor will be to facilitate and advise the group to achieve its research objectives, rather than telling them what to do. A group can number anything from three upwards and a size of four to five is common, although much larger groups are possible. Advantages of small groups include greater opportunity to define research problems and establish equal relations between team members, but they require greater supervisory resources. Groups may be selected directly by teaching staff or they may be self-selected by students; there are arguments for and against both approaches, though self-selection can become socially exclusive.

Group projects give students an opportunity to apply knowledge of sociological methods to "live" research problems. Almost anything may qualify as a topic so it's a chance to pursue your interests; it makes learning research methods rather more enjoyable than just reading textbooks! You gain experience of research as a total process, from defining a topic or problem to production of a final report. It encourages creativity, planning and organization, making choices between methods and strategies, setting targets, putting practical skills into operation, and working to deadlines. Working as a team emphasizes both co-operative and communications skills. Importantly, each team member will have something to contribute and it is an opportunity to learn from one another.

Where group project work is not part of formal study requirements, there may still be opportunities for students themselves to adopt a team approach on an informal basis, for example, tracking down information on a particular sociological topic, contacting outside bodies or conducting a literature search.

One key issue to be resolved by the team is the research topic. Sometimes this will be determined by tutors – they may be able to arrange projects linked to community organizations and other outside bodies – but often it will be the group's first task to define the project. Everyone will have a view so arriving at agreement involves negotiation; a danger here is that you can end up with a compromise that no-one really wants. You need to be realistic: choose a topic that is feasible and can be completed in the time available. This usually means relatively small-scale projects, avoiding settings where access may be difficult to obtain or methods that involve substantial costs (e.g. printing many questionnaires). Don't spend too much time on planning: as a rule allow one third for preparation, one third data gathering, and one third for analysis and report writing.

You will have to agree some ground-rules about how the group will operate. It is essential that these matters are discussed openly and explicitly so that everyone shares the same expectations; this process of negotiation will usually strengthen the team. Immediate decisions concern when and how often the group is to meet and where. Is this convenient for everyone? What happens if individuals don't attend? It is particularly important that everyone is clear what commitment is required; teams can get into serious difficulties when individuals do not participate equally and this can cause great resentment. You need to agree what sanctions apply in these situations, especially if the group is to be assessed on a collective basis. This sort of issue should be raised with a tutor if the team is operating under supervision.

How is the group to be structured? If non-hierarchical, how will decisions get made if the group cannot agree? Sometimes particular people emerge as leaders and this can work fine, but you need to guard against some members dominating proceedings while other views are ignored. It's important that everyone is given a hearing, but how will conflicts be handled? The group will need to develop a degree of mutual tolerance and trust.

You will need to draft a timetable for each stage of the project week-by-week. How are the tasks to be divided? Will they be shared equally or does it make more sense to divide tasks according to individuals' skills and expertise. Certain tasks require special attention: it's essential to keep a record of what's discussed and decided at team meetings; there will also be more general administrative tasks. Someone may be willing to act as "secretary" or perhaps these duties can be rotated.

Data analysis and writing the report need careful thought. It is desirable to include everyone in these important tasks but difficult to achieve in practice. There's a risk that the final report can be disjointed (or even contradictory!) when separate parts are contributed by each member. The team may need to agree on some form of editing, undertaken either collectively or by a particular individual, to ensure that the final account is well integrated and reads coherently. Alternatively, your tutor may ask each student to produce a separate report, perhaps concentrating on a particular aspect of the project.

There is a considerable amount to be negotiated in team research, but the emphasis on making each aspect of the research process explicit is a great strength. As well as enhancing your ability to work with others, participation in a group project can sharpen your appreciation of sociological methods and practical research issues. With the right choice of topic and an effective team, it can be a stimulating way of learning to "do sociology".

References

Burgess, R. G. 1984: *In the Field*. London: Allen & Unwin.

Fielding, N. G. and Fielding, J. L. 1986: *Linking Data*. Sage University Paper series on Qualitative Research Methods, Vol. 4. Beverly Hills, CA: Sage.

Harding, S., and Phillips, D. 1986: *Contrasting Values in Western Europe: Unity, Diversity and Change*. Basingstoke: Macmillan/EVSSG.

Kellaher, L., Peace, S., and Willcocks, D. 1990:

Triangulating Data. In S. M. Peace (ed.), *Researching Social Gerontology: Concepts, Methods and Issues*. London: Sage.

Ramazanoglu, C. 1990: Methods of working as a research team. Women Risk and Aids Project (WRAP) Paper 3. London: The Tufnell Press.

39

Research Ethics

Roger Homan

One Sunday afternoon in the early 1930s two American social scientists, Henle and Hubble, equipped themselves with clipboards and torches and concealed themselves under the beds of students in university dormitories and waited. Their purpose was to record the conversations that were to take place above the mattresses. There are, of course, serious operational hazards attending such a method of collecting data. The environment they chose is known to be prone to dust and they were in danger of blowing their cover – metaphorically as well as literally – by sneezing. Such methods are today less practised by sociologists than by ornithologists – but this is for ethical as well as for pragmatic reasons.

In its day (1938) the work of Henle and Hubble may not have seemed irregular. The invasion of private space in the course of academic research was not always the sensitive issue that it now is. Nor was their use of covert methods, nor their failure to seek and inform the consent of their human subjects. These and other ethical scruples have developed and been formulated in response to a series of pieces of research which for one reason or another got a bad press for sociology and its related disciplines. There is now a professional consensus which inhibits some now disfavoured approaches to the field, though there are new opportunities and new ethical problems.

Leon Festinger's work (1964) is reported in the book *When Prophecy Fails* and relates to his theory of cognitive dissonance: this partly concerns the way in which, when an expectation is disconfirmed, a revised form may be embraced with even greater conviction. Festinger used his graduate students to gain access to the apartment of a group of spiritualists who were expecting at Christmas time a visitation from outer space. Over a period of time before Christmas, Festinger's students took up positions in the community of the sect and were present at Christmas to witness the simulated advent of heralds from outer-space. Festinger moved in to study how sect members came to terms with their disappointment when they found that they had been misled.

Laud Humphreys (1975) chose to investigate homosexual encounters in men's lavatories in the USA, called "tearooms". This started as a non-participant study but Humphreys became more involved in the course of his research taking on the role of lookout-voyeur or "watchqueen". His book *Tearoom Trade* gives detailed reports of what he observed, interest in which would not be confined to a sociological readership. He noted the registration numbers of his subjects' cars, obtained their addresses and adopted a disguise to visit them at their homes on the pretext of a social health survey.

The Festinger study was an instance which evoked explicit disapproval of social science from within the arts. It attracted considerable publicity outside the literature of social science and is the basis of Alison Lurie's novel *Imaginary Friends* (1967) which plays on some of the problems implicit in his methods. In a similar way the studies of authority and obedience by the psychologist Stanley Milgram (1974) became the subject of concern outside the profession as well as within it, and prompted the playwright Daniel Abse to write *The Dogs of Pavlov* (1973). (In Milgram's study subjects were urged to inflict pain on others – or, rather, they believed they were inflicting pain.) Their concerns have had to do with the invasion of private space, with the practice of deception and with the disruption or harm done to the equilibrium of the lives of those observed. But ethical dilemmas also arise when covert methods are used to expose the practices of institutions or individuals in positions of power: such a use is close to the methods and purpose of investigative journalists and the work of Rosenhan and his collaborators is a case which highlights these issues.

Rosenhan's study (1982) is an example of research where the investigator pretends to be a medical patient. Its purpose was to illuminate screening procedures for the admission of patients to mental hospitals in the USA. Rosenhan and his collaborators reported to a number of mental institutions in the USA feigning symptoms which were diagnosed as those of insanity. They then gained admission and were able from the inside to study screening procedures and other aspects of institutional life. By prior agreement among themselves they could not declare to doctors that they were in fact researchers. With that constraint their purpose was, by acting sanely, to gain release as soon as possible, but they had the utmost difficulty convincing medical staff that they were fit to be released. The only persons who suspected them of being sane were the other patients. On average Rosenhan's collaborators were hospitalized for 19 days and one of the eight took 52 days to convince the hospital authority he was sane. While the work of Rosenhan may have had a long-term benefit in contributing to medical wisdom and procedures for the diagnosis of insanity, there are serious questions about the ethical justification of the subterfuge involved, not to mention the taking of hospital beds that might have been occupied by others in genuine need.

The experiments of Stanley Milgram, to which passing reference is made above, have prompted among psychologists a concern for the enduring effects of participation in research upon subjects and investigators. This concern is much more evident in ethical codes of psychologists than of sociologists. However, social scientists would do well to heed the implications of the Milgram study and to be sensitive to comparable hazards in their own procedures. Some of those undertaking participant observation have taken more drastic measures than Humphreys to settle unobtrusively in the environment of their human subjects. John Howard Griffin (1977) wanted to study empathically the treatment of blacks in the southern states of America and had the idea of controlling a single variable, the colour of his own skin. He took advice from a dermatologist who recommended some tablets to be taken in conjunction with exposure to a sun-ray lamp. The experience was a deeply disturbing one. He wrote:

The transformation was total and shocking. I had expected to see myself disguised but this was something else. I was imprisoned in the flesh of an utter stranger, an unsympathetic one with whom I felt no kinship. All traces of the John Griffin I had been were wiped from existence. Even the senses underwent a change so profound it filled me with distress. (Griffin, 1977, p. 11)

The effects for which he did not bargain included the hostility to himself and his family that ensued when his experiment was given television coverage. Further, he found he could not remove the colour once his fieldwork had been completed.

The possibility that participation in research acts may have enduring effects on investigators has been variously illustrated by the Milgram experiments and the Griffin study. The involvement of students in schemes which in later years they may regret places a special responsibility upon the directors of research projects, many of whom may be under pressure to publish but not under obligation to take part. Both students and their supervisors need to consider carefully all projects, especially those that are innovative in the methods proposed.

These and similar cases raise a number of issues, mainly bearing upon the reputation of social research. Social scientists will want to be, not only for the sake of their discipline but also for the sake of their humanity, responsible, considerate and respecting of fellows. To do harm or injury to human subjects or to collaborators is abhorrent. The pressure to publish or to deliver a thesis does not justify negligence of the welfare of other human beings. And even those like Henle and Hubble who have used unobtrusive methods of which their human subjects may have been unaware may get research a bad name. The future of research depends on a public confidence in its methods and the validity of its data: social researchers therefore have a professional responsibility so to act and report that cooperation and credibility will still be afforded investigators who follow in their footsteps. So they have a further duty to be honest and rigorous: it must never be said of social enquiries as it is of statistics that anything can be proved by them.

Professional Codes

So the desirability of moral behaviour and the need to conserve the reputation of the profession are in practice closely related principles. Institutions of higher education often operate rules, codes or guidelines and feature these in their methods courses, not merely as an element of moral education but because without certain standards and assurances the cooperation of other agents such as schools and employers may be jeopardized. In a frequently used phrase the risk is that the research environment becomes "contaminated".

So it is with professional associations. The regulation of sociological research is the subject of a number of formulations of guidelines and codes of conduct. These are issued by the major professional associations including in Great Britain the British Sociological Association, the Social Research Association and the Market Research Society; and in the USA the American Sociological Association and the American Anthropological Association. Most American and many British universities have formulated ethical codes which are usually expressed to govern a range of types of research of which the sociological is only one.

Codes, criteria and guidelines everywhere have their limitations. For the purpose of the reputation of the profession, they are standardized procedures that will protect human subjects as well as those undertaking research. There are disagreements over the force of such guidelines, although it is recognized that an individual operating against the spirit of a professional or institutional code does so at his or her peril. That said, there are cases in which it may be necessary to set aside one ethical guideline in order to safeguard another value.

The principle that is widely accepted is that researchers should seek and secure the informed consent of subjects. That human subjects should be invited to give consent implies that research is overt and participation is voluntary. Relatively little social research is conducted with legal force, the population census being the obvious exception. That this consent should be informed then means that human subjects should be appraised of such hazards as may beset them, of the purpose of the research, of any risks involved and of the use that will be made of findings. Since subjects are made aware that a research act is taking place, covert methods are precluded by the principle of informed consent.

Such comprehensive appraisal as is given to inform the voluntary consent of human subjects is normally required to include an assessment of the consequences of participation. There may be immediate effects upon the well-being of the subject. The code of the British Psychological Society makes more provision for this possibility than that of the British Sociological Association: but there are such hazards in sociological research too, as when the cooperation of individuals may estrange them from peers. Responsibility also resides with the investigator to predict the consequences of publication. Clearly publicity had implications for the freedom of Laud

Humphreys' subjects as a community, even though their individual identities were not given. In another case, the American small town pseudonymized as "Plainville" was in for a surprise when its identity became known: it lost its innocence overnight and turned into a destination for tourists (Gallaher, 1961).

Ethical principles of confidentiality and anonymity are widely commended but in practice fragile. The protection of identities may mean changing clues in statistics and other details: the author of the Plainville study even published under the assumed name of "James West" (1945) but the secret still got out.

It is sometimes argued that human subjects may be given some control over the form in which they are represented in any research report if they are granted ownership of or entitlement to data. Researchers like Helen Simons (1984) have operated a "democratic" relationship with subjects, giving them the right to check field records and vet papers before publication. Simons' work has often been action research in school classrooms and she has given teachers the opportunity to contribute to her interpretations and reports, if need be by editing them. Teachers are relatively in tune with the purpose and method of research but the democratic principle may work less effectively with other kinds of subject – such as those in management positions who are already skilled in massaging minutes to their advantage, and groups who have special reasons for wanting the truth to be misrepresented. There is a hazard besetting democratic procedures in that time spent in the field could come to nought if subjects were to disapprove at a late stage before publication.

In the other extreme the ownership of data is claimed by some sponsors, especially those which are government departments (Social Research Association, 1980; Boddy, 1981; Homan, 1991, pp. 135ff). Whether sponsor or subject claims rights over data, there is an implicit risk of inviting the obstruction of reporting of a project which may have occupied the researcher for a long time. In case of screening by government sponsors, there is also a threat to intellectual freedom: social

research will soon lose its credibility if it is recognized that the only cases that are published are those that accord with policy intentions.

Further, there is a respect for privacy, more in countries like Britain than in those like Sweden. The notion that human beings are entitled to guard their own space and personal details is in tension with another principle which inheres in much social research, the public right to know. The obverse of the subject's promise of confidentiality is the researcher's agreement to deny information to the public which the subject has been allowed to define as private. A sociologist who assures subjects that nothing that is said or observed will go beyond four walls in a recognizable form may well have second thoughts about that assurance on discovering a paedophile racket.

Problems with Ethical Controls

Codes have a function not merely of control but of education. Investigators do well to check codes at the design stage and to take stock of the issues that may arise in their own projects. They have the further potential of such professional regulation as might assure human subjects that due precautions are being taken.

There are, however, a number of problems with codes, both in principle and in practice. While claiming the moral high ground they license practices which are quite contrary to their intended spirit; while purporting to protect human subjects, they are more directed to the protection of researchers and the reputation of social research; and they relieve the social researcher of the sense of personal moral responsibility.

In questioning the ethical legitimacy of certain practices such as covert research, they implicitly endorse other kinds of research, where the ethical dilemmas, though less immediately obvious, are no less real. This may be illustrated in the cases of interviewing and the administration of questionnaires. According to the standard principle of informed consent the subject is advised at the outset that participation is voluntary and may be discontinued at any time. Consent having been informed, the defence of privacy is made the responsibility of the subject, thus relieving the researcher of any further moral obligation. Indeed, if the investigator wants to ask any intrusive questions he or she will have been trained how to introduce them strategically, after rapport has been established, ideally at the end when the subject will not want to negate all that has gone before. This breaking down of the defences is widely commended in research methods manuals (Homan, 1992). Moreover, an investigator may use a subject as a surrogate or spy to give confidential details about another person: enquiries about sexual behaviour often feature the role of partners and Shere Hite (1977) even asked women responding to her questionnaire to draw diagrams.

The principle of informed consent is satisfied by the use of phrases that are often anodyne and elusive. Investigators may talk of a health survey when they really want to know about drugs. "We are interested in your views", they will say, as a foil to an interest in your habits. In practice, only the barest insight is imparted, perhaps because investigators know that information can prompt anxieties and affect response rates.

It is further arguable that covert methods, which are widely disapproved, are more sensitive of the needs of certain kinds of subject and require a more moral and protective attitude by the investigator. To ask participants in a prayer meeting for permission to watch them while they are praying is to render them self-conscious and thereby to deprive them of a valuable dimension of their behaviour. To ask a group of child pornographers for permission to observe is to invite a refusal and thus to deprive the public of its arguable right to know. But because data gathered by covert methods have not been willingly yielded, it is incumbent upon the investigator to treat with caution and not to compromise the reputation of subjects unless there are important reasons for doing so. So there are ethical reasons of various kinds for conducting covert observations: on the one hand, covert methods may be more sensitive of the rights of subjects and on the other they may be more likely to yield the kind of data to which the public is arguably entitled.

The problem of framing realistic principles relates in part to the force with which they are to be uttered and to the persistence of debate. A professional body which publishes a code as a basis of disciplinary procedures assumes that the sanctions it can impose, such as dismissal from membership, will somehow affect the culprit. It also assumes a level of professional consensus that may not yet have been achieved and which may be eternally elusive: issues such as the problem of covert methods, deception as a means of access to prohibited environments, whether subjects must always be told what is going on, are the themes of a debate among sociologists which may yet defy resolution.

References

Abse, D. 1973: *The Dogs of Pavlov*. Valentine Mitchell.

Adelman, C. (ed.) 1984: *The Politics and Ethics of Education*. London: Croom-Helm.

Barnes, J. A. 1979: *Who Should Know What?* Harmondsworth: Penguin.

—— 1993: Lying: a sociological view. *American Journal of Forensic Science*, 15, 152–8.

Boddy, A. 1988: *DHSS Research Contracts*. London: Society for Social Medicine.

Bulmer M. (ed.) 1980: *Social Research Ethics*. London: Macmillan.

Festinger, L., et al. 1964: *When Prophecy Fails*. New York: Harper & Row.

Gallaher, A. 1961: *Plainville: Fifteen Years Later*. New York: Columbia University Press.

Griffin, J. H. 1977: *Black Like Me*. Boston, MA: Houghton Mifflin.

Henle, M. and Hubble, M. B., 1938: Egocentricity in adult conversation. *Journal of Social*

Psychology, 227–34.

Hite, S. 1977: *The Hite Report: A Nationwide Study of Female Sexuality*. London: Tammy Franklin.

Homan, R. 1991: *The Ethics of Social Research*. Harlow: Longman.

Homan, R. 1992: The ethics of open methods. *British Journal of Sociology*, 43, 321–32.

Humphreys, L. 1975: *Tearoom Trade: Impersonal Sex in Public Places*. Chicago, IL: Aldine.

Lurie, A. 1967: *Imaginary Friends*. London: Heinemann.

Milgram, S. 1974: *Obedience to Authority*. London: Tavistock.

Rosenhan, D. L. 1982: On being sane in insane places. In M. Bulmer (ed.), *Social Research Ethics*. London: Macmillan, pp. 15–37.

Simons, H. 1984: Guidelines for the conduct of an independent evaluation. In Adelman, C. (ed.), *The Politics and Ethics of Education*. London: Croom-Helm, pp. 87–92.

Social Research Association 1980: *Terms and Conditions of Social Research Funding in Britain*. London: Social Research Association.

West, J. (pseud.) 1945: *Plainville USA*. Columbia University Press.

40

Using Computers in Sociology

Millsom Henry

Introduction

Due to the growing use of computers in the home, schools and colleges and in popular culture more generally, students entering higher education now tend to have a significant knowledge of computers and associated technologies. Despite the fact that sociologists have used computers for years, particularly in the field of quantitative data analysis, the pervading image is that sociology is not a technologically literate discipline. Fortunately, however, both the image and reality of technology in sociology has begun to change. This has been due to a number of factors: the shift from mainframe to microcomputers; the developments in new forms of storage media, artificial intelligence and the possibilities opened up by the Internet and the World Wide Web. These shifts have led to new forms of student learning which encourage the role of exploration, discovery and reflection. The aim of this chapter, therefore, is to inform the student of sociology about the current range of computer resources and to assess the potential benefits for student learning.

Computers and Peripherals

At the moment, there are two common types of computers. The Macintosh made by Apple – the "Mac", as it is colloquially called, has a very friendly graphical userface which has made it particularly attractive to graphical designers and non-computer technicians. The other type is the personal computer (PC), which originated from IBM but which is now made by many firms. The PC and its many clones were essentially microcomputers which had reasonably good processing power on the desktop and a range of generic software with a rather crude and unfriendly userface based on the disk operating system (DOS). In the 1980s, the computing giant Microsoft developed a windows system (similar to the Mac) to improve both the interface and the range of fully integrated software (Microsoft Office), which cornered the market. Microsoft's latest release of Windows 95 aims to improve their market position even further. Apple Macintosh now also has the Microsoft range of integrated software and the new generations of Macs – the PowerMacs – which can also read PC-formatted disks. Nevertheless, it is the case that PCs, not the Macs, are dominating the computer market in schools, universities, at home and in industry.

If students want to fully utilize the benefits of the new developments in technology, there are a number of key pieces of equipment in addition to the computer monitor and hard-disk which are necessary. These pieces of equipment are called "peripherals" and they include: laser printers which produce high-resolution copies of documents at a good speed; compact disk (CD-ROM) players which are usually built into the computer and act as an additional resource; and multimedia equipment such as sound (including speakers, microphones) and video cards (for digitized cameras and film) which enable the user to

Figure 40.1 Most people now have a long familiarity with the use of computers.

manipulate sound and video directly from the computer.

Technological developments are very rapid, so it is wise that students review the most up-to-date impartial information from computer magazines and newspapers and seek advice from local computer centres. This is important as there are cost implications not only for the initial purchase of computers and peripherals, but also for the on-going maintenance of such equipment. Students should be aware that there is sometimes a misplaced emphasis on acquiring the latest new developments irrespective of genuine need and should be prepared to do some serious homework to ensure that sensible choices are made.

Using Computers for Word-processing

Gazing at a blank screen/window can seem quite daunting at first to students who are used to getting their ideas down on paper, but the process of writing on screen gets easier over time and many users eventually find it more effective and creative. Word-processing programs such as Microsoft Word or Word-Perfect enable the student to type text on a screen, alter the layout, save it as a file to a floppy or hard disk, retrieve, edit, print and store files. These programs are extremely valuable for students wishing to redraft or update essays/projects, design standard letters and forms, merge letters with mailing lists and devise the all-important *curricula vitae*. In addition, most word-processing programs provide immediate access to a spelling checker, grammatical aid and an on-line thesaurus. Students can insert graphics, figures and tables into documents and, depending on the sophistication of the program, utilize attractive desk-top publishing features. More and more departments of sociology are requesting that students submit essays/projects as word-processed documents. Using a word-processing program effectively also provides students with an invaluable opportunity to gain a set of skills which can be used both, across and outside the higher education curriculum.

In addition to the word-processing programs, another useful and related development for the student, are the range of bibliographical/referencing software. Popular programs on the Macs and PCs, respectively, are EndNotePlus and Pro-Cite (also available on the Mac). Essentially, these are specialized databases which are used for indexing and referencing. For students these are useful when devising a bibliography for the large-scale project/thesis. The key features of these programs are that they usually allow annotation in the text, can sort references in any order quickly and can adopt a number of types of house style for the final bibliography. In some cases, some programs can be used for parts of qualitative data analysis, namely, coding and indexing. Students should learn to use this type of software as a way of developing good practice for keeping information and references in a logical order.

Spreadsheets

The easiest way to think of a spreadsheet is like that of a large piece of paper which is divided into columns and rows. At the intersection of each row/column is a cell where information is entered. Spreadsheets can be edited on screen, saved to a file, retrieved and amended at any time.

The spreadsheet program can be used to manipulate data and perform calculations. Spreadsheet programs are devised largely to deal with numbers and mathematical formulae, but they also allow information in text or alphanumeric form to be entered. In addition, most spreadsheet programs have the facility to output the information as graphs or tables, to import drawing objects and to export the data as a raw file for use in other programs such as SPSS. Microsoft Excel and Lotus 123 are two of the most common spreadsheets that are currently available. For the student of socio-

logy, the spreadsheet can be used to devise budgets, calculate statistical information, create and display charts and graphs and even develop population models. Spreadsheets then, are more than just forms for maintaining financial records; they are very versatile and can be used to explore a number of "what if" demonstrations. As Timms (1992) pointed out "spreadsheets can be used to illustrate the differing levels of maintenance provision or vacancy rates on rent setting in social housing or . . . the effects of changes in voting intentions on the strength of parties." Using spreadsheets offers another set of transferable skills to students of all backgrounds.

Databases

A computer database comprises a set of "records", usually broken down into "fields", which the user can rapidly search and sort in different ways – edit, save and/or print. For example, records in a bibliographic database contain entries in fields for book titles, author, date of publication and so on. Other types can contain information about datasets, mailing lists and actual survey data. These records can then be sorted by alphabetically, in date order and can be searched by using a number of Boolean operators (and/or/not) to answer specific queries. Two of the most popular are Microsoft Access and Fox Professional.

Specific Computing Resources for Students of Sociology

There are a growing range of computing resources available for the student of sociology, from the generic programs outlined above to the more specific range of quantitative and qualitative data analysis programs, CD-ROM, modelling and simulation packages, electronic mail and conferencing systems and the Internet/World Wide Web. (For a more comprehensive overview, refer to Garson and Nagel 1989, 1991 and the *SSCORE* journals 1988–96.) Students simply need to learn how to use them effectively. What follows is an introductory guide to how students can find and use some of these computing resources.

Quantitative Programs (including Surveys and Questionnaires)

Despite the lack of good quality course content materials in electronic form social sciences, there actually is an extensive range of quantitative programs on offer, from simple programs designed to teach the fundamentals of statistical analysis to full-blown packages for more professional use. The most popular type of quantitative data analysis programs used by professional social scientists are large-scale statistical programs such as SSPS-X or SAS. However, due primarily to their size and cost, these programs were considered to be too expensive and cumbersome for students. As a result, SPSS have developed a Windows version for which students can purchase key modules or access the modules on-line from their institution who will have paid the appropriate site license. SPSS and others (BMDP, GLIM and SAS) have also developed a useful introductory front-end to the programs, making them much more user-friendly. Students should be aware of a number of medium-size programs, such as Minitab or Instat which also provide a good introduction to quantitative data analysis, and the emergence of textbooks which incorporate relevant examples on enclosed disks. (For further information refer to Cramer, 1994, 1996a, b; Bryman and Cramer, 1996; Hinton, 1995; Levitas and Guy, 1996.)

The development of questionnaire-design programs, some with complete design, input and analysis features such as SurveyIt and PinPoint, are good examples for students. They encourage the user to examine the ways in which questionnaires are designed, questions phrased, the advantages and disadvantages of open, closed or multi-choice responses, the coding process, how the data are summarized, and the best ways of displaying/presenting the report. Such pro-

grams are very useful for small-scale projects or essays and are of direct benefit to students who want to explore and practise the core skills of social scientific research.

Qualitative Programs

Computers can also be used effectively for qualitative research, despite the traditional divisions between the two main sociological research traditions (as outlined by other chapters in this *Companion*). Fortunately, such debates have moved on and consequently, over a period of time, the ground between the two opposing traditions has shifted. Denzin's (1970) essay on triangulation was particularly influential here as he argued that a number of methods, both quantitative and qualitative, may be employed in the social sciences. Each tradition had both its own strengths and weaknesses. By combining these traditions, one could provide a more robust way of seeking to understand the social world.

Against this background, there have been developments in using computers in the actual qualitative research process. Computer-assisted-personal interviewing, for example, enables researchers to use portable computers in a face-to-face interview setting, and computer-assisted telephone-interviewing focuses on the use of electronically recorded telephone surveys. The key features of such systems are the fact that the questionnaire is automated; there is provision for safe checks; and there is a faster input of responses which leads to speedier analysis. Some of the most popular programs are: *Blaise*, *Cases* and *Quancept*. These methods are now being widely employed for large-scale government surveys in several countries. The next stage of development in this area is computer-assisted self-interviewing which does not need the actual presence of an interviewer.

Nevertheless, some qualitative researchers still resist what they regard as attempts to fit qualitative data into quantitative methods and some quantitative researchers stress the need for a more traditional scientific approach where data can be treated in the same way as numbers.

There is some middle ground emerging where qualitative researchers insist that their methods are scientific, but maintain that it makes sense to exploit some of the computational powers of technology to assist in performing key functions, but not to use these to define or shape the essence of the data. As a result, in recent years there have been great advances in the methods used to analyse documents such as interview transcripts, diaries, letters and newspapers, many of which can be employed effectively with the use of specialized computer packages. Programs such as *NUD.IST, Ethnograph, HyperQual, HyperSoft* and *TextBase Alpha* have taken many of the labourious aspects out of qualitative study, notably indexing, coding and analysis and have made it easier for students to use. There is still some debate about the use of such programs today, but it is clear that students will need to learn how to use these programs effectively as part of the necessary range of skills required as a social scientist for the next century. (For a fuller review of qualitative analysis packages, refer to Dey 1993; Tesch 1990; Fielding and Lee 1991; Miles and Huberman 1994; Denzin and Lincoln 1994 and Burgess 1996).

Social Science Databases and Archives

Within the social sciences there are a number of useful bibliographical databases which contain abstracts of academic journals. For example BIDS (Bath Information and Data Services) provides a service to databases such as ISI and IBSS which provide access to social science citation indices with over 7000 journals. Accessing these databases is usually via the university library or a host agency. The other main type of database in the social sciences is that which lists and contains datasets housed in data archives. Here information and the actual data about key official surveys (for example, the Census, the General Household Survey, the Family and Expenditure Survey and the British Social Attitudes Survey) as well as other commissioned research are kept in a series of databases, which the user can access, search using key terms, print and get details of data on and off-line. The main repositories for the social sciences in the UK are the ESRC Data Archive based at the University of Essex; the University of Manchester Computing Centre and the new qualitative data archive also at the University of Essex – QUALIDATA.

Other useful social science data archives can be found at the ANU – Australian National University (Canberra); the SSDA – Social Science Data Archive; the DDA – Danish Data Archives World Wide Web server; the BDSP – Banque de Données Socio-Politiques; the German ZA – Zentralarchiv für Empirische Sozialforschung; the Hungarian Social Research Informatic Society (SRIS/ TARKI); the Israeli Social Sciencies Data Archive, Hebrew University; the Dutch SWIDOC – Social Science Information and Documentation Centre; the Norwegian NSD – Norwegian Social Science Data Services; the Swedish SSDA – Swedish Social Science Data Service; the American ICPSR – Inter-university Consortium for Political and Social Research (Michigan); the SSDC – Social Sciences Data Collection (University of California) and the National Data Archive on Child Abuse and Neglect – (Cornell). These global archives are increasing all the time and most now are accessible via the Internet (for details, refer to the ESRC web site: http ://www.esrc.ac.uk/).

For students of sociology then, these datasets provide useful access to a range of information and resources that are available in the social sciences in an easy and convenient manner. Part of the core skills for the sociology student is the ability to search, find, retrieve and utilize a number of tools and techniques for summarizing and analysing information. Learning to be proficient with a variety of databases is an essential skill for the student of sociology.

CD-ROM (Compact Disk-Read Only Memory)

The CD-ROM is like any music compact disk. The difference with this type of CD is that it is pressed to be read directly into a computer. CD-ROMs store a lot of information, around an average of 500 books per text-based CD-ROM. Information can also be scanned, searched and analysed very quickly at a time that is convenient to the user. There is now a large market in textual resources such as national newspapers on CD-ROM, (for example, *The Times* and *The Guardian*), which are replacing the fragility of microfiches, offer space to university libraries and provide a robust way to manage databases.

In addition, the CD-ROM is capable of storing a range of media in pictorial, video and sound formats. Bill Gates of Microsoft slowly bought the rights to famous works of arts before the potential of CD-RM was known to the market and has since successfully been able to press them into attractive and popular CD-ROM encyclopaedias. Other organizations and government departments have realized the potential of CD-ROM technology and now a number of government surveys and datasets are available in this format. For example, the small area statistics from the British 1981 Census complete with digitized map of census areas from enumeration districts upwards; the British Social Attitudes Surveys from 1983 to 1989; the Election Surveys from the ESRC Data Archive; and Sociofile, the CD-ROM for all abstracts of sociology journals from 1974.

For the student of sociology these CD-ROMs provide access to a wide range of resources which would have previously been difficult or expensive to obtain. In addition, the ability of CD-ROMs to store a range of media formats makes it essential for students whose work cuts across text, graphics, sound, video and animation. The promise of large-scale multimedia programs and CD-interactive systems in the social sciences has not yet been fulfilled and in fact may no longer be required. Instead, the emphasis seems to be shifting to encouraging students to create and modify (with guidance), the plethora of resources and formats that CD-ROM technology has to offer, rather than developing fixed computer-assisted learning programs. There may well come a time when students will be asked to submit their work throughout their degree and/or their actual doctoral thesis on CD-ROM. This technology will be here for some time to come.

Simulation Programs

Attempts to simulate real-life scenarios date back a long way in the social sciences. The difference today is that there are new forms of technology which can make this process easier and appear more real. Simulations and other role-playing exercises can also involve students in decision-making activities and help to foster more collaborative ways of student learning. For example, The Poverty Game, Ethics and SimCity are examples of computer programs, exploiting the range of technology which place the user in key decision-making roles and explore ways of demonstrating how such decisions have a number of intended and unintended consequences which must be weighed up. Projections based on modelling programs or basic spreadsheets also allow students to explore alternative scenarios reflecting, for example, the impact of AIDS or a change in fertility patterns. Developments in virtual reality are more sophisticated versions of these, where the user can begin to "feel" and "see" environments as if they are actually there. (For a good exposé of some of the key issues, refer to the special edition of the *SSCORE* journal, Volume 6, No. 1, 1988 and Kulver, 1996.)

Electronic Mail and Conferencing

Developments in computer-mediated-communications (CMC) represent a key area on two fronts for sociologists. Firstly, it offers a useful set of new tools which should provide more opportunities for interaction, and secondly it raises a number of issues about the implications of technology. CMCs take many forms and each have their own special nuances. Here are a few. Electronic mail refers to the use of computers to transfer messages (usually textual) between users from local/

regional/national/global site to site. It does not require both parties to be on-line at the same time, or to be in the same time zone. It is also fast, flexible and sophisticated. Other forms of CMC include electronic bulletin boards where information is electronically "posted to a noticeboard"; electronic discussion lists and newsgroups where messages are sent to all users on the list/newsgroup who can then take part in static and on-going debates; and electronic conferencing where one can simultaneously link up with a number of people regardless of geographical space and see/read responses live. All higher education institutions should be linked up to the JANET (Joint Academic Network) or SUPERJANET where a number of "gateways" to filter information according to subject areas can be found. (For more information, refer to SOSIG – the Social Science Information Gateway: http://www.sosig.ac.uk   and SocInfo: http://www.stir.ac.uk/socinfo/.)

In addition, a range of discussion lists and news groups are also available. In the first instance, students should obtain a username and password from the computing centre at their local institution and then follow the on-line instructions or the accompanying documentation from the library/computing centre. There are also new forms of electronic publishing, such as SOCRESONLINE, the first fully refereed electronic journal of sociology in the UK and the *Electronic Journal of Sociology* in the USA. These offer the reader and the contributor all the benefits of the Internet in terms of exploiting many different formats in combination in one article; wider dissemination than paper journals; more opportunities to work collaboratively and greater access to wider knowledge and information.

This new electronic medium for communication has shifted a number of boundaries, in terms of physicality as well as convention. It is possible to speak/send messages to anyone linked up to a modem and computer regardless of status and without having any visual cues to their behaviour. Students can converse easily and in a less formal manner with renowned professors and users can remain relatively anonymous. However, new rules of behaviour have emerged ("netiquette") which ensure some order, but these are mainly to do with being polite. These new ways of communicating also exclude those without access to the technology and raises questions about knowledge, power and ethics, all classic hallmarks of sociological thought (Glastonbury and LaMendola, 1992). This will undoubtedly be an area of critical interest for students of sociology.

The Internet and World Wide Web

Simplistically, the Internet is a global system of networks more commonly referred to as the World Wide Web. Students can access the Internet/web through a browser. This is a program which enables the user to read the combination of text, graphics, video and audio on the Internet. The web contains a vast network of information and so it is easy to get lost. Fortunately, the browsers have a useful set of tools to enable the user to get back to the starting point (home), to retrace their steps and to record/bookmark their path for future explorations. Each institution should now have its own home page and this is the point from which most students start. Look at the structure and explore the links on this page. The best way to learn is by doing. Students should at first simply browse. Once confidence has been achieved, students should be more selective and use one of the many search engines available such as *AltaVista, Lycos, Webcrawler, Yahoo*, etc. to look up material by using key terms. The average speed and accuracy of the returns are impressive. The Internet provides an invaluable resource where students can exploit all the technologies of computer, CD-ROMs, e-mail and bulletin boards free (at point of use), at a time that is convenient and usually quite quickly. Knowing your way around the Internet will undoubtedly be a very useful skill to acquire as a student and for a long time afterwards.

Future Techologies: The Role of Sociology

In the future, developments in technology will expand in the areas of virtual reality and artificial intelligence which should be of great interest to the student of sociology. These developments in technology are so rapid that it would be foolhardy to make any predictions here. However, it is possible to argue that the role that sociology will play should increase as there will be more emphasis on CMC. As a discipline, sociology will also need to take a critical and engaging look at the impact of the technologies in society in ways which highlight both its pleasures and perils. For students of sociology there remain a number of key skills which need to be acquired and updated regularly. The new forms of learning which are being engendered by technological developments will encourage more exploration, discovery and reflection in sociology which must be regarded positively. In addition, the advancements in technology and the role these new students will play can only ensure that sociology will not again be viewed as a technologically illiterate discipline.

References and Further Reading

Bainbridge, W. S. 1995: Sociology on the World Wide Web. *Social Science Computer Review* (*SSCORE*), 13(4), 508–23.

Bryman, A. and Cramer, D. 1994: *Quantitative Data Analysis for Social Scientists*. London: Routledge.

—— 1996a: *Quantitative Data Analysis with Minitab*. London: Routledge.

—— 1996b: *Quantitative Data Analysis with SPSS for Windows*. London: Routledge.

Burgess, R. (ed.) 1996: *Computing and Qualitative Research*. London: JAI Press.

Cramer, D. 1994: *Introducing Statistics for Social Research*. London: Routledge.

—— 1996: *Basic Statistics for Social Research*. London: Routledge.

Denzin, N. K. 1970: *The Research Act*. Chicago: Aldine Atherton.

Denzin, N. K. and Lincoln (eds) 1994: *Handbook of Qualitative Research*. London: Sage.

Dey, I. 1993: *Qualitative Data Analysis: A User-friendly Guide for Social Scientist*. London: Routledge.

Fielding, N. and Lee, R. (eds) 1991: *Using Computers in Qualitative Research*. London: Sage.

Garson, G. D. (ed.) 1988–96: *Social Science Computer Review* (*SSCORE*), Volumes 1–14. California: Sage.

Garson, G. D. and Nagel, S. (eds) 1989: *Advances in Social Science and Computers*, Vol. 1. London: JAI Press.

—— (eds) 1991: *Advances in Social Science and Computers*, Vol. 2. London: JAI Press.

Glastonbury, B. and LaMendola, W. 1992: *Integrity of Intelligence – A Bill of Rights for the Information Age*. London: Macmillan.

Henry, M. S. (ed.) 1990–6: *SocInfo Newsletters*. SocInfo Publications, University of Stirling.

—— (ed.) 1996: *Using Computers Effectively in the Social Sciences*. London: Taylor & Francis.

—— (ed.) 1997: *Computers for Sociology and Political Science Students*. Oxford: Blackwell.

—— 1997: The role of computers in social policy. In *SPA Student's Companion to Social Policy*. Oxford: Blackwell.

Henry, M. S. and Rafferty 1995: Equality and CAL in higher education. *Journal of Computer Assisted Learning*, 11, 72–8.

Hinton, P. 1995: *Statistics Explained*. London: Routledge.

Kluver, J. 1996: Sociological discourses in virtual reality. *Social Science Computer Review* (*SSCORE*) 14(3), 280–92.

Lee, R. (ed.) 1995: *Information Technology for the Social Scientist*. London: UCL Press.

Levitas, R. and Guy, W. (eds) 1996: *Interpreting Official Statistics*. London: Routledge.

McCartan, A. (ed.) 1991: *Computer Literacy for Every Graduate: Strategies and Challenges for the Early Nineties*. Oxford: CTISS Publications.

Miles, M. B. and Huberman, A. M. (eds) 1994: *Qualitative Data Analysis: An Expanded Sourcebook*. London: Sage.

Richards, L. and Richards, T. 1991: The transformation of qualitative method: computational paradigms and research processes. In Fielding, N. and Lee, R. (eds) *Using Computers in Qualitative Research*. London: Sage, pp. 38–53.

Tesch, R. 1990: *Qualitative Research: Analysis Types and Software Tools*. London: Falmer Press.

Timms, D. W. G. 1992: Computers and the teaching of sociology and the policy sciences. *Computers and Educational Journal* 19(1/2), 97–104.

PART V
Directory and Resources

Chapters in the previous part indicated some of the ways in which you can learn through active reading and researching. In this part, guidance is given on *where* you might turn for information. In Chapter 43 Speight introduces you to just a few of the major sociological journals and explains their function. Academic journals contain a wealth of information and analysis, but you will need to learn which ones contain material that is accessible to you at your current level of sociological knowledge for, although there is no easy route to intellectual growth, it can be confusing and disheartening if you struggle with an article that is quite beyond you. Scarrott's chapter is a wide-ranging guide to the use of library and other data sources, emphasizing the *methods* by which you can search effectively. The advice in this chapter will pay close and repeated attention throughout your time as a student, as enhancing your library skills will enable you to tackle more ambitious projects effectively.

The two other chapters in this part are useful to refer to as the occasion arises. Fisher's "biographical dictionary" begins with an account of how sociology has been institutionalized in academic departments and then goes on to give brief biographical notes on frequently cited sociologists. Besides indicating some of their most notable publications, this chapter usefully shows where and when they lived, and identifies their significance in the history of the discipline, so you can more easily locate the chains of influence and debate between them.

If you intend to study sociology at an advanced level you will doubtless wish to attend sociological conferences and join your national sociological association. Chapter 44 (Morgan) provides information on some of the most important associations and discusses their role in the institutionalization of sociology.

41

Biographical Dictionary

David Fisher

Introduction

If sociology has a long intellectual pedigree, it has a relatively short institutional history as an academic discipline. The first sociology course in the USA was taught by William Graham Sumner at Yale College in 1875. Conditions were peculiarly favourable to sociology's development in the USA at this time. An expanding higher education system receptive to this new discipline, forged in the reform movement, enabled sociology to make its way on to the curricula of many colleges and universities. The transitional nature of American society, its growing urban and industrial regions and culturally diverse immigrant population, ensured a rich source of sociological material. It is no surprise, therefore, that sociology established itself first in Chicago, the epitome of American urbanization. Until the mid-1930s, Chicago University boasted the country's, if not the world's, most influential sociology department and published the only major journal, the *American Journal of Sociology*. From the 1940s onwards, other universities – Harvard, Columbia and California at Berkeley – dominated, but by then sociology was firmly established in American academic and cultural life.

The same cannot be said of the British experience. The Sociological Society of London, established in 1903, was Europe's first national sociological society. In 1907, the country's first Chair in sociology was created at the London School of Economics. But subsequent progression stalled and no further sociology departments were established until after World War II. Philip Abrams (1968, p. 4) suggests the main problem for sociology was that for it to develop "an existing thought world had to be reconstituted. But that thought world had an institutional as well as an ideological existence". There was simply no place for an unproven, upstart academic discipline in the existing social order. Established institutions such as government and the church, dominated by the gentry, effectively channelled the efforts of those of a reformist disposition. The Oxbridge-led university system, itself part of the establishment, was intellectually antagonistic towards sociology, and assumed it was already covering the field with courses in social philosophy. The discipline fared better in the flux of post-war Britain with its crumbling old guard and emergent welfare state. Social issues were high on the political agenda and at last there was a role for sociologists to play in planning for social reform. A. H. Halsey, for instance, became an influential government adviser on education. Sociology was also building itself a tentative institutional footing within the intellectually adventurous civic universities, spreading first to Birmingham, Edinburgh, Leeds, Leicester, Liverpool and Nottingham. In the 1960s sociology was adopted by the new universities including, Essex, Kent, Lancaster and York, and so finally came of age.

L. L. and Jessie Bernard's *Origins of American Sociology* (1943) remains the classic study of nineteenth-century sociology. For an overview of the discipline's formative years during the first half of the twentieth century, see Lewis A. Coser "American trends" in Tom Bottomore and Robert Nisbet, *A History of Sociological Analysis* (1979). *Sociological Traditions from Generation to Generation: Glimpses of the American Experience* (1980) edited by R. K. Merton and M. W. Riley offers detailed analyses of individual American sociologists. The history of sociology in Britain is well served by Philip Abrams' *The Origins of British Sociology 1834–1914* (1968) and John Eldridge's *Recent British Sociology* (1980).

This chapter attempts to reveal the people behind the theories by offering biographical sketches of some of the most notable sociologists. Such a selection is necessarily controversial and I doubt whether any two sociologists would arrive at the same list. To ensure a degree of objectivity, the majority of entries are based upon names most commonly cited in American and British undergraduate textbooks, and so should be ones students are likely to encounter. But we have also selected individuals whose work continues to be relevant today, and contemporary European and American sociologists who are developing the discipline in original directions.

Biographical Dictionary

Jane Addams (1860–1935) pioneering American sociologist and social reformer. Born in Cedarville, Illinois, she went to Europe after finishing college, to study the settlement movement. In 1899 she founded Hull House, America's first major settlement house. In addition to offering shelter for the homeless, child care and health education, Hull House became an intellectual centre for female sociologists, excluded from the male-dominated university departments. Addams and her colleagues developed the methods of applied sociology, including case study and demographic mapping techniques, later used by the men of the Chicago School of sociology. A tireless campaigner for the rights of women and children, Addams was the first American woman to be awarded the Nobel Peace prize in 1931. Major works

include *Democracy and Social Ethics* (1902) and *Twenty Years at Hull House* (1910).

Louis Althusser (1918–1990) French Marxist philosopher, studied and taught at the École Normale Supérieure. Tremendously influential in the 1970s, he saw a break between the early "humanist" Marx (writing on alienation) and the later "scientific" Marx (writing on political economy). Critical of crude economic determinism, he gave his name to a school of structuralist Marxism which stressed the "relative autonomy" of political and ideological structures. Personal tragedy, depressive illness culminating in his killing of his wife, has secured Althusser an infamous reputation for posterity. Major works include *For Marx* (1966) and *Lenin and Philosophy* (1971).

Earl Babbie (1939–) born in Detroit, Michigan, he took his AB at Harvard (1960) and MA (1966) and PhD (1969) at the University of California, Berkeley. He is Professor of Sociology at Chapman University. Well known for his books on methodology, *The Practice of Social Research* (1973, 7th edn 1995) and *Survey Research Methods* (1973, 2nd edn 1990), he is also the author of several sociology textbooks including *Society By Agreement* (1977, 1983).

Michelle Barrett (1949–) studied at the Universities of Durham and Sussex. A past president of the British Sociological Association, she is Professor of Sociology at the City University, London. Interested in the relationship between Marxism and feminism, she uses a Marxist feminist perspective to analyse the ideological nature of family and gender relations. Major works include *Women's Oppression Today* (1980) and with Mary McIntosh *The Anti-social Family* (1982).

Ulrich Beck (1944–) Professor of Sociology at the University of Munich. His works *Risk Society: Towards a New Modernity* (1986, English translation 1992) and *Ecological Politics in an Age of Risk* (1988, translation 1995) are having a major impact throughout the German *speaking world and the social sciences generally. A dominant influence on German ecological politics, Beck writes regularly for the newspaper Frankfurter Allgemeine Zeitung.* His conceptions of risk society and reflexive modernization offer an original recasting of modernism/post-modernism debates.

Howard S. Becker (1928–) born in Chicago, where he attended university (PhD 1951), he is Professor of Sociology at the University of Washington. A renowned symbolic interactionist, famous for his development of labelling theory, he has written on a wide variety of topics including: music, methodology, youth culture, education, art and hypertext fiction. One of the few sociologists with a home page on the Internet. Major works include *Outsiders: Studies in the Sociology of Deviance* (1963), *Sociological Work, Method and Substance* (1970) and *Art Worlds* (1982).

Daniel Bell (1919–) American sociologist and journalist, studied at CCNY and Columbia University. Currently divides his time between Harvard and the Academy of Arts and Sciences. Known for his bold predictions, he announced the demise of class conflict in *The End of Ideology* (1960) and the arrival of the information society in *The Coming of Post-industrial Society* (1973). He subsequently qualified his optimism in *The Cultural Contradictions of Capitalism* (1976).

Peter L. Berger (1929–) born in Vienna, he has held professorships at several American universities and is currently at Boston. A noted sociologist of religion, he provided a contemporary interpretation of phenomenological sociology in *The Social Construction of Reality* (1966). He has written introductory texts including, *Invitation to Sociology* (1963), an exploration of "the first wisdom of sociology . . . things are not what they seem".

Jessie Shirley Bernard (1903–) educated at the Universities of Minnesota and Washington, she researched and taught at Pennsylvania State University. Co-founder and past president of the Society for the Study of Social Problems. Moving from a functionalist to a feminist perspective, she has written extensively on women, the family and marriage, arguing men gain most out of the latter institution. Major works include *Women, Wives, Mothers: Values and Options* (1975) and *The Female World* (1981).

Basil Bernstein (1924–) studied at the London School of Economics and University College, London. He is Emeritus Professor of the Sociology of Education at the University of London. He pioneered research into the relationship between language, social class and school achievement (*Class, Codes and Control*, 1971–75, and most recently, *Pedagogy, Symbolic Control and Identity: Theory, Research, Critique*, 1996). Latterly, he has been concerned, more generally, with the interaction of knowledge, language, power and social control.

Pierre Bourdieu (1930–) Professor of Sociology at the College de France, Paris. Widely known for his Marxist influenced cultural capital theory of education, which he developed with colleagues at the Centre de Sociologie Europeene, he has also contributed to the agency/structure debate within sociological theory. Major works include *Reproduction in Education, Society and Culture* (1977) and *In Other Words: Essays Towards a Reflexive Sociology* (1990).

Harry Braverman (1920–76) American Marxist and social theorist. Unable to afford to complete his studies at Brooklyn College, he left to work in the steel industry before entering publishing. He co-founded and edited *The American Socialist* during the 1950s. His reputation within labour process theory rests with one book *Labor and Monopoly Capital* (1974), in which he argued that under capitalism jobs have been deskilled by employers to control the workforce. This thesis has inspired decades of debate.

Randall Collins (1941–) studied at the University of California, Berkeley and is Professor of Sociology at the University of California,

Riverside. Working within conflict theory, he has focused on a variety of topics including the family and education. His work is a good example of what he sees as "the speciality of sociology . . . the study of processes that do not turn out to be rational" (*Sociological Insight: an Introduction to Non-Obvious Sociology*, 1992).

Auguste Comte (1798–1857) read natural sciences at the École Polytechnique, Paris and later worked for Claude-Henri de Saint-Simon. Comte coined the term "sociology" in his *Cours de Philosophie Positive* (1830–42). He regarded sociology as the most important of all sciences. His theory of scientific positivism was influential in sociology's early development.

Ralph Dahrendorf, Baron (1929–) German sociologist, he adopted British nationality in 1988 and is Warden of St Anthony's College, Oxford. He was Secretary of State in the German Foreign Office, 1969–70 and a European Commissioner, 1970–74. His main sociological work has been within conflict theory, explaining class conflict in terms of differential authority within organizations, rather than a Marxist notion of class exploitation. Major works include *Class and Class Conflict in Industrial Society* (1959) and *Life Chances* (1979).

Jacques Derrida (1930–) French post-structuralist philosopher, born in El-Biar, Algeria. He studied at the École Normale Supérieure in Paris, where he later taught. He is currently based at the École des Hautes Études en Sciences Sociales, Paris. A primary developer of the "deconstruction" perspective, Derrida argues language cannot express absolute truths, but is socially constructed and, as such, in a state of flux. Meaning is constantly shifting and never fully realized. Sociologically, his work is interesting because it exposes the use of language in the maintenance of cultural inequalities and suggests a dynamic and fluid concept of self. On the negative side, Derrida's ideas have been used to highlight the impossibility of really knowing anything. Major works include *Writing and Difference*

(1967, English translation 1978) and *Dissemination* (1972, translation 1981).

William Edward Burghardt Dubois (1868–1963) attended universities at Fisk, Harvard (PhD, 1895) and Berlin. Professor of Economics and Sociology at Atlanta University (1897–1910). He conducted a major study of black life in *The Philadelphia Negro* (1899). Active in the black rights movement with the National Association for the Advancement of Colored People and as organizer of the Pan-African Congresses, he finally settled in Ghana, where he edited the first African encyclopaedia.

Émile Durkheim (1858–1917) born in Epinal, France, he studied at the École Normale Supérieure. He taught the country's first sociology course at the University of Bordeaux and later became Professor of Education and Sociology at the Sorbonne. Durkheim was influential in establishing sociology as a discipline in its own right, asserting it must "treat social facts as things", an approach he demonstrated in *Suicide* (1897). His efforts to understand the function of social facts paved the way for functionalism. Major works include *The Division of Labor in Society* (1893) and *The Rules of Sociological Method* (1895).

Norbert Elias (1897–1990) German-born sociologist, studied at Breslau and Heidelberg, later becoming Karl Mannheim's assistant at Frankfurt. He left Germany at the onset of Nazism and taught at universities in England, Ghana and Holland. In *The Civilizing Process* (1939), he demonstrated links between the development of nation states and changes in individual behaviour. He devised "figurational sociology" to express his belief in the reciprocal nature of social interaction.

Amitai Etzioni (1929–) received his PhD from the University of California, Berkeley in 1958. He is First University Professor and Director of the Center for Communitarian Policy Studies at George Washington University. A former Senior White House Advisor

(1979–80) and past president of the American Sociological Association. Founder and Director of the Center for Policy Research, a not-for-profit corporation dedicated to public policy, he appears regularly on television and frequently contributes to *The New York Times, The Washington Post* and *The Wall Street Journal*. A key figure in organizational sociology, Etzioni is also a prime mover within the American communitarian movement which promotes the importance of community values, bonds and responsibilities. Major works include *Modern Organizations* (1964) and *The Spirit of Community: Rights, Responsibility and the Communitarian Agenda* (1993).

Janet Finch formerly Professor of Social Relations at Lancaster University, she is currently Vice-Chancellor of Keele University. She is a member of the Board of the North West Regional Health Authority and Chair of the Research Board of the Economic and Social Research Council. She has made valuable contributions to the sociology of the family, particularly in her examination of the often hidden roles played by wives. Recent research has included an ESRC funded study on inheritance, property and family relationships. Major works include *Married to the Job: Wives' Incorporation in Men's Work* (1983) and *Family Obligations and Social Change* (1989).

Herbert J. Gans (1927–) born in Cologne, he emigrated to the USA at the age of 13. Trained as a sociologist and city planner, he is Professor of Sociology at Columbia University. Often working within a broadly functionalist perspective, he is noted for studies on a variety of topics including urbanism, poverty and ethnicity. Major works include *People and Plans: Essays on Urban Problems and Solutions* (1968) and *The War Against the Poor: The Underclass and Anti-poverty Policy* (1995).

Michel Foucault (1926–84) French post-structuralist philosopher, studied philosophy and psychology at the École Normale Supérieure. After a chequered career, he created his own title in 1970 as "Professor of the History of Systems of Thought" at the Collège de France. His writings on diverse topics – madness, medicine, penology and sexuality – are infused with original analyses of knowledge, language, power, social control and self. Major works include *Madness and Civilization* (1965), *The Archaeology of Knowledge* (1969) and *Discipline and Punish* (1975).

Harold Garfinkel (1917–) studied under Talcott Parsons at Harvard (PhD, 1952). Emeritus Professor of Sociology, University of California, Los Angeles. Founder of ethnomethodology, a term he coined while working on a study of jurors between leaving Ohio State University and joining UCLA. Influenced by Schutz, Garfinkel is interested in "how society gets put together", in the methods people use to construct social reality. Major works include *Studies in Ethnomethodology* (1967).

Anthony Giddens (1938–) educated at Hull, the LSE and Cambridge (PhD, 1974), where he was Professor of Sociology from 1985 to 1996. He became Director of The London School of Economics in 1997. A prolific writer, three main strands to his work are discernible. Interpretations of the founding fathers (*Capitalism and Modern Social Theory: an analysis of the writings of Marx, Durkheim and Max Weber*, 1971), analyses of the institutions of industrialised countries (*A Contemporary Critique of Historical Materialism*, three volumes, 1981, 1985 and 1994) and the development of structuration theory (begun in *New Rules of Sociological Method*, 1976).

Erving Goffman (1922–1982) born in Canada, after gaining his PhD (Chicago, 1953), he taught at the Universities of California, Berkeley and Pennsylvania. A major figure within micro-sociology and often labeled a symbolic interactionist, although he eschewed association with any one perspective. Goffman studied face-to-face interaction in "everyday" and "deviant" settings, enriching sociology's vocabulary with his dramaturgical analysis. Major works include *The Presentation of Self in Everyday Life* (1959), *Asylums* (1961) and *Frame Analysis* (1974).

John Harry Goldthorpe (1935–) Official Fellow of Nuffield College, Oxford since 1969, was educated at the Universities of London, Oxford and Cambridge and the LSE. Stratification is his main area of work. Together with David Lockwood and others, he carried out the *Affluent Worker* studies (1968–9). Goldthorpe's neo-Weberian theory of class (*Social Mobility and Class Structure in Modern Britain*, 1980 and 1988) has been very influential within British sociology.

Alvin Ward Gouldner (1920–80) educated at Columbia University (PhD, 1953), he taught at universities in America, Jerusalem and Berlin. After initial work on bureaucracy, his main contribution has been to sociological theory, attacking both functionalism and Marxism in *The Coming Crisis of Western Sociology* (1971), arguing for a more reflexive approach.

Jurgen Habermas (1929–) German social theorist, studied at Gottingen and Frankfurt's Institute for Social Research. Professor of Philosophy at Johann Wolfgang Goethe University. Grounded in critical theory, his work synthesizes perspectives from the social sciences, philosophy and linguistics. Habermas developed legitimation crisis theory to explain contradictions in late capitalist societies. Underpinning this and all his other writings is a concern with the role of knowledge in society. Major works include *Legitimation Crisis* (1975), *The Theory of Communicative Action* in two volumes (1986 and 1989) and *The Structural Transformation of the Public Sphere* (1989).

Stuart McPhail Hall (1932–) educated at Jamaica College and Oxford University. Professor of Sociology at the Open University and President of the British Sociological Association. Always working within "shouting distance" of Marx (his own phrase), he was a founding editor of the *New Left Review* (1957–61) and one of the founding fathers of Cultural Studies. He was Director of the Birmingham (England)-based Centre for Contemporary Cultural Studies (1972–79).

Through his own writings on crime, race, and nationalism he has explored the challenges facing the Left in a post-industrial age, arguing that politics must appeal to people's sense of identity as well as their economic interests. Major works include *Policing the Crisis* (1978) and *Politics and Ideology* (1986).

Albert Henry Halsey (1923–) educated at Oxford and the LSE Emeritus Professor of Social and Administrative Studies, University of Oxford. A well-known believer in the social democratic perspective, he has written extensively on education, class and social mobility. He has contributed directly to post-war educational reform in the UK both as advisor to the Secretary of State for Education (1965–8) and as promoter of comprehensive and compensatory education. Major works include *Social Class and Educational Opportunity* (1956) and *Change in British Society* (1978).

Paul F. Lazarsfeld (1901–76) Viennese-born sociologist. After obtaining a PhD in mathematics, he became interested in mass media research which he undertook at the Universities of Newark, Princeton and Columbia, founding the Bureau of Applied Social Research at the latter institution. Lazarsfeld had a major impact on quantitative and mathematical sociology. He was instrumental in establishing survey research as a sophisticated method of sociological analysis. Major works include *The Language of Social Research* (1955) and *Latent Structure Analysis* (1968).

David Lockwood (1929–) educated at the LSE (PhD, 1957), he has been Professor of Sociology at Essex University since 1968. Lockwood has made perceptive contributions to sociological theory (*Solidarity and Schism*, 1992) and is widely known as the author of two classic neo-Weberian studies of social stratification: *The Blackcoated Worker* (1958) and with John Goldthorpe et al., *The Affluent Worker* studies (1968–9).

Michael Mann (1942–) British sociologist, read history at Oxford University. Professor of

Sociology at the University of California, Los Angeles. Interested in social stratification, he has been pursuing an ambitious historical analysis of power (*The Sources of Social Power*, vol 1 and 2, 1986 and 1993), arguing it has four, equally important, sources: military, political, economic and ideological.

Karl Marx (1818–83) born in Trier, Germany. Studied law, philosophy and economics at the Universities of Bonn and Berlin. Social theorist, journalist and activist, he spent much of his life in London, supported financially by Friedrich Engels. Marx's contributions to sociology include analyses of capitalism, alienation, ideology, economy, social class, class conflict and social change. Major works include *The Communist Manifesto* (1848), *Grundrisse* (written 1857–8, published 1939–41) and *Capital*, three volumes (1867, 1885 and 1894).

George Herbert Mead (1863–1931) studied under Josiah Royce and William James at Harvard and Wilhelm Wundt in Germany. Invited by John Dewey to Chicago University's Department of Philosophy in 1893, he remained there until his death. A charismatic lecturer rather than a writer, his reputation has grown from posthumously published lecture notes. Stressing that the self evolves through social interaction, his ideas were influential in the development of symbolic interactionism. Major collections of his works include *Mind, Self and Society* (1934), *The Philosophy of the Act* (1938) and *The Philosophy of the Present* (1959).

Robert K. Merton (1910–) graduated in philosophy and sociology from Temple University (1931) and studied under Parsons at Harvard. Emeritus Professor of Sociology at Columbia University. He has made significant contributions to functionalism and sociologies of science, deviance, mass communications and bureaucracy through his "middle range theory" approach. Major works include *Social Theory and Social Structure* (1957) and *The Sociology of Science: Theoretical and Empirical Investigations* (1973).

Robert Michels (1876–1936) sociologist and economist, born in Cologne, educated in England, France and Germany. His early socialist beliefs precluded an academic career in Germany and he taught mostly in Italy. He wrote on many topics including, nationalism, fascism, democracy and imperialism. He is most famous for formulating the "iron law of oligarchy", which reflected his disaffection with socialism and the belief that elite rule is inevitable. The "iron law" was promulgated in *Political Parties* (1911).

Charles Wright Mills (1916–1962) educated at the Universities of Texas and Wisconsin, he joined the Bureau for Applied Social Research at Columbia in 1945. The author of studies on stratification and power (*White Collar*, 1951 and *The Power Elite*, 1956), he was critical of American society and orthodox sociology, attacking both functionalism and empiricism. Mills advocated a more interventionist sociology, appreciative of both agency and structure, in his most famous work, *The Sociological Imagination* (1959).

Robert Ezra Park (1864–1944) after graduating from the University of Michigan, he spent twelve years as a newspaper reporter before resuming his studies at Harvard (MA) and Heidelberg (PhD). At the age of 50 he began his sociological career at Chicago University. An inspirational teacher, his interest in urban, community and race issues became central to the development of the Chicago School. With Ernst Burgess he wrote an early influential textbook, *An Introduction to the Science of Society* (1921) and helped promote empirical research, especially the use of participant observation.

Talcott Parsons (1902–1979) took his AB at Amherst College and DPhil at Heidelberg University. He accepted a post at Harvard in 1927, where he remained for the rest of his career. A major contributor to functionalism, he wanted to create a general theory based upon his systemic view of social action. His influence faded in the 1960s and 1970s when his consensus oriented theories were challenged both by political events, such as the US race riots, and the emergence of alternative interpretive sociologies. Major works include *The Structure of Social Action* (1937), *The Social System* (1951) and *Societies: Evolutionary and Comparative Perspectives* (1966).

John Rex see his Personal Account in Chapter 1.

Alice S. Rossi (1922–) Emeritus Professor of Sociology, University of Massachusetts, Amherst. Her 1964 article, "Equality Between the Sexes: an Immodest Proposal" (*Daedalus*, 93, Spring), has acquired classic status because of its women-oriented analysis and departure from the prevailing functionalist perspective. Rossi has continued to focus on gender relations arguing, controversially, for more importance to be given to the biological basis of gender differences. Major works include *The Feminist Papers: From Addams to de Beauvoir* (1973) and *Seasons of a Woman's Life* (1983).

Alfred Schutz (1899–1959) Viennese-born philosopher and sociologist, emigrated to the USA in 1939. He maintained a dual career for most of his life, as Husserl put it, "a banker by day and phenomenologist by night". Schutz was a primary contributor to the development of phenomenological sociology, concerned with how individuals make sense of and construct social reality. Major works include *The Phenomenology of the Social World* (1932).

Georg Simmel (1858–1918) studied history, philosophy and psychology at Berlin University, where he taught until gaining a Chair in Philosophy at Strasbourg. He was one of the first to try to establish sociology as a unique discipline. A pioneer of interactionism, his work was integral to the development of the Chicago School of American sociology. Major works in English include two collections of essays, *The Sociology of Georg Simmel* (1950) and *Conflict and the Web of Group Affiliation* (1955).

Carol Smart (1948–) formerly Director of the National Council for One Parent Families, is Professor, Department of Sociology and Social Policy at Leeds University. Working within a feminist perspective, she has written extensively on women, law, crime and social policy. Recent research includes a study of single mothers' response to the Child Support Act 1991. Major works include *The Ties That Bind: Law, Marriage and the Reproduction of Patriarchal Relations* (1984) and *Feminism and the Power of Law* (1989).

Alain Touraine (1925–) French sociologist, he has taught at universities in North and South America and most recently at the École des Hautes Études en Sciences Sociales, Paris. He has made a significant contribution to our understanding of social movements and social change. He was one of the first sociologists to use the phrase "post-industrial society". Major works include *The Post-industrial Society* (1974) and *The Voice and the Eye: An Analysis of Social Movements* (1981).

Sylvia Walby (1953–) studied at the Universities of Reading (BA) and Essex (MA and PhD). She is Professor of Sociology at Leeds University and President of the European Sociological Association. An original voice within feminist sociology, she has been developing a sophisticated theory of patriarchy (*Patriarchy at Work*, 1986 and *Theorizing Patriarchy*, 1990) which she uses for historical and contemporary analyses of women in American and British societies.

Immanuel Wallerstein (1930–) American sociologist and historian, educated at Columbia University (PhD, 1959). Since 1976 he has been Distinguished Professor of Sociology at the State University of New York, Binghampton. President of the International Sociological Association (1994–8). Having spent the early part of his career researching in Africa, he developed "world system theory" as a means of explaining unequal relationships between different regions of the globe. Major works include *The Modern World System* (1974) and *The Capitalist World-economy* (1979).

Max Weber (1864–1920) born in Erfurt, Germany, he studied at the Universities of Heidelberg, Gottingen and Berlin. A professor of economics at 30, he suffered a mental breakdown in 1897 which precluded occupation of full-time posts until his acceptance of a Chair in Sociology at Vienna in 1918. A key figure, Weber made insightful contributions to the study of methodology, religion, capitalism, class and bureaucracy. Most significantly, he demonstrated the centrality of meaning for sociology, his theory of social action providing a touchstone for myriad sociological perspectives. Major works include *The Protestant Ethic and the Spirit of Capitalism* (1904), *Economy and Society* (1922) and *The Methodology of the Social Sciences* (1949).

William Julius Wilson (1935–) Professor at the Kennedy School of Government and member of the Department of Afro-American Studies, Harvard University. An influential figure in the study of race and urban poverty. Until recently a promoter of the term "underclass", he has become increasingly concerned by the right-wing's prejudicial use of the word. Major works include *The Truly Disadvantaged: the Inner City, the Underclass and Public Policy* (1978) and *The Ghetto Underclass* (1989).

Erik Olin Wright (1947–) studied at the Universities of Harvard, Oxford and California. Professor of Sociology at the University of Wisconsin. Best known for his neo-Marxist theories of class, he has attempted to account for the complexities of class relations through the development of the concept of "contradictory class locations" in *Class, Crisis and the State* (1978) and *Classes* (1985).

References

Bernard, L. L. and Bernard, Jessie 1943: *Origins of American Sociology*. New York: Thomas Cromwell.

Coser, Lewis A. 1979: American trends. In T. Bottomore and R. Nisbet (eds), *A History of Sociological Analysis*. London: Heinemann, pp. 287–320.

Merton, R. K. and Riley, M. W. (eds) 1980: *Sociological Traditions from Generation to Generation: Glimpses of the American Experience*. Norwood, NJ: Ablex.

Abrams, P. 1968: *The Origins of British Sociology 1834–1914*. Chicago, IL: University of Chicago Press.

Eldridge, J. 1980: *Recent British Sociology*. London: Macmillan.

A Select Bibliography of Sociological Dictionaries and Encyclopaedias

Abercrombie, N., Hill, S. and Turner, B. S. 1995: *The Penguin Dictionary of Sociology*, 3rd edn. Harmondsworth: Penguin.

Borgatta, E. F. and Borgatta, M. L. 1991: *Encyclopedia of Sociology*. Chicago, IL: University of Chicago Press.

Jary, D. and Jary, J. 1995: *Collins Dictionary of Sociology*, 2nd edn. Glasgow: HarperCollins.

Johnson, A. 1995: *The Blackwell Dictionary of Sociology: A User's Guide to Sociological Language*. Cambridge, MA: Basil Blackwell.

Lachmann, R. (ed.) 1991: *Encyclopedic Dictionary of Sociology*, 4th edn. Guilford, CT: Dushkin.

Magill, F. (ed.) 1995: *International Encyclopedia of Sociology*. Chicago, IL: Fitzroy Dearborn.

Marshall, G. (ed.) 1994: *The Concise Oxford Dictionary of Sociology*. Oxford: Oxford University Press.

World Biographical Index of Politics, Social Sciences & Economics: Politicians, Sociologists, Economists, Political Scientists & Psychologists. 1996: Kent: K. G. Saur.

42

Information and Data Sources

Martin Scarrott

This chapter aims to offer a general introduction to some of the basic information sources available to sociology students. Most sociological research at undergraduate level will be undertaken in the university library and your ability to use the library resources available to you efficiently and effectively will impact directly upon your ability to demonstrate your full academic potential in your coursework. During the early stages of your studies you can expect to be given essential and recommended reading by academic staff, but as you progress and are asked to produce longer, more in-depth and more specialized work so the information skills that you need to support this will also have to be developed. This chapter offers some advice about the skills you need to obtain and the information sources you will need to use.

Using Libraries and their Catalogues

The university library will provide the materials needed to support basic coursework and academic staff will provide guidance with regard to appropriate reading. Some of this will be considered essential reading and some will be recommended background reading. There may be a special collection of essential course material in the library which has been separated from the main stock and has special conditions governing its use. Some course material may be made available on the university computer network. You will have to find out how the system operates in the library which you are using.

Most university libraries offer some kind of information skills training which will begin with basic orientation. This may simply be a guided walk around tour of the library or it may take the form of an independent study pack which is an assessed part of the degree. Such activities are often organized during the first week or so of a university career when there are many other demands on students' time and learning how to use the library may seem relatively insignificant. However, make sure that you check to see what is available and take full advantage of it. The aim of such activities is to empower you to locate and use information and reduce dependency on academic and library staff for basic information needs. A small amount of time invested early on could save you a lot of effort when you begin preparing for your first essay or presentation.

In general you should aim to achieve the following basic information skills as a minimum during the early stages of your course.

- An understanding of the physical layout of the library; the location of books, journals and computer equipment that you will be expected to use; any rules relating to the use and loan of material, including those relating to the use of computer equipment.
- The ability to use the library catalogue to identify material which has been included on a reading list; you should also be able to locate material by subject so that you can find additional material that is not given on reading lists.

- The ability to interpret information given on reading lists, including the ability to distinguish between a reference to an article in a journal and that to a book.
- Basic computer keyboard and mouse skills.

The Library Catalogue

Almost all university libraries have catalogues which are computerized. Such a catalogue is often referred to as an on-line public access catalogue (OPAC). When attempting to locate a particular item always begin by using the catalogue. Do not simply browse on the shelves even if you think you know the correct area to look. Even fairly small university libraries are much larger than even the largest bookshops (where one would normally locate material merely by browsing the shelves) and are arranged in a much more sophisticated way. Material is indexed and classified according to its subject and in most (but not all) university libraries material is arranged on shelves in a classified order again according to subject. There are various classification schemes in use but in general they all attempt to organize knowledge in a relative and logical way.

Library catalogues can vary tremendously between libraries but in general they enable users to:

- identify whether the library holds an item they are seeking;
- identify where that item is located, how many copies there are and whether they are available for loan.

In addition users may be able to:

- place a reservation for an item which is on loan;
- check to see which items they have borrowed and when they are due for return;
- renew items they have on loan;
- access the catalogues of other libraries.

Computerized catalogues enable material to be accessed in a number of different ways. When you have the full author and title details

(known as the bibliographic details) of a book you would normally search for it on the catalogue using these details. If, however, you do not know the author and title of a particular book you can search by subject. Normally you will be able to use keywords which describe the subject you are looking for. You will have to think of the words that best describe the subject. Often, it is possible to use more than one word and either narrow the search down by finding items with all of the words you choose or broaden the search by finding items with either one word or another. There may also be a subject index where the library has used particular words or phrases to describe the subject content of an item. You can then identify all items which have been assigned a particular subject description.

When using library catalogues it is important to remember:

- they do not normally contain references to articles in journals or chapters in books;
- they are general search tools, e.g. the catalogue will not indicate if a book about the sociology of work contains a critique of Fordism.

Secondary Statistical Data

What percentage of unskilled manual workers' children obtain a university degree? How does alcohol consumption vary by social class? How does the participation rate for soccer compare with that for cricket? Secondary statistical data can be a useful and interesting source of information and these are examples of the kinds of questions which can be answered by referring to it. Every government produces statistical information which is available in a variety of forms. All countries, for example, have a national census which provides valuable information for the sociologist. In the UK the General Household Survey (Office of Population Censuses and Surveys) provides annual data about household expenditure and activities whilst data from a wide variety of sources is brought together in an annual publication *Social Trends* (Central Statistical Office). In the USA useful data can be found in the *Statistical Abstract of the US* (Bureau of the Census, 1995). Many university libraries have separate statistics collections and they often produce brief guides on how they are used. There are a number of published guides to statistical sources available for most countries and examples include the annual *American Statistics Index* (Congressional Information Service), the annual *Statistics Canada Catalogue* (Canada: Statistics Canada Library) and the *Guide to Official Statistics In Britain* (Central Statistical Office, 1995). Increasingly, such material is being made available electronically and some of it is freely accessible on the Internet.

The Internet

The Internet is simply a network that connects tens of thousands of computers across the world. The World Wide Web (often referred to as "the web") is one of the most useful features of the internet. It provides access to documents which include both graphics and text (hypertext) with seamless links to documents which can be held on different computers. These documents all have a unique address called a universal resource locator (URL). There are numerous books available which provide an introduction to using the Internet (Glister, 1995). The Internet is certainly not the answer to all your information needs and it is possible to spend hours "surfing the net" without finding anything of academic value. Perry (1995) surveyed Internet users and cites one user who commented that the Internet is "extremely interesting but not the panacea proclaimed in the press". Perry concludes that "the Internet has a long way to go before it becomes the 'ideal' information resource".

So the Internet isn't a panacea but it can provide access to some interesting sources of information for the sociology student including, for example, data from the American census (Bureau of the Census, 1996). There have been attempts to provide subject access to documents on the web. One example is the Social Science Information Gateway

(Economic and Social Research Council, 1996) which has a "subject tree" with direct links to resources located worldwide. Find out how to access the Internet from within your university.

Abstracts and Indexes

As you progress through a course and your understanding of sociological theory and concepts develops, so you will be expected to produce more advanced work which will involve more independent study. Many undergraduates are required to produce a dissertation or term paper, often during the final year of their course. The dissertation may be based entirely on secondary research or it may involve doing some primary research, but it will always involve conducting a literature search and review. A literature search involves trawling the published literature systematically for relevant material using information search tools. Make a record of all the references you find. There are numerous books available which offer advice on this process (e.g. Bell, 1993, Chaps 3 and 4). Abstracting and indexing journals are tools which can help in conducting a literature search.

An index enables material to be located by subject. Some indexes also include abstracts which are brief summaries of publications. Note that even in electronic form such databases do not contain the full text of the publications they index. There are numerous abstracting and indexing journals of value to sociology students. Three very general examples are listed here. There are many others some of which, such as *Sociology of Education Abstracts*, are much more specialized. Many such publications are available in electronic form.

Sociological Abstracts (Sociological Abstracts Inc.)

This is a collection of non-evaluative abstracts of journal articles and conference proceedings and it also provides an index to book reviews. It indexes three categories of journals: those produced by sociological associations and university departments containing the word sociology in the title; those from related disciplines such as anthropology; those of more general interest which publish articles on sociological topics. This publication is also available on a CD-ROM called *Sociofile* which is available in some libraries.

International Bibliography of the Social Sciences (British Library of Political and Economic Science)

IBSS is an annual publication in four volumes covering the social sciences in the broadest sense. The sociology volume is called "The International Bibliography of Sociology". Together the four volumes index around 100,000 articles from 2,500 journals and 20,000 books per annum. There are no abstracts. Most universities in the UK provide access to this database electronically via BIDS (Bath Information and Data Services).

Social Science Citation Index (Institute for Scientific Information)

SSCI indexes around 4,700 journals in sociology and related disciplines and it includes conference proceedings and book reviews. In printed form there are four volumes including a "permuterm subject index". SSCI is also used to identify material by citation. Once a key paper has been identified it is possible to identify subsequent papers which have cited it. Hence it can be used to trace how a particular theory has been received or developed as well as simply to identify other material on a similar subject. SSCI is also accessible via BIDS from most UK universities.

....

Ask for advice in the library about the most appropriate indexes to use for a particular topic. It may be possible to access indexes

which are not held in printed or electronic form in the library. Imagine that a student is researching the leisure activities of retired females and *Leisure Recreation & Tourism Abstracts* (Commonwealth Agricultural Bureau) has been identified as a likely tool for locating published material, but the library does not hold it in either printed or electronic form. In common with most other university libraries it can access the data in this publication on a remote computer system. It is paid for by a combination of the length of time connected to the computer and the amount of references retrieved so the student is not given unlimited access to it. Instead a librarian searches the database with the student present. This is called an on-line search.

Once sufficient references have been obtained it is necessary to check the library catalogue to see if the material is held. If not it may be possible to obtain some of it through a document delivery or inter-library loan service. Find out about any such services available in your library. It is very important to plan work well in advance since material obtained may take a considerable amount of time to arrive. Consequently, it is normally possible to use such services only when engaged in a major piece of work.

To conclude, this chapter has attempted to give some indication of the kinds of resources available. These resources are many and varied and it is essential that you familiarize yourself with the resources available within your particular university. Take full advantage of any classes, study packs or guides to information sources that may be available. The library is still the place where most sociology students will do most of their research. For the majority of students print on paper will be the main medium through which they gain information and develop their knowledge although, increasingly, this will be supplemented by using electronic sources of information.

References

Bell, J. 1993: *Doing Your Research Project: A Guide for First–Time Researchers in Education and Social* *Science*, 2nd edn. Buckingham: Open University Press.

British Library of Political & Economic Science. *International Bibliography of the Social Sciences*. London: Routledge.

Bureau of the Census 1995: *Statistical Abstract of the US*, 115th edn. Austin, TX: Reference Press.

—— 1996: *Census Bureau Home Page* URL: *http://www.census.gov*

Central Statistical Office 1995: *Guide to Official Statistics*, No. 6. London: HMSO.

—— *Social Trends*. London: HMSO.

Commonwealth Agricultural Bureau *Leisure Recreation & Tourism Abstracts*. Wallington: CAB.

Congressional Information Service *American Statistics Index*. Washington, DC: Congressional Information Service.

Economic and Social Research Council 1996: *Social Science Information Gateway*. URL: *http://sosig.esrc.bris.ac.uk*

Glister, P. 1995: *The Internet Navigator*, rev. edn. New York: John Wiley.

Institute for Scientific Information *Social Science Citation Index*. Philadelphia: ISI.

Office of Population Censuses and Surveys *General Household Survey*. London: HMSO.

Perry, C. 1995: Travellers on the internet. *Online*, 19, 2, 29–34.

Sociological Abstracts *Sociological Abstracts*. San Diego, CA: Sociological Abstracts Inc.

Sociology of Education Abstracts. Abingdon, Carfax.

Statistics Canada Library *Statistics Canada Catalogue*. Ottawa: Queen's Printer.

43

Major Journals in Sociology

Simon Speight

The number of titles listed under the subject "sociology" in any journals directory (Ulrich's 1996; Benn's 1996) is enough to make even the most conscientious student blanch with fear! Miller noted 72 "major" sociological journals, and supplemented this with a list of over 320 further titles relevant to sociology. Even then, many potentially useful journals in the fields of economics, education, law and politics were excluded (Miller, 1991, 644–52). This chapter is intended to make a little sense out of this confusion, and provide an introduction to some of the major journals.

The main aim of most sociology journals is to report new research and theoretical developments. Different journals aim for different audiences (e.g. academic sociologists, researchers, policy-makers in specific fields), and this should be noted when selecting journals to read, since it influences the presumptions authors and editors make about the readers' prior knowledge. Although there are few academic journals designed specifically to meet the needs of undergraduate students, with skilful use there are many titles of value to your studies. Many journals contain book reviews, together with news, updating or review articles, all of which tend to be reasonably understandable. A sensible strategy for developing your ability to read journal articles is to begin with those recommended by your tutor in lectures and seminars, since these should be more accessible items. Another useful strategy is to follow up debates on major articles you have read by looking through subsequent issues of the same journal for comments and replies.

Most of the journals considered in this chapter have been selected on the grounds that they are amongst the more accessible titles. At postgraduate level, or in the later stages of an undergraduate degree, most of the articles published should be understandable and, with tutor support, even students relatively new to sociology should be able to increase their knowledge. Whatever stage you are at, remember this simple advice: journals are there to help you, and by selecting a journal article carefully, you will increase your understanding of sociology. However, if you come across an article you don't fully understand, don't be disheartened – just because you don't *yet* have sufficient background knowledge to make sense of it, doesn't mean that you won't in a few month's time!

A good starting point are the journals published by the American Sociological Association (ASA) and the British Sociological Association (BSA). The *American Sociological Review* was established in 1936 as the official journal of the ASA. It is published bi-monthly and, according to Miller (1991, p. 668), is ". . . the journal most widely read by sociologists". Founded in 1967, and published quarterly, *Sociology* is the official journal of the BSA. Both journals publish articles of interest to the whole discipline and encourage debates, thus providing a range of different perspectives. Extensive book reviews are also printed, allowing students or researchers to keep up to date with new publications in their areas of interest. Both journals are highly respected by academics and, over the years, have included contributions from many leading sociological researchers.

Another internationally respected journal is the *Australian and New Zealand Journal of Sociology*, published by the Sociological Associations of Australia and New Zealand. Articles of general interest are published, making this accessible for postgraduate students and those in the later stages of an undergraduate course.

Established in 1885, as the first American scholarly journal for sociology, the *American Journal of Sociology* presents articles concerning the history and practice of sociology. In particular, the journal seeks to apply methods used in other, related disciplines, and regularly publishes articles written by practitioners in psychology, economics, history and political science, thus providing a cross-disciplinary perspective.

The *Canadian Journal of Sociology/Cahiers Canadiens de Sociologie* also encourages a cross-disciplinary approach. Founded in 1974, and published quarterly in English and French, it has established an excellent reputation internationally. Although considerable emphasis is placed on Canadian society (particularly politics and history), new trends in international sociology are reported, and articles and book reviews covering a wide range of sociological issues are published.

There is an increasing trend for publishers to make information and articles available over the internet. For example the *American Journal of Sociology* and the *Canadian Journal of Sociology* have on-line versions – and there are some journals which are dedicated to the Internet such as the *Electronic Journal of Sociology* and *Sociological Research Online*.

These, then, are a few of the major journals. However, in a field as fragmented as sociology, there are inevitably research areas not covered by the major journals, and many specialist titles have evolved. *Ageing and Society* is an example of such a title. This is a quarterly journal, co-sponsored by the Centre for the Policy on Ageing and the British Society of Gerontology. It covers aspects of ageing worldwide, including issues such as lifestyle, work and retirement, and other articles which contribute to an understanding of the ageing process. Review articles are also printed, allowing students to keep abreast of new publications and developments. Although reasonably accessible, some of the articles published are quite demanding, and aimed at readers with a good understanding of ageing (e.g. health-care professionals, geriatricians). It remains, however, a key journal on an increasingly important subject.

There are hundreds of similar specialized journals – far too many to be listed here. However, a few examples of the sorts of titles available are *Sociology of Education*, *Rural Sociology*, *Social Problems*, *Feminist Review*, *Sociology of Health and Illness*, and *Population Studies*. Although these journals deal with specific subjects, they are widely read and internationally respected, and are useful for gaining more detailed knowledge of subjects which may be covered only briefly in other journals.

Review Journals

Most of the journals discussed so far are "traditional journals", containing a number of short articles on a variety of subjects. However, some journals focus more specifically on certain areas. *Current Sociology* and *Contemporary Sociology* are two examples.

Whilst many journals devote some space to reviews, *Contemporary Sociology: A Journal of Reviews* is devoted to them. Book reviews, critical surveys and discussions of new or recent important works in sociology are published. Books selected for review reflect current concerns.

Since *Contemporary Sociology* is dedicated to reviews it is, perhaps, of less use to new students, since it provides few basic facts. However, for postgraduates or academics, it is an invaluable source of new publications, and an important means of keeping abreast of developments in a constantly changing field.

Current Sociology/Sociologie Contemporaine is closer to a traditional journal. Published three times a year in English and French, it examines aspects of sociology worldwide. Unlike most journals however, each issue has a trend report, devoted to a single subject, and written by a different author/editor. Articles are, therefore, more like a short book on a subject, rather than a journal article. This provides an excellent introduction to a subject, whilst an annotated bibliography directs interested readers to other sources of information. Since coverage is wide-ranging, across the social sciences, it is an ideal source for new students and academics alike.

Although this brief survey has covered only a tiny proportion of the many journals relevant to sociology, it has hopefully provided some clues as to good starting places for information. As your studies progress, you will undoubtedly find other sources which are also useful. The journals listed above, however, are the major journals which you should consult time and again.

References and Further Reading

Benn's Media Directory 1996. London: Miller Freeman.

Miller, D. 1991: *Handbook of Research Design and Social Measurement*, 5th edn. London: Sage.

Publishing Options: An Author's Guide to Journals. Washington, DC: American Sociological Association, (occasional publication).

Ulrich's International Periodicals Directory 1996. New Providence, NJ: Bowker.

44

Associations and Conferences

Steve Morgan

As with any dynamic area of study it is important that students become familiar with the current trends and debates, the leading players and the research activities within the relevant fields of the discipline. It is mainly through this process of familiarization that participation in research and the dissemination of results become possible. Students who are committed to the study of sociology at an advanced level, especially if they intend a professional life which involves sociology, would therefore gain enormous benefits from joining an appropriate association. Such associations or societies – whether regional, national or international – offer a wide variety of services to the research community (and often services appropriate to the needs of students). These include journal titles, regular newsletters, conferences and, increasingly, their own electronic services on the World Wide Web. However, the major benefit which they offer nascent or practising sociologists is the opportunity to participate in and learn from sociological debates.

Most associations have a code of ethics which provides members with guidelines for behaviour in relation to research and professional conduct.

For the purposes of this chapter I have concentrated on the major national and international organizations, giving brief details of their aims, conferences and membership. The Appendix gives details of postal and e-mail addresses, where available.

American Sociological Association (ASA)

Founded in 1905, the ASA is a voluntary association which aims to advance sociology as a scientific discipline and profession serving the public good. It has a distinct role in promoting sociology as a vibrant, stimulating and diverse discipline. It has a network of regional associations whose conferences tend to provide greater opportunities for students and practitioners to participate in since competition for the acceptance of papers is less fierce. The ASA publishes a number of prestigious journals including its flagship publication the *American Sociological Review*. Its membership of over 13,000 includes academics, researchers, practitioners and students. Currently there are four categories of membership – regular, associate, emeritus and student. Undergraduates or graduates who are studying in accredited institutions may belong to the association for the duration of their course at a reduced fee. The benefits of membership include the choice of receiving one of the association's journals, subscription to their newsletter, calls for papers for the annual meetings, and a variety of discounts. The annual meetings take place during August. In 1995 the ASA launched its own Internet service, ASANet, which provides information for members and the general public.

British Sociological Association (BSA)

Founded in 1951, the BSA's aims are to promote interest in sociology and to advance its study and application. Its activities and services include the annual conference which takes place in April, a network of study groups, a book club and an information service. It publishes a regular newsletter called *Network* together with two journals *Sociology* and *Work, Employment and Society*. Membership which currently numbers over 2,000 is open to all who are interested in the advancement of sociology. Subscription is income-related although students are entitled to reduced rates.

Canadian Sociology and Anthropology Association (CSAA/SCSA)

The overall goal of the CSAA is to develop and promote the interests of those involved in sociology and anthropology in Canada. This process involves the articulation of social policy concerns expressed by the membership and the preparation of briefs for presentation to government or other organizations. Particular emphasis is placed on the promotion of research, publication and teaching. Membership, which includes those in education, government and business, students, and individuals from other disciplines, currently stands at around 2,000. The CSAA publishes a professional journal the *Canadian Review of Sociology and Anthropology/La Revue canadienne de sociologie et d'anthropologie*, and their newsletter *Society/Société*. All members receive these publications. The association organizes an annual conference in conjunction with the meetings of the learned societies.

The Australian Sociological Association (TASA)

TASA was founded in 1960, with New Zealand sociologists who have since formed an association of their own. It has more than 500 members, including a large postgraduate membership. Student membership is encouraged by a sliding scale of subscriptions reflecting income level. The Association publishes a journal *The Australian and New Zealand Journal of Sociology* (ANZJS) which is issued three times a year and reflects the diversity and scope of sociology in Australia. It also publishes a quarterly newsletter *NEXUS* which deals with current issues, the various sociology departments in Australia, the activities of the TASA executive, conference news and brief book reviews. TASA holds an annual conference, often in early December at the close of the Australian academic year. The Conference is hosted by different universities. There are very active "health" and "women's" sections – both of which hold additional activities at the annual conference. There is also a postgraduate group. A series of mini-conferences run on a state-wide basis has recently been initiated.

Sociological Association of Aotearoa (New Zealand) (SAANZ)

In 1988 the New Zealand Sociological Association changed its name to the SAANZ to reflect the Maori name for the country. The Association aims to encourage the development and dissemination of sociological knowledge and to provide a forum for communication and exchange of ideas between members. Membership offers a number of benefits including a regular newsletter, listings of members' research and work interests, organization of the Annual Conference and reduced subscriptions to *New Zealand Sociology* and *Australia and New Zealand Journal of Sociology*.

International Sociological Association (ISA)

The ISA was founded in 1949 under the auspices of UNESCO. Its overall goal is to advance sociological knowledge throughout the world. It aims to represent sociologists worldwide regardless of their ideological opinion or scientific approaches. The association undertakes a wide range of activities such as research committees (covering 50 different areas of sociology), thematic and working groups, organization of the world congress, as well as holding regional conferences. The ISA publishes two prestigious journals – *International Sociology* and *Current Sociology* – and is co-sponsor of *Sociological Abstracts*. The association also runs a "Young Sociologists" competition which provides encouragement and wide dissemination for those trying to make their name in the discipline. Membership, which currently stands at 3,600 from 91 countries, is open to scholars and professionals of sociological teaching, research or practice.

European Sociological Association (ESA)

The ESA was formed in 1992 following the major changes in East–West relations. Its main aim is to facilitate sociological research, teaching and communication on European issues. It seeks to fill a gap between the national and the international associations. The ESA focuses particularly on sociological analysis of Europe rather than acting as a forum for sociologists in Europe. The activities of the Association include the publication of its newsletter *European Sociologist* and also *Research Networks* which covers specific themes. It organizes a biennial conference. Membership is open to *bona fide* scholars who contribute to the development of sociology within Europe or about European issues.

Appendix

American Sociological Association
1722 North St, NW
Washington, DC 20036
e-mail: executive.office@asanet.org

British Sociological Association
Unit 39, Mountjoy Research Centre
Stockton Rd
Durham DH1 3UR
e-mail: BSA.admin@durham.ac.uk.

Canadian Sociology and Anthropology Association
1455 de Maisonneuve Blvd
West, LB–615
Montreal
Quebec
H3G 1M8
e-mail: CSAA@VAX2.CONCORDIA.CA

The Australian Sociological Association
c/o Dr Marilyn Poole
School of Social Inquiry
Deakin University
662 Blackburn Road
Clayton, Victoria 3168
Australia
e-mail: marp@mail-b.deakin.edu.au
Internet: http://www.faass.newcastle.edu.au/tasa/tasa.htm

Sociological Association of Aotearoa (New Zealand)
Henry Barnard
NZ Social Research Data Archives
Faculty of Social Sciences
Massey University
Private Bag 11–222
Palmerston North
New Zealand
e-mail: NZSRDA@massey.ac.nz

International Sociological Association
Secretariat: Facultad C. C. Politicas y Sociologia
Universidad Complutense
28223 Madrid
Spain
e-mail: isa@sis.ucm.es

European Sociological Association
Bernard Kruithof
ESA
SISWO
Plantage Muidergracht 4
TV Amsterdam
Netherlands
e-mail: kruithof@siswo.uva.nl

Although the above associations have their own World Wide Web sites, it is advizable to obtain their adresses from your university library. Unfortunately, electronic addresses are prone to frequent changes.

Acknowledgement

Thanks to Marilyn Poole for information on the Australian Sociological Association.

PART VI
What Next?

"What next?" is not a question that students ask only as they near the end of their course. It is a question that, for many, is a constant background accompaniment to their studies and, for others, a question that led them into sociology in the first place. You may have come into higher education for one or many reasons – to satisfy your parents, in the hope of a personally stimulating experience, or as preparation for a specific career. It may have been a conscious and deliberate choice (this is almost always the case with mature students – see the chapter by Freeland), or the result of "drifting" into the next stage after school. Equally, a decision to study sociology may be reached in a variety of ways. Perhaps it sounds interesting because it is "about people", or addresses social and political issues perceived as important, or is seen as a means to helping people, or is thought – wrongly! – to be an easy way to get high grades (Osborne, Patel and Hammond). Snoopy, the cartoon dog in *Peanuts*, once reviewed all these possible reasons for doing sociology and rejected them all. He wanted to do the subject because he was "just plain nosy!".

The choices we make at one stage of our lives are conditioned by how we anticipate their consequences, and for most students that means prospects for employment. Each graduate will be looking for a job with some combination of preferences in mind with regard to pay, security, location, opportunities for travel, job satisfaction, worthwhileness of the occupation and so on. Some flavour of the kind of work sociologists do is provided in the chapters by White; Osborne, Patel and Hammond; and Freeland. Given a competitive market for jobs and the current high levels of graduate unemployment, students are bound to consider what their chances are of realizing their career hopes, whether studying sociology is a good bet in this respect, and what they can do to enhance their job opportunities.

There are two opposite responses to the uncertainties of the graduate labour market and the fact that so many jobs are unsatisfying. One is for students to go down the route of vocationally-oriented study, selecting subjects that they think will lead to a good job but in which they have no real interest. The other is to ignore vocational considerations altogether. "Since there is little chance of a good job whatever subject I study, I might as well select the one which most interests me and will best develop me as a person". Perhaps few students dare to take such an uncompromising stand yet there are two important kernals of truth in it. Life it not only about employment; and being interested in your studies is crucial to the quality of your learning, and your ability to summon the energy and enthusiasm to work hard and even to complete your course.

In any event, studying sociology in no way lessens your prospects in the labour market. Far from it. Sociology characteristically provides you with the opportunity to develop a wide range of skills and abilities – and it is important for you to become fully aware of the qualities you are able to offer prospective employers and know how to present them to best effect (Miles).

But after completing your initial introduction to sociology (as an undergraduate in the UK, perhaps as a graduate student in the USA) you may decide you wish to develop your abilities further. Thus you might consider higher graduate studies in sociology or closely related fields (Johnson, Middleton) or training directed towards a professional career (Cross). Another possibility is to widen your experience, perhaps through travel and employment abroad (Eglin). The *Companion* is a travel guide too!

Advice on Employment and Further Study

45

How to Present your Sociological Education to the Labour Market

Sheila Miles

"You've got an 'ology – you're a scientist!"

On the phone to his doting, but overbearing, grandmother Anthony has been defensive about his string of exam failures and low grades. But she cheers up immediately when she hears of his modest grade in sociology. She is highly impressed by the sound of an "ology".

This scene from an award-winning television advertisement will be familiar to most British students. But doting grandmothers are one thing. The challenge for sociology graduates is to have the same effect on prospective employers!

Outside research and teaching within sociology itself, there is usually no *direct* vocational pay off from your degree. But you may be better equipped for the graduate labour market than you realize. This chapter attempts to show you how to:

- identify the skills and abilities you have acquired during your sociological education for inclusion in your *curriculum vitae* (CV)
- use your sociological training to analyse job requirements
- draw on your training to present your achievements and personality to the best advantage.

I am suggesting, then, that your specifc training *as a sociologist* can be made a selling point, and can also assist you in the process of job hunting. I call this your "sociological capital".[1]

Recognize the Value of Your Sociological Education

Your CV provides a record of your education and achievements up to the present time, but it also needs to provide a vignette of you as a person. Your aim should be to:

- capture all the relevant experiences and skills you have accumulated
- show you understand how your learning can be applied in practical ways
- convey a sense of the kind of person you are.

Large employers increasingly use criterion-based methods for shortlisting (where marks are accorded to each candidate under a series of predetermined headings – see Fig. 45.1). Your combined CV and application form must therefore provide evidence of abilities and achievements across a range of skills. But the third point is important too. Your application needs to show that you have broad interests, a fair degree of self-knowledge, and a commitment to the type of work for which you are applying. Your CV should therefore draw on all aspects of your life experience including voluntary activities, membership of organizations, clubs and societies, sports and recreation, etc. to give a broader picture of the sort of person you are.

This chapter, however, focuses specifically on your sociological education, during the course of which you will have acquired abilities that are relatively subject-specific and more general skills – often called "transferable" or "core" skills. The first steps then are to *recognize* the skills you have acquired, and design a CV showing how these can be applied in employment contexts.

General Skills

Many large employers base their initial selection on their own test procedures as well as your application form. The skills or "competences" which they seek are usually of a generic kind, as exemplified in the extract relating to a management training scheme – the sort of vocational training for which many sociology graduates apply (Fig. 45.1).

These kinds of generic skill, alongside others such as problem-solving and decision-making, numeracy and computer skills, are common to most job specifications. So in constructing your CV it is a good idea to look back through your courses to identify, in a systematic way, all the activities in which such general skills were developed. Collate all the basic information you can, then sift through and structure it under headings such as those listed above.

There are two complementary ways of approaching this task systematically. One is to analyse each *skill* into its constituent parts and see how your various activities feed into it. The other is to carry out a similar breakdown of your *activities* and see how different aspects are relevant to different skills. Let me give an illustration of each strategy.

Analysing the constituent elements of a job specification

Take "communication" as an example from the list above. This concept covers a variety of forms of written communication (e.g. essays, reports, summary reviews), verbal (presentations, group *rapporteur*, interpersonal) and, sometimes, visual (practice with audio-visual aids). Having analysed "communication" in this way you can reflect on how you have improved your communication skills in various settings. Think beyond "obvious" occasions, such as a formal class presentation, to less obvious ones too. For example, you may have developed good interpersonal skills through involvement in qualitative research where you acquire the ability to listen attentively to different views, and to probe interviewees' answers with pertinent questions.

Analysing your activities for the skills involved

You might perhaps have been involved in a team project which you can immediately put down as evidence of "teamworking". But don't stop there. Reflect on the nature of your particular contribution to the project, and you will realize that it helped you develop qualities that fall under other headings in the list above. Did you take a leadership role or deliver a presentation on behalf of the group, and did you find you were good at it? Did you help resolve conflict in the group? Did you help coordinate the project – taking minutes, arranging meetings, etc.? Did you take a major part in analysing the findings and writing up? Why did you choose/were you chosen to perform these roles? You will see that you gained experience not only in "teamworking", but also perhaps in leadership, managing people, organizational, analytical skills, etc.

Your suitability for the scheme will be assessed against the following eight areas of competence:

- communication
- team working
- managing people
- conceptual skills

- analytical skills
- judgement
- values and drives
- organizational skills.

Figure 45.1 Extract from job description details issued to applicants for a Management Training Scheme in the UK National Health Service.

Sociological Skills and Abilities

Sociological education is not just, or even mainly, about the acquisition of a body of knowledge. Rather it is about developing "ways of thinking".

For anyone wanting cut and dried answers, answers "off the peg", sociology is certainly not the subject to take up. For it is a subject area best characterised by its lively disputaciousness, its conflicting approaches and versions, and vitally, by its questions. (Cuff et al., 1990)

At first sight an education that feeds off conflict and dispute might not sound like the ideal qualifications to set before a prospective employer! The point is however that, given the "essentially contested" nature of the discipline, sociology students learn to cope with differing perspectives from an early stage. They do not expect black-and-white answers, and are unlikely to be "thrown" when there is no quick fix to a problem. A sociological education trains you how to analyse situations from a range of diverse and often conflicting viewpoints, and equips you to reflect critically and dispassionately on each. It teaches you to live with complexity and uncertainty, and to move between bodies of abstract knowledge and practical outcomes. In your learning you will have encountered social processes operating both at the macro-level of global forces and the micro-level of interpersonal relations, and will have developed a specific body of background knowledge about the way social relations are structured and how organizations work. These are essential qualities in the development of the "flexible" worker which I discuss below.

Just as importantly your sociological education will have introduced you to research skills: library skills to keep abreast of current research, and the analytical tools with which to evaluate it; statistical skills for the analysis of large datasets, and a methodological understanding of the limits to their validity; and skills in qualitative methods such as observation and interviewing.

Your CV

Your CV should be updated regularly. It is advisable to start shaping it well before you start applying for jobs, as the process of writing applications is time-consuming and often has to take place just when your course is at its most demanding stage (exams, completing coursework, etc.)

Analysing the Job and "Presentation of Self"

Familiarizing Yourself with the Graduate Job Market

The graduate labour market is changing rapidly. Less bureaucratic organizations are emerging which seek to recruit a more flexible and adaptable workforce (see Brown and Scase, Chapter 20). Not all firms have as yet taken the "flexible" route, though the pressures on them to do so are clearly considerable. But at the current time there are many different kinds of organization "out there", and it is an important part of your task as a job-seeker to "suss out" what kind of organization it is that you are applying to. Your sociological training should help you do this systematically.

First familiarize yourself with the kind of job market you are entering, by reading *recent* sociological writings on changing organizations and employment markets, and specifically on the industry or profession you wish to enter. Next, familiarize yourself with the skills and personal qualities required in different occupations, and levels of work and salary. Find out where the kinds of job you are interested in are advertised (your Careers Centre will advise you) and familiarize yourself with the language of their job specifications. Learn how to interpret them accurately by comparing different job advertisements.

Focusing Your Application

You have found a post that attracts you and obtained an application form. The next stage is to focus your application so that it relates to the requirements of the specific job.

First, you need to identify what the employer is looking for. Read all the information you have on the job (the original advert, the job specification and the application form) and *highlight* its key requirements. This is sociological detective work, applying skills in content or textual analysis that you have acquired in your training – being sensitive to the language used, and spotting the emphases and repetitions which provide clues as to the employer's requirements. Make a list and then examine your CV to identify those aspects of your experience which "match" the requirements of the job specification.

In your letter of application, or the "open" section of an application form, your "presentation of self" should be structured around the key points derived from your analysis and the "match" you have identified, making cross-references to the appropriate sections of your CV. Present yourself positively in as clear and succinct a way as you can, so that the shortlisters do not have to plough through a mass of detail. But you need to show that you have *thought* about your suitability for the job and your interest and commitment to the kind of work it entails so the "matching" should not be presented too mechanically.[2]

If you have time it is worthwhile conducting some background research on the firm, company or organization before committing yourself to paper. At the initial stage this may have to be restricted to a library trawl, but researching the firm becomes far more important if you are called for an interview.

Researching the Firm or Organization

I once applied for a research job looking at housing provision in an inner-city authority. I possessed the required research skills, but had no knowledge of housing. The terminology used in the job specification was foreign to me. But on being invited for an interview I approached my local housing department and spent a whole morning reading reports and committee minutes so as to familiarize myself with the relevant language and issues. The research paid off, and it could for you in similar circumstances. It is perfectly acceptable to write

to the firm for information about its management structure, mission statement and policies. This will help you to "suss out" its organizational culture – for example, whether it is a "traditional" firm (dress formally for the interview!) or one with a more informal management style.

Researching the background achieves two things. It obviously bolsters your confidence and improves your chances of performing well in an interview. But it also conveys a latent message to the interviewing panel that you are sufficiently enthusiastic about this particular job to invest time and effort in order to secure it.

The Interview

This trawling is excellent preparation for the interview as it enables you to show you have a clear understanding of the job requirements and how you might fit into the organization. It will also help you prepare intelligent questions to ask during the interview.

> A tried-and-tested strategy for preparing for the interview:
>
> - think of five key points why *you* are the person for *this* job
> - rehearse these points with a critical friend
> - filter them in at suitable opportunities in the interview.

Your sociological training can also help you negotiate the interview itself. I have found Goffman's work on the presentation of self (1958) especially helpful in understanding the social processes at work in interview-type situations. He compares social interaction with theatrical performances where actors play a multiplicity of roles to different audiences. The interview setting is one such "stage". You need to be aware that the panel may represent different interests, levels of power, areas of bias and vulnerability. The panel members may be concerned to make an impression on each other (as part of their own performances) as well as hearing your answers, and being alert to the nuances of their interaction may help you "play" the scene more effectively. Share your attention (through eye contact or direction of answers) with all the members of the panel at different times. Try to generate enthusiasm without being overbearing, to be relaxed without being too "laid back". If your mind goes blank, it is perfectly reasonable to ask the chairperson to clarify the question. Take time answering; it is better to reflect carefully before committing yourself to an answer, but keep your answers to the point. It may be necessary to answer questions from a variety of perspectives, bearing in mind the different receptions your responses will have, and your sociological background should stand you in good stead here.

Keep in mind the five key points you want to make.

You have a very short period in which to present yourself and convince the panel that your sociological capital is a worthwhile investment. But I hope I have helped you appreciate how you can draw on that capital at every stage of the application process to build a convincing case.

Notes

1. This chapter focuses specifically on sociological aspects of your search for employment. But you should also consult general books on careers advice, job searching, the applications process and interviews.

2. Make several photocopies of a formal application form, so that you can experiment with the clearest way of completing it. Clear presentation is essential.

References

Cuff, E. W., Sharrock, W. and Francis, D. 1990: *Perspectives in Sociology*, 3rd edn. London: Unwin Hyman.

Goffman, E. 1958: *The Presentation of Self in Everyday Life*. Harmondsworth, Penguin.

46

Opportunities for Professional and Vocational Training

Sheila Cross

Sociology's fascination often lies as much in the questions it asks as the answers it provides. But in the increasingly competitive world of work, employers are looking for more than an enquiring mind. There is a growing requirement for specific competences and expertise in addition to the general skills of statistical analysis and ability to communicate effectively that so many sociology graduates can offer on the job market.

Consequently many sociologists nowadays are moving on to postgraduate training as and when they can afford to. The patterns vary between the different English-speaking countries. Even the vocabulary is different, with Americans referring to "graduate" study and Britons calling it "post-graduate". In Britain the uptake of graduate courses is still increasing whilst in the USA the level seems to have plateaued. In Britain and Australia graduate study takes less time: there are more one-year vocational diplomas, and master's and PhD schemes tend to be shorter than in the USA. Funding for graduate students differs too.

The books in the Further Reading section at the end of this chapter give comprehensive lists of all the graduate courses in the respective countries, so it will be necessary to consult them carefully to identify what is available on the area of study and in the country of your choice.

Professional Options

Sociology graduates enter a diverse range of occupations. However, for professional status careers it is increasingly essential to undergo graduate or vocational study. In some cases, graduates will choose to specialize in an area of their programme of study which they had especially enjoyed on their degree. The sorts of issues which frequently appeal include: women's studies, criminology and deviance, international affairs, public policy, demography and population studies, gerontology, environmental policy, Third World or other area studies (e.g. African-American, Latin American), and communication studies. MA's or other graduate studies in these areas generally offer in-depth analysis rather than a specifically vocational training. However, many of these issues are increasingly significant in policy terms so an MA or PhD may enhance your opportunity to obtain a career in a related field, as would a master's course in research methods.

There is a wide range of professions that attract sociologists and for which vocational training is available. Many sociologists interested in the "personal troubles" dimension are attracted to the challenging career of social work. In the USA you are likely to need an MSW, Master's degree in Social Work (obtainable in over a hundred universities). In Britain you are also likely to register on one of the 40 two-year postgraduate courses offering a Diploma in Social Work but, as a graduate, you can also obtain a master's qualification from most of these courses if your academic achievement merits it. Relevant social work experience is essential for admission to the course, and all courses include approved practice placements. Field placements are also a crucial ingredient for a social work qualification in Australia, which requires four years at degree level, integrating social work theory, and practice.

Equally challenging as a career is counselling. In the USA a master's degree approved by the Council for the Accreditation of Counselling may be necessary to practise as a counsellor – including educational counselling. In Britain the situation is complex, since proven experience over a period of time is very important. Whilst master's courses in counselling are an advantage, the crux is a qualification recognized by the British Association of Counselling, which may be at diploma or even certificate level. The new counselling division of the British Psychological Society is gaining in importance. However, if you have a straight sociology degree, you will need a conversion course in psychology (the Open University offers an excellent conversion diploma).

Other careers attracting graduates that require further training include careers guidance (one-year diploma needed in Britain, graduate certificate in Australia) and youth and community work (one-year postgraduate diploma in Britain, or MAs – often at post-experience level – in community studies in Britain and in community development in Australia). Some graduates are attracted to occupational therapy, a career which increasingly engages in social work-related practice: a full three-year degree is necessary in Britain and Australia. Prior relevant experience is necessary for many of these careers, and funding may be difficult to obtain in both countries

Moving away from the caring careers, many sociology graduates enter some of the more traditional professions. Some apply to law, which in Britain would involve a very expensive two-year period tackling two intensive courses without – currently – any firm guarantee of a job. Sociologists might be especially attracted to specializing in family or trades union or equal opportunities issues in law.

More commonly still, some decide to take qualifications in personnel management. In Britain a postgraduate diploma at one of the new universities might be sufficient, in Australia you can take a graduate certificate or diploma in human resource development, but in the USA you are likely to need a master's degree. A more specialized, and arguably more political, aspect of personnel work is industrial relations. Both Britain and the USA have interesting MAs in this subject.

Less contentious, yet equally problematic in Britain in the current social climate, is housing management, for which there are an increasing number of postgraduate courses, often with funding attached if full-time or employment based (part-time). A related career is urban or regional planning. In Britain it is more commonly geography majors who enter this, but in the USA over 80 colleges and universities offer accredited two-year master's courses, to which many sociologists apply. In Australia there are postgraduate certificates, diplomas and master's degrees.

Sociologists with a more entrepreneurial leaning are attracted to marketing or public relations (PR). In the USA you will need a master's degree in marketing or a master's degree in business administration specializing in marketing, whilst in Britain and Australia there are postgraduate certificates, diplomas and master's degrees. For PR, and other media-related subjects such as journalism, an internship will be a major advantage (a period of intensive work experience in a relevant organization). In Britain a one-year postgraduate diploma will be advisable, although not absolutely necessary, but proven relevant experience may be essential even to gain a place on a course. In Australia you can take a one-year graduate cadetship or a graduate diploma.

Your Next Steps

This brief chapter has necessarily only offered you a taste of some of the careers requiring further training which are most commonly chosen by sociologists. You owe it to yourself to do further research – after all your future is at stake! So you will need to consult the directories listed in the Further Reading section to find out more about what the careers actually entail, what level of qualifications they require, and what internship or work-placement experience is essential or desirable. Early planning will really work to your advantage. The longer the lead time, the more you can think through what you want to do, and the better able you are to gain any necessary experience. If you want to go directly on to graduate training from your degree, you will need to apply well in advance. In Britain you need to apply a year ahead of your planned start date, but for the USA or Australia you will need to apply at least 18 months before the start of your proposed graduate study.

Unfortunately one consideration may be if and when you can afford the graduate course. The Further Reading section includes books that give advice on funding and other forms of financial support. Many universities operate an "assistantship scheme" where you work as a tutor in order to help pay your way through your studies. You may even have to consider working for a couple of years to save enough to put yourself through the study, or you may be able to find a suitable part-time master's degree, enabling you to support yourself by paid work during your studies. The key thing is to research which career and course of study is right for you, what you need to be successful . . . and then go for it!

Action Planning Your Future

- Read the books listed, consult your advisor, to analyse which career matches your needs and interests best.
- Decide which courses of graduate study will help you achieve your career objective.
- Check if you need relevant internship or other work experience: if so, organize it.
- Find out when and how you need to apply, and ensure you brief your referees carefully.
- Sort out what the financial position will be – apply for funds – set up paid work.

Further Reading

Directories of Postgraduate Courses

UK

Postgrad: The Directory of Graduate Studies. Annual. Cambridge: CRAC.

USA

Peterson's Graduate Programs in the Humanities, Arts and Social Sciences. Annual. Princeton, NJ: Peterson.

Australia

Directory of Postgraduate Study. Annual Balgowlan: AVCC/GCCA/The Graduate Connection.

Canada

Directory of Canadian Universities. Biennial. Association of Universities and Colleges of Canada.

Commonwealth

Commonwealth Universities Yearbook. Annual. London: Association of Commonwealth Universities.

General

Study Abroad. Biennial. UNESCO
Postgraduate Arts, Humanities and Social Sciences Studies in Europe. Annual, London: Edition XII.
The World University Year Book. Annual.

Publications advising on Financial Support

UK

Directory of Grant Making Trusts. Biennial. Tonbridge: Charities Aid Foundation.

USA

Grants for Graduate and Postgraduate Study. Annual. Princeton, NJ: Peterson.

Australia

Directory of Postgraduate Scholarships. Annual. Balgowlan: AVCC/GCCA/The Graduate Connection.

Commonwealth

Awards for Postgraduate Study at Commonwealth Universities. Biennial. London: Association of Commonwealth Universities.

General

The Grants Register. Biennial. London: Macmillan.

Directories of Career Opportunities

UK

Occupations. Annual. Bristol: Careers and Occupational Information Centre.

The Penguin Careers Guide, 1992. London: Penguin.

USA

Occupational Outlook Handbook. Annual. US Department of Labor, Bureau of Labor Statistics.

Leape, M. P. and Vacca, S. M., *Harvard Guide to Careers*. Harvard University Press.

Australia

Australian Careers Guide, 1992. Redfern NSW: David Royce.

47

"Sociologist – Will Travel": Career and Work Opportunities in the USA and Canada, European Union, Eastern Europe and Australasia

Janice Eglin

Introduction

The prospect of working abroad can be an exciting one. As a sociologist, overseas travel will provide the opportunity to deepen and expand the skills you have gained from your course of study. It will expose you to different social and cultural arrangements, giving you a different perspective on your own society. Any job abroad can be eye-opening – what matters is how you reflect on your experiences of travel and work.

As a sociologist you will already have many skills that overseas employers will be interested in such as analysing complex texts, devising questionnaires, interviewing, working in teams and using computers to write research reports. Possessing these skills and having knowledge of welfare systems, social inequalities and cultural change should increase the opportunities of gaining more interesting work abroad. Furthermore, prospective employers in your own country are interested in candidates who have that "something extra" and travelling abroad can enhance such transferable skills as communication, teamwork, motivation, using your initiative, commitment, organizing ability, interpersonal skills, leadership and foreign languages. These skills will complement those already obtained through academic study of sociology and will therefore make you more employable. However, gaining as much information as possible well in advance of your travels would be advisable in order to make the experience worthwhile and enjoyable. This chapter should give you some

ideas on opportunities available, but you should also read other books on travelling and working abroad. These are available from bookshops, careers departments and libraries. Some useful addresses are listed at the end of the chapter.

Preparation

Before travelling you will need to investigate work permits/visas. Different rules and regulations operate depending on your residency status and the agreements your country has with other countries. You are usually required to obtain a work permit prior to entering a country in order to work legally, but not in every case. Always check the regulations with relevant embassies/consulates/high commissions prior to travelling and be prepared to pay a fee.

Whether you plan to obtain work before travelling or hope to find work when you arrive, it is essential to have prepared your *curriculum vitae* to take with you, and to have thought about how you are going to present yourself (including, where relevant, the skills acquired in your sociological education) to prospective employers. You should also take at least two references, ideally from past employers, showing that you are responsible, intelligent and hard-working, and an academic reference from your tutor outlining the skills acquired on your sociology course. It may be useful to learn/brush up on foreign languages (for some countries, competency in the native language is a prerequisite for employment). Skills not necessarily associated with your sociology qualification will always be useful such as a driving license or, if possible, a larger vehicle license; computing skills; experience of working with children; a Teaching English as a Foreign Language Certificate (TEFL); sporting qualifications, e.g. swimming, canoeing; even experience of working in bars and restaurants. Plan ahead and gain relevant skills before you travel and take proof of qualifications and experience with you.

If the thought of working abroad seems daunting, there are a number of recognized schemes which will help you find employment before you travel, although be prepared to pay for costs and, in some cases, travel expenses. Further information is available from your university careers centre. However, if you prefer not to use these schemes there are a variety of other useful sources to check: newspapers and trade journals, particularly overseas newspapers found in larger newsagents; embassies, consulates and high commissions; libraries and careers centres where overseas directories and reference books on travelling and working abroad can be found; government employment offices (Jobcentres in the UK) which have access to overseas vacancies held on the National Vacancy System (NATVACS); and some private recruitment agencies may also assist you. A listing of international companies can also be found on the World Wide Web – http://www.dicr.com. Friends and relatives abroad may help with useful contacts. Tutors may also have contacts abroad, especially if you want to explore the possibility of getting work with sociological research projects. Remember, if you write to prospective employers abroad, always use their own language and, if you wish to receive a reply, always include an international reply coupon, available from a post office, so that your prospective employer does not have to pay for postage.

If you intend to find work while abroad, it may be possible to use the local equivalent of government employment offices where these exist (some specialize in specific job markets). Hostel notice boards may have local job in-formation while private recruitment agencies may assist with temporary work such as office/computing and domestic work. Recognized schemes also have access to employer directories.

What Type of Work?

If you want to obtain some experience building on your sociology degree there are a number of organizations which arrange for students and graduates to undertake practical work experience (internships). The Council on International Educational Exchange (CIEE) international work programmes offer internships for up to 12 months (usually paid) in the USA and Canada, and international placements (usually unpaid) in the UK, France and Germany for students and recent graduates. CIEE will provide support, administration and will organize placements, but for internships expect to find your own employment although CIEE will assist you. Be prepared to pay towards costs, travel and accommodation, which vary accordingly. Contact CIEE for further details and application forms. The Fulbright Commission also has information on approved exchanges and internship programmes and has offices in the capital cities of many countries including west and east Europe, USA, Canada and Australia. You may also be able to find career-related work through your own efforts; check employer and internment directories available from libraries and career centres.

However, you may want or have to try some other form of work such as TEFL, working as an "au pair" or casual employment. Summer camps offer opportunities to care for children (using your sociology skills) during the vacation period. Contact the International Voluntary Service (IVS) or Service Civil International (SCI) for a list of work camps. Voluntary work can offer other opportunities in community programmes, where you may use and expand your sociology skills, and in some situations you will be provided with accommodation and an allowance. The Quaker International Social Projects (QISP) offer exchanges with partner organizations abroad. Obviously, the main reason for doing such work will be to help you "pay your way", but it is a good idea to keep a diary of your experiences and observations which can be of considerable advantage later on when you wish to convey to a prospective employer just *how* you have benefitted from your foreign travels. Everyone can claim (truthfully) that travel broadens the mind, but you will make a bigger impression if you can show that you have made connections between your studies and your experiences abroad.

USA and Canada

USA

To work in the USA you must obtain a relevant visa before you travel. "H" or temporary work visas can be issued if you have arranged employment and your potential employer in the USA has filed a petition for you to be approved. "J-1" or exchange visitor visas are issued by officially approved programmes for the purpose of participation in schemes designed to encourage international understanding, educational visits, practical work experience (internships), and student exchanges. They may operate in the summer period or follow the academic calendar.

Schemes organizing employment on the numerous summer camps where many US children spend their school vacation may be worth considering. Two major operators are Camp America and British Universities North America Club (BUNAC) – BUNACAMP/KAMP. BUNAC's Work America scheme also assists full-time students, to find employment. Check for details and application deadlines well in advance.

Voluntary work within a variety of community programmes is organized by groups such as Winant Clayton Volunteers Association although you would be required to have had practical experience working with people (paid or unpaid) and be a UK resident. Check voluntary directories and reference books for further contacts.

Canada

As with the USA, to work in Canada requires the appropriate visa which may be obtained from your local Canadian Consulate, Embassy or High Commission. To qualify you will need to provide a written job offer from a Canadian employer. USA residents, however, may apply for employment authorization at a port of entry. Like the USA, internships are also accepted in Canada.

There are a number of work experience schemes available, but these are often only available to citizens of certain countries and are usually for students or recent graduates. Australian students should contact STA Travel's Student Work Abroad Programme (SWAP), USA students should contact the CIEE's Student Work Exchange Programme and British students should contact BUNAC's BUNACAMP and Work Canada Programmes.

Another Canadian possibility is the live-in caregiver programme, which employs live-in only staff to provide unsupervized care of children, the elderly or disabled in a private household. Employment must be arranged prior to entering Canada but as jobs are advertized via the Canadian Employment Centre (in Canada) you should contact your nearest Canadian Consulate/Embassy or High Commission for further details and selection criteria.

Canada also has a vigorous immigration programme for skilled and professionally trained people. Although sociologists are considered it does help to have a further professional qualification, e.g. in social work. Selection is based on specific criteria including your age, qualifications, experience and ability to communicate in English or French.

European Economic Area

There are a total of 18 countries participating in the European Economic Area (EEA), including the European Union (EU). EU/EEA nationals have the right to move freely within the area, enjoying the same rights as any citizen of the country where they stay. This opens up opportunities for jobseekers, self-employed persons and students. If you are a national of an EU/EEA country you are entitled to work and live in any other member state for up to three months without a work or residence permit, provided you have the finances to support yourself. If you find employment within three months you may remain in that country, but if not then you must leave. The EEA countries are: Belgium, Denmark, France, Germany, Greece, Ireland, Italy, Luxembourg, The Netherlands, Portugal and the UK (all EU) and Austria, Finland, Iceland, Liechtenstein (free movement of persons as of 1998), Norway and Sweden. To be eligible to work in an EU/EEA country you may be required to speak the relevant language of the country.

Non-EU/EEA citizens must arrange employment prior to entering a member country and be in possession of a work permit, application for which must be made by a prospective employer. As competition for jobs throughout the EU/EEA can be high you may experience difficulty finding work. However, there are a number of schemes which organize employment, documentation and travel to the UK. The Training and Work Experience Scheme (TWES) allows foreign university graduates to work in the UK in their academic field for up to a year with the possibility of extension for a further 12 months. You will need to contact the Overseas Labour Service of the UK Department for Employment and Education (DfEE). Residents of Commonwealth countries may come to the UK for a working holiday but may not pursue a career or engage in business. Australian and Canadian students may utilize the Students Work Abroad Programme (SWAP). Contact the Canadian Universities Travel Service (Travel CUTS) or STA travel in Australia. USA students may contact the CIEE and voluntary community work can be organized by Winant and Clayton Volunteers. The Central Bureau also provides information and advice on all forms of educational visits and exchanges including opportunities through voluntary service and seasonal work.

Eastern Europe

If you wish to work in an eastern European country you would usually need to obtain a work permit prior to entering. You will need to obtain a written promise of employment and the employer may need to apply for your application to be approved. Contact the relevant embassies/consulates to obtain regulations on the country you wish to travel to. You may be asked to show you have sufficient funds to cover your living costs.

The main types of work available tend to be in teaching or within international work camps, enabling you to utilize your sociology skills in a voluntary capacity. All eastern European countries have opportunities for qualified English teachers. Usually agencies will require a TEFL qualification but it may be possible to obtain employment without one. The pay is generally low and accommodation can be a problem. It may be more beneficial to travel as a "volunteer" where you may have your travel, insurance and other benefits paid for. Organizations can be found in directories and travel reference books in libraries and careers centres.

Australasia

Australia

You may undertake a working holiday providing you obtain the correct visa prior to entry. However, eligibility for visas varies according to your country of origin. The procedure for obtaining the visa also varies and UK, Irish, Canadian and Dutch passport holders can apply in any country they happen to be in at the time. All other nationals need to apply in their own country.

Various organizations exist to help you find work and offer general guidance support in exchange for a fee covering costs and travel. For people holding British, Irish and Dutch passports, BUNAC's Work Australia Programme will arrange documentation, travel and provide support, while US students should contact the CIEE, New York, which organizes working holiday programmes in Australia. The World Travellers Network programme, Sydney, specializes in finding work for those holding work permits.

It is also possible to undertake occupational training, building on your sociology degree, which may include work experience with a sponsoring organization for 12 months (sometimes longer). You will need to apply directly to the Australian organization and also apply for a visa before you enter Australia.

New Zealand

If you obtain a job offer in writing before entering New Zealand you may apply for a temporary work visa. The UK Citizens' Working Holiday Scheme enables British citizens aged 18–30 years to travel for a working holiday of up to 12 months, but there are a limited number of places which are allocated on a first-come-first-served basis. You will need evidence of your return travel ticket and living expenses. US students are eligible to apply for a six-month work permit from CIEE, New York. Travel CUTS in Canada administer a similar work abroad scheme for Canadian students.

Before you take up employment make sure you have all the necessary documents such as a passport, visa, work permit and residence permit; check all terms and conditions of your contract, particularly those relating to pay; sort out your travel arrangements; plan your accommodation; obtain travel and health insurance; and have enough money to live on until you get paid and to cover the cost of a return ticket home. Make sure people at home know how to contact you in an emergency.

The following is a list of some useful addresses. For further information contact your university careers department.

Useful Addresses

BUNAC, 16 Bowling Green Lane, London EC1R 0BD. Tel. 0171-251 3472.

Central Bureau, Seymour Mews House, Seymour Mews, London W1H 9PE. Tel. 0171-486 5101.

Council on International Educational Exchange (CIEE), 33 Seymour Place, London W1. Tel. 0171-706 3008.

Council on International Educational Exchange (CIEE), 205 E 42nd Street, New York, NY 10017.

Fulbright Commission, Australian/American Education Foundation, Garden Wing, University House, Australian National University, ACTON, GPO Box 1559, Canberra, ACT 2601.

Fulbright Commission, Foundation for Educational Exchange between Canada and the US, 350 Albert Street, Suite 2015, Ottawa, Ontario K1R 1A4.

Fulbright Commission, Institute of International Education, 809 United Nations Plaza, New York, NY 10017.

Fulbright Commission, 62 Doughty Street, London WC1N 2LS.

IVS (International Voluntary Service), SCI (Service Civil International) South Office, Service Civil International (SCI) Old Hall, East Bergholt, Colchester, Essex CO7 6TQ. Tel. 01206 298215.

Quaker Social Responsibility and Education, Friends House, 173–177 Euston Road, London NW1 2BJ. Tel. 0171-387 3601.

Student Work Abroad Programme (SWAP), STA Travel Department, PO Box 399, Carlton South, Melbourne 3053.

SWAP Canadian Programme administered by Canadian University Travel Service (Travel CUTS).

(TEFL) RSA/UCLES, Syndicate Buildings, 1 Hills Road, Cambridge CB1 2EU.

(TESOL) Trinity College, 16 Park Crescent, London W1N 4AH.

Training and Work Experience Scheme (TWES), Overseas Labour Service, Employment Department, W5 Moorfoot, Sheffield S1 4PQ. Tel. 0114-259 4074.

Winant Clayton Volunteers Association, The Davenant Centre, 179 Whitechapel Road, London E1 1DU. Tel. 0171-375 0547/0181-986 7045.

Winant Clayton Volunteers, 109 E 50th Street, New York, NY 10022.

World Travellers Network Programme, 14 Wentworth Avenue, Sydney NSW 2010, Australia.

YFC Centre, National Agricultural Centre, Kenilworth, Warwickshire CV8 2LG.

Recommended Reading

There are many useful books for you to read which are available from bookshops, libraries and university careers centres. The following are just a selection of these.

De Vries A. 1993: *The Directory of Jobs and Careers Abroad*, 8th edn. Vacation Work.

Griffith S. 1994: *Teaching English Abroad*, 2nd edn. Vacation Work.

—— 1995: *Work Your Way Around the World*, 7th edn. Vacation Work.

Hempshell, M. 1995: *Do Voluntary Work Abroad*. How-To Books.

Internships 1996. Peterson's Guide (in USA); Vacation Work (in Europe).

Jones, R. 1992: *How to Get a Job in America*. How-To Books.

Vandome, N. 1994: *Find Temporary Work Abroad*. How-To Books.

Woodworth, D. 1993: *The International Directory of Voluntary Work* 5th edn. Vacation Work.

—— 1996: *The Directory of Summer Jobs Abroad*. Vacation Work.

—— 1996: *The Directory of Summer Jobs in Britain – 1996*. Vacation Work.

48

Postgraduate Studies in Sociology in the USA and Canada

G. David Johnson

Introduction

Substantial opportunity for postgraduate study in sociology exists in North America. Two-hundred-and-seven universities and colleges in the USA, and another 25 in Canada, offer doctoral and/or master's degrees in sociology (American Sociological Association 1995). Programs range in size from the very large, with more than 200 postgraduate students in sociology at a time (as at the University of Wisconsin–Madison or the City University of New York–Graduate Center), to the very small, with less than 10 (University of Missouri–St Louis). As a discipline, sociology is either blessed or cursed, depending on one's point of view, with a plethora of theoretical orientations, meth-

odologies, and areas of specialization. This great variation in the discipline is reflected fully in the range of postgraduate training available at North American departments. Some programs tend to specialize training in a small number of substantive areas, while many others have faculties of sufficient size to offer concentrated training in more than a dozen subdisciplines.

The Structure of Postgraduate Programs

Postgraduate education in the USA and Canada, as elsewhere, typically begins with the master's degree, and continues to the PhD. In some cases for sociologists, it may also include one to two years of postdoctoral study. Most programs require the completion of a Master's degree prior to admission for PhD study, but many others allow for entrance into the doctoral program directly after completion of an undergraduate degree.

Master's and PhD degree requirements in the USA and Canada differ from those of the UK and other countries which follow British or other European models. In the USA, particularly, postgraduate degrees always require a substantial amount of taught coursework, often including a series of required courses, usually including theory, methods, and statistics. Additional courses (for example, social psychology or social organization) may also be required. Elective courses, chosen by the student, complete coursework requirements.

A Note on Terminology

The terminology used by North American and British universities can be very confusing as identical terms can mean different things. Thus the word "dissertation" which is used exclusively for PhD level work in the USA, refers to undergraduate or master's level work in the UK. The word "thesis" is used in the reverse order, i.e. it refers to work below PhD level in the USA, but only to PhD level work in the UK!

Please note that in this chapter US terminology has been used.

Most PhD and some master's programs, also require that the student pass comprehensive exams (written and/or oral) prior to earning the degree. All PhD programs require a dissertation, and many master's programs require a thesis. Master's degrees typically take two years to complete, PhDs usually require a minimum of four years, with the average student taking approximately seven years to complete his or her doctoral education.

Postgraduate programs in Canada tend to be structured in a fashion which combines characteristics of British and American systems. Canadian programs, like those of the USA, require that a specific amount of coursework be completed for each degree, frequently including required courses in theory and methods. The number of taught courses tends to be somewhat smaller in Canadian universities, with greater emphasis on independent study, performance in comprehensive exams, and the production of a master's thesis and doctoral dissertation.

The Applications and Admissions Process

The admissions process is structured and therefore fairly straightforward. Matriculation (registration) typically begins in the fall term (late August or early September) of the academic calendar, and admissions and funding decisions are made the preceding spring (as early as 1st February). The most important concern in applying to a program is to plan well in advance. Initial contact with prospective programs should occur at least one year prior to the term postgraduate study is to begin. The student should plan on applying to a number of programs. Most universities require an application fee, and thus financial considerations must be part of the decision on where to apply. Nonetheless, I recommend applying to as many good-quality programs as practically possible. Many students apply to five or six programs, and some students apply to even more.

The application process includes the following steps.

(1) The student contacts the sociology department and requests information including application forms for both admission and financial support.

(2) Applications are completed and submitted. Admissions applications are typically returned to the graduate admissions office of the university – the student usually does not apply directly to the department. Some universities require that applications for financial support be returned to the department; others require submissions to another university office.

(3) The student sees to it that official transcripts are mailed directly from his or her undergraduate institution to the admissions office of the university to which he or she is applying.

(4) The Graduate Record Examination (GRE) is taken and official scores are submitted directly from the Educational Testing Service (ETS), the organization which administers the GRE. Virtually all US universities, and some Canadian, require the "general test" of the GRE, which measures verbal and quantitative skills. Some departments also require an "advanced" exam in sociology. The "pencil and paper" GRE exam is offered in many countries, but frequently on a limited schedule – two to three times per year is common. The exam must be scheduled in advance, and six to eight weeks allowed after the test is taken for the results to be mailed. In some countries (currently including Australia, England, New Zealand, Canada, and the USA), the GRE may be taken at designated sites on a microcomputer, with results submitted electronically to ETS. Information on the GRE may be obtained by contacting the Educational Testing Service (see end of chapter for addresses).

(5) Recommendations are solicited by the student from professors who have knowledge of the applicant's academic strengths and weaknesses. Because of recent changes in the law, applicants to most US universities have a choice as to which kind of recommendation to submit: either confidential, in which case the student waives the right to examine its contents, or non-confidential, in which case the student maintains right of access. In the former (in Britain commonly called a reference), the recommendation is mailed directly by the professor to the applying university. In the latter (in Britain commonly called a testimonial or an 'open reference'), either the student or the

professor may make the submission. Although the student usually has the right to choose either option, it should be noted that confidential references are more influential in the admissions committee decision, and therefore I recommend this choice to most students. Some departments require that a form, which is supplied by the university, be used for the recommendation. Others simply require a personal letter.

All application materials must be received prior to the deadline for the student to be considered for admission and financial support. In most departments, admissions and funding decisions are made by a committee of faculty. Criteria are similar for both decisions: undergraduate grades, quality of undergraduate institution, letters of recommendation, and particularly in the USA, GRE scores. In some cases, special abilities or experiences of the applicant may be considered. To be admitted and awarded funding, applicants to better programs must be strong in all categories. Some applicants submit writing samples, for example a copy of their best undergraduate research paper. In addition, some students submit a letter of application, which states concisely their intellectual ambitions, and how the particular graduate program fits their plans. If the student writes well, and has well articulated plans, these documents can increase the likelihood of a positive decision.

Financing Your Postgraduate Studies

Financial support is available at most North American universities on a competitive basis. Students from abroad typically compete on an equal basis with domestic applicants. The most common form of support in the USA is a teaching or research assistantship. Assistantships frequently include a tuition waiver and a stipend for part-time work in the department. Although it is doubtful any stipend will be large enough to yield a lavish lifestyle, the size of awards varies tremendously among departments. Note, however, that the standard of

living in North American cities varies as well, so the largest stipend awarded is not always the most economically valuable.

Assistantship responsibilities may include assisting faculty (staff) members in their teaching and research, or the student may be asked to teach his or her own course. In fact, all PhD students should take advantage of the opportunity to teach if it is given, since the experience can be useful in the job market after the degree is earned. Fellowships, which award a stipend and carry no work requirement, are also available at some US institutions, although these are more rare, and more competitive, than assistantships. In Canada, graduate scholarships, which are analogous to US fellowships, are somewhat more common than teaching assistantships, particularly for the first few years of postgraduate education.

Once the student settles into a graduate program, other part-time employment possibilities may become available, particularly teaching opportunities at nearby colleges. Students should always be careful, however, of overcommitting time which might better be used for the completion of degree requirements.

Choosing the Right Program for You

Choosing the right program is very important. Several criteria should be used in making the decision, including program quality, fit between student interests and program strengths, and sponsorship. If any of the student's undergraduate professors are known to faculty members of the postgraduate program, the student's chances for admission and funding may be enhanced. There are some useful published guides to graduate programs in the USA and Canada. The first, available from the American Sociological Association (ASA) is the *Guide to Graduate Programs in Sociology*. This is a very important source. It lists details, including all graduate faculty members' names and specialties, for nearly every postgraduate program in North

America. Also valuable are two titles which rank the quality of doctoral programs in the USA. The first is *The Student Guide to Research Doctorate Programs in the United States*, and is available from the National Academy Press. The rankings published in this guide were developed by a distinguished committee of the National Research Council. The most recent rankings of 92 PhD programs in sociology were published in 1995, and are recalculated every 10 years or so. A separate, annual ranking of the top 25 doctoral programs is published by *US News and World Report* (a news magazine published in the USA), and is entitled *America's Best Graduate Schools*. By and large, the latter two guides report similar rankings for the top institutions.

It should be noted, however, that the graduate programs ranked highest in prestige will not necessarily be the best programs for every student. Students have different interests and needs, and programs have different strengths. Often it is desirable to identify particular faculty members, who have conducted interesting research in one's area of interest, and apply to the programs where these professors teach. A couple of warnings about this strategy are in order: First, some listed faculty members only maintain a nominal presence in particular departments, spending most of their time elsewhere on campus, or on other campuses altogether. Second, professors occasionally change departments, and changes in affiliation may not show up in the published guide for a year or two. A phone interview with the postgraduate coordinator or the departmental chair can be instructive. Also, many postgraduate programs have e-mail addresses, which are listed in the ASA *Guide to Graduate Programs*, and if the student has Internet access, communication with program representatives may be conducted electronically. Many sociology programs are also developing home pages on the World Wide Web, and many facts about program requirements and faculty research interests can be accessed through a web browser. Finally, although it is certainly expensive, a visit to prospective programs would provide the most complete information to aid the student in making a wise choice. Every student should use the resources available to him or her to learn as much as possible about prospective programs in advance of what will certainly be a major life decision.

Resources[1]

American Sociological Association 1995: *1995 Guide to Graduate Departments of Sociology*. Published annually. Available from American Sociological Association, 1722 N Street, NW, Washington, DC 20036, USA. Tel: 202-833-3410. E-mail: executive.office@asanet.org. World Wide Web: http://www.asanet.org.

Educational Testing Service 1996: *Information and Registration Bulletin*. Published annually. Available from GRE-ETS, PO Box 6000, Princeton, NJ 08541-6000, USA. Tel: 800-473-2255. E-mail: gre-info@ets.org. World Wide Web: http://www.gre.org.

National Research Council 1996: *The Student Guide to Research Doctorate Programs in the United States*. Available from National Academy Press, 2101 Constitution Ave., NW, Box 285, Washington, DC 20055, USA. Tel: 202-334-2000.

US News and World Report 1995: *America's Best Graduate Schools*. Published annually. Available from *US News and World Report*. Tel: 800-836-6397.

Acknowledgement

The author acknowledges the helpful advice of John Manzo in preparing this chapter.

Note

1. Contact information is accurate at the time of printing, but is subject to change.

49

Postgraduate Studies in Sociology in the UK

Chris Middleton

There has been a rapid increase in the number of postgraduate students in the UK over the past ten years, as well as in the number and variety of sociology programmes offered. There are more opportunities for postgraduate study than ever before but, at the same time, the life of a postgraduate student has become considerably harder – particularly in financial terms. This chapter offers initial guidance on what to expect, and on how to maximize your chances of success.

The Structure of Postgraduate Programmes

Postgraduate studies come in two basic forms: taught courses leading to qualifications at master's degree, diploma or certificate level, and research degrees leading either to a "doctorate" (PhD) or MPhil.

Taught Courses

The range of taught postgraduate programmes is vast, and the situation complicated by the fact that course designations (MA/MSc, diploma, etc.) do not give a consistent indication either of the length of the course or its intellectual demands. You need to check carefully what kind of course you are signing up for.

There are essentially five kinds of master's course of interest to graduates in sociology.

- *Conversion courses*. Primarily for students who lack a UK undergraduate qualification in sociology (or its foreign equivalent), these courses may still appeal to students who wish to consolidate their sociological training – especially if their undergraduate programme was in combined studies.
- *Social research courses*. Vocational in orientation, leading to careers in social research. They contain a substantial research methods component.
- *Specialization courses*. Advanced sociology courses specializing in a specific area of the discipline such as social statistics; sociology of race or gender; sociology of development, etc.
- *Interdisciplinary courses*. For example, criminology, women's studies, media studies, area studies. These draw on a range of disciplinary perspectives, although sociological perspectives are often dominant. It is sensible to check the particular slant of the course before applying.
- *Vocational courses* leading to a specific professional qualification, such as an MA or Diploma in Social Work, Journalism, etc.

Some key terms have different meanings in the USA and the UK. In this chapter UK terms have been used.

UK	US equivalent
• postgraduate	• graduate
• dissertation (master's level)	• thesis
• thesis (PhD)	• dissertation

In some universities students are required to attain a master's degree before they can embark on a PhD programme, and elsewhere it will normally be considered an advantage.

Typically master's programmes last one year (full-time) or two years (part-time), although some may last longer, especially vocational courses accredited by outside professional bodies. In fact, in addition to the taught element, a master's degree will invariably require, as a significant component, a dissertation based on your own independent research. A diploma may sometimes be obtainable by passing the taught element alone, especially if the course is "credit-based". On some courses you may not be able to proceed to master's level unless your coursework reaches a minimum standard of excellence. Check the regulations beforehand.

Research Degrees

To attain a PhD you must submit a thesis of some 80,000 words (the precise length varies) which demonstrates you have made an *original* contribution to knowledge. Full-time students are typically registered for three years (five to six years for part-time students) and this is also the standard duration for student awards. The thesis has to be completed within four years from starting if you are studying full-time. Completion dates are rigorously enforced, and there are usually financial penalties for late submission.

In many universities you register initially for an MPhil. Assuming you wish to advance to the PhD programme your progress will be reviewed at the end of your first year and, if satisfactory, you will be allowed to proceed. This review procedure has been considerably tightened up in recent years.

Most PhD programmes in sociology include a strong training (instructional) element in the first year of study accounting for as much as two-thirds of the total. Training invariably covers research methods (qualitative and quantitative), and usually advanced sociological theory and the philosophy of social sciences. There may be additional optional

courses. Exemptions may be provided if you can demonstrate previous achievement to the required standard in a particular field.

The rest of your first year is spent conducting a thorough literature review, and honing your research proposal with your supervisor's help. As a PhD student you will be allocated a personal supervisor. This person will be an expert in your general research area and will provide regular one-to-one supervision throughout your years of study. By the end of that period your specialist knowledge may be far greater than that of your supervisor – which is why most academics enjoy supervising postgraduate students. They can learn as much from their students as they teach them.

PhD Applications: Improving your Chances of Success

Choose the University that's Right for You

Normally, when we apply for anything, we ask ourselves: "Am *I* good enough?". But the key to successful PhD work also lies in the quality of supervision, a fact that has been recognized by the research councils (the main providers of student awards) who will be as concerned about the university's capacity to offer high quality supervision in the field of your research as they are interested in the details of your proposal.

How do you find out about the strengths of the various departments?

- Check the directories listed at the end of this chapter to see which universities offer suitable programmes.
- Each university produces a prospectus of its postgraduate programmes, and most sociology departments publish their own graduate handbooks. These handbooks tell you about the department's research strengths and interests, and give lists of academic staff and their research interests. Many departments now provide this information on a home page on World Wide Web. Study these carefully.

- The academic grapevine can be a source of information. Your lecturers are likely to know where key researchers in their specialist field are working, so ask them for advice.
- You may be attracted to a department specifically to work alongside a particular individual. But, if this is your intention, make some preliminary enquiries with the departmental postgraduate admissions officer. Some high-flying researchers may not be readily available to research students – they may, for example, spend much of their time away from the university. Wherever possible it is sensible to apply to a department that has strength-in-depth in your general research field – that way you won't be stranded if, for whatever reason, your relationship with your supervisor breaks down.

Departments vary enormously in size ranging from the large and internationally renowned departments through to small departments offering only a small number of places. Big postgraduate departments offer access to a wide range of leading researchers and visitors, research seminar series and a large group of fellow graduates with whom to share ideas and problems. But smaller research departments can offer closer contacts with staff and more certain opportunities for work as tutors and teaching assistants.

Work on your Research Proposal

Many students apply for a research degree with a proposal that merely outlines a general area of interest. This will not make a good impression. Use the techniques described by Lyons and Wilson (in Chapter 35) to formulate a project, think about suitable methods, and even work out a tentataive timetable. Think about how your proposal can be made to mesh with the research interests of the department to which you are applying – they will be looking for evidence that you are seriously engaged with your intended research field. Obviously this kind of preparation takes time and may be difficult to fit into your final, pressured year of undergraduate study. An increasing number of students now take a one-year "taught" MA/MSc in order to help prepare for advanced research study, and

some universities require this qualification before allowing you to embark on a PhD.

Send your proposal to the department where you wish to study. Research students are recognized as an asset to the department's research reputation, and they may well ask a potential supervisor to liaise with you in order to maximize your chances of a student award. They will help you tighten your proposal and clarify its links to the department's existing research strengths.

Admissions Procedures

Admissions procedures are set out in university and departmental brochures, but most work to a similar timetable. Your main consideration should be to plan ahead and apply in good time. Create a time-line working backwards from your intended start-date and stick to it (see Box 49.1).

Financial Support

Funding is far harder to come by than a place on a postgraduate programme, a fact which accounts for the very sharp rise in the number of part-time postgraduate students. Find out about funding possibilities when you apply for a prospectus.

By far the most valued source of funding for sociology students is an award from a government-financed research council. For most UK sociology students this means applying to the Economic and Social Research Council (ESRC) though, depending on your research proposal, some may be eligible for a Medical Research Council (MRC) award. Competition for these awards is very stiff. You will need a first class degree or, at least, a very strong upper second class honours – together with a carefully framed research proposal and evidence that your intended department can offer high quality supervision in your research area. The great advantage of an ESRC award is the security it provides: it covers the whole of your period of study.

Many institutions offer a limited number of postgraduate awards, teaching assistantships, scholarships or bursaries (again on a competitive basis), but these are not usually sufficient to

12–18 months before start	• Further study or employment? • If study: by research, master's or vocational? • Find out about the different *kinds* of courses that are available.
October/November	• Browse through postgraduate directories. • Write for prospectuses, application forms and information about funding. • Decide on where to apply. • Approach your referees.
December	• Mail completed application forms.
January–March	• Interviewing takes place. • If you are applying for a PhD, clarify your research proposal in discussion with potential supervisors. • Choose which offer to accept. • Clarify funding arrangements. If you are applying for an award check the department is preparing its documentation in good time.
Around 30th April	• Deadline for ESRC award applications. (Check the exact date – no excuses are accepted for late submission.)
June/July	• Notify the department of your degree result.
September/October	• Registration (matriculation).

International students should plan even further ahead, especially in the early stages when getting all the information you require may not be straightforward.

Box 49.1

finance the whole of your studies. (Check prospectuses and departmental brochures for details.) The majority of students, in fact, have to put together an "income package" from a variety of sources in order to get by. Most departments will offer their research students the chance to take some undergraduate classes, but in the recent financial climate they will rarely be able to guarantee this teaching in advance. It is also worth enquiring about opportunities for teaching in neighbouring colleges; some universities are entering into formal arrangements with local colleges whereby maintenance and tuition fees are paid in exchange for an agreed teaching commitment over three years.

Ultimately you may have to be prepared to self-finance your postgraduate studies to a considerable extent, by other forms of employment or taking out a bank loan (see leaflet on career development loans). Self-financing students are normally allowed to pay fees by instalments.

Postgraduate study can be an immensely exciting stage of your intellectual development – a time when you acquire increasing confidence in your ability to think independently as a sociologist. But it requires initial commitment and a determination to see it through.

Sources of Further Information

The main series of guides are published by Hobsons Publishing plc (address below) and are available in careers services throughout the UK, university and college libraries, British Council offices, and major overseas universities.

- *The Students' Guide to Postgraduate Studies*
  A quick and easy reference guide to use when searching for postgraduate courses and research opportunities in the UK.
- *Postgraduate – The Directory*
  A comprehensive and detailed guide to postgraduate courses and research programmes.
- *The Directory of Graduate Studies on CD-ROM*
  On screen cues guide you through searches by subject, research topic, qualifications and modes of study to find suitable postgraduate options.
- *The Update* to *The Directory*.
  A quarterly publication featuring new courses, changes in funding and application procedures, impending deadlines and current news. *The Update* is available on the Internet: http://www: hobsons.ac.uk.
- *Postgraduate: The Magazine*
  Annual – contains articles offering useful information and advice to potential postgraduate students in the UK (both home and overseas students).

Other reference works include:

- *British Universities' Guide to Graduate Study*
  A directory of taught postgraduate courses in UK universities
- *How to get a PhD: Managing the Peaks and Troughs of Research* by Estelle M. Phillips and D. S. Pugh (1987): Milton Keynes, Open University Press. Provides valuable advice from an occupational psychology perspective.
- *The Postgraduate Book 1995–6*
  Updated regularly. Published by National Postgraduate Committee. (Address below.) Contains useful background information on postgraduate studies in the UK.

For international students *Postgraduate Study UK* is available from

- overseas universities: study abroad advisors and departments
- British Council officers
- consulates
- overseas public libraries, government departments, and overseas companies, or from Hobsons Publishing.

Addresses

Hobsons Publishing plc
159–173 St John Street
London EC1V 4DR

National Postgraduate Committee
Brandon House
Bentinck Drive
Troon
Ayrshire KA10 6HX

Sources of Information on Funding

Postgraduate Training Division
Economic and Social Research Council
(ESRC)
Polaris House, North Star Avenue
Swindon SN2 1UJ

Student Awards Agency for Scotland: Postgraduate Section
Gyleview House
3 Redheughs Rigg
Edinburgh EH12 9HH

Career Development Loans

Leaflets available from participating banks,
and from careers advice centres, Training and
Enterprise Councils (TECs) and Local Enterprise Companies (LECs). Your local Job
Centre may be able to help. If in difficulty ring
0800 132660.

Directory of Grant-making Trusts

Available from public and university libraries,
and from Careers Advice Centres.

Acknowledgement

I should like to thank Professor Nigel Gilbert for helpful advice on this chapter.

50

Postgraduate Studies in Australasia

Chris Middleton

Chris Middleton

The opportunity to study abroad is particularly valuable to sociology students as there is no better way of discovering the "contingent nature" of social structures and relations than to experience cultures other than one's own. Obviously, for a student from the UK or North America, the culture shock of studying in Australia and Aotearoa/New Zealand will not be too extreme, but the differences are sufficiently great to provide a novel perspective on the taken-for-granted realities of social life "back home".

To undertake PhD research in Australasia you will need a first class or good upper second class honours degree. You need to plan well ahead (note that the academic year in Australasia runs from February to December), and it is important to make some preliminary inquiries into the research interests and strengths of different university departments. It is worth going about this systematically.

The best source of information for sociologists is *Sociology in Australian Universities* (edited by Katy Richmond) which is published on a biennial basis. It lists all universities in Australia and New Zealand which teach sociology – not all of which are called sociology departments. It lists staff, their research interests, their e-mail addresses, full postgraduate information including contact staff, and recent lists of staff publications, research grants and thesis topics. Another useful source is the *Commonwealth Universities Yearbook*. But for more detailed information you need to write direct to each university for their general prospectus and the departmental graduate handbook. The latter will provide up-to-date details on staff members and their current research interests. Many departments will have a home page on the World Wide Web where you can obtain this information, but it is still worth making direct contact with departments for the full range of information on offer. The next step is to read some of the recent publications of people whose work interests you – and start thinking about how your own research interests might mesh with theirs. When you submit your research idea you will then be able to relate it to the interests of the department and the work of individual members within it. In Australia there is a move towards asking postgraduate applicants to provide a research proposal (one or two pages) which shouldn't be prepared in advance, but "negotiated" with a suitable supervisor who sounds broadly interested in a student pursuing a particular field of research. This will greatly improve your chances of securing a place and, importantly, your chances of being funded will be that much greater if you have the backing of an individual staff member in the department to which you are applying.

Overseas student fees are very high in both countries which, together with living costs, effectively rules out the self-funded route to PhD research. You will need to obtain an award or scholarship to cover fees and at least an allowance towards living expenses. Applicants with publications and a first-class honours degree should be in a good position to get a scholarship. The deadline for PhD scholarship applications in Australia is

31 October. (Enrolments for people not wanting scholarships are not tied to a particular date.) The main sources of support are:

- **General**. *Commonwealth Scholarships*. Awarded to graduates with first class and, occasionally, good upper second class honours degrees. Covers fees and living and travel allowances.
- **Australia**. *Overseas Postgraduate Scholarship Scheme (OPRS)*. A limited number of scholarships funded by the Australian government for postgraduate students from developed countries. Awarded to students working in research priority areas as established by the university. *University Scholarships*. Most universities award a number of scholarships to full-time research students on a competitive basis (open to Australian and foreign students). Additional allowances and fee waivers may also be available. Check with each university for details.

As in other countries it is usually possible to supplement your income with some paid teaching.

Admissions Procedure

Having discussed your research proposal and possible sources of funding with the department you need

- to contact the nearest Australian/New Zealand Embassy or High Commission to obtain a student visa and check immigration requirements.
- to apply formally to the university for admission.

Publications

UNESCO, *Study Abroad*. An annual directory providing information on courses, scholarships and financial assistance, and student employment possibilities.

K Richmond (ed.), *Sociology in Australian Universities* (biennial and covers New Zealand). Available from: Dr Marilyn Poole, TASA Secretary, School of Social Inquiry, Deakin University, Rusden Campus, Clayton, Victoria, Australia 3168. E-mail: marp@deakin.edu.au, fax: 613 9543 1484, price: A$28 plus postage and packing.

The addresses of the sociological associations can be found in Chapter 44.

Acknowledgement

Thanks to Katy Richmond for helpful advice on postgraduate study in Australia.

From Sociological Study to Employment

51

Viewpoints from Three Sociology Graduates

Jackie Hammond, Joanne Osborn and Meeta Patel

*Jackie Hammond, Joanne Osborn
and Meeta Patel*

In this chapter three recent graduates discuss their experiences of studying sociology and what gaining sociological knowledge has meant for them in their working and personal lives.

....

Joanne

I started to think about studying sociology after I left school. Originally, I wanted to teach but, finding that the course was not what I had expected, took a job in an insurance company instead while contemplating my next move. I came around to the idea that I would like to work in publishing, to be involved in the production of books. In my investigation into credentials necessary to enter publishing, it was obvious that even the most junior posts needed a degree, and also that, unless you particularly wanted to edit within a certain subject area, the degree choice was very open. As I have always liked learning new subjects, and I had never studied sociology at school, I decided to go for a degree in which I was interested rather than continue on from my earlier studies of drama, French, and geography.

Jackie

I discovered sociology by accident during my "A"-level study. My third subject was supposed to be French but, as it was unavailable, I chose sociology as a replacement, not really knowing what it was about.

At first I found the Marxist, Functionalist and Interactionist perspectives hard to come to grips with, but they became easier as my understanding grew. The aspect of sociology that I found extremely interesting was that of research. Having never questioned characteristics of society before, I found it fascinating to learn how societies are organized in such different ways. This interest carried over into my undergraduate study and I discovered that, rather than being a chore, studying for essays which required me to do research or read research studies was really absorbing.

Joanne

At university, the individual courses were of varying interest to me. Some in particular stand out as having helped to form my opinions and provide me with a much more tolerant and open view of society. At first, the issues tackled such as race, feminism and poverty gave me an unexpected cynicism about the world, but also made me more aware of different issues and the difficulties facing individuals within society. I feel that I learnt an awful lot about people and the structures within which we live. A focus on the workings of contemporary society has provided me with an insight which I feel has improved my understanding of the world.

Figure 51.1 Joanne, Meeta and Jackie.

Meeta

There were a selection of modules offered, and each one could have lead to a totally different career. For example, the computing element gave me an insight into this field and the confidence to join the world of computers. Indeed the confidence I gained has made me feel I can turn my hand to anything I desire. If I had pursued the research element of sociology, my career would have taken a completely different turn. The module that attracted my attention most was the *Sociology of Health and Illness* which introduced me to the world of "alternative therapies", the field in which I am now working. This illustrates how the career opportunities that sociology offers are quite diverse.

Jackie

Since finishing my degree I have worked in the administrative field, and I have gained a Postgraduate Certificate of Education in primary school teaching. I am now working for Barnardos as a residential social worker.

I did not think of my sociology degree as being specifically vocational and in my administrative positions a sociological outlook was not relevant for actually doing the job. It did, however, give me a better insight into societal forces, and helped me to understand wider issues. This was especially useful when I worked in an unemployment benefit office as it made me more appreciative of clients' varying situations and the difficulties that they faced.

Joanne

After my degree, I returned to my publishing ambitions and, taking the advice of a professional, I enrolled on a postgraduate printing and publishing course for four months. After this I secured a job as an Assistant Production Editor for English Language Teaching books, followed by one as a Production Controller for children's books. These first two years in the industry were not as satisfactory as I had hoped – I was mainly involved in the setting and printing of books which was not as stimulating as I had expected. I decided that I had been mistaken in my career path and that I would find editing more worthwhile and satisfying. The move from production is quite a leap, but I was lucky and found work as a Desk Editor for Geography Education books, which I am still doing almost three years later. This is where my sociology has proved relevant again. As well as making me very aware of the need to express unbiased and open views throughout the books, human geography relates closely to sociology and so reinforces my knowledge continually. I am glad that my degree has proved far more useful for my career in terms of subject matter than I ever anticipated.

Meeta

Learning about culture, race, class and sex has been invaluable during every step of my working life. Although I have worked mostly in administration and computer support, what I have learned from sociology has taught me that there are so many inequalities. Recognizing and understanding how they arise does actually help to confront these challenges in a positive and constructive manner.

Jackie

When I did my teacher training, I realized how much sociology contributed to my understanding of education and its function in society. It took me back to one of the first things that I learned about in sociology – the socializing process. It was a new departure for me to realize that people in societies do not behave the way they do by nature only, but they also *learn* behaviour. In my training, it was apparent that education was not just concerned with academic, but also with social learning. When teaching children about acceptable ways to behave, I could see that I was part of the socialization process.

As a social worker, I continue to be part of this process as I act *in loco parentis* to the children with whom I work. Some of these children are estranged from their families. Again, I have found that a sociological outlook has helped me to appreciate the various forces and pressures at work in society and this has helped me to be less judgemental in my work and more understanding of my clients' situations.

This view has also been useful in my general life. I would say that studying sociology has made me more open-minded, more accepting of difference, and more able to question societal norms.

Meeta

Initially, I chose sociology because it had the least lecture hours! However, it has taught me so much about life from every possible aspect that, given my time again, I would make the same choice – although, knowing what I do now, it would be for very different reasons.

My degree has also been used on a daily basis in my personal life. Being aware of the behavioural patterns of people in different situations gives a better all-round understanding of their feelings and reactions, and this in turn results in richer relationships. The ties that I made at university are the strongest yet and, without these people in my life, I would not be the person I am today. I believe that this is not only due to the fact that we shared three intense years, but also that our relationships have been enhanced by the knowledge acquired during our studies.

Joanne

On a personal level some of the most important friendships that I have now were formed during and through my sociology studies at University. Jackie, Meeta and I started on the introduction to sociological research course together and, through Meeta, we met Margit who also studied some sociology courses. Throughout university, and to the present day, these friendships have continued and are un-usual in both their consistency and closeness. For so many reasons the subject has proved beneficial to me on both a personal and professional level.

52

A Sociology Graduate in Employment

Kay Freeland

Recently I completed a master's degree in sociology. My career, however, lies outside of traditionally defined sociology. I am a college financial aid administrator. Approximately 12 years ago, with a bachelor's degree in psychology (minor in sociology) and no related experience, I, rather accidentally, happened into the financial aid office of the local university, and have been helping needy students fund their postsecondary educations ever since. As with most major institutions of service in the USA, the business of higher education administration has become a classic bureaucracy, and I can think of no better example than a university's financial aid office. To understand and accept that I work within this bureaucratic system, without losing sight of my personal and professional desire to be of service to both individuals and society at large, has proven to be one of the most satisfying challenges of my career, and I feel that sociology has been important in helping me toward such an appreciation.

How did I come to earn an advanced degree in sociology? I love what I do and currently have no plans to change jobs. However, advancement in this career, as in most others today, requires education beyond the bachelor level, the qualification itself being more important than the field of study. Thus, about five years ago I found myself contemplating entry into a master's program. I wanted the credential and I wanted to select a discipline which would intellectually challenge me and for which I would be well suited. The social sciences had captured and held my interest throughout my undergraduate education. Therefore, despite some colleagues' advice to broaden my perspective and study business (something obviously different from psychology and sociology but certainly fitting to my career), I chose to stay with what I knew and loved. The choice of sociology over psychology was, perhaps, serendipitous, although guided most strongly by two personal factors: the physical proximity of a good program and the motivating influence of a close personal friend who had previously completed the program.

Since I did not choose sociology because of any perceived direct relationship to financial aid administration, I was quite pleasantly surprised to find that, indeed, there was a connection! In learning to look at the world with C. Wright Mills' "sociological imagination" (1959), I could see myself, my career, and my institution from a new perspective. I was often able to apply sociological concepts to better understand my own working environment. Knowledge of such topics as organizational sociology, social stratification, and sociology of education afforded me the opportunity to "step back" from my deep day-to-day involvement in financial aid administration, and take a look at it through a sociologist's eyes. For example, I could see the financial aid office as a component part of a system, a "people-processing organization," similar in certain crucial respects to hospitals and prisons. It was almost as if the job of college administrator were a mannequin on whom I could try many different outfits (sociological perspectives), all of which fit, to an extent; some much better than others. Thus, it made sense to view my role more as "people processing" than that of simply providing services to students. I found such insights valuable because they allowed me to connect my experiences in the sociology program to my career.

In my graduate degree program in sociology I was able to channel my enthusiasm into a research project. I studied the relationship of students' financial need to persistence in their studies at a two-year college. This project taught me a great deal about the social forces that help to shape our educational and life choices. I have been better able to answer such questions as: "Who enrolls?", "Who drops out?", "Who persists?", and "Why do two-year colleges in the USA have higher drop out rates than four-year colleges?" I learned that people from the lower socio-economic levels matriculate to two-year colleges, and that fewer two-year college students persist through degree-attainment than do those at four-year colleges and universities. Sociological theories abound to explain why the two-year college drop-out rate is so high. I tend to agree with the conflict theorists, Karabel (1972), for example, who see two-year colleges as part of a system that perpetuates the existing class structure in the USA. Because of the nature of the students they attract (poorer, less physically healthy, less well academically prepared, lacking well-developed personal support systems), the two-year colleges experience low rates of student persistence. Failure to attain one's educational goals usually leads to difficulties in raising one's socio-economic status.

This perspective has helped me to do a better job administering financial aid. If I can understand, from a sociological standpoint, what sorts of people my clients are, and from what sorts of cultural milieus they come, then I can better assist them in persisting and attaining their educational and life goals.

Sociology has provided me with the understanding that we, as human beings, are not simply individuals existing in a vacuum, but rather individuals functioning as part of an increasingly complex socio-cultural environment. This understanding has made my work

more difficult because I am more aware of its complexities. I am, perhaps, less naive than I once was. The sociological perspective has led me to the realization that, despite such personal assets as opportunity, self-motivation, individual intelligence, financial support, and willing facilitators, many of my clients will not succeed. Statistics show that more than half of these students will not complete their educational goals, and, therefore, will fail to raise their socio-economic status. Cultural forces exist that are often stronger than any given individual's will or desire to achieve. These include such factors as poor precollege intellectual training, indifference or, even, opposition from families and peers, and prejudicial treatment by college professors and prospective employers. Although the Protestant ethic (Weber, 1905) is alive and well in the hearts and minds of my students, what they don't understand, that the sociologist in me does, is that, while hard work can *help* us prevail and we are all unique individuals, we *do not* come into this world with equal opportunities for success, happiness and creature comforts. Rather, we come into the world at the socio-economic levels of our parents, and are likely to remain there.

Knowing this about our world, I have to guard against a pessimistic, defeatist attitude at work. After examining a first-generation college student's financial statement (thus inferring socio-economic status) and his or her previous academic record, it is often difficult to feel much more than helplessness and resignation about my ability to improve the student's chances for post-secondary success. However, to do my job effectively, I must be continually mindful of my tendency toward cynicism and strive to avert it. This is usually not difficult, for two reasons. First, I am, by nature, optimistic and idealistic. Secondly, sociology has also taught me that, while any given individual may have difficulty overcoming the social forces that govern our world, there are successes achieved everyday (some small, some large), in combating the dual problems of poverty and ignorance. Prior to my study of sociology, I experienced no such pessimism, but I do believe that having a clearer insight into the harsh realities facing my students, and the kinds of factors that enable some to overcome these obstacles enhances my ability, as a bureaucrat, to intervene in ways that might make the difference between a student staying in school and dropping out. I do not take for granted this aspect of bureaucratic power. On a daily basis, at work, I use sociology to help students gain access to the financial resources needed to continue their educations.

The greatest benefit of the sociology degree, I think, has been the deep, abiding understanding and acceptance of higher education as a bureaucracy. Many who have done well in financial aid administration have left prematurely due to burnout. The job is extremely stressful; bound, as it is, by the existence of countless, ever-changing federal and state regulations. Many who get into the field see it only as a human service position, rather than a human service position *within* a huge organizational bureaucracy. Consequently many of these new professionals leave the career, frustrated that they cannot *just* be helping professionals. They must also be bureaucrats. To those many, the word bureaucrat is a "dirty" word! Thanks to my education in sociology, I understand both the formal and informal structure of the bureau-

cracy in which I must function. I can, indeed, provide service to my students and society *because* I see the bureaucracy as a part of our culture and because I know it is not going to disappear anytime soon. By learning as much about it as possible, I can work *within* it, to guide my students through it and try to change it for the better. I certainly cannot help needy young people further their educations if I leave the profession. Therefore, I stay, do the best I can, and am literally thrilled, almost to tears, when I attend graduation ceremonies. This is what my career is all about, and if that means being a bureaucrat, then that's okay with me! The study of sociology, time, and the wisdom that time affords, has fostered this attitude in me. Not all of this knowledge is attributable to a degree in sociology; experience has played a major role in how I work.

My study of sociology has been positive, for the most part, not only intellectually and professionally, but also personally. The most valuable insight gained has been the realization that I love to learn. Whether it is sociology or something else, I am happiest when I am learning new things and facing new challenges. It is interesting that it took me more than 40 years and two post-secondary degrees to know this about myself!

References

Karabel, J. 1972: Community colleges and social stratification. *Harvard Educational Review*, 42(4), 521–62.

Mills, C. W. 1959: *The Sociological Imagination.*

London: Oxford University Press.

Weber, Max. 1905: *The Protestant Ethic and the Spirit of Capitalism* (trans. Talcott Parsons, 1958). New York: Scribners.

53

Being a Sociologist Employed in Public Agencies – A Personal View

Tricia Lain White

It was something of a shock three months after completing my undergraduate studies in 1988 to see a job advertised in the local paper that I thought I could do, knew I wanted to do and felt I even had a chance of getting. It read:

SOCIAL SCIENTISTS
Opportunities in research
"Working as a member of a professional team in the Department of Employment,[1] you will carry out internal research and provide support on projects contracted to outside research bodies."

And all I needed was a good degree in a relevant discipline, while "experience of research, research management and computing skills would be an advantage". I had some experience of working with a keyboard and monitor in previous jobs and although I had no experience of research *management* I thought that anyone who had just written a dissertation and about 50 essays in the past three years at university could surely claim experience of research.

I still think I was fortunate to get a job as a social researcher, although it had not been my ambition until I saw this post advertised. My career strategy – if it can be called that – was "ready, fire, *aim!*" which was not as haphazard as it may sound since the labour market I hoped to enter after graduating almost certainly would not be the same as the one I had left to go to university. Miraculously, it had improved, but I am not sure even economic forecasters understood completely why. Mainly I wanted to do something that mattered in a job that gave me the chance to use my degree.

My preparation for the interview was more focused. I read as many leaflets produced by the ED as I could lay my hands on and scoured the press for a grasp of the current employment issues. This helped my confidence and inspired a few sensible questions to ask the panel of interviewers I faced. Of more interest to them, however, was what I had learned in the course of studying sociology for three years at university, why I wanted to do research and how I felt about working in a large government department.

It was very helpful to be able to say (truthfully) that I was interested in a number of labour market issues, and had a special concern for people disadvantaged in the labour market such as the older worker. Also, while acknowledging the scarcity of resources, I was also interested in a more flexible system of higher education that recognized the need to extend the franchise to all.

I explained that any job but this would be second best, and that working in a government department held no fears for me, but looking back, that may have been because I did not know very much about it. I have since discovered that more is expected of a researcher in a government department – or, for that matter, in a commercial organization – than was suggested in the advertisement that first caught my attention.

Social Research in the Public Sector

An outstanding strength of working as a social researcher, in either the public or private sector, is that it offers the opportunity to use and develop the knowledge and understanding you have begun to form as a student of sociology. In the public sector you are positively encouraged to set aside time to keep up with your subject discipline by reading the latest books and relevant journals and by attending seminars and presentations, often given by people whose names appeared on your reading lists as a student. It is also considered important to develop links with other social scientists by joining professional associations and attending their conferences.

It is recognized that learning takes a lifetime, and time is allowed each year to acquire or improve knowledge and skills. As a researcher these may relate to the research process, to statistical techniques, to information technology, to the management of people and resources, to enhancing personal effectiveness or to achieving an understanding of the relationship between parliament, government and the civil service.

All these skills are required because, whether conducting or managing research, the duties of a researcher in both the public and private sectors are many and varied. You may be involved in five different research projects at any one time, from the stage of design to dissemination. Projects can be as diverse as a national postal survey that provides a snapshot of thousands of people on one day, but that takes a year to complete, and a multidimensional case study of a small group of people that is finished within weeks. You may be required to give an oral presentation of your findings, consider the feasibility of particular projects or the rationale of particular policies, attend or chair numerous meetings, provide briefing and advice and draft answers to parliamentary questions.[2]

Considering that this is a job and we are being paid to do it, researchers in the public sector are reasonably autonomous. You are judged not by the way you choose to order your work or your day, but by what you accomplish. And the principal measure of that is your success, or otherwise, in finding the golden mean between the quality and quantity of what you research or commission.

The research programme each year, and the funds to support it, are collectively agreed at a senior level by the department and the treasury, but individual researchers are able to express an interest in the projects they wish to undertake and to advise on how these should be approached. Often this is done in consultation with researchers, economists and statisticians from within the division, but team work in a government department is not of the same order as that practised by management consultants in commercial organizations. When we produce a research report the name on the cover is that of the author, whereas with theirs it is the name of the organization. While the seamless uniformity of their style and standards could not be achieved without a division of responsibilities and emergency reserves of labour on stand-by, we often have only ourselves to rely on. Sometimes our freedom can seem illusory as we realize it is the freedom to work a 12-hour day, but I still count it as important.

If there are problems in being a social researcher in a government department they arise from the tensions of operating in three spheres, each with competing demands that must be balanced. First, we are professionals but, unlike doctors, lawyers and accountants, we are without a professional body to set and enforce standards and provide support should it be needed. A conflict of interests may never arise, but the feeling is inescapable that the possibility of it cannot be excluded. Since this has implications for the ownership of research, as professionals we must be concerned. In principle, researchers are encouraged to write books or contribute articles to journals, but in practice official approval must first be sought and obtained. What would happen if approval were to be withheld is something I have never put to the test. But it can be imagined that opposing one's employer, especially when that employer is an institution as powerful as the government, is not a decision that would be taken lightly. Power does not have to be exercised, it has merely to exist. Equally, while it is recognized that ownership resides with the author of a report written for the government, authors are likely to be respectful as they would to any major sponsor of research.

Second, we work in a vast bureaucracy that has its own time-honoured language, culture and ways of doing things. The personnel "handbook", alone, runs to five volumes. The duties of a civil servant entail obsessional copying of letters and "minutes", completing forms and amassing huge files. Commercial organizations seem more concerned with charting the future than recording the past, but they may not need to account for themselves in the same way as public servants. This may not be the most vital way of working, but it is *safe*. Thirdly, we serve the public through their representatives, government ministers, the policy-makers. Our aim may be to produce flawless research, but its purpose is to assist the policy-makers in their work. They have their own agenda and timescales: ministers must consider what is socially acceptable, and possibly, on occasion, what is politically expedient. One of the effects of this is that they need immediate evidence of the value of their policies and we need to work to tight deadlines to provide it, sometimes assessing the effects and impacts of measures when they are still nascent. A politician's world is volatile and for us that means planning can only ever be provisional.

At one time the government's research needs were met solely by its own researchers. Now, this has become the exception and, unless it can be argued that, for instance, disclosure would endanger the security of the nation, research projects are offered to external organizations and awarded on the basis of competitive tendering. Now, although there are exceptions on each side, the major difference between researchers in a government department and in a commercial organization is that we are buyers of research services, whereas they are suppliers. Because we are not alone in having demands made on us – the

academic researcher is required to publish and the commercial consultant to make a profit – our respective concerns call for an element of accommodation. As civil servants we are bound by statute to a life-long duty of confidentiality. Those contractors we commission to undertake research on behalf of the department are contractually bound to confidentiality, with similar effect.

Influencing Public Policy

The second real strength of a career as a researcher in a government department is the opportunity it provides to become engaged in influencing the course of events and effecting change for the better.

The civil service itself is presently undergoing change on an unprecedented scale. The previously monolithic and monopolistic service has been broken up into *agencies* headed by chief executives on limited-term contracts with performance-related pay, and with separate arrangements for recruitment of staff, differing pay scales, grading structures and conditions of service. The different agencies have their own mission statements, logos and loyalties.

The intention has been to be make the public sector more business-like, more like the private sector, and what could not be privatized has been commercialized. But it remains to be seen whether the public sector can ever be like the private sector without being motivated by the maximization of profit, whether a "code of conduct" will ever provide the same inspiration to selflessness as the ethos of public service it replaces. It is also unclear how representative democracy will be affected by making chief executives, who are appointed and not elected, directly accountable for operational matters – especially as there is no clear distinction between operational and policy responsibilities. But whichever party is in government after the next election, it has been made clear that there is no going back for the civil service. As Sir Robin Butler, Secretary of the Cabinet and Head of the Home Civil Service, has said, "However far we have come, we will have further to go. We have entered the world of continuous development".

In parallel to the actual and potential changes in the civil service, are changes in the way the future of research is being viewed. In the past the role of researchers in the policy process has been twofold:

- to define options;
- to pronounce judgement *ex post facto* and, with Olympian detachment on the impact of past policy, with a view to influencing future policy.

But a sea change seems to have taken place.

Policy-makers are less inclined to take the medicine they are prescribed if it arrives in the form of a thick and unappetizing research report, containing a mass of qualifications but few action points. It is being recognized that if it is to be relevant and timely, research must be integrated into the policy process from the outset, and researchers must be directly involved in the process of policy formulation. Where previously there were aloof researchers and resistant policy makers, it is now possible to achieve agreement and commitment through continuous dialogue.

Notes

1. In 1988 the Department of Employment (ED) was the branch of central government whose aim it was to create a more flexible and efficient labour market by helping people in jobs, by encouraging enterprise and by facilitating training. It was also responsible for the payment of state benefits to the unemployed. The ED was merged with the Department for Education in 1995.
2. Parliamentary questions or "PQs" are a daily feature of parliamentary affairs that give Members of the House of Commons, our elected representatives the opportunity to raise and publicly air subjects of their choosing that relate to a particular minister's portfolio. Ministers answer by providing a personal account of the work and conduct of their officials and the exercise of their own powers and responsibilities in the context of the issue raised.

Postscript: Potentials and Predicaments

The Editors

Troubled Times

The potential for developing and satisfying human needs has never been greater. Modern transport, communication systems and commerce have mutually influenced or even merged the cultures of societies around the globe. Knowledge grows exponentially, as embodied in print and electronic media – and, especially, in educated persons. The applications of this knowledge feed into the continuous transformation of what and how we produce and consume – and how we organize our personal lives and public institutions. Our capacity to produce more goods and services with proportionately less labour constantly increases. The means exist to protect us from or ameliorate the adversities of nature – whether storm, disease or crop failure. We also have a fantastic potential in the modern world for attending to our social and emotional needs. Thus, universal literacy in a largely urban society generates massive possibilities for creativity and enjoyment of the arts, density of social interaction and civil relations between strangers.

Yet, this potential is far from being attained and, indeed, is often frustrated by the means that could promote it. Interacting and intermeshing cultures all too often relate to one another in hostility rather than conviviality. Our century has seen countless ghastly wars, persecution, brutal dictatorship and genocide – all executed with terrible effectiveness due to the application of modern social and technical knowledge. The human and material resources expended on means of coercion contrast starkly with those going into the relief of famine. Indeed, we have poisoned rivers, polluted the atmosphere and spoiled the land. Fantastic waste and opulent plutocracies stand in marked contrast to the squalor and poverty in which millions live, even in supposedly "rich" countries. Many areas of our cities are experienced as dangerous, soulless and isolating. How terrible it is, in modernity, that homeless people can be left to die in city streets.

That such potential can be frittered away cries out for explanation – and remedy.

Understanding our Troubles

Nearly 40 years ago C. Wright Mills wrote memorably of the desperate need for *sociological imagination*, by which he meant an understanding of the broad social scene in terms of the lived experience of individuals – and an understanding of this lived experience in the context of the broader social scene. The personal troubles which so many of us experience *or fear* – being unemployed, trapped in joyless work, a victim of crime, in hostile family relationships, lonely, impoverished as a result of illness – are all products of social rather than individual pathologies, such as anarchistic market competition, privatized consumption, bureaucratic forms of organization, ideologies and social norms that legitimate oppressive behaviour towards minorities and the vulnerable, and so on. But one person's troubles may be rooted in another person's opportunity for gain, the constraints upon them the result of choices made by others – especially those with wealth and power. The discernment of such connections is therefore dangerous knowledge, their exposure threatening to the powerful. The better we can understand the sources of predicament in our lives and those of our friends, the more there is a chance of breaking out of fatalism and tackling the causes of social ills. The sociological imagination, thus understood, is not some esoteric body of knowledge or skills, but a way of looking at things which is accessible to all.

Studying Sociology: Skills and Quality of Mind

Doubtless some of our fellow sociology teachers will disagree with the following attempt to specify criteria for a good sociological education. That is only to be welcomed, for dispute is the lifeblood of social sciences!

- A sociological education should build on students' social inquisitiveness as well as their intellectual curiosity, so that they become driven by the desire to know what is really going on behind the veil of appearances.
- The budding sociologist needs to acquire the intellectual capacity for both abstract thought and immersion in nitty-gritty description – and, most challengingly, to move between them.
- Sociology students must learn *to use* the "tools of the trade" (not just read or hear about them) such as questionnaire design, interviewing, observation, note-taking, report writing, construction of cross-tabulations and so on. However, even more important than acquiring a command over techniques is the capacity to assess the *significance* of what research reveals. The most important skills the sociological craftworker can acquire are imagination, especially empathy with the experiences of others, creativity in forming explanatory accounts, and analytical rigour. Together these form the basis of *sociological theorizing*. Note we claim these skills can be learned: they are not capacities with which some fortunate individuals happen to be endowed.
- The sociologist has to learn to live with contestation. This is because there are usually alternative theories that could explain what we observe. Indeed, what we observe is affected by alternative prior theories. That does not mean that any view is as good as any other, but rather that as a sociologist one must be prepared to respond to the arguments of others, argue one's own case with vigour, yet keep a sufficiently open mind to recognize that the positions one defends may subsequently have to be revised. Moreover, because rival theories often put different groups in a good or poor light, there are temptations to adopt accounts which are most comfortable in the existing structures of power and legitimacy. So, as well as the argumentative disposition, a good sociological education should foster the courage to stick by or modify one's conclusions without concern for personal consequences.

The Degradation of Sociological Education

Unfortunately, there are many factors that work against the prospects of the sort of sociological education described above. They derive in large part from more general ills of the universities – inadequate resourcing for expanding student numbers, standardization (and routinization) of course content, bureaucratic modes of monitoring and controlling student performance (which encourage instrumental and rote learning) and so on. One significant symptom of alienation in mass higher education is the decline in personal face-to-face relations between teachers and students, to be replaced by interactions with computer screens. Moreover, staff actions and attitudes are significantly influenced by the culture of the institutions and career hierarchies within which they work and, for many, by the insecurity of their terms of employment. The search for tenure and promotion, or simply for status-recognition by one's peers, may lead, however unwittingly, to self-censorship so as not to offend funders or potential patrons, to the downgrading of teaching because academic status and rewards are geared to research grants and publications, and to the loss of overall vision as the search for a "niche" in the intellectual market drives people into over-specialization and esoterica. All this can have deleterious effects on the form and substance of teaching and student learning.

There are also some negative features specific to sociology as currently researched and taught in universities. Some of the commonly voiced criticisms are accurate in the case of some sociological practice: there *is* a substantial amount of teaching and research that uses unnecessary jargon to give the impression of profundity; statistical calculations *are* sometimes needlessly complex to give the impression of technical sophistication, and so on. You have probably come across some examples of these. However, in our opinion, more pernicious failings derive from attempts to accommodate to (largely unjustified) criticism that sociology is subjective, subversive and "left-wing". These accommodations include a tendency to ape theory-testing modalities supposedly characteristic of natural sciences, and to bend efforts to "useful" policy-oriented research (adopting frameworks defined by the sponsors who finance it).

Those who are studying sociology need not take the tendencies to degradation lying down. The sociological imagination allows students to see these processes as due, not to the inexplicable ill-will or incompetence of teachers and university bureaucrats (although such failings may also be present), but rather to the larger structural processes mentioned above. Such recognition can galvanize students out of that sense of fatalism that comes from feeling gripped by remote and ineffable forces; a good sociological education encourages students to take active control of their own learning and to negotiate their own agenda, exploiting the resources of university libraries and teachers in ways beyond those specified in the curriculum. Often students will find even hard-pressed teachers delighted to give of their time to help and encourage initiatives fuelled by genuine interest.

The Limits of Sociology

In the above paragraphs we have sought to portray the sociological imagination as crucial to an understanding of the interaction between contemporary public issues and personal troubles. But we have not sought to idealize sociological education, seeking rather to portray it "warts and all" by recognizing structural conditions that negatively constrain its development. That said, there are great personal benefits to be gained, and social benefits too, if the quality of mind and skills that characterize the "educated sociologists" become more widely diffused. As noted, sociology is sometimes charged with being subversive. This is an accusation it should proudly admit to. A sociology that is afraid to challenge conventional assumptions and vested interests is not worth the candle.

This does not mean that sociology is inherently "left-wing" – or "right-wing" for that matter. Rather it can provide an arena in which alternative diagnoses and solutions are debated. Sociology cannot tell us how to act, but it may alert us to a realization that what is legal is not necessarily right, and that what is normal is not necessarily fair. Of course, it will take more than talk to realize those potentials of modernity now so cruelly frustrated – and thus move beyond sociology to forms of political activity in which debate is just one element. Sociology cannot resolve what such activity should be, but it may help you to think through the issues for yourself.

The Editors

Index